The Compensation Handbook

A State-of-the-Art Guide to Compensation Strategy and Design

MILTON L. ROCK
Chairman MLR Enterprises, Inc.
Philadelphia, Pa.

LANCE A. BERGER
Managing Director
MLR Publishing Company
Philadelphia, Pa.

Editors in Chief

Third Edition

McGraw-Hill, Inc.
New York   St. Louis   San Francisco   Auckland   Bogotá
Caracas   Hamburg   Lisbon   London   Madrid
Mexico   Milan   Montreal   New Delhi   Paris
San Juan   São Paulo   Singapore
Sydney   Tokyo   Toronto

Library of Congress Cataloging-in-Publication Data
    The Compensation handbook : a state-of-the-art guide to compensation strategy and
design/Milton L. Rock and Lance A. Berger, editors in chief. — 3rd ed.
        p. cm.
    Rev. ed. of: Handbook of wage and salary administration.
    Includes bibliographical references and index.
    ISBN 0-07-053352-0
    1. Compensation management—Handbooks, manuals, etc.   I. Rock, Milton L.
II. Berger, Lance A. III. Handbook of wage and salary administration.
HF5549.5.C67H36 1990
658.3'2—dc20   90-40324 CIP

*IMPROSHARE, Scanlon, Rucker, Identifying Criteria for
Success (ICS), and Hay ACCESS are registered trademarks
of Mitchell Fein, Scanlon, Rucker, Development Dimensions
International, and The Hay Group, respectively, and are
used with permission.*

*For their assistance in the production of the finished manu-
script we thank Joan Harrison, copy editor; Margaret Daly,
word processor; and Betty McHugh, coordinator.*

    234567890 DOC/DOC 987654321

ISBN   0-07-053352-0

*The sponsoring editor for this book was Barbara B. Toniolo,
the editing supervisor was Jim Halston, the designer was
Naomi Auerbach, and the production supervisor was
Suzanne W. Babeuf. It was set in Baskerville by McGraw-
Hill's Professional Publishing composition unit.*

*The first and second editions of this book were published un-
der the title:* Handbook of Wage and Salary Administration.

Printed and bound by R. R. Donnelley and Sons Company.

Contents

Part 1. Introduction

Part 2. Wage and Salary Administration: Theories, Approaches, and Practices

iii

Part 4. Executive Compensation

Part 5. Computers and Compensation

Part 6. Performance and Compensation

Part 7. Corporate Culture and Compensation

Contributors

Claudio Belli President and Chief Executive Officer, Europe, Middle East and Eastern countries, Hill & Knowlton, Milan, Italy (CHAPTER 43)

Lance A. Berger Managing Director, MLR Publishing Company, Philadelphia, Pa. (CHAPTER 2)

Renae F. Broderick Ph.D., Senior Research Associate, Center for Advanced Human Resource Studies, School of Industrial and Labor Relations, Cornell University, Ithaca, N.Y. (CHAPTER 3)

Peter T. Chingos National Practice Director, Performance and Compensation Management Consulting Services, KPMG Peat Marwick, New York, N.Y. (CHAPTER 23)

David J. Cichelli Executive Vice President, The Alexander Group Inc., Irvine, Calif. (CHAPTER 20)

Jerome A. Colletti President, The Alexander Group Inc., Scottsdale, Ariz. (CHAPTER 20)

Richard A. Connelly Ph.D., Active Management, Inc., Newtown Square, Pa. (CHAPTER 35)

Frederic W. Cook Frederic W. Cook & Co., Inc., New York, N.Y. (CHAPTER 38)

Michael R. Cooper Ph.D., President and Chief Executive Officer, Opinion Research Corporation, Princeton, N.J. (CHAPTER 39)

Trudy Downs School of Communications, Information and Library Studies, Rutgers University, New Brunswick, N.J. (CHAPTER 29)

Charles H. Fay Associate Director, Institute of Management and Labor Relations, Rutgers University, New Brunswick, N.J. (CHAPTER 32)

Mitchell Fein President, Mitchell Fein, Inc., Hillsdale, N.J. (CHAPTER 12)

W. Fred (Duke) Fuehrer Ph.D., Director of Organization Development, Pentair Inc., St. Paul, Minn. (CHAPTER 18)

Peter Gelfond Director, U.S. Operations, Research for Management, Hay Group Inc., Philadelphia, Pa. (CHAPTER 40)

Luis R. Gomez-Mejia Research Professor, Management Department, College of Business, Arizona State University, Tempe, Ariz. (CHAPTER 17)

George G. Gordon Ph.D., Associate Professor of Management, Department of Business Administration, Rutgers University, Newark, N.J. (CHAPTERS 28 AND 41)

Ike Greenspan Director of Compensation, GTE Corporation, Stamford, Conn. (CHAPTER 19)

Monroe J. Haegele Ph.D., Institutional Funds Group, Provident National Bank, Wilmington, Del. (CHAPTER 25)

Marsha Cameron Haller Principal, National Practice Leader, Salary Management, TPF&C, a Towers Perrin Company, New York, N.Y. (CHAPTER 31)

Michael E. Hora Vice President, A. T. Kearney, Inc., Chicago, Ill. (CHAPTER 34)

Jeffrey S. Hyman Partner, Hewitt Associates, Lincolnshire, Ill. (CHAPTER 24)

Bernard Ingster Consultant, Human Resources Management, Philadelphia, Pa. (CHAPTER 9)

Thomas W. Jacob Vice President, Compensation Information Center, Hay Group Inc., Philadelphia, Pa. (CHAPTER 30)

Alan M. Johnson Managing Director, Executive Compensation Practice, Handy Associates, New York, N.Y. (CHAPTER 22)

Jill Kanin-Lovers Vice President and Manager, Compensation Services, TPF&C, a Towers, Perrin Company, New York, N.Y. (CHAPTER 6)

Ira T. Kay Director, U.S. Compensation Practice, and Worldwide Director Compensation Design, Hay Group Inc., New York, N.Y. (CHAPTER 40)

Norman R. Lange Managing Director, Job Measurement Practice, Hay Group Inc., Philadelphia, Pa. (CHAPTER 5)

Edward E. Lawler III Ph.D., Director, Center for Effective Organizations, Graduate School of Business Administration, University of Southern California, Los Angeles, Calif. (CHAPTER 42)

Gerald E. Ledford, Jr. Senior Research Scientist, Center for Effective Organizations, Graduate School of Business Administration, University of Southern California, Los Angeles, Calif. (CHAPTER 15)

D. Terence Lichty Director, Research & Development, Cole Surveys, a Wyatt Data Services Company, Boston, Mass. (CHAPTER 7)

John M. Linton Chicago Office Practice Leader, Executive Compensation, TPF&C, a Towers Perrin Company, Chicago, Ill. (CHAPTER 21)

Jerry L. McAdams Vice President, Performance Improvement Resources, Maritz, Inc., Fenton, Mo. (CHAPTER 16)

Robert P. McNutt Project Manager, Compensation, Fibers Department, E. I. du Pont de Nemours and Company, Wilmington, Del. (CHAPTER 14)

George T. Milkovich M.P., Catherwood Professor, Center for Advanced Human Resource Studies, School of Industrial and Labor Relations, Cornell University, Ithaca, N.Y. (CHAPTER 3)

Johannes M. Pennings Department of Management, The Wharton School, University of Pennsylvania, Philadelphia, Pa. (CHAPTER 26)

Linda E. Rappaport Esq., Partner, Shearman & Sterling, New York, N.Y. (CHAPTER 27)

Milton L. Rock Ph.D., Chairman, MLR Enterprises, Inc., Philadelphia, Pa. (CHAPTER 1)

Robert H. Rock D.B.A., President, MLR Enterprises, Inc., Philadelphia, Pa. (CHAPTER 37)

Ruth Ann Ross Co-Director, Ross Gain Sharing Institute, Chapel Hill, N.C. (CHAPTER 13)

Timothy L. Ross Co-Director, Ross Gain Sharing Institute, Chapel Hill, N.C. (CHAPTER 13)

Thomas S. Roy, Jr. Director, Salaried Compensation, Armstrong World Industries, Inc., Lancaster, Pa. (CHAPTER 8)

Marvin Schiller Ph.D., Managing Director, North America, A. T. Kearney, Inc., Chicago, Ill. (CHAPTER 34)

Craig E. Schneier Ph.D., Managing Principal, National Director, Human Resource and Organization Effectiveness Practice, Sibson & Co., Inc., Princeton, N.J. (CHAPTER 36)

Jesse Sherman Vice President, Research for Management, Hay Group Inc., Philadelphia, Pa. (CHAPTER 40)

Lyle M. Spencer, Jr. Ph.D., President, McBer & Co., Partner and Technical Director, HRPD Practice Worldwide, Hay Group Inc., Boston, Mass. (CHAPTER 33)

Arnold A. Trillet Vice President, Human Resources, BOC Group, Murray Hill, N.J. (CHAPTER 10)

Marc J. Wallace, Jr. Ph.D., Professor and Ashland Oil Fellow, College of Business and Economics, University of Kentucky, Lexington, Ky., and Consultant, Sibson & Co., Inc., Chicago, Ill. (CHAPTER 11)

Theresa M. Welbourne Division of Strategy and Organization Management, Graduate School of Business Administration, University of Colorado, Boulder, Colo. (CHAPTER 17)

Martin G. Wolf Ph.D., CMC, Vice President, MAS Management Advisory Services Inc., Glenside, Pa. (CHAPTER 4)

John Yurkutat Senior Survey Consultant, Compensation Information Center, Hay Group Inc., Philadelphia, Pa. (CHAPTER 30)

PREFACE

The Compensation Handbook is a road map to modern compensation strategy and design. It describes the entire process a practitioner should follow in order to put together a totally effective compensation program according to the best contemporary standards. There is a common body of knowledge in the field that almost everyone has lived with since 1972, and readers who wish to refamiliarize themselves with this material can refer to the second edition of this handbook, entitled *The Handbook of Wage and Salary Administration*. This historical base remains the foundation of a modern compensation program and provides the basis for the more advanced approaches contained in this third edition.

However, the focus of the new edition is on performance-based approaches to compensation that will help managers and human resources professionals create state-of-the-art programs that support a company's broad-based strategic needs. To achieve this focus, the third edition has been almost totally rewritten by the leading experts within the field. These experts provide the most advanced thinking on job analysis and documentation, job evaluation technologies, compensation surveys, contingency-based compensation plans, current executive compensation practices, productivity measurement, and the use of computers in compensation. Thus *The Compensation Handbook* is the indispensable desktop reference for making informed practical decisions on new policies and procedures affecting today's compensation issues.

Milton L. Rock
Lance A. Berger

ABOUT THE EDITORS

MILTON L. ROCK, Ph.D., is chairman of MLR Enterprises, Inc., a publishing and information services company based in Philadelphia. He is the former chairman and chief executive of The Hay Group, a worldwide management consulting firm. He has written extensively for both professional and business publications in his 40-plus years in the consulting profession. He is the editor of *The Mergers and Acquisitions Handbook, Corporate Restructuring: A Guide to Creating the Premium-Valued Company*, and the first and second editions of the *Handbook of Wage and Salary Administration*, all published by McGraw-Hill.

LANCE A. BERGER is managing director of MLR Publishing Company, which publishes *Mergers & Acquisitions* in the United States and Europe, and the *Medical and Healthcare Marketplace Guide*. The company also produces the M&A Data Base and provides marketing support to professional services firms. Mr. Berger is the former vice president and managing director of The Hay Group's worldwide compensation practices. He has written numerous articles and is a former speaker on human resources issues.

PART 1
Introduction

1
Looking Back on Forty Years of Compensation Programs

Milton L. Rock, Ph.D.

Chairman, MLR Enterprises, Inc.

Introduction

When the *Handbook of Wage and Salary Administration* first appeared in 1973, the compensation profession was in the throes of a heady period of development and innovation. From a somewhat ill-defined activity in the 1930s, salary administration was evolving into a systematic process replete with its own technologies and internal checks and balances. For the first time in history, employers and employees could speak in a shared language about what a job was worth. And, after a protracted struggle, personnel managers had earned recognition as valuable members of the overall management team.

Our purpose in creating the book was to capture the state of the art in salary administration—to present the issues, methodologies, and technologies in sufficient depth to ensure a widespread understanding of the field and, to the degree then possible, to lay a scholarly foundation for the compensation professional.

Our perception that such a handbook was necessary was validated

3

soon after the book's publication when the *Handbook* became the most widely read book of its kind. Within five years it was revised for a second edition, which was also translated into Spanish.

The decision to launch this third edition came from our conviction that we have reached a watershed in compensation activity. Compensation managers' understanding of the globalization of business, the information revolution and its applications, the insurgence of knowledge workers, and differing social values has matured. At the same time, corporate restructuring has given birth to a variety of special compensation needs—including components for leveraged buyouts, management buyouts, ESOPs, and mergers and acquisitions—arising from corporate restructuring. Because compensation systems, in many ways, are a continuum, this third edition of the *Handbook* builds on the first two, carrying us up through the present and offering a glimpse of the future.

Though superficially transformed by a number of new communications and information technologies and applied to a host of unforeseen managerial issues, the underlying precepts of salary administration—internal equity, external competitiveness, pay for performance, and rewards based on job worth—have changed little over the years and today are well accepted by management and investors alike. While most innovations have come from the field itself (from those practicing professionals whose daily focus is the design and management of compensation), the discipline today is studied and taught in all graduate schools of business and scholars are making important contributions to the field.

The Rise of the Compensation Professional: A Short History

The ideas and information presented in the chapters that follow represent the most advanced thinking in an ongoing process of salary-administration experimentation and development. To place these contributions within the broader historical framework, we believe a short history of the compensation profession and the changing role of its practitioners is appropriate.

Professional Origins

Though compensation has always stood at the heart of the employer-employee relationship, systematic salary administration is by and large a twentieth-century phenomenon, the product of a complex web of corporate, social, economic, and political forces. Its evolution from an agent of internal equity to a powerful, strategic management tool parallels the rapid expansion of American industry, and its history is, therefore, rich with insights into the changing landscape of corporate America.

The primary catalyst for the emergence of the compensation profession and its pool of singular technologies was the changing relationship between the business owner and the white-collar employee, which shifted from one of daily interpersonal contact to a more distant chain of command within the space of just a few decades. Most nineteenth-century proprietors, of course, were personally familiar with their employees' individual contributions and, therefore, positioned to judge what a job should pay. Twentieth-century managers, removed from their staffs by expanded corporate hierarchies, did not share this advantage. In the early years, many sought to overcome this dilemma by establishing general minima and maxima for specific jobs and allocating pay according to the individual jobholder's efficiency, courtesy, accuracy, speed, length of service, and organizational loyalty.

Such customized consideration became less feasible in the corporation's next stage of development, as the rise of specialized divisions made it increasingly difficult to assess how the contributions of one individual in one department compared with those of others in an entirely different department. The arrival of World War II further complicated the question of salary administration by imposing a series of external wage restrictions and guidelines. The National War Labor Board wage freeze, which fixed wages and salaries at September 15, 1942, levels, and the 1942–1943 Little Steel formula effectively limited individual salary increases that did not conform with a definite plan of salary rate changes. Those corporations that had not established a consistent method for regulating internal rate changes were thus placed in the rather untenable position of denying their workers the anticipated annual raise.

Although civil service wage scales and union wage proposals began to appear in the late nineteenth century, the private sector did not begin to study systematic job evaluation until the post-World War I years. It was then that articles with such forward-looking titles as "Wage Scales With a Reason" first appeared in the press, that the American Management Association discussed job evaluations for nonunion personnel, that salary guidelines for clerical and blue-collar workers were put forth, and that organizations like the Philadelphia Rapid Transit Company surveyed jobs and pay with the then novel objective of establishing proper rate bases and relationships. Some organizations went so far as to adopt the factor-comparison method of job evaluation as early as 1926.

In 1938 First Pennsylvania Company for Insuring Lives and Granting Annuities, no longer equipped to fairly administer pay to its growing cadre of employees, undertook a comprehensive review of alternate job-evaluation systems for the specific purpose of determining a fair rate of pay for each and every company position. Spearheaded by the bank's personnel officer, Edward N. Hay, it was this study that in many ways laid the foundation for the modern era of salary administration.

First Pennsylvania's desire for objectivity, for a wage and salary program that was blind to interpersonal relations, race, creed, or gender, required the introduction of a scientific method. This, in turn, meant beginning with the facts: What is a job? What are the jobholder's duties? How does the job relate to what others do? What are the supervisory responsibilities? What skills are required for performing the job? How are those skills acquired? What native abilities must be brought to the job? What is the size of the jobholder's responsibility?

These data, captured in a standardized job description, enabled the bank's job analysts to systematically compare one job with another. Five factors—mental requirements, skill requirements, physical requirements, responsibility, and working conditions—were introduced to help discern the fine distinctions among jobs, and the resultant web of job comparisons made it possible to establish salary grades and very specific wage minima and maxima. By the time Edward Hay established his own consulting practice in 1943, organizations across the United States were recognizing the need for a reliable salary-administration system that would facilitate the analysis, grading, and pricing of jobs.

Quantifying Human-Resource Factors

When I think back on the technical concerns we at Hay Associates harbored in the formative days of the 1940s and 1950s, I am amused to realize that the Hay guide charts were developed not so much as a means of evaluating jobs, but rather as a means of explaining the concept of job evaluation to boards of directors and management. The guide chart's rapid transformation into a method of evaluation resulted from a growing recognition that this measurement system could indeed be used as the process to achieve results. The thesis that something that can be measured has value while something that can't be measured has none was thereby reaffirmed. The guide charts began with two basic building blocks: know-how and its use and accountability. At the lower-job level two variables, working conditions and physical effort, were added to facilitate a more accurate measurement. Now a standard component of the guide charts, the problem-solving chart was actually developed somewhat later.   •

For the creator of the guide charts, determining the value of the variables and the relationships among them became an interesting challenge, one ultimately resolved through profiling. Essentially, profiling reflects the fact that, whereas an executive position is relatively high in accountability and a technical job is relatively high in problem solving, a production job is predominately linked to know-how. Within this system, a vice president of manufacturing might be profiled as 43-25-32 (43 percent know-how, 25 percent problem solving, 32 percent accountability), a vice president of technology as 37-30-33, and a CEO as 29-26-45. Not only did profiling ensure a logical relationship among the three variables, but it also provided compensation specialists with an easily comprehended shorthand by which to discuss differences between and among jobs.

The process was further systematized when we applied the standard measurement from Webber's Law, "just noticeable differences," to clarify separations among variables. Determining the size of a just noticeable difference was, of course, dependent upon how well committees could differentiate steps of the three variables. Because we found all committees could differentiate 15 percent intervals, we ultimately decided on the 15 percent interval as the standard.

Having settled on variables, profiling, and intervals, our next task was to construct a reasonable approach to numbering the charts. We ardently debated the pros and cons: Should we begin with 50 (a good, round number) and step up to 57? Or should we begin with 100 and step to 115? Interestingly, even after we agreed to use 50 as our starting point, many subsidiaries of parent companies insisted, in acts of true independence, that their charts be numbered differently than those of their headquarters. In Canada, similarly, the guide charts were numbered differently for quite a long time—a reflection, I am sure, of Canadians' feelings of nationalism.

Who Decides?

Yet another key decision demanded careful deliberation, this one concerning committee composition: Who should be entrusted with the evaluation of jobs? To ensure the acceptance of the final evaluation results, we argued for multirepresentational committees composed of members from the company's varying occupational areas and disciplines.

Then, to ensure an effective committee process, we studied committee chairperson leadership styles. These studies indicated that an autocratic leader produced a more acceptable standard number of jobs evaluated per session than a democratic one. Further studies suggested that the arts of negotiation, conciliation, and consensus on the part of committee members were also critical to the overall success of the evaluation process, and thus these skills were introduced and emphasized throughout the evaluation training programs.

Compensation Databases

As long as organizations were focused on internal equity, compensation surveys and databases had no place in the world of compensation management. Corporate curiosity (interest in how much the competitor was paying) and a heightened sense of fiscal responsibility soon, however, brought the issue of competitive data to a head.

Hay Associates began its exploration of intercompany compensation comparisons in the mid-1950s. Our starting point was the recognition that if it were possible to evaluate every job from every company on the same guide charts and if we could place these scatter points on the same plot, a direct comparison of all salary lines would be possible. The outgrowth of our theorizing was the Eight Company Chart, a manually evaluated and processed database product that placed eight clients' lines of central tendency on the same chart and thereby facilitated intercompany comparisons.

Within short order, spurred by a surging interest in the salary marketplace, the Eight Company Chart, along with other competitive databases, burgeoned. Succored by the mainframe computer, which greatly simplified the data-collection, quantification, and storage processes, these databases quickly grew into sophisticated tools that enabled survey analysts to investigate more thoroughly the relationships among various corporate practices and to discern human-resources trends.

As compensation databases multiplied in size and sophistication and as corporations grew more diverse and far-flung, compensation analysts began to rely on one of the computer's most basic and important functions, the sort function, to build an array of functional and industry- and geography-specific databases and survey results. The structure of these relational databases, in many ways, mirrored the structure of the participating organizations, which were increasingly shedding hierarchical ladders in favor of networks, entrepreneurial venture units, and job sharing.

Motivating Employees Through Careful Communications

Completing evaluations, attaining committee approval, and plotting points and salary lines were all essential steps leading to the basic objective of salary administration: motivating employees through trustworthy and reliable rewards systems. Attaining employee buy-in depended on that most intangible of all human relations skills: communications.

Although conveying the message that job evaluation was in fact fair, equitable, and accessible sounds easy today, one must recall that in the early days, employees were not by and large aware of what their coworkers earned. Compensation was a very secret business, and pay scales and salaries seemed to come from on high.

A broader understanding of corporate compensation practices became possible when compensation specialists began to prepare brochures detailing philosophies and procedures for the various job-evaluation boards and when the boards, in turn, elected to distribute these pamphlets to all employees. Today, there is practically no major company that does not conscientiously communicate its compensation practices, either through written manuals or videotapes.

Broadening the Focus of Compensation Specialists

The emergence of the sunshine laws and the communications revolution that marked the 1970s had a deep-seated impact on corporate human relations in general and on compensation in particular. Dissatisfied with simple explanations of internal and external salary scales, employees began to demand explanations as to why jobs were paid the way they were and, through insistence on job posting, equal access to available positions. Finally, with the widespread acceptance of systematic job evaluation processes, whose backbone, of course, was equal pay for equal work, employees also began to argue for the fundamental right to equal pay for comparable work.

These and other issues eroded the old, somewhat detached relationship between compensation specialists and employees. The era of secrecy was firmly left behind as employees looked to personnel managers for information and insights into the factors governing job assignments, remuneration, and opportunities, as well as the overall ability of the company to pay.

The Handbook: Content and Structure

The fact that it has been the practitioners and not the scholars who have made the greatest contributions to the compensation field is reflected in the slate of authors chosen for this book; over 20 percent of this edition's authors are university-based, as compared with fewer than 10 percent in the second edition, and even less in the first.

Here, as in past editions, we draw upon those who are truly expert in applying established techniques or promulgating change. Whereas the earlier editions related the step-by-step processes associated with building a total reward system, this third edition is designed to help managers create compensation processes that will effectively support present and future requirements. Its structure reflects our belief that the merger mania of the 1980s has bred a new group of owner-managers (analogous to the captains of industry of the late nineteenth century) whose needs are somewhat different from those of the professional managers who rose in the post-World War II years.

Part 1 begins with the basics. Featuring job analysis and documentation, job evaluation technologies, salary surveys, and the like, Part 2 ensures an understanding of the processes by which fair and equitable base-salary systems are established. Contingency-based approaches to compensation—with techniques ranging from IMPROSHARE to nonmonetary rewards to team incentives—are highlighted in Part 3, while Part 4 reviews current executive compensation practices, long-term incentives, contracts, tax treatments, and related issues.

Complementing the more traditional fare are three new subject areas. Part 5 details the use of the computer in job documentation, evaluation, pricing and salary structure, and budgeting and planning and reflects on the way managers reach decisions through information analysis. Drawing from the extensive reliance on, and interest in, the relationship between executive and corporate performance, Part 6 brings pay for performance and productivity-measurement systems into close focus. Finally, Part 7 reviews corporate culture, a fitting topic for today's generation of administrators who are charged with the responsibility of creating a resilient corporate climate that can survive internal and external financial upheavals.

The incorporation of overviews to each section satisfies yet another goal: it enables the reader to acquire quick glimpses into each subject area and thereby gain a broad understanding of the complex fabric of salary administration.

It is hoped that the structure and content of this third edition, *The Compensation Handbook*, will empower the reader with a greater appreciation of the shifts that have occurred in compensation philosophy since the 1940s and the implications of these changes for the compensation practitioner. It considers the transformation of personnel into a major department whose core functions embrace labor relations, salary administration, and organizational design. It highlights the strategic and tactical aspects of compensation planning in an era of corporate raiding and restructuring. It reveals how the changing mix of compensation devices—base salary, long-term incentives, stock options, perquisites—have become accepted and meaningful implements of strategic management. It looks at the sensationalization of executive compensation data by both business and popular media, and it examines the widespread implications of a society that now knows, more than ever thought possible, about how and why people are paid to do just what they do.

2

Trends and Issues for the 1990s: Creating a Viable Framework for Compensation Design

Lance A. Berger
Managing Director, MLR Publishing Company

Human-resource management was once a relatively placid profession—a profession operating in a world in which rapid expansion, rising productivity, and large market opportunities were commonplace and in which pay was seen more as an expense than an investment. Year upon year, employees climbed the corporate ladder, collected generous benefits packages, and reaped yet another merit-pay salary increase.

Stability and security went hand in hand. It was not long after World

War II that Americans' basic belief in prosperity and a growing sense of entitlement were translated into an unwritten quid pro quo, an informal employee-employer contract. At its core, this contract assumed that the employee would be loyal to the organizational enterprise, serve with long-term commitment, and perform the tasks requested by management. For the employer's part, the contract implied employment stability, promotional opportunities, and annual increases. Large base salaries were part and parcel of the contract terms.

By the 1970s, however, social and political uncertainty, a fluctuating economy, growing challenges to United States technological supremacy, and the itch of entrepreneurship had turned the quiet waters into a still churning whirlpool of change. Compensation professionals were jolted by the force of events as the age of entitlement drew to a close and the performance era began. It was a new environment demanding a new portmanteau of methodologies and tools.

Forces of Change

To comprehend just what happened and what it means for the future management of compensation, seven basic forces of change—slow growth, globalism, technological advances, corporate restructuring, growth of small business, value shifts and market segmentation, and changing demographics must be considered.

Slow Growth

According to many economic forecasting firms, worldwide growth will be no more than 3 percent for the foreseeable future. Although some industries—aircraft and aircraft parts, office equipment, plastic products, electronic components, communications technologies—will most likely surpass this mark, the general economic reality cannot be ignored.

Short-term fiscal management and uncompetitive levels of productivity have weakened the United States. Having cut its spending for education, technology, development, and training its international peers, having allowed the national debt and trade imbalance to soar, and having lagged behind in the race for improved productivity, America looks ahead to a period of very modest growth and a GNP that will, according to the Bureau of Labor Statistics and the Department Commerce, hover between 2 percent to 3 percent between the years 1989 and 2000.

Globalism

Globalism, a term much bandied about in the past few years, describes both the increasing interconnectedness of the world economy and the rise of international competition. The evidence is everywhere. Today, Japan is suffused with brands like Nike, Kleenex, and Kellogg cornflakes; the United States is flooded with Japanese automobiles, cameras, and electronics. And, around the clock, via electronic channels, the world's currencies are moved from continent to continent. International corporate acquisitions, mergers, joint ventures, and licensing arrangements are slowly reducing business to a trade enterprise, while the covers of today's annual reports reflect a growing concern about the international marketplace.

The rise of multinational subsidiaries and other off-site manufacturing and processing centers offers further proof that the national border is no longer synonymous with the national boundary. To complicate the picture, previously minor players in the international arena—South Korea, Thailand, and the Philippines, to name a few—have become very major factors in the economic scene, heightening, by their very presence and success, the intensity of international competition.

Technological Advances

Technology's impact on the world of work has been pervasive. The advent of smart manufacturing technologies and production processes, for example, has had the two-fold impact, in areas of problem solving and team playing, of eliminating some routine positions while demanding more from those who remain. The shift from mainframe information technologies to networked personal computers has transformed traditional communications processes and decision-making tools. And the proliferation of advanced telecommunications systems has provided immediate access to once distant corners of the globe.

The blurring of traditional distinctions between job functions has spawned job redesign—featuring expanded individual accountabilities, fewer job levels and classifications, and emphasis on work teams and interdependency—around the new technologies. Others are taking a close look at the man-machine interface—painstakingly matching human skill levels to technological mandates—to ensure maximum returns from the new generation of automated processes.

Technology has forced modern corporations to redesign their organization structure and management process in order to compete in a global marketplace. The value systems created by the entitlement mindset of the 1970s are also feeling the effects of the new technologies.

Corporate Restructuring

In the 1960s and 1970s many American corporations, lured by perceived market opportunities and hoped for economies of scale, pursued an aggressive policy of diversification. Multidivisional conglomerates, structured along traditional staff and line hierarchies, sprouted up across America.

Slow growth, globalism, volatile financial markets, the threat of corporate raiders, and the rise of advanced information and manufacturing technologies have forced managers to rethink the policy of diversification and realign corporate resources. One by one, the conglomerates of yesterday are shedding the weight of unrelated business lines, refining their market foci, and shrugging off the quest for diversity.

Hand in hand with elimination of business lines has come a reduction in the large corporations' work forces. Much of the trimming has come in the managerial and administrative ranks; those who have remained have found their job accountabilities redefined to facilitate increased flexibility, decision making, and creativity. Vulnerable and insecure, blocked from traditional routes of corporate advancement, today's employees wear the battle scars of this environment, revealing, in various employee-attitude surveys, a growing lack of trust in the business community, an increasing reluctance to bond with their corporate employers, and a flagrant skepticism in their ability to advance into the corporate ranks.

Paralleling this trend to downsize has been a rise in merger and acquisition activity. Every public company is, by definition, up for sale or "in play," and thus very few of today's organizations can be certain that they will be spared the current feeding frenzy. The pace of this change has placed even greater pressure on corporations to build effective new structures and redefine their employees' roles.

Growth of Small Business

As cost-conscious corporations implement leaner management structures and traditional promotional opportunities decline, one aspect of enterprise—the small business—continues to take a great step forward. *Inc.* magazine's David Birch reports that virtually all of the more than 10 million jobs that have been added to the American economy since 1980 have come from companies with fewer than 100 employees. In ever greater numbers, top executive talent is fleeing to entrepreneurial environments. Drawn as much by the opportunity for challenge and creativity as by the desire to be treated with respect, this new breed of risk-taking executives is participating in a change process that many believe will redefine how and where the business of the future takes place.

Value Shifts and Market Segmentation

Two generations ago, employees and their employers could draw a clean line of distinction between the hours of work and the hours of leisure; product development and marketing professionals could readily identify and define consumer populations and attitudes. Not so today. Not only is the work week now about 20 percent longer than it was in 1973, commuting aggravated by the rise of "urban villages," but also the dual-career family is on the rise. In addition, corporations are stepping over traditional boundaries with work-at-home requests and employee-assistance and wellness programs.

Furthermore, we are ensconced in an era of somewhat confusing value shifts. It is a time characterized by strategic consuming and a search for stability, a time of muddy ambiguities. It is also a time that is far from homogeneous, encompassing several wholly different sets of values, attitudes, and expectations.

Embodying both tradition-bound individuals and change agents, today's diversified culture poses enormous challenges for employers and marketing strategists alike. Fitting the right person to the right job and assembling a mutually reinforcing project team have become increasingly complex sciences. Product positioning, brand management, and value enhancement are equally difficult imperatives.

Changing Demographics

It is a well-known fact that the postwar baby boom has swollen the ranks of those workers between the ages of 23 and 41.[1] This has created a highly competitive environment for an increasingly smaller array of upper-level job opportunities. Less well known, perhaps, is the baby-bust phenomenon, which threatens employers with a forecasted dearth of entry-level workers.

Not only are the size and value set of the work force changing, but so also are the demographic characteristics (the gender, ethnic background, and age) of the individuals actually doing the work.

The most obvious change has been the increasing entrance into the

---

[1]*Forging New Relationships Between Companies and Employees: Work in the 1990s,* Environmental Scanning Association, October 1987, p. 8.

work force of women, whose educational attainments, experiences, and career mindedness qualify them for a full spectrum of positions previously dominated by men. Though still hemmed in at the uppermost executive levels, the female factor and all the attendant issues of child rearing and career pathing can no longer be ignored.

The increasing presence of minorities in the work force, many of whom adopt English as a second language, is a demographic phenomenon of similar importance. Here, work force issues vary significantly by ethnic group, and the gap between required and available skills continues to grow. Increasingly, human-resources professionals will be called upon both to develop minority training programs to fill entry-level jobs left vacant by the white baby-bust and to proactively eliminate those implied and overt barriers that prevent skilled minority workers from moving up the corporate ranks.

The greying of the American work force also poses challenges. The population over the age of 65 is increasing, and more workers are retiring earlier, either by personal choice or corporate mandate. Though surveys suggest the majority of those approaching retirement would prefer to continue working, this employee group appears to face age discrimination, to perceive jobs as unavailable, and to harbor concerns regarding the safety of Social Security benefits. Unless organizations plan to incorporate older Americans into their work force, a skilled and committed employee group will go largely underutilized.

Compensation Implications

The need to balance economic and demographic realities with corporate imperatives and individual expectations has tossed many organizations on the sea without a compass. The forces of change have shattered familiar frameworks, rendering traditional approaches to compensation management irrelevant. Instead, a number of important new programs and approaches have grown up.

Contingency-Based Approaches to Compensation, Benefits, and Job Evaluation

Before the winds of change blew across corporate America, personnel and reward management was a rather straightforward process. Jobs were evaluated and ranked in accordance with organizational hierarchies, pay scales were established by applying market data to more evaluations and rankings, and the entire company's pay scale was then fine-tuned in accordance with the organizational pay policy. People received pay raises based on promotion, automatic merit, or cost-of-living increases.

But the worldwide forces of change and competition sparked, in the 1980s, a growing need for contingency-based approaches to compensation, benefits, and job evaluation. The simple world of internal equity and market measurement began to dissipate as affordability and performance, the needs of new employee groups, and the strategic objectives of the parent company were factored into the human-resources equation. Differentiation became the battle cry.

The speed at which these programs are being developed is mind-boggling. On the compensation side, there are emerging (or, in some cases, reemerging) tools such as gain sharing, risk sharing, profit sharing, hiring bonuses, two-tier systems, differential market pricing, uniform lump sums, skill-based pay, knowledge-based pay, individual incentives, team incentives, and group incentives. Each has been designed to address a specific need—for example, cost containment, retention of top performers, performance motivation, or team playing—and a specific set of employee values and expectations. The impact on contingency-based compensation programs is now felt in almost every corporate strata. More and more, compensation is being tied to individual, team, or business-unit performance. Even administrative and production workers are having part of their pay placed at risk through bonuses and other variable compensation plans.

Job-evaluation professionals are likewise employing a broader spectrum of alternatives. Originally introduced as a means of establishing equity in internal pay systems, job measurement has matured into a full-fledged management tool, a powerful technique for analyzing organizational structures and job relationships, improving understanding of job requirements, and managing performance. The current range of choices—manual or computer-assisted job evaluation that make use of either classification, whole-job ranking, factor comparisons, point-factor analyses, cross-sectional evaluation committees, or expert job analysts—permits organizations to select the technology that best fits their strategic objectives and culture.

Today's benefits managers also can pick and choose from a variety of programs, such as flexible spending accounts, flextime, and in-house training and tuition-refund programs, to meet their corporate goals and satisfy their diverse employee populations. Employees can expect to share more in the costs of their benefits, to witness the benefits programs of small and large organizations converging into a no-frills core package, and to see the trimming of executive-level benefit supplements.

But, like a penny-wielding child in a candy store, this plethora of choices brings with it the dilemma of selection. Managing the alternatives means digging deeper into the corporate mindset; analyzing the organization's strategic objectives; evaluating the expectations of employee groups, determining affordability levels and appropriate pay markets; identifying key people resources; quantifying team and individual output; and building an appropriately differentiated and cost-effective reward, job evaluation, and benefits structure that can simultaneously answer to both budgetary and motivational concerns—all of which, ultimately, expand the responsibility and visibility of the human resources professional.

Cultural-Readiness Profiles

The mainstreaming of contingency-based approaches has enabled the human-resources professional to learn more and more about the way both overall organizations and particular employee groups respond to various reward programs. Whole databases have grown up around the success and/or failure of relationships between specific compensation systems and specific cultures, making it possible to gauge an organization's "cultural readiness" for a particular compensation approach.

The ability to compare cultures of companies that have successfully introduced a form of contingent compensation to the profile of an organization currently considering the same approach allows companies to close key cultural gaps prior to plan implementation. For example, by strengthening group orientation, encouraging initiative, enhancing the levels of trust and commitment, or improving the clarity of direction, an organization on the verge of installing a new incentive program can take a proactive step toward ensuring its success.

Creating the Small-Company Environment

As alluded to earlier, tensions between today's larger, hierarchical corporations and their individualistic, entrepreneurial managers (many of whom bring the expressive values of the 1960s to their jobs) threaten corporate America. Squeezed by tight margins, international competition, and an ever-changing business environment, the hierarchical corporation has been forced to look for alternate organizational structures, to emphasize value-added knowledge, and to encourage innovative employee behavior. The entrepreneurial manager, conversely, feels threatened, grows increasingly discontent, believes the marketplace affords greater opportunities, and yearns for the dynamic, entrepreneurial culture of the small company. Many of the larger organizations have met these tensions head-on by restructuring along the lines of their smaller competitors. Through a combination of redesigned jobs and at-risk incentive programs, executives are being encouraged to think and act like owners, to focus on long-term performance, take calculated risks, work effectively in teams, and put forth a broad-based commitment to the business operation.

At the same time, to reduce costs and facilitate improved market responsiveness and decision making, organizations are shedding themselves of midmanagement positions and eliminating span breakers and coordinators in favor of skilled professionals who can add value to the corporate enterprise. Jobs are being redesigned across the board. Reflecting the old adage, "If you want someone to do a good job, you have to give them a good job to do," human-resources professionals are creating both intrapreneurial and entrepreneurial positions, venture capital units and skill-based teams, and horizontal and vertical career paths. Small work groups, from the shop-floor level all the way up to senior management, are being designed and put in place.

More variety and flexibility is being built into the work scope of the single jobholder, shared accountabilities and freedom to act are being encouraged, and, in the absence of traditional routes to the top, "developmental" jobs are being created to groom young talent for executive positions. The job descriptions of the 1990s reflect these shifts, incorporating language that emphasizes empowerment over control, knowledge application over acquisition, problem solving over procedure, and linkages over discrete functions. Words like *lattice, adhocracy, wagon wheel,* and *statocracy* are also becoming part of the job-description vernacular.

Organizations' willingness to enhance the entrepreneurial nature of the enterprise is, additionally, evident in the new reward systems. As we have seen, long-term incentives have been introduced into lower echelons of the organization to more closely tie employees to the overall performance of the corporate entity. Closer attention is also being paid to the design of reward systems to ensure their ability to instill a sense of pride, support participative cultures, encourage innovation, balance short- and long-term priorities, and preserve management and technical continuity.

In all cultures, however, the principal thrust will be to relate the variable compensation element to those measures that truly reflect performance. By pushing those measures further down into the organization, the spirit of the small company will more likely be achieved.

Managing Performance Through Employee-Employer Partnerships

Despite corporate America's recent strides in developing contingency-based rewards programs and mirroring the successful qualities of the small business, the linkages between performance and pay remain, at best, tenuous. In *Achieving Competitive Advantage Through the Effective Management of People, 1986–1987*, the Hay Group's Strategic Management Associates and Yankelovich Clancy Shulman point out that only a small minority of today's employees see a clear relationship between the performance of the company and their own salary increases. Part of the problem stems from the growing work force malaise referred to earlier—the breach in employee-employer loyalties and a widespread pessimism regarding opportunities for advancement.

There are, however, other factors at work. *Achieving Competitive Advantage Through the Effective Management of People, 1986–1987*, cites the discrepancies between top executive and senior-management viewpoints as one critical problem. The report maintains that whereas executives must steer the organization's strategic course according to changes in the business environment, senior managers must operate within a more controlled environment in order to satisfactorily implement and support decisions already made. More often than not, this basic incongruity between short- and long-term decision making renders effective, consistent performance measurement and management a near impossibility.

A few significant techniques have developed in response to this performance-management dilemma. One approach centers on the conscientious implementation of small-group employee-employer partnerships in which the employee's sense of control and belonging is enhanced through the delegation of some decision-making powers. The quality circles introduced in the automobile industry in the 1970s are prime examples of this type of partnership; employers would encourage and then reward employee ideas that improved the quality of products.

Use of the Computer to Administer Tasks and Codify Replicable Functions

Since the 1970s computers have been used to support job evaluation in a variety of cost- and time-efficient ways, ranging from record keeping to job-evaluation calculations to the refinement of the statistical foundations of job evaluation. (Computers have been used, for example, to alter factor weightings based on elaborate mathematical criteria.) In addition, by relieving individual evaluators from the greatly repetitious task of preliminary analyses and decision making, the computer has enabled evaluators to spend more time considering unusual job needs or special refinements.

Of course, no two computerized job-evaluation programs are created equal, and none should be considered an absolute substitute for human judgment. While some programs merely capture the current practice of an organization (with little regard for reasonableness), others have been designed to reflect and act on organizations' specific job-measurement value systems, emphasizing managed effectiveness of an organization as well as efficient production of job evaluations.

The increasingly computerized compensation environment has catapulted practitioners into yet another realm and has placed the burden of a wholly different kind of responsibility on their shoulders—that of selecting, installing, and maintaining computer-assisted job evaluation, salary administration, and executive compensation technologies that support administrative expectations, strategic organizational goals, and human-resources philosophies. Many practitioners are pursuing systems that not only link to an existing evaluation system and pricing database, but also yield sound job descriptions; facilitate factor-by-factor reviews; and satisfy standards of speed, ease of use, and internal consistency.

The Road Not Yet Taken

With the day of the automatic merit and cost-of-living increases now firmly behind us, the demand for contingency-based approaches to compensation and benefits will require human-resources professionals not only to secure a firm grip on the fundamental rationale of pay for performance, but also to exercise creativity and flexibility in program design as well. Developing unambiguous measures for individual and corporate performance, especially in the nonmanufacturing sectors, will stand as one of the great human-resources challenges long into the 1990s.

Differentiation, of the overall marketplace, the organizational entity, and the employee population, is likewise certain to demand increased attention from the human-resources professional in the coming years. Once again, skill in identifying issues—be they the need to realign in response to global pressures or the need to manage (even capitalize on) conflicting value systems—will be ensured through the effective application of the new tools and technologies at the professional's command. The art and science of human-resources management has always revolved around the insight to perceive the pressing issue of the day and the creativity to develop management frameworks, philosophies, and tools that can meet these changing circumstances head-on. On the road not yet taken, human-resources professionals will no doubt rely on these critical building blocks as they carry on the unceasing process of refining and implementing job-measurement technologies and affordability-based pay systems for tomorrow's work force.

3

Developing a Compensation Strategy

George T. Milkovich

M.P., Catherwood Professor
Center for Advanced Human Resource Studies
School of Industrial and Labor Relations
Cornell University

Renae F. Broderick, Ph.D.

Senior Research Associate
Center for Advanced Human Resource Studies
School of Industrial and Labor Relations
Cornell University

The management of change remains the challenge of the 1990s. The objectives of this change are to foster better performance, control costs, and enhance flexibility—all necessary to successfully compete in fierce markets. All managers are challenged by the pace and magnitude of this change. Human-resources managers are not excepted, being confronted daily with questions about how to manage employees to support changes in technology, changes in organization structures, and changes in business strategy. And employees themselves are changing in their values and expectations, their demographic diversity, their education, and their willingness to accept change.

When confronted with the need for rapid and large-scale change, human-resources managers, like their counterparts in marketing, finance, and production, tend to adopt strategies that enable them to manage their work forces effectively in the face of uncertainty. Developing a human-resources strategy requires *defining* the work force performance goals needed to support the organization's overall business strategy and the human-resources implications of these goals, *diagnosing* the organization's internal and external environment to pinpoint human-resources strengths and weaknesses relative to these goals, and *designing* the mix of human-resources policies and programs that exploits strengths and downplays or corrects weaknesses. The aim is to shape a work force that is focused on strategic performance goals and capable of achieving them.

Compensation is a critical piece of overall human-resources strategy. Because compensation is both visible and important to employees, a compensation program designed to communicate and reward strategic goals increases the probability that employees not only will understand what those goals are but also will achieve them. Because employees also understand that compensation dollars are important to the organization, the strategic intent of other human-resources efforts, such as performance management, recruiting, career development, and the like, is also clearer if their designs are consistent with the compensation program. In short, realization of compensation strategy requires that the money match the message.

Developing a compensation strategy requires the same process of definition, diagnosis, and design described above for human-resources strategy. This chapter provides some guidelines for beginning this process.

Which Compensation Decisions Are Strategic?

Strategy refers to the fundamental directions of an organization. Strategies serve to guide the deployment of all resources, including compensation expenditures. But not all compensation decisions are strategic. Only those decisions that are critical to the success of the business are strategic, such as those that affect labor costs and performance. Decisions about techniques, such as which job-evaluation plan to use or where to slot the compensation manager in the pay structure, are probably not strategic. Policy decisions, such as linking a portion of pay increases to corporate and unit performance and determining the competitive position in the market, probably are. We propose five basic decisions, shown in Figure 3-1, as a place to begin. These decisions are considered strategic by those who manage compensation systems.

1. Compensation's Role in Total Human-Resources Strategy
   - Initiate, on the point
   - Follow-supportive

2. Competitiveness
   - Market position
   - Mix-base, benefits, incentive forms
   - Percentage of guaranteed pay

3. Internal Structures
   - Sensitivity to internal and market factors
   - Number of levels in hierarchy
   - Size of differentials between levels

4. Employee Contributions
   - Pay increase criteria: objective/subjective performance, experience, inflation
   - Level of measurement: corporate, division, facility, team, individual
   - Size, frequency of payout
   - Renewal, proportion not added to base
   - Number, mix of increase programs

5. Administration
   - Communication: detail and type of pay information provided
   - Centralization: extent of employee participation in design and implementation of business unit
   - Formalization: extent of written rules, manuals, budget procedures, and so forth

Figure 3-1. Strategic compensation decisions.

Compensation's Role in Total Human-Resources Strategy

Compensation is only part of the policies and programs that organizations use to manage employee relations. Decisions regarding employment security, development and training, career opportunities, employee-assistance programs, and organization design, along with compensation, form patterns of human-resources policies. These patterns may be well integrated or so disjointed as to work at cross-purposes. Compensation can act as an instrument of change or simply act as a support of the overall human-resources strategy. The implementation of profit-sharing plans, for example, acts to signal competitive environments, to encourage employees to identify with corporate performance, and to support corporate values. Alternatively, other human-resources initiatives, such as transforming organization structures, forming work teams, and developing other flexible arrangements, may act as the change agent in the overall human-resources strategy. In such cases, compensation's role may be to support, rather than be on the cusp of, human-resources strategy.

Determining compensation's role in the larger human-resources picture is a familiar message. All managers nod in agreement but often neglect it when making decisions. Compensation decisions are part of the pattern of human-resources decisions; they do not operate in a vacuum. The rush to implement pay programs, particularly incentive pay, without first examining their role in the total human-resources strategy, often results in failure and employee distrust. Hence, determining compensation's role in the overall human-resources strategy is a strategic decision.

Competitiveness

What level of pay—base, benefits, incentive, perquisites—should be offered relative to competitors? What mix of these forms should be offered—base, flexible benefits, stock options, cash bonuses, stock-appreciation rights, and so forth? What should be the proportion of guaranteed compensation (base, benefits) relative to riskier returns (incentives)? Choices on market position, mix, and the proportion of guaranteed compensation directly affect managers' abilities to meet strategic performance goals. The competitive position managers choose affects the quality of the work force and its overall costs.

Choices about competitive position also communicate to both prospective and incumbent employees. Savvy employees, for example, can discern the organization's ability and willingness to recognize their needs based on the flexibility and tax protection offered in benefit plans or the opportunity to share in the firm's success through stock- and performance-based plans.

Internal Structures

Decisions on internal structures determine the distribution of base pay to different jobs or skills. In some cases this distribution is determined by market pricing, through matching competitors' structures reported in the market. In others, the number and uniqueness of jobs and skills and the strength of organizations' values dictate sensitivity to both internal and market factors.

Figure 3-1 lists several decisions associated with the internal structure of compensation systems. These range from the number of structures (national and local, technical and nontechnical, and managerial, and so forth) and the number of levels in each pay structure to the size of differentials among levels. Objective data show that these decisions differ among organizations in different industries and in vastly different markets with no reference to business strategies. For example, businesses that are highly labor-intensive, such as space and defense contractors, tend to exhibit more levels, smaller differentials, and greater emphasis on internal norms and traditions. In contrast, business units with less labor-intensive technologies, such as chemicals and plastics, tend to have fewer levels and wider differentials. However, even business units competing in the same industries and markets may exhibit very different internal pay structures consistent with their particular business strategy.

Internal structures let employees know the relative value of their jobs and skills and delineate career paths. Consequently, dual ladders, technical and managerial, are believed to signal the technical contributors' value to an organization. The extent to which employees view these decisions as equitable—with reference to either market values or internal norms—will influence their sense of fair treatment and their motivation to perform. Structural decisions also influence the flexibility managers have in reassigning employees without changing their pay. For example, General Electric Co.'s plastics division adopted an exempt-pay structure with only four levels: executive, director, leadership, and technical and professional. Managers believe that it provides greater flexibility to move employees without requiring pay changes. It also communicates to employees a relatively egalitarian philosophy about the value (base pay) of different skill groups. However, to be successful, the increased flexibility must be managed effectively. Inconsistencies within levels can result in anarchy and quickly will lead to employee dissatisfaction and distrust.

GE's competitors typically opt for more meritorious, hierarchical-based structures, with more levels and/or larger pay differentials linked to employees' jobs and skills. The circumstances under which these egalitarian versus hierarchical structures may be most effective is currently under study. Without such evidence, structural decisions seem to be based more on following fads, beliefs, and conventions than on strategic considerations.

Employee Contributions

Determining the whys, hows, and whens of employee pay increases is perhaps the most important strategic pay decision. Increases in pay are powerful communicators. For example, bonus plans tied to exceeding annual operating plans, such as those recently adopted by Du Pont Co., Union Carbide Corp., Scott Paper Co., and others, are believed to focus employees' attention and efforts on the unit's performance. Across-the-board increases based on a cost-of-living index, on the other hand, make inflation more salient, and merit increases make performance appraisals and competitors' practices important. The nature of pay increases signals what an organization values. Retaining experienced and talented employees, rewarding their contributions, recognizing unit performance, and even offsetting inflation are all, to some degree, objectives of pay increases. The art of strategic management involves choosing the pay increase plans that best serve the unit's business strategy and complement its overall human-resources strategy.

Administration

Decisions about how to administer pay may also be strategic. They can influence managers' sense of ownership and employees' views of the fairness of their pay. Both ownership and fairness are thought to be achieved through decentralization, participation, and communication. For example, one currently popular axiom is that deciding "how best to compete" rests with business unit managers; hence, ensuring that pay systems help them compete should also be their responsibility.

Decentralization, however, is not a universal good—more is not necessarily better. Determining which decisions should be decentralized and to which organization level involves experienced judgment. Benefits seem to be best managed corporatewide; incentives are best managed at various levels, depending on the type of plan; and choices about structures and competitive positions seem to depend on the skills and product markets in which units compete. Hence, decentralization decisions probably must be customized to fit each organization's unique situation.

Employees' sense of fairness regarding their pay is thought to be heightened if its administration is internally consistent, if communication is perceived as open, and if employees believe they have the opportunity to participate. Thus, while many decisions involved in the administration of pay are operational, the basic policies underlying the nature of the administration seem critical to employee performance and the success of the business.

These five basic decisions—compensation's role, competitiveness, internal structures, employee contributions, and administration—only serve as a starting point. Tailoring to each organization's unique situation is required. The choices made affect every organization's success.

Key Steps in Developing a Compensation Strategy

Developing compensation strategies is a simple process. One familiar to any manager is the generic decision-making model: Analyze compensation implications, establish objectives, compare actual conditions with objectives to identify gaps, develop actions to close gaps, and follow through.

Figure 3-2 shows this model applied to developing compensation strategies. It involves four key steps:

1. Analyze the compensation implications of the organization's business strategy, external environment, and internal human-resources conditions

2. Establish the desired strategic compensation position involving the five strategic choices discussed earlier

3. Determine any gap between the desired strategic position and the

---

1. Analyze compensation implications.
   - Business strategy
   - External environment
   - Internal human-resources conditions

2. Develop a strategic compensation position.
   - Compensation's role in total human-resources strategy
   - Competitiveness
   - Internal structures
   - Employee contributions
   - Administration

3. Determine any gap between the strategic position and the analysis of conditions, and design a compensation strategy to close it.

4. Follow through.

Figure 3-2. Key steps in developing a compensation strategy.

implications derived from the analysis, and design compensation programs to close the gap and to translate the compensation strategy into practice

4. Follow through.

Analyze Compensation Implications

The changing forces of the external environment through which organizations must navigate were examined in the previous chapter. Here, we only reemphasize that they are crucial to developing compensation strategies. Perhaps a major issue is whether these environmental forces allow any room for managers to adopt different compensation policies in support of their business strategies. Legislation on health benefits, pensions, and deferred contributions have reduced the viable choices for executive and manager compensation. Yet, we do know that firms pursue different options in responding to changes accompanying advances in technology, to changes in population demographics, and to shifts in regulatory concerns. Again, managers charged with developing compensation strategies must innovate compensation strategies that offer competitive advantages within the changing pressures that operate in the external environment.

Implications for a business's compensation strategy reside in the work force's performance and the sustainable labor costs associated with its successful implementation. For example, the decision to enter a new market requires a work force that is willing to take risks, put in long hours, and quickly solve problems not previously encountered. At the same time, especially for new ventures, cash flow is often restricted. A compensation strategy that attracts and motivates the necessary work force while dealing with cash limitations—all else being equal—will increase the new venture's chances of success.

Proponents of compensation-strategy development maintain that different business strategies vary in their work force performance requirements and sustainable labor costs and, thus, in the compensation strategies that best support them.

Develop a Strategic Compensation Position

Two related levels of business strategy need to be considered when developing a compensation strategy: the corporate unit and the business unit. Compensation strategy is most directly related to the business unit's strategy, but, as depicted in Figure 3-3, both the corporate and

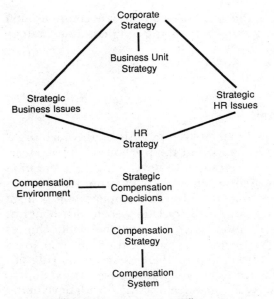

Figure 3-3. Strategic perspective: an illustration.

human-resources strategies also influence compensation-strategy development.

Business-unit strategies are designed to answer the question, "How should we compete in this particular product or service market?" Many approaches exist, but most classify business-unit strategic types in terms of two predominant strategies. One is labelled "Growth," the other, "Maintenance." The discussion of both these strategies is idealistic in the sense that actually very few organizations completely exhibit the patterns to be described. However, these two types do serve to guide the development of compensation strategies under different business strategies.

Managers pursuing a Growth strategy make high investments and take significant financial risks to expand their market shares. The ideal organization design allows for maximum flexibility in dealing with new markets and technologies. Division of labor is product- or service-centered with little job or functional specialization. Decision making is decentralized; there are few formal controls such as budget, inventory, or even human-resources programs. Hierarchies, supervision, and work rules are minimal. Information flows freely and informally throughout the organization. Performance criteria focus on market outcomes, such as expanding sales and market share.

A Maintenance strategy emphasizes maintaining current market shares while minimizing costs and improving customer satisfaction. Here, the ideal organization design exploits the organization's past learning and success in dealing with a particular market and technology. The division of labor is functional with relatively high job specialization. Decision making is more centralized, and more formal control, hierarchy, supervision, and work rules exist here than in the Growth strategy. Information flows through well-established communication channels and is more restricted. Performance criteria focus on cost savings, quality, and customer satisfaction.

The strategic compensation decisions thought to best support the Growth and Maintenance strategies are shown in Table 3-1 and are derived from studies of compensation strategy in Growth and Maintenance organizations. The logic underlying these results is readily apparent when considering the performance and labor-cost implications associated with each strategy. The Growth strategy, for example, requires heavy investments in marketing and development without the benefits of high cash income—at least over the short term. This means that dollars are not available for high base salaries and benefits, but significant performance and ownership incentives can be offered. In order to realize incentive potential, employees must be willing to take risks, work long hours, creatively solve problems, and focus on the market outcomes critical to Growth strategy success.

Compensation plays a dominant, lead role in the overall human-resources strategy. It serves to signal the climate of risk and reward. Incentives tied to the organization level and market outcomes with high, annual payout potential help attract and direct the types of employees needed. Internal structures and administrative decisions that allow maximum flexibility are also consistent with the organizational design and administrative style thought ideal for Growth-strategy success.

One study of the relationship between human-resources strategies and business-unit strategies showed that units successfully pursuing Growth were more likely to emphasize the importance of compensation programs than those pursuing Maintenance strategies. While the results of one study are not conclusive, they suggest that when making choices about developing a compensation strategy for several business units, those pursuing Growth strategies should take precedence because pay appears to play a more dominant role.

Research also confirms that the internal structures and administration of pay are related to the cultures and management styles used throughout the organization. It follows that any shift toward either a Growth or Maintenance strategy must be supported by similar changes

Table Table 3-1. Suggested Compensation Profiles for Business-Unit Strategic Types

	Business-unit strategic types	
Strategic compensation decisions	Maintenance	Growth
1. *Role in Human-Resources Strategy*	Support or subordinate	Lead signals, risks and rewards
2. *Competitiveness*		
Market position	Emphasize base, benefits	Emphasize incentives
Pay mix	Variety and choice in benefits	Variety in incentives, choice in benefits
Percentage of guaranteed pay	Higher	Lower
3. *Internal Structures*		
Mix internal and market pay values	Internal and market-sensitive	Market-sensitive
Number of levels in pay hierarchy	More	Fewer
Differentials	Larger	Smaller
4. *Nature of Pay Increases*		
Criteria	Experience, inflation, performance appraisal	Objective performance
Level of measurement	Individual, group	Unit, individual
Size of payout	Smaller	Larger
Renewal	Added to base	Not added to base
5. *Administration*		
Communication	Restricted	Open
Centralization	High	Low
Formalization	High	Low

in the organization itself. A compensation strategy at odds with the organizational culture is futile.

Designing a Compensation Strategy to Close Any Gap

The compensation systems of most organizations will not look exactly like either of the Maintenance or Growth profiles. The Maintenance and Growth profiles shown in Table 3-1 really serve as polar guideposts for managing strategic change and development. A simple example illustrates how these profiles can be used to guide strategy development.

The current compensation-system profile shown in Table 3-2 comes from a unit whose market orientation, structure, and administrative style place it closest to a Maintenance type. The unit's business strategy is to continue its current market orientation: maintenance of market share. It also anticipates, however, that increased levels of market competition mean that minimizing costs and increasing quality and customer service are no longer enough. Internal structure, administrative style, work force performance, and labor costs all need to be more flexible in order to accommodate changes in market demand. Flexibility of the order recommended to support a Growth strategy is not desired. The Maintenance unit just wants a little more flexibility and maybe some correction of past problems: redundant jobs and employees, lackluster performance standards, and overspecialization of jobs.

In order to develop a compensation strategy that promises more flexibility, the compensation profile of the Growth type offers a guide. Table 3-2 shows the unit's current compensation profile, the ideal Growth profile, and the recommended compensation strategy.

The recommended strategy infuses a little more risk into the system and potentially lowers labor costs. The role of the pay system in the total human-resources strategy shifts to the role of a change agent. The shift toward a Growth strategy requires a competitive position more sensitive to market pressures and less to internal traditions and norms. A higher proportion of incentives in total compensation is proposed; there is less guarantee that these incentives will be paid. A profit sharing plan ties about 10 percent of potential pay increases to unit performance, and, if realized, this amount will not be added to base salary. Also, more information will be shared with employees. In particular, the profit sharing plan calls for employee education in basic financial concepts, employer's markets, and the like.

Table 3-2. Illustrated Comparison of Current and Compensation-Strategy Profiles

Strategic compensation decisions	Compensation-system profiles		
	Current/actual	Growth	Recommended
1. *Role in Human-Resources Strategy*	Support or subordinate	Lead signals, risk and rewards	Shift to higher profile, pay system
2. *Competitiveness*			
Market position	Lead in base, benefits	Lead with incentives	Meet in base, benefits, and incentives
Pay mix	Variety of benefits	Variety of incentives	No change
Percentage of guaranteed pay	High—90 percent	Low	Moderate—85 percent
3. *Internal Structures*			
Mix internal and market sensitivity	Both used	Market	No change
Number of levels in pay hierarchy	25 levels	Fewer	Reduce
Differentials	Large	Flat	No change
4. *Employee Contributions*			
Criteria	Performance appraisals & seniority	Financials	Mix of both
Level of measurement	Individual	Unit individual	Unit and individual
Size of payout	Small	Large	Moderate—15 percent of total pay
Renewal	Added to base	Not added	Not added
Mix	Merit, seniority-based plans	Incentives only	Merit (5 percent); profit sharing (10 percent)
5. *Administration*			
Communication	Restricted	Open	More open: Information relevant to profit sharing
Centralization	High	Low	No change
Formalization	High	Low	No change

Follow Through

Implementation of these strategic changes is tricky. Compensation changes cannot take place overnight, but most can be accomplished within a time framework associated with shifts in most business-unit strategies. The key is to identify which changes should happen first in order to ensure that success. For the recommended strategy changes in Table 3-2, the profit-sharing program might have enough visible impact in year two to carry internal support for reductions in job levels, changes in the merit plan, and increased emphasis on external market pressures.

The Payoffs From Developing a Compensation Strategy

Why spend the time developing compensation strategy? One recent estimate assessed the development time at about six months. The underlying premise of any strategic perspective is: If managers make pay decisions consistent with the organization's business strategy, responsive to external and internal conditions, and consistent with the overall human-resources strategy, then the organization is more likely to be competitive. This statement is based on belief, not systematic evidence. No studies link the implementation of compensation strategy with business success. Indeed, there are so many factors unrelated to compensation that can influence business-strategy success that disentangling the effects of compensation strategy is a difficult task.

Recent studies do offer guidelines on the effects of certain decisions, specifically pay-for-performance plans, on firm performance. It has been documented, for example, that gain sharing plans are related to between 10 percent and 17 percent improvement in performance. Performance in these studies included rates of absenteeism, suggestions, and safety as well as cost and production measures. The longest period covered by any study was 18 months. It has also been shown that firms distinguish themselves through decisions on incentive pay plans more than they do through decisions about the competitive level of base pay. Thus, the conventional competitive decisions, such as leading or meeting competition, may be obsolete. Rather, firms seem to establish competitive positions based on the nature of their incentive plans. Furthermore, studies show that greater use of bonuses and long-term incentives is associated with better firm performance. Specifically, according to one study of over 250 firms, an increase of 10 percentage points in the bonus/base ratio is associated with 0.21 to 0.95 greater return on assets.

Some evidence also suggests that such plans are more successful when they are part of a total, or strategic, approach to compensation.

A note of caution: Negative results and failed compensation plans are seldom reported. Consequently, much of the work in this area needs to be treated with some caution. However, a conservative conclusion is that empirical evidence does support the proposition that performance-based pay, as part of an overall strategic approach, does contribute to firm performance.

There are also some potential side benefits of developing a compensation strategy. It provides a business-related rationale for compensation system changes that may be useful in explaining decisions to both employees and outside regulators. The process of compensation-strategy development requires the managers involved to stretch their understanding of all aspects of the organization and the environment in which they are competing and their relationship to pay. The process may spark ideas for much needed change in pay systems that are often overly bureaucratic.

There are many questions on compensation strategy that remain unanswered. As we gain more experience with strategy development, the steps needed to make development efforts pay off will become clearer.

Suggested Readings

Balkin, D., and L. Gomez-Mejia. "Toward a Contingent Theory of Compensation Strategy," *Strategic Management Journal*, Vol. 8, 1987, pp. 169–182.

Broderick, R. "Pay Policy, Organization Strategy and Structure: A Question of Fit," in R. Niehaus (ed.), *Strategic Human Resource Planning Applications*, Plenum Press, New York, 1987, pp. 43–58.

Carroll, S. "Business Strategies and Compensation Systems," in D. Balkin and L. Gomez-Mejia (eds.), *New Perspectives in Compensation*, Prentice-Hall, Englewood Cliffs, 1987, pp. 343–355.

Cooke, F. *Strategic Compensation*, Frederick W. Cooke Associates, New York, 1986.

Dyer, L. "Strategic Human Resource Management and Planning," in K. Rowland and G. Ferris (eds.), *Research and Personnel and Human Resources Management*, Vol. 3, JAI Press, Greenwich, 1985, pp. 1–30.

Dyer, L., and R. Theriault. "The Determinants of Pay Satisfaction," *Journal of Applied Psychology*, Vol. 61, No. 5, 1976, pp. 596–604.

Ellig, B. "Compensation Elements: Market Phase Determines the Mix," *Compensation Review*, Third Quarter, 1981, pp. 30–38.

Gailbraith, J., and D. Nathanson. "The Role of Organization Structure and Process in Strategy Implementation," in D. Schendel and C. Hofer (eds.), *Strategic Management: A New View of Business Policy and Planning*, Little, Brown & Co., Boston, 1979, pp. 249–283.

Gearhart, B., and G. Milkovich. *Organizational Differences in Managerial Compensation and Financial Performance.* Working Paper No. 89-11, Center for Advanced Human Resource Studies, School of Industrial and Labor Relations, Cornell University, Ithaca, 1989.

Kerr, J. "Diversification Strategies and Managerial Rewards: An Empirical Study," *Academy of Management Journal,* Vol. 28, 1985, pp. 155–179.

Lawler, E. *Pay and Organizational Development,* Addison-Wesley, Reading, 1981.

Miles, P., and C. Snow. *Organizational Strategy, Structure and Process.* McGraw-Hill, New York, 1978.

Milkovich, G. "A Strategic Perspective on Compensation Management," in K. Rowland and G. Ferris (eds.), *Research in Human Resources Management,* Vol. 6, JAI Press, Greenwich, 1988, pp. 263–288.

Milkovich, G. *Gain Sharing in Managing and Compensating Human Resources.* Working Paper No. 87-03, Center for Advanced Human Resource Studies, School of Industrial and Labor Relations, Cornell University, Ithaca, 1987.

Milkovich, G., and B. Rabin. "Firm Performance: Does Executive Compensation Really Matter?" in F. Foulkes (ed.), *Executive Compensation in the 1990s: A Strategic Approach,* Harvard Business School Press, Boston (forthcoming).

Ochsner, R. "Customized Contingent Compensation: The Wave of the Future," in C. Fay and R., Beatty (eds.), *The Compensation Sourcebook,* Human Resource Development Press, Amherst, 1988, pp. 38–40.

Schuster, M. *Gainsharing: Issues for Senior Managers.* Working paper, School of Management, Syracuse University, 1985.

Wallace, M. *Alternative Reward Strategies: Improving Productivity and Competitiveness,* Certification Course 12, The American Compensation Association, Scottsdale, 1988.

Weiner, N. "Determinants and Behavioral Consequences of Pay Satisfaction: A Comparison of Two Models," *Personnel Psychology,* Vol. 33, 1980, pp. 741–757.

Wils, T., and L. Dyer. *Relating Business Strategy to Human Resource Strategy: Some Preliminary Evidence.* Paper presented at the 44th Annual Meeting of the Academy of Management, Boston, 1984.

PART 2

Wage and Salary Administration: Theories, Approaches, and Practices

4

Theories, Approaches, and Practices of Salary Administration: An Overview

Martin G. Wolf, Ph.D., CMC
Vice President
MAS Management Advisory Services Inc.

Job evaluation and salary administration are nothing new, although there is some new technology used in the field (see Part 5, "Computers in Compensation"). From the beginning of time, all groups have used some form of job evaluation. The earliest recorded history indicates that there was a division of labor (different jobs existed) and that different levels of reward were given out based on this division. Anthropological evidence suggests that a formal division of labor existed even in prehistoric times. Our word *salary* comes from the Latin *salarium*, meaning "salt money"; soldiers and workers were paid at least in part with salt, a precious commodity then. Our expression *not worth his salt* derives from the same roots. While to the victor goes the spoils, not all soldiers got equal choice of the spoils. The Roman army, although fairly large, was not all that complex. It made do quite nicely with a simple system of job evaluation—leaders of 10, leaders of 100 (centurions), leaders of 1000, and so forth. It was only as organizations became both large and complex that formal job evaluation became necessary.

Job-Evaluation Systems

All job-evaluation systems, formal or informal, essentially are based on three things: what you know, what you do, and, to a degree, what you have to put up with. These three things are the primary compensable elements, that is, the things for which employers pay people. Particularly in statutes and regulations, the three primary compensable elements are often broken down into four categories: skill, effort, responsibility, and working conditions. All formal job-evaluation systems represent an attempt to define the compensable elements in a fashion that allows them to be measured as easily and as consistently as possible. Some systems have preestablished compensable elements, while others develop the compensable elements to fit the value system of the organization. Some have only a few compensable elements, others have dozens. Despite this, all formal job-evaluation systems look pretty much alike because they all come down to some variation of the three primary compensable elements.

Adequacy of Coverage

One aspect in which formal job-evaluation systems differ meaningfully is in the adequacy of their coverage of the relevant compensable factors for a broad range of jobs. It is relatively easy to develop the relevant factors for jobs that are similar in content. For example, to differentiate between and among plant managers and production supervisors, one can rather quickly develop measures of size (how much is produced of what) and of complexity (the nature of the tasks performed by subordinates) that will sort the positions into a ranking that is perceived as being appropriate by all concerned. It is much more difficult to develop scales that will properly rank a mixed group of production supervisors, accountants, engineers, and personnel managers.

Type of Measurement

Another aspect in which job-evaluation systems differ is the type of measurement they employ. Job-evaluation systems all fall into two broad categories: qualitative and quantitative. The qualitative systems are easier to use but are limited in precision. Quantitative systems can be either point-factor systems or factor-comparison systems. Point-factor systems have a series of predefined levels on each compensable factor. Each level of each factor is associated with a point value. Factor-comparison systems compare jobs one to another on a variety of compensable factors. While factor-comparison systems often provide rudimentary guides to the meaning of the different levels, the organization essentially expresses its value system by its placement of jobs on each factor. Where the slipping of jobs from one level to another is usually a source of error in a point-factor system, it is precisely this that is the essence of a factor-comparison system—the inherently subjective nature of all human judgment is structured and is employed as part of the evaluation process. The various approaches to job evaluation and their relative strengths and limitations are developed in Chapter 6, "Job-Evaluation Technology."

Scaling

Yet another difference among formal job-evaluation systems is in the rigor of their measurement. The process of scaling human judgments, referred to as psychophysics, has been studied extensively by psychologists. One would never know that psychophysical research existed from looking at some job-evaluation approaches that violate concepts of equal-appearing intervals yet treat the results as if the intervals were equal, and so forth. Both point-factor and factor-comparison systems need to be properly scaled, although the effect of improper scaling is greater in point-factor systems.

The Job-Evaluation Process

No off the shelf job-evaluation system can match the value system of all organizations, so many organizations elect to develop their own custom system, selecting the compensable factors and developing their scaling and weighting. If one has the resources (lots of knowledgeable staff and/or plenty of money for consultants), such an approach can result in a job-evaluation system that fits the organization's values very closely. The price to pay for any unique expression of an organization's values, however, is that the evaluation process becomes very time-consuming. If one wishes to have an evaluation system that expresses the organization's unique value system, it is necessary first to articulate a formal statement of the organization's values and then to develop a logical and consistent way to represent those values via the evaluations. Because of this, many organizations prefer to select a job-evaluation system that is structured around a system that mirrors the values held by a broad cross section of organizations.

Understanding the Job

This first step in any job-evaluation process is job understanding. The use of a formal job-evaluation system amplifies the need for comprehensive understanding of all the relevant aspects of the job, since each position must be similarly analyzed and compared versus the measurement instrument. Since job evaluation exists not for its own sake but rather as a guide in compensation decisions, there is also a need for record keeping. As in any other financial process, it is highly desirable to have a good audit trail. The combination of the need for increased job understanding and an audit trail results in the adoption of formal processes for studying jobs (job analysis) and of recording the bases for job evaluation (job documentation). The issues associated with these topics are discussed in detail in Chapter 5, "Job Analysis and Documentation."

Compiling Information

As was suggested above, job evaluation exists only to improve compensation decisions. Since information is power, the most powerful means to improve compensation decisions is to gain good information. In today's world this is typically accomplished via the use of formal compensation surveys, the topic of Chapter 7. However well they are executed, salary surveys provide only data, not information. To become information, the data that comes from the survey on the pay practices of others must be interpreted in terms of each individual organization's needs and desires.

The best compensation decisions result from the simultaneous translation of both job-evaluation results and survey data into a salary policy based on the organization's compensation strategy. An effective compensation strategy must include questions of mix (the relative amounts of base salary, short- and long-term incentives, and benefits and perks at various job levels) as well as the issue of the level of competitiveness (how high to pay as compared with the outside world). While questions of mix are outside the scope of this section, the determination of a base-salary posture is the subject of Chapter 8, "Pricing and the Development of Salary Structures."

Budgeting

Even after the jobs have all been analyzed, documented, and evaluated and the salary survey results have been translated into a salary structure, the task is not yet over. The resulting salary levels for each position must be budgeted for, the application of compensation policies and procedures by the various users (managers) must be audited, and controls must be implemented to protect the fiscal integrity of the organization. This is no small task, and the advent of the computer has helped significantly. Chapter 9 looks at how several of today's leading organizations go about the process of developing and administering budget, audit, and control systems for salary administration. The determination of a salary budget, like all budgeting, is a prospective exercise. That is, one sits down in advance of the start of the year and forecasts how much one is going to spend in total, and then one allocates that amount in accordance with compensation policies. Typically, the salary budget drives various salary-increase mechanisms (merit guidelines, general increases, and so forth) that determine the spending plan.

If the financial results during the year fall significantly short of expectations, the spending plan may be changed at midyear. This usually results in internal inequities between those who got increases under the initial plan and those who get increases under the reduced plan. If the financial results during the year significantly exceed expectations, the salary budget for the following year may be increased. (In union situations, there is often considerable pressure to do just this following a good year.) In today's rapidly changing world, organizations find it ever more difficult to predict the future accurately. It is this increasing level of uncertainty about what next year will bring as well as a desire to improve employee involvement in business results that has led to the widespread use of contingent (incentive) compensation, the subject of Part 3 of this handbook. However, it is possible to have a contingent base-salary program even without the use of one of the techniques discussed in Part 3.

A contingent approach would begin just as the typical prospective-salary budgeting process does. There would be a forecast of the upcoming year's business results and of the most appropriate salary budget in light of both the expected business results (what the organization can afford to do) and the interpretation of survey results within the framework of the organization's compensation strategy (what the organization would like to do). Based on this process, a salary-budget estimate would be prepared, just as it is typically done today. However, at this point the contingent approach would diverge from today's norm. The contingent approach would reduce the targeted amount (that developed by the above-described budgeting process) by about one-third, developing the salary-increase mechanisms based on this reduced amount. The communications to employees and to managers about the new year's salary-increase program would identify the targeted amount as well as the reduced amount. These communications would stress that the targeted amount is what the organization would like to do for its employees but that the reduced amount is all that the organization is sure it can afford. These communications would also stress that the organization will retroactively adjust the increases granted based on actual business results for the upcoming year. If the organization achieves the results on which the targeted amount was budgeted, the difference will be allocated proportionately to employees based on the increases they received under the reduced program. Should the organization's results exceed the amount on which the target increases were based, the total increase budget would be greater than the targeted amount. Whether the organization's increase program is based on merit, tenure, position in the salary range, or some combination of factors, all the aspects of differential reward are preserved by making the additional amounts granted proportional to the amounts given out under the reduced program.

For example, assume that the targeted amount was a 6 percent increase in budget, with the reduced amount being 4 percent. All increases would be granted via mechanisms designed to spend 4 percent. If the organization achieved its business targets, each employee would receive at the end of the business year a second salary increase equal to 50 percent of the increase they had received through the standard increase program. These amounts could be paid in a lump sum and would reflect the time between the date of the original increase and the date of the end-of-the-year award. This approach will work whether either or both the standard increase program or the year-end program adds to permanent base-salary levels or is only onetime lump-sum amounts. This approach offers significant advantages to the organization. In addition to virtually eliminating the risk of either spending more than is affordable or of having to change in midyear and create inequities, the delay in awarding part of the merit increase until the end of the year has a cash flow advantage. This approach involves a limited type of both profit and risk sharing for employees. It is neither as leveraged nor as potentially powerful a motivational force as the programs described in Part 3, but it is simple to administer and easy for employees to understand. It represents a step up from the traditional, noncontingent approach to salary budgeting and might be used as a first step in preparing the culture for more sophisticated contingent approaches.

Effective budgeting and salary administration will better realign compensation costs with affordability. Chapters 10 and 11 focus on the implications of managing compensation programs in line with organizational goals.

5
Job Analysis and Documentation

Norman R. Lange
Managing Director, Job Measurement Practice
Hay Group Inc.

Job analysis is the term used to describe the series of activities undertaken to systematically obtain, categorize, and document all relevant information about a specific job. (The important word here is *systematically* since the objectives of the analysis must be clearly related to the process used.) Jobs don't exist in a vacuum. Job analysis is really part of an extended communication process, between a jobholder and his or her organization, that articulates a series of mutual expectations. It describes a particular job context in order to clarify perceptions, and when properly done, the analysis should provide an understanding of the job, the outcomes of acceptable performance by the jobholder, as well as the skills and abilities required to produce those results. There are several reasons for doing job analysis. First, managers should know their organization, jobs, and employees. Job analysis contributes to a clear understanding of job responsibilities, required employee skills, and competencies thereby enabling a manager to make the most appropriate work assignments, identify training needs, and achieve unit objectives.

Second, most processes of job measurement rely on summary information derived from job analysis, usually provided as job descriptions, questionnaires, or written commentary about the nature and scope of job activities. Some estimates suggest that over 90 percent of job analysis is done for job measurement purposes. The information gained from the measurement process may also be used for salary administration, job classification, or reclassification studies.

Third, determining what jobholders currently do in their present jobs is the necessary first step in understanding how duties and whole jobs can be realigned or eliminated or job content enhanced. The job-analysis process is the basis for determining the kinds of information to be collected and documented. Most importantly, job analysis creates an understanding of the relationships and hierarchies within an organization.

Fourth, recruitment and staffing activities within companies rely on job-analysis processes for information about the nature and content of the jobs involved as well as information about jobholder requirements for education, training, and experience. This information may also be required by trainers or course developers in establishing training and development programs for employee groups or functional specialties.

Fifth, managers and supervisors often utilize job descriptions or summary documents about job duties as the starting point for discussions with employees about current plans and objectives and performance measures. The job-analysis process establishes the kinds of information that would have to be collected and how such information should be presented to facilitate the performance planning and review applications.

Sixth, federal regulations against discriminatory employment practices now require employers to validate their actions in those areas with accurate job and employment information. Meeting the requirements of the Fair Labor Standards Act on exempt and nonexempt classification requires supporting job-analysis information. Issues and controversies over equal pay, comparable worth, and age discrimination issues and controversies can only be resolved with accurate job information and documentation.

Few would agree that job analysis, as practiced today, regularly provides the right kind of information. Too much, as well as inappropriate or irrelevant, information is being collected by those involved in the process. Users of this information, including managers, human-resources professionals, even prospective jobholders, are not likely to gain an understanding of actual job content based on a review of today's job documentation. The objectives of the job-analysis process (for example, performance appraisal, training, job evaluations) must be clearly articulated before the methods to be used can be determined. Too often, decisions about the kinds of information to be collected are made on the basis of immediate need. Too little thought is given to other needs which will affect the usefulness of the undertaking over the long term.

Because of pressures to operate with smaller staffs, organizations are increasingly relying on jobholders and supervisors to perform the job-analysis tasks and no longer relying on skilled job analysts. Without the benefit of training or proper instruction, these individuals do not consistently provide pertinent, current, and workable data, or they may furnish far more data than is necessary. Because of natural concerns about the consequences of excluding important information, they tend to include information about everything done on the job. Conversely, because of lack of understanding of either what constitutes key job content or of the purposes and uses of the job description, they disclose little or no information. The design of the data-collection process or instrument should take these factors into account. Tightly drawn questionnaires, in some cases, may be better than descriptions which rely on prose and writing skills.

Job analysis is a labor-intensive activity that makes demands on jobholders, supervisors, managers, and human-resources professionals. It is an intrusive process that inquires into what people do in their jobs, how their jobs interact with other jobs, the nature of their supervision, and so forth. It may provoke anxiety because of uncertainty about management's intentions, thereby undermining the very basis of trust that management is trying to create. It requires time to determine what information is to be collected, processed, analyzed, and documented. It is focused on an intangible thing called a "job," functioning in a dynamic, constantly changing environment called "the workplace." The information collected often has a limited useful life. Even if the job is considered stable and unchanging, it is usually necessary to verify that a year or more later when questions arise about the job.

Preparing for the Job-Analysis Program

Developing Criteria

The first step in preparing for a program of job analysis is the development of design criteria to provide guidelines for planning and decision making. Criteria serve as standards to check against, regardless of what the objective of the job-analysis program may ultimately be. The following are appropriate criteria:

Credibility. Will the process be viewed credibly by the various employee groups affected? Does the process require direct employee intervention and participation, or is job information best obtained from supervisory personnel? Is there a preexisting condition of employee suspicion about the proposed program? Is this viewed as just another human-resources department project that management does not totally support and endorse?

Timing.   Is there a best time to undertake this job-analysis program? Is the organizational area already undergoing extensive and perhaps unsettling change? Are jobs newly designed or evolving, or is structure constantly changing? Have conditions stabilized?

Cost-Effectiveness.   Are there economic constraints that restrict the choice of approaches to the job-analysis program? These might occur when computer aids, which require software development or the purchase of software packages, are being considered or when use of contract employees or consultants is being considered for data collection or documentation activities. Does the proposed approach seem to be the most cost-effective way of doing this particular project?

Reliability.   Does the proposed process capture the information required to meet the purpose of the program? Does the proposed program include the necessary safeguards to ensure that the results are replicable? Is the methodology being proposed going to produce comparable results the next time it is done?

Sustainability.   Are the outcomes of the process, whether they are documented products, such as job descriptions, questionnaires, or duty lists, easily maintained? Are they prepared by experts whose skills are not easily replicated in the organization or available to maintain the documentation? What process will be used to check the current accuracy or validity of the documentation?

System Compatibility.   Should the job-analysis process be linked to other existing human-resources information systems? Should it be structured as a stand-alone module or as part of a system that helps to maintain and ensure that it remains current?

Understanding the Organizational Context

The second step in preparing for the job-analysis program is understanding the organizational context of jobs to be studied. Too often, job-analysis projects become focused on the immediate objectives of identifying and acquiring the kinds of information needed to meet project activities, and they lose sight of the fact that jobs operate within an organization that significantly controls and shapes all aspects of the job's life. Jobs do not exist in a vacuum, and incumbents cannot just "do their thing." Jobs have a purpose, and jobholders are expected to achieve results. Jobs are grouped into work units, clusters, or teams for communication, support, coordination, or symbiosis. The grouping usually has a clear rationale and may be based on functional similarity, skills, hierarchies, common objectives, and so forth. Quality circles are examples of recent efforts at rationalizing the structure of work groups. It is particularly necessary to gain an understanding of these aspects of the organization if the job-analysis effort is to have validity.

If one observes the behavior of external consultants who have been asked to undertake a job-analysis program, their work usually begins with fact-finding and data gathering about the organization. The consultants frequently interview senior executives to gain an understanding of the overall enterprise philosophy and the strategic goals and objectives of the corporation, its important functions, and its business units. These interviews become a diagnostic tool for understanding how the job-analysis process is influenced by many factors, such as an organization's stage in its life cycle; the structure and management process; compensation philosophy and practice; culture, values, and attitudes; and employee groupings.

An organization that is new and emerging in its life cycle presents a different set of conditions for job analysis than does an organization that is mature with well-established jobs and structure. Jobs in the new organization are constantly evolving, structure is fluid, new incumbents are regularly being added and influencing the nature of jobs, and incumbents are frequently used on an ad hoc basis in which their skills are most needed at the moment. The risks are that information gathered today will not be appropriate tomorrow.

An organization that is centralized and particularly focused on managerial integration and control presents different conditions than a decentralized organization. Some analysts have found that it is useful to spread functional information about the organization (as shown on Table 5-1, "Fields of Management") to gain an understanding of the organization. This information identifies major activity areas, their functional elements and subfunctions, and, ultimately, work sections or groups.

An organization that administers compensation conservatively, restricts movement within salary ranges but provides promotional increases, or responds to apparent job change or enhancement may tax the resources of the job analysis and challenge the process. Employees may have learned that to "beat the system," job descriptions should be rewritten and embellished in order to justify review.

Table 5-1. Fields of Management

	Activity areas basic to getting the work done				Activity areas that influence the working environment		
			Activity Areas				
	Research & development: Designing the product or service	Production: Making the product or performing the service	Marketing: Selling the product or service	Financing & control: Handling financial matters and controlling costs and profitability	Personnel administration	External relations	Secretarial & legal
Functions	1. • Research 2. • Development 3. • Product engineering	1. • Plant engineering 2. • Industrial engineering 3. • Purchasing 4. • Production planning & control 5. • Manufacturing 6. • Quality control	1. • Marketing research 2. • Advertising 3. • Sales promotion 4. • Sales planning 5. • Sales operation 6. • Physical distribution	1. • Finance 2. • Control	1. • Employment 2. • Wage & salary administration 3. • Industrial relations 4. • Organization plan & development 5. • Employee services	1. • Communications and information 2. • Public activities coordination	1. • Secretarial 2. • Legal
Subfunctions	1. • Basic research • Applied research • Advanced development • New product development & product improvement • New process development & process improvement	1. • Utilities design & operation • Facilities design & specification • Maintenance • Plant equipment control 2. • Methods study • Plant layout • Work measurement • Materials handling • T-l-f-Ptn manufacturing & repair study 3. • Buying • Purchase expediting • Purchase records & files • Purchase research • Salvage sales	1. • Market analysis • Product requirement determination • Distribution problems analysis • Campaign planning • Copy preparation • Media selection • Production 3. • Program development	1. • Financial planning • Tax management • Financial relations • Custody of funds • Credit and collections • Insurance 2. • General accounting • Cost accounting • Planning and budgeting	1. • Recruitment • Selection • Indoctrination • Promotion & transfer • Separation 2. • Employee classification • Rate determination • Merit ratings • Supplemental compensation • Work-schedule control	1. • Attitude & opinion appraisal • Employee information exchanges • Creditor & investor communications • Public communications	1. • Stockholder affairs • Board of directors affairs • Corporate affairs

Table 5-1. Fields of Management (Continued)

Activity areas basic to getting the work done		Activity areas that influence the working environment	
	Subfunctions		
• Product redevelopment for cost reduction 3. • Product design • Engineering test • Factory follow-up • Sales assistance 4. • Traffic • Factory receiving • Factory shipping • Materials procurement • Operation scheduling • T-C-F-Gage procurement • Production instruction distribution • Dispatching • Production expediting • Performance reporting • Storekeeping • Stores control 5. • Part manufacture • Subassembly • Final assembly • Service & repair 6. • Control methods development • Gage control • Inspection & test • Customer complaints • Salvage	• Sales aids 4. • Sales-policies determination • Budgeting • Pricing • Buying • Packaging 5. • Salesperson procurement • Salesperson training • Salesperson direction • Salesperson compensation • Order service • Selling 6. • Warehousing • Shipping • Product service • Internal auditing • Systems and procedures	3. • Communications • Collective bargaining • Employee discipline • Personnel research 4. • Organizational planning • Employee development • Training 5. • Medical services • Recreation • Personal services • Safety • Protection & security 2. • Civic affairs participation • Association & society relations	2. • Corporate affairs • Employee affairs • Financial affairs • Patent affairs

NOTE: The foregoing groupings are typical for a manufacturing industry. The level, location, and importance of functions may vary with industries and specific companies.

Activity Area: A group of specialized management functions that, because of common objectives, common skill requirements, or merely tradition, are usually directed by a member of top management with specialized knowledge of and experience and training in that area.

Function: A more or less arbitrary subdivision of the total activity area, which, when the size or nature of the business justifies it, can best be performed by a specialist.

Subfunction: A more or less arbitrary subdivision of a function.

55

The culture and values that characterize an organization should be considered in the job-analysis process, particularly concerning the sources of information to be tapped. Should employees be asked to directly participate in the data-collection process by writing their own descriptions, giving interviews, or completing questionnaires? Is this an organization characterized by loyalty, trust, and security or by highly competitive employee groups, distrust, poor communication, and low morale? What processes should be instituted to verify or validate job-content claims?

Consideration should also be given to the nature of jobs within the classes of jobs being studied. There are observable differences in content, responsibilities, and controls among production jobs, service jobs, and clerical support jobs. These may be different in technician jobs and exempt jobs, such as accountants, engineers, and planners. Management job content differs noticeably by job level and designated responsibility. Supervisors, middle managers, senior executives, and corporate officers have jobs whose characteristics are sufficiently different and may warrant different modes of data collection, analysis, and documentation.

Jobs with multiple incumbents present different job-analysis considerations than single-incumbent jobs. Should data be collected from each employee? How should differences in information be processed? Should generic approaches be considered? Jobs within a job family in which incumbents progress through different classification levels based on skill differences or maturity differences present separate issues for identification, collection, and documentation of job information.

Integrating Organizational Insights Into the Job-Analysis Process

The Job-Analysis Diagnostic Profile shown in Table 5-2 may prove useful as a model for displaying the insights gained about the organization. These insights, in turn, may suggest the type of conditions that may seriously hinder a program's success and that modifications are called for. Let us examine how this information can be organized and analyzed in order to provide the appropriate process and documentation solution. Consider the situation of Company A, a relatively young, fast-growing organization that the CEO wants to keep lean, flat, and responsive. He recognizes, however, that the organization has become sufficiently large and that he must rely more on management process than on personal intervention. He also believes that a more focused process of job analysis should be considered in order to create the basis for introducing a

Table 5-2. Job-Analysis Diagnostic Profile

Job-documentation diagnostic	Employee-completed questionnaire	Analyst-prepared questionnaire	Focus group	Analyst-prepared job description	Employee-prepared job description	Computer-assisted quantitative questionnaire
Stage in business cycle Growth	X					
Organizational structure Constantly changing	X					
Compensation practice Base salary only		X				
Value system Competitive		X				
Employee groups Only middle management (with 150 incumbents)		X				

more performance-oriented compensation practice among his middle management employee group.

When the data is arrayed on the Job-Analysis Diagnostic Profile, the most appropriate documentation approach becomes clearly evident.

Structuring the Job-Analysis Program

Establishing the objectives of the program is the first step in structuring the job-analysis program. Program objectives will dictate the kinds of data to be collected. If the purpose is to collect data in order to prepare job documentation to be used in a benchmark job-evaluation project, the job-evaluation method and compensable factors will determine the nature of the information needed. This includes information about or requirements for each of the compensable factors used in the plan or system. If the data is to be used in a benchmark job-evaluation project for all employee groups, data-collection processes must be geared to collect the data that is group-specific or key to job evaluation of those jobs. Executive and/or managerial jobs, for example, may be valued as a result of organizational positioning characteristics—positioning relative to the CEO or to a function head, comprehensiveness of functions managed, and special skills that are utilized. Company- or job-specific numeric data and scope data are important data elements.

Supervisory jobs generally are positioned to provide administrative and technical direction of work effort by professional, support, or hourly workers. To understand the supervisor's job, information must be collected about the nature and purpose of the work unit, its relationship to other work units within the same functional area, the special skills and composition of the members of the work unit, and the role served by the supervisor, for example, trainer, mentor, coordinator, discipliner, controller, and so forth.

To understand the job of individual contributors, one needs to understand the nature and purpose of the work unit of which they are an integral part, what the roles are, what products or outputs result from the work effort, and what special skills are required to do this work. Employees in this grouping would include exempt individual contributors, nonexempt clerical and support employees, and hourly paid craft, factory, service workers, and technicians.

Sources of Data

Direct Contacts With Workers.   There is normally an advantage to face-to-face meetings with the jobholders when collecting information about a job. Historically, this meant that data on factory jobs was best collected by observation of the jobholder at work. Factory jobs and many clerical jobs often consist of short-cycle tasks that are repeated over the course of a working shift and, therefore, permit the observer to see the full nature of the job.

Other jobs are more varied in the tasks performed, or some duties are performed irregularly. Direct observation is, therefore, less efficient as a process for collecting job information. Job incumbents can be taught how to prepare job documents, such as job descriptions, or how to most appropriately respond to the questions posed in a structured question-naire. The use of trained job analysts to interview job incumbents and prepare job descriptions or summary documents generally produces the highest-quality job documentation. It can, however, be expensive and disruptive to the organization if not handled through effective manage-ment and communication processes.

Many data-collection processes collect far more data than is required in the immediate application. This may be done as a precaution to min-imize return contacts with the jobholders. It may occur because of un-certainty about the relevance of some data, or because the collection of information was open-ended and permitted the job incumbent free li-cense to provide all information considered potentially useful. The risk of collecting all information, regardless of direct relevance, is that the jobholder might consider the final document deficient since it left out much of what was provided.

Supervisors.   Supervisors of jobholders are another source of informa-tion about the nature and content of jobs, because a supervisor is ex-pected to know what each jobholder does. The credibility of this ap-proach is dependent on employee review of and agreement with the content of the information.

Methods of Data Collection

Quantitative Methods.   These methods appear to be most often con-sidered by large employers with significant numbers of employees in job classifications, all requiring the collection, organization, and analysis of large amounts of data. There are a number of practical applications of the techniques being used in quantitative job analysis for smaller organizations, among them, the preparation of a document that may serve as a job description. One example of this application uses inventories of activity statements for a job family or function, such as marketing and sales. Job-holders select the prenumbered statements and record them on an activity inventory that also includes a number of other questions about education, experience, supervision, and so forth. The personal computer-oriented process then lists all the statements selected and prepares a summary document which lists the activities in order of importance. The supervisor's intervention in a review and approval process would still be required. This approach is also useful for determining the similarity of activities performed by employees within a given job title or job family in order to determine if there are job-classification or evaluation issues. Among the potential problems stemming from the inventory approach is the amount of data included in the final document. To guard against the output taking on the characteristics of a computer dump, the technique described earlier restricts the number of activities listed and requires the jobholder's judgment about each item's importance. Figure 5-1 shows examples of quantitive methods.

Qualitative Methods.   This term will be used for questionnaires and job descriptions prepared by job incumbents, supervisors, or job analysts that combine data collection with judgmental processes to distill, synthesize, or summarize information to enhance meaning and understanding.

Executive and/or Managerial Jobs.   Figure 5-2 shows an approach being used to collect appropriate organizational and job information for executive jobs. This device requires an understanding of the specific characteristics and content elements of a job (in this instance, the head of a function).

Individual-Contributor Jobs.   Figures 5-3 and 5-4 show a job family-specific questionnaire used to collect data, and a description document to enable job-evaluation ranking or comparison processes. This questionnaire is tailored to the characteristics of the jobs under study and would need modification for other families. Figure 5-4 is a job description that is analyst-prepared with commentary provided about the major compensable factors. The job content was obtained through analyst interviews and then summarized by a skilled job analyst. While this document could be subsequently updated by a job incumbent, experience has shown that a gradual deterioration in quality occurs over time.

Hourly and Clerical Jobs.   Figure 5-5 is representative of a job description prepared for a painter job. It shows the information pre-

ACTIVITY INVENTORY

NAME: _____ DATE: _____

JOB TITLE: _____

SOCIAL SECURITY NUMBER: _____ POSITION NUMBER: _____

DEPARTMENT: _____ LOCATION: _____

SUPERVISOR'S TITLE: _____

I. JOB SUMMARY: Briefly summarize the purpose of your job by completing the following:
   This job is responsible for:

II. PRINCIPAL ACTIVITIES: List the number for up to 25 of the most important activities of your job
   as described in the accompanying Job Activity Library. For each entry, indicate the typical
   responsibility you have in performing the activity and the importance of the activity relative
   to your other activities. "Direct Others" should be used only if you directly supervise an
   immediate subordinate in performing the activity.

ACTIVITY NUMBER	RESPONSIBILITY LEVEL (Circle one) a.Direct Others	b.Personally Perform	c.Both a. and b.		IMPORTANCE LEVEL (Circle one) 1.Important	2.Very Important	3.Critical
1.	a	b	c		1	2	3
2.	a	b	c		1	2	3
3.	a	b	c		1	2	3
4.	a	b	c		1	2	3
5.	a	b	c		1	2	3
6.	a	b	c		1	2	3
7.	a	b	c		1	2	3
8.	a	b	c		1	2	3
9.	a	b	c		1	2	3
10.	a	b	c		1	2	3
11.	a	b	c		1	2	3
12.	a	b	c		1	2	3
13.	a	b	c		1	2	3
14.	a	b	c		1	2	3
15.	a	b	c		1	2	3
16.	a	b	c		1	2	3
17.	a	b	c		1	2	3
18.	a	b	c		1	2	3
19.	a	b	c		1	2	3
20.	a	b	c		1	2	3
21.	a	b	c		1	2	3
22.	a	b	c		1	2	3
23.	a	b	c		1	2	3
24.	a	b	c		1	2	3
25.	a	b	c		1	2	3

(a)

Figure 5-1. (a) Quantitative method.

10000 Achieve sales goals for assigned products.

10001 Achieve sales goals for assigned services.

10002 Coordinate the design and implementation of advertising programs developed by an advertising agency.

10003 Identify technology needs, and recommend products to fill these needs.

10004 Analyze results of market tests.

10005 Prepare economic and sales forecasts.

10006 Approve print, radio, and/or television advertisements before release.

10007 Identify and select distribution channels.

10008 Analyze legislation impacting company products or marketing.

10009 Ensure effective deployment of sales force.

10010 Negotiate contracts with foreign sales representatives.

10011 Recruit and hire salespeople.

10012 Plan and implement warehousing and sales-distribution programs.

10013 Manage new product introductions.

10014 Develop and produce advertisements.

10015 Arrange transportation for customers or suppliers.

10016 Analyze the financial, engineering, and manufacturing implications of new product development.

10017 Negotiate contracts with foreign customers.

10018 Develop point of sales materials.

10019 Initiate modifications to existing products.

10020 Analyze market trends to determine profitable opportunities.

10021 Establish sales budgets and quotas.

10022 Establish and maintain contact with top management of important customers.

10023 Implement marketing plans for assigned product lines.

10024 Coordinate product distribution and availability with sales force and manufacturing.

Figure 5-1. (*b*) Quantitative method.

NAME: Pat R. Smith   DATE: 05/09/90

JOB TITLE: Supervisor, General Accounting

SOCIAL SECURITY NUMBER: 394-05-1972   POSITION NUMBER: 11111

DEPARTMENT: Accounting   LOCATION: Northwest

SUPERVISOR'S TITLE: Manager, Accounting Operations

Job Overview

This position is responsible for the preparation of all financial statements, the recording of all accounting transactions, and the conduct of accounting analyses to support management requests and comply with regulatory requirements.

Job Dimensions

This position supervises 8 exempt employee(s), 2 nonexempt employee(s), and manages a budget of $360,000.00.

Nature and Scope

This position would be competently filled by someone with a bachelor's degree and 3 to 5 years' experience.

Activities are subject to standard precedents and established practices; supervision is normally of completed tasks only.

This position manages multiple units, each with its own supervisor or manager, and is responsible ultimately for selection, training, discipline, salary changes, and other personnel actions within these units.

This position supervises the following positions:

Accounting Clerk I	1
Accounting Clerk II	1
Accountant I	1
Accountant II	1
Accountant III	1
Programmer I	1
Programmer II	1
Programmer III	1
Secretary I	1
Receptionist	1

Figure 5-1. *(c)* Quantitative method.

This position interacts frequently with other employees and with external individuals and groups.

This position works significantly with both employees in the immediate work group and with employees outside that group.

Major Activities	*Importance*
This position directs others in performing the following:	
Determine accounting treatment of company transactions.	3
Prepare monthly, quarterly, or annual financial reports for external reporting.	3
Maintain general and subsidiary ledgers.	3
Prepare SEC and other regulatory agency reports.	2
Conduct special accounting analyses and studies.	2
Prepare shareholder quarterly and annual reports.	2
Prepare monthly, quarterly, or annual financial and operating reports for management.	2
Verify cash and other assets, such as Accounts Receivable.	1
This position personally performs the following:	
Select, train, and motivate subordinate employees.	3
Develop and/or revise accounting procedures.	3
Prepare balance sheets and income statements for organization.	3
Direct and supervise the work activities of assigned unit or units.	3
Review and/or verify journal and ledger entries.	2
Decide on personnel actions for subordinates, including promotions, transfers, discipline, raises, etc.	2

Figure 5-1. (c) *Continued.*

```
                                        _____    _____
                                                Company Name              Code
                                        Date Completed: _____/_____/_____


                              Position Scope Form
                            Corporate Human Resources


Basic Function:    Corporate employment ☐, training ☐, labor relations policy ☐, labor negotiations ☐, compensa-
                   tion ☐, benefits ☐, EEO ☐, organization ☐, employee  planning ☐, management development ☐,
                   health ☐, safety ☐, OSHA ☐, international functions ☐.

Title: _____

Reports to: _____

Level in Organization: _____

Exclusions/Additions to Basic Function: Check if none ☐

Exclusions:    1. _____      3. _____

               2. _____      4. _____

Additions:     1. _____      3. _____

               2. _____      4. _____

Subordinates:
    Corporate Unit:   Exempt _____   Nonexempt _____

    Functional (Groups, Divisions, Plants):  Exempt _____   Nonexempt _____

Board Member:   Yes ☐    No ☐              Hard Core:   Yes ☐    No ☐

Board Committees:   Executive ☐,   Financial ☐,   Other ☐,   specify: _____

Top Management Committees: _____

_____

_____


Department Budget                         $ _____ million

Total Company Personnel Costs — Pay and Benefits    $ _____ million

Total Employees: U.S. _____  Overseas _____

Number of Union Contracts: _____

Data Effective Date _____
```

Figure 5-2. Method for executive and/or managerial position.

FIELD SYSTEMS ENGINEER SURVEY
POSITION CONCEPT QUESTIONNAIRE

NON MANAGEMENT

Company_____   Position Title __ Assistant Systems Engineer ____

Company Code _____   Survey Job Code _____ 026 _____

                                    Job Population Total _____ 92 _____

Hay Evaluation		Date Eval.
KH	EN2 175	
PS	D3(29) 50	
Acc	C2C 43	
Total	268	

                                    Active Entire Period   Pop. Total _____

I. TRAINING and EXPERIENCE

A. Formal Education Required ____ Technical degree from high-level college. _____

B. Nature, Content and Length of Training (Classroom, Self Pace, O.J.T.) Formal classroom plus OJT –
   13 months. Completion of formal and informal training process required for
   qualification as Associate SE.

C. Time in Position to Achieve Competence ____ 6 months _____

D. Typical Time in Position Before Promotion to Next Position 6-9 months _____

II. PRODUCT / PROCESS COMPLEXITY

A. Typical Hardware Utilized ___ All equipment of the DP division which is the 370 system
   including teleprocesing/telecommunications peripherals.

B. Typical Systems Applications Simple to very complex real time multi-program, virtual, etc.
   systems in OJT mode while at the same time providing support for customer systems
   applications.

C. Exposure to Leading Edge Applications None

D. Job/Skills Orientation (By Product, Market, Industry, Geography) Team member – customer-oriented.

III. CUSTOMER ACCOUNTABILITY

A. Level of Contact Customer operating/Systems/Programming personnel.

B. Interaction with Sales Function _____ Supports sales effort in systems applications as required.

C. Average Number of Assigned Accounts _____ None

D. Annual Account Revenue $ _____ None

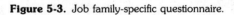

Figure 5-3. Job family-specific questionnaire.

Customer Accountability (Cont.)

E. For Account Growth

(Surveys, Feasibility Studies, Selection and Configuration, Proposal Preparation, Benchmarking and Demonstration). Prepares surveys, selection and configurations, benchmarks and demonstrations, and assists in proposals and customer presentations all under close supervision.

F. Product Installation

(Installation Planning and Management, Design, Programming and Coding, Problem Diagnosis, Customer Training). Assists higher level Systems Engineers in programming and detailing design of standard and complex systems. Performs billable services under close supervision.

IV. ORGANIZATIONAL RELATIONSHIPS
(Indicate Company Titles that Apply to Generics)

Generic 3rd Level Mgr.	Company Title Code

Generic 2nd Level Mgr.	Company Title Code

Generic 1st Level Mgr.	Company Title Code

Company Title

Trainee	Novice	Minimum Qualified	Fully Qualified	Senior	Professional
025	Assistant SE 026	125	225	325	425

V. LEADERSHIP ROLE:
(Project, Trainer, Scheduling, etc.) None

VI. OTHER COMMENTS: A combination job incorporating final formal training with beginning customer applications efforts.

Figure 5-3. *Continued.*

		JOB NUMBER: 289
POSITION TITLE: Chemist		DATE: 3/3/90
LOCATION: R&D Center	DEPT.: Vinyl	SECTION: Coatings Research
INCUMBENT: R. Thomas	APPROVED: FDR	ANALYST: Williams

Function: Under supervision of a Section Head, in Coatings Research, *conducts* investigational and experimental work for the development of new, or improvement of existing, coating and backing systems for vinyl products.

Know-How: This position is concerned with the development or improvement of coating formulations, and the technical aspects of their production and their application, in the manufacture of vinyl siding. The principal objective is to find means for reducing the number of coats required, for cost savings and increased equipment output, while maintaining or in providing product quality. The principal problems are to increase the percent of solids (by weight) per coat, maintain viscosity and "recovery rate" essential to processing, and retain necessary compatibility with characteristics of decorative coatings subsequently applied to the material. While this is currently the primary assignment of this position, other projects of a similar or equivalent nature are occasionally undertaken. The work is performed under guidance of the Section Head as to approaches to be taken, and with his or her specialized technical consultation and advice available on key aspects of the experiments and their evaluations. But the Chemist's assignments include the need for perceptive and critical evaluations of the reliability of existing experimental techniques and test methods and the ability to devise (or recommend) new or improved techniques as appropriate.

As intermittently requested, the position also provides technical assistance and advice to the production organization, such as color dispersion, roughness of backing applications, etc., and also in the writing of formal process specifications for paint production and application.

The position requires a thorough knowledge of organic chemistry, supplemented by specially oriented training in vinyl technology and also familiarity with the technical and practical aspects of the plant processes, and of the capabilities and limitations of the principal equipment utilized in the manufacture and application of coating and backing. Direction of the work of 2 technicians and plant contracts during factory test runs and/or investigation of production difficulties, require the ability to communicate instructions and/or advise clearly and effectively.

Figure 5-4. Analyst-prepared job description.

Principal activities include:

1. *Receives* assignments from Section Head; *contributes* suggestions on details of work to be done.

2. *Evaluates* components of present and potential formulations; *devises* and *specifies* new or modified formulations for experimental purposes; *directs* the making of experimental batches, and *observes* same as considered advisable; *makes* or *directs* evaluations and tests of same; *reformulates* for further experiments as need is indicated; *informs* Section Head of progress and/or problems, and *secures* advice as needed.

3. *Plans* and *writes* factory test requests; *observes* and *directs* technical aspects of running of tests; *evaluates* results; *reports* results and conclusions to Section Head and to Manager of the Section.

4. *Devises* and *recommends* new or improved techniques of experimentation and testing.

5. *Provides* technical assistance and advise on production and process problems as requested.

6. *Keeps abreast* of technical developments relating to assigned field of work through reading of appropriate technical literature and other available means.

Problem Solving: The problem solving of this position consists primarily of determining and planning the specific vinyl formulations for experimental purposes, achieving necessary "flow" properties and compatibility of systems so defined, and translating results of experiments into practical product formulation and processing terms.

Accountability: This position is accountable for applying a maximum degree of proficiency in developing new or modified formulations, and related processing techniques or methods, within assigned product area.

Key End Results:
1.
2.
3.
4.

Figure 5-4. *Continued.*

CLASSIFICATION NO._____

DEPT. NO._____

JOB TITLE__Painter_____

WORKS _____

DEPT. __Maintenance_____

Primary Functions of the Job

Prepare for and apply protective and decorative coatings to buildings, fixtures, and equipment.

Materials Used, Processed, and Handled

Various coatings, paints, stains, epoxies, and varnishes.

Paint removers, cleaners, solvents, and pigments.

Fillers, glazing, plaster, caulking compounds, preservatives, and insulating materials.

Sandpaper and steel wool.

Tools and Equipment Used

Hand tools common to the trade. Brushes, rollers, and spray equipment.

Scrapers, wire brushers, sanders, strippers, heating torches, steam cleaning, blasting equipment, drop cloths.

Putty knife, glass cutters, and caulking equipment.

Measuring equipment.

Ladders, scaffolding, block and tackle, cranes, trucks, and hoists.

Direction Exercised

Occasional.

Duties and Working Procedures

Prepare surface for coatings by scaling, scraping, brushing, burning, sanding, or blasting; and applying fillers, putty, primers, and caulking.

Apply all types of coatings and paints by brush, roller, or spray, including finishing and decorative work.

Determine material requirements.

Mix paints or other coatings for proper color and consistency.

Make or paint signs.

Apply and repair plaster.

Cut and install glass.

Use material-handling equipment in conjunction with assigned work.

Erect and disassemble scaffolding and rigging.

Figure 5-5. Job description.

sented, including materials used, tools and equipment, and so forth, in a brief and concise manner. This summary document usually also includes information that is factor-specific to the points used in the job-evaluation method.

Generic Questionnaires. Questionnaires that provide a common set of questions for all employee groups are used by a number of organizations. In practice, no employee group is well served by this approach, which is usually manually completed by employees, produces uneven answers, suffers from excessive length, requires review by supervisors for clarification and verification, and varies in its utility.

Summary

The processes of job analysis and documentation are being performed far less effectively today, partly because of problems in managing and organizing far more data about all aspects of our human resources. Yet, the need for an effective means of communication between the employee and his or her management is even greater. In an era of employee participation, the job document is implicitly a contract with management. Therefore, management must find an effective way to handle this key process. The computer increasingly has been made a part of the information system about employees, but to date it has not been effectively used to analyze and evaluate appropriate information. Management increasingly is reliant on the human resources professional to be more selective in the clarification and collection of job-relevant information, based on insights gained from more diagnostic and analytical approaches to the collection of job-content information.

6
Job-Evaluation Technology

Jill Kanin-Lovers

Vice President and Manager
Compensation Services
TPF&C, a Towers, Perrin Company

Is job evaluation simply a means to an end? Is it a way to create order out of confusion? Is it true that the technique you use to evaluate jobs is irrelevant because you will wind up with the same relative ranking anyway? The answers to these questions depend on you and your organization. You can approach job evaluation simply as an *administrative* tool. In this case, its only purpose is to develop a hierarchy, or ranking, of jobs to reflect their relative value to the organization. Having done this, the job-evaluation system has accomplished its function.

However, you can also use job evaluation as a management tool. If this is your goal, the process and the methodology employed become critical. The job-evaluation system should support management values and business objectives. A well-designed system can help build consensus, communicate corporate values, and manage payroll dollars. As with any personnel program, though, you get out of it only what you put into it.

Selecting a Job-Evaluation System

All job-evaluation systems rank positions based on one or more criteria. Plans differ in the criteria used, the method of evaluation, and the degree of reconciliation between internal worth and market value.

Because selecting a job-evaluation system is one of the most important decisions a human-resources manager can make, he or she must understand the differences among the various systems. Implementing a new job evaluation system is a costly proposition. Job evaluation can help bring an organization together, or it can create more political maneuvering than a presidential campaign. The effectiveness of any job-evaluation system depends largely on its acceptance by all those involved in and affected by the process. The system most likely to be accepted is the one that is carefully chosen to reflect the special needs and environment of the organization.

There is no such thing as a universal system, that is, one that is right for all companies. The factors to consider in determining the right job-evaluation system for your organization include:

- Company size
- Number and diversity of jobs to be included
- Company structure (for example, centralized, decentralized, or multiple locations)
- Business-cycle stage (for example, fast-growth phase or stable, mature phase)
- Industry characteristics (for example, types of employees, occupational groups, union or open shop)
- Short- and long-term strategic plans (for example, expansion, merger, or diversification)
- Values and culture
- Management style (for example, participatory or dictatorial)
- Employee expectations (internal equity or external competitiveness)
- Legal and regulatory environment
- Internal resources for implementation and system maintenance (for example, available staff and data processing systems)

Selecting the right system requires a thorough understanding of the organization and what it is trying to achieve through the job-evaluation process. The most practical and least complex plan that meets an organization's objectives is the one most likely to succeed. If chosen correctly, a job-evaluation system can serve as the mechanism that links the many elements of a successful pay program.

Job-Evaluation Systems

Traditional job-evaluation methodologies fall into two categories: quantitative and qualitative. Quantitative plans attach numeric values to the degree to which a job possesses a specific evaluation criterion. Qualitative plans can also consider specific job criteria, but positions are generally slotted or classified into a hierarchy without any specific documentation as to the extent to which a criterion determines final job value.

Many companies consider job evaluation such an important management tool that they customize a traditional system to ensure that it conforms to their needs. These hybrid plans, which combine the attributes of several traditional systems, are becoming much more common. If, however, a simple ranking is all that's required from job evaluation, customization may be unnecessary. In general, it's not a good idea to overengineer your system. Organizations that are fluid or are experiencing change will not tolerate inflexible systems for very long.

Market Ranking

Market ranking is probably the most straightforward of all job-evaluation systems. Positions are evaluated primarily in terms of their value in the marketplace. Selecting a suitable comparator group and judging your organization's relative position in the market represent the two key decisions.

You can determine a suitable comparator group by considering such criteria as:

- Company size
- Industry
- Geographic location
- Prestige
- Pay philosophy

For market ranking, jobs must be defined clearly and then matched against similar positions in the comparator group.

Human-resources managers can obtain data from one or more

sources. A customized survey of pay rates among a closely defined comparator group will yield the most precise results, but publicly available survey data or subscription-fee surveys can also be used. It is important to employ a consistent methodology to price the jobs so that the final ranking reflects a defined marketplace strategy rather than a hodge-podge of data sources.

Based on the survey data, the human-resources manager can determine salary rates or ranges in one of several ways, including:

- Simple market averaging
- Percentiles generated from the pay data to reflect the desired pay philosophy (for example, 60th percentile, 50th percentile)
- Adjusting market rates to account for differences in position due to company size or a position's scope and range of responsibilities
- Using single or multiple regression analysis to relate market data to such factors as position-related sales, number of employees supervised, and reporting level

Market-ranking plans are generally easy to implement. They do, however, require consistent, reliable market data and the ability to match with some degree of accuracy your organization's jobs to similar jobs elsewhere. The strength of the system is its direct market relatedness, but this can also be its greatest weakness. You must have access to high-quality market data that will be relatively stable over time and that truly reflect your organization's business situation. Temporary market conditions can affect internal consistency. The quality of the approach is dependent upon the amount of job responsibility or job-scope data provided by surveys to help refine the job matches. If you pick the wrong comparator group, survey source, or pay-policy target, you can wind up with skewed pay rates and, as a result, face either high turnover or excessive labor costs.

Furthermore, you must be careful in assessing female-dominated jobs under this method. Title VII permits the use of market data as a defense in pay discrimination suits; the Equal Pay Act does not. Although the courts have not interpreted each case in the same way, too much reliance on market data can result in claims of perpetuating existing pay discrimination. Using market data or "business necessity" as a defense may not work in sex-bias cases.

Market-ranking plans also have the advantage of being relatively easy to communicate to employees. They are comprehensible and let employees feel that they are being paid competitively. Because it is usually impossible to match every position in an organization to the marketplace, companies generally use market ranking in conjunction with some other system. Such an approach will enable you to account for internal differences that may make a position in your organization worth more or less than one at another organization, without appearing to manipulate the data.

Market ranking is most frequently used by smaller organizations and by any organization interested in evaluating a number of clearly defined top executive positions. It is the most commonly used approach for valuing or determining a CEO's base pay and that of his or her direct reports. The expense of implementing and maintaining a market-ranking system directly relates to the cost of obtaining quality survey data. Depending upon your definition of the market, this can be expensive or inexpensive.

Whole-Job Ranking

Many human-resources managers employ whole-job ranking along with market ranking for jobs that cannot be appropriately priced. Whole-job ranking determines the worth of a position by measuring its overall content against all other positions in the organization. You can use simple ranking or a paired-comparison technique to establish the hierarchy. In simple ranking, jobs are placed in a high-to-low continuum based on managers' judgments about the overall value of positions. Many organizations manage this process by putting the title of each job on a separate index card and then manipulating the cards to reflect ranking decisions.

Typically, management uses certain guidelines or criteria for assessing whole-job worth. These can include:

- Department size
- Job responsibility and/or complexity
- Necessary qualifications or skills
- Importance to the company

You can use paired comparisons to systematize the ranking process by comparing each position to every other position and scoring it "greater than," "equal to," or "less than." As with simple ranking, managers will generally make evaluations informally. Guidelines or criteria can also be provided. The scores are then analyzed or tallied (manually or by computer) to determine an overall high-to-low continuum or pyramid. This final hierarchy is reviewed against market data to establish an appropriate salary structure.

If whole-job ranking is used in conjunction with market ranking, you should slot unmatched jobs into the hierarchy developed from market data. Another alternative is to whole-job rank all positions first and then modify the rankings based on market input. Once again, you must monitor this process carefully to make sure that male- and female-dominated jobs are being treated consistently. If the relative ranking of male jobs is elevated due to market conditions, then female-dominated jobs should also be elevated, if the survey results show a similar discrepancy.

As jobs are assigned to the salary structure, whole-job ranking provides some degree of reconciliation between a position's internal worth and its external price. The ranking process, however, is subjective and, generally, undocumented. It is subject to criticism that job content or work-related dimensions are not adequately considered. Although it is relatively easy to administer, managers and employees may not readily understand or accept the results of the whole-job ranking process. Because the "magic" used to reconcile internal and external values can be difficult to explain, credibility can be an issue in implementing the system.

Despite its subjectivity, whole-job ranking has great appeal because it is simple to implement and administer. It can be an effective job-evaluation approach for small organizations and/or self-contained divisions or departments in which jobs are clearly defined and understood by the managers doing the ranking. It is also a good first step for organizations that have never had a formal job-evaluation system.

Classification

Classification systems begin with clearly defined job families, such as engineering, accounting, and secretarial. For each readily identifiable job family, you must prepare written classification charts that define the continuum of jobs in that career progression in terms of such elements as:

- Responsibility
- Typical duties
- Degree of decision making
- Supervision received and exercised
- Minimum entrance qualifications

Positions are then slotted or ranked relative to others in the same family and placed into the appropriate levels. You should customize the classification charts to reflect the specific dimensions of the job family in your organization. In fact, a number of organizations use classification charts such as mini job descriptions. Classification requires specific knowledge of the positions under study. Evaluations, therefore, are typically conducted in conjunction with function heads, with a final review by a management committee.

After classifying all positions, you can establish a salary structure by gathering market data for as many job families and levels as possible. Each career progression is assigned to the salary range that best matches the market rates for jobs slotted for or classified on that level. Through this process, the system treats each job family as a distinct hierarchical group.

One of the major advantages of classification is how closely it is linked to the market. Because of its flexibility, a classification system can respond quickly to external supply-and-demand fluctuations. Thus, you can easily adapt salary ranges and job-level placements to reflect sudden marketplace shifts without affecting the basic evaluation system. In a sense, classification provides the external pricing advantages of market ranking while imposing some structure based on job-family career progressions.

The system's external focus can help promote acceptance among employees and managers. Managers of clearly defined functional areas find this job-evaluation technique particularly appealing. Because the system is so functionally driven, it serves, in effect, as a separate tool for each clearly defined job family. Managers can feel that the jobs specific to their units are being evaluated separately.

However, the system's sensitivity to the marketplace also represents a serious disadvantage. Classification does not address the issue of internal equity among job families. Although the same salary structure can be used for all job families, there is no means of bridging among the classification assessments within the organization. The only bridge is the marketplace. This can be a significant drawback if delineations among certain occupational groups are unclear. In these situations, the resulting salary structure may be ambiguous and difficult to defend.

Classification depends heavily on having reliable market data for *all* job families. You must be able to price an adequate number of jobs at each career level to have confidence in their final placement within the salary structure. The federal government and some municipalities and state governments use classification systems. In the private sector, classification is most commonly used for secretarial and clerical jobs and for distinct occupational groups. If the system is to be used for the entire organization, it is best suited for midsize companies with clearly defined job families (that is, groups of jobs in which career ladders can be readily distinguished). These job families should be diverse and distinct. As classification is only concerned with the relative ranking of positions within a job family, intergroup or cross-career ladder comparisons should be a secondary issue for organizations selecting this method of traditional job evaluation.

Factor Comparison

Factor comparison is a relatively sophisticated evaluation technique that measures job content in terms of several specific factors. Although any well-defined factor can be used, this method typically employs four widely accepted compensable factors to compare jobs. They are:

- Skill
- Effort
- Responsibility
- Working conditions

Factor comparison involves ranking each job against every other job—with respect to each factor—to arrive at a hierarchy. Most companies accomplish this by focusing on a single job family, one factor at a time. Positions are clustered together based on the degree to which they possess particular job criteria relative to other jobs in the organization. For example, a given position might rank "4" in skill, "5" in effort, "3" in responsibility, and "2" in working conditions. The score depends on a relative comparison of this job against all others. To facilitate comparisons, you should identify benchmark or crossover jobs that can be used to compare positions across families. Another approach is simply to rank the jobs by factor and then cluster them together into "baskets" based on relative comparability or significant breaks in the data.

To ensure consistency, a number of benchmark positions are usually evaluated first, thereby creating a useful yardstick against which all other jobs can be compared. You should try to identify the top or bottom jobs and a group of midlevel positions to serve as the benchmarks. Other positions can then be evaluated based on their relationships to these jobs. Most companies do not attempt to define the criteria for each level (for example, how much effort is required to be a level 4 versus a level 5). Rather, the clustering of the jobs themselves becomes the yardstick against which other jobs are contrasted. In this sense, the application resembles whole-job ranking. As you evaluate each job by factor, you should involve line mangers who know about the relevant job relationships.

When all positions have been evaluated and clustered by level, the relative importance, or weight, of each factor is determined. You can do this subjectively, based on the organization's value system. For example, your organization may value skill and responsibility as the most important job criteria. Using your own judgment, these factors could be assigned a weight of 35 percent each, while effort is given a 20 percent weight, and working conditions a 10 percent weight. The appropriateness of these judgmental weights can be determined by reviewing the resulting job hierarchy to see whether it makes sense.

You can also calculate weights for each factor by correlating the relationship between unweighted evaluation results and market data. This process provides a link between internal equity and external competitiveness. Based on these factor weights, points are assigned to each ranking and total points are calculated for each job. This creates a job hierarchy within which jobs with comparable total point scores can be grouped into grades. Salary ranges are developed using the market rates of the jobs assigned to each grade.

Factor comparison enables you to rank jobs consistently across functional lines in terms of the compensable factors selected. It works for both exempt and nonexempt jobs. You should customize both the factors used to evaluate the jobs and the weights applied to those factors to reflect your organization's value system. Using market rates to weight the factors can provide a strong link to the competitive environment.

Because factor comparison takes into account internal equity and external competitiveness, it can be explained easily to employees. Communicating the compensable factors used to evaluate jobs should help to reinforce the organization's value system. Since this single approach applies to all jobs, regardless of level or function, it can also communicate a one-company philosophy. The link to the marketplace reinforces the company's commitment to be competitive in its pay practices. Employees may, however, have trouble understanding the subjective ranking process and the statistical weighting of the factors.

Organizations that have a large number of disparate jobs (more than 100) will have a hard time using factor comparison. Midsize, homogeneous companies usually find this job-evaluation system effective because it can measure job content across functional lines and is easier to implement and maintain than point-factor systems. Documentation can be difficult, however, because it usually involves a great deal of subjectivity.

Point-Factor

Point-factor job-evaluation systems use compensable factors and a scale of defined degrees within each factor to determine the relative value of jobs. Degree levels carry point values from low to high that reflect noticeable differences in how defined factors are present in any given job. Positions are evaluated with respect to each factor and assigned a degree (and eventually a corresponding point value). The job hierarchy is determined by totaling the assigned points for each factor.

Most point-factor plans contain between 3 and 7 distinct compensable factors, although some companies use as many as 15 factors in their job-evaluation systems. The number and type of factors will depend upon the jobs under study and the organization's value system. Ideally, each evaluation factor will represent an independent, measurable job-content requirement or characteristic that is present in varying degrees in all jobs. Each factor should be clearly defined, nondiscriminatory, and a measure of only *one* basic dimension of job worth, Regardless of the label, most plans include such factors as knowledge and skills, complexity and judgment, and responsibility. Contacts and working conditions are also commonly used factors.

As a rule of thumb, you should try to use as few factors as possible to adequately measure the job content of the range of positions to be evaluated. Additional factors may be needed for "face validity." For example, key line managers may not feel that the breadth of their positions can be captured using only three factors. Although statistically you may be able to account for 90 percent or more of the variations in job content with these three factors, politically you may need to add additional evaluation criteria. For face validity purposes, you may also need to add factors that overlap with other job criteria but need to be included because of a newly communicated value system. A factor like "intrapreneurialism" could fall into this category.

However, using as few factors as possible is advantageous because:

- Statistical analyses of various evaluation plans reveal that there are rarely more than five or six independent measures of job worth in any factor-based plan. Additional factors tend to be highly correlated with other factors, which means that you are measuring the same thing more than once.

- The time required to evaluate jobs relates directly to the number of factors used in the plan. Additional factors mean a greater time commitment and, therefore, greater expense in implementing and administering the program. If the factors are highly related to one another, it may also cloud the reason for differentiating among jobs.

- Most organizations do not usually apply equal weight to all factors. If a plan uses ten factors, then, on average, the overall weight of each factor would be 10 percent. If, however, the organization decided to emphasize the importance of a particular factor by raising its weight to 20 percent or 25 percent, for example, this would necessitate lowering the relative weights of other factors to insignificant levels. This makes the extra expense of maintaining a system with excessive factors difficult to justify.

Implementation of a point-factor plan depends on whether the plan is generic (that is, uses standard factors, degree descriptions, and point values) or customized (that is, uses individually selected factors, degree definitions, and factor weights). In a generic plan, positions are measured against each factor, assigned appropriate point values, and placed in an overall hierarchy based on their cumulative scores. This hierarchy is then reviewed against market data to establish an appropriate salary structure. An organization considering such a system must determine whether the generic factors are indeed relevant. By far, the most commonly used generic point-factor system is the Hay Guide Chart-Profile Method of Job Evaluation. It employs a number of dimensions that merge into three factors—know-how, problem solving, and accountability.

Because compensable factors vary from organization to organization, many companies choose to develop a customized plan. This can be a time-consuming process, but having a job-evaluation system that incorporates your organization's own value system can be well worth the effort. Designing a custom point-factor plan involves:

- Selecting the appropriate compensable factors that management considers relevant, credible, and valuable
- Defining factor degrees that are understandable and applicable to the range of jobs being evaluated
- Evaluating a series of benchmark positions using unweighted factors and degree definitions
- Determining factor weights and point progressions through regression analysis, management judgment, or a combination of the two
- Evaluating nonbenchmarks using the plan designed for the benchmark positions

Selecting and defining the compensable factors and degrees are the most critical steps in developing a customized point-factor plan. Interviews with top executives and senior management should help identify what the company values most, thereby permitting selection of compensable factors. These interviews should produce information on perceptions about the current job-evaluation method, the organization's value system, the criticality of skills and responsibilities, and future business plans. Such information will ensure that the factors selected represent management's current values and will support the organization in the foreseeable future. In this sense, it is a communications tool that tells employees what the company values. Interviews with senior management should also add credibility to the system and foster buy-in from the key players.

In addition to defining compensable factors, you must establish degree levels to cover the range of responsibility of jobs under study. The degree levels of each factor should:

- Be specific and applicable to the organization and positions evaluated
- Define or explain key terms using examples
- Be consistent in language and sentence structure, and reflect a clear progression in job worth (market value)

The number of levels necessary depends on the market-value range of the positions to be evaluated.

For added flexibility, a number of point-factor plans allow you to evaluate jobs that are between two clearly defined levels. This feature is often called "windows," "shadings," or "pulls." Language is not always as precise as job evaluators would like, and "plussing up" on a degree level can be an alternative to tightly defined degree levels. Shadings are sometimes introduced after the evaluation process has begun, when the committee or system users become frustrated because a level is missing.

Once all benchmark jobs have been assigned degree levels or placed into baskets according to the degree-level definition, you should determine point progressions and factor weights. Although this can be done judgmentally, the most precise way is to use regression analysis and market data. In this fashion, you can link internal equity and external competitiveness. The procedure involves:

- Developing a database for benchmark positions, including a market pay rate and the factor-level ratings
- Reviewing factor correlations to determine potential overlap
- Developing single regressions for each factor, using market data as

the dependent variable and the degree levels as the independent variable

- Identifying the best fit by looking at a constant change between levels and the market, an increasing rate of change between levels and the market, and a decreasing rate of change between levels and the market
- Converting degree levels to points, using the resulting equation from the best curve
- Using multiple regression analysis to weight factors against the market, thus determining the most significant factors and minimizing the overlap in what the factors are measuring
- Reviewing results and modifying them, if necessary, based on conceptual judgment

The point-factor method is considered the most rigorous and quantitative of all traditional job-evaluation techniques. Because it appears to minimize subjectivity, it has become the most frequently used formal plan. Point-factor provides a detailed systematic approach for comparing positions against criteria that the organization has identified as appropriate measures of job value. It enables organizations to compare jobs across functional areas and, if so designed, can include all levels of jobs (exempt and nonexempt) under the same umbrella.

The point-factor approach seems most appropriate for midsize and large organizations. It is especially suitable when there is a broad range of positions (staff, line, and specialist jobs) and when the sheer number of jobs requires specific guidelines, as provided by factor-degree definitions for accurate comparisons. Organizations with numerous jobs that are difficult to price externally also prefer point-factor systems.

Even if point progressions and factor weights are customized based upon market data, point-factor job evaluation retains a very strong internal focus. Because of this, it may be inappropriate for organizations or jobs that must respond quickly to unusual or frequently changing market conditions. Point-factor may also be unnecessarily complex for small, fast-growth companies. It requires a greater expense and time commitment for implementation and administration than any other of the traditional job-evaluation methods.

Other Considerations

If job evaluation is to be more than just a way to slot jobs into a salary structure, it cannot stand alone. Support systems are essential to the success of your job-evaluation system. These systems include:

Management Buy-In

All job-evaluation systems require the backing of senior management. Although we discussed management interviews only as part of a design for a point-factor plan, they can facilitate the implementation and ongoing administration of any system. For example, in market ranking, top management can play a major role in selecting the appropriate comparator group. In whole-job ranking or factor comparison, interviews with senior management can help identify the most relevant criteria to use in ranking positions.

Evaluation Committees

Job-evaluation committees are most frequently used in conjunction with point-factor systems. They can, however, be used with any of the traditional job-evaluation approaches. Such committees provide a valuable service irrespective of the job-evaluation system adopted. Job-evaluation committees broaden the input and the buy-in you receive. They help build consensus and ensure consistency over time. Because committee members function as a team in evaluating jobs and establishing guidelines and protocols, replacing individual members should not significantly affect evaluation results.

Using a job-evaluation committee or review team that includes line representation expands the program beyond the boundaries of the human-resources department. (Some organizations put employee representatives on the committee too.) This frees the human-resources department from the role of police officer for the program and allows it to function as part of a management or organization team that has established consensus on the criteria for determining job values. The advantages of using a job-evaluation committee are not limited to the initial implementation process. The committee can have an ongoing role in evaluating new jobs and in serving as an appeals court if employees challenge their job rankings. The committee can also monitor the consistency of the program over time by participating in system audits.

Documentation

A method should be established to document implementation and administration of the job-evaluation system. An audit trail provides guidelines for future evaluations and can be used as protection against discrimination suits. Documentation should include:

- A description of the evaluation criteria

- An annotation of the decisions made when evaluating specific jobs
- An explanation of any refinements or modifications (for example, adding new factor levels in an existing point-factor plan)

Keeping records of this type will enable you to go back and trace the decision-making process. This can be a valuable tool if the ranking of a job is questioned.

Appeals Procedure

No system is perfect. Therefore, you need some procedure for reviewing plan results. Employees and managers should feel that the system is flexible enough to deal with possible changes in job content or in the marketplace. Establishing a procedure up front can minimize pain and suffering down the road. Policies and procedures should also be set up for valuing new jobs and auditing the program.

Conclusion

Job evaluation is not a science. Although some systems are more quantitative than others, job evaluation should be viewed as a management process. It ranks positions in an organization based on one or more selected criteria. Job evaluation also tells employees, either formally or informally, what the organization wants to pay for. Use the opportunity to reinforce the message you want to give.

7

Compensation Surveys

D. Terence Lichty

Director, Research and Development
Cole Surveys, a Wyatt Data Services Company

Information sharing—surveys—provides data that can be a cornerstone of your compensation communications efforts. Through participation in and competent analysis of good surveys, your organization can be ensured solid information that will develop credibility, not only with those whose pay is being administered but also with the management who has to foot the bill.

Pay Environment

Compensation surveys are typically designed to examine the external pay levels of positions in a given industry or geographic sector. In fact, recent scholastic enterprises have shown that market-compensation surveys carry more weight in pay-scale determination than do organizationally sensitive job-evaluation schemes. Salary-range midpoints or ranges may also be studied to provide a broader look into an organization's pay policy for a given job.

The Legal Question of Information Sharing

Many people are reasonably concerned with the legality of passing around salary information. You have probably heard of class action suits—such as the *Nine-to-Five* organization v. the *Boston Survey Group*, a coalition of large-area employers—brought for potential area "wage setting" in violation of antitrust laws. In fact, salary surveys are not inherently illegal: even the United States government conducts area wage surveys. Limited information sharing, such as telling a neighboring company what your company's average wages are for a single position, may seem innocent. However, sharing substantial amounts of information directly with competitors and making decisions based on that data can present problems. Whether true or not, using another company's specific compensation data to establish salary levels can be perceived as wage setting. For this reason, one of the safest and often most efficient ways to obtain survey data is through a disinterested third party—such as a trade organization, consultant, or survey company—thereby preserving the individual participants' data confidentiality.

Survey Purposes

In formulating and administering your pay structure, you have several goals: Avoid inappropriate pay expenses—paying too much (or too little) to too many (or too few); be aware of what the bigger (or smaller) organizations are doing, as well as those of your own size in your own part of the country; and keep on top of line-managers' interests in their particular areas or lines of business. To assist you in meeting those goals, salary surveys should:

1. Help shape and increase the accuracy of management pay decisions.
   a. Develop market data from which to make and support individual practice and broad-based salary policy recommendations; and
   b. Develop information on other, broader human resources and operating data for decision making.
2. Give you timely, needed answers to questions about competitive rates.
   a. Respond to inquiries from management about appropriateness of pay; and
   b. Respond to outside inquiries from professional sources and counterparts.

3. Provide continuity and consistency of information.

4. Provide a vehicle with which to define and communicate what market and what pay is being compared (for example, base salary only, commissions and other variable pay, total cash compensation, or other combinations, including long-term incentives, perquisites, and benefits).

Defining the Pay Market

The basic idea behind compensation surveys is to answer this question: What is the market paying? A fundamental starting point, critical to sound management decision making, is answering this question for your organization: What is the competitive labor market for this particular group of positions? Certain complexities can cloud the market picture. For example, most medium and large companies don't have one market but several—exempt and nonexempt; local, regional, national, international; functional and/or line-of-business markets; and so forth. Also, some organizations may *think* their market is limited to the company down the street and the bank on the corner. But, whatever your circumstances, define comprehensive markets *before* developing salary structures, and keep abreast of market-data sources and market changes to keep your program current.

Once the market has been defined, the next questions are: What data should I compare? Should I only compare base salary levels or also examine total compensation? What about looking at competitors' midpoint structures or comparing our midpoints to their base salaries? The answers are: Compare everything, show how your organization stands up in each instance, and draw your primary comparisons to complement your organization's business plans and objectives.

Survey Techniques

Several survey techniques exist. *Telephone surveys*, though generally not the most accurate or sophisticated, are probably the most prevalent form of surveying today. In the compensation departments of large companies, rarely a week goes by without another company calling and asking what a particular job is being paid. Often this type of study is of the "short-fuse" variety and is used to support an out-of-the-ordinary, imminent hiring decision. While the personal touch can be helpful in gathering information quickly, telephone surveys often yield marginal results, forfeiting quality for immediacy; questions are likely to be inconsistently phrased, and answers are likely to be inaccurate. Don't forget that while answers to your questions are important to you, they are rarely of any interest to the person at the other end of the line. In addition, calls often interrupt whatever the person was working on when you called. The data you seek may not be readily available, and you may be getting a "best-guess" response rather than one that is studied and researched.

A second survey technique involves a *mailed questionnaire*. This approach is often used by trade associations, personnel consultants, and survey companies to maximize the size of their databases in a given information area. Compared to the telephone survey, this method achieves far more consistent results, though rarely is this vehicle capable of providing a quick turnaround answer. The mailed questionnaire can be particularly effective when used in conjunction with telephone surveys and/or personal interviews. To solicit participation and show the extent of data required, the questionnaire is mailed to the potential respondent. The survey questionnaire serves as a recording instrument, increases the chances of collecting consistent data, and gives the prospective respondent the opportunity to complete it at his or her convenience. At a specified time, data is returned to you or you contact the participant, who has had time to complete the survey. The data can be collected and qualified over the phone or in person.

Personal interviews provide, perhaps, the best opportunity to obtain accurate survey data. During an on-site visit, the surveyor can probe for qualifying or disqualifying information on position comparability, check the appropriateness of components being collected, and even alter the focus of survey questions and data being sought. The time and travel expense for the surveying company and for the companies whose data is being solicited is a limitation with this survey approach. But for insight into the broader environment and for clarification of finer points (as opposed to just the numbers), the personal interview gives the best results.

Survey Scope

The scope of surveys varies significantly. Many are limited to average salary information on a single job. Others, such as job-family and line-of-business surveys, may include more data on a given position or related group of positions, such as an examination of an entire accounting department's positions and compensation levels. Job-family surveys can provide an excellent view of compensation within a particular field or line of business, but participant lists are often inconsistent from family to family, making an integrated analysis of a specific group of companies difficult. Base salaries are collected in some studies; others, such as noncash surveys, run a more complete gamut, including employee expense, staffing levels, total cash, long-term incentives, and benefits.

Finally, *benchmark surveys* include key industry jobs common to most organizations. A good benchmark survey will include higher and lower levels, and multi- and single-incumbent positions representing all major functions of an organization. Because the survey's participant base is constant across a whole range of jobs, benchmark surveys give their users a framework for comparison, not just among individual jobs but among job families. Scope measures, such as number of employees managed, sales volume, budget size, and the like, are a means to determine the relationship between pay and magnitude of responsibility. The competent practitioner will collect data from all of these sources, assess the data's value, and use it appropriately.

Quantity and quality of information, as well as cost, can vary significantly. Some of the most common surveys and the results you can expect from them are:

- Irregular survey requests from counterparts: Costs incurred as a participant in surveys of a limited scope are typically zero, although protocol warrants the return of favors granted. If they give you information today, expect to give them information tomorrow. Output? Unless you are concerned enough to ask "What's everybody else paying?" expect no information on the subject.

- Group or association (club) surveys: Most often, other than club or association dues and perhaps a small charge to offset processing costs and materials, no costs accrue here either. The survey instrument is usually developed by a committee, completed by the membership, and forwarded to a delegated member of the group or the association headquarters for collection and production. Your time and interests are the chief concerns. Depending on how tight or small the club is, your participation may be solicited but not required. A printed report with your data included in the averages is the typical output.

  Groups concerned about the issues of legality and ego regarding direct information sharing with contemporaries often hire a consultant or survey company to serve as the "back room" for data collection, processing, and publication needs. When third party resources are employed, some costs may be expected if you want a copy of the survey results, though often the group or association will subsidize the study as a benefit of membership.

- One-time, custom surveys: These are often conducted by consultants engaged by you or a competitor in your industry or labor market to develop particular market data for specific purposes. For example, custom surveys can be part of job-evaluation and/or salary-structure program development. If you commission them, you can expect to receive (and pay for) very precise data, data that may be difficult to recreate or carry on from year to year. If you are a selected participant, expect a complimentary copy of the results with your data included in the averages.

- Third party annual surveys (consultants): These studies serve a host of interests and virtually cover the gamut of compensation information. Relative to custom surveys, annual consultant-conducted surveys are less expensive. The consultants' objectives are to make an impression as a competent consultant and to research speeches and articles as well as background and comparative data for the next year's consulting reports. Profit is rarely a concern. Expect output to be printed, although you can always buy a "special cut" of the data if you are really interested.

- Third party annual surveys (survey companies): Most often, these surveys cover certain functional areas (such as data processing or accounting positions) or levels of management (such as middle management, supervisory level, and so forth). Some concentrate on particular industries, such as financial services, health care, or advertising. Some combine functional areas and management levels to give a broad-based study with depth in a number of lines of business. The companies that administer these surveys are in business to make a profit by selling information to participants and other interested parties.

Data Displays and Terminology

Surveys appear in myriad forms and formats. Some reports will extensively slice and dice the data provided; some adopt a minimalist stance. A good survey will return some information on everything collected, consistent with the quality and quantity of data received. Remember, though, the underlying value of a survey is not in the numbers it presents but in the answers you are able to derive from its use.

60.0

58.7

75th Percentile/3rd Quartile → 55.2 ⎧ 58.3

55.0   Data in this range
is within one
standard deviation
Median (50th Percentile) → 55.0 ⎨ of the mean.
Approximately 67
55.0   percent of the data
appears within this
25th Percentile/1st Quartile → 52.1   range.

⎩ 49.9

48.6

47.1

n =   9
Standard Deviation =   4.2
Weighted Average (Mean) =   54.1

Figure 7-1. Array.

Table 7-1. Frequency Distribution
of Figure 7-1

Range	Frequency
45.0–47.9	1
48.0–50.9	1
51.0–53.9	1
54.0–56.9	4
57.0–59.9	1
60.0–62.9	1

Basically, most data is presented in one of three fashions: tabular (numeric) displays, graphic (visual) displays, or regression analysis (containing formulas and chart lines which project compensation levels).

Tabular Displays

Tabular displays (see Figure 7-1 and Table 7-1) include arrays, statistical reference points, and frequency distributions.

Arrays.   Arrays are high-to-low listings of all data collected in a given category. Arrays allow the analyst to inspect each data point reported and to see how the data distributes through the range.

Statistical Reference Points

Weighted average: Also called the arithmetic mean, the weighted average is the sum of all salaries (or other compensation values) divided by the number of incumbents reported. For example, the $47,000 weighted average salary for a production manager is based on 88 salaries (reported by 23 companies). The weighted average is the best indicator of the real market for a given survey position.

Simple average: The simple average is the sum of the averages for each participating company divided by the number of companies participating. For example, the $50,000 average midpoint for a production manager is based on 23 companies' average midpoints (reported on 88 incumbents). The simple average can be used to compare company policy on, for example, midpoint levels.

Standard deviation: The standard deviation is a number that, if added to and subtracted from the mean in a normal distribution, yields the middle two-thirds of the observations (the data within one standard deviation of the mean).

Median: Also called the 50th percentile/5th decile/2nd quartile, and so forth, the median is the middle of all the data points reported. Focus on the median when data is erratically distributed, especially when you have a small sample.

Quartiles, percentiles, and so forth: These refer to locations in an array below which a certain portion of the data lies. The 75th percentile, or 3rd quartile, is that point below which 75 percent (3/4) of the data points are found. Some analysts like to look at the data between the 1st and 3rd quartiles instead of using the standard deviation. This approach gives them the middle 50 percent instead of the middle 66.7

percent of the data viewed when using standard deviations.

N: This refers to the number of observations of data (data points) in a given sample.

Frequency Distributions.   These are often used in lieu of arrays if presenting individual data points strains the confidentiality concerns of the participants. Table 7-1 shows how many times a salary is reported within a certain range of salaries; actual salaries are not shown.

Graphic Displays

Graphic displays include a multitude of charts (line, pie, bar, and so forth) that can be used effectively in presenting data, especially to top management, when the big picture is more desirable than all the detail (see Figure 7-2).

Regression Analysis

Regression analysis (see Figure 7-3) is a powerful form of data presentation that relates two or more data elements and shows by formulas and charts the central data tendencies. Regressions project where, based on one measure (such as company sales), another measure (such as total cash compensation) will be found. Regression analysis correlates the reliability of the information to its dispersal around the line of central tendency. Regression charts often use logarithms because the range of data covered can be so great and because the formulas often are more accurate when the data is so transformed. A few words of caution: Regression analysis infers that if the one condition exists, then the other exists, and when looking at a chart, the eye and mind can lead the untrained observer to conclusions that may or may not be valid. The assumption that you should pay your CEO a base salary of $416,483 because your company has $10 billion in assets and because the regression formula says so is no more valid than if you were to conclude that you should pay $416,483 because that's the average salary of your peer group.

Regardless of format, "above average" does not equal "overpaid"; "below average" does not equal "underpaid." "Average" is not necessarily the proper pay posture for your organization versus your market. Remember the pay environment in which you operate: Performance, internal organizational values, and other issues come to bear on what's right for you. If your compensation policy is to pay at the 75th percentile, you may consider someone at the average to be underpaid.

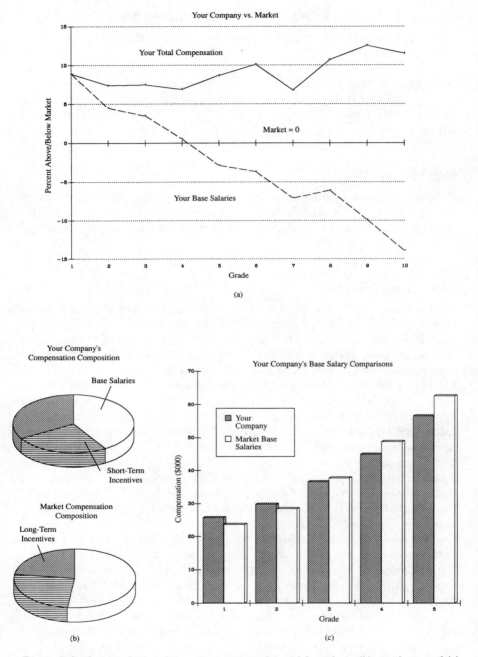

Figure 7-2. Graphic displays for use in presenting data: (*a*) **line chart,** (*b*) **pie chart,** and (*c*) **bar graph.**

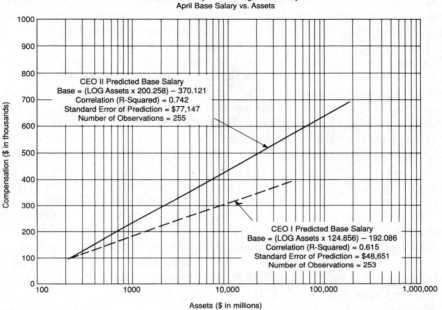

1988 Cole Survey — CEO Regression Analysis
April Base Salary vs. Assets

CEO II Predicted Base Salary
Base = (LOG Assets x 200.258) − 370.121
Correlation (R-Squared) = 0.742
Standard Error of Prediction = $77,147
Number of Observations = 255

CEO I Predicted Base Salary
Base = (LOG Assets x 124.856) − 192.086
Correlation (R-Squared) = 0.615
Standard Error of Prediction = $48,651
Number of Observations = 253

Compensation ($ in thousands)

Assets ($ in millions)

Figure 7-3. Regression analysis.

How to Use a Survey

Without exercising caution, those responsible for providing compensation recommendations can fall into one of two categories: (1) those who use every bit of survey data available without regard to its validity and (2) those who fail to fully exploit the data sources at their disposal. The following paragraphs give you some pointers on what constitutes worthwhile information and how to use the data. (In-depth quantitative analysis and methods of developing salary structures from survey data are not treated here.) The effective practitioner assesses a survey's reliability and the efficacy of the data before incorporating the information into a thought process; all survey numbers may not be as meaningful as you would like them to be. Because people are people and because organizations differ so widely in the way jobs and people in them relate to each other, data quality can vary markedly and should be checked before deciding to base one of your management decisions on it.

Understand that at the foundation of all surveys is the need to compare similarities, not differences. The surveyor tries to identify areas of similarity and jobs that are consistent from year to year and to include the same companies annually. The hope is that the individuals submitting the data follow directions. Unless the survey participants see how their jobs and the surveyed jobs are alike, little data will be forthcoming. When the survey results are published, that is the time to ask two questions, in this order: (1) How can I be sure that the data is correct? and (2) How similar is our job to the market comparison position?

You can feel comfortable that the data is correct by following a few guidelines. Choose annual survey sources that contain the majority of the positions and competitors in which your top management is chiefly interested. Don't shortchange yourself or your organization by getting only free survey information from recruiters (with their own interests to cultivate) or from magazine articles. Survey costs represent only a fraction of the payroll costs being administered that use the information the surveys generate. In short, good surveys can be a real investment.

To begin, participate in a quality, omnibus benchmark survey as a fundamental data source. This allows you to see how all the major job areas and functions relate to each other, drawing on a relatively consistent set of organizations and data preparers. Augment your chief data source with other data and other surveys; don't limit yourself to one source of information. Also, don't overlook the opportunity to compare compensation data from different sources. After all, surveying is a comparative process. Increasing the number and variety of weapons in your information arsenal increases your coverage and understanding of positions, organizations, and other industries.

So, what if you've taken these steps and the numbers don't agree or if you have only one source? How do you know that the data is reliable? You can assess the number of data points. If only a small, unrepresentative sample appears on a given position, you should consider devaluing its importance in your structure development or not using the information at all. The more tightly packed the data distribution is, the more confident you can feel that the comparison is a valid one. Realize, however, that aberrations are common in compensation. One organization will buy talent to use in a start-up or turnaround situation, and the individual's pay will be out of line with the size or profitability of the unit managed. Another organization will pay an individual very high or very low total compensation because of performance. Rare is the survey that can capture the relationship between pay and targeted, actual performance, except when viewing top management compensation in light of corporate performance.

In addition, rates for positions in the same job family should relate to each other. Case I (Table 7-2) shows a reasonable salary progression from entry to junior level ($7,300 difference), from junior level to medium level ($11,000 difference), and from medium level to senior level

Table 7-2. Salary Progression by Position

	Number	Case I average salary	Case II average salary
Senior-level position	12	$57,000	$57,000
Medium-level position	15	40,700	40,700
Junior-level position	2	29,700	37,900
Entry-level position	27	22,400	22,400

($16,300 difference). Although the junior position is sparsely populated, its salary level seems plausible, given the surrounding job-family data. In Case II, however, the data is skewed so that the junior-level job is $15,500 higher than the entry-level job, and just $2800 below the medium-level position. Therefore, data about salary levels in Case II is not as reliable as that presented in Case I.

If your survey source covers a broad spectrum of positions—upper- and lower-management levels, staff and line functions, multi- and single-incumbent positions—most of the position pay relationships should be consistent with the compensation program of your organization. Most companies try to have overall pay practices within plus or minus 10 percent of "their market." Be cautious of data skewed by one or two large companies weighting much of the data upward or downward. However, before discounting data affected by such circumstances, consider the following: If the job being surveyed is teller, for example, and one company employs 60 percent of the tellers in the state, shouldn't a pay decision on teller positions be heavily influenced by the pay average that includes the one large company?

The participant sample should also represent your industry or labor market. Then, regardless of how odd pieces of data appear in relation to your own, if all of your company's direct and indirect competitors are submitting data, you may have to admit that *you* are out of line with the overall market. On a similar theme, realize that the more consistent the sample of participants is from year to year and the better the survey covers your competitors, the greater the survey's value to you. Finally, the survey should describe positions that correspond closely to those in your organization so that you feel confident using the results.

Getting the Most out of Your Survey Efforts and Dollars

Assuming that you are the individual responsible for using salary surveys to develop compensation programs:

Start by creating a survey library. Set aside a file, a file drawer, a diskette, a closet, or a shelf for all of your organization's survey data. Alert others in your organization to forward all surveys and requests for survey participation to you so you can respond to them most efficiently.

Choose your surveys. Limited resources and day-to-day work requirements often preclude participation in every survey in which a company is asked to participate. You must balance your current needs, your future needs, and the ability to get what you want from others. In other words, participate not only in those studies from which you get information but also in those that your competitors need to satisfy their information demands. Unless you help them get their data, you may well not get theirs when you need it.

Use the data you have. Take the time to examine each survey in your library. Only by using the data you have will you benefit from the investment of time and money you expended to procure the data in the first place. Categorize surveys and their data by position, or family type, and by year. Don't retire a survey until you have its replacement; even a three-year-old study of a specialized, infrequently surveyed job stream can be useful if updated by prevailing salary-increase rates.

Consolidate your data onto a spreadsheet. Surveys are often consulted many times each month to respond to specific questions from a variety of interested parties. Some practitioners consolidate qualified position data from multiple survey sources onto a single spreadsheet— either on analysis paper or on a personal computer—for more convenient consultation. By arranging all of your data this way, you will have the best possible view of your organization's overall competitive pay markets and you will save time and effort during your annual compensation planning and structure review.

Derive a single answer from each set of numbers presented in a survey. If you consolidate data from multiple survey sources or have several views of the data presented in one source, you have a decision to make: Of the data available, of the different numbers purporting to be "the market," what is the single number that best represents "the market" for your organization? Some practitioners simply average all the data available from each source, throwing out odd data. Some feel that the data from one source is more valuable than that from others and weigh that data more heavily. (For example, one source will provide 50 percent of the answer and the second and third sources will supply 25 percent each.)

Answer all survey questions to the best of your ability. The survey designer is responsible for requesting data that are relevant to the survey output. Assume that all data have value in the quality of the results and that without certain data from you the survey will be delayed or reduced in value to you and to others. In other words, share requested information to the best of your ability. After all, that's what you expect of others. Remember, as no two companies are alike, no two sets of information needs are identical. Don't be an informational black hole.

As you develop your data, two criteria should guide the way. First, be realistic. Find your market answer first, and then describe how your situation differs. You and others will find many reasons why your organization's situation is different from the market and why, therefore, your incumbent's salary level is too high, too low, or just right. Let the market give you an answer first, then decide whether or not you like the answer. Don't become obsessed with finding matches and survey data on all positions. Remember organizational differences. A good analyst can determine three reference points relative to an undefined or dataless position: one surveyed position obviously higher in your organizational hierarchy, one obviously lower, and one perceived to be of a similar job value.

Second, be creative. While some organizations and managers will require you to produce information in a certain format, don't allow your thinking to stop there. Compensation information is like a bolt of cloth—you should see patterns of numbers within a function, from function to function, and across the entire organization. You should notice the different hues and textures from area to area, division to division. Then, from this combination of highs and lows and positive and negative variances, you should be able to fashion your organization's pay garment.

How to Conduct Your Own Survey

The preliminary thought process is critical in a good survey of any sort. You must know what the questions are and how you plan to present the answers before you involve anyone else. Only then should you concern yourself with targeting the appropriate markets, soliciting and securing their participation, ensuring good data, and presenting the data in a meaningful manner. Keep in mind four fundamentals in the business of surveying: People gain by getting information; people gain nothing by giving information; people are the companies with whom you must deal; and people have their own agendas that are different from yours.

With the fundamentals in mind, start by choosing a survey type that is appropriate to your need for speed and comprehensiveness. Different circumstances may dictate different approaches. You may have extra time available just for this survey, or you may need to conserve your energies and resources (data processing support, costs, and so forth). An outside agent may be more cost-effective. Always have a report format in mind when you conduct a survey—that is, know specifically what information you are seeking. This way, you won't miss asking for a particular piece of important information. Too often, especially with phone surveys, follow-up calls have to be made to fill in additional data elements. Always construct a questionnaire, even if you're collecting data on just one position from just a few companies. A questionnaire helps you to ask the same questions of all participants, and it serves as a record of responses. Keep your survey simple and focused on the final product. Don't collect extraneous data that is irrelevant and takes extra time to input and analyze.

Keep your survey brief or use a check-the-box format. Asking for narrative answers reduces the ability and interest of the potential participants to input data. Few executives and even fewer organizations are particularly altruistic. They want to get something for their time and energy. As a minimum, always plan to give your survey participants a copy of the results of the study. Try to fashion your survey so that it answers your questions and provides value to others as well. For example, add a job or two, ask for another component, or change your description a bit. Finally, ensure that you have enough "hooks" in your survey to allow you to merge it into a larger body of survey data. In other words, collect enough comprehensive data to allow you to compare the results to other data you have received in this particular area, as well as broader market or evaluation data you have.

Where to Find Survey Data

Survey sources are growing, and the field is becoming very competitive, so the following list is by no means exhaustive. Consider this a starting point in your quest for information. All of the major compensation and/or human-resources consulting firms have surveys conducted on a regular or semiregular basis—The Wyatt Co., and its survey units, Cole Surveys and ECS; Hay Group Inc.; Towers, Perrin, Forster & Crosby;

Mercer-Meidinger-Hansen; Hewitt Associates; to name a few. The major accounting firms—KPMG Peat Marwick; Deloitle & Touche; Ernst & Young; and so forth—also have survey interests.

The United States government is one of the largest surveyors in the country. Contact the Bureau of Labor Statistics (BLS), Wage and Hour Division of the U.S. Department of Labor. Most major cities have BLS offices. Check your telephone book under the federal government listings. Your state may also produce survey data of some value.

In addition, many local or regional personnel and compensation associations conduct surveys. Trade organizations and local consultants are other good sources. Also contact the American Compensation Association, Scottsdale, Ariz.

Every few years Dr. Steven Langer of Abbott, Langer & Associates, Crete, Ill., produces a comprehensive list of surveys in *Available Pay Survey Reports: An Annotated Bibliography*. This is an excellent resource.

8

Pricing and the Development of Salary Structures

Thomas S. Roy, Jr.
Director, Salaried Compensation
Armstrong World Industries Inc.

Compensation Strategy

Salary structures should be developed within the context of the total compensation strategy of the business. The intent of a total compensation strategy is to support the overall organization, its mission, and its strategic and tactical plans. The total compensation strategy should be an integral part of the human-resources strategy and should support the human-resources plans of the various business units. Thus, the compensation strategy recognizes the total environment in which the organization exists.

There was a time when the development of a salary structure was little more than establishing a base salary midpoint line for the company that was at the median or average of the survey information. Therefore, the policy of the company's salary program was to be competitive with other base salaries. Progressive companies today recognize that there are various compensation components that comprise the total compensation program. These components typically include base salary, short-term incentives (for example, sales incentive, bonuses, and so forth), long-term incentives (for example, stock options, performance shares, and so forth), and perquisites and benefits. Each of these components, while individually designed and often competitively measured in and of themselves, should be looked upon as tools to achieve one or more compensation objectives in support of the overall, total compensation strategy.

The use of specific compensation elements is affected by many considerations. These include the needs and resources of the company, competitive practices, regulatory factors, fixed versus variable costs, short- versus long-term goals, organizational culture, and administrative considerations. Thus, the design of the total compensation program weighs and measures all of these considerations and strives to achieve a desired balance of the various compensation components. Simply stated, the base salary structure should be developed within the context of all forms of total compensation and, quite particularly, within the context of total direct compensation.

Progressive companies also recognize that not all businesses necessarily have the same competitive posture, business profile, or strategic needs. Thus, separate compensation strategies are developed to support specific business-unit objectives. The decisions on such matters as the use of a desired balance of the components of total compensation, the definition of the competitive market, and the desired positioning of the compensation program within the marketplace are key policy decisions that should be made at the highest levels of the company.

Developing a Policy Line

In developing the specific policy line, the company initially looks to the defined external, competitive marketplace to assemble survey data. A scattergraph of survey data, illustrating the relationship between job size and pay, is thus plotted for the jobs that have been evaluated or are included in the study. Then a line of best fit through these scatterpoints is developed. Technically, this line of best fit is one that minimizes the sum of the squares of the vertical deviations around the line. The line or lines can be straight or curved. The technique for achieving this line can be as sophisticated as a computer-generated least squares line or approximated through the use of a rubber band. Several popular spreadsheet programs today make the job relatively easy. The trend line in Figure 8-1 represents an approximation of the competitive market.

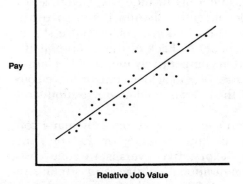

Figure 8-1. Scattergram with a trend line of external pay data.

On a similar graph (pay versus job size), internal pay rates are plotted and a line of best fit is developed. By an examination and comparison of the respective data, an analysis can be made of the relative competitiveness of current internal pay versus the defined market. This analysis is shown in Figure 8-2. The actual positioning of the company's salary structure midpoint line relative to the defined external, competitive market (referred to as the "policy line") is one of the key policy decisions referred to previously.

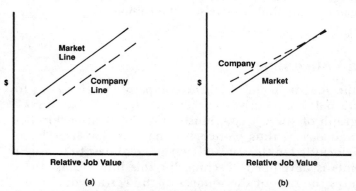

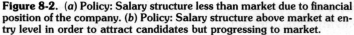

Figure 8-2. (*a*) Policy: Salary structure less than market due to financial position of the company. (*b*) Policy: Salary structure above market at entry level in order to attract candidates but progressing to market.

A more comprehensive approach, one that is used by more sophisticated firms, involves the comparison of the targeted total direct compensation versus the defined competitive market. This comparison is shown in Figure 8-3. Under this approach, the development of the salary structure does *not* begin with a comparison of salary range midpoints. Rather, the analysis focuses on the policy decision regarding the desired positioning of the firm's total compensation policy and the targeted components of the compensation program versus the external market. After these policy decisions have been made, the salary structure becomes the *result* of total compensation less targeted incentives.

For example, assume for a given position that the policy decision is to have a $50,000 total, direct compensation package composed of (1) no long-term incentive; (2) a short-term incentive plan targeted at 25 percent of base salary; and (3) the balance to be base salary. Under this scenario, the $50,000 total direct compensation has a resultant base salary structure midpoint of $40,000 and a $10,000 targeted bonus.

Once established, the specific values of the plotted base-salary policy line are utilized as the assigned policy objectives of the structure or structures being computed. It is important to note that there is no theoretical reason why the policy line must be a straight line. It could be curvilinear, disjointed, or of varying slopes, all depending on the total compensation policy objectives of the unit.

Determining Pay Grades

After determining midpoint or policy-line rates for the company or business unit, attention is then turned to developing job grades. Job

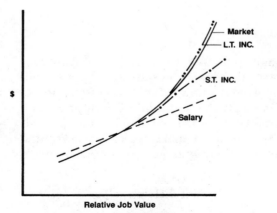

Figure 8-3. A comparison of total direct compensation versus the defined competitive market.

grades are often used for administrative simplicity. They are groupings of a variety of positions of similar internal job ranking, and these may provide a convenient means to attach an internal worth to each position. There are a number of techniques for developing job grades.

1. Develop grades by dividing the X or Job Value Axis, and maintain an equal or progressive point spread for each grade.

Points	Point spread	Grade
Up to 49	50	1
50–99	50	2
100–149	50	3
150–225	75	4
226–300	75	5

The table below shows a variation, where an equal or progressive percentage spread for each new grade is maintained.

Points	Percent spread	Grade
Up to 99		1
100–115	15%	2
116–132	15%	3
133–156	17%	4
157–184	17%	5

2. Develop grades by a midpoint to midpoint progression Y Axis. Under this technique, grades are developed by starting with a certain midpoint value and then progressing upward in a successive, predetermined manner. In this manner, the midpoint of each grade is a constant (or an increasing) percentage greater than the one preceding it. This midpoint to midpoint differential is typically 5 percent to 15 percent. Mathematically, the midpoints are computed by using the formula:

$$\text{Midpoint} \times (1 + \text{midpoint differential})$$

Thus, $10,000 × (1 + 10%) = $11,000. An example is illustrated below:

Dollar midpoint		Midpoint progression	Grade
$10,000	(starting point)		1
11,000		10%	2
12,100		10%	3
13,550		12%	4
15,180		12%	5

3. Develop grades as a continuum. Some firms develop grades as a continuum whereby each point or reference job value has its own corresponding pay value.

Regardless of the technique employed for determining job grades, several key factors must be considered in the design of the pay grade system and the number of grades to be used. These include:

- The interfamily relationship within the organization
- The number of jobs in the business
- The number of pay structures to be used
- The organizational hierarchy
- The distinctions that are evident in the marketplace

Pay-Structure Characteristics

As illustrated in Figure 8-4, pay structures often have many common characteristics. Some of these include:

A minimum, midpoint, and maximum. Within a pay grade there is typically a minimum (a), a midpoint (d), and a maximum (e). The midpoint usually represents the control point for administration of pay and the series of midpoints (d, g, j) represent the policy line of the company.

Pay grades. Although a single rate of pay for each job is not uncom-

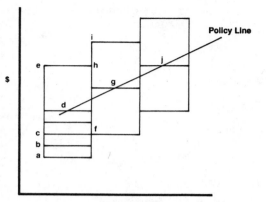

Figure 8-4. Pay structure characteristics.

mon, particularly in a factory environment, pay grades often provide for a pay range. This is illustrated as the width between (a) and (e).

Steps or limits. A number of steps or control points add various points through the width of range. Thus, points (b) and (c) may be prescribed steps or limits, for example, based on seniority or performance.

Midpoint progression. The midpoint progression (from d to g to j) provides an adequate progression from grade to grade. The smaller the difference between midpoints, the more pay rates are available to assign to jobs. On the other hand, too narrow a difference may not offer sufficient differential among grades, particularly as it involves a relationship between a supervisor and subordinate, or a promotion progression. Generally speaking, at the lower end of the job grading system, a relatively small difference in midpoint of 7-½ percent to 10 percent is satisfactory, whereas at the upper end it would typically be 15 percent to 20 percent.

Overlap. An overlap of grades (that is, the area f to h) may be desirable, particularly in a pay-for-performance system that stresses the opportunity to earn added compensation based on merit. While some overlap is desirable, excessive overlap should be avoided.

Range Width

The policy decision or decisions on the width of pay ranges center on the theories of the relative independence offered in the job and the desired impact of reward systems. Thus, this range typically is quite narrow (20 percent to 25 percent) for nonexempt factory or service positions, progressively larger for nonexempt clerical (25 percent to 40 percent), and typically larger still (50 percent to 60 percent) for professional through executive levels.

The technique for mathematically calculating the desired range width from a predetermined midpoint is as follows: To determine the minimum, divide the midpoint by one plus 1/2 of the desired range spread; to determine the maximum, either subtract the minimum from the midpoint and add the difference to the midpoint, or multiply the minimum by one plus the desired range spread. For example, for a 50 percent range spread with a $10,000 midpoint:

$$\text{To calculate the minimum: } \$10,000 \div 1.25 = \$8000$$

$$\text{To calculate the maximum: } \$10,000 - 8000 = 2000$$

and

$$\$10,000 + 2000 = \$12,000$$

or

$$\$8000 \times 1.50 = \$12,000$$

When pay steps within grades are used, they may be applied arithmetically or geometrically in a variety of ways. For example, after determining the midpoint and a spread of a pay grade, various steps can be calculated within the grade. As illustrated in Figure 8-5, each step is a constant $500. It is quite common to calculate the steps as a constant percentage, for example 3 percent per step.

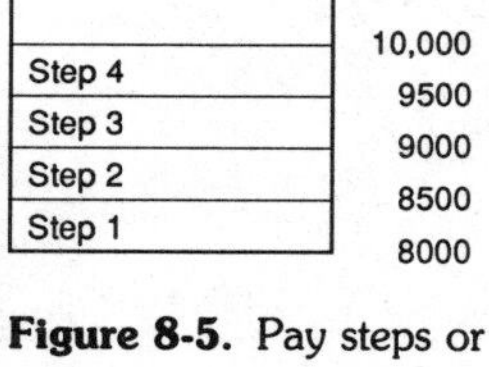

Figure 8-5. Pay steps or control points.

Number of Structures

It was stated earlier that a policy line need not be a straight line. So, too, a salary structure need not be a single structure. The use of multiple structures becomes more common as the compensation program becomes more comprehensive. Separate and distinct structures may be used, for example, for nonexempt versus exempt personnel, high- versus low-wage areas, bonus versus nonbonus positions, and so forth. It is vitally important, however, that such multiple structures be designed with an acute awareness of internal equity issues and within the context of the total compensation-plan design.

9

Budgeting, Auditing, and Control Systems for Salary Administration

Bernard Ingster

Consultant, Human Resources Management

Most organizations recognize that forecasts and budgets of wages and salaries can be primary tools for estimating and controlling these specialized forms of personnel costs. But, too often, organizations fail to realize that wage and salary planning can also become an instrument for developing skills in human-resources management as well as being an instrument of financial management. (The distinction between wages and salaries is maintained here because very few companies have eliminated the hourly-wage concept and converted to a fully salaried work force.)

The focus on the financial management aspect of salary planning is particularly intensified when annual or merit wage or salary increases are granted on a *single date* for all employees in a business unit. This popular tradition has deep roots, particularly among employers with large numbers of hourly wage workers, unionized or not. This practice is asserted to have significant administrative benefits: (1) It concentrates the time demands of salary administration into a single, limited period of a fiscal year and thereby relieves managers of the need to be concerned with most matters of wage or salary increase throughout the year, as is the case with compensation programs using the staggered, individual anniversary dates of employees as the time frame for regular pay adjustments; and (2) it greatly simplifies the annual process of forecasting and budgeting personnel expenditures, particularly with regard to their impact on cash flow. Defenders of once-a-year salary administration who incorporate formal performance appraisal into the program also claim the benefit of being able to rate employees against each other as well as in terms of their accomplishments against individual objectives.

In general, it is true that the use of variable increases of base salaries in a program of merit pay, administered on anniversary dates, gives rise to complexities in budgeting, auditing, and controlling compensation changes. However, it is also true that those same complexities provide opportunities for broader human-resources management improvements. Therefore, it is on the issue of variable, merit-based increases for salaried employees that this chapter places its emphasis.

There is one variable of substantial significance among organizations using an anniversary-date model of salary administration. In governmental and health care organizations, which are very labor-intensive, between 65 percent and 80 percent of the total operating budget is based on personnel costs. Thus, the consequences of salary planning in those organizations will be readily apparent. On the other hand, the personnel costs of high-technology process industries, such as chemicals or pharmaceuticals, constitute a relatively small percentage of their operating budgets, and the consequences of the planning process may be more subtle. Despite these differences, however, the concepts of effective salary planning and control are the same in all economic sectors.

General Concepts of a Salary Budgeting and Control Process

Salary planning should be a component of the general program of financial planning in an organization, and it should be conducted within the regular company cycles for planning an operating budget. The salary forecasting should cover at least a two-year period—the current fiscal year in which the budgeting is done and the fiscal year immediately following. Some organizations attempt to project to a third year or beyond, but when that is done it is generally recognized that the projections are very soft. Beyond a two-year salary-planning cycle, the budgets for additional future years are understood to represent at best an early-warning system forecasting that certain significant changes might occur. Thus, this chapter concentrates on a two-year cycle.

Salary planning and budgeting are best done by each employee responsible for the work of others. The process is an iterative one in which each level of supervision completes a budget proposal that is then integrated upward in the organization, usually to the department level of a function. At that level, all of the earlier judgments are tested against each other and against the departmental and business unit objectives. A consolidated departmental budget is then shared with all who have contributed to the process, with particular highlighting of higher management changes made to original entries of the contributors. Opportunity should exist for final reconciliation of different managerial judgments.

Salary budgeting is best performed using at least two major planning cycles in each budget year. Assuming a fiscal year starting January 1, a May-June preliminary budget and an October-November final budget should be prepared. The planning for the preliminary budget document, which will be discussed in detail later, should include the actual, current-year salary budget plus forms to supply data for at least the next immediate fiscal year. Opportunities to reflect possible budget changes for the second half of the current fiscal year should also be provided as part of this process. The October-November budget should represent the best and final judgments of supervisors of the actual operating conditions they anticipate that they will face in the next fiscal year. The budgeting process should utilize total base-salary costs, not merely the incremental costs of adjusting base salaries.

The Human-Resources
Management Challenge

A special challenge for the human-resources professional exists during the period of the announcement and explanation of preliminary budgeting. This is the time during which supervisors should be influenced to examine the human-resources management issues that are the foundations for the salary decisions they will be forecasting. They should be encouraged to ask themselves general questions, such as:

- Do I have the best organizational design for the achievements expected during the current and future years of the budgeting program?

- If the organization design is right, are the individual jobs structured in optimal fashion? Are there opportunities for job-content revisions that would improve overall unit performance and/or efficiencies?

- Who are the star performers in this unit? Am I providing effectively for their continuing development and success within the organization? Are compensation rewards appropriate?

- Whose performance is below expectations? Is discharge a likely outcome? What provisions have been made or must be made to help such employees succeed? Are compensation rewards consistent with the performance level? (In particular, are they too generous, thus communicating conflicting messages?)

- What are the likely employment needs during the years covered by the budgets? What are the likely replacement hiring and/or new hiring needs?

- Will there be significantly large numbers of new hires? Will there be a significant number of reductions in the staffing of the unit?

- What are the likely needs for granting leaves of absence during the periods covered by the budgets (personal, education, military, or maternity)? Is anyone planning retirement?

- What promotions and/or reclassifications are likely to be made during the periods covered by the budgets?

The process of salary budgeting should formally encourage all supervisors to examine at least annually the full range of issues associated with the management of the people for whom they have leadership responsibility. It is a highly useful vehicle for portraying a composite of the human-resources management needs of a working unit. If the process does not clearly illuminate the paths of necessary management action but emphasizes the quantitative indications of a budget, its value for the management of the enterprise is substantially diminished.

Variable Base-Salary Increases

In those organizations that have replaced the uniform progression of salary increases with variable increases in base salaries reflecting differing levels of personal accomplishments, a merit matrix has usually been developed as a guide for managers. The matrix is an important component of salary planning and usually attempts to relate several variables: the size of a base salary increase, generally expressed as a percentage of the base; the location of the current base-salary in the salary range, commonly expressed as the ratio—called the compa-ratio—of the base salary to the range midpoint; and the frequency of time over which the base-salary increases should be given, although many companies are eliminating this variable and offering salary reviews for everyone at 12-month intervals. A merit matrix based upon uniform 12-month reviews might look as shown in Table 9-1.

Table 9-1. Merit Matrix

Performance rating	Base salary	
	Below midpoint	At or above midpoint
Distinguished	9%–11%	7%–8%
Exceeds expectations	7%–8%	5%–6%
Meets expectations	4%–6%	3%–4%
Deficient performance	0	0

The merit matrix establishes the boundaries within which management may grant merit salary increases. In good practice, these matrices should be reviewed annually to ensure the continuing competitiveness of the levels of reward.

Some organizations exercise control over the total cost of merit increases by either mandating or suggesting that managers limit the numbers of staff eligible for a particular performance rating. For example, the company might distribute guidelines with the salary-planning and budgeting documents that suggest limiting 15 percent of the departmental work force to the rating of "Distinguished," 20 percent of the work force to the rating of "Exceeds Expectations," and 55 percent to 60 percent of the work force to "Meets Expectations." (Usually, it is not anticipated that more than 3 percent to 5 percent of a given departmental staff will exhibit deficient performance.)

Some organizations exercise control over the total cost of the merit increases by establishing a separate merit budget that cannot be exceeded for the fiscal year in which it is established. For example, managers are told that the total of all merit increases proposed for a given fiscal year may not exceed 6 percent of all base salaries of employees in a department at the start of that fiscal year. In most cases, managers in these organizations are also provided with additional guidelines for salary increases such as those found in the merit matrix.

Components of a Preliminary Salary Budget

In almost all organizations using effective techniques for salary planning, the necessary data exists in computerized human-resources information systems (HRIS) that are also integrated with the computerized financial-reporting databases. It would be difficult, but not impossible, to establish and maintain the salary-budgeting, audit, and control practices described in this chapter in the absence of such a computerized capability. Typically, the worksheets provided for the preliminary salary budget consist of at least two sections. One section provides detailed information about the salaries of employees for the current fiscal year during which the planning is being done. For each current employee, this section should at least include:

- Employee name and identification data
- Position title
- Salary class, including minimum, midpoint, and maximum salaries of class
- Current base salary
- Current compa-ratio
- Type, date, and amount of last salary increase
- Planned salary change for the current year (forecasted in previous year), including type, date, and amount

In addition, this section should include a total of all staff in the unit (a head count) and the totals of all current and all proposed base salaries. The net increase cost of the planned salary changes for the current year plus the percentage increase this represents over the total base salaries of the previous year should also be shown. Managers should also affirm or propose modifications to the current-year plan in this section of the preliminary budget. This constitutes one additional opportunity to reconsider plans for the balance of the operating year.

A second section of the worksheets for the preliminary budget should allow managers to enter a variety of codes (preferably those of the existing HRIS) reflecting planned salary changes for the next immediate fiscal year. The forms should also provide space for the entry of certain variable data, such as the percentage award of the merit increase. Thus, in addition to entries for merit increases, there should be available codes for personnel actions such as:

- Promotions and/or reclassifications
- Planned leaves
- Planned transfers
- Planned retirements

The second section should also provide space for the entry of planned increases in staffing for the future year, including the designations of salary classes. The system should calculate projected costs of a new hire using the midpoint of the salary class. Dates of all planned changes should be identified, usually using the first or last day of each month in the year.

All of the proposed changes in the budgets for the current year and all of the changes forecasted for the future year should be automatically calculated by the computer and reported to each contributing manager. In printed form, the format and content of the preliminary budget reports for both the current and future year should be the same. The accuracy of the printed reports should be affirmed by the contributors.

The Final Salary Budget

Toward the close of the current fiscal year, usually in October or November, the budget for the current and future year and the planning summaries should be redistributed to all contributors. These summaries should be accurate with regard to all salary and other personnel actions taken to date in the current fiscal year. The budget summary for the future year might now reflect proposed changes in salary ranges adopted as a result of salary surveys. Such range changes might have impacts upon the originally proposed levels of salary increase because of compa-ratio changes. These should be highlighted by the computer for attention by the managers making the original submissions. Managers should affirm or modify their proposals.

Once more, there should be an upward organization process of integration of budgets to the department level of the function, with opportunities for reconciliation of differing managerial judgments.

Summaries of Reports

All organizations attempt additional integrations of budget planning data to increasingly higher functional levels. This process is usually accompanied by summaries of selected information. For salary planning and forecasting, it is useful to have at the department level at least summary data such as:

- Total base salaries (current year)
- Total base salaries (future year)
- Actual net change of base salaries for the current and future year
- Percentage of the net change in base salaries from the current year to the future year
- Head count and base-salary expense in major functional groups
- Projected changes in head count and base-salary expense in major functional groups
- Totals of base salary and personnel actions by type (that is, merit increases, promotions, reclassifications)
- Compa-ratio comparisons for current and future years

Ongoing Audit and Review of Salary Budgets

In highly labor-intensive organizations, the monthly measurement of actual performance against operating budgets primarily will be a report of performance against the salary budgets previously prepared. In these situations, month-to-month analysis of variances between planned and actual base-salary expenses is useful and necessary because in these organizations, cash flow planning is fundamentally built upon salary costs. However, in nonlabor-intensive organizations, a quarterly review of performance against salary planning is generally adequate and the cash flow impacts of changes in the base salary may not be seen as particularly significant.

In good practice, the function of compensation administration is responsibility for the independent audit and review of the salary budgets. While managers are primarily accountable for ensuring that plans and actual performance are fully congruent, the human-resources function should also ensure that the budgeting objectives are being met. Should that not be the case, it is anticipated that direct consultations would occur between a human-resources professional and the manager affected.

Additional Considerations

Some organizations find discrepancies between planned and actual total personnel costs because salaries for certain groups of people are not included in the salary-planning and budgeting programs. For example, part-time employee salary costs might be aggregated at an organizational level above that at which the part-timers work. Or, of greater frequency, there is the problem of discovering at the end of a year that a large number of temporary employees have been utilized to fill needs for which regular, full-time employment requisitions would not be approved. This also tends to be the result of aggregating the costs for per diem employees hired from a contractor for a limited time at an organizational level remote from that at which the work is performed. It is in the interest of an organization that the salary planning process identify the expenses for part-time employees, temporary workers, and consultants in the salary budgets of each budget unit.

However, with regard to the costs of bonus payments of various kinds, most organizations do not attempt to forecast those expenses in the planning processes described in this chapter. There will usually be accruals for the bonuses that are allocated to departmental budgets by the finance function. In like manner, costs for employee benefits tend to be budgeted at the macro level of an organization and subsequently allocated to each organizational unit on the basis of the numbers and kinds of employees in that unit.

If the HRIS capability is particularly strong and well integrated into the financial computing systems, salary planning can be greatly facilitated through the automatic modification of budgets when various unplanned salary or personnel actions occur. For example, transfers into or out of the budget unit, hirings, and terminations are routinely recorded on the company's computer files. The computer system should also routinely amend the budgets of affected departments and alert the managers of the new conditions on the worksheets used in the preparation of preliminary and final salary budgets and on the monthly or quarterly statements of budget performance.

Finally, it must be understood that salary planning and budgeting are tools for effective general management, not artifacts of the human-resources administrator. For greatest benefit, these processes must be institutionalized within the general planning programs of an organization, and they must be perceived as equally necessary with other forms of budgeted expenses. But most importantly, the best forms of salary planning and budgeting must be understood to be symbols of the best practices of human-resources management.

10
Cost Containment

Arnold A. Trillet
Vice President, Human Resources
BOC Group

Cost containment in human-resources practice no longer means what it did ten years ago—incremental attempts to limit the growth of the payroll or benefits adjustments. Today, cost containment and reduction is one of the principal weapons in a fight for survival in many American businesses. Faced with global competition, maturing products, and pricing squeezes, industry has only three possible responses: (1) Get a technical or product edge through innovation, (2) be the quality leader, or (3) cut costs and be the cost leader. Often, it takes all three to save a business and keep a local economy healthy.

The human-resources executive has been thrust into this new environment, and he or she has become potentially the most important factor in restricting costs in most businesses. He or she must be a member of the team that, based on clear-headed, zero-based strategic thinking, makes most efficient use of the available human-resources dollars. No longer can the human-resources professional view people costs as a fixed base, linear function, subject only to good administration and minor tinkering. We are in an era in which only double-digit improvements in overall cost efficiency and in productivity will ensure continued health for many businesses.

Cost containment is a result, not a process. The only valid way to achieve cost containment is through the process of matching business objectives to worker needs in the most cost-efficient way possible. Although this process usually results in substantial cost reductions, the temptation is to look only for ways to slash costs, and this almost always is a disaster for both human relations and business objectives.

The winners of the 1980s (and the probable winners of the 1990s) are those managers who know how to meet the competitive situation head-on and who treat the human-resources function with the same strategic importance as the cost of raw materials or product pricing. It's clear that the winning human-resources managers are those who know how to get on the strategic team and boldly use the restructuring tools available—such as delayering, unbundling, multiple tiering, and rigorous pay for performance—to achieve cost leadership.

The Need for Cost Containment

A company may have one or more of the following reasons for requiring major cost containment in its total compensation:

- Maintain or improve cost and pricing competitiveness
- Contribute to a change in company culture (for example, an improved bottom-line focus and pay for performance) without negatively affecting productivity or competitiveness
- Obtain more compensation impact on employees for the same cost
- Respond to economic factors
- Respond to the changing market position of the company, from the maturity stage to the return-to-growth stage

Broadly speaking, the most common areas for application of cost containment have been in the downsizing of employment, flexible staffing, health care, and, of course, compensation, on which we will focus much of our attention.

A simple and effective way to measure the need for more compensation cost efficiency is to compare the company's market position, in terms of both share and profitability, with its comparator ranking in compensation levels and costs. Later in this chapter is a case study that illustrates the need for compensation cost containment. The company had only average profitability, was ranked third in market share, but had a pay structure that exceeded that of 75 percent of its competitors.

It is clear that, given other equivalent costs, the salaried costs were too high, and an opportunity existed for major restructuring.

Reduced to its simplest terms, cost containment may be viewed simply as bringing corporate performance into line with its compensation position. When compensation programs are part of a strategic market repositioning of the company, the new target market ranking is the ranking against which compensation is balanced (see Figure 10-1).

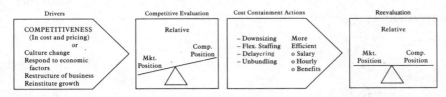

Figure 10-1. Flow process: compensation cost containment.

Setting the Stage

The more urgent the need for cost containment, the more important it is that it be given sufficient attention at the highest levels. Cost containment is effective, understood, and accepted only when it is driven by and positioned as part of an overall business strategy. Perhaps the most valid long-term way to view cost containment is to define it as "making the total compensation package congruent with business strategy and objectives."

Competitive strategy often involves improvement or new positioning of the company relative to its competitors on price and/or product/service. It usually involves one or a combination of the following elements: operating cost reduction, operating efficiency or productivity improvement, or innovation in setting product and/or service apart from that of competitors.

The competitive strategy generates the establishment of company objectives regarding the organization, the company's culture, and overall financial results. Each company's strategy, objectives, needs, and culture are unique and require a customized human-resources and compensation solution.

Arriving at the objectives and converting the objectives to specific tactics and plans involves the consideration of numerous internal and external factors. Some of the most important internal factors bearing directly on human-resources objectives and plans are labor costs (absolute and relative to competition), company culture, quality of talent relative to projected goals and requirements, and the stage (in market cycle) of development of the company. Some of the most important external factors are economic conditions (present and forecasted), available work force (size, quality, and location), major societal trends, and business environment (particularly, relative position versus that of competitors).

Development by human resources and top management of congruent tactics and plans often includes changes to some or all of the following: organization design, job design, job specification and employee selection criteria, objectives and performance standards for groups and individuals, and the total compensation system.

In designing or redesigning a total compensation system, particularly when cost containment is a key objective, some of the major considerations are:

- Identification of competitors for talent and their practices and projected strategies
- Determination of elements most likely to attract, retain, and motivate top performers
- Determination of what compensation elements in what mixes will be most effective in supporting company objectives
- Extent of emphasis on pay for performance in determining the degree of leveraging of compensation
- Company affordability (internally and relative to competition)
- Current and projected employee needs and preferences
- Existence or nonexistence of a union and its relationship to pay
- Administrative capability for complex or simple, single or multiple programs that vary by strategic business unit, location, and employee group or level

The Role of the Human-Resources Executive

Seeing one's job in the proper perspective is one of the keys to success in human resources and an absolute necessity for any human resources executive setting out to achieve cost efficiency for the company. The typical job responsibility and accountability has increased enormously from

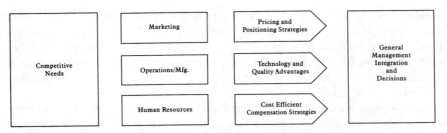

Figure 10-2. HR integration into the strategic team repositioning strategy.

administering and improving an existing system to having accountability for organizational and cost effectiveness.

The executive with the large perspective steps back from a new job and asks the most basic and broad questions, such as, "What kind of value are we getting for the dollars we are spending on people?" Then he or she gets management's attention with related questions, such as, "Are we happy with the value received for our dollars?" "Can you see that only a minor-to-moderate restructuring of the budget could result in a major savings to the bottom line?" "Are we focusing on the right people?" "Do the really critical people have a good deal here?"

Once a human-resources executive gets the attention of senior management on issues this big, it often becomes hard to be left alone. Then the human-resources professional needs the resources and knowledge to carry off the restructuring in the face of almost certain opposition. To be an effective influence in cost containment, the human-resources executive must be an integral part of the top management team and participate in the development of strategy, objectives, and performance goal-setting processes.

The human-resources executive must provide leadership in establishing the appropriate top management perspective and ensuring the meaningful integration of his or her own role into the management system (see Figure 10-2). It requires:

- That management of employees and their costs be shared by management and the human-resources department

- A constant awareness of the total costs of keeping an employee on the payroll and of the relative costs of comparable employees of key competitors

- An understanding that, like raw materials, the costs of employing people are inherently connected with the resulting company productivity and performance
- That the desired pay-for-performance mentality must be communicated, understood, and reflected in the management system and in the day-to-day working environment for all levels of employees
- Providing for an appropriate level of employee participation in the development of the performance and compensation systems
- Using or creating critical times in the business cycle to shape and justify major changes to top management and other employees
- Planning and facilitating the effective communication of the management system (and the pay system) throughout the organization
- Ensuring that the resulting reward systems are, in perception and reality, critical, tangible evidence of the importance management places on its performance expectations and that the reward systems clearly are supportive of these expectations
- Providing a change agent in assessing and changing company culture when required (In doing so, the culture must be congruent with the current strategy and objectives. Compensation may be the most critical tool to do so. There are many difficulties in identifying needs for a change in culture and for determining the alternative courses, the probability of success, the costs, and the risks.)
- Providing management with timely, reliable data that is properly focused on the market, the competitors and geographic information and that is analyzed on both a quantitative and qualitative basis to facilitate the right compensation decisions
- Enthusiastically joining the management team in the institution of cost containment measures to maintain maximum cost efficiency on an ongoing basis

Airco: A Case History

In the mid-1980s, the author examined a situation with classic, high potential for cost savings from improved compensation management. Factors considered in the initial evaluation are shown in Table 10-1.

Table 10-1. Initial Airco Evaluation

Factor	Profile
Characteristics/Culture	
• Size	$750 million+(over 3000 employees)
• Industry	Commodity (stable, long-term)
• Management style	Traditional
• Organization climate	Innovative
• Attitude toward cost containment	Need not be recognized
• Profitability	Moderate
• Employment security	Very high
• Competitive strategy	Expand through acquisition
• Work force age/quality	High seniority and age/competitive quality
• Organization structure	Centralized
• Turnover	Very low
• Union influence	Diminishing
• Work force as percentage of total costs	25 percent
• Morale	Guarded
External Factors	
• Economy	Unstable, low inflation
• Industry status	Flat
• Competition	Growing, cost competitive, foreign and domestic
• Competitive position	Losing market share
Performance factors	
• Costs/pricing vs. competition	Costs/pricing too high
• Goal-setting process	Not vital, critical process
• Commitment to objectives/results	Unclear
• Appraisal system (results or behavioral)	Behavioral
• Pay linked to performance results	Very indirectly
• Performance differentiation	Minimal (95 percent rated satisfactory or better)
• Focus of existing incentives	Not focused, primarily long-term return on investment
Compensation	
• Market data basis	Informal—based on high demands of new hires
• Fixed/variable ratio	Fixed virtually 100 percent
• Employee perception	Pay too low, entitlement/cost-of-living mindset
• Competitive pay level	Third quartile
• Salary structure	Single pay structure based on high-pay market
• Range penetration	Very high (averaged over 60 percent)
• Distribution of salary increases	90 percent of increases within 3 percent range
• Incentive/base ratio	Very low
• Incentive participation	Limited to executives and direct sales representatives
• Perquisites	Moderate to low
• Position descriptions/evaluations	Outdated
• Benefits suitability	Common plans for all business units with little change in several years

The first approach to handling this challenging set of factors was implemented by general management and the human-resources team working in close coordination. The approach consisted of the following steps:

- Repositioning the business mix
- Disposing of several unprofitable business units
- Restoring acceptable margins and returning to a moderate growth stage, partially through increasing cost effectiveness of people
- Restructuring the organization from three highly vertical units into seven decentralized strategic business units (SBUs) and implementing more direct reporting (see Figure 10-3)
- Fully developing the human-resources planning process to be a vital contributor to the process
- Implementing a plan to phase out employees whose performance was not consistent with new standards (This plan included voluntary retirements and resignations.)
- External hiring of key contributors who fit the new specifications and standards

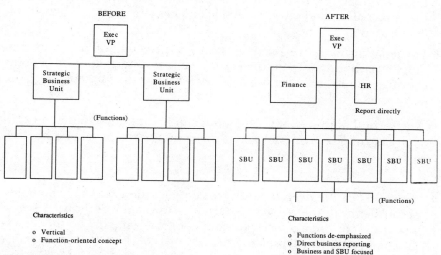

Figure 10-3. Airco organization structure.

- Developing an improved business planning process and a performance results-oriented management system
- Introducing a more highly leveraged pay-for-performance approach on a short-term basis, which was the keystone to attaining higher profit goals
- Acting on the need for short-term results improvements, which suggested a restructuring of compensation programs and a relatively limited amount of employee participation in the program development (The lack of employee involvement in program development results in a more difficult rate of acceptance.)
- Initiating the necessary culture changes by instituting a compensation plan based on performance and subsequently reinforcing development programs, such as quality circles, with training
- Separating "performance results" ratings, which result in rewards, from "potential ratings," which are attributable to the human-resources succession planning process
- Selecting compensation as the major means of stimulating both individual and strategic business-unit performance, extending the use of incentives deeper down into the organization, and using compensation as a key element in achieving cost-containment objectives
- Taking advantage of the existing desire among management for increased compensation opportunity by establishing lower fixed pay targets, greater differentiation in appraisal ratings and resultant merit increases, and more extensive eligibility for results-oriented incentive pay
- Formulating incentive plans around the principle of company and employee sharing of both the costs (negative results) and the benefits (positive results) associated with a performance-pay system

The second approach was operational in nature. Maximum cost efficiency can only be achieved when three important principles are followed:

1. The costs of the overall executive compensation package should be reconciled with the relevant external factors, such as industry sector practices, positioning or repositioning of the company on the life cycle curve, and the current and desired market share and profitability of the company.

2. The selection of the mix of elements should correspond to the culture, management style, and external factors of the business.

3. Compensation should be rigorously connected with individual performance, reducing the "automatic" elements (cash and noncash) to a practical minimum.

Attacking the challenge of cost efficiency in compensation challenge was begun by commissioning a consulting organization to do a comparator survey. More than 100 exempt job titles (a 25 percent sampling) were selected to be evaluated. After an extensive study, 21 companies and two direct competitors were identified as valid comparators. Factors that were considered included size, growth rate, similarity of structure, and comparable pay market.

The comparison of Airco with 21 other companies yielded many surprises to general management. It showed Airco was paying in the 75th to 90th percentile of its industry, and that payment to staff people was in a higher percentile than payment to line people. In contrast to the industry in general, the survey showed that a higher proportion of total compensation went into fixed salaries and a lower proportion into incentives. These findings led to the following steps to achieve cost efficiency in compensation and to restore cost efficiency of people.

- Reevaluating all jobs based on a point-factor system
- Unbundling the nationwide percentage-based pay system and replacing it with industry geographic scales
- Implementing a performance-appraisal system linked to the objectives and results achieved by groups and individuals
- Developing and implementing a plan to bring all employees' salaries into proper relationships with performance over a three-year period, driving total compensation close to a 50 percent position in market comparator data
- Communicating and training managers at all levels in new performance concepts (for example, eliminating pay entitlement mindset)

The third approach was managerial and administrative in nature and consisted of:

- Capturing the performance dimensions of each job so they could be correctly measured (These performance dimensions must be accepted by employees as appropriate, and trust in the system must be developed.)
- Developing human-resources information systems to report and ana-

lyze performance-rating distributions and merit-increase recommendations

■ Developing training and communication vehicles, including compensation planning worksheets

■ Discussing, evaluating, and adjusting ratings and compensation at the executive, managerial, and supervisory levels, as well as on an individual and group basis

It is worth looking at the results of the changes in compensation strategy in more detail. They can be found in Table 10-2. As stated before, it was based on a strict appraisal system and a plan to bring all employee salaries into proper pay-for-performance relationships over a three-year period and to put overall company compensation levels back in line with company performance. Total compensation targeted for professional and supervisory employees was the 50th percentile, middle management at the 60th percentile, and senior levels at the 75th percentile, as shown in Table 10-3.

It is important to understand the mechanism by which some of the rather substantial results were achieved in salary cost containment. One of the most important concepts in the restructuring of salaried compensation was the performance zone.

In the performance zone concept (see Figure 10-4 and Table 10-4), the size of any employee's performance increment is determined by the distance between the compa-ratio (CR) and the performance ceiling and the number of years required to achieve the performance ceiling. Thus, the performance award will be individually calculated for each employee. It will result in a planned salary progression over one to four years based on the compa-ratio (see Figure 10-5).

Annual salary-scale changes are a function of competitive pay changes that incorporate market movement, productivity, and industry economics. Compensation based on compa-ratio progression toward a performance ceiling over a specified period is easy to communicate and understand.

The two examples that follow illustrate the use of the performance zone in two different circumstances—first, using a three-year time frame, to develop salaried employees' base pay to the targeted performance ceiling (see Figure 10-6), and, second, using a three-year time frame, to bring an employee exceeding his or her performance ceiling back into line.

Table 10-2. Airco Compensation Program Changes

Change	Results
• Performance award (merit) increments based on each employee's performance rating, position in range, and two-to-three-year plan to bring individual salaries into proper relationship to performance	• Reduced overall compensation position from high third quartile to low third quartile in two to three years; overall merit budget expenditures reduced to below-market-movement level
• Increased the number of employees receiving no merit award and froze their salaries until performance evaluations reached realistic levels based on business results	• Brought costs under control
• Geographic salary structure	• Focused on local market levels (a shift away from basing pay on highest levels)
• Narrower rate ranges for nonexempt and low-exempt employees	• Increased overall range penetration
• Performance zones established within the individual rate range	• Increased the high performers' merit potential
• Ninety percent midpoint control for commission-eligible positions	• Put base salaries and incentive pay for sales personnel into better balance
• Selective lump-sum merit increases	• Provided lump-sum increases to very high performers who exceeded performance zone
• Increased number and amounts of promotion increases	• Intensified the rewards for promotion
• Hourly rate structures adjusted to eliminate fixed increments and COLA provisions, replacing them with productivity-related increases in order to maintain or reduce unit labor costs	• Brought costs under control
• Lump-sum contract wage increases not tied to COLA	• Strengthened competitive position in all geographic areas
• Benefits-to-wages ratio held constant or reduced; employees to participate in benefits cost increases	• Brought costs under control
• Selective application of two-tier wage systems	• Retained experienced workers yet hired new ones

Table 10-3. Ranking of Pay Practices by Percentile Against 21 Comparator Companies

Employee group	Before	Three-year target
Nonexempt and lower management	80th percentile	50%
Middle management		
Base salary	70th percentile	50%
Total compensation	65th percentile	60%
Senior management		
Base salary	75th percentile	75%
Total compensation	50th percentile	75%

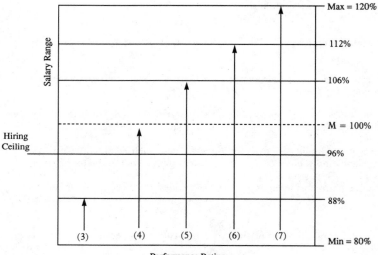

Figure 10-4. Performance zone salary range defined.

Table 10-4. Guidelines and Objectives of Performance Zone Base Salary Administration

Performance rating	Distribution guidelines	Performance ceiling (% of midpoint)	Competitive compensation objective
7 (Outstanding)	5%	120% (max)	90th percentile
6	10%	112%	75th percentile
5	15%	106%	60th percentile
4	40%	100%	50th percentile
3	20%	88%	40th percentile
2	5%	N/A	N/A
1/0	5%	N/A	N/A

- Compa-ratio is greater than performance ceiling.
  Management judgment. Consider:
  1. Freeze salary
  2. 2%–3% increase (versus 4% range adjustment)
  3. Lump-sum award

- Compa-ratio is less than performance ceiling.
  Base salary increase to performance ceiling based on:

If the difference between actual CR and ceiling is:	Then the number of years to consider is:
Below 8 points	1 year
8–14 points	2 years
14–20 points	3 years
Over 20 points	4 + years

Figure 10-5. Guidelines for administration of performance zone concept.

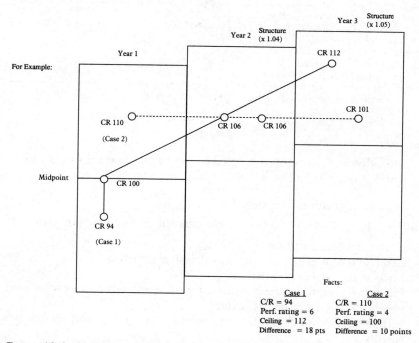

Figure 10-6. Objective: to bring the employee, over a three-year time frame, to the targeted performance ceiling.

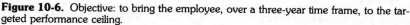

To illustrate this point, suppose an employee has a current compa-ratio of 94 and performance appraisal rating of 6 (ceiling of 112) on a scale that increases by 4 percent in Year 1 and 5 percent in Year 3. This employee's actual salary progression would be in the area of 6 percent for Year 1, 10 percent for Year 2, and 11 percent for Year 3. The second illustration is of an employee already at a compa-ratio of 110. Over the next three years the employee is repositioned into his or her proper performance zone.

Another key concept in the salaried cost containment effort was the creation of geographic salary scales from a formerly national system (Table 10-5). These many compensation changes were implemented in less than a year's time. The effects on the culture of the company were dramatic. For example, performance appraisal changed from a five-level system, in which 93 percent of employees were rated in the top three categories, to a seven-level system with a normal forced distribution curve (see Figure 10-7).

Table 10-5. Effect of Geographic Salary Scales

	Typical nonexempt position	Low-mid level exempt position
Midpoint—National (former)	$20,000	$40,000
Midpoint—South Area (new)	$17,600	$35,200
Former Compa-Ratio—South	80	80
Geographic Compa-Ratio—South (new)	92	92
Former Indicated Merit Budget	7%	8%
Geographic Actual Merit Budget (new)	4%	5%

NOTE: Estimated annual savings nationally: 1.5% of payroll.

Summary

The methodologies presented yielded a significant amount of change in the organization. Overall company results include:

- Boosted organization morale
- Improved employee acceptance and trust of the new organization
- Facilitated communication:
  1. Established goal-setting process (boss/subordinate)
  2. Linked incentives to business goals
  3. Facilitated management communication of desired results and ways that they can be achieved
  4. Enhanced feedback to the organization on group and individual results
- Dramatically increased profits

Initial Distribution (before)		Resulting Distribution (after)	
		1. Does not meet most objectives	1%
1. Unsatisfactory	0.3%_____	2. Does not meet some	4%
2. Marginal	4.3%_____	3. Meets most	20%
3. Standard	55.9%_____	4. Meets all	41%
4. Exceeds standards	37.2%_____	5. Meets all—Exceeds some	26%
5. Outstanding	2.3%_____	6. Meets all—Exceeds most	8%
		7. Far exceeds all	1%

Figure 10-7. Results of performance review/compensation changes.

- Improved profits and sales per employee or per payroll dollar
- Reached planned turnover at target levels, starting from very low levels in the previous undifferentiated environment
- Diminished unplanned turnover of high performers
- Lowered overall payroll costs by 7 percent

Incentive Compensation

Incentive compensation practices today are undergoing a revolution. As in most revolutions, the principles underlying the growth in the many forms of variable compensation to employees are not new, but they are increasingly being rediscovered and extended through the corporation. High-performance sales operations have always known that the concept of incentive pay is more than added pay for performance. Incentive pay, as it is increasingly being used, is "an optional percentage of total compensation that is directed as a tool to meet specific objectives of the company." Far from being an "adder," incentive compensation today is actually a valuable tool in cost containment.

Some of the parameters through which incentive compensation can steer an organization include:

- Retention of top performers
- Organization "pacing" changes
- People-recognition measures

- Individual productivity enhancement
- Profit and revenue enhancement
- Organizational productivity

When it is understood how incentive compensation can affect all these parameters positively, it is easy to see how it can be a cost containment tool rather than an added pay burden. Just as incentive compensation can affect these basic factors, it can also directly affect most key financial measures. In a corporation in which variable compensation is expertly designed and applied, average cost per employee can actually go down, and has, in the author's experience. During difficult years, it offers the company more flexibility so that, although sales may be declining, costs go down as well. But incentive compensation has even more leverage in good years in which performance gains from the right incentive plan can far outstrip additional compensation, reducing the average cost per sales or profit dollar ever further.

How It Works

A typical unrenewed corporate situation is a sales-oriented organization in which only direct sales representatives are on any kind of variable compensation, and that compensation is tied directly to sales volume. In good times and in bad, one of the company's biggest cost components, people, is fixed, and inexorably destined to creep upward while human-resources professionals try to hammer them down and top executives complain about what they're not getting for their people dollar.

Contrast that with a situation in which a substantial portion of the organization is on some form of variable pay that is targeted to the business objectives of the company, for example, productivity in administrative components, return on capital, profitability in sales components, and even specialized objectives such as market share in unique situations.

The new system is funded out of planned increases in salary scale, with little net effect on total compensation costs. The people effects are even more dramatic. The company's best performers are being paid above the market level in almost every case, resulting in high retention rates; average contributors are being paid at the market level; and below-average performers are being paid under the market level. Some of the latter have departed; many of the average contributors have improved their productivity to the extent that head-count requirements have been reduced. The incentives are paid on an annual basis, three months after the close of the fiscal year, and this becomes in itself a retention factor for high performers since they have already earned variable compensation into the following year. If an employee terminates employment prior to receiving an award, it is forfeited.

In addition, the culture has shifted subtly toward team recognition and performance against objectives and away from the previous focus on individual performance.

Although this may seem to be an idealized situation, in the author's experience, it is one that has worked out largely in the manner described. Widespread variable compensation may not be the solution for every situation, but it is an underutilized tool in today's corporations.

Guidelines and Cautions

As has already been pointed out, incentive compensation is a tool that must be applied with considerable expertise just because it has such strong leverage to help or exacerbate a strategic situation. The top human-resources professional must begin with a review of objectives, agreed upon by senior management, and proceed to outline strategy and to have that strategy communicated to line organization, preferably before any implementation begins. Furthermore, the strategy must be tailored to the objectives of each operating unit. Some fundamental considerations in designing an incentive compensation plan are:

- Eligibility (How far down into the organization?)
- Standards
- Plan award maximums
- Percentage of base pay
- Measurability and its communication
- Type of reward
- Degree of customization versus standardization

The type of organization must also be considered very carefully. Is it a low-ticket, high-volume sales organization? Is it a contract operation? Is it a deal-making, one-time transaction environment? Is it a customer service or support operation? Or is it a staff or administrative function?

To illustrate just how important this consideration is, three very different divisions within one organization, Airco Gases, are discussed below. You will see how Airco Gases changed from using largely fixed pay or volume-driven incentive to a more specific and focused pay system.

Guaranteed Pool. The first division, Airco Industrial Gases, is a group that supplies industrial gases nationwide in large volume on a contract basis to such disparate customers as steel mills (oxygen) and poultry processing (liquid nitrogen for flash freezing). It is an industry leader and was paying well in comparison to the market. But there was dissatisfaction in the ranks of sales representatives because pay, although good, had little movement upward. Management was concerned about controlling future costs and maintaining industry leadership. Sales representatives wanted incentives, but short-term incentives were not possible under a long-term sales system with multiyear contracts. There were strengths. Sales swings from year to year were not dramatic, and retention of good performers was already good but could be better.

The challenge was not fixing something that was already highly dysfunctional. Rather the challenge was productivity, cost leadership, and positioning for the future. The solution chosen was unconventional: a guaranteed bonus pool with defined costs, a structure well-tailored to the long-term characteristics of the business.

During the first phase of the program, the bonuses were awarded through a point system, in published rankings called group standings (see Figure 10-8), and the individual rankings were done on sophisticated, objective-driven division parameters. Factors included both volume and pricing, a profit modifier, referrals accomplished, and equipment sales, as differentiated from gas contracts.

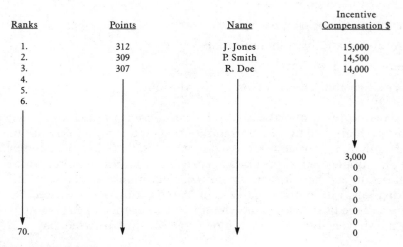

Ranks	Points	Name	Incentive Compensation $
1.	312	J. Jones	15,000
2.	309	P. Smith	14,500
3.	307	R. Doe	14,000
4.			
5.			
6.			
			3,000
			0
			0
			0
			0
			0
			0
70.			0

Figure 10-8. Group standing.

The program was designed to phase in over a three-year period and to incur less incremental cost to the group. The program was funded the first year by forgoing any base salary increase and setting aside 10 percent of total salary for bonuses. In the second year, 100 percent of bonuses were able to be funded from previously planned salary increases. The third year and succeeding years created a semipermanent arrangement with funding coming from competitive market movement and improved performance. The target mix of fixed and variable pay had been achieved.

The net effect of the plan was that most sales representatives acquired an altered view of their performance against division objectives from the group standings list. Some saw their performance less valued than they had imagined; others saw it more valued. The pace and performance of the group began to change dramatically as its features appealed to the competitive nature of the sales force. There was little turnover of high-potential employees, but there was more turnover in the middle- and lower-performance ranks because of the higher-performance expectations of the organization.

As some personnel left, it became apparent that not all would have to be replaced, since productivity had increased. And it was then that a second independent phase of the program began. A focused-selection approach to replacement made a significant contribution to work force quality. It became clear that a combination of selection, training, and incentive plans were bringing new hires to full parity and productivity in half the time than had been the case under the old system. When all these factors were added up, the company had gained millions of dollars and was approaching its goals of cost leadership and productivity leadership in its industry.

One possible objection to a closed-end, guaranteed pool system is that if performance becomes uniformly outstanding or uniformly poor, the incentive system no longer works because the wide differentiation can no longer be motivated or provide performance-based pay. This is a valid objection in theory, but the author has never seen it happen in actuality. If it did, a reevaluation of the system would definitely be required.

Retail Plan.   A second example starts with a very different set of business parameters. Airco Retail Operations consisted of locally run businesses that were short-cycled, primarily selling lower-cost items with a high emphasis on customer service. There are no long-term contracts present as there were in the previous example. Cylinders of gas are sold under two basic conditions: inside sales (over the counter and on the telephone) and outside sales. Also included in the evaluation project were branch managers. Some sales incentives were in place, based on sales volume only, but the strategic situation called for reevaluation in the face of increased competition.

The methodology was the same as that which was used in the first example: define objectives, define the measures to be used, and set the mix of variable and fixed compensation accordingly. In this case the measures to be used needed to shift dramatically in the direction of profitability and away from volume in order to avoid, for instance, long-distance deliveries to unprofitable accounts simply to build volume. The measures settled upon were gross profits from the sales representatives' customers, return on capital, and some individual and team objectives.

The mix of variable to base pay was set differently than in the former example to compensate for business characteristics. Base pay was set relatively lower, and the incentives were relatively higher to account for greater upside bonus potential. Total compensation remained comparable, as shown in Table 10-6.

Table 10-6. Retail Incentive Plan—Outside Sales

Old plans		New plans	
Objective	Measure/reward	Objective	Measure/reward
1. New customers	Small new-account bonus	New accounts	New-account bonus scaled to number and net profitability of each new customer and weighted to importance of new accounts vs. current customers
2. Sales volume growth	Commission-basis percent on year-to-year volume growth	Territory net profit	Net profit vs. target, scaled with high threshold and high cap
3. Gross profit	Limited group award	Individual performance objectives	Tailored objectives for individuals and territories, fixed dollar amount for achievement
		Team incentives for key area profit or other improvement goals shared among all sales and support	Scaled to performance vs. target

The result was similar to that of the contract business example in one respect. Movement started, productivity rose, and overall costs declined. It also was different in one respect. Individual income varied more widely, resembling more closely the actual fortunes of the market and business. Today, morale and work force quality are both up, in part as a result of a tailored application of incentive compensation.

Staff Plan.   The third example occurred in an area which formerly had almost no incentive pay—middle management. The objectives in these staff ranks were cost containment and more pay to high performers.

The solution was a matrix approach. The money that had been budgeted for the normal annual salary increases in the first year was put into the incentive plan to be distributed according to two parameters (see Figure 10-9). Bonuses were tied to overall performance of the business unit and to individual contributions to that performance.

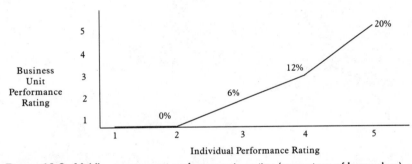

Figure 10-9. Middle management performance incentive (percentage of base salary).

That led to investigation of possible innovative group incentives even lower in the organization. Employees in this third group have indicated a willingness to put certain portions of pay at risk in return for higher potential. This had to be designed carefully, since discretionary income is less in this group.

Summary

The totally revised pay system at Airco tied performance tightly to salary for the first time, linked salary to company affordability, and gave managers a system that has clearly accomplished two objectives: It contained costs and it reinforced the concept of performance-based pay at Airco.

Incentive plans reach further down into Airco's organization than ever before, and the results illustrate the potential for well-designed plans. The overall projected compensation costs have actually been reduced about 7 percent since the plan was implementated, and profits and productivity have increased. Average person costs per sales or profit dollar went down.

There has never been a time of more opportunity for the human-resources executive who has all the tools of cost efficiency firmly in his or her grasp and has the courage and persistence to get them implemented. Change has brought opportunity. The broader application of incentive plans is benefiting many of today's corporations.

PART 3

Contingent Compensation

11

Sustaining Success With Alternative Rewards

Marc J. Wallace, Jr., Ph.D.

Professor and Ashland Oil Fellow
University of Kentucky

Overview

Clark Equipment's Materials Systems Technology decides to design and implement an incentive program. The model includes four standards: budgeted cost per unit, quality, on-time customer delivery, and inventory. The incentive plan ignites the organization. It attracts the attention of all employees—hourly workers, office staff, and managers—who learn more about the business's priorities and how they can each make a difference. Groups start working smarter to resolve the challenges of quality and efficiency.

Year-end results at Clark Equipment show the plan has had a positive impact. Production costs per unit have been reduced by almost 10 percent. Quality performance has consistently met the challenge of increasingly tougher standards. On-time delivery goals have largely been met, and inventory levels have dropped. The plan clearly succeeded as a driver of strategic performance, and the total payout per employee was about $317, averaging 1 percent to 2 percent of the typical employee's annual base pay.

A power utility rolls out an incentive plan to motivate innovative and risky decision making. The plan is the brainchild of a new CEO. Under the rules, managers are encouraged to look for exceptional cases of this kind of innovative behavior from among their direct reports and reward them with lump-sum awards of as much as 20 percent of a person's annual base pay. Although the program is designed to be discretionary, there are some guidelines: a maximum of 20 percent of the eligible population can receive awards in a given year and the minimum award is 5 percent. The plan falls flat on its face the first year. Although the maximum 20 percent of the eligible population receive awards (each at 5 percent), the CEO is disgusted by the results. He spent more than $1 million implementing the plan and considers that he has nothing to show for the investment. The program is quietly dropped.

Why do some companies succeed with incentive programs while others fail? Clark Equipment and the utility company are 2 of 46 organizations that I have been tracking over the past several years to answer that question. The effort, supported in part by the American Compensation Association, has studied organizations that made the transition to alternative rewards. We've learned a great deal from the experience of the 46 companies, and the results of the study are presented in a report, *Rewards and Renewal*.[1] The purpose of this chapter, however, is to report on a follow-up analysis. During the past year I have revisited a number of the original 46 organizations to see how things are going. Specifically, I was concerned with the following questions: After one has successfully implemented an alternative-rewards program, what does it take to *sustain* that success? Are there additional factors of which an organization must be aware to ensure that an alternative-rewards program continues to deliver results?

Experts on strategy have long recognized that what it takes initially to establish a competitive advantage in a business venture and what it takes over time to sustain that advantage are often quite different.[2] Rewards strategy is no exception to this rule. Those organizations that enjoy continued success over time with their reward programs have adapted and modified them as conditions change and the business grows. They have

---

[1]Marc J. Wallace, Jr., *Rewards and Renewal: America's Search For Competitive Advantage Through Alternative Rewards*, American Compensation Association, Scottsdale, Ariz., 1989, p. 1.

[2]Michael Porter, *Competitive Advantage: Creating and Sustaining Superior Performance*, The Free Press, New York, 1985, Chap. 1.

been willing to break the rules and question conventional wisdom that has grown up around specific reward techniques.

Successful Plan Implementation

We found that five factors were crucial in determining whether or not an implementation of an alternative-rewards program would succeed:

A Clear Vision

Those organizations with successful alternative-rewards programs did two things differently from those companies that had unsuccessfully implemented their alternative-rewards programs. First, they took the time necessary to plan and prepare their companies for the change. They took the time to design the new program to fit their organizational strategy and culture. They took the time to involve people in the new design and prepare them for its introduction. They took the time to establish buy-in for the concept of the new plan among all key opinion groups. Second, these organizations had their yardsticks ready. They were familiar enough with what they expected to accomplish with the new pay system to have explicit measures and base lines established. They were prepared to track and evaluate the program before and after implementation.

Discretionary Content

In addition, the owners of the organizations sufficiently valued the peak performance that occurred as a result of discretion to pay extra for it. Peak performance was valuable enough to warrant budgeting additional money for incentives. In contrast, the companies with unsuccessful alternative-rewards programs still operated under a budget mentality. The managers in these firms still viewed compensation as a cost center, like electricity or water. It was something to be used sparingly and not to be wasted.

Sunsets

Surprisingly, the successful plans in this study were those with definite terms. Those firms that did not place definite terms on their plans found themselves strapped with incentive schemes that continued paying out but ceased to have a positive impact on business performance. They quickly degenerated into another entitlement vehicle. Successful plans, in contrast, were those that had a definite expectation that they would run in concert with a specific business plan.

Decentralized Design

Did the corporation allow individual divisions and business units to do their own thing? Traditionally, corporations have imposed a great deal of centralization on pay design. Such policies ensure consistency and internal fairness throughout the organization. When it comes to alternative pay, however, companies like FMC and General Electric have found that it is impossible to find the gain sharing formula or the skill-based pay system that will work in very different types of businesses.

These and other firms that have succeeded with alternative rewards have found it necessary to allow for a variety of different reward designs throughout the corporation. Allowing for decentralization, however, does not mean giving up control and accountability. Control has been achieved by requiring each business unit to use the same set of principles and protocols to plan the specific design that will support their business. Accountability has been ensured by requiring each business unit to track its programs against these design principles and assure the corporation that the plan continues to achieve results related to the business. Unsuccessful plans either required every unit to do the same thing or gave up control entirely and never held specific business units accountable for achieving business results with their pay systems.

Separation of Incentive Pay From Base Pay

Those companies that were successful with alternative pay separated the incentive payment from the base pay. The incentive payment does not roll into base pay and, therefore, must be reearned each year or period. This separation of incentive pay accomplishes two objectives. First, the practice enhances the incentive value of the reward because it underlines a clear connection between performance and pay. Second, the practice prevents base pay from becoming an impossible fixed cost. Rolling incentives into base pay compounds over time, and many of the firms in this study reported that they simply had too much cost rolled into fixed cost. In addition, the practice led to a compression in earning.

The companies could not make significant enough pay distinctions between outstanding performers and merely acceptable performers.

Business Incentive Plans

The most popular alternative-rewards program implemented among the 46 organizations was business incentives, or gain sharing. Forty-five percent of the organizations in this study implemented such plans. All of the firms in this group continue to face some uncomfortable realities about gain sharing.

A great deal of experience has developed and been documented about classical gain sharing approaches, including the Scanlon, Rucker and IMPROSHARE plans.[3] Most experts agree that certain conditions must exist for gain sharing plans to succeed over time.[4] These conditions are as follows:

- Relatively small size in terms of employment and operations
- Mature operation that has stable standards based on past performance
- Simple, accurate performance measures with a stable history
- Stable product mix—no new products planned
- Stable, good technology—no changes planned
- Stable capital investment

Every one of the 21 organizations that tried gain sharing had fundamental difficulties in satisfying these conditions. Not one of the them reported a stable product mix, for example. Every one of the organizations was in the process of introducing new products and phasing out old ones. Although many of the businesses faced growing markets, demand was anything but stable. They were trying to improve their market share but faced very uncertain competition. None of the firms in this group could be characterized as very far up their learning curves and therefore could not be characterized as a mature operation. Each of them was introducing new technologies, or there were new start-ups. In either case, without a stable history past measures were irrelevant, and

---

[3]See, for example, Brian E. Graham-Moore, and Timothy L. Ross, *Productivity Gainsharing*, Bureau of National Affairs, Washington, D.C., 1989.

[4]Edward E. Lawler, III, *Pay and Organizational Development*, Addison-Wesley, Reading, Mass., 1981.

that made it impossible for management to improve on past performance. One of the executives in the study ruefully noted that if all he did was repeat past performance, his unit would go out of business.

Experimentation

Each of the firms in this study experimented with the traditional gain sharing formulas. In fact, their experience suggests that gain sharing is evolving beyond the first-generation Scanlon, Rucker, and IMPROSHARE plans.

First-generation plans focused almost exclusively on financial or physical productivity as the goal for the business unit. They also tended to set those standards in terms of history. The first-generation plans also were set into place with indefinite terms; they had no sunset. The expectation was that they would continue with current standards, measures, and payout formulas indefinitely. Also, first-generation plans tended to isolate production workers from indirect employees.

The experimentation encountered among the 21 firms is leading to a new generation of incentive models that should not be called gain sharing because they are so different in a number of key aspects. First, the new models measure a much broader reach of business goals. The Clark Equipment plan mentioned at the beginning of this chapter serves as a good example of this new generation. Going beyond a productivity standard, it incorporated other measures that are also critical to business performance, including product quality and responsiveness to the customers. Second, the new models are no longer based on history. In contrast, they are driven by future-oriented goals derived from business plans. The specific goals frequently emerge from highly participative goal setting involving owners, managers, and employee teams. The goals are tentative and subject to change over time. Clark Equipment, for example, set increasingly tougher standards for quality throughout the year. What was considered incentive performance in January was considered unacceptable by midyear. The model created incentives for movement up a learning curve. Third, these newer models have definite terms. The volatile nature of business in the 1990s will not allow organizations to repeat history. Successful business incentive plans, therefore, are those that establish an expectation of change and constant improvement. Fourth, the ready distinction between direct and indirect labor has disappeared in each of the 21 firms. Management and staff functions have been incorporated into teams as most of these firms adopted socio-technical system approaches toward high employee involvement. The new plans do not make distinctions between direct and indirect labor—they include all groups of employees.

Skill-Based Pay

Fifteen of the 46 firms in this study, or 33 percent, implemented skill-based pay or pay-for-knowledge plans. As in the case of gain sharing, several conventions have been widely accepted since the experiment at General Foods' Topeka plant.[5] They include:

- The system pays for what people know about their work.
- Skills are arranged in a hierarchy of four to five skill blocks.
- The work performed by the group is relatively homogeneous and can be learned by everyone in the group.
- Everyone progresses to the top block and receives the top pay rate in about two to three years.
- The system is expensive because everyone is paid the highest rate.
- The system is a natural for a *greenfield* investment (building a new plant from scratch) in which rapid learning is needed.

Several Counterpoints

The experience with skill-based pay provides some interesting counterpoints to conventional wisdom. The surprises involved three issues: what the company is purchasing in regard to skill-based pay systems; how to handle bottlenecks, or slowdowns in movement, through the system; and how similar must work be to be included in a skill-based pay system.

First was the issue of what the organization was purchasing in regard to skill-based pay systems. Those organizations that thought of the system as one that pays for knowledge correctly saw it as an expensive system. Once they became experienced with the system, however, many of the firms noted that it wasn't so much a system that pays for knowledge as it was one that rewards people for being flexible. Several of the managers in the study reported that skill-based pay maximized their ability to deploy a work force in the most efficient and effective way possible. In these cases, skill-based pay more than paid for itself through the fi-

[5]Ibid., p. 120.

nancial returns realized by being able to absorb more production with fewer people. In addition, a flexibility mindset among work teams allowed the organization to more effectively enhance quality and responsiveness to customers. There was no longer the concept in these organizations of a narrowly defined job that provided the basis for workers to define what they don't or won't do.[6]

The second issue had to do with a problem that plagued most of the skill-based pay implementations: bottlenecks, people being unable to move through the skill blocks on a timely basis. One type of bottleneck was created by immediate production demands. Because manufacturing managers were faced with daily demands for output in a start-up situation, they could not or would not allow individual employees to take time away from their immediate work to learn new activities or tasks. Another type of bottleneck emerged when there were just four or five hierarchical skill blocks. If an employee did not have sufficient time to complete qualification of all the elements in a given skill block, he or she might have to wait more than a year to qualify for the higher block and to receive the adjustment in his or her base pay.

Those firms that dealt successfully with bottlenecks did three things. First, the top managers of the organization balanced short-run pressures against long-run needs. They provided the time and monetary resources to allow employees to develop work-related skills, even in the face of short-run production pressures. Second, successful organizations enforced a true team concept of operation in which everyone continues to perform all activities. Thus, more senior team members who were qualified in higher skill blocks still performed activities in the lower skill blocks, thus allowing more junior members the opportunity to learn and practice in the higher skill blocks. In a true skill-based pay system, being more senior does not mean that one only performs higher-level work. Ultimately, every team member performs every activity. Third, they broke down the four or five skill blocks arranged in a hierarchy (each with its own wage rate) and replaced them with a system of eight or ten smaller steps. That practice provides much more frequent movement in skills acquisition and pay rates, even though the lowest rate and highest rate remain the same.

The third issue focused on the frequent assumption that commonly accepted functions or job families could not or should not be mixed or combined into the same skill-based pay system. Thus, manufacturers in the study who tried skill-based pay often started out by isolating identifiable functions in the skill-based system. It was common to find, for ex-

[6]Edward E. Lawler, III, "What's Wrong With Point Factor Job Evaluation," *Compensation and Benefits Review*, Vol. 18, No. 2, American Management Association, New York, March-April 1986, pp. 20–28.

ample, that production employees, maintenance electricians, maintenance mechanics, and warehouse employees would have their own separate skill-based plans. If the office staff—finance/accounting, quality assurance, administration—were ever even thought of, they too would be in a separate skill-based system. Similarly, banks adopting skill-based systems treated back-room functions, such as accounting, differently from front-office functions, such as customer service.

Successful firms broke the rules of convention and pushed the skill-based pay concept of flexibility as far as possible. In several cases, manufacturers found that they could unbundle as much as 90 percent of the activities historically restricted to maintenance mechanics and invest them in upper-level skill blocks for operating technicians. The same firms found that many of the activities performed by first-, second-, and third-level managers could similarly be invested in the operators' skill blocks. The key factor is to break down the barriers. Once this was done, much greater operating efficiency resulted.

Indications for Success

It is important to note that skill-based pay is not so much a compensation system as it is a radical departure from traditional organizational design. It works best in work systems where there is a high level of employee involvement, where work has been organized into self-managed teams, where traditional functions beyond operations (for example, sales, accounting, quality assurance, human resources, administration, planning) are conducted in large part by the teams, and where there is a commitment to high levels of investment in human capital.

Additional Factors for Successful Plan Implementation

Earlier in this chapter, I identified five factors that are critical in determining the success of an alternative-rewards program. Five additional factors have emerged that I believe are necessary in ensuring that the alternative-rewards system continues to support strategy and competitive advantage.

Flexibility

It's not only important that the reward program have a definite term at the outset, it must also adapt and change as the business grows and conditions alter. Successful reward programs are living beings. Because they are not onetime events, the measures and standards of the program change as the business, goals, and people change. The programs that failed were those that were not adaptive. They tended to lock in measures and standards. Employees covered under them developed expectations that incentives would be owed every time the standards were met. Successful programs were managed by people who understood that the primary purpose of the incentive plan was not to deliver extra pay but to contribute to business achievement. Firms with successful plans reviewed their incentives continually and made sure to adjust them as the business changed.

Tracking

A vivid finding in this study was that every time an organization failed to track and evaluate its program in an open, formal, and systematic fashion, the program died. The organization didn't stop paying, but the reward program lost its impact. It no longer got attention. It no longer focused individual and group interest on business measures and performance. It no longer resulted in performance improvements. The experience of the 46 firms in this study underscores the importance of tracking pay programs to ensure that they continue delivering results of importance to the organization and employees. Pay programs should be treated as ongoing management initiatives that require continual review and redirection.

Removal of Barriers

When skill-based pay was successful, the most frequently cited benefit was that the program broke down barriers. All of the firms that introduced and switched to skill-based pay from more traditional systems reported that the transition was certainly not easy. The prospect of training operating employees to perform maintenance tasks, to carry out quality tests, to screen and interview new team candidates, to conduct meetings, to confront fellow team members, to perform accounting calculations, and to manage relationships with customers often meets with incredulity. In fact, it's threatening to many, especially to senior crafts persons. The absence of the traditional job titles, however, forced people to become more flexible and adaptable. One no longer had a handy job title to delimit what one did from those things one need not worry about. With the barriers broken down, teams of individuals could concentrate on the work at hand.

Simplicity

Breaking down barriers makes organizations simpler, and simplicity has become a major contributor to competitive advantage among manufacturers and service providers in North America. Interestingly, not only were the 46 organizations trying to become simpler, but also many found advantages to making their alternative-rewards programs simpler. Gain sharing serves as a good example of this trend. Many of the business incentive plans in this study began as rather complex models. They contained explicit measures of productivity for several different product lines or production centers. They contained adjustments for conditions beyond the employees' control. They had formulas for estimating the impact of indirect labor on the production process.

Ironically, several of the firms quickly became dissatisfied with their first models. They were too complex, and that made them difficult to communicate and discuss. In each of these cases, the firm moved to a simple model that resembled a simple profit-sharing formula. The premise of the strategy was a value judgment: Why not develop a program that accurately reflects the business with all its upside and downside risks? Why not develop a model that people can influence but not influence perfectly. Why not generate a plan that reinforces a sense of partnership among those with a stake in the organization—owners, managers, employees, and customers. The result may be something as simple as a profit-sharing formula.

Celebration

Finally, those managers who were particularly successful with alternative rewards intuitively recognized that rewarding people is, in part, an act of celebration that underscores business necessity and yet still allows people to relax and enjoy themselves. These organizations departed from the traditional custom of delivering pay in a very serious, no-nonsense, quiet fashion. They did just the opposite. They made noise. They talked about the success throughout the organization and made a public celebration of how much had been earned and why it had been earned. It was a time to bang the drums and ring the bells.

12

IMPROSHARE: A Technique for Sharing Productivity Gains With Employees

Mitchell Fein
President, Mitchell Fein Inc.

An Overview

The term IMPROSHARE is derived from "improved productivity through sharing." This incentive plan encourages employees to increase productivity in order to share in the gains. It incorporates a philosophy of managing that is significantly different from the traditional view that productivity improvement is a unilateral responsibility of management. When employees share in productivity gains, they accept management's productivity goals. The "we-they" adversary relationship changes so both the organization and its employees gain as they cooperate to produce more product or services per employee hour. Productivity impediments and losses affect both groups. IMPROSHARE consists of three components:

1. A philosophy of managing that encourages employees to cooperate in raising productivity and to share the productivity gains
2. A formal work-measurement system to ascertain productivity changes
3. An involvement program that establishes productivity teams of employees and management to help promote improvements in operations and product that will benefit both the employees and the organization.

IMPROSHARE was developed by Mitchell Fein and was first installed in 1974; parts of the plan were used previously for over 20 years. IMPROSHARE productivity measurements use traditional work-measurement standards and practices of a selected base period. The IMPROSHARE plan is quite different from the Scanlon and Rucker plans, which measure productivity gains as a ratio of dollar labor payroll to sales dollar; Rucker is based on "value added," which is sales less purchased materials. IMPROSHARE measures productivity by the employee hour value of completed product compared to the hours worked by all employees in the plan.

Employee Involvement

Numerous experiences in small and large companies have demonstrated that when employees are involved in the production process, substantial benefits and improved productivity are obtained. In many instances, employees know more about their operations than do their supervisors and others in management. The IMPROSHARE plan is designed to encourage employees to cooperate with management to improve productivity and reduce costs. IMPROSHARE rewards employees for their efforts. Shared benefits increase take-home pay, and reduced production costs create more secure and better jobs.

Plantwide Productivity Measurement

A plan to share productivity gains must measure the contributions and inputs of the employees and processes being measured and exclude factors outside their control. Money values should not be used in productivity measurement because many factors that affect money costs do not affect productivity.

Traditional work measurement establishes the time it should take to perform a given task under prescribed conditions, not how long it took to perform the work in the past. Such normal or fair day's work standards are established through performance rating with a stopwatch time study or through predetermined standards against a defined measurement base. This leveling or normalizing of observed data is the keystone of traditional work measurement; it must be employed for that approach.

The differences that arise between employees and management in setting traditional time standards are avoided under IMPROSHARE by measuring productivity against the average level of an agreed-upon base period. Using a method called "measurement by parameters,"[1] standards are set at the average time of the past, using historical data within a place of work, with no need to performance-rate the observed data. The rationale for this approach is that yesterday's performance is established as the Accepted Productivity Level (APL). Measurements in the future will be made against this APL base.[2]

Traditional measurement and measurement by parameters are two different gauging systems; one has no bearing or influence on the other. Not performance-rating the data in measurement by parameters does not obviate the need to performance-rate data in traditional measurement. It is as valid to use the past average productivity against which to measure as it is to establish any other level that may be determined by altering the past average or by performance-rating the observed data obtained from time studies, provided the measurement base used is defined. The past average is a valid base if that is the base management decides to use; it is the APL.

IMPROSHARE is a macro measurement system that measures productivity by comparing the labor-hour value of completed production to the total labor-hour input. This approach is indisputable and valid; only acceptable product, ready for shipment, is counted. Everyone in the work force can be included. This overall measurement of productivity avoids the arguments and rationalizations that occur with conventional accounting practice that separates workers into two categories—those who work directly on product and those who do support and service work. It is unlike traditional work measurement, which is micro-oriented. Engineers traditionally follow accounting practice and measure production

[1]Mitchell Fein, *Establishing Time Standards by Parameters*, Proceedings of the American Institute of Industrial Engineers 1978 Annual Conference, May 1978.

[2]Mitchell Fein, *Work Measurement Today*, Industrial Engineering, American Institute of Industrial Engineers, August 1972 and September 1972 (two-part article).

operations mainly to establish traditional incentives. Labor that goes into services, product repairs, maintenance, and other such work is usually not measured.

Productivity Measurement for IMPROSHARE

When measuring groups or a plant under IMPROSHARE, a reliable measurement base is the average productivity over a past period. Considering the total output of the group against the total hours worked by the group permits the establishment of valid measures that include all employees.

This principle of measuring and sharing productivity is shown by a simple example. Assume a single-product plant of 100 employees produced 50,000 units over a 50-week period; the employees worked a total of 200,000 hours. The average time per unit is 200,000/50,000 = 4.0 hours. This would become the measurement base. Suppose an IMPROSHARE plan is introduced and the employees and management share productivity gains 50/50 below the past average of 4.0 hours per unit. In a given week, if 102 employees worked a total of 4080 hours and produced 1300 units, the value of the output would be 1300 × 4.0 = 5200 hours. The gain would be 5200 − 4080 = 1120 hours, within one-half or 560 hours shared by all the employees. Translated into pay, this would be 560/4080 = 13.7 percent additional pay to each employee based on each employee's weekly pay. Management also would gain 560 hours. Where originally the unit labor value of the product was 4.0 hours, the new unit time including productivity-sharing payments is (4080 + 560)/1300 = 3.57 hours. Thus, the unit time after productivity-sharing payments to the employees has been reduced.

Similar results could have been obtained by using labor and production data in dollars, but, as changes are made in wage rates and selling prices, the data would have to be adjusted to equivalent dollars or the employees will gain or lose due to factors beyond their control. This occurs with the Scanlon and Rucker methods which use dollars to measure productivity change.

In plants with multiple products, a measurement base must be established to reflect the past average productivity for all products and of the entire plant. This was done for a company with 350 factory hourly employees, not including those who were salaried, that produced 475 different products made of machined-metal and sheet metal components. The plant operated under measured day work; no incentives were used but conventional, engineered time standards measured the productivity of individual employees. Since these standards included only the work of production or direct employees and omitted the work of those who did all sorts of so-called nonproduction work (about one-third of all employees), it was necessary to compute the composite productivity of the entire plant.

The engineered time standards for all the operations needed to produce each product, established using traditional work-measurement methods, were totaled to obtain the overall, engineered standard time by product; this included all direct labor and excluded all nonproduction labor. Working from records of finished product transferred from production to the warehouse, the total was obtained for each product made during the prior year. These totals were then multiplied by the respective overall standard time for each product to obtain the total standard hours produced for all products. Then, the total hours worked by all employees in the plant for the year, including all the indirect workers, was obtained from the payroll ledgers.

In that year, the workers produced 367,500 standard employee hours based on product time standards and worked a total of 700,000 hours. The hours worked are much higher than the produced hours because the time standards did not include the time for receiving, shipping, maintenance, materials handling, machine set-ups, waiting for work, rework and salvage, and so forth. The actual time is in excess of standard time because the performance of the measured employees was below the 100 percent standard level. To convert the engineered standards to reflect the previous year's productivity and to factor in all actual time, a Base Productivity Factor (BPF) is computed:

$$\text{BPF} = \frac{\text{total hours worked}}{\text{total standard hours produced}}$$

The BPF represents the relationship, in the base period, between the hours worked by all employees and the value of the work in hours produced by these employees, as determined by the measurement standards. In effect, the BPF is a means to "use up" all hours worked and to factor into the original standards all occurrences that were not included in the standards. This approach is equitable to both employees and management when management is willing to use the past-average productivity as the measurement base from which to measure improvements. Auditors agree that this approach produces valid measurements of all labor-hour costs and reflects the productivity of the base period. In this example, the BPF = 700,000/367,500 = 1.905 hours.

Multiplying all engineered product time standards by 1.905 creates base standards to be used for the IMPROSHARE plan, which groups the entire plant. All 350 hourly workers were included in the product standards and the productivity measurements. The BPF states the total clock hours required during the base period to produce a 1.0 standard hour of work. The same result could be obtained by using the accounting department vs. product standard costs, expressed in hours per unit of product. A BPF would be calculated, as described above, to develop product standards for the IMPROSHARE plan.

Relationship of the BPF to Time Standards

Standard time multiplied by the BPF will reflect fully the average operating conditions and productivity that prevailed in the base period. These modified standard times, called IMPROSHARE "product standards," then are used to measure productivity in any other period. The BPF adds all plant labor hours not included in the standard times, excluding holidays, vacations, and nonworked time.

Productivity measurement must be made against a defined base or the measurements will have no meaning. This requires that measurement standards be frozen, or at least clearly identified as to the base. For example, suppose overall productivity of a plant is raised by 10 percent. If the measurement standards are updated at the end of the year and multiplied by 0.909 (1.0/1.1 or 100 percent divided by 110 percent), the plant productivity will show no improvement. Productivity measurements for IMPROSHARE must be made against frozen measurement standards at the beginning of the IMPROSHARE program. The accounting department will continue to update its standard costs following accepted accounting practice, but the standards used as the basis for the IMPROSHARE product standards must not be changed.

In the previous example, the BPF was calculated as 1.905, based on 700,000 total hours worked and 367,500 hours transferred to finished goods, representing standard time. Suppose the time standards in this plan were cut in half; the calculations would be:

$$BPF = \frac{700,000}{367,500/2} = 3.810$$

The BPF would be doubled, but the IMPROSHARE product standards would be the same, reflecting the average operating conditions and productivity that prevailed in the base period. Once the BPF is established, it is carried on into the future with no change. The assumption is that the relationship between standard time and total IMPROSHARE product standards is fairly constant.

Standards for new operations and products in the future must be set to the same work performance base used to set standards in the base period. Reducing either time standards or the BPF will tighten the measurement system; such tightening is not proper under IMPROSHARE. Exceptions are new capital equipment and technology, which are specifically defined. The BPF established for different plants cannot be compared because each plant has its own base-period characteristics and measurement practices. The BPF in one plant can be quite different than that in another plant, depending on the products, how the time standards are set, and so on.

Once established, the BPF concept can be used to measure productivity changes from one period to another by calculating the Operating Productivity Factor (OPF) for a period, just as the BPF was calculated. Suppose the OPF of a period is 1.89 and the base period BPF is 2.0. The change in productivity is calculated as $(2.0 - 1.89)/2.0 = .055 = 5.5$ percent improvement. Conversely, if the base period BPF is 1.89 and the new period OPF is 2.0, the change is $(1.89/2.00)/1.89 = -.0582 = 5.82$ percent reduced productivity.

Essentials of the IMPROSHARE Plan

An IMPROSHARE plan can be developed for all sorts of operations. The plan can be applied to one person or a thousand, to groups or to an entire plant. It can be used to supplement incentive plans or to replace them. Several plans can operate in a company. The versatility of IMPROSHARE comes from the way productivity is measured: hours of input against output, expressed as hours.

A full IMPROSHARE plan contains details of how to establish measurement standards and calculate productivity changes and how to make calculations under changing conditions. The main features of the plan are:

- Increased productivity is shared by employees in the group, usually the entire plant or company.
- The input is the total hours worked by the group.
- The hour value of the output of the group is the total good units produced multiplied by the respective past average-hour standards.

- Productivity improvement is shared 50/50 between employees and the company.

- Gains are usually calculated weekly, with a moving average to span several weeks to create a stable output level. Productivity is usually shared and paid weekly. Some companies pay monthly.

- The average productivity level of a base period is the measurement base. The average labor hours required during a base period to produce a unit of product is established as standard. This includes all indirect and so-called nonproduction time, such as materials handling, set-up, inspections, delays, rework, and so forth, as well as the direct labor time.

- Employee hour standards are frozen at the average of the base period. Standards are not changed when operations are changed by either management or the employees; exceptions are capital equipment and material changes, which are specifically defined. Increased productivity is shared with no attempt to pinpoint whether employees or management created the improvements.

- An agreed-upon ceiling is established on productivity-sharing earnings. The excess over the ceiling is carried forward to future weeks; eventually the standards may be "bought back" from the employees by cash payments.

The main constraints on the plan are:

- Total unit time under the plan cannot exceed unit time in the past. Time must decrease as productivity is raised.

- Management rights are not changed. All changes in methods and quality must be approved by management. Production levels, schedules, assignment of employees, and so forth, are vested in management, as they were before.

- Union contractual agreements are not altered.

The plan limits management to following a set of rules but puts few restrictions on employees. It is an unusual agreement in a technical sense because the employees are not held to any conditions. The IMPROSHARE plan does not require the signature of union representatives or that employees follow any new rules. The plan's ground rules specify how productivity will be measured and shared, who will be included, how various types of production changes will be handled, and other such details. All of these are binding only on management.

Placing the responsibility on management does not make the arrangements more or less favorable to the employees. The proposition to share does not obligate management to make any payments unless productivity actually increases as measured by management's yardsticks and records. The plan clearly provides that management's rights are not changed. Management does not enter a blind arrangement or give up any traditional prerogatives and rights. Employees' interests are protected since all productivity records by operations and products are open to inspection by employees. Current working conditions, benefits, and wages are protected; no one can earn less than before.

The IMPROSHARE plan measures only final results, usually as finished product ready for shipment. The system encourages employees to become concerned with matters they previously ignored. Employees will not take on management's responsibilities and start running the plant. However, to make more good product per hour, they will use skills and abilities that today may not be utilized. They will voluntarily do things they would refuse to do if ordered to by management without the plan. When employees become oriented to the bottom line, a new world of potential improvements opens up.

Control Over the IMPROSHARE Plan

The greatest difficulty in controlling the operation of traditional incentives is that the time standards deteriorate over time. This occurs as employees use their ingenuity to improve their incentive earnings. To obscure the looseness, employees hold back on production and often work less than a full day to maintain a level of incentive earnings that will not alert management to the loosened standards. In some plants, this process seriously retards overall productivity. The IMPROSHARE plan creates opposite conditions. Employees are encouraged to use their ingenuity, make changes in how the operations are performed, and keep raising their output. The goal is to raise overall productivity and share the gains.

The IMPROSHARE plan provides that measurement standards are frozen at the average of the base period and are not changed except for capital equipment and material changes or a buy-back of standards. Control over the IMPROSHARE plan is maintained by:

1. A ceiling on productivity improvement, generally set at 160 percent, which is 30 percent in earnings

2. A cash buy-back of measurement standards when productivity exceeds the ceiling

3. An 80/20 share of improvements created by capital equipment

The IMPROSHARE plan establishes a ceiling on earnings. When productivity exceeds the ceiling in any measurement period, the excess hours produced are banked and moved ahead to the next period. Banking the excess is an inducement for the employees to produce as much as they can in order to create a cushion for subsequent periods when productivity may be lower than the ceiling. Should productivity rise above the ceiling and continue at a high level, the IMPROSHARE plan provides a simple formula for a one-time cash buy-back equivalent to 50 percent of one year's savings created by the changed standards. The process is voluntary, and employees and management must agree to the buy-back. The ceiling and buy-back provision does not limit productivity, but it provides an extra inducement to employees to raise output further and rewards the company for contributing the efforts of its experts and specialists to help the employees gain half the improvements.

The ceiling and buy-back works as follows: Suppose productivity averages 180 percent and the ceiling is 160 percent. The excess hours produced, represented by the 20 percentage points, are banked for future periods. If productivity remains over the ceiling, the standards can be bought back with the employees' agreement to the 160 percent level, or any other level, reduced by a factor, so that, in this case, 180 percent becomes 160 percent. The employees receive a cash payment of 50 percent of the 20 percent, projected for a year, at their regular pay. A $10-an-hour employee would receive a cash payment of $10 × 2000 hours × 50% × 20% = $2000. Simultaneous with the buy-back, all time standards are reduced by a multiplier of 1.6/1.8 = 0.8889.

Capital equipment and material gains are also shared. Expenditures for equipment of $15,000 or more (varies by plant) are identified as capital change. Eighty percent of the savings attributed to the equipment are removed from the measurement standards, and 20 percent are left in. Since productivity gains are shared 50/50, management retains another 10 percent, so management received 90 percent of the gains created by the equipment. Employees share 50 percent of all gains from equipment that costs less than $15,000 and 10 percent of all gains from equipment costing more than $15,000. Material changes are treated the same way. Over several years, the shared gains from capital equipment can be substantial.

Employees may question why gains should be shared 50/50, when, they claim, they do all the work. In introducing an IMPROSHARE plan, management revises a cardinal rule on how time standards are established. Under traditional work-measurement practices, when changes are made in methods, procedures, tools and dies, or other factors that affect how operations are performed, new operation time standards are established and the company gets all the gains. This occurs even when employees create the changes, as when a suggestion plan operates.

Under IMPROSHARE, operation standards are frozen at the base-period level and are not changed when operations are changed by either management or the employees, except for capital equipment and technology changes or for buy-backs of standards. Increased productivity is shared with no attempt to pinpoint whether employees or management created the savings. Since management personnel continually make operations changes when the IMPROSHARE plan goes into effect, even if the employees make no contributions, they still receive 50 percent of the 100 percent gains that the company always had retained in the past.

Establishing an IMPROSHARE Plan

Since valid output and input measurements are essential to establishing an IMPROSHARE plan, one of the first steps in designing a plan is to develop the measurement system following the IMPROSHARE principles.

Output is measured by counting finished product ready for shipment. Parts and subassemblies used in the production process are not counted; no credit is given for work in process. When parts and subassemblies are shipped as spare parts, these then are designated as products. Under the plan, product is anything that is packed for shipment. For output measurement under IMPROSHARE, the total hours required to manufacture product must include the hours of all employees involved in the plan, as reflected in the IMPROSHARE product standards, at the average productivity level prevailing in the base period. When direct labor standards are not available, the direct labor content of each product can be estimated and then the BPF can be calculated. Various estimating procedures can be devised. Some plants list the operation sequence by part and obtain, or estimate, the direct labor by operation. Other plants develop matrix charts with two or more variables from which to determine the labor content.

Measuring Job Shops With
IMPROSHARE

Job shops and low-volume production are the most difficult operations to measure using traditional work measurement practices. Job shops usually estimate and bid every job. IMPROSHARE can use the labor content of the estimate as the standard. All sorts of contract and one-time jobs can be handled this way, including diversified work such as the preparation of computer programs, the fabrication of structural steel, and construction projects; there is no limit.

The goal is to beat the hours estimated in the quotation and share the gains. The money quotation includes figures, such as material costs, overhead, markup, and so forth, that will not affect or be used in the measurement of productivity.

IMPROSHARE for
Nonmanufacturing

IMPROSHARE can be applied to any work for which unit work counts can be developed. For example:

Bank operations; check encoding: The total hours required to process checks during a base period is the standard. Include hours of service people, trainers, supervisors, batch totalers, and others.

Surface mine: Two standards are required: one for removing and replacing overburden and the other for removing the mineral or coal. Use hours per cubic yard of overburden and hours per ton of mined materials. Include all employees in one or the other. Pool total input and output.

Warehouse: Hours per case or line item shipped is usually the standard. Include hours of all employees. If receipts are out of phase with shipments, set hours of receipts separate from shipments.

Using IMPROSHARE With
Traditional Incentives

An IMPROSHARE plan can be designed to operate in conjunction with traditional incentives, or the incentives can be replaced by IMPROSHARE. The following alternatives are possible:.

1. The incentive plan can be discontinued and replaced by IMPROSHARE.

2. All or some of the incentives can continue, and only employees who do not participate in the incentives are included in IMPROSHARE.

3. The incentives can continue, and an IMPROSHARE plan can cover all employees, including those on incentive. Several variations are possible.

Concept of Charged Hours

When a plant operates without incentives, the average productivity during the base year is reflected in the BPF. Dividing the hours worked by all employees included in the plan by the total produced hours at standard provides a BPF that reflects the base-period productivity. When an incentive plan operates before introduction of an IMPROSHARE plan, in calculating the BPF it is necessary to include in the BPF numerator the incentive premium hours earned by all employees on incentive and to include the total hours worked by all employees. The sum of hours worked plus hours earned as incentive premium is termed "charged hours." The time standards used to generate the standard hours produced for the base period would show standard productivity at the level where incentive earnings start. Since the employees earned incentive pay in the base period, the actual productivity level was higher than standard; the amount by which it exceeded standard is calculated for the base period for all employees on incentive (expressed in hours). Incentive premium is paid in dollars and converted to equivalent hours earned by dividing the total dollar premium incentive pay by the average hourly rate of all employees on incentive.

This is illustrated by an example. For purposes of the example assume 100 hourly employees, 52 incentive and 48 nonincentive; incentive employees are at 125 percent average productivity.

Incentive direct labor hours	(52 × 40)	2080
Nonincentive hours	(48 × 40)	1920
Total hours worked		4000
Incentive premium hours	(25% × 2080)	520
Charged hours (total hours worked + premium hours)		4520

The rationale for the concept of charged hours is that if the employees were all at 100 percent, instead of 52 employees at 125 percent, to maintain the same output there would have to be (52 × 125%) 65 employees. The total hours worked would then be (48 + 65) × 40 = 4520 hours, which is the same as the calculations above in which the incentive premium hours were added.

In calculating the BPF for a plant in which incentives will be retained or replaced by IMPROSHARE, the numerator of the fraction must be the charged hours, equal to the total hours worked by all employees in the plan, plus the premium incentive hours earned during the base period by all incentive employees. In calculating productivity after the plan is established, the charged-hours concept must also be followed.

IMPROSHARE to Replace Traditional Incentives

A traditional incentive plan can be discontinued and replaced by IMPROSHARE. To protect the employees who have been on incentive against reduced earnings, they are guaranteed their former average premium hourly earnings as a personal red-circle add-on. All employees, those formerly on incentive and those not, will then receive the same percent share from productivity improvement on their base earnings, not including red circles. The company is protected against loss by the charged-hours concept; all red circles paid each period are added to hours worked as charged hours. Output hours must exceed the charged hours for productivity sharing to pay off.

IMPROSHARE for Nonincentive Employees Only

When incentives are retained and IMPROSHARE will involve only non-incentive employees, the productivity calculations are the same as for the entire plant, except that only the nonincentive employees share in the gains. Productivity of the entire plant is calculated by total product made. The input hours are the charged hours of the entire plant, which includes all hours worked plus incentive premium hours. In calculating the productivity share to all employees eligible to share, which includes only those who are not on incentive, divide the 50 percent hours gained by the hours worked by only the nonincentive employees.

Sharing Material Savings

Establishing productivity sharing with measurement only of completed product always saves materials yields. Employees become quality conscious because, to save production labor, they produce fewer defects. Inevitably there are savings in materials.

Labor savings and material savings can be shared in separate plans.

Labor savings are usually measured weekly on a moving average with gains included in a regular pay check. Material savings are generally distributed several times a year. When materials usage can be calculated in short periods, improved yield can be reflected as equivalent hours and integrated into the labor-productivity calculations. Most companies have records of materials and maintenance supplies consumed. Using the records of several years' usage, the dollars spent on materials per standard hour produced can be established as standards for the various items. Since material prices change, a constant dollar base must be established using a suitable producer price index published monthly by the U.S. Department of Labor. Each month, the actual usage is compared with the standard usage, and the difference is posted on a spreadsheet. The cumulative gain or loss for the month is carried forward to following months so that all in the plant can see the gains accumulating in the material plan. At the end of the period, 50 percent of the total dollar gains are divided by the total pay of all eligible employees and the fund is distributed to each employee in relation to his or her annual pay.

IMPROSHARE for Hourly and Salaried Employees

Managers who see the potential for productivity improvement through IMPROSHARE readily agree that all hourly employees should be included in the IMPROSHARE plan. Many also agree that supervisors of hourly employees are important to the success of a program and that they should be included. However, there are differences on whether to include other salaried employees.

Proponents of including salaried employees believe that:

- All employees can contribute to productivity improvement. The argument that direct employees make a greater contribution than indirect employees is unsound. Higher productivity will be attained when all employees are involved.

- Offering earnings gains to hourly and not to salaried employees will cause resentment on the part of the latter. In union plants, salaried employees may believe management favors the union members. Labor relations are improved when everyone is included.

- The wage structure is preserved when all employees share in the gains. Permitting increases only to hourly employees will compress earnings between the two groups.

- Salaried employees are drawn closer to the production operations and will be more effective in their work.

Reasons for not including salaried employees are that:

- Salaried employees are traditionally expected to represent management's interests in the we-they adversary relations of managing the plant. Many are in managerial positions and are expected to perform effectively without extra compensation.
- Salaried employees do not affect factor productivity to an appreciable extent; pieces are produced mainly by hourly employees.
- Extra compensation paid to the salaried employees will increase costs if increased productivity could be attained without the extra pay.

There are valid arguments for and against each position. The contention by some managers that professional employees, supervisors, and others in higher positions are well paid to perform their work and should not have to be paid extra for doing superior work does not match the widespread practice among top management of paying substantial bonuses for improved performance by top management. A cogent argument favoring the inclusion of salaried employees is that as hourly earnings increase, the relationship between hourly and salaried employees is compressed, inevitably forcing management to raise salaried wage scales. Increased take-home pay earned by increased productivity is not a wage increase. Wage increases are permanent, with no tie to productivity.

Mechanics of Including Salaried Employees

Salaried employees can be included in an IMPROSHARE plan by using one of two methods: (1) include salaried hours in calculating the BPF and in measuring productivity or (2) do not include salaried hours and pay the average of the plan. When salaried are included with hourly, their productivity is also measured and the BPF is calculated the same way as it is for hourly employees only. In measuring productivity for hourly employees in a previous example, the BPF was calculated based on:

Employees: 350

Total hours worked by hourly for year: 700,000

Total direct labor standard hours produced for year: 367,500

$$\text{Hourly BPF} = \frac{700,000}{367,500} = 1.905$$

Assume 60 salaried employees will also be included in the plan:

$$\text{Hourly + Salaried BPF} = \frac{(350 + 60) \times 2000}{367,500} = 2.231$$

The BPF for hourly employees only is 1.905; including the salaried workers increases it to 2.231. When salaried employees are excluded from an IMPROSHARE plan, the supervisors can be included by adding their hours to the BPF or paying them the average percent earned by the plan. Paying salaried employees the average of the plan is the more appropriate method to use if the salaried employees can affect plan productivity but their hours are expected to remain fairly constant.

Including the Total Company

When hourly and salaried employees are included in the IMPROSHARE plan by including them in the BPF, care must be used to account for fixed and variable employees. When only the factory hourly employees are included, the BPF is fairly constant at different volumes of business. When fixed salaried hours are included in BPF future calculations, variations in volume can distort the productivity measurements; with increased volume, the fixed employees are overabsorbed, and the reverse occurs with reduced volume.

To measure the entire company of hourly factory and salaried employees, an effective approach is to include hourly factory employees plus variable nonfactory employees in the BPF. For illustration, assume that a company has 350 factory hourly employees; 21 salaried fixed factory supervisors in administrative, engineering, accounting, purchasing, personnel, and so forth; 60 variable employees; and 53 fixed employees. Calculate the BPF on the factory hourly employees and only include the administrative variable. Also, assume the total produced standard or measured hours for all product made in the year was 367,500 hours. The BPF calculations would be:

$$\text{BPF} = \frac{(\text{hourly } 350 + 60 \text{ variable}) \times 2000}{367,500 \text{ std. hrs}} = 2.231$$

All 484 employees would be included in the plan, although productivity measurements would be calculated on 410 employees. The 21 supervisors and 53 fixed salaried employees would also share in the productivity gains. They would be paid the average of the plan, but their hours would not be in the BPF or charged to the productivity calculations. One approach is to include only the hourly and nonexempt salaried employees (nonexempt as defined by wage and hour regulations of the Department of Labor) in the BPF calculations and omit all exempt employees. The hourly and nonexempt employees are usually variable with respect to production volume. Exempt employees are more likely to be fixed. All employees, including the exempt, would participate in the plan. Exempt employees would receive the same percent sharing paid to the hourly and nonexempt employees, but the exempt hours would not be included in productivity calculations.

Summary

The success of the IMPROSHARE plan depends on the involvement of the employees in efforts to raise productivity. Employees and management must be dedicated to creating more effective operations. An important element in the success of IMPROSHARE is that employees share directly in productivity gains; they see the fruits of their efforts in their paychecks. The entire work force is involved. Since productivity losses affect them, employees speak up and propose ways to reduce costs and facilitate output. Most importantly, they participate actively in raising productivity. Managers should consider utilizing the skills, efforts, and knowledge of the work force. Traditional managing, which relies completely on the abilities of management's experts, has enabled productivity to reach high levels. Even higher productivity levels will be attained by encouraging the entire work force to assist in raising productivity and reducing costs.

13
Gain Sharing: Sharing Improved Performance

Timothy L. Ross

Co-Director
Ross Gain Sharing Institute

Ruth Ann Ross

Co-Director
Ross Gain Sharing Institute

What Gain Sharing Is

The concept of sharing gains with employees is certainly not new. The term *gain sharing* was used as early as 1889 in an article written by Henry R. Towne, even though the word is not a formal dictionary term. In a very broad context, most companies use some form of gain sharing, even if limited to higher management. Some consultants and writers promote packaged plans; others say that only narrow employee-controlled measures work; and still others say that only a broad-measurement plan, close to and including profit sharing, works.

In its most elementary form, gain sharing is a group bonus plan that shares improved performance with most or all employees of a unit. In its broadest form, it is a plan that includes profit sharing, individual and/or small group incentives, management bonus plans, and so forth, all under the banner of gain sharing.

In earlier days, these boundaries were much more clearly defined since many applications were packaged approaches known by names such as Scanlon, Rucker, and IMPROSHARE. Scanlon, which emphasizes heavy employee involvement, Rucker, which promotes value added as a calculation, and IMPROSHARE, which uses a standards-based calculation and does not require a formalized employee-involvement system, are still being installed. However, the trend today is moving toward more customized plans that meet the needs and sophistication of a particular organization, although some people still promote narrow- or broad-packaged plans as a panacea to solve most, if not all, problems. Frankly, we don't know which system works best in all situations; research generally studies successful plans, which tells us little about unsuccessful ones. There are, however, some common characteristics of gain sharing about which most people agree. They are as follows:

Performance Improvement-Related

A goal of all gain sharing plans is to improve performance by changing employee behavior. Performance can be measured narrowly, by using total actual time versus standard time or physical measures of output versus physical measures of input (for example, 40 tons of coal in 40 hours), or broadly, by using calculations based on *improving* profits or return on investments.

Based Upon Something

Historically, most gain sharing plans were based on some measure of past performance, from periods as short as a few months to as long as several years. There seems to be a trend today toward basing the bonus on a combination of past and expected performances. The advantage of using past performance is its ease of building trust; employees can more easily accept what the desired performance is and that it is attainable since they achieved it in the past. Some "experts" promote using the most recent past year.

Shared With All or Most Employees

In the past, gain sharing has included select groups of employees, such as hourly or factory employees, but the trend today is toward including almost everyone. Double-dipping into two bonuses is discouraged, so some executives or sales-commissioned people may be excluded on all or part of their wages. In fact, the idea of including most people and basing it upon past performance pretty much excludes all managerial bonus plans from gain sharing.

Employee Involvement-Related

Most, but not all, plans include considerable employee involvement since the emphasis is on developing better cooperation, communications, teamwork, and goal attainments. In fact, gain sharing would have a hard time surviving in the long run without extensive employee involvement and communications. Most consultants of gain sharing are behaviorally oriented and often view gain sharing as a fairly refined form of organizational development that marks significant employee self-control as its ultimate goal; much time is spent in developing the concept of working smarter, not just working harder.

Not Individual-Oriented

Since gain sharing is group-oriented, individual-oriented systems are typically excluded. Before installation, most, but not all, firms eliminate individual-oriented systems, such as piece-rates and pay-for-suggestion systems, neither of which seem to work well after a period of time for a variety of reasons.

Site-Specific

Although exceptions can be found, most plans are site-specific and, therefore, generally exclude companywide plans, such as the Ford and General Motors profit-sharing plans. These companywide systems do little, if anything at all, to change behavior by themselves.

Long Term-Oriented

Most gain sharing plans are not installed for short-term results; the employee involvement aspect makes this difficult. Few are installed on a pilot, small-department basis for the same reason. It is hard to isolate the group because of the emphasis placed on interdependency within the organization.

Not Part of Wages

Traditionally, gain sharing has been maintained separately, set apart from market-based pay systems. That is, it has not been considered part of normal compensation. Consequently, it has almost always been excluded from union contracts, for example.

Paid Frequently

Most gain sharing plans pay earned bonuses more than once a year. Monthly, quarterly, bimonthly, and even weekly payouts are being made in gain sharing plans today.

Why Companies Install Gain Sharing Plans

The outcomes of a successful gain sharing plan can be numerous. These include: increased competition; more emphasis on quality and cost reduction; more knowledge and assistance to help; more "healthy" knowledge and experience about employee involvement; and more responsive managers. The reasons for installing a gain sharing plan are as numerous as the plans' potential results, but most interested companies can be grouped into one of three broad categories.

Troubled Companies

Their need to change is apparent. A variety of problems are often present: low or no profits, poor labor relations, limited trust, declining business, and so forth. In these situations, gain sharing leads the organization through a change process. Major change is expected. Gain sharing has been proven to change behaviors and performance in a very short time period. In fact, one of the fathers of modern gain sharing, Joe Scanlon, was hesitant to install it in other than troubled companies.

Successful Companies

These companies install gain sharing plans because they believe in sharing, capitalism, more employee self-control, and employee involvement.

They install gain sharing plans because they *believe* in it, not because they *have* to. A large number of successful firms, such as Motorola, General Electric, and 3M, have installed gain sharing plans for these reasons. In these situations, gain sharing follows organizational change.

Contingent-Compensation Situations

More firms are starting to tie pay, or part of it, to business performance. The greatest push for this probably has been made by unionized organizations, but it is rapidly spreading into nonunion situations. Traditionally, the gain sharing bonus was paid *over and above* normal and equitable wages, but this is no longer true in all situations. Because of increased competition, particularly from foreign countries, many organizations can no longer afford the automatic pay increases rewarded to employees in the past. Companies now look to gain sharing plans to help instill in employees the notion that more pay results when the company makes more profits or has improved other performance. As the Japanese have discovered, increased identification with the company is built into a system that ties pay to firm performance; such identification is implied by this approach to gain sharing. Unions, in general, are not big proponents of gain sharing because firms may and have used gain sharing as a substitute for normal wage increments.

Types of Organizations Installing Gain Sharing Plans

Most gain sharing installations are made by manufacturing firms with 100 to 1000 employees, although several have over 1500 employees; about 40 percent of these are unionized. Most of them are plants or divisions of larger companies rather than small, privately owned companies, as was true in the past. Gain sharing plans are slowly gaining acceptance by service sector organizations, such as hospitals, banks, and insurance companies. This trend is likely to accelerate in the future.

The government is also installing some gain sharing plans at various local, state, and national levels. Various initiatives at these levels are expected to continue at an increasing rate.

Gain Sharing's Relationship to Profit Sharing

Most gain sharing plans stop short of sharing profits with employees, but about one-third of the plans are profit-oriented and many experts heavily promote such an approach if coupled with extensive employee involvement. We believe that some people will include profit sharing as one form of gain sharing and others will exclude it. For those organizations that base their bonus on profit improvement (that is, a hurdle rate) and include the other components discussed earlier, such as including most employees as eligible bonus recipients, promoting employee involvement, making payments more than once a year, and being site-specific, there is no difficulty in classifying their plans as gain sharing. To summarize, some people classify profit-oriented systems based on improvements, not just a percent of profits, as a form of gain sharing and others do not. To say that employees cannot understand profit-oriented calculations is erroneous; comprehension just requires a little more effort.

Why Gain Sharing Works

Many successful companies already do or should espouse the tenets of gain sharing. Gain sharing integrates communications, teamwork, goal orientation, improvement in quality and performance, employee involvement, and financial rewards into one system. There are no secret tenets, and successful firms work on them continually. The benefits of gain sharing include more long-term identity with the company, improved communications, employee involvement, and shared rewards from improved performance. We do not believe that management would install gain sharing without expecting to get something in return for both the company and hopefully all employees. Possible benefits for management include: emphasis on improved performance through cooperation, rewards tied to improved performance, use of a goal-oriented system, a structured approach to the change process that is needed, and getting people to relate to economics and identify with the company. Possible benefits for employees include: improved long-term employment security; a way to make changes and get things done; learning more about the company; a way to get recognized for performance; improved communications, teamwork, and cooperation; a way to get involved with the company in many ways; and the possibility of more money.

Key Issues Underlying Gain Sharing

If you were to read the more than 100 articles and books written on gain sharing, you would find that most deal with the two issues outlined in Figure 13-1.

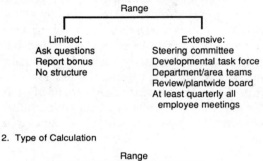

1. Involvement (Includes Teamwork/Communication/Recognition)

Range

Limited:
Ask questions
Report bonus
No structure

Extensive:
Steering committee
Developmental task force
Department/area teams
Review/plantwide board
At least quarterly all
   employee meetings

2. Type of Calculation

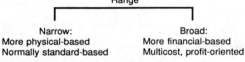

Range

Narrow:
More physical-based
Normally standard-based

Broad:
More financial-based
Multicost, profit-oriented

Figure 13-1. The two key issues of gain sharing.

A relationship exists between these two major issues. For example, if a coal miner produces 40 tons of coal in 40 hours in the first week and 44 tons in 40 hours in the second week, physical performance has increased by 10 percent (1 ton per hour to 1.1 tons per hour). This increase could be caused by capital improvements, the person's working harder, easier coal to mine, and so on. If between the first week and the second week the price of coal decreased by 25 percent, the financial performance has decreased. No doubt, most employees relate more to physical performance, but financial performance is most important to the long-term success of the company. The two key calculation issues are to what degree you need employee involvement, education, and communications if you want to change behavior, and what the company wants to pay for.

Involvement

Does a company need a major commitment to employee involvement? Although some people may disagree, most successful long-term gain sharing plans require a considerable amount of employee involvement in some form. This amount may vary from relatively limited and informal involvement to a fairly elaborate and extensive one that utilizes the overlapping-team concept to build long-term identity and changed behavior.

A fairly typical overlapping-team concept of employee involvement in its installation and operation is outlined in Figure 13-2. The approach shown in Figure 13-2 seems to work quite well. It has been used for many years and could probably be called an intermediate level of employee involvement. It may not materially change the daily operations of a department. Although many other options can be found in practice, many consultants recommend this type of approach.

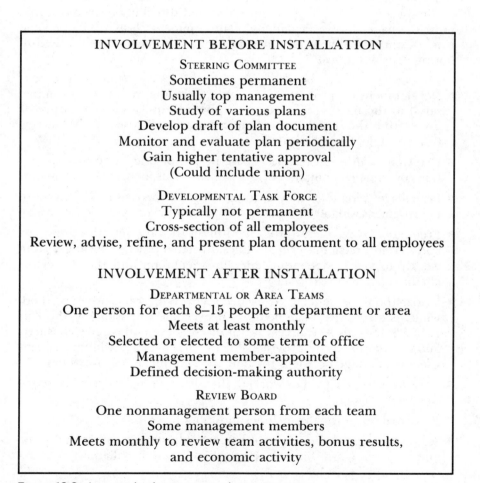

INVOLVEMENT BEFORE INSTALLATION

STEERING COMMITTEE
Sometimes permanent
Usually top management
Study of various plans
Develop draft of plan document
Monitor and evaluate plan periodically
Gain higher tentative approval
(Could include union)

DEVELOPMENTAL TASK FORCE
Typically not permanent
Cross-section of all employees
Review, advise, refine, and present plan document to all employees

INVOLVEMENT AFTER INSTALLATION

DEPARTMENTAL OR AREA TEAMS
One person for each 8–15 people in department or area
Meets at least monthly
Selected or elected to some term of office
Management member-appointed
Defined decision-making authority

REVIEW BOARD
One nonmanagement person from each team
Some management members
Meets monthly to review team activities, bonus results,
and economic activity

Figure 13-2. An example of an organization's team structure.

Types of Calculations and Payment Issues

In actual practice, one can find a wide range of calculations from physical measures of output (for example, board feet of lumber, standard time earned, documents processed) as related to hours of labor input to much more profit-oriented calculations. Some successful gain sharing plans measure improvements in return on investment. The ultimate success of any calculation will depend on several common factors. It must be perceived as fair by the employees, company, and customers; it must meet management's objectives; and it must be understandable and relatively easy to administer. Several examples will be discussed after outlining some of the key measurement and distribution decisions that must be made. Most calculations relate inputs, such as labor, to some ratio of outputs. When deciding on calculations, keep in mind the following considerations:

- Development of a measure of output from the broad (for example, sales) to the narrow (for example, physical units) and a measure of input from the broad (for example, most or all costs) to the narrow (for example, labor hours)
- Determination of an historical base period or one based on expectations or some combination of the two (which is increasingly common)
- Percentage going to employees (ranges from 10 percent to 75 percent of improvement with 50/50 being fairly common for narrow calculations)
- Frequency of payment (often monthly with some set aside for year-end to reinforce long-term attitudes; in actual practice, it ranges from weekly to yearly depending on the orientation and the degree of changed behavior expected)
- Distribution (percentage to each employee or some other method, which is a sensitive issue because of overtime provisions of the Fair Labor Standards Act; unless profit-oriented, one must give consideration to the overtime provisions of the act, which is why most firms use a percentage of wages for time worked, including overtime)
- Basis of pay (time paid or worked; this also is a sensitive issue in actual practice)
- Participation (normally includes most employees)
- Adjustment procedures (some require adjustment for capital, mix, and so forth, which have to be specified before installation)

- Separate check or not (most pay as a separate check)
- Moving base or not (some experts are strongly against moving the base and some do not believe that one should pay for a one-shot improvement in performance—obviously, a very sensitive issue)

The developmental task force previously outlined *may* be allowed an important say in some of these decisions.

Although many calculations are found in practice, we have outlined three of the most common forms: one based on a broad measure of performance, one based on physical performance, and one based on a multiple pool concept.

Multicost-Calculation Example (Broad Measure of Performance):

	Period A
1. Output (could be revenue, total standard cost, or some other measure)	$1,000,000
2. Costs allowed (assume 80 percent of line 1 from history or targets)	$ 800,000
3. Actual costs	770,000
4. Bonus pool (line 2 minus line 3)	$ 30,000
5. Employee share (assume 50 percent of line 4)	$ 15,000
6. Reserve for year-end (assume 1/3 of line 5)	5,000
7. Net bonus (line 5 minus line 6)	$ 10,000
8. Participating payroll (all participating payroll)	$ 200,000
9. Bonus percentage (line 7 divided by line 8 or $10,000/$200,000)	5%

This calculation is fairly broad, and the more costs included, the closer one gets to profit sharing. Line 1, output, is generally a broad measure of output, such as sales or sales plus or minus changes in inventory to make it more production-oriented. From line 2, allowed costs in this orientation, usually felt to be those over which employees have more control, are determined from which actual costs are deducted. The bonus pool is on line 4. If the employee share of the improvement is 50 percent (line 5), one-third is set aside for the year-end (line 6) to protect against normal ups and downs and reinforce long-term attitudes (distributed at year-end if positive and normally absorbed by company at year-end if negative) to yield the net bonus (line 7). When divided by participating payroll (line 8), one arrives at the net bonus percentage (line 9).

Allowed-Labor Calculation Example (Physical Performance):

	Period A
1. Allowed labor (for example, standard hours allowed or physical units times hours per unit, generally from history)	5000 hours
2. Actual hours	4600
3. Performance improvement	400 hours
4. Hours to employees (assume 50 percent or 1/2 of line 3)	200
5. Percentage improvement (line 4 divided by line 2)	4.3%

If there is no reserve, each employee would typically receive a 4.3 percent increase in the hours paid for the period; overtime hours normally count at 1-½ of normal hours. This is similar to the IMPROSHARE type of calculation based on more physical measures of performance. It has been used by gain sharing companies for over 30 years, including some Scanlon-oriented systems.

Expanded Labor-Calculation Example (Multiple Pool Concept):

POOL 1—LABOR PRODUCTIVITY   Period A

1. Allowed hours (based on historical standard hours earned)		5,000 hours
2. Actual hours		4,600
3. Performance improvement		400 hours
4. Percentage improvement (line 3 divided by line 2)		8.7%
5. Participating payroll (assume)	$ 100,000	
6. Net addition (line 4 times line 5) before split and reserve	$ 8,700	Pool 1

POOL 2—OTHER COSTS OR QUALITY

7. Examples of costs allowed as a percentage of revenue, or standard hours, or standard cost (based on history or targets): scrap, overtime, material quantity variance, supplies, travel	8%	
8. Revenue (as an example)	$1,000,000	
9. Allowed costs (line 7 times line 8)	$ 80,000	
10. Actual costs	$ 75,000	
11. Net addition (line 9 minus line 10)	$ 5,000	Pool 2

Pool 1	$ 8,700
Pool 2	$ 5,000
Total bonus pool	$13,700

Decisions are needed for how the split should be apportioned to employees, reserve, and so forth. One could distribute a different percentage of each pool, which is common. Three pools are fairly common: labor productivity, quality and/or customer service, and expenses. This is an expansion of the allowed labor calculation and may well become the most common gain sharing calculation in the long term because of its flexibility. For those firms so inclined, profit goals can be easily tied into the year-end reserve to develop an even closer tie to total performance.

Conditions Supportive of Success

If one assumes that a major, long-term change process is desired with significant changes in employee behavior, some specific areas among others are important for success.

1. Management commitment (this must be fairly specific)
2. Need to change or strong desire to improve or continue to improve (one or the other is strongly needed)
3. Management acceptance and encouragement of employee input and education
4. High interaction and cooperation
5. Lack of major threats to job and employment security or lack of major problems with business volume
6. Adequate information on productivity and costs
7. Goal setting
8. Commitment on part of all people to the change or improvement process
9. Agreement on a calculation that is relatively simple, perceived as fair, and meets management objectives

What the Evidence on Gain Sharing Shows

Dozens of case studies and government studies document the merits of gain sharing. Perhaps the most comprehensive study, done by the

American Productivity (and Quality) Center,[1] included over 200 gain sharing companies. Some of the results from the study are:

1. The reason for implementing gain sharing was that performance improvement was important or very important to 92 percent of firms.
2. Bonuses seemed to average around 7 percent to 8 percent, depending on the plan.
3. The percent reporting a positive effect on productivity and costs ranged from an average of 98 percent (Scanlon) to 84 percent (custom plans) and somewhat lower for profit sharing; many other variables also improved.
4. Gain sharing companies disclosed much more information to employees than non-gain sharing firms.
5. Percentage of pay was the most common bonus-payment method.
6. Respondents expected major growth in such systems in the future.

How to Start the Gain Sharing Process

Perhaps the most common approach is to start with a presentation for top management or someone attending a seminar. Frequently a steering committee, made up of higher management, is then formed to:

1. Evaluate the different plans.
2. Visit locations and read materials.
3. Decide on the need for involvement of outside consultants.
4. Develop a draft of a plan including:
    a. Purpose and goals
    b. Involvement system
    c. Calculation
    d. Policy issues.
5. Consider the timing of union involvement, if applicable (sometimes on a steering committee).
6. Formulate a corporate-approval process.

---

[1]Carla O'Dell, *People, Performance and Pay*, American Productivity and Quality Center, Houston, Tex., 1987, pp. 33–45.

This process varies greatly by firm. Packaged plans obviously do not include all of these steps, but all interested firms should keep an open mind in deciding what might be best for them.

The Outlook for Gain Sharing

If current trends are any indication, gain sharing applications will continue to grow, but for many different reasons. Some firms will install a gain sharing plan because they are in trouble, which is how the concept really got started. Others will use it to help eliminate a deteriorated individual incentive system. Still others will install it as a form of contingent compensation to totally or partially offset wage increases. And some will implement it because they truly believe in employees and in sharing financial and other improvements with them. Gain sharing will also show significant application in service-sector firms and periodically will be applied in government units. As over 41 million Japanese have shown, organizationwide bonus plans can help build long-term identity, communications, and positive attitudes. We expect these trends to continue.

14

Profit Sharing: A Case Study of the Fibers Department at E. I. du Pont de Nemours and Company

Robert P. McNutt

Project Manager, Compensation
Fibers Department
E. I. du Pont de Nemours and Company

To many people profit sharing means one of two things: a deferred capital accumulation plan for retirement or a plan that will share its profits with its employees. Interest today in profit sharing is a movement toward reaching a profit threshold and then sharing those earnings. The idea of creating stakeholders or owners in a business is very important as companies move from entitlement pay to pay linked to the success of a business.

The Fibers Department of E. I. du Pont de Nemours and Company embarked on a new cash profit-sharing program for its 20,000 United States employees. What follows is a case study based on more than two years of experience in which a task force developed, gained acceptance of, and implemented a new variable pay plan for the department. This chapter will address:

- Why the largest and one of the most successful business segments of du Pont (the Fibers Department had 1988 sales of $5.8 billion) moved to variable pay for all its employees

- How du Pont made such a significant change in the way its employees in the Fibers Department were paid

- Which elements of the new program applied to all 20,000 employees

Option to Investigate
Alternate Pay Programs

In the mid-1980s, du Pont, as well as many other companies, was facing global competition, confronting competitive pay practices, and inheriting new pay systems as a result of acquisitions. For example, in the pharmaceuticals area, du Pont, with its merit pay system, was competing with many companies that had commission-sales pay programs. When it acquired American Critical Care, a pharmaceuticals firm, the company inherited a commission pay system.

Du Pont recognized that for businesses to win in the marketplace, business units needed to have the flexibility and the capability to put alternate pay systems in place. In late 1986 the corporation gave its business units the option to look at alternate pay systems. The Fibers Department at du Pont had the interest and commitment to exercise that option. Even though the culture or value system within the Fibers Department had changed and continues to change, the department continues to value quality leadership, continuous improvement in everything it does, teamwork, prudent risk taking, and a self-directed work force.

Revenue from the department grew from $4.5 billion in 1984 to almost $6 billion in 1988. During the same period, earnings grew from $285 million to more than $700 million. Over this same five-year span, total employee levels within the department dropped from 27,000 to 20,000. The culture had to change in lockstep with business success. As a result, employees had to approach their jobs differently and more effectively in order to deliver record sales and earnings.

Self-management, increased span of control and reduced management layers, and the idea that personal security is related to winning in the marketplace have contributed to a shared destiny among employees. Personal security under the old culture would have meant lifelong employment, routine pay increases, and a retirement plan.

When matched against the new culture and its values, the pay system was lacking. The merit pay system for salaried employees is based on a competitive frame of reference with 15 other major United States companies. There is no relationship to business success. Also, local pay determination (pay based on the competitive labor market) at the plant sites is not linked to business success. Simply put, the existing compensation system had not kept pace with the changing culture. It was time to evaluate the system and possibly change it.

Task Team Formed

Once the energy and commitment to study compensation had been confirmed, a multifunctional task team, made up of representatives from research and development, manufacturing, marketing, business units, human resources, and corporate compensation, was formed. A person was selected from the line organization to lead the task team full-time. Task team members were selected in two ways. First, they were asked whether they had interest in working on compensation. Second, if the interest was there, they were asked if they were committed to devoting sufficient energy to the task. Would they make a contribution?

After an interview process, 12 people representing the businesses and functions in the fibers department were selected.

Task Team Process

Initially, task team members considered themselves experts on pay or compensation. Each had a preconceived notion of how people should be paid. Therefore, developing a process for analyzing the task was essential. This disciplined, systematic process for thinking and organizing was a key ingredient in producing a successful product.

The process involved developing beliefs—things the team held to be true about pay systems. A philosophy, a collection of beliefs followed by a set of principles, was created that provided the guidance for development of a pay system. Based on their beliefs, philosophy, and principles, the team members agreed to a concept leading to a design.

The task team, representing all of the functions within the Fibers Department, used sounding, or focus, groups to test the thinking of more than 1000 people in the department. Input and upgrades from employees were received at the same time that beliefs, philosophies, and principles were tested and understood.

During this process, more than 50 outside companies active in evaluating variable pay were analyzed. Many companies were willing to share their successes and failures in terms of how they pay people. The team initially worked without a consultant. Before a consultant was retained, team members wanted to shape their early thinking toward a product that was consistent with the department's developing beliefs, philosophies, and principles.

A pay system that reinforced or supported the emerging culture and value system was necessary. It was felt that the new pay system should not drive a culture change; culture change should drive a new pay system. Also, it was essential that the pay program be equitable and effective and, most importantly, perceived as fair by the employees. It could be the most equitable and fair system as assessed by the team, but if it would not be perceived as fair by employees, acceptance would become difficult. The product should enable the business to maximize the return it gets from its human resources.

Achievement-Sharing Program Design

Achievement Sharing, as the Fibers Department program is called, was based on two fundamental premises. First, it would be an enabler, a supporter, and a reinforcer of the department's business vision to increase earnings in real terms an average of 4 percent a year. Second, it would include all 20,000 employees who were based in the United States. The time had come to remove the barriers among employees. Since business success could be attributed to all employees, it was important to include everyone.

As the team began to think about the design for an alternate pay program, one of the things that the members said was needed was to give employees a stake in the business. Since the culture within the Fibers Department values success and winning, the team members thought that employees needed a form of ownership in the business. The Fibers

Department earnings performance would be linked with the individual; and in that way the employee would be identified with the department.

As the team was looking for ways to reinforce the new culture, they wanted to distinguish between competitive reality and entitlement. People were accustomed to being paid for simply coming to work, whether or not the business was successful. That is not competitive reality. Job or personal security for the 1990s and beyond should be a shared destiny toward business success.

The team also thought it would be important not to have wages or salaries reduced under Achievement Sharing. Therefore, a portion of future pay increases would be tied to the Fiber Department's success. The Achievement-Sharing program is not a cost-reduction or cost-neutral program because if the annual earnings objective is exceeded, employees will get more money than they could get under the current pay system. And consistent with the concept of cash profit sharing, an annual cash bonus will be paid to the employees based on the success of the business.

Design Specifics

As merit pay or our local frame of reference pay moves to variable compensation, the design specifies a compensation target rate made up of a 94 percent base pay rate and a 6 percent variable pay rate (see Figure 14-1). Participating employees will have 6 percent of their pay at risk but will have the opportunity to earn back 3 percent when the Fibers Department reaches 80 percent of its earnings objective and will get another 3 percent when the department fully reaches its objective. In ad-

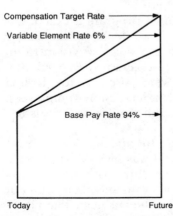

Figure 14-1. Achievement sharing.

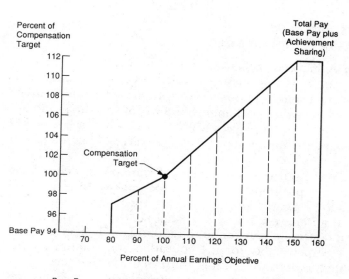

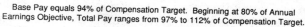

Base Pay equals 94% of Compensation Target. Beginning at 80% of Annual
Earnings Objective, Total Pay ranges from 97% to 112% of Compensation Target.

Figure 14-2. Total annual pay at 6 percent variable element.

dition, another 12 percent, for a total payout of 18 percent, is available
if earnings exceed the objective by 50 percent (see Figure 14-2).

Future employee pay increases, a portion of which would become variable
until an employee reaches the 6 percent variable, is the transition step in
moving to variable pay in the Fibers Department. Participating employees
move to variable pay by using a portion of their future increases (up to an
annual 2 percent maximum of their target compensation to a total maximum
of 6 percent at risk at the end of a three-to-five-year period).

At the end of a three-to-five-year period in which employees have
had pay increases, they should achieve a 6 percent at risk variable pay
component. Any future pay increases would be at 94 percent of what
they would have been in order to maintain the 94/96 percentage split of
fixed/variable components of pay.

An Employee Pay Example

If a Fibers Department employee with 6 percent of pay at risk has a base
pay of $28,200 a year, the pay for a counterpart du Pont employee that
is not in the Fibers Department Achievement-Sharing program would
be $30,000 a year. Therefore, for the Fibers Department employee,
$1800 is at risk. Depending upon the Fibers Department's perfor-
mance, the employee can earn between $28,200 and $33,600 or between 94 percent and 112 percent of the counterpart's $30,000 salary.

Educating for and
Communicating a Pay Change

As the design of Achievement Sharing started to take shape, the education and communication strategy planning began. Thorough employee education and communication are very important elements to the management of a successful pay change. Simply "downloading" and announcing a pay change to employees will not work when a business is making a step change from entitlement pay to variable pay or pay at risk.

A team was formed ten months prior to the announcement of the Achievement-Sharing program to develop the strategy for education and communication. Again, potential team members were asked whether they had an interest in and a commitment to developing and implementing an education and communication plan. The team members had specific responsibility for the education and communication process and wanted to do it well within a sufficient time period.

The education and communication strategy addressed the Fibers Department's vision and the role of its business with regard to the needs of du Pont. It began with the vision and then assessed the status of the department culture, the things that were valued in the organization. Finally, it addressed the pay change in relation to the vision. In the department culture, continuous improvement and a demonstration of the ability to win were fundamental in making the change that links pay to business success.

The team started with the broad issues around the education and communication strategy, but as it defined the tasks it put in place an education and communication core team at every one of the 20 Fibers Department sites. A short video was shown, and an introductory brochure was given to the employees when Achievement Sharing was announced. At follow-up meetings at the plants, sales offices, and r&d facilities, employee booklets were distributed, and additional meetings were held to help employees understand, question, and think about the movement to variable pay. A very detailed education and communication manual addressed all the issues and questions that employees had raised over two years.

The process of educating and communicating is ongoing. In 1989 refresher education was begun to ensure that people continued to understand the key aspects of the variable pay program. In addition, the need for broad business understanding was addressed. If employees are asked to be stakeholders in a business, they need to have more than a superficial knowledge of it. Each quarter employees are advised as to business performance compared with objective.

In summary, it is crucial to design the best possible education and communication process *before* a pay change is instituted. The time, effort, and resources expended are significant and instrumental to the long-term success of a new pay program.

Administration

At the time that the education and communication task force for Achievement Sharing was formed, a team of key people in the administrative systems area were identified. The administrative systems for variable pay tracked pay for each individual in two ways. First, pay for every individual was tracked as if Achievement Sharing had never existed. If an individual was transferred out of Fibers, his or her salary returned to what it would have been if he or she had never been part of Achievement Sharing. A second tracking of employee pay included the base pay plus the variable pay (equaling target pay) for each individual in the program. It is important to keep track of variable pay and base pay, both under the program, as well as pay not under the program.

With regard to impact on benefits, the decision was made that all gain sharing programs would not impact benefits and, therefore, would not be benefit bearing. On the other hand, all variable pay programs would be benefit bearing and would be impacted by business performance. An individual in Achievement Sharing could put more into the savings plan and have a higher pension calculation during times that business is very good. But, on the downside, he or she could experience a few years of poor departmental earnings performance without a payout and the pension calculation. Contribution to the savings plan as well would be negatively impacted. In the area of long-term disability and life insurance, the payout would be at target pay—the sum of base pay plus variable pay.

Systems are complex and require people and resourcing to ensure that they are appropriate for the successful introduction of a new pay plan. In summary, an effective systems design is a very important ingredient in a pay change if it is to be perceived as fair and credible.

Conclusion

There are four summary points to keep in mind as corporations begin to move toward profit sharing or variable pay from the normal compliance or entitlement pay programs.

- A change in how people are paid must be compatible with and supportive of a changing or emerging company culture. To use a pay change to drive a culture change would be a serious mistake.

- Employees have valid input and points of view. Processes must be in place to listen to and record their inputs so that they and a variable pay program can make a difference in the bottom line.

- The need to educate and communicate a change, rather than just communicate or announce it, is critical. There must be a process for educating and communicating change over time rather than in a single announcement event.

- Successfully linking a portion of employees' pay to business success should expand employees' capacity to contribute in a way that they have never contributed before.

Progressive and innovative businesses that want to survive in the 1990s and beyond will be seriously evaluating pay systems linked to business success. Moving away from entitlement pay to some form of pay at risk tied to business success is a move in the right direction.

15

The Design of Skill-Based Pay Plans

Gerald E. Ledford, Jr.

Senior Research Scientist
Center for Effective Organizations
Graduate School of Business Administration
University of Southern California

In skill-based pay systems, employees receive compensation for the range, depth, and types of skills they possess. They are paid for the skills they are capable of using, not for the job they are performing at a particular point in time. This is a fundamental departure from traditional job-based pay plans, which pay employees for the jobs they hold. Because little research has been conducted on skill-based pay, there are many questions about the forms skill-based pay can take and about the strengths and weaknesses of it. One of the most important practical limitations of the available literature is that it offers little information about how to develop skill-based pay plans. This chapter addresses this shortcoming by reviewing the key issues and options in designing skill-based pay plans.

We begin by discussing the nature of skill-based pay systems and considering three types of skill-based pay. Then we review the use and effects of skill-based pay. We also consider some of the reasons why designing a skill-based pay plan is more difficult than designing a traditional job-based pay plan. Next, we offer a framework for understanding skill-based pay design issues. Finally, we explore in detail the key design issues in skill-based pay and their associated design options.

Types of Skill-Based Pay

Skill-based pay also is called pay for knowledge, pay for skills, and multiskilled compensation. There is no generally accepted distinction among these terms, and we do not make distinctions among them here. More important to understanding skill-based pay is indicating the types of skills that can be rewarded in a skill-based pay system. Skill-based pay systems can be designed to reward at least three types of skills. These types are depicted as different skill dimensions in Figure 15-1.

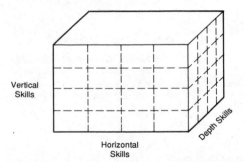

Figure 15-1. Types of skills that skill-based pay can reward.

The first dimension is *depth* of skill. That is, employees may be rewarded for knowing more and more about a particular specialized area. Although not usually recognized as such, some depth-based skill-based pay systems have been common for decades. The blue-collar skilled-trades system typically provides pay increases for employees who progress through the steps of apprentice, journeyman, and master craftsman in a given trade, such as electrician, pipefitter, or millwright. Among white-collar employees, the technical ladder is used in many companies to reward scientists or engineers for becoming more and more expert in their field, even without advancement through different levels in the management hierarchy.

The second dimension is *breadth* of skill. That is, employees may be rewarded for learning skills that are upstream, downstream, or parallel to their original job in the production or service delivery process. In most cases, this would include learning other jobs within the employee's work group or department. In other cases, employees may be rewarded for learning every job in a manufacturing plant or other work location. Pay systems that reward breadth of skill are a more recent innovation than depth-based systems. The first manufacturing plants that used such skill-based pay systems were built in the 1960s by Procter & Gamble Co.

The final dimension is *vertical* skills. These are self-management skills, such as scheduling, leading group problem-solving meetings, training, communicating, and coordinating with other groups. In traditional organizations, these skills are expected of supervisory and managerial employees, not nonexempt employees.

Any particular skill-based pay plan may make use of one or more of these three dimensions. Whether acquiring the skills represented by any given dimension is rewarded and how much emphasis is placed on the dimension should be a function of the goals of the plan. In turn, the goals of the plan need to be determined by the technology of the organization, business needs, and the desired culture of the organization. For example, organizations that rely on self-managing work teams may find it especially desirable to encourage employees to acquire vertical skills, which in other organizations might be reserved for supervisors or higher-level managers.

Who Uses Skill-Based Pay and Why

Skill-based pay is an increasingly prevalent pay innovation. Previously, skill-based pay was used mostly with nonexempt manufacturing employees. Recently, however, skill-based pay has spread to service organizations in such industries as telecommunications (American Telephone & Telegraph Co. and Northern Telecom Ltd.), insurance (Shenandoah Life Insurance Co.), hotels (Embassy Suites), and retailing (Dayton Hudson Corp.). It also has been used with white-collar professionals, most notably with information-system professionals in several companies, who are given incentives to broaden their skills and remain current in a rapidly changing field. Polaroid Corp. is attempting to become the first large corporation to pay virtually all employees on a skill-based pay system.

Three studies have attempted to assess the prevalence of skill-based pay in the United States. The most sophisticated study was a national sample survey of corporations listed on the New York and American stock exchanges for the U.S. Department of Labor.[1] The researchers found that 8 percent of these companies used pay-for-knowledge plans. A survey of large United States organizations by the American Productivity Center and the American Compensation Association (ACA) found that 5 percent used skill-based pay plans with production and/or service workers, and of these, 68 percent had adopted their plans within the previous five years.[2] The study projected a 75 percent increase in future use of skill-based pay. Both studies found that current skill-based pay usage is concentrated in blue-collar manufacturing jobs, but that it also is used in a wide variety of job types and organizations. A more recent study of Fortune 1000 firms found that 40 percent claimed to use skill-based pay, broadly defined, with at least some employees.[3]

There is evidence from several case studies that employees often feel high levels of pay satisfaction when they are paid on skill-based pay plans.[4] Also, two studies in particular found that the overwhelming majority of firms using skill-based pay plans believed them to be effective overall in enhancing organizational performance along virtually every dimension considered.[5] However, little hard research evidence is available so far to confirm or disconfirm these opinions about the performance effects of skill-based pay. Indeed, it is difficult to conduct well-controlled research on the organizational effects of skill-based pay plans. This is because organizations that adopt skill-based pay also tend to adopt a number of other practices that are designed to encourage high levels of employee involvement. It is hard to separate the effects of the pay-plan innovations from the effects of such practices as self-managed work teams, high levels of training, extensive sharing of business information, and many other innovations. Therefore, a discussion of the advantages and disadvantages of skill-based pay is somewhat speculative.

The potential advantages and disadvantages of skill-based pay plans have been considered elsewhere. Briefly, under some conditions skill-

[1]N. Gupta et al., *Exploratory Investigations of Pay-For-Knowledge Systems*, Department of Labor Technical Report (BLMR 108), U.S. Department of Labor, Washington, D.C., 1986.

[2]Carla O'Dell, in collaboration with Jerry McAdams, *People, Performance, and Pay*, American Productivity and Quality Center, Houston, 1987, pp. 8–19.

[3]Edward E. Lawler III et al., *Employee Involvement in America: A Study of Contemporary Practice*, American Productivity and Quality Center, Houston, 1989, p. 22.

[4](a) Gupta, pp. 121–138.

[4](b) Gerald E. Ledford, *Skill-Based Pay: Some Implementation Issues in New High-Involvement Plans*, paper presented at the Academy of Management Annual Meeting, August 1985, San Diego.

[4](c) Henry Tosi, and Lisa Tosi, "What Managers Need to Know About Knowledge-Based Pay," *Organizational Dynamics*, Vol. 14, No. 3, 1986, pp. 52–64.

[5](a) Nina Gupta et al., "Paying for Knowledge: Myths and Realities," *National Productivity Review*, Vol. 5, No. 2, 1986, pp. 116–119.

[5](b) O'Dell, p. 14.

based pay can lead to higher performance, including lower staffing levels, greater productivity, improved quality, faster response to customer orders, more effective problem solving, lower absenteeism and turnover costs, and other benefits. These benefits can be the result of greater employee flexibility and the facilitation and support of a high-involvement management style. Greater flexibility is the obvious result of having employees who can perform multiple jobs. Multiskilled employees can be moved to where they are needed, such as to bottlenecks in the production or service system, and they can cover for each other when employees are absent due to illness, transfers, or training. Multiskilling also reinforces a high-involvement management style, in which employees are given a high level of responsibility for self-management. It makes self-management more effective by giving employees a broader understanding of the overall production system, emphasizes the value placed on employee development, and makes leaner direct labor and management staffing possible.

Skill-based pay also carries with it some potential disadvantages. It leads directly to increased wage and training costs, which may or may not be offset by cost savings. Pricing jobs in the marketplace may be more difficult if there are no competitors or other organizations in the area that pay on a skill-based pay plan. Skill-based pay is more complex and difficult to administer than job-based pay. This is because employees must understand a pay system that involves advancement through and certification on a series of jobs, not just one pay rate associated with the one job they hold. Finally, some employees do not have the ability or the desire to learn multiple jobs and, as a result, they may resist skill-based pay.

The Difficulty of Designing Skill-Based Pay Plans

Methods for designing traditional job-based pay plans are institutionalized in contemporary organizational practice. Standard textbooks codify these practices. Universities and the ACA offer courses that teach design methods to compensation professionals. Organizations can hire nationally prominent consulting firms, such as Hay Group Inc., to design job-based systems. The net result is that the procedures for designing job-based pay systems are widely understood and the expertise needed to design and administer such systems is widely available.

Designing a skill-based pay plan is more difficult. Compensation textbooks give little or no attention to skill-based pay, and there is no college course on the subject. Although some ACA courses touch on skill-based pay concepts, the ACA does not yet offer any course on methods of skill-based pay design. No large consulting firm has much experience with skill-based pay. There also has been very little academic research or theory on skill-based pay, and there are few articles offering practical advice on it. This makes it difficult to know the key characteristics of skill-based pay plans, what design variations are possible, or what the design process should look like.

Virtually the only published research on the design of skill-based pay plans has been conducted by a group of researchers at the University of Arkansas. They examined the degree to which the perceived effectiveness of 19 skill-based pay plans was related to a wide variety of design factors, including number of skill blocks, maximum and minimum number of skill blocks required of employees, period of time required to learn skill blocks, period of time employees must remain within skill blocks before learning new ones, and so forth. The only design factor that the researchers found to be related to effectiveness was the number of skill blocks. Their data indicated that the higher the number of skill blocks, the lower the effectiveness—presumably because the greater the complexity, the harder it is for employees to understand and be motivated by the plan. They argue that the specific mechanical elements of the skill-based pay plan generally are unimportant compared to the organizational context, such as whether the organization supports and is suitable for a skill-based pay plan and whether the skill-based pay plan is supported by management and by organizational factors such as training practices.[6] However, I do not share the view that the mechanics of the plan are unimportant in determining effectiveness. There is no reason to expect that most of the factors examined by the Arkansas researchers, such as minimum and maximum number of skill blocks, would be important in the same way across different organizations and skill-based pay plans. Thus, they do not serve as good predictors in a correlational or multiple regression sense. Rather, these features need to be tailored to specific organizational conditions and the goals of the plan.

Key Issues in Skill-Based Pay Design

In developing a sound skill-based pay plan, a wide variety of design issues must be considered. There are three general categories of skill-based pay design issues:

- Global issues—designing skill-based pay to fit its organizational context

---

[6]Gupta et al., *National Productivity Review*, pp. 114, 119–122.

- Mechanics—working out the nuts and bolts of the skill-based pay plan
- Transitions—dealing with issues concerning the transition from the existing pay system to a skill-based pay system

These categories can be thought of as a range of issues that must be addressed before a skill-based pay plan is complete.

Global Issues

Global issues concern the big picture, that is, how skill-based pay is designed to fit into its organizational context. Many of these issues are not explicitly considered when designing job-based pay systems in traditional organizations. This often is not a problem because, in general, job-based pay systems fit within the context of traditional organization designs rather well. They emphasize the importance of hierarchy, specialization, and seniority, which are cornerstones of traditional organization designs. Skill-based pay plans are designed for different purposes and fit different organizational contexts than job-based pay. Thus it is important to review explicitly the following issues of fit with the organizational context.

Organizational Culture. Companies that adopt skill-based pay for all employees should be or have been moving toward a participative organizational culture. Generally, the flexibility advantages of skill-based pay can be gained more cheaply in other ways, such as by cross-training a group of utility workers. The cost of skill-based pay for all employees is justifiable only if it is an integral part of a high-involvement management system that has the potential to offset the cost of increased wages per employee with greater productivity and other performance advantages.

It is especially important for organizations using a participative management style to encourage breadth skills. Breadth skills allow employees to gain perspective on the technical system, improve employee problem solving, and help employees appreciate their common fate. These are critical aspects of a high-involvement culture. Many high-involvement organizations also find it useful to reward vertical skills in the skill-based pay plan, for example, through a team-leader skill block that all can earn. By contrast, a skill-based pay system that is oriented only toward depth skills encourages a narrow, parochial focus that works against self-management.

Organizations need not already have a participative culture for skill-based pay to succeed. Indeed, skill-based pay can be a powerful force in helping an organization live up to a commitment to become a high-involvement organization. This is because employees, acting in their own self-interest, begin to exert pressure for greater training, information, and control over job rotation and other key decisions. In short, they begin to demand that the organization behave more like a high-involvement organization.

Technology and Business Objectives.   The skill-based pay plan is effective only if it reinforces business objectives, as constrained by the technology and work design. This is often easier said than done because there can be multiple, competing objectives that are difficult to support simultaneously. Nevertheless, we can point to examples of how skill-based pay may support business needs.

In continuous process technologies, such as food processing or chemical refining, the key to business success is tight control of the production process. Interdependent employees from throughout the facility must respond quickly and accurately to quality and production problems that may appear anywhere in the process. Thus, skill-based pay plans in these plants often reward employees for learning skills *through-out* the facility.

Manufacturing cells typically combine different functions, such as machining and assembly, into self-contained units that make one set of products and serve specific customers. In these systems, skill-based pay may reward employees for learning as many skills as possible *within* the cell, but not for learning skills in *other* cells or departments.

In customer service operations, the critical need may be to have employees who can respond to all common customer queries without referring the queries to other departments. This avoids the familiar and aggravating situation in which no single employee knows enough to help a customer with a problem. Thus, employees may be rewarded for learning all the skills they need to serve customers effectively.

Employee Involvement in the Design Process.   Because organizations that install skill-based pay usually attempt to encourage high levels of employee involvement in general, it follows that in these organizations there should be some level of employee involvement in the design of the pay system, which can affect employees profoundly. Employee involvement in pay-system design potentially offers the same advantages as employee involvement on other matters: greater employee understanding and acceptance of the change and better decision making.

In practice, it is common to design a skill-based pay plan using a task team that includes several representatives of nonexempt employees. A more limited form of participation is sometimes used in the case of new organizations, in which the essentials of the pay system may be determined before nonexempt employees are hired. In these cases, employees nevertheless may be involved in the design of specifics such as skill evaluation tests and procedures. In unionized firms, a form of representative participation—collective bargaining—is the norm.

Employee Groups to Be Covered. A conscious decision should be made about which employee groups will be covered by skill-based pay. All else being equal, it is probably better to include all employees in the same facility on the same type of base-pay plan. Covering some employees on skill-based pay and other employees on job-based pay can create tensions over pay equity. This is especially true in the case of an organization in which the pay plan is changed from job-based pay to skill-based pay for only some employees. The job-based pay employees who do not have opportunities for earning greater pay through skill-based pay can be expected to lodge inequity complaints.

Nevertheless, skill-based pay plans often apply to some but not all employees in the work location. In manufacturing plants, it is common to include all nonexempt factory employees in the plan but to omit other groups, such as managers and office workers. In principle, however, there is no reason that skill-based pay plans could not be extended to all groups.

Alignment for Local and Industrial Equity. Any pay plan must take into account the wages that are paid in the surrounding community and by competitors in the industry. Paying wages that are too low leads to high turnover, especially by experienced and talented employees who are most in demand. Paying wages that are too high leads to excess labor costs.

Skill-based pay plans often are difficult to price in the market. There may be no other firms in the local area or in the industry that pay using a skill-based pay plan. The skill blocks or steps in a skill-based pay plan rarely translate well to job classifications in a traditional job-based pay plan.

In practice, organizations with skill-based pay usually make no attempt to peg each step in the plan to particular jobs in the external market. Rather, they are most concerned about pricing the entry rate and the top end of the pay system in the market. The entry rate is set just high enough to get qualified applicants from the community to accept jobs in the organization. The high end often is pegged to multiskilled utility-operator jobs in the market, or is based on management's estimate of what it can afford to pay if a significant proportion of the work force eventually reaches the top of the skill-based pay ladder. Once a top and bottom are set, the available pay in between is allocated to skill blocks in a way that maintains equity within the skill-based pay system.

Managers considering skill-based pay often become alarmed at the prospect of all employees earning top wage rates. Two points are worth noting in this regard. First, even if all employees reach the top of the pay scale, this will not happen for a period of time (usually several years). If the plan is well-designed, the plan should be returning performance benefits to the organization that offset the added costs. Second, data from a U.S. Department of Labor study indicate that a majority of employees tend to stop advancing before reaching the top of the pay scale if they are not required to reach the top.[7]

Plan for Review and Renewal. Most skill-based pay plans undergo substantial revisions after initial implementation for three reasons. First, errors may be made in the design of the plan. Design mistakes are common in organizational changes of all kinds, particularly when the changes are innovative. Second, some skills for which employees are being paid may become obsolete due to changes in technology or work methods, the loss of certain types of business, or other reasons. In this case, employees who are being paid for obsolete skills usually are redcircled to maintain their pay level for a period of time. During this time, they can learn other skills, such as operating the new technology, that allow them to avoid a loss of pay. Third, the objectives of the skill-based pay plan may evolve over time as business conditions change and as the organization matures. For example, the initial pay system in new plants may encourage the acquisition of all the skills within an employee's first work team. This ensures that employees have basic technical knowledge that they need to perform efficiently. Over time, however, the focus of the plan may shift to rewarding the acquisition of additional skills in other teams. This can improve coordination and cross-functional problem solving as employees gain a better perspective on the production process.

Changing the pay plan creates problems only if skill-based pay is oversold and employees are led to expect that the original version of the plan will solve their pay problems once and for all. It is better to create the opposite expectation: that no pay plan is perfect and that the plan will need to be modified periodically in the future to learn from experience and to ensure that the plan continues to meet the needs of em-

[7]Gupta, *Exploratory Investigations of Pay-For-Knowledge Systems*, pp. 88–91.

ployees and the organization. This is consistent with the self-design approach to implementing organizational change.[8]

The self-design approach requires that systematic data be collected in order to monitor the implementation and effects of the change. This is essential to the learning process. Thus, the skill-based pay implementation plan needs to include provisions for the renewal process, including what type of assessment data will be collected, when and by whom data will be collected, and how the data will be used to make any needed modifications in the plan.

Mechanics

Skill Levels or Blocks. A skill block is a cluster or set of skills that the organization is willing to reward with extra pay. There are no hard and fast rules on what is included in a skill block and what pay is attached to it. However, well-designed skill blocks are critical to the design of the plan for two reasons. First, the structure of the blocks determines how well the pay plan fits with the organizational technology, management style, and business needs. Second, the pay blocks are the skeleton of the plan which is fleshed out by attaching pay levels, certifications, training, and communication methods. A skill-based pay plan with poorly designed skill blocks usually is ineffective, no matter how well other aspects of the pay plan are handled.

An important question to ask is whether the skill blocks should be built around specific work stations or steps in the production process. If there is little redundancy in the skills required at different work stations, they may serve as skill blocks or parts of skill blocks. This is advantageous because the blocks can be easily defined and communicated to employees. However, if the skills between different work stations overlap to a significant degree, they may not make a good basis for skill blocks. This is because employees in effect would be tested and paid over and over for learning the same core set of skills. It then would be better to repackage specific job skills into more abstract, generic skills, such as material handling, inspection, machine operation, and so forth, that cut across different work stations.

It is important to define the order of progression through different skill blocks. It may be necessary to learn skills in a certain sequence. If a specific sequence is not needed, it should not be mandated because do-

[8]Thomas G. Cummings, and Susan A. Mohrman, "Self-Designing Organizations: Towards Implementing Quality-of-Work-Life Innovations," in Richard W. Woodman and William A. Pasmore (eds.), *Research in Organizational Change and Development*, Vol. 1, JAI Press, Greenwich, Conn., 1987.

ing so unnecessarily clogs job rotation and limits advancement possibilities.

In order to control job rotation, to ensure that employees are spending enough time on the job to fully learn new skills, and to maintain organizational performance at reasonable levels, it is customary to insist that employees remain within their skill blocks for a minimum period of time. Three to nine months is a typical period of time that employees remain within a skill block. The time period (and pay increase attached to the skill block) usually varies with the difficulty of the block. In any case, it is important that the time period attached to each skill block permits mastery of the skills by employees who have completed that block. Many organizations set maximum times within a skill block as well to facilitate job rotation.

Some organizations set minimum and maximum numbers of skill blocks that all employees can learn. The logic behind a minimum number of blocks is that the organization design may rely on employees who have enough technical skills to be self-managing. Minima are much more common in new plants, where everyone can be told from the start of the hiring process that they will be required to learn, for example, every job in their team or every job in the plant. Maxima are set to ensure that employees are not paid for more skills than they can retain at an acceptable level of proficiency.

Skill Assessment or Certification. Often one of the most contentious issues in skill-based pay systems is the assessment or certification of employee skills. This issue has no counterpart in job-based pay systems, since no elaborate process is necessary for determining which job the employee holds. However, skill assessment is central to the concept of skill-based pay; it is the basis for setting pay levels. When base pay levels are involved, employees pay close attention to the fairness and adequacy of the assessment process. Assessment issues to consider include assessment criteria and methods, personnel, timing, and reassessment policies.

The criteria and methods used to determine skill attainment need to follow from the nature of the work. Obviously, the criteria used should be closely linked to the skills that are represented in the skill blocks. Testing methods can include work samples, paper and pencil tests, and oral tests. The best method to use, all things being equal, is the work sample. It is the most objective testing method and the least subject to claims that test anxiety led to failing the test. A work sample may be a simple demonstration for a tester, or a longer-term demonstration that, for example, the employee can operate a machine at a high rate of efficiency for several weeks. Work samples are not always enough to certify skills, however. For example, the skill block may include knowledge of emergency safety procedures or knowledge of how to handle unusual situations that cannot be re-created for purposes of a work sample. These may need to be tested with written or oral tests. Written tests permit efficient coverage of a wide range of issues but can be a problem if literacy levels are low. Oral tests have the advantage of permitting follow-up questions that prevent employees from simply memorizing study material by rote without understanding it. Whatever testing method is used, it is common to provide employees with some type of skill-based pay manual that permits them to study for the tests they will take.

Skill assessments may be conducted by supervisors or managers, staff personnel (engineers or human-resource staff), fellow employees, or some combination of these. In traditional organizations, employee responsibility for pay decisions about co-workers usually is resisted by both management and employees. However, employee teams in mature, high-involvement organizations may assume most of the functions of first-line supervisors, including hiring and firing. In these organizations, it may be highly appropriate to make skill assessment a team responsibility.

The certification process is time-consuming. In fact, it may become one of the most time-consuming supervisory duties. Thus, the timing of skill assessments needs to be determined as part of the skill-based pay plan. May employees be tested at any time upon request or only at certain times? If an employee fails a certification, must he or she wait before being retested? Is there any queuing of certification opportunities within the work group?

Finally, a plan for periodic recertification may be desirable. This depends partly on the nature of the skills being certified. Some skills are like riding a bicycle; retesting them is a waste of time because they are rarely lost once gained. Many other skills, however, such as computer skills, can be lost rapidly unless the skills are reused. If there are no recertifications, the firm may be paying for skills that have been lost through disuse.

Training Plan.   Skill-based pay plans cannot succeed without training. Training gives employees the learning opportunities that are essential to advancement in the system. Because skill-based pay creates such strong incentives for employees to learn new skills, managers should expect the demand for training to increase greatly following the adoption of skill-based pay.[9]

[9]Dale Feuer, "Paying for Knowledge," *Training*, Vol. 24, No. 6, May, 1987, pp. 57–66.

Because more training will be needed, it is desirable to create a solid training plan. The content of the training can be linked closely to the content of the skill blocks and certification tests. The training plan needs to go further, however. It should indicate what specific training courses will be provided according to what schedule. The training plan also should indicate who will do the training. Will it be provided by trainers, training vendors, peers, managers, or others? Finally, the training plan should identify any conditions attached to the training. For example, training may be on company time, on employee time, or on some combination of the two.

Job rotation, which is essential to training job skills, has the potential to be the source of much controversy and hard feelings. It is desirable to decide in advance how decisions will be made about rotation. For example, will it be done on an inflexible timetable, or will ongoing decisions about rotation be made by team members or the supervisor? It is also desirable to think through in advance how two common problems will be handled. First, how will short-term production needs, which exert a pressure to slow down rotation and training, be balanced with long-term organizational needs for a more highly skilled work force and employee preferences for more training? Second, how will slow learners and those who refuse to rotate be handled? Such employees reduce training opportunities for others if they can lock up certain jobs indefinitely. There are a variety of options for addressing this problem, but all the options are more palatable if they are agreed upon or at least understood in advance.

Communication Plan

Skill-based pay is far more difficult than job-based pay for employees to understand. In job-based pay, employees really must know only their job classification and the pay is attached to their classification in order to understand how they are paid. Skill-based pay is far more complex, and employee understanding is critical to the effectiveness of the plan. Employees need to understand a whole ladder of skills, the certification-standards process, and how to obtain training in order to advance in the system. Moreover, changes in the pay system also tend to affect far more people in skill-based pay plans. If a change in technology leads to a new job classification in job-based pay, only the job incumbent is affected directly by the change in the pay system. In skill-based pay, the change affects every person who is eligible to earn a skill block that includes that job.

Thus, it is imperative for the organization to do a good job of communicating to employees about the nature of the skill-based pay plan, how it affects them, and how they can advance in the system. Because the information that must be communicated is complex and because some employees may be very emotional about it, it is best to plan on intensive, multichannel communications. Written materials that employees can study are especially important. One common form of written communication is a notebook of skill-based pay rules and certification tests that each employee receives as a study guide.

Transitions

Transitional issues are those that involve moving from the existing pay system to skill-based pay. These issues usually are present but less intense in new organizations, where the skill-based pay system replaces only a single entry rate pay structure. However, these issues can be critical in retrofits, where there is a conversion from job-based pay to skill-based pay.

Initial Assessment of Skill Levels.   Organizations that are converting from job-based pay face the prospect of testing virtually everyone who will be converted by the skill-based pay system to determine where they will fall on the skill-based pay ladder. There is no obvious way to avoid a costly and time-consuming crush of skill-based pay certifications. One organization I have worked with, however, stretched out the testing process by announcing that employees would be converted from job-based pay to skill-based pay and that testing needed for the conversion would be conducted, on the employee's hiring anniversary date.

Credit for Prior Education and Skills.   An issue can arise about whether the skill-based pay system should credit the education and skills that new hires bring to the organization. This is most likely to be an issue if the organization must hire people who have needed technical skills that are in short supply in the labor market. In a labor shortage, applicants may refuse to take a job at the organization's entry pay rate, even if they have opportunities for advancement, when they can make much higher starting pay elsewhere.

There are various options. Some jobs requiring scarce technical skills may be exempted from the skill-based pay system in order to set pay rates high enough to attract workers to those jobs. Alternatively, employees may be hired for some jobs at a rate on the skill-based pay system corresponding to their apparent skills. Then they are red-circled at that rate for a specified period of time until they can pass the certifications that justify their higher initial pay rate. Also, it may be possible to hire contractors for a period of time long enough to train employees as permanent replacements.

Role of Seniority in Skill-Based Pay.   Skill-based pay is not a seniority-based pay system. It does not assume that people who have worked in an organization longer have more skills. Skill-based pay rewards the skills that people can demonstrate, not their longevity in the organization. Nevertheless, there may be instances in which seniority appropriately can play a minor role in skill-based pay. For example, it may serve as the basis for queuing when training or job rotation opportunities are limited.

Dilemma of Highly Paid, Low-Skilled Employees.   Employees who are relatively highly compensated do not necessarily have higher levels of skill in traditional pay systems. Under traditional pay systems, employees can reach higher levels of pay by seniority or by bidding into jobs that are rated highly. As a result, a certain percentage of the work force in job-based pay systems is likely to be high in pay but low in skills.

Depending on the number of these employees and their social status, this can be a very divisive issue for organizations converting to skill-based pay. Job title and loyalty as indicated by length of service, which were valued under the old system, may suddenly become unimportant compared to skill level. Older employees who benefitted under the old system may resist skill-based pay, while skill-based pay may be endorsed by younger employees who see opportunities for advancement at a much faster pace than would otherwise be possible. The two types of pay systems thus may be seen as having different winners and losers, and the losers may oppose the new pay plan.

There may be no easy solutions to this problem. One alternative is to red-circle employees who are at pay levels well above that warranted by their skills. This promises that their pay will not be cut while they gain the skills needed to reach and surpass their current pay level. Depending on the structure of the new plan, however, some employees may go for years without a pay increase while they gain new skills. A second alternative is to preserve one or more pockets of the organization in which employees are managed and/or paid in a traditional way. If employees can bid into these parts of the organization, it may become unnecessary for highly paid/low-skilled employees to change. On the other hand, this option may not be feasible or desirable in light of the overall organization design, and it may maintain tensions in the work force. A third option, which can be used in combination with the other two, is to offer early retirement incentives for these employees. In some situations, however, there may be no acceptable solution, and the divisions caused by the skill-based pay plan may be so severe as to foreclose skill-based pay as an option.

Interim Training Delivery. Increased training becomes an ongoing obligation of organizations that adopt skill-based pay. The most intense demand for training, however, comes at the beginning of the plan. As the material to be covered in the certifications becomes known, employees realize that they can be certified in additional skill blocks simply by closing a few gaps in their knowledge or by brushing up on skills that were learned once and later lost through disuse. A special interim training plan is needed to find ways to respond to intense short-term demands for training.

We have considered design issues concerning the global context of skill-based pay, the mechanics of the plan, and transitions from job-based pay to skill-based pay plans. This list of issues may be useful as a checklist of issues and options. However, designing a skill-based pay plan is not a simple matter of going through the list of issues one at a time. The actual process inevitably is much less linear and much more complex. Inevitably, there is much going back and forth between issues and revising earlier conclusions.

Installing Skill-Based Pay in New and Old Organizations

An increasingly important issue in skill-based pay design is whether skill-based pay is equally suitable to new organizations and to existing organizations that have a long history of using job-based pay. Early skill-based pay plans tended to be found mostly in new, high-involvement plants. More recently, however, there appears to have been a sharp growth in the use of skill-based pay in existing organizations that originally had a job-based pay plan. Companies such as General Motors Corp., Eaton Corp., Northern Telecom Ltd., and General Mills Inc., have installed plans in existing operations. It does not appear that even the presence of a union is a barrier to skill-based pay. There are now many unionized, retrofit installations.[10]

New plants and other new organizations have advantages over existing organizations when implementing skill-based pay. On the positive side, there is a very easy transition to skill-based pay in new organizations. New plants using skill-based pay typically pay all employees at the

---

[10]Bureau of National Affairs, *Pay for Knowledge: A BNA Plus Report*, Washington, D.C., June 1988.

entry rate until the skill-based pay plan can be developed and installed. Thus, employees want to see the plan installed as quickly as possible; it is really the first pay plan they will see. It is no accident that the fastest installations of skill-based pay I have seen are in new plants. It typically requires 9 to 12 months to design and install skill-based pay in a new plant.

On the negative side, new plants also face adverse conditions in designing a skill-based pay plan. These include chaotic start-up conditions, very long working hours, a technology that often does not work very well (making skill analysis difficult), and the lack of an established training function.

These conditions contrast with conditions in existing organizations, which often enjoy such luxuries as a known technology, training and other resources that are already developed, and the available time to "do it right" in making organizational changes. Thus, it is probably no accident that the best communication packages, the most thorough training materials, and the most carefully designed skill-based pay plans that I have seen are those developed in conversions rather than in new organizations. In general, conversions tend to take longer to complete the installation process but adopt more careful pay plans and support for skill-based pay.

There is another difference between new organizations and existing ones that adopt skill-based pay. It is often possible to offer more of a skill-based pay incentive in new organizations, in the form of a greater spread between the bottom and top rates. In new plants, all new hires can begin at a relatively low entry rate and then progress through the system at an appropriate pace. Existing organizations cannot take away pay by starting everyone at the entry rate in the new skill-based pay system. People will move from their existing pay rate, which on average may be well above the entry rate, to the new skill-based pay structure. Thus, if a new and old organization have the same top pay rate, there will be less incentive built into the old organization's plan because people will not be able to advance as far under skill-based pay.

Conclusion

This chapter reviews a number of issues in the design of skill-based pay. Much remains to be learned about how to design effective plans. Research on skill-based pay is needed to help identify the variables that are most important in the success or failure of skill-based pay plans. In the meantime, the issues and options identified here can help managers ensure they have thought through the key design issues as we presently understand them.

Certainly, much will be learned about skill-based pay in the future. There has been tremendous growth in skill-based pay installations in recent years. One trend in particular suggests why this growth is occurring: the increased used of skill-based pay in existing organizations that are converting from traditional job-based pay plans. As long as the use of skill-based pay was limited primarily to new plants and other new organizations, the overall usage of skill-based pay was bound to remain low. Now, however, evidence is accumulating that skill-based pay can be successful in conversions. As more is learned about how to implement skill-based pay in conversions and as more examples are publicized of companies that have gained a competitive advantage through skill-based pay, the overall use of skill-based pay no doubt will accelerate.

16
Nonmonetary Awards

Jerry L. McAdams
Vice President
Performance Improvement Resources
Maritz Inc.

If you are considering alternative reward strategies, consider alternative award types. Ask employees what type of award motivates them, and the answer will probably be "cash." Compensation professionals, consultants, and practitioners rarely consider any other type of award. We think of and design for cash awards because it is how we pay and get paid. It is not, however, the only effective type of award; ask anyone who has earned a special holiday or a new stereo system for outstanding performance.

We also understand the power of a pat on the back as social reinforcement from people we respect. In fact, recent surveys show that being recognized for a job well done is the most often mentioned motivator to do a better job.[1] Also listed as important were "challenging work" and "knowing that my opinions matter"; cash is usually lower on the list. (These surveys, as well as this chapter, assume that the respondents are presently being fairly compensated.)

To begin with, you should appreciate the difference between performance-improvement plans and recognition plans. Performance-improvement plans identify what needs to be accomplished, engage

[1]American Productivity and Quality Center, "What Motivates Center Members," *Consensus*, Houston, Tex., Vol. 1, No. 4, July 1988, p. 1.

people in the work, and reward on performance. Recognition plans recognize outstanding performance after the fact and are designed for awareness, role modeling, and retention of the recipients. To improve performance, a reward plan must be behaviorally sound, measure performance improvement and its value, provide measurements that can be affected by the people, and use awards that are perceived as valuable by the recipients. These nonmonetary awards are unique in that they do double duty: They are of sufficient value and attractiveness to motivate people to improve performance, and they provide the recognition that is increasingly important to today's work force.

Reasons for Using Nonmonetary Awards

1. *Supplements a fair compensation plan.* If people generally believe they are being fairly compensated and you don't want to change your compensation plan, consider using nonmonetary awards for reinforcing performance against specific objectives. If people do not believe they are being fairly compensated, fix the basic compensation plan before you try to add new objectives with nonmonetary awards.

   If you have an existing cash-incentive plan, it is generally not a good idea to replace the cash with nonmonetary awards. You can create an additional plan with different criteria using nonmonetary awards or stop the cash plan for a time (at least a year) and introduce one with nonmonetary awards and different objectives and performance measurements.

2. *Eases the transition to a gain sharing plan.* There is ample evidence that a properly designed performance-improvement plan will work effectively using nonmonetary awards. You can test all aspects of the new strategy, get the bugs out, and refine it without upsetting employees. After a two- to three-year period, conversion to a cash plan can be easily done, if you chose to make it permanent. Obviously, if you decide not to make it permanent, you can withdraw without a significant negative employee reaction.

3. *Helps introduce an objective-driven or cost reduction/gross profit enhancement plan (CR/GPE).* If you have an established cash gain sharing plan, both CR/GPE—team-based programs to generate ideas from employees to reduce costs or enhance gross profit—and objective-driven plans-group—based programs that reward for group performance in reaching an objective or objectives and that are often operated in conjunction with gain sharing—can be run very effec-

tively using nonmonetary awards. In fact, using cash as an award in these situations is probably not as effective as using nonmonetary awards. The special attention and focus that nonmonetary awards bring with them will allow the employees to differentiate more easily between the productivity objective of your existing cash gain sharing and the other objectives. Using cash for everything reduces the ultimate effectiveness of all the plans.

If you are introducing gain sharing with nonmonetary awards, you can also introduce an objective-driven or CR/GPE program using nonmonetary awards. This approach has been done successfully in manufacturing, health care, service, and white-collar organizations. When introducing new plans, mixing award types (cash for gain sharing, nonmonetary for objective-driven and/or CR/GPE programs) is not a good idea. Most organizations cannot adjust quickly enough to absorb and act upon new plans and different types of awards all at the same time.

4. *Recognizes outstanding performance.* Nonmonetary awards carry the element of recognition. They can be shown with pride to peers, family, and neighbors; the awards are visible.

5. *Works well with most employee populations.* In the private sector, nonmonetary awards do well with nonsales, individual or group, exempt or nonexempt, with any existing incentive plans, except piece rate; sales, individual or sales team, with existing salary, salary-plus-commission or straight-commission plans; sales support, individual or group, with any compensation plan; and service or technical support, with any compensation plan.

And in the public sector, symbolic awards are frequently used, but there is little use of merchandise, travel, or earned time off (the nonmonetary awards of significant value). Public hospitals, however, have used merchandise and travel awards with success to improve productivity, patient-care quality, attendance, and cost reduction. The limited use of nonmonetary awards in the public sector does not mean that they cannot or should not be used. It probably reflects the sector's limited use of any form of incentive for improving performance.

Types of Nonmonetary Awards

There are a few companies that specialize in full-service performance improvement, whether the performance to be improved is that of employees or the company's customers, such as dealers, distributors, or jobbers. These agencies offer research, training, communications, promotion, and reward-systems design and implementation. They supply merchandise, travel, and symbolic awards. The largest of these agencies are Maritz Motivation Company (a division of Maritz Inc.), E. F. MacDonald (a division of Carlson Companies), S&H Motivation & Travel Company, and Business Incentives.

A distinction should be made between these full-service performance-improvement agencies and those that are limited to supplying awards, known as a fulfillment source. An example of a merchandise fulfillment source would be a local retail store or the incentive division of a merchandise manufacturer. An example of a travel fulfillment source would be a local travel agency, and a local broker of promotional and advertising items is an example of a symbolic-award fulfillment source. The decision of whether to use a full-service agency or a fulfillment source depends on how much you want to accomplish with your alternative reward strategy—the more you want to accomplish, the more services you will need—and how much of your internal staff you want to dedicate to the design, implementation, and administration of the strategy.

The five basic types of nonmonetary awards are social reinforcers, merchandise awards, travel awards, symbolic awards, and earned time off (see Table 16-1).

Table 16-1. Types of Nonmonetary Awards

Social: Involvement, listening, pats on the back, respect, feedback, training, activities (picnics, tailgate sales, charity days, etc.). Should be an integral part of all management practices. Most of these are a function of management's style and can be used for morale and acknowledgment of the value the organization puts on its people.

Merchandise: Preselected items or a broad offering earned through the accumulation of points applied to a catalog; of "significant" financial value, generally totalling over 2 percent of annual salary as an award for improved performance. Merchandise certificates can be issued and used at a local branch of a national retail chain.

Travel: Trips awarded to an individual, family, or group from the organization; generally valued from $250 to $4000 per person. Certificates of $10 to $100 in travel are also used. These certificates are accumulated over a period of time and applied to a trip's costs.

Symbolic: Awards with more "meaning" than financial value: often referred to as "recognition awards." Examples are plaques, rings, pins, desk sets, publicity, free lunches, jackets, hats, reserved parking places, memberships in advisory councils, etc.

Earned Time Off: Time off with pay. This is in addition to time off with pay as a result of sickness, vacation, or disability. These are considered an entitlement or part of the agreement for employment, not as an award.

The most popular nonmonetary awards for improving or recognizing outstanding performance are merchandise, travel, and earned time off with pay. Symbolic awards are most popular for awareness (focus on a specific objective or message) and role modeling.

Social Reinforcers

These should be an integral part of all management practices. Examples of social reinforcers include a pat on the back, respect, training, and various activities (picnics, tailgate sales, charity days, and so forth). These awards can be used as morale boosters and acknowledgment of the value the organization puts on its employees.

Merchandise Awards

These are given for improved performance, and they can be pre-selected items or a broad offering of merchandise. The merchandise award is of significant financial value, usually totalling over 2 percent of the employee's annual salary. Merchandise certificates that can be used at a local branch of a national retail chain often are used as awards, although merchandise awards, in general, are most effective when delivered via an awards catalog.

There are two types of merchandise awards catalogs: an awards catalog and a general-purpose catalog. Books of awards come in various sizes. Some catalogs offer 1800 or more items of the highest quality, selected as appealing awards for a broad range of tastes. While it offers a broad selection of functional items, its intent is to focus on items with special value to the individual or family. The next smallest catalog generally has about 800 items. The smallest catalogs are really booklets that are made up of 10 to 15 items, each in value groupings of $25, $50, to $500.

Accompanying the catalog is a price list in points or award credits. When a plan is introduced, levels of performance are directly related to the award value in points. Checks are issued by the agency for the appropriate number of points. The employees can redeem them immediately or accumulate them for a larger award. About 90 percent to 95 percent of employees accumulate the checks to get the award they have selected. An awards catalog itself also enhances the merchandise as an award by providing an attractive and exciting promotional vehicle. Of the two ways to offer and promote merchandise as awards, the awards catalog is the most popular and has the highest motivational appeal.

Awards catalogs are supplied by full-service performance-improvement agencies. They issue and mail the point checks, based on performance information supplied by the company or directly from the participants. They handle lost checks and refunds (when participants send in more points than necessary for their order). All record keeping, tax and management reports, order entry, shipping, customer service, auditing, and billing is also handled by the agency.

Some agencies also offer a bank-account system. This system deposits the points into an account in the participant's name, issues balance statements, and allows for ordering by telephone or mail.

To award earners, service is a critical element. People have higher expectations in product quality, delivery, and customer service than when they purchase something for cash. They have earned the award, and they want it as soon as possible and without problems. If there are any problems, they demand quick, fair, and empathetic service. A good agency will stock items that make up from 60 percent to 75 percent of their orders. Some items, such as clothing, furniture, and large appliances, have to be shipped from the factory. The size and buying power of the agency has a strong influence on the service that an award earner will receive on these "drop" shipments. If the desired item is not in the awards catalog, a special ordering service is also offered by some agencies.

People earning merchandise awards feel that they have been cheated if they have to pay taxes on the awards. For this reason, firms "gross up" the award value when reporting it on each W-2 form and pay the federal tax, usually based on 20 percent withholding. Assuming this does not move an employee to a higher tax bracket, there is little or no tax cost to the employee. Many firms extend this practice to cover state and local taxes as well.

Agencies usually bill the firms for the award points *redeemed* plus transportation and sales tax. This gives firms a cash flow benefit unique to merchandise incentives. The vast majority of merchandise-award earners save their checks until they have enough to get their selected (and often larger) award. This time lag between the actual performance improvement and the billing for awards can be as much as eight months to a year. The performance has improved and the company has the benefit of that improved performance without the cost of an award until redemption and billing. Depending on the interest rate, the positive cash flow can be significant. Obviously, there is no cash flow advantage when the award is made in cash. Bank accounts are generally billed on point issuance, providing no cash flow advantage.

The second type of merchandise awards catalog, a general-purpose catalog from a traditional department store, is designed to meet everyday, functional needs. These catalogs provide a range of items within each category, from the basic TV to the expensive, big screen models. The majority of the catalog items, however, are low-end merchandise and would not be considered as awards. While the individual may find a number of desirable items in the catalog, the catalog is not designed to be an award vehicle.

Firms using this type of catalog issue merchandise certificates redeemable at the store. As opposed to the award-points approach, merchandise certificates are essentially directed cash and lose much of the award appeal. Little goal setting is done.

Most retail stores with catalogs do not offer administrative services for certificate issuance, record keeping of participants' performance, stop payments, tax reporting, and all other administrative demands of a program. If a company arranges its fulfillment directly with a retail store, the company handles all administrative duties. Also, the tax considerations are not the same as those associated with the book of awards program. Merchandise certificates are billed on issuance, eliminating the cash flow advantage over cash. The service the employees get from the store is purely a function of the store itself. As with the agency approach, the service, good or bad, will be perceived as the responsibility of the sponsoring firm.

Companies can also buy merchandise awards directly from a manufacturer. Many major manufacturers of popular consumer goods (GE, Motorola, Sony, Thomasville, and so forth) have an incentive division that focuses on selling a limited selection of their products directly to companies for their incentive plans. The buyer, in this case the company, has to decide what will be most appealing to the targeted population. A common approach is to create a booklet of a few items (TV, VCR, camera, golf clubs, and so forth), at least one of which will be of interest to anyone in the audience.

The risk of preselected items is that they might not be appealing to the people who are targeted. If you have three TVs, it is hard to get excited about earning another. Trying to guess what is valuable to people is a frustrating and often hopeless task. Offering a broad range of awards is the safest approach.

Agencies are generally not involved in the incentive plan when companies purchase their merchandise awards, although brokers often represent a number of manufacturers for the incentive market. Generally, they do not offer any additional services.

If a company decides to purchase merchandise from a manufacturer, then the company handles all the administrative work. This may not be very burdensome if the number of items is limited and all merchandise is drop shipped. If the company buys a number of items and stocks them for redistribution, it must take all of those costs into account when designing the alternative reward strategy. Because of the complexities involved, few firms take this approach, at least not the second time around.

The tax considerations are the same as described for the award catalog approach, and unless the purchasing arrangement is drop shipped only, there is little cash flow advantage with this approach because award payment is made when shipment is made to the company's stock.

Demands for good customer service exist with a preselected merchandise approach and when the company's staff is responsible for providing the service.

Travel Awards

Trips can be awarded to an individual, family, or to a group from the organization, and are generally valued from $250 to $4000 per person. Certificates of $50 to $100 for travel are also used. These certificates are accumulated over a period of time for a trip. Travel awards have a special motivational appeal to people, particularly when delivered as a group incentive.

Group-Incentive Travel. In group-incentive travel, all earners of a travel award go to the same location and are entertained as a group. A sales force is the most common user of this form of incentive. While some trips are for the earner only, the majority are for the award earner and spouse or guest. Everything is arranged in advance: airline tickets (often including charters), ground transportation, hotel accommodations, cocktail parties, group dinners, sightseeing, sports activities, and so forth. The program can be as deluxe or as economical as the company wishes.

The appeal of a travel award is hard to overstate. An all-expense-paid trip to Hawaii (still the most popular destination), Europe, the Caribbean, the Far East, or a cruise offer what many consider the "giant carrot" for motivating people to improve performance. It is not unusual for people to extend travel awards into vacations that they could not otherwise afford.

One of the most overlooked benefits of group-incentive travel is the good feelings that naturally develop on a trip. It is a relaxed opportunity to lay the groundwork for networking and company loyalty. It is not unusual for the highlight of the trip to be the announcement of the next year's destination and how it can be earned. If the spouses are also there, the company has more motivators on its side for future incentive plans.

Because of the logistics involved and the importance of quality service for the earners, most companies use a full-service performance-improvement agency rather than a local travel agency (fulfillment source). Although most travel agencies claim to offer incentive travel, few have the staff, resources, experience, and buying power necessary to guarantee a successful group-incentive travel experience. These full-service agencies design how the award trip operates; recommend des-ignations; customize the activities to the firm; handle all ticketing, char-ters (if appropriate), hotel arrangements, receptions, on-site travel directors; and handle the myriad of other necessary services.

Because of deposits and payment schedules required by the hotels and airlines, the cash flow aspect of group-incentive travel is not as at-tractive as that of the awards-catalog approach. The Internal Revenue Service generally has established that group-incentive travel programs are taxable to individuals. Consultation with the firm's tax attorney is strongly recommended. If the trips are taxable, most firms gross up the trip value (as with merchandise awards) and factor this increased cost into the financial rationale of the plan itself.

Group travel, with all its motivational appeal, is a sensitive business. Weather, strikes, and airline operations, for example, are often out of anyone's control. The sponsoring company, however, is held account-able in the minds of the award earners. The power and experience of the full-service agency is the firm's insurance policy. Most companies have learned the hard way to use the major agencies for consistent per-formance because they are in the business of working with the same ho-tels, airlines, and local service suppliers on a yearly basis.

Individual-Incentive Travel. Individual (or family) travel awards are becoming more popular because they feature many benefits of an awards-catalog plan. Travel awards operate in two ways:

1. Travel certificates can be issued in various denominations of "travel value" ($10, $25, $50, and so forth) according to a preannounced schedule that relates levels of performance to a number of certifi-cates. A book of travel destinations is given to the employees at the beginning of the program. Certificates are accumulated by the award earners and redeemed for the travel awards. The certificates may be used to pay for any part or all of the cost of the award.

2. Points earned for performance improvement could be used for indi-vidual travel. The certificates are given a point value. The rest of the process is the same as above. This approach allows a company to of-fer both merchandise and travel awards without the expense of group-incentive travel or having a lot of people out at one time. (Nonsalespeople often prefer to travel with family than with a group of co-workers.)

Both approaches have a high motivational appeal because they offer the glamour of travel customized to individual needs and desires. Individual-incentive travel also has a great appeal to the family.

It is possible to use local travel agencies for individual-incentive travel. Local travel agencies rely on a collection of brochures or a stock airline promotional piece for your company to use with your participants. If your participants are located in offices in other than the local area, the agency must be staffed to handle these travel arrangements as well.

One of the appeals of this approach is its ability to offer a wide range of destinations (100 or more) in a promotional kit to the participants. All administration services, including redemptions and all arrangements, are generally made by the individual award earner directly with the airlines, hotels, and other travel suppliers. The certificates are used in payment directly to the supplier for the travel-award cost.

Full-service agencies offer a catalog of award travel destinations designed to promote the resorts and locations. Their primary award-travel business is to serve participants from any part of the nation or world, and they are staffed to deliver this service. Customer service is a function of the travel supplier (hotel, airline, and so forth) with the support of the agency. In either case, the sponsoring company will be held responsible in the participant's mind for the quality of service.

Taxes can be handled by grossing up. Billing for the cost of the travel certificates is done on issuance, so there is no cash flow advantage over cash. If the certificates are issued in exchange for points, however, the cash flow advantage is the same as with the awards-catalog plan.

Symbolic Awards

This type of award includes plaques, coffee mugs, photographs, mementos, T-shirts, hats, rings, pins, and so forth—the list is endless. These awards have symbolic but little financial value to the employee. That does not mean that these awards have to be inexpensive. Company rings or pins can cost hundreds of dollars, but the average symbolic-award budget per person is $8 a year.

Symbolic awards are used for two purposes: awareness and recognition. Awareness is acknowledging the importance of an objective or goal. A company could have program themes printed on selected items to distribute to all members of the organization, regardless of their performance. These items are excellent communication tools and tangible, ever-present reminders of the company's focus.

The more common use of symbolic items, however, is as recognition. Offering a T-shirt or coffee mug to each employee who reaches a pre-established goal is an inexpensive way of getting focus. Few would argue that this award is significant enough in financial terms to get people to improve performance, but there are a number of cases in which group dynamics and pride take over. The symbolic award is a way for employees to publicly display their accomplishments. Most companies have some form of individual recognition for display in the workplace—plaques, pictures displayed in the cafeteria, and so forth.

Membership in advisory councils, upgrades in company cars, reserved parking places, free lunches, special business cards, and so forth, are also used extensively as symbolic awards for recognizing individual outstanding performance. A word of caution about such programs as "Employee of the Month": the concept is great, but the execution is generally poor. Nominations from management of their employee population often degrade into a lottery or rotation. Credibility and the reinforcing power of these programs tend to erode. Unless you truly can identify and defend the nominations to the rest of the employees, the worth of such programs is questionable.

There are hundreds of advertising specialty and promotion brokers that supply symbolic awards. Full-service agencies offer symbolic awards as an accommodation to their clients. They also offer artistic symbolic awards rarely available elsewhere. These awards are often limited edition sculptures, designed and produced just for the company and/or event. As with the awards catalog approach, these full-service agencies offer the design, communication, promotion, and distribution services not available with fulfillment sources.

Administration of symbolic awards is much the same as described in the awards-catalog plan. Because the value of each item tends to be low, many firms stock the awards and handle most of the administration themselves, particularly if the awards are issued throughout the year. If the plan is to send out the awards all at one time, it is considerably easier to have the full-service agency or fulfillment source handle the distribution from a mailing list supplied by the company.

Generally, symbolic awards are valued at less than $25 each and are tax-free to the employee. Under certain conditions, such as with the cost of service awards, the tax-free allowance goes up to $600. The tax law tends to be interpreted differently over time, so be sure to consult your firm's tax attorney.

Earned Time Off

Americans value their leisure time more than ever. With the increasing demands of work, time off can become an award in itself. Having an unplanned day off is becoming a very attractive award. Vacations, of course, are an entitlement and are planned in advance.

Most companies make the time off with pay because they feel it is hard to consider it an award otherwise. Time off without pay, however, can be a positive way of capturing productivity improvements. There are lots of employees who would be quite happy to get a day off without pay if it would not jeopardize their job status.

Selectively used, earned time off can be a very powerful group incentive. Earned time off has been used as a group incentive in two ways. One way is for all employees to take a day (or days) off when a specific goal or objective has been reached. Some companies allow employees to accumulate days for additional vacations or extensions. There could be, however, a philosophical conflict with earned time off. What message does such a plan send? Do we really want to reinforce the idea of not coming to work? Some believe such a plan should only be applied in organizational units in which attendance is not a problem or customer contact is not part of the job.

A second way to use earned time off is through company celebrations that take people, as a group, off the company premises. Most of these activities are considered entitlements, such as company picnics, but they can also be effective awards. When goals are met, everyone gets to celebrate. If your company already has traditional events that are not considered awards, it would be unwise to try to convert them into awards. Some creative thinking, however, can bring a company real benefits through group activities. One firm uses special team-building training as an award. The event takes place in the Rocky Mountains, lasts a week, and is highly prized both as a benefit to the company and as an award to the employees. To be the latter, however, participation must be purely voluntary. Even implied pressure to participate eliminates any award aspect of such an activity.

Administration for this type of plan must be handled by the company and tends to be more complex with nonexempt and shift workers than with the exempt and professional ranks. Unlike the other types of awards described, the cost of this award is something to consider.

Because of the limitations of accounting systems, the real cost of this award gets lost in the system. Many firms consider professional, exempt, and management earned time off to be of no cost to the company, depending on how much time off is given. Nonexempt and shift worker's earned time off is generally considered to carry a real cost. Earned time off is probably most effective when used on a limited basis, driven by the nature of the operation, timing, work load, and how critical the individual is to the organization. Also, earned time off generally has no tax consideration to the employee.

Plan Design

Regardless of the type of award, the plan must be effectively designed to meet the strategic objectives of the organization. This sounds rather obvious, but it is common to become wrapped up in mechanics of the plan and have little consideration of whether or not the plan is the right type to meet the company's objectives. Too many plans have been installed because "it seemed like a good idea" or "everyone else seemed to be doing it." The strategic objectives of each organization must be fully explored to develop and create plans that motivate employees to meet and exceed those objectives.

The report by the White House Conference on Productivity, *Reward Systems and Productivity*, describes the elements of a productive organization, which are also critical elements for a well-designed performance-improvement plan.[2] They are:

- A high degree of information sharing, including business, financial, competitive, performance, and planning information. Not to be overlooked is a consistent plan for feedback to management.

- A general sense of employment security. This does not mean lifetime employment guarantees but regularly communicated statements of the relationship between business realities and employment. These statements have legal considerations, particularly with recent court decisions on employee rights. The point, however, is that you cannot expect employees to work cooperatively to improve performance if they live with the constant fear of losing their jobs. As our labor pool continues to shrink, this element will become increasingly important.

---

[2]White House Conference on Productivity, *Reward Systems and Productivity*, American Productivity and Quality Center, 1985.

- A mechanism for involving employees in meeting business objectives. If the employees really can make a difference, a productive organization must provide an easy way for them to make a contribution to improve performance. Quality circles, labor-management teams, multifunctional task forces, advisory councils, and cost reduction/ gross profit enhancement teams are but a few examples of such mechanisms. Employee involvement often requires a proactive, program-based process. The answer is not just to install quality circles, for example, but to make it easier for all employees to make a contribution by offering all-employee programs focused on specific objectives. It is a dynamic process, requiring effort and commitment at all levels of the organization.

- A reward system that rewards for performance. It is unfortunate that most pay plans do not effectively pay for individual performance improvement. Across-the-board increases, most individual merit-increase plans, and even some sales-commission plans have become entitlements.

- A behaviorally based plan design. An effective plan incorporates the basic behavioral science rule: "Behavior is a function of its consequences."

Recognition Plan Versus Performance-Based Reward Strategies

Most compensation professionals relegate nonmonetary awards solely to recognition programs. The most common recognition-plan design involves picking out the top 5 percent to 10 percent of your sales force and recognizing them with a trip or merchandise awards. Nonsales-recognition programs include "Employee of the Month," "Customer Service Person of the Year," and "President's Award." Plaques, publicity, and memberships to councils are also used as awards. Although large lump-sum bonuses are common for this kind of plan, they are almost always accompanied by such symbolic awards.

These types of recognition plans are important to creating role models, retaining outstanding performers, and motivating these performers. They do little, however, for the majority of the employees. In fact, when the plan includes an organization-sponsored competition for the top slots, it can be counterproductive. Organizationally imposed competition will not encourage teamwork and can pull focus from the real competition in the marketplace. Within an organization you want everyone to be winners. To accomplish this, design plans in which everyone understands what it takes to become a winner or earner by improving his or her own or his or her group's performance.

Figures 16-1 through 16-3 provide a comparison of three basic plan designs—recognition plan for top performers, earning threshold for performance improvement and recognition of top performers, and a performance-based reward plan. The recognition plan for top performers defines winners as a top percentage of the eligible population, rather than those who reach a specific goal. An example would be that the top 10 percent of work force would win, rather than that everyone with 120 percent of objective would earn. In the top 10 percent (or "Employee of the Month") case, people compete with each other rather than focus on the more important competition in the marketplace or against previous performance. This is an effective plan for retaining and motivating winners, but it has little effect on the rest of the employees, as indicated in Figure 16-1 by the relatively small area defined as people likely to be motivated.

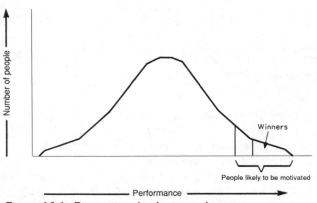

Figure 16-1. Recognition plan for top performers.

With a plan for earning threshold for performance improvement and recognition of top performers, the message is clear: Do this, get that. The focus is on improvement over past performance or toward a new

goal. In this case, everyone with 120 percent of objective would earn
rather than just the top 10 percent. Winners become earners, determined by achievement of a goal. The earning threshold could be set to
generate the top 10 percent of the people as earners. For example, if
last year the lowest performance of the top 10 percent was 120 percent
of the objective, then 120 percent could be the earning threshold. As
indicated in Figure 16-2, this plan design motivates a larger portion of
the population.

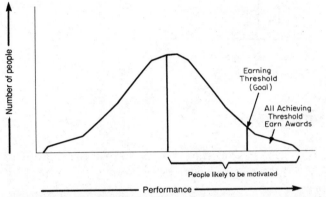

Figure 16-2. Earning threshold for performance improvement and recognition of top performers.

In a performance-based reward plan, thresholds are set for each individual (usually salespersons) or groups (work groups, organizational
units, or the whole organization). Everyone is engaged in improving
performance. As shown in Figure 16-3, this plan design offers the
greatest opportunity for improvement by moving the whole performance curve to the right.

Most organizations have installed versions of either of the first two
plans—the recognition for top performers or earning threshold for
performance improvement and recognition of top performers—primarily because they are relatively easy to implement. Unfortunately, management often believes these plans are improving the performance of
everyone in the organization. This is clearly not the case. The greatest
performance-improvement opportunity (and highest return on investment) is achieved with a performance-based reward plan.

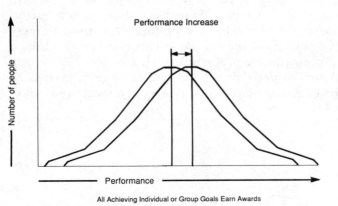

All Achieving Individual or Group Goals Earn Awards

Figure 16-3. Performance-based reward plan.

Why Nonmonetary Awards Work

In *People, Performance, and Pay*, Carla O'Dell and I reported on why organizations using nonmonetary awards chose them over cash.[3] The reasons are as follows:

- *Trophy value.* Every time a person looks at the award, a TV, VCR, furniture, and so forth, or remembers the trip to Hawaii earned for being a top performer or for improving performance, it motivates the person to continue to improve.
- *More promotable than cash.* It is easier and more effective to promote the value of a nonmonetary award than its cash equivalent. There is an excitement and recognition factor built into nonmonetary awards that is not present with cash.
- *More flexible than cash.* Because nonmonetary awards are clearly not cash, they cannot be confused with the compensation plan. There is little or no entitlement. The use of nonmonetary awards allows the organization to adjust the measurements and objectives, within reason, without argument from the people who believe that their cash income standard of living may be reduced.
- *Less expensive than cash.* Performance generally increases the same amount whether cash or nonmonetary awards are used, assuming

[3]Carla O'Dell, in collaboration with Jerry McAdams, *People, Performance, and Pay*, American Productivity and Quality Center, Houston, Tex., 1987.

that the award is consistent with the degree of performance improvement required.

Also in *People, Performance, and Pay,* we asked sales managers who have the most experience in using nonmonetary awards to tell us how cost-effective they were versus cash. There was about a 13 percent performance improvement using either nonmonetary awards or cash awards. The cost of cash was nearly 12 cents for every dollar of increase. The cost of nonmonetary awards was 4.1 cents for every dollar of increase. This reflects a significantly better return on investment with nonmonetary awards than with cash.

These data pertain to sales, but my experience in nonsales is about the same. The three-times return on investment advantage of nonmonetary awards over cash in sales populations may slip to 2.0 or 1.5 in nonsales populations, but the point is the same: When organizations want increased performance, the return on investment is often better using nonmonetary awards than cash.

- *Promotes family involvement and goal setting.* Nonmonetary awards have the unique attribute of getting the family involved. A catalog at a family's home provides the opportunity for everyone to participate in the award selection. The catalog is used for the family members to pick out what they want and as encouragement for the employee to make his or her personal goals. The family focus and involvement provided by nonmonetary awards are important advantages to consider when choosing this award type.

Conclusion

This chapter is an argument for a broader mix of awards to complement the broader mix of reward strategies that will be installed in the 1990s. It is a suggestion that there are many types of awards as well suited as cash to meet the performance-improvement challenge. In many situations, nonmonetary awards are more suitable than cash and can provide a better return on a company's investment.

17

Team Incentives in the Workplace

Theresa M. Welbourne
Division of Strategy and Organization Management
University of Colorado

Luis R. Gomez-Mejia
Research Professor, Management Department
Arizona State University

A growing number of corporations are moving away from the long-held belief that individual achievement and success, often through brutal competition with fellow workers, is to be encouraged and reinforced. Instead, there is an emerging emphasis on a more cooperative environment in which employees learn to share their talents and information with each other by working as a team on common tasks. Increased foreign competition, more educated employees, excessive turnover and absenteeism, the aftermath of the social revolution in the 1960s and 1970s, and fewer management positions are some of the key factors often cited for this trend.

Redesigning work using a team concept provides the organization with flexibility to blend employees with unique skills and backgrounds to tackle common projects or problems. It also provides workers with more freedom, greater independence, and the ability to improve skills and use talents that might not have otherwise been tapped in a narrowly defined position. For example, General Foods Corp. created a network of interfunctional work teams as part of a new strategic direction emphasizing greater cooperation and integration in the work force.[1] The multidisciplinary teams were formed to encourage maximal performance from every member. Although trained in a particular area of specialization, such as finance or marketing, these individuals in the new system are expected to cross boundaries within the team and contribute in those areas in which they had not previously worked. The result of the experience at General Foods is what M. Bassin describes as peak performance of each and every employee.

Another example of team performance, reported by M. S. Fisher, indicates that even within three months of employing a team concept one can observe improved productivity, reduction in costs, fewer employee grievances, and improved turnover.[2] Fisher reports that after four years with the team design one plant calculated a 69 percent improvement in productivity and after five years the figure had jumped to 92 percent. The nature of the work in this plant required extensive, cooperative work relationships among employees, and changing from an individual- to a team-based work environment allowed this plant to achieve remarkable improvements in productivity. Examples of companies employing teams within their manufacturing operations include General Motors Corp., TRW Inc., Digital Equipment Corp., Shell Oil Co., and Honeywell Inc.

Like any other personnel program, team-based management approaches do not function in a vacuum; they need the support of other human-resources systems to be effective. By putting your money where your mouth is, compensation can play a leading role in communicating the organization's commitment to the team concept. As Bassin noted when describing the experience of General Foods, "In terms of support for team activity, nothing is symbolically more important than compensation."[3] Therefore, in addition to the institutional mechanisms by which team-based pay programs are coordinated with other compensation methods, the way group rewards are linked to performance will be pivotal in establishing and maintaining effective team arrangements.

How the Team Is Defined

The terms *team* and *group* are constantly found in popular management journals, and both words are frequently connected with gain shar-

---

[1]M. Bassin, "Teamwork at General Foods: New and Improved," *Personnel Journal*, Vol. 67, No. 5, May 1988, pp. 62–70.

[2]M. S. Fisher, "Work Teams: A Case Study," *Personnel Journal*, Vol. 60, No. 1, January 1981, pp. 42–45.

[3]Bassin, pp. 62–70.

ing and profit-sharing plans. In order to provide a frame of reference, four levels of analysis will be discussed below. They are the organization, business unit, team, and individual. This is intended to clearly differentiate what is being referred to in this chapter as "team incentives" from other pay-for-performance systems.

Table 17-1. Compensation Programs Broken Down by Payment Criteria and Unit of Analysis

Criteria for rewards	Unit of analysis			
	Organization	Business unit	Team	Individual
Pay for performance	Profit sharing Stock plans	Gain sharing Bonuses Awards	Bonuses Awards	Merit pay Piece rate Awards Bonuses
Pay for skills/ knowledge			Skill-based pay Team awards	Skill-based pay Suggestions /Seniority

As shown in Table 17-1, pay plans can be designed to reward the performance of the entire organization, the business units, teams, individuals or any combination of these. The choice should be made based on the firm's strategy, goals, and objectives.

At the most macro level, organization performance can be measured by a variety of accounting criteria such as sales, revenue, return on investment, and profitability. Profit-sharing plans reward all employees participating in the program when the business realizes a profit or when accounting indicators of performance (for example, return on investment) exceed a specified amount. Because the performance measure is so aggregate, organizationwide incentive plans provide a tenuous link between the individual employee's performance and the outcome measure. A worker cannot be assured that his or her outstanding performance today or for the entire year will have any impact on corporate profits. Many interceding factors exist, including the performance of co-workers, government regulations, input costs, accounting adjustments, and a host of market factors far beyond the employees' control, that contribute to the final profit figure.

Business units are represented by divisions, departments, manufacturing plants, or strategic alliances within an organization (such as a group of manufacturing, marketing, and engineering workers assigned to develop a new product). While the business unit may be composed of a large number of employees, it is only one of many segments within the corporation. At this second level of analysis, the firm may reward employees based on business unit performance. This smaller scale may allow the organization to tie rewards to criteria that are more directly influenced by the individual employee. Business unit plans, such as gain sharing programs, are becoming popular due to their ability to differentially reward employee groups that are responsible for profits within a particular unit without compensating those who have not contributed to that unit's success. Quantitative performance measures for the business unit are generally available and tend to be perceived as objective in the employees' eyes.

Unfortunately, business unit measures can also suffer from the same dilemmas haunting organizationwide performance plans. The measures utilized for the bonus formula might be too obscure to motivate an individual employee. In spite of the popularity of gain sharing programs in recent years, there is no convincing evidence that demonstrates the incentive effect of such plans on the work force. For instance, it is unknown whether outstanding performers or superstars work well when the fruits of their efforts are distributed to fellow employees who do not adhere to similar performance standards.

A number of firms are gravitating toward team-based rewards in an effort to circumvent problems associated with rewarding performance on the organizational level, business-unit level, and individual level. A team is defined as a smaller group of workers (in which several teams comprise a business unit) who have common goals and objectives, work closely with each other, and are dependent on each other for the team's outcome. As the interdependencies among tasks increase, team success becomes a crucial determinant of organizational performance. Therefore, linking rewards to both team outcomes and effective team processes facilitates the achievement of corporate goals and objectives.

At the most micro level, firms attempt to link pay with individual performance. Plans requiring the identification of unique employee contributions for pay purposes are the most widely used pay-for-performance programs in industry. If companies were to successfully link the rewards program to individual work performance, the pay plan may become an effective communication device to employees and a positive motivation force for continued performance. In practice, however, these programs frequently fail. Individual performance is typically assessed by supervisory ratings that are used in merit-pay plans to reward employees, in most cases, on an annual basis. This results in programs that are linked to budgeting processes but are inconsistent in timing the reward with actual performance. Numerous perceptual and psychometric errors also plague the entire process and result in employees who often are unsure of what type of performance deserves an increase in pay. In many cases, it has been found that merit-pay programs result in pay raises based on seniority and cost of living rather than performance.

Rewards Tied to Team Performance

Team incentives can be based on the concept of either pay for performance or pay for skills and/or knowledge. Pay for performance is the more common design in which outcomes of team effort are used as payment criteria. Objectively measured consequences might include cost savings, number of products manufactured, meeting agreed-upon deadlines, parts rejected, or the team's successful completion of a new product design and successful patent. The goals, methods of measurement, and bonus amount can be determined in advance and communicated to group members, thereby serving as an incentive for the entire team.

Bonus payments can be made in cash, corporate stocks, or through noncash items such as trips, time off, or luxury items. Payment may be distributed equally to all team members or differentially in an effort to reward those who made greater contributions to the team's objectives. If rewards are to be distributed based on the individual's contribution to the team's goals, then the organization must employ a method of individual-based performance measurement. Rather than granting a lead or supervisor the responsibility for evaluating individual contributions, team members may rate each worker's performance, and the group's consensus can be employed for distributing rewards.

When team rewards are distributed differently to individuals, the element of competition among team members creeps into the team concept. Team bonus payments can easily evolve into simply just one more method of merit pay, and the processes of dividing bonus money among individual members can then be contaminated with the multitude of errors cited in traditional pay-for-performance systems. One may also have the added problem of differentiating between true performance and the results of a popularity contest when using peer evaluations.

Team-based pay for skills and/or knowledge is a second approach. It is important to differentiate this from other pay-for-skill plans based on individual performance. Manufacturing plants are experimenting with skill-based pay plans in which members of the organization increase their pay when they acquire additional skills and can master new tasks within the plant, usually as a result of extensive cross-training efforts within their team. Although the members might be working in teams, each individual increases his or her pay by improving personal skills. This form of knowledge-based pay is individual-oriented rather than team-based and reinforces individual accomplishments in the same manner that merit pay traditionally rewards workers for self-improvement.

Skill-based pay at the team level, on the other hand, rewards group members for increasing their ability to work as a team. Cooperation with other teams might be an important criteria for payment; ability to work effectively together on problem-solving assignments might be another. The important distinction is that all team members are rewarded when the skills of the entire team, not just the skills of specific individual members, are improved. Corporations experiencing problems with competition among various teams might find this type of incentive useful by employing the criteria of cooperation among teams as a basis for pay.

This same approach can be used to reward the team when each member has attained new skills. Rather than rewarding one person for learning a new job, the entire team might be compensated when all team members are satisfactorily cross-trained or the team's evaluation can be dependent upon its ability to bring each team member up to speed. This provides incentives for the more competent employees to assist the struggling employees. It also motivates team members to evaluate each other's performance in a more open, honest environment. Because team members are aware that one person's nonperformance can hinder the rewards to all members, a poorly performing employee is likely to be quickly discovered and dealt with by members of the team.

Reasons for Choosing Team Incentives

Rewards based on team performance will affect the business' ability to attract, retain, and motivate employees and will mold the corporation's culture. Team-compensation plans should be chosen when they are consistent with both the nature of the work and the goal setting of the organization and the team.

Nature of Work

Recent efforts to redesign jobs have focused on enhancing cooperative work relationships among employees to attain desired outcomes, such as improved quality, increased quantity, enhanced communication, and lower costs. Manufacturing programs, such as just-in-time inventories, require constant communication among sales representatives, field engineers, and inventory personnel. Since the nature of much work today requires cooperation among team members, incentive plans that reward the team's performance provide workers with feedback that will reinforce the organization's goals and strategies.

A cooperative work environment was defined by M. Deutsch as one in which the objectives of individual employees are mingled together in such a way that there is a positive correlation among the group member's goal attainment. In other words, no one individual can achieve success without the willingness of co-workers to contribute to the desired performance outcome. This type of work requires compensation programs that emphasize group outcomes rather than individual outcomes.

The concept of individual pay programs stems from economic theories that indicate individual contracts between employees and the organization are formed in a working relationship. Thus, the sum of all individual employment contracts forms the corporation. This concept has a number of problems associated with it due to the intercorrelated nature of most work. A group of employees independently working on separate goals and objectives is inefficient in an organization that does not have a number of individual goals but rather one objective that requires cooperation among individual workers.

An often-cited example of failure of this concept can be found in traditional sales-commission plans. The sales representative is commonly paid strictly for units sold, representing an individual contract between the salesperson and the employer. Unfortunately, the contract only delineates the amount of money the sales representative receives based on the quantity of goods sold rather than on the quality of information delivered to the customer. This may create a tremendous customer-relations problem that is only realized after the sale. The customer service representatives and field technicians are often extremely frustrated due to the salesperson's disinterest and inability to effectively relay information to either the customer or to headquarters offices. The employment contract between the salesperson and the company specifies only units sold. Therefore, the contractor is not concerned with cooperating with the customer service group, home office, or field representatives. By narrowly defining the jobs, the firm's goal of effective sales and service is not realized. The result is confusion within the organization and a poor image conveyed to the customer. This type of work is intrinsically team-oriented, and team rewards could assist in realizing the organization's true goals, which are both volume and quality.

Goal Setting

There has been an abundance of research suggesting that goal setting leads to improved performance.[4] Most of the studies have focused on individual goal setting and resulting individual performance, although a few studies have considered the issue of group goals and subsequent group performance. In general, it appears that group goal setting does lead to improved group performance when the goals are accepted by the group members.[5] The goals should be difficult, therefore providing a challenge for the team members, but not unattainable.[6] It has also been suggested that group goal-setting processes persuade individuals within the team who have not accepted the team's goals to personalize the group's goals.[7]

Research has also found that linking group rewards to the achievement of group goals has a positive effect on team performance.[8] When combined with consequences, such as rewards, it appears that goal setting has a long-term effect on the team's performance.[9] Compensation programs provide an essential feedback link for the goal-setting process. Pay related to the goals set by the team signifies that the organization is committed to the program, and the feedback provided when rewarding the team provides employees with positive reinforcement in addition to an incentive to continue pursuing the team's goals.

Two Examples: Self-Managed Work Teams and Research and Development Teams

As the traditional corporate hierarchy continues to evolve into a more egalitarian structure with emphasis on participative management, new organizational forms are being introduced. Self-managed work teams are currently utilized by manufacturing and nonmanufacturing firms

---

[4] G. P. Latham, and E. A. Locke, "Goal-Setting—A Motivational Technique That Works," in R. M. Steers and L. W. Porter (eds.), *Motivation and Work*, 1987.

[5] C. R. Gowen, "Managing Work Group Performance by Individual Goals and Group Goals for an Interdependent Group Task," *Journal of Organization*, 1985.

[6] J. Forward and A. Zander, "Choice of Unattainable Goals and Effects on Performance," *Organization Behavior and Human Performance*, Vol. 6, 1971, pp. 184–199.

[7] J. T. Austin, and P. Bobko, "Goal Setting Theory: Unexplored Areas and Future Research Needs," *Journal of Occupational Psychology*, Vol. 58, 1985, pp. 289–308.

[8] R. D. Pritchard and M. Curtis, "The Influence of Goal Setting and Financial Incentives on Task Performance," *Organization Behavior and Human Performance*, Vol. 10, 1973, pp. 175–183.

[9] Austin and Bobko, pp. 289–308.

that have found the traditional form of supervisor, lead, and worker ineffective in promoting autonomous decision making and high levels of
cooperation.

Self-managed work teams are formed by a group of employees, usually all at equal status within the hierarchy, who work together in identifying goals and objectives, solving problems, and completing stated
performance objectives. The team's responsibility can also encompass
personnel matters such as hiring, disciplining, evaluating, rewarding,
and firing team members. Such teams are currently being used in many
manufacturing firms in which individuals need to closely cooperate to
perform tasks. The Sherwin-Williams Co., for example, emphasized
work teams in an effort to allow employees to more effectively handle
the numerous product changes required in their plant while also maintaining high quality standards.[10] A flat organizational structure with
emphasis on operators' contributions to their teams' tasks was developed and complemented by an open-plant design allowing workers access to all stages of the production process.

Moving to the concept of team management versus individual workers reporting to a supervisor enhances an environment of close cooperation and allows workers to contribute more effectively to job completion. Employees are more committed to the goals of the group than
when individuals are competing under traditional systems.

The effectiveness of these teams has been greatly enhanced with the
employment of compensation mechanisms that reward the team for accomplishment of team objectives, whether these be performance-based,
such as meeting a stated output goal, or process-based, such as improving management skills. The pay system that rewards team members for
accomplishment of team goals delivers an important message to workers that management supports team performance and team goals are
important to the corporation.

Luis Gomez-Mejia and D. Balkin studied 175 scientists and engineers
and found that aggregate rewards were more effective for research and
development teams than individual rewards. The nature of research
and development work requires teamwork and cooperation by scientists
and engineers who often have competing personal goals due to their
scientific training and interest in pursuing strictly research-oriented activities versus customer-oriented projects. Aggregate incentive plans
help bring their personal objectives into alignment with the organization's needs.

These authors found that an additional reason for the effectiveness

---

[10]E. J. Poza, and M. L. Markus, "Success Story: The Team Approach to Work Restructuring," *Organization Dynamics*, Vol. 8, No. 3, 1980, pp. 2–25.

of team incentives was the absence of adequate individual measures of performance for these professionals. Research and development teams make progress in leaps rather than gradually, and it is hard to measure the contributions of one individual to the team's success in ventures such as designing a new product or creating a unique technology. Team-based bonus programs were also found to provide the organization with more flexibility in timing the reward to match team accomplishments.

Two primary advantages of using team incentives for research and development work rather than individual-based programs or organizationwide plans such as profit sharing were uncovered by Gomez-Mejia and Balkin. First, compensation is more closely tied to performance of the workers within teams that control both the quantity and quality of their research results. Second, pressure can be exerted on individuals to perform their best in alignment with the team's goals.[11] Gomez-Mejia, Balkin, and George Milkovich describe the case of a Boston-area high technology firm that allows engineers to earn up to 25 percent of their salary as a result of successful team performance. The program is administered competitively, and each research and development team is required to submit a written report showing how the team's efforts resulted in significant cost savings or other benefits to the firm. A committee of technical and nontechnical supervisors and managers reviews the proposals and may or may not grant bonus money.[12]

The team approach may also be used to motivate the research and development department to work more closely with individuals within the marketing department. These two divisions have traditionally been in conflict due to their responsibilities and training; research and development is interested in pursuing technology while marketing focuses on selling products based on consumer needs and perceptions. Although these two goals are not always in alignment, pay mechanisms can be used to create teams of technical and marketing personnel. The result can be products that are both technologically advanced and marketable.

Integration

Team incentives can be combined with individual, business unit, and organization rewards programs. The key to success is integrating all of

---

[11]Luis R. Gomez-Mejia, and D. B. Balkin, "The Effectiveness of Individual and Aggregate Compensation Strategies in an R&D Setting," *Industrial Relations*, in press, 1989.
[12]Luis R. Gomez-Mejia, D. B. Balkin, and G. T. Milkovich, *Rethinking Your Rewards for Technical Employees*, working paper, 1989.

these compensation methods so that they are consistent with the organization's strategy. If they are not developed to be consistent with the business strategy, then each individual method of payment can conflict with each other or the corporation's objectives, therefore transmitting extremely mixed signals to employees. When team incentives are utilized, individuals continue to possess personal goals in addition to their incorporated team goals. The rewards system can be effective in ensuring that individual and team goals are consistent rather than in conflict with each other.

Rewards programs are important for supporting or developing either hierarchical or egalitarian business structures. If the firm is primarily hierarchical and if individual employees know that success comes only after rising through supervisory and management levels, there will continue to be a struggle among team members in an effort for the high achiever to ensure that his or her performance is noticed by upper management. Incentives, in addition to promotional opportunities, must be carefully tailored to anticipate the needs of individuals who desire successful movement within the organization. Tall, hierarchical structures are consistent with individual rewards. Therefore, firms that desire flat organizations must change their rewards methods to be consistent with the desired structural goals.

Organizations must also consider the desired relationships among teams. Teams can work in either a competitive environment, in which teams are competing with each other for performance outcomes and subsequent rewards, or they can work cooperatively on common objectives. The atmosphere will be reflective of the corporation's goals and culture. Team membership can be designed so that only individuals within one department work together on a team, or department members can cross over their traditional boundaries to join teams that are multidisciplinary. Again, the form of the team is dependent upon the goals of the business.

Individualism as a Cultural Value

Although many organizations are moving to the team concept, relatively little attention has been given to the nature of the American worker in a team environment, which is foreign to the basic culture from which the employee has emerged. G. Hofstede, in a comprehensive study employing a database with over 116,000 questionnaire responses, found that the United States ranked number one on a construct that he called individualism. High-individualism countries are characterized as places where the culture emphasizes the individual rather than the group. Each individual is expected to care for himself; the organization is not committed to care for individuals on a long-term basis. Pay policies within these countries tend to emphasize individual rather than group performance.

An employee's ability to demonstrate his or her successful individual achievements to others is important and evidenced by the accumulation of rewards for performance, such as salary, company cars, job title, number of subordinates, and other rewards found in traditional compensation systems. As team concepts are employed, one must ask how the mentality of individualism, which is typical of the American worker, can survive in this atmosphere. The compensation program can be one tool for satisfying both individual and group needs. Awards for outstanding individual performance cannot be ignored in a society so insistent on individual accomplishment, but they must be carefully incorporated within an organizational environment whose survival depends on team rather than individual effort. Turnover should be carefully monitored when a business moves from individual to team programs. This will provide feedback on the types of personnel who are challenged by the team concept and those who are not satisfied within the environment. This information will be essential for future recruitment efforts, succession planning, and program evaluation.

Creative compensation management, in which pay is tailored to the needs of the organization, the nature of work, and the characteristics of the work force, is playing an important strategic role in organizations. The team concept is rapidly gaining popularity due to the positive outcomes that many organizations have experienced after implementing such programs. Team-based, rather than individual, criteria for pay should be used when the goals of the business are to strengthen the team's performance not only the individual employee's performance within the team. In a culture so dominated by individual goals and objectives, organizations must strive to be creative in their deployment of effective team-incentive programs that communicate to the worker that group, rather than individual, performance is critical to success.

18

Practical Approaches to Gain-Sharing Design

W. Fred (Duke) Fuehrer, Ph.D.
Director of Organization Development
Pentair Inc.

Introduction

Gain sharing is probably not a new term for the readers of this book. However, like most people in management, and even most with a compensation background and work history, you probably haven't designed, installed, and managed a gain sharing program. Experience brings the enthusiasm and confidence to try a new approach when a good set of management practices are already in place within the organization. When do you proceed and when do you not? This chapter is directed to the practitioner who conceptually understands gain sharing and needs the nuts-and-bolts help that comes from the successes and failures of many real gain sharing experiences.

Gain sharing has survived as an employee reward system for 50 years. There have been glowing long-term successes and miserable short-term failures during this history. Both the successes and failures have been attributed to the same variables: culture, management, employees, business cycles, competition, lack of employee involvement, and the list goes on. And, although these variables impact the success or failure of a gain sharing program, the most impacting determinant of success is the view or perception of gain sharing as an intervention taken by the organization's management and other employees.

Gain Sharing as an Intervention

Gain sharing is viewed as a compensation or shared-rewards add-on to another, more basic and primary (base) compensation plan. Frequently, consideration of gain sharing is a result of:

- Increased competition
- The desire for giving an incentive for harder work
- The desire for giving an incentive for smarter work
- Concern for a sagging economy
- Concern for poor company performance
- A runaway individual incentive plan

In more than 80 percent of the times that management considers gain sharing as an intervention, it is a result of the items noted above.

The somewhat more liberal manager may also see gain sharing as an opportunity to involve employees and solicit their ideas. Successful gain sharing programs have provided methods for providing shared rewards and involving employees. As gain sharing plans have been designed over the past five decades, employee involvement has been a critical design element in nearly every type of plan (at least this is true of the Scanlon plans). Furthermore, it is usually important and included with Rucker (value added) plans, but it is less of a design feature with IMPROSHARE plans. It has been from both practice and theory that the following definition of gain sharing has developed:

> Gain sharing is a compensation and involvement system designed to reward employees for improving the productivity of their organization through better use of important resources—labor, capital, materials, and energy. Gains resulting from improved productivity are shared between the company and the employees according to a predetermined formula.

This definition has been used by several consultants and organizations. Its initial origin is unknown. The consultants employing it's theory and components have had both successes and failures. The failures are likely a result of the instability built into the definition's design. A solid plan design requires emphasis on more than the two components of employee involvement and shared rewards [see Figure 18-1(a)].

When gain sharing is viewed only as a method to speed up work or solve the financial problems of an organization, its long-term success is unlikely. As will be seen later, management must be solidly behind the philosophy of gain sharing, and thus my definition:

> Gain sharing is a compensation, employee-involvement, and *management-practices* system designed to reward employees for improving the productivity *of their team and organization* through better utilization of important resources—labor, capital, materials, and energy. Gains resulting from improved productivity are shared between the company and employees in accordance with a predetermined formula.

The added component, management practices, adds stability and a "way of life" within the organization that supports and makes possible the success of the other components [see Figure 18-1(b)].

Many gain sharing and organization development consultants approach an organization with the questions, "Could gain sharing have some positive impact?" and "Will the present style of management be sufficiently supportive to reasonably guarantee a program's success?" With a 50/50 positive response to those questions, the consultant suggests moving forward with the design process. At this point, gain shar-

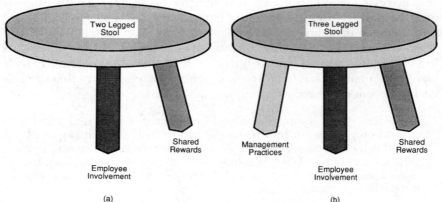

Figure 18-1. Gain sharing components.

ing becomes an organization development intervention to improve the organization.

Organization development is a process of planned evolution and change in the total functioning of an organization through the improvement of individual functions and systems. However, organization design is comprehensive and integrates systems and functions to create synergy and maximum performance from the organization. It is this organization design, when compared to the above definitions, that brings to light the need for an integration of the organization's systems to achieve a synergy.

The most significant point in the design of a gain sharing plan is to not settle for a program that is a single intervention that may or may not fit with the existing tasks, rewards, communication, decision process, and structures already in place. Rather, the organization should be viewed from the perspective of its many systems, and the gain sharing plan should be designed to integrate all of its systems for it to achieve its full potential. When the organization's systems are deemed to be homogeneous or congruent with the philosophy and goals of gain sharing and the components of gain sharing are supported by shared rewards, employee involvement, and a set of management practices that will support the philosophy, then it is time to proceed with the design in full confidence of forthcoming success.

Requisites for Plan Design

Conditions Favoring Success

Many companies in many environments with a wide range of demographics have been successful with gain sharing while others with a similar size and demographics have failed; there is a range above or below which success becomes less likely. The following are recommendations based on experience. A single item or two outside of the limits will not guarantee failure but, rather, raises a cautionary flag that must be addressed.

Business environment: Relatively stable with the expectation that the first plan year has no unforeseen swings

Age: Old enough to have established some historical baseline measures

Management team: Knowledgeable and supportive of the philosophy, articulate of the goals, and able to answer detailed questions concerning the plan and its design

Size: More than 50 and fewer than 2000 participants

Union: Open to the philosophy and willing to be an active participant in the design and implementation

Employees: Well trained and competent to perform the tasks necessary to provide quality products and services; able to achieve higher
limits with additional training

Data: Good historical data—financial and operational

Company stability: Soundly managed company with financial health
or backing

Communications: Open and willing to share operational and financial information with employees

Climate/culture: Open, trusting environment in which employee involvement is a natural phenomenon

Although these items are important to success, there are other requirements that are imperative for it. The most critical factors for success include:

- Corporate support
- Top management's total commitment
- Knowledgeable and supportive middle management and team lead-
  ers or front-line supervisors
- Adequate base compensation and benefits

Custom-Designed Plans

As was noted earlier, gain sharing as a group-level incentive has been
with us for nearly 50 years. Yet, of all the gain sharing plans in existence
today, 70 percent were installed within the past five years. And until recently, most true gain sharing experts and consultants were associated
with a specific formula; for example, Joe Scanlon, Carl Frost, and Fred
Lesieur with the Scanlon plan; Allen Rucker and Robert Scott with the
Rucker plan; and Mitchell Fein as designer of the IMPROSHARE plan. The
few other known consultants tended to support one of the above philosophies. From a review of these three philosophies and plans, one easily notices the strong differences that distinguish each plan from the

others. Each plan has its advantages and shortcomings. There are situations (environments) for each plan in which it may or may not fit. And, this fact has created a dilemma.

The early organizations exploring gain sharing did so because of success discovered with other companies. Probably an executive of Company Y heard of the great productivity achievements by Company X and rushed to contact the same consultant used by Company X. Regardless of the environmental difference between Companies X and Y, the consultant would apply the off-the-shelf plan design because it had become known as the "X plan" expert. Failures began to pop up because not every plan fits every environment. Companies X and Y had different products. Their manufacturing processes were different, so were the number of employees, union statutes, cultures, and philosophies. Different organizations have different needs and problems. The gain sharing plan that met the needs of Company X was custom-designed to specifically address that company's issues. A plan for Company Y should also be specific to its needs and custom-designed for it.

Gain sharing plans should get people involved and share rewards for changed behavior. Thus, plans must be strategic in their approach to incentive for behavior change. In the design process the question must be asked, "What must change for the organization to achieve its mission and financial goals?"

One continuous-process organization had $4 million a year in scrap loss. Their gross sales were slightly over $40 million. Their newly designed gain sharing plan formula leveraged waste. Another company had experienced unusually high lost-time accidents and workers' compensation costs. Their formula included an add-on to the bonus pool for reduced accidents that were below goal and a take away from the pool for lost-time accidents that were above the goal. The company calculation from historical data showed that each lost-time accident cost $20,000. As dollars were added or subtracted from the pool in $20,000 bites, it created lots of attention and discussion, followed with a renewed emphasis on safety. Behavioral changes resulted, large gain sharing pools were generated, and everyone won!

Each organization must be assessed to determine the need, readiness, and appropriateness for a group-level incentive plan. Most importantly, off-the-shelf prescriptions are unlikely cures, and prescription without diagnosis is malpractice whether in medicine or management. Most off-the-shelf plans lead to quick implementations and equally rapid failures.

The Design Process

Each gain sharing plan should be designed to fit the specific conditions of the organization. The quality of results achieved may be directly attributable to the quality of the process. I have found that there are ten steps that are critical in achieving successful designs.

Ten Critical Steps

Select a Consultant.   Few people today have firsthand experience at gain sharing plan design. Much trial and error and certainly many mistakes can be avoided. Someone from the school of hard knocks can avoid many mistakes. More importantly, all employees in the organization must perceive and believe that an objective and experienced third party is handling the consideration and implementation of a plan. A third party can say things to both management and labor that the other couldn't say and get away with saying. The most controversial discussions frequently involve evaluating baseline data and establishing a formula. Management personnel, usually the controller, will be viewed as far too conservative, while other employees, usually union members, are pegged as being too liberal and too eager to establish an easily attained target. The third party consultant is a "friend of the plan" and thus wants everyone to be successful.

Assess the Needs of the Organization.   Gain sharing is an organization development intervention that should be prescribed after a diagnosis has been done. If existing levels of productivity or employee involvement or management practices are not concerns of the organization, then gain sharing probably isn't a need.

Assess the Readiness of the Organization.   If there is need, then is the organization ready for gain sharing? Readiness should be viewed from the environmental, organizational, and change congruence perspectives. As discussed previously, there are key variables that load a potential gain sharing plan for success or failure. Assessing readiness can take a variety of forms. The consultant must understand the organization and how it fits in the competitive marketplace. What are the goals and missions, and how are they planned for and achieved? Is there a fit between the company's approaches and those of gain sharing? And, what are the programs and processes already under way in the company? The consultant gains this information through sensing activities and survey techniques. The present climate and the attitudes of employees also are important readiness factors, and so is management's initial and sustained support.

Environmental congruence occurs when certain internal and external key variables affecting the organization are compatible with the proposed gain sharing implementation. Several organizational congruence variables can influence the predictable success or failure of a proposed gain sharing plan implementation. Those variables may include the following: management's risk-taking tendencies; management's tendency to support the long-term execution of programs; management's style or approach to leading and guiding employees; relations among management, employees, and the union; strategic fit; and organization size.

An initial sensing by the trained observer may suggest that the consultants are ready to begin designing a program. Yet some feedback about poor communications and trust levels may lead to interviews, which may lead to a survey, which may lead to follow-up discussions, which all might point to strong mistrust between management and employees and a culture that begins new projects every month and seldom finishes any. Assessment is a series of paths that ultimately lead to moving ahead or setting up roadblocks. Knowing when to put up roadblocks and when to charge ahead will mean the difference between the plan's success and failure. This knowledge and experience should reside with the consultant.

Determine the Mission, Goals, and Objectives.   An organization that does not have good planning processes is unlikely to see the value of thoroughly preparing for gain sharing. Gain sharing should support and help achieve the organization's goals. Traditionally, gain sharing held narrowly formed goals to provide incentives for employees to improve primary productivity ratios. Today, more creatively designed plans are encouraging a variety of other improvements: attendance, safety, health-care costs containment, workers' compensation, expenses reduction, and so forth. The gain sharing design must become both compatible with and supportive of the company's mission and goals. There must be congruence if gain sharing is to achieve its greatest potential.

Determine Whether Gain Sharing Should Be a Strategy.   There are situations in which gain sharing will be an improper strategy for helping to reduce costs or to improve quality, productivity, and service:

- Where existing productivity standards are far too low. Initiating a gain sharing plan would pay for productivity improvements that are better achieved through good management practices. Companies should clean up sloppy methods and practices before initiating a gain sharing plan.

- When upcoming market dynamics are likely to be extreme and the only good productivity gain sharing measure is sales dollars.
- When substantial layoffs are planned. The success of gain sharing should not be directly identified with people reductions.
- When a change in management personnel is forthcoming and the philosophies of gain sharing and the new executive or executives conflict.

These examples may suggest other strategic mismatches that can hinder, or even ruin, an otherwise good design.

Appoint a Representative Study and Design Team.   When one company president heard the recommendation to choose an eight- to ten-person gain sharing design team representing a cross section of the entire company, he had two reactions: First, "We're paying a consultant to design a plan," and second, "Most of our employees don't understand our business and certainly don't understand gain sharing programs." He was basically correct on both counts. However, to get a smoothly operating plan from day one, employees have to believe that the plan is fair, understand more about the business, and believe that management will, in fact, practice the principles inherent in a good gain sharing design. They must believe that improved management practices, employee involvement, and sharing improvements from gains will be forthcoming.

The best way to ensure that management will change and that employees will learn is to get them started immediately practicing and developing the desired behaviors—involvement. A favored design-team composition would include a location general manager; controller; a human-resources manager; a first-line supervisor; five to seven others representing manufacturing, engineering, purchasing and materials management, and customer and quality assurance; others according to the organization structure; and union representation, when appropriate.

Educate the Design Team.   Equipping the design team with knowledge of gain sharing and of how the business operates, its competition, markets, and where it must spend its money will prepare the team to begin making decisions and solving problems. This is a critical step that takes time and a willingness to invest in people resources.

Design and Model a Plan. Two components of the design process are especially important, and if they are not completed thoroughly, they will lead to many regrets after a few weeks of plan operation. First is a plan document, and second is computer modeling of formula design alternatives.

Prepare a plan document (summary plan description) to ensure that detailed interpretation is always possible. Never rely on your memory or the memories of others on the design team. The most distressing recollections of a plan will be the arguments over unrecorded plan variables. The absence of a plan document will forever be a haunting experience. Similarly, don't rely on logic or mental mathematics to guarantee that the gain sharing plan design will deliver exactly the expected payout results under given conditions. Every custom formula I've seen computer-modeled has generated surprises. So, you can imagine the surprises that would be generated when the formula is not computer-modeled. There are enough uncontrollable variables inherent in a plan design without the formula being one of them.

Historical modeling should review three to five years of the following kinds of data:

- What would have happened if the plan had been in place?
- How would the plan have paid bonuses if we had only achieved our business plan?
- How far have we missed our business plan projections each year?
- What are the monthly, seasonal, or yearly business cycles that would have affected the plan?
- Have capital expenditures, for example, new equipment, affected productivity, and how quickly was it affected after installation?

Forward modeling should consider the following similar conditions:

- What are the upcoming market trends or new entries into the market that may affect demand, pricing, or productivity?
- Are there planned technology changes?
- What does the formula pay if productivity increases 1 percent to 15 percent?
- Are there conditions where the formula will pay for gains while the company is experiencing severe profit losses?
- Is one input or output measure overly influencing the formula?

These are only types of many questions and what-if modeling that are necessary.

Even the very best formula design will generate results that do not always motivate or reward goal performance. However, eliminating most of the surprises today will save headaches tomorrow. The front-end planning, design, computer analysis, and training will not be wasted time or effort.

Design a Training and Involvement System. Asking employees to improve productivity and make the gain sharing plan successful without providing training is like throwing darts at a bull's-eye when you're blindfolded. Employees must understand the plan and see the target. Initial training should include information on the company, its competition, markets, goals, and strategies. To work toward achieving goals, departments and individuals must understand the goals and perceive how their efforts can affect success. Employees may need help determining techniques or methods of measuring performance. They should also help identify appropriate measures and target criteria.

If employees have been discouraged in the past from communicating and achieving results in a team environment, additional training may be necessary. Such training might cover listening, communicating, presenting materials in group sessions, keeping records, resolving conflicts, and making decisions.

These training needs will vary in intensity, but they will exist. The training should be custom-designed in each situation after analysis and diagnosis have been completed.

Certainly, training must ensure that each employee understands the gain sharing plan and how the formula is computed. The intent is not to make every employee capable of computing the formula each month. Rather, each employee must understand how his or her actions affect the formula.

Implement. Many successful programs are kicked off with great fanfare—dinner, champagne, balloons, stickers, buttons, caps, jackets, and a host of other souvenirs and motivators that help associate positive and fun happenings with the program. On the other hand, many successful programs also begin with management and the design team's meeting with employees and describing the program, how it works, and how management promises to support employees. Then, management fulfills that promise.

The first approach is probably too flamboyant and could backfire because management may have a hard time maintaining the momentum and excitement of the kickoff. Many quiet and logically thinking employees might rather have had the party expenditures used to improve productivity and subsequent gain sharing rewards. Any approach should be carefully planned, well-timed, and congruent with other changes in the organization. If a big kickoff is used, management must be prepared to maintain the high level of excitement and expectations.

Most important is continued communication and follow-through on all promises and plan design elements. The moment the plan document is typed is not necessarily the best time to sever ties with the consultant. Insist on an implementation plan, then execute it. Have the consultant return frequently and near the end of the year fine-tune the plan. Revisions are likely and appropriate. Continuous improvement is appropriate with gain sharing as with other programs and functions.

Formula Guideline

As was previously noted, there are many factors to consider before beginning the design of a gain sharing plan. The perception is that a gain sharing plan is the formula. Although there are many critical elements, the formula is the one of most interest and sometimes the least understood. I've found the following set of guidelines to be helpful in judging or critiquing a formula and determining its appropriateness, given the organizational environment. The formula should:

- Reflect the philosophy of the organization
- Be perceived by employees as a good measure of performance
- Be perceived as fair
- Be relatively stable over time, given the competitive industry
- Be understandable by employees
- Include key factors in the business
- Be composed of factors or variables employees can influence

It is important to note that two of the guidelines deal with perception. This only emphasizes that the formula must actually be fair (in the eyes of the consultant) and be believed to be fair by management and employees. Perception is truth, even in gain sharing plan design.

The seven guidelines might be more accurately entitled "Principles In Formula Design." They present the basis for creating a congruence between the company and the plan and its employees. The reader should not be misled to believe that designing a formula around those seven, seemingly simple statements is easy. Surrounding each statement is a hidden complexity that has created conflict in many design meetings. A good example can be drawn from the last two guidelines, that is, that the formula should include key factors in the business and that the formula be composed of factors that employees can influence as opposed to those uncontrolled by employees, such as taxes. However, if the formula encompasses one or two key factors that employees can affect, but those factors (utility usage, for example) represent only 2 percent of the variable costs of the business, then the opportunity for gains is small. Such a design affects the company and employees negatively. The employees' opportunity to build a large bonus pool is nonexistent, and the company, through giving incentives to employees to work on such a small portion of variable costs, is limiting the impact of savings potential. Conversely, including all variable cost-line items that employees could affect raises the question of how large the bonus pool could become.

This discussion should further focus attention on the importance of having a total compensation philosophy that differentiates between fixed (base) and variable compensations. How much of the employee's total compensation opportunity should be put at risk? Of course, this discussion also points to the importance of computer modeling the one philosophy that is established.

Many employee gain sharing design teams have been fooled by believing that one type of gain sharing plan is better because the sharing percentages were larger with one plan than another. For example, one union representative was enthralled by the sales presentations made by the consultant because the formula shared gains 50 percent for employees and 50 percent for the company. Under IMPROSHARE, the formula, the shared 50 percent of the savings from labor productivity improvement only, and labor dollars in the particular company in question represented only 9 percent of the company's cost of production. So the pool of opportunity for the employee was only 4.5 percent of viable production costs (50 percent times 9 percent).

Another consultant had suggested a formula that shared only 25 percent of the savings with employees. However, the opportunity was included in the formula to affect 96 percent of the company's costs. The saving opportunities included raw materials, energy, labor, scrap, contract labor, and so forth. In this example, the employees could potentially earn a much larger bonus pool by affecting 96 percent of the business times a 25 percent share, or 24 percent of all savings. So the employee was misled in believing a 50/50 split was much better than a 25/75 split. In this instance, the company could have been misled if there had been a need to affect and motivate more than labor productivity. This example represents only one of many complexities that must be considered in formula and plan design. Would-be gain sharing users are well advised to proceed carefully and consider the intricate details that will definitely influence success.

Design Issues

Payment Frequency

Gain sharing plans pay earned bonuses on some frequency, sometimes weekly, monthly, or quarterly, depending on formula type and payout philosophy. IMPROSHARE or physical-type formulas pay more frequently, whereas financial and multicost plans usually pay less frequently.

One variable in determining payout frequency is data availability. Most formulas contain data that the organization rolls up on a monthly basis, thus contributing to a monthly payout. Yet philosophically, the gain sharing plan designers want the payout amount, after taxes and deductions, to be sufficient for the purchase of an appliance or personal gift that will be psychologically identified with gain sharing. Small weekly payouts are too frequently viewed as extra grocery money. The appliance or gift will be remembered as coming from gain sharing long after the food is gone.

Payouts require accounting, check printing, distribution, and other administrative support that are costly yet reinforcing to employees. Many companies pay monthly but will not cut checks under a fixed dollar amount so the small earned bonus is carried forward and added to the next payout period. Each organization has variables affecting a preferred payout frequency. This issue should not be taken lightly or as a minor point. There are strategic issues involved that affect plan success.

Payment Method (Determining Share)

There are five primary methods used to determine the amount of the total pool to be paid to each employee:

1. The *percent-of-payroll* method identifies each employee's monthly payroll as a percent of the total eligible payroll. That percentage is then multiplied by the pool to determine the employee's share. This is a commonly utilized method.

2. The *equal-share* method merely divides the number of eligible participants into the pool amount to determine each share. This method does not take overtime into consideration and thus fails to meet all the criteria of the wage and hour laws.

3. The *hours-worked* method totals the hours worked by all eligible employees, and each participant's hours worked is divided into that total. The percentage is then multiplied by the pool amount to generate each participant's share.

4. The *hours-paid* method differs from the method above only in that more emphasis is given to overtime hours. A person working 43 hours would have straight-time equivalent pay equaling (3 hours overtime) 4.5 hours. Thus, the hours-worked method would receive 43 hours of credit. But under the hours-paid method, the employee would receive 44.5 hours of credit.

5. *Team achievement* has been used as a payout split method to encourage achievement of goals. There are several versions of this concept to qualify teams for payment of a companywide pool. In some instances, teams are disqualified from earning a bonus or may earn greater percentages of a bonus based on the team's contribution compared with some goal or standard.

It is important that certain derivations of these methods may be considered illegal under the wage and hour laws.

Formula Adjustments

The gain sharing plan document or summary plan description mentioned earlier needs language describing when and how the plan may be charged. Failure to recognize the reality of likely plan modifications only represents naïvety. Accommodating the realities of change will make that otherwise emotional time and event a smooth transaction to an improved design.

The most difficult changes usually come within the formula itself. Some of the more typically justifiable reasons for modifying the formula are major capital input by the company that significantly affects productivity and the baseline data in the plan, the introduction of new products, radical modifications to the production or service process, and a significant change in the price of raw materials or product pricing.

Some examples of when formulas are not modified include large productivity improvements resulting from employees' ideas and efforts, normal costs and changes of wages or other inputs, and normal fluctuations in the selling price.

Various adjustment methods are used: IMPROSHARE plans have "buyout" language that allows the company to purchase "formula tightening" after productivity enhancements have been achieved over some specified level. The preferred adjustment method is a "ratcheting" algorithm that treats yearly trends in a fair way for employees and the company.

These formula adjustments may be fairly complex or complexly fair. They may be as simple as adjusting the baseline data each year by one-third of the average three years' experience, or the adjustments may be complex. Some companies ask their consultant to recommend the appropriate new baseline. Whatever method fits your organization, it should be reduced to language in the plan document. Then everyone understands in advance the changes that will be happening. Formula adjustment language eliminates surprises, and it is surprise that generates trauma.

Payment During Periods of Loss

The theory behind gain sharing is that employees achieve a bonus (share rewards) as a result of improved productivity. Consistent with the formula, employees may significantly affect productivity over the plan's baseline while the company is deep in red ink. This may result from market price or some other variable not included in the formula and outside the employees' control.

Early gain sharing plan designs paid employees regardless of profits because that's the gain sharing philosophy! However, a conservative client along with a particular environment within the organization led the writer in 1984 to a paper mill gain sharing plan design that incorporated a secondary formula component accommodating profitability, or lack there of. Since 1984 the concept of a trailing profit formula has grown in use. This is another issue that ties to company philosophy, environment, and so forth. The secondary or trailing profitability formula built into the design provides a greater assurance for the company that payouts under gain sharing result only when there is black ink on the profit and loss statement.

Payment Schedule

In which of the four situations (shown in Figure 18-2) should employees get paid under a gain sharing plan? The obvious answer is "no" in the lower right quadrant because there are no productivity improvements and no profits. The upper left quadrant shows productivity improvements and profitability, so the obvious answer is "yes," the plan should pay. But what about the other alternatives? The answer is determined by environment and philosophy, and the plan design must be congruent. This issue has

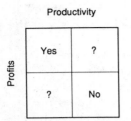

Figure 18-2. When should a plan pay employees?

been a driving force in creating the trailing profit formula mentioned in the previous section. Companies must be guided to assess their philosophy and design a plan that fits their philosophy, environment, and needs.

Costs and Benefits of Gain Sharing Plans

There are companies that view and enter into gain sharing as the quick fix or panacea. Neither is further from the truth. Gain sharing is not a quick fix. There are benefits but there are also costs. Some of the costs include:

- Substantial time to design and implement
- Consultant expenses
- Substantial management time to administer
- Employee and management education and training
- An orientation for new managers and employees
- Accurate and timely production and cost data
- A shift to participative philosophy and behaviors
- Increased employee involvement
- The education of employees to better understand the business

These costs are real and must not be overlooked or taken lightly. They are necessary. They determine success, and their absence may guarantee failure.

These are the benefits, however, that offset the costs:

- Improved productivity
- A shared sense of values and cooperation
- Employee involvement in the plan

- A broader base of communications with the motivation to listen
- Employee involvement in the total operation
- Improved job satisfaction
- Increased employee participation in problem solving and decision making
- Improved labor-management relations

The costs are large and so are the benefits. Managed properly, gain sharing helps create a win-win environment.

Summary

Gain sharing is a useful compensation program that may be a viable alternative and organization development intervention for many organizations. As an organization development intervention, gain sharing has been most successful when combined with two other components that almost ensure a successful plan—namely, employee involvement and a discrete set of management practices. As a compensation component, gain sharing can give incentive for hard work, smart work, improved productivity, and some changes in short- and long-term behavior. The plan design can determine these variables that are affected most.

The greatest impact of gain sharing comes when management follows a set of practices that demonstrate a philosophy that people are important and are the experts in those areas where they were trained and function on a daily basis. Such a philosophy and the accompanying practices naturally encourage employee involvement—and the synergy begins. When the synergy of the three components are equally stressed (shared rewards, employee involvement, and appropriate management practices), the program shares the strength and stability of a three-legged stool. Gain sharing as a compensation and organization development intervention can be successful and a powerful tool. Gain sharing integrated as a prescription within a total organization design process will impact even more.

There are numerous practical and legal issues surrounding the design, development, and implementation of a gain sharing program. Many, but not all, of those issues are addressed here. The smart and fainthearted are advised to seek experienced help early if you see gain sharing as a potential alternative reward system for your organization.

19
Short-Term Incentives

Ike Greenspan
Director of Compensation
GTE Corporation

The late 1900s undoubtedly will be regarded as a time when our country's post-World War II economic hegemony disappeared and a time when an aggressively conservative government sought to, among other things, deregulate various aspects of economic activity while resisting trade protectionism. It will be recognized as a period that severely tested the mettle of many United States companies and a period when the management of major corporations, in response to unprecedented global competition, took drastic steps in reducing costs and modernizing plants and operating methods in an effort to reestablish preeminence, or at least avoid further erosion. Many management processes and tools were employed in this struggle. Looming large among these was the emergence of compensation practices that suppressed entitlement and accentuated a direct tie-in to measures of productivity, profitability, and other operating results.

In many ways this emergence follows a predictable pattern evident throughout the twentieth century. On several occasions there was an apparent convergence of factors—economic, political, and societal—whose combined influence lead to, or at least coincided with, the advent of new or rebuilt uses of incentive pay. What may be different

Table 19-1. Characteristics of the Commitment Model

- Focus on customer and employee (shareholder gains as a byproduct)
- Emphasis on quality, not as something that costs money but as something that is worth an investment
- Common fate and the long-range view
- Sharing of power, information, problem solving, and gains
- Total career, not just total compensation perspective
- Cultural values—emotional ownership, not just intellectual involvement
- Contractual commitment, not just psychological compliance

about the 1900s is the breadth and depth of the migration toward incentives.

The shock of unrelenting global competition of the 1980s in combination with a new organizational ideal—the so-called Commitment Model (the characteristics of which are shown in Table 19-1)—had led to numerous changes in the American workplace, including renewed interest in incentive pay. As corporations struggled to shed dysfunctional overhead, they also looked to undo certain employee expectations—that had built up over the years but which could no longer be sustained. Some of these expectations included unlimited promotion, free health insurance, and an entitlement to annual pay adjustments as good or better than the rate of inflation, regardless of company performance.

Generally, short-term plans today can be classified as falling into one of two categories—*individual* or *group* and tend to be of an incentive rather than a bonus nature. As implied by these designations, the individual incentive emphasizes personal accomplishments whereas group incentives look at collective performance.

The shift to incentives at the expense of bonuses is a byproduct of objective-based and commitment-oriented work environments.

In this environment, incentive pay, which is tied to predetermined, mutually agreed upon objectives and for which the risk element and upside potential are known to the participant, would be favored over bonuses, which inherently are fashioned on after-the-fact assessment of contribution and for which payouts are highly discretionary. In general, as shown in Table 19-2, all incentive designs share certain strengths or weaknesses. Each specific design, in turn, also has certain strengths and weaknesses (see Table 19-3).

Table 19-2. Characteristics of the Prevailing Incentive Designs

Principal strengths	Principal weaknesses
• The organization can more easily focus on employee effort and attention.	• Unhealthy rivalry and contention can occasionally be produced.
• A closer linkage is established between specific rewards for specific contributions.	• Excessive concentration on specific objectives at the expense of recurring responsibilities can result.
• An impression of common fate or destiny is enhanced.	• Problems can arise regarding allocation formula and participant selection.
• A sense of sharing in company success is provided.	• Managers may have a more difficult time in selecting the winners than they do under merit process.
• Nonrecurring costs and potentially reduced expenses are typically involved.	• Increased costs are associated with communication, installation, and effort.

Table 19-3. Characteristics of Specific Incentive Designs (*Continued*)

Principal strengths	Principal weaknesses
Individual incentives:	
• There are no recurring costs and potentially no benefits roll-up.	• Narrowing employee focus and hurting teamwork is a possibility.
• Improved pay-performance perception is a possibility.	• Supervisors are additionally burdened.
• There is congruence with many existing organization cultures.	• Individual performance measures are fallible.
• Attention is focused.	• There is a dilemma over a public versus a concealed award.
• The organization can specify desired individual deliverables and reward or punish according to results.	• There is a participation controversy (for example, eligibility rule contentions and job- rather than performance-based).
• Potential award levels are known in advance.	• The administration process (that is, nonfinancial objectives, payout algorithm, and so forth) is demanding.
Spot recognition (discretion awards, and so forth):	
• There are no recurring costs.	• Overall impact on the organization is uncertain.
• Recognition is not applied to benefits.	• Recognition is highly dependent on trust in selection process.
• Fast response time and possible frequent payouts should strengthen pay-performance perception.	• As currently used, recognition is often too small and narrowly distributed to influence performance-pay perception.
• There is a surprise value.	• Recognition does not focus on effort but rather recognizes the event.
• There is a publicity value; employee is publicly acknowledged.	
• Flexibility allows manager discretion; recognition can be tailored to department.	
Team or Small Group Incentives:	
• There are no recurring costs and potentially no benefits roll-up.	• Individual pay-performance is more weakly perceived.

Table 19-3. Characteristics of Specific Incentive Designs *(Continued)*

Principal strengths	Principal weaknesses
Team or Small Group Incentives:	
• There is less culture change; administration is easier than gain sharing	• Unhealthy interteam rivalry and a focus on functional objectives only are possibilities.
• Team or department objectives can be more meaningful and measurable than individual objectives.	
• Managers are less burdened than with individual awards.	
Profit Sharing:	
• There are no recurring costs, and profit sharing is generally not included in benefits.	• There is a weak individual pay-performance perception, especially in lean years.
• Installation is relatively easy.	• Profit may be affected by factors extraneous to employee effort—for example, accounting practices. This may be difficult to communicate.
• Profit sharing is directly linked to company success.	• The allocation formula is problematic, for example, what organizational level to measure.
• A common destiny—identification of the employee with the company—is perceived.	• Profit sharing is not particularly appreciated in a regulated environment (for example, rate commissions) and by shareholders.
• Profit sharing is perceived well during a low-inflation era.	
Gain Sharing:	
• There are no recurring costs, and gain sharing is not applied to most benefits.	• There is little history on use with management and/or professionals where quantifiable group performance measures are difficult.
Gain sharing is well suited for production environments.	• There is a weak individual pay-performance perception.
• Well-defined and concrete measures of unit performance can be used.	• Extensive installation time is usually needed.
• A common destiny—teamwork and employee involvement—is perceived.	• Profit sharing is usually part of a larger culture change effort.
	• Research suggests difficulties when unit size exceeds 500.

Common Characteristics of
Incentive Plans

There are many types of short-term incentive plans. Yet they all share certain basic design characteristics. On a macro level, incentive programs deal with the reward mechanism itself, including whom we pay, how much we pay, and how we pay. Plus, they generally contain a measurement mechanism that gauges what we are paying for, what the lower and upper limits of expected performance improvement are, and how this performance improvement translates into the reward.

Interestingly, the measurement part of the design process, despite serving as the plan backbone, often gets short shrift. This perhaps is not by accident, because getting the measurement system right usually requires more effort and thought than designing the reward mechanism. The organization, the supervisor, the employee, and other interested parties, such as shareholders, regulators, unions, and so forth, need to know what the incentive program is paying for specifically and, perhaps just as important, what it doesn't pay for.

The universe of potential measurements is infinite, with a depth and breadth only limited by the vision of the incentive program developer. However, to be effective, the measurements need to possess certain basic properties. They must be congruous with the reward piece of incentive design, be sufficiently individualized to allow the sense of personal influence and impact, be reasonably easy to track, have credibility, be externally sensitive, and have a certain timelessness to them.

A telecommunications company recently introduced a team incentive program in one of its service organizations covering some 5000 management employees that were divided into 50 teams. The effort to pinpoint relevant, competitively sound measures, and the subsequent identification of meaningful performance thresholds and targets against the measures turned out to be an immensely complex yet worthwhile undertaking—one that, for the first time, crystallized in the minds of the management group the way in which the various work groups interrelate, what the "handoffs" are like, and how each group influences ultimate outputs.

The Individual Management
Incentive Plans

Although subtle variations abound, there are common threads that run through most contemporary individual management incentive plans (note the term *incentive*, and not *bonus*) in industrial United States corporations. This fact is no accident, given the role that boards of directors play in both the design and administration of such plans and the intricate nature of board service among United States companies. These threads revolve around considerations that management takes into account when looking into a specific plan and certainly involve reward and measurement issues. These considerations are also ultimately manifested in various approval, governance, and communication documents that are typically drawn up, and they include:

- Shareholder approval
- Eligibility rules (nomination, approval, notification)
- Size of targets and minimum or maximum opportunities around them
- Objective-setting process (formalized objective-setting, including measures and milestones)
- Performance tracking and assessment (individual and aggregate)
- Fund determination (formula or discretionary approach, and carry-forwards)
- Payment form (cash, stock, or stock equivalents)
- Timing of payments
- Proration of payments
- Deferral
- Application of payments toward benefits

On the whole, it can be safely said that no optimum combination of features has been identified in American incentive plans. We cannot point to a definitive study that has identified the characteristics that decidedly predetermine the ultimate success or value of a plan. Generally, corporations make choices regarding their own plan design that are in sync with their corporate culture, organizational structure, stage in life cycle, industry norms, senior executives' preference, and competitive needs. What follows should serve as a broad framework for developing an individual management incentive plan.

Plan Authorization

Shareholder approval is not mandated by federal law, although the commercial statutes of several states do have this requirement. Regulatory bodies, such as the Securities and Exchange Commission, require written disclosure, usually in the proxy, as do some of the stock exchanges, particularly when company stock would be used as a means of payment (even if it is partial). In addition, almost without exception, company bylaws require the board of directors or a pertinent committee (for example, a compensation committee) of the board to approve such plans. The board, or its pertinent committee, may also annually approve various administrative elements of the plan, for example, eligibility, payout opportunities, and actual awards.

Eligibility and Participation

The most common eligibility criteria are as follows:

- Minimum grade
- Minimum dollar midpoint, or salary
- Minimum job-evaluation points
- Minimum organizational level
- Reporting-relationship rule
- Specific rules relating to type of job (for example, nature of influence on operating results, and so forth)
- Combination of the above
- Discretionary approach
- All management with specific ratio of actual recipients determined annually

With the exception of the last item, it is highly likely that no matter what criteria are used and no matter how airtight the specific stipulation language is, it will be deemed arbitrary by someone, someplace in the organization. This has to be considered as an inevitable consequence of having an employee plan that, by its very nature, distinguishes among people. In developing the plan text and in administrating participation, the compensation practitioner must be mindful of related ground rules affecting nomination, approval, notification, and proration due to entry in the middle of the cycle and the eventual exit from the program.

Award Targets and Limits

The use of payout targets is commonplace. The typical means of expressing target levels is to do it on the basis of percentages, either in relation to salary or midpoint, thus permitting the resulting dollar award levels to be adjusted automatically whenever the underlying basis is changed. The percentages are then converted to dollars for ease of communication. The targets can also be expressed in fixed dollars at each grade, thereby avoiding the automatic "creep" factor associated with the percentage method. Other less frequently used means attempt to denominate job-evaluation points, specific title, or reporting relationship.

In addition to targets, many companies set upper limits on the awards. These are typically factored as a percentage of salary (for example, 50 percent of salary, 75 percent of salary, and so forth), or as a percentage of target award (for example, 150 percent of target, 200 percent of target, and so forth). Targets are generally scaled so that the larger the job, the higher the target. Target awards are generally communicated to participants. The disclosure occurs at various times in the incentive plan year, with the most frequent one being the start of the fiscal year. Some companies also establish official minimum limits on awards. If a minimum (as a sort of a threshold) is warranted, then it can be represented as some percentage of the target. However, care should be taken in the drafting of plan documents to allow the company an outlet should it elect in selective cases to make minimal or no payments.

Award targets are set by most companies based on desired competitive positioning and a mix of salary and incentive. Considerable thought enters this process since the company's practices can affect the ultimate expense of the program and participants' perception of the strength of its commitment to incentive pay, not to mention the ultimate and perhaps difficult explanations to all interested parties if the awards' size should become too large. Then too the competitive benchmarking process can prove tricky in a rapidly fluctuating economy. To the extent that corporate profitability is affected by economic cycles and in turn affects the relative level of incentives awarded, compensation practitioners must examine several years' worth of payout history to ascertain a trend. This trend data needs to be fine-tuned to provide a scale of awards that matches the participation demographics. (For an organization using evaluation points or grades this is relatively straightforward.)

Objective-Setting Process

Objective setting is closely intertwined with the performance measurements—financial, operating, and other—used by the corporation. The objective-setting process is generally multistage and often two directional. The corporation's overall short-term operating strategies and financial performance goals are translated into business-unit goals and, in turn, depending on organizational structure, diffused into suitable quantitative individual objectives. Conversely, certain types of objectives, those related to functional and more qualitative efforts (for example, successful integration of acquired businesses, development of new products, financing or refinancing efforts, reorganizations, and so forth), may originate with participants and roll-up.

The writing of high-quality objectives often involves considerable effort. To ensure the best quality possible, organizations often do a variety of things. Guidelines issued by one company the author is familiar with can be found in Figure 19-1. Additionally, companies may require review of objectives at various organizational levels to ensure that the necessary congruity and stretch exists up and down the organization in order to maximize the probability that overall goals will be accomplished.

Most organizations prefer to deal with a limited number of well-developed key objectives of a demanding nature rather than numerous objectives that capture the more routine aspects of a job. Formalized weighting of individual objectives can be found in some companies' plans. However, given the dynamic business environment of most organizations, such weighting can encumber the overall process.

Performance Tracking and Assessment

Generally, at the end of the performance cycle each participant's results would be measured against objectives. This may or may not include a self-assessment. Results are subsequently reviewed at one or more higher organizational levels for corroboration and consistency. This is particularly important in situations in which the measured activities require internal handoffs. Assessments are also often conducted at various stages during the plan cycle. Recapitulation of year-to-date performance and the outlook regarding completion of the balance of objectives are also conducted by many organizations.

Fund Determination

The vast majority of organizations employ some type of funding mechanism, and, of these, most settle on some financial measure or expression of the participants' stake in the plan (for example, total targeted awards, some percentage of participants' salaries, and so forth). Occasionally, organizations employ dual formulas—financial and nonfinancial. When financial measures are used, they typically denote the maximum allowable expenditure (X percent of pretax net income). Often the formula also contains a threshold that forbids payment unless

The number of objectives each participant develops should generally range between three and six, and be written in short and simple sentences. When done well, the objective should reflect the translation of a complex consideration into precise and specific terms.

Objective statements should reflect and define:
- The critical areas requiring attention
- The results expected in these critical areas
- How the results will be achieved
- How long they will take to achieve
- The cost in dollars, resources, and so forth to accomplish them

Following is a checklist, divided into two sections, on the characteristics each objective statement should possess. The first section explains the essence of an objective statement. The second section qualifies what it should and should not do. Examples of objective statements meeting these requirements are included.

SECTION 1: Characteristics of an Objective Statement

1. The statement deals with only one central theme or purpose. By limiting each statement to one objective, there is less possibility for ambiguity in understanding it and in knowing what action steps are needed to attain it.

2. Action-oriented language is used. Verbs such as "increase," "install," "initiate," "complete," "conduct," "design," are examples. Using these action-oriented verbs improves your ability to identify action steps and helps to ensure that your objective will be measurable.

3. The statement describes the specific results required.

4. Results are described in measurable or observable terms. ("The plant is operative," "the new product line is on-stream," "sales have increased by X percent.") When results are measurable, it is possible to intermittently gauge progress and identify when you have met your objective.

5. The statement includes the time by which the results will have been achieved. A specific time frame helps in planning the rate of progress necessary to achieve the objective.

Figure 19-1. General guidelines and checklist for writing objective statements.

SECTION 2: Qualifications of the Objective Statement

In addition to the characteristics listed in Section 1, each objective statement, as a whole, should be checked for the following:

1. It should be consistent with and supportive of your organization's short- and long-term objectives. Attainment of the objectives must provide a significant contribution to the company's strategic or tactical plans.

2. It should be a challenge. A stretch factor is implied in the objective statement—it encourages new thinking and new approaches to important problems. Objectives that are challenging are also stimulating.

3. It should be attainable within its time and cost limits. Only realistic objectives are useful to you and to the organization, unrealistic objectives are counterproductive.

4. The result should be within your ability to control. There is no point in setting an objective for yourself that is beyond your area of influence.

5. The outcome should help to bridge the gap between where you are now and where you want to be. The objective specifies the difference between the current and the preferred situation and serves to direct your future course of action.

6. It should provide you and the company with new information about your plans for the future or suggest new plans. The process of objective setting clarifies thinking, and additionally can suggest alternative courses of action. It should not merely state the obvious.

7. The objective should be worthwhile. Choosing which objectives to include implies rejecting others. Are the ones you have chosen the most important challenges facing you in the time period?

8. It should be supported by value added, payback, or other investment analysis when new expenditures are involved.

9. It should not describe routine tasks. Because you will do these tasks in the ordinary course of events, they do not require special planning. Execution of them is routine.

Figure 19-1. (Continued)

some minimal performance is achieved (for example, return on investment must exceed Y percent). Occasionally, companies using dual or tandem measures develop grids that formally reflect the expected returns or growth rates and the proportion of targeted awards that the incremental returns or growth rates would drive. An increasingly common approach is to state these measures in relation to benchmark company performance. These benchmarks can be spelled out in absolute terms, that is, to match the return on investment of companies X, Y, and Z, or, on a relative year-over-year change basis, can exceed the rate of improvement in the benchmark groups' net operating profit by 2 percent.

Formal measures can also be applied at the individual business group level, particularly if such businesses (in a diversified organization) have fundamentally different operating and financial characteristics, face different economic climates, or are in different stages of evolution. Whatever the measures, it is important that they are well communicated and acceptable to all concerned parties.

Since companies generally want to ensure sufficient funds for future awards, and perhaps even the accommodation of expansion of either participation or award targets, it is very common to see funds formulas that generate excessive funds. These excesses are often booked and carried forward as a form of insurance to allow for payouts even during years of depressed business and financial conditions. Such carryforwards must be used judiciously since they may be criticized by shareholders, unions, regulators, and nonparticipating employees. However, if the incentive philosophy of the organization is such that it emphasizes the individual's contribution and if the total compensation philosophy (that is, the incentive component) is not a piece on top of generous base salary but rather an integral part of the overall competitively determined pay program, then the use of carryforwards can typically be justified.

Fund Allocation and Individual Award Determination

At the end of the performance cycle, the organization must disburse the incentive awards. In many companies this process is two-dimensional. On one hand, bottoms-up individual performance, which often is stated in a rating form and then applied against the individual's targeted award, and self-assessed operating unit numbers are aggregated. These aggregated numbers can be further rolled up through as many hierarchical levels as necessary. On the other hand, the corporate headquarters (typically the finance, planning, and compensation departments) develop performance numbers for the corporation and often for individual units.

Unless contrary to plan language or to the management style of the organization, a reconciliation between unit and corporate assessment of performance, including degree of difficulty experienced and the standing against competitors, is likely to ensue. The time and effort devoted to the reconciliation can be considerably shortened if the performance measurement contains certain safeguards or step savers. These safeguards include minimizing the use of qualitative, difficult to standardize measures; maximizing the use of external benchmarks; upfront mentioning and identification of extraordinary circumstances under which measures can be adjusted; and using a weighting process that assigns degrees of importance to the objectives.

The decision regarding specific participants' payouts against this backdrop of organizational performances can be made rather complex. Some companies prefer tightly strung matrices in which the performance of successively lower organizational entities is calibrated through a weighting process and the individual performance is factored in.

For example, Company A is looking at the performance of a division controller for whom the performance against objectives and the respective importance of each are carefully monitored (see Table 19-4).

Table 19-4. Performance Evaluation of Division Controller in Company A

	Corporate performance	Group	Division	Division controller	
Performance rating (1.00% = norm)	1.00	.90	1.10	1.20	
Weight of each	20%	20%	20%	40%	
Product	.20	.18	.22	.48	= 1.08

This rating can then be compared against the target award to develop a specific recommendation:

Target award	= $25,000
Rating	= 1.08
Payout	= $27,000

All the participants' potential payouts can be computed as in the table and aggregated, and the obligation can be compared to the available fund. Other variations on this theme and other degrees of detail can be employed, right up to where the organizational and individual performance is obscured by a single performance measure that does not allow demarcation between individual and business unit performance. Whatever the degree of formality and specificity the organization is looking for, the invariable reconciliation and sanity checks are going to take place. These will ensure that the funds are being disbursed in a manner that safeguards the corporation's interests and fulfills key executives' and board of directors' views of what is right.

Payout Form and Deferral

The vast majority of short-term incentive plans in the United States, particularly those for which deferrals are not offered, pay out in the form of cash. Stock or stock equivalents are also used, but more often only when deferral is permitted or required. Given the personal financial outlook of most managers in the aftermath of tax reform (no advantage to capital gains and the lowest tax rate in modern history), while mindful of continuing stock disposition restrictions under Security Exchange Act, Section 16(b), and personal liquidity difficulty, the use of stock in nondeferral arrangements would appear passé. The use of stock or stock equivalents in deferral arrangements, particularly ones aimed at estate building, might continue to make sense.

Payment Timing and Proration

Payments under incentive plans are generally annual and are made as soon as practicable after the end of the fiscal year. Proration of payments may be allowed under the plan and may occur in a variety of circumstances, including retirement, disability, death, separation for the convenience of the company, movement to a job that is normally not eligible for incentive, and so forth.

Benefit Applications

The posture of companies on the issue of including incentive awards in determining benefit levels (for example, life insurance coverage as multiples of salary plus incentive, as opposed to only salary) varies considerably. Often, however, in view of the unpredictable year-to-year track of payouts and the concern for meeting the discrimination tests in qualified plans, companies elect not to include incentive payments in benefit calculation. The only common exception relates to pensions that are taken care of through separate, nonqualified supplemental executive retirement plans (SERPs).

Change in Control

With the explosion during the late 1980s of hostile corporate takeovers and raids, many organizations, in the interest of safeguarding employees' rights, turned to various change-in-control measures. These safeguards are generally set off by double triggers, one being the hostile takeover itself and the other the loss or detrimental change in the manager's job. The safeguard often calls for a prompt payment, either on a prorata or whole basis, of the incentive based on some prearranged formula, such as the average of the previous three years, the incentive target, and so forth.

Team Incentive Program

Recently a large telecommunications company, with the help of Booz Allen & Hamilton Inc., introduced a team incentive plan in one of its big divisions. The company, like the rest in the industry, had a few years earlier begun doing business in a deregulated, highly competitive environment and had set on a course of transforming many operating and employee-relations efforts. The basic objectives for the team incentive program were outlined as:

1. Focus the entire management population on specific problems, and mobilize them to develop solutions.
2. Send strong, clear cultural messages and signals regarding the fostering of teamwork vertically and horizontally.
3. Make performance targets difficult yet achievable.
4. Help reduce cost through remixing compensation, shifting from salary only to a desired variable/fixed ratio.
5. Continue to recognize individual contribution, and meaningfully reward superior performers—reward pockets of excellence.
6. Integrate with other employee involvement and reward efforts across the company.

In designing the program, the company had in mind an ulterior motive, that being the need to break down certain historical management processes that were deemed to impede rapid improvements in performance. One of the chief villains in this regard was a tradition-bound, departmentalized organization and allegiance. All prior efforts, including many employee involvement efforts, to get people who worked in different departments to truly work with each other did not live up to expectations. A review of past failures indicated that the causes were basic:

- Diffusion of effort rather than focus on specific objective
- No specific competitive benchmarking (that is, who do we have to beat and by how much?)
- Insufficient understanding of how the work of various departments integrates and the specific handoffs that are required to maximize outputs
- Insufficient understanding of how the efforts of individual segments within the company aggregate (roll-up) to ultimately deliver specific overall outcomes
- Inadequate attention to a variety of problems, partly because of imperceptible personal risk associated with organization's failure to improve.

The program set out to correct all of the above failures and took on a multistage evolution. It included:

- Identification of essential business objectives (initially these were to be cost- and quality-oriented)
- Identification of absolutely essential processes (transactions) that can lead to improvements in cost and quality
- Identification of natural work groups that best fit the essential process model
- Ways to integrate and improve competitive intelligence gathering to not only know what competition is doing and where its results exceed those of the division, but also find out how they got there
- Development of the means for determining how the work of the new work teams integrates to get at overall results
- Identification and development of the specific performance measures that the teams will concentrate on and that drive toward attainment of overall company results

- Development of the compensation mechanism to get attention and reward or penalize in accordance with contributions results
- Development of the system infrastructure for performance tracking and reporting and for incentive calculations
- Communication

The effort to focus on cost and quality led to identification of two aggregate-cost and five aggregate-quality measures that cumulatively captured all the essential goals of the division. The effort to map out how the business processes work lead to flow charts like the example in Figure 19-2.

The identification of natural teams led to grids like the one in Table 19-5.

The effort to improve benchmarking intelligence led to greater use of certain competitive analysis tools, including certain customer satisfaction surveys available in the industry and the development of other sources.

The effort to trim the numbers of teams to the most realistic number is shown in Figure 19-3.

The desire to develop team measures that could drive overall division objectives lead to identification of specific measures for each team. These were also externally benchmarked (see Figure 19-4).

The statistically based model for determining how much annual improvement can be expected, given where the division and team performance stood at base point, was currently arrived at by using competitive information as shown in Figure 19-5.

Based on the principle that recognizes that the higher the existing performance, the more difficult the incremental performance improvement becomes, a handicapping approach was applied. This handicapping would permit teams, that were thought to have difficulty in meeting their goals, to have an equal shot at rewards.

The reward mechanism itself was the product of numerous iterations and was set up as follows. Basically, a portion of the merit budget (50 percent) was reserved to act as seed money for the overall fund. The fund would grow based on the degree to which the overall various cost and quality measures were achieved or exceeded. An example is shown in Figure 19-6. At target, the originally withheld funds are reinstated; above target, the fund can grow to three times the original amount. The overall allocation diagram can be found in Figure 19-7.

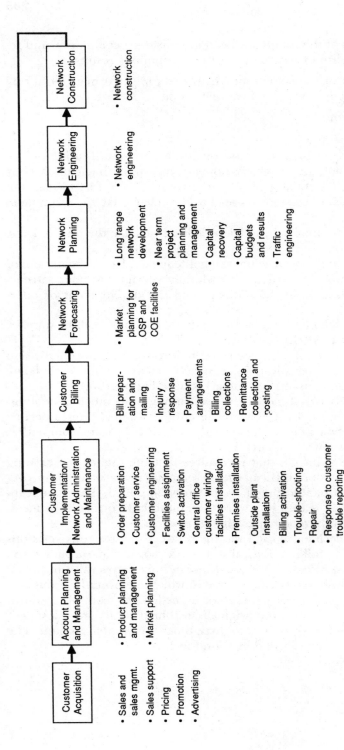

Figure 19-2. How the network business works.

Table 19-5. Communications Business Summary

Team		Communications business					
	Marketing planning	Product management	Access services	Consumer operations	Business operations	Public communications	Total
Communications Business Staff Team	47	17					64
Access Services Team	5	7	106				118
Mass Market Team	6	6		51			63
Major Accounts Staff Team	6	17			93		116
Major Accounts East					33		33
Major Accounts North					42		42
Major Accounts South					43		43
Network Planning Northern Team	8						8
Network Planning Southern Team	9						9
Total Subteam*	81	47	106	51	211	0	496	91%
Corporate Team*	0	0	0	0	0	47	47	9%
Total Mgmt. Empl.*	81	47	106	51	211	47	543	100%

*Levels 1–12 only.

285

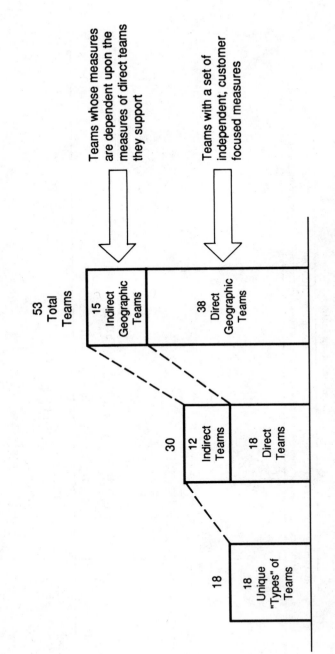

Figure 19-3. Grouping the proposed teams into fewer than 20 team types with unique sets of measures.

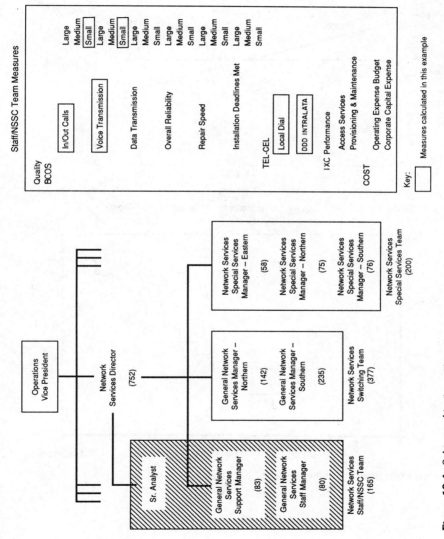

Figure 19-4. Subteam objective setting.

287

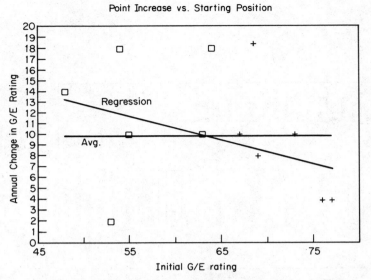

Figure 19-5. Telcel overall quality: point increase versus starting position.

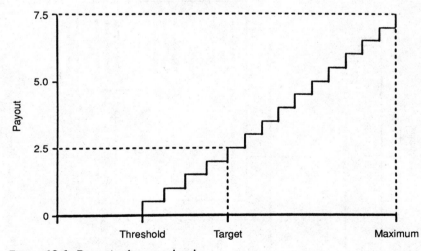

Figure 19-6. Payout/performance bands.

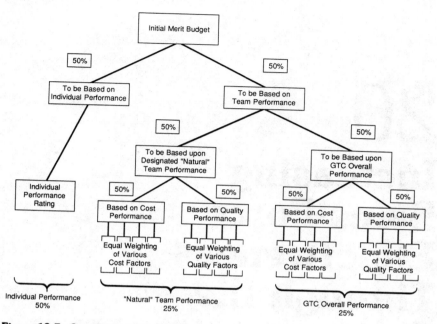

Figure 19-7. Overall allocation of budget.

Every member of a team would receive an equal percentage of his or her own midpoint, which would be a product of both the team's and division's performance. At the end, the organizational unit recognized that any number of other payout mechanisms, besides the one adopted, might have sufficed. The one selected, however, contained the right blend of measurements and rewards that fit with the organization's expectations and needs.

20

Increasing Sales-Force Effectiveness Through the Compensation Plan

Jerome A. Colletti,
President, The Alexander Group Inc.

David J. Cichelli
Executive Vice President, The Alexander Group Inc.

Introduction

Today many companies are faced with rapidly changing sales environments. A slower growing economy, increased competition from overseas producers, and rising marketing costs all contribute to top management's concern about the effectiveness of their sales organizations. One of the consequences of this situation is that many companies have been compelled to examine the effectiveness of their sales forces, with a particular focus on existing compensation arrangements. It is not surprising that sales compensation is one of the first places management looks when there is a concern about sales effectiveness. Depending on the industry, our research shows that sales compensation makes up between 50 percent and 70 percent of the selling expense budget. Additionally, top management asks for an examination of the sales compensation plan because these executives intuitively know that how the sales force is paid is not consistent with recent changes in business strategy. Our experience suggests that changes to a sales compensation plan lag behind changes in business strategy by one to two years.

The overall objective of this chapter is to discuss how to design an effective sales compensation plan. First, we describe the key business factors that cause companies to reexamine their sales compensation plans. Second, we outline a model, with related techniques, to help ensure that the compensation plan supports the marketing strategy. Third, we introduce several incentive formula approaches. Fourth, we discuss how to manage the compensation plan in the future.

Key Business Factors

Sales executives have come to learn that three major business factors directly affect the effectiveness of the sales compensation plan. A change in any one of these factors requires a proper response regarding the design of the sales compensation plan.

Customer Coverage and Development of Sales Resources

The sales department needs to serve the customer base. Cost-efficient customer coverage is a widespread concern among sales managers. Should a direct salesperson call on all accounts? Or, should he or she call on small- and medium-sized customers while the large-sized customers are called on by national or major account sales representatives? These are important questions of customer coverage.[1]

Each customer segment has a best-coverage strategy, but this strategy will shift over time. The results of these changes should be reflected in the reallocation of the sales resources. Frequently, sales management's response is to create or redefine new sales jobs. In turn, changes in cus-

[1]Jerome A. Colletti and Gary S. Tubridy, "Effective Major Account Sales Management," *Journal of Personal Selling & Sales Management*, Vol. VII, August 1987, Pi Sigma Epsilon National Professional Fraternity, Hartland, Wis., pp. 1–10.

tomer coverage models will affect the design of the sales compensation program significantly.

Priority of Objectives

As markets become more complex, sales objectives change. Certain markets require volume growth. Normally, more sales help reduce unit costs, thus increasing profits. In other markets, better pricing and less volume leads to higher profits. The priority of objectives, such as volume, profitability, product mix, and account objectives, change. As these priorities change, so must the sales compensation program to reflect the new priorities.

Labor-Market Realities

Attracting and retaining qualified sales personnel remains a constant challenge. Simply providing more money does not necessarily meet this challenge. First, sales personnel should not be overpaid. The economics of the sales channel, such as the direct sales personnel costs, must be consistent with competitors' cost profiles. High pay practices may cause the company to either raise prices to cover costs or keep prices competitive and accept more modest profits. Both of these are unacceptable results. On the other hand, too low pay levels cause the company to employ less qualified sales personnel. Again, this is unacceptable. Tracking labor market practices must be ongoing. Adjusting target compensation levels will keep pay levels competitive.

Design Model and Supporting Techniques

The sales compensation plan needs to support the company's business strategy. For that reason, the design effort should trace a series of decision-making steps that give direction to a sales compensation plan design and make sure it is consistent with corporate objectives. Figure 20-1 presents this decision-making process. At each step of the model there are several key questions intended to guide the design process.

As this model suggests, the design of an effective sales compensation plan begins with an understanding of the business objectives of the

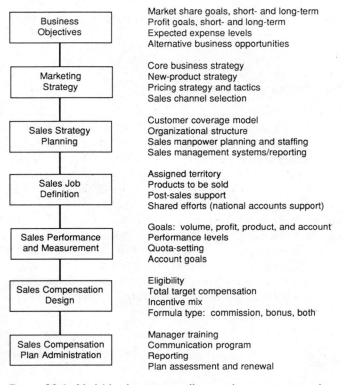

Business Objectives	Market share goals, short- and long-term Profit goals, short- and long-term Expected expense levels Alternative business opportunities
Marketing Strategy	Core business strategy New-product strategy Pricing strategy and tactics Sales channel selection
Sales Strategy Planning	Customer coverage model Organizational structure Sales manpower planning and staffing Sales management systems/reporting
Sales Job Definition	Assigned territory Products to be sold Post-sales support Shared efforts (national accounts support)
Sales Performance and Measurement	Goals: volume, profit, product, and account Performance levels Quota-setting Account goals
Sales Compensation Design	Eligibility Total target compensation Incentive mix Formula type: commission, bonus, both
Sales Compensation Plan Administration	Manager training Communication program Reporting Plan assessment and renewal

Figure 20-1. Model for designing an effective sales compensation plan.

company. Each level of design activity and decision making provides more information. This information contributes to the development of an effective sales compensation plan design.

Designing a sales compensation plan is a derivative process. That is, the design of the proper plan is *derived* from the circumstances and objectives unique to that company.

Most companies are committed to sales growth and increased profitability as the essential objectives of their business plan. Typically, the marketing function is responsible for charting a course of action to achieve these financial objectives. Marketing defines markets and advocates the delivery of products to meet customer needs. In many companies, marketing also determines the sales channels used to reach customers. After marketing selects the sales force as a sales channel, sales management then needs to translate the marketing strategy into sales programs and tactics. This effort involves what is known as sales strategy planning.

Management of Sales Strategy Planning

A sales strategy is a plan of action for guiding the use of sales resources. The sales strategy outlines all the efforts the sales department will use to accomplish the marketing strategy. This is the richest point of investigation for the sales compensation plan designer.

Some organizations have a formal sales strategy planning effort; others do not. Regardless of the approach, a close effort between marketing and sales management is necessary to define the role of the sales force in achieving the marketing strategy.

The activities of the sales department determine the success or failure of major business objectives. The sales compensation plan must reflect these key business objectives. A helpful diagnostic technique to properly identify the role of the sales department, illustrated in Figure 20-2, is a sales strategy matrix[2]

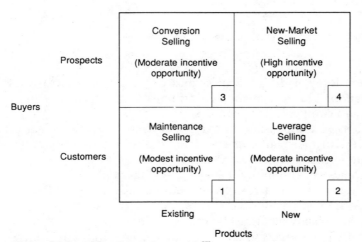

Figure 20-2. AGI's sales strategy matrix[sm].

[2]Jerome A. Colletti, "The Sales Strategy Matrix: A Tool for Finding and Fixing Sales Problems," *The Sales Management Bulletins*, Summer 1987, The Alexander Group Inc., Scottsdale, Ariz., p. 2.

As the Matrix shows, there are two types of variables: buyers and products. Buyers fall into two groups—customers and prospects. Products also fall into two groups—in-line and new. The two-by-two matrix defines different types of selling circumstances. Selling circumstances such as new-market, leverage, conversion, and maintenance selling suggest different types of sales compensation plan designs.

Maintenance selling. This job sells to existing customers who are re-ordering a product. Little persuasion is needed in the sales effort. As a result, little incentive opportunity is offered in the incentive plan.

Leverage selling. Selling the same product to different buyers provides a new challenge to adapt sales messages. Effective training can assist in this process. Such jobs are eligible for moderate incentive opportunity.

Conversion selling. Getting competitors' customers to switch to the company's products is a challenge. Again, such jobs are eligible for moderate incentive opportunity.

New-market selling. This type of selling requires individual sales initiative as the primary source of sales excellence. Aggressive incentive opportunities should reinforce this sales process.

The degree of incentive opportunity in a sales compensation plan can be represented as the *mix* between base and incentive pays and expressed as a percentage of the total target compensation. A mix of 70/30 means that 70 percent of the total target compensation is base salary; the remaining 30 percent of the total target compensation is incentive pay available for expected performance. In practice, the greater the mix, that is, the higher the incentive component (the second half of the ratio) as a percentage of 100 percent total target compensation, the more upside pay is available for outstanding performance. As a general rule, the implications of the type of selling for incentive opportunity are highlighted in each cell of the matrix.

Most companies would like to favor one of the four selling types presented in Figure 20-2. In such cases, the design of the sales compensation plan is relatively simple. The measures are clear-cut, the selling behaviors are predefined, and the results, hopefully, are easily measurable. However, most companies ask their sales force to perform all four types of selling. In such cases confusion often arises. Documenting the selling model must occur before work can proceed on the design of the sales compensation plan. As part of this analysis, management might find that more than one type of sales job exists and the need for a field product specialist or a field market specialist emerges.

Definition of the Sales Job

Identifying the sales strategy leads to the definition of the sales job. At this stage, more specifics about the exact role of the sales job become evident. For sales compensation plan purposes, the following factors about the sales job are most important:

Sales prospects.   The degree of independence in selecting sales prospects is an important sign of the role of the salesperson in the selling process. The more latitude given to the sales representative, the more independent the sales effort. Consequently, there is a need to reward successful prospecting and selling through the sales incentive compensation opportunity.

Product sales.   The selection of products or services to sell is another area that can be either well defined or left to the salesperson's judgment. Again, more independent decision making allows for the use of enhanced incentive opportunity.

Sales purchase terms.   Other sales elements, such as the transaction terms, installation, and service supports, are extensions of the sales process. The more extensive these elements are, the less independence the sales representative has. In such cases, the use of high incentive opportunities should be limited. This would allow for the proper balance of sales, service, and support.

Shared efforts.   The fourth factor is the degree of interaction with other selling and sales support personnel. Less use of enhanced incentive opportunity is necessary when selling actions are collaborative. For example, collaborative selling exists between the national account sales force and the territory representatives.

After determining the type of selling to be done and the role of the sales job in the sales process, the next step is to identify the appropriate measures of sales performance upon which to base incentive compensation.

Sales Performance: Measures and Goals

This is the most critical step in the sales compensation design process. The selection of performance measures is essential to the success of the sales compensation plan. Senior management must reach a consensus when selecting the most important performance measures for the sales force. Balance must be given to volume, profit, product, and account objectives. Having four or fewer than four objectives is best. Also, establishing the relative weights among the measures is important in helping the sales force understand how to deploy its time. For example, where volume may account for 70 percent of the importance in the incentive plan, new product sales might account for 20 percent and new customer sales might account for the remaining 10 percent. These weightings help the sales force understand how to best allocate selling time. Additionally, the weights will guide the designer of the sales compensation plan in providing the proper levels of incentive payout for sales achievement relative to each of these performance measures.

Many companies assign goals to the sales force for the selected measures of performance. These goals are frequently referred to as *sales quotas*. The process used to arrive at sales quotas varies widely by industry and even differs among companies within the same industry. For example, in some companies the sales representatives' quota is last year's sales result plus a price increase plus a national growth factor. In other companies, sales quotas are allocated to sales representatives based on market growth and market share within the territory.

Regardless of the practices, many firms find quota setting to be difficult and express deep frustration with their process. Nevertheless, our experience suggests that giving proper attention to quota assignments is essential to the success of a sales compensation plan. Properly assigning sales quotas provides the opportunity to manage for sales results. When supplemented with appropriate sales data analysis, territory planning, and account planning, a company's quota-setting practices can be an important contributor to the effectiveness of the sales compensation plan.

Another key management concept is the span of expected performance, known as *performance levels*. The sales compensation plan has varying degrees of payout depending on performance levels. Below a certain level of performance, no payout should occur. Above a certain level of high performance, the plan should provide the highest payouts. While avoiding ceilings, the plan may make earnings beyond this level more difficult to achieve. Shown in Figure 20-3 is an illustration of the general rules covering the relationship between performance level and sales compensation payment.

Excellence	Only 10 percent of all sales personnel should achieve this level of performance. Provide top pay for this level of performance.
Target	Most employees should achieve target performance. Specifically, at least 60 percent of all employees should achieve this level of performance and thus receive target incentives.
Threshold	At least 90 percent of all sales personnel should achieve this level of performance. Performance below this level earns no incentive pay.

Figure 20-3. Performance levels for sales compensation.

Design of Sales Compensation

The steps in the plan design process include determining eligibility, total target compensation, incentive mix, and plan type.

Eligibility for participation in the sales compensation plan rests on the degree of persuasion and independent sales action required of the job incumbent. The more persuasion and independence of action necessary to accomplish the sales results, the more likely a job will be eligible for plan participation. New-market selling is an ideal example of a sales job that should participate in the plan. However, jobs that are order taking in nature, that require complex involvement of multiple parties, or that have long sale cycles most likely should be considered for base-salary treatment only.

While most sales organizations profess a desire for sales personnel to earn what they are worth, planned earning levels help to properly manage the cost of the pay program. Establishing a *total target-compensation* level is the starting point. Total target compensation is the level of expected earnings for sales personnel who achieve expected results. How does a company establish its total target-compensation level? The process involves collecting market data (from published surveys or a custom survey) and adjusting that data to reflect the company's preferred market position. Some companies want to pay above market rates. Others want their pay levels to match competitive practice. Once documented, the total target-compensation level acts as a reference point for future judgments about the appropriateness of incentive-plan payments. Periodic examination of market data is necessary to ensure that the total target-compensation level remains consistent with the preferred market position.

The *incentive mix* is the ratio of base salary to incentive opportunity for expected performance, expressed as two portions of 100 percent. As discussed earlier, the first portion of the ratio is the base salary and the second portion is the incentive opportunity. A mix of 90/10 reflects a base salary component of 90 percent and an incentive opportunity component of 10 percent. Both portions added together equal 100 percent of total target compensation. Selecting the proper mix is a function of several factors, although the three most significant factors are as listed in Table 20-1.

As the sales strategy matrix in Figure 20-2 demonstrates, the factors affecting incentive mix vary by sales job. Table 20-1 below illustrates that jobs that have broad independence, rely on extensive skills of persuasion to close the sale, and sell within relatively short sales cycles are candidates for a high-mix incentive plan. The opposite is also true. Jobs with minimal independence, limited persuasion skills, and long sales cycles should consider a low-mix incentive design.

Table 20-1. Factors Affecting Incentive Mix

Range	Factors			Incentive mix (base salary/incentive)
	Independence	Persuasion	Sales cycle	
High	Broad	Extensive	Short	0/100
•	_____	_____	_____	50/50
•	_____	_____	_____	60/40
•	_____	_____	_____	70/30
•	_____	_____	_____	80/20
Low	Minimal	Limited	Long	100/0

Plan Types

One of the final steps in designing the sales compensation plan is the selection and development of the plan type. There are four types of sales compensation plans.[3]

1. *Base salary only.* Many sales jobs receive a base salary only. Occasionally, sales management will promote and reward sales efforts through sales contests and sales recognition programs as the only form of sales incentive.

2. *Commission only.* A commission plan is a specific calculation tech-

[3]Jerome A. Colletti, *Handbook of Human Resources Administration*, 2nd ed., McGraw-Hill, New York, 1986, pp. 31–5.

nique that ties the sales performance, for example, sales volume, units sold, or profit dollars, to a payout calculation. The higher the sales results, the higher the pay. The payout amount reflects the true, absolute performance of the individual. In commission-only programs, a draw provides minimal cash flow. The draw is offset from actual earnings.

3. *Base salary plus commission.*   Known as a combination plan, a base-salary-plus-commission plan provides a guaranteed base salary regardless of sales results. Depending on the mix of the incentive plan, the commission element can affect sales behavior significantly or minimally. A 50/50 plan would cause sales personnel to focus on achieving sales objectives. A 95/5 plan would act primarily as a performance reminder.

4. *Base salary plus bonus.*   A bonus formula is different than a commission formula. A bonus formula always uses a performance quota for payment purposes, and the payout is expressed either as a percentage of base salary or as a fixed dollar amount. A bonus program allows management to better control the compensation program. A quota allows for recognition of territory potential. Payouts tied to a quota can reflect the degree of sales difficulty for a territory.

Base-salary-only plans are appropriate for complex and nonpersuasive selling circumstances, perhaps with a long sales cycle. Generally, commission-only plans are best used in new-market selling circumstances in which an individual's sales initiative and persuasion skills work best to close short sales-cycle opportunities. Base-salary-plus-bonus programs are used in more mature sales environments, particularly those in which multiple objectives are to be served.

Once the plan type is selected, the incentive formula is devised. There are three major types of incentive formulas: unlinked, adjusted value, and linked. In an *unlinked* incentive formula design the various performance measures stand alone. Incentive pay is earned by the sales representative for accomplishment measures regardless of what occurs on the other performance measures. In a sense, each performance measure—volume, profit, or product mix—acts as its own incentive plan. Obviously, too many unlinked performance measures will induce the sales representative to "shop the plan." This behavior occurs when sales personnel maximize their earnings by doing what is easiest for them to accomplish rather than what management prefers to have accomplished.

Adjusted value plans change the value of the sales results to reflect its importance. For example, with the use of point systems, values can be selected to underscore the importance of a desired sales result. Product A may be worth more for each dollar of sale than Product B. In such a case, the point value for each dollar of Product A sales may be worth 10 points, while each dollar of Product B sales may be worth only 5 points. In this manner, sales personnel are paid more to sell Product A than Product B because of the strategic value of Product A to the company.

The third type of incentive formula design is the *linked* formula. The linked formula ties together two or more different performance measures. Linking together performance measures ensures that sales objectives are served in the order of importance that has been determined by management. In turn, there are several types of linked incentive formulas:

Hurdles. Hurdles are the simplest form of a linked incentive formula. A hurdle is a stated level of performance needed on one measure before another measure can be activated. For example, the statement that sales volume must be at target levels before the new account bonus can be paid demonstrates the use of a hurdle on sales volume.

Matrix. A matrix incentive formula links together two competing measures. Payout rewards are constructed so that outstanding performance on both measures provides the highest incentive payment. The two measures are aligned along the two axes of the grid shown in Figure 20-4.

Multiplier. The third and final linked incentive formula is the multiplier. Multipliers are used to calculate a second incentive payment from the results of the primary incentive earnings. For example, the primary incentive formula may be a commission on sales volume, paid monthly. A second incentive payment, such as a quarterly award, may be provided for the sale of emphasis products. The summation of monthly commission earnings could be used as the basis for calculating the quarterly award. Higher levels of emphasized product sales would provide higher percent multipliers. But, these multipliers would be applied against the summation of three months' worth of commission payments. The logic here directs the salesperson primarily to sell volume. More monthly volume provides a higher reward basis for calculating the payout of the emphasis products. The sequence of sales performance is obvious: Sell volume first then improve the sale of emphasis products as much as possible.

As shown in Figure 20-4, the actual development of the payout formula requires coordinating the total target compensation, the incentive mix, and the performance measures. Selection of a plan type (base, commission, or a combination plan) and the incentive formula (unlinked, adjusted value, or linked) is the final step to determining the incentive rates. Modeling with the use of a spreadsheet helps facilitate the fine-tuning of the payout schedules.

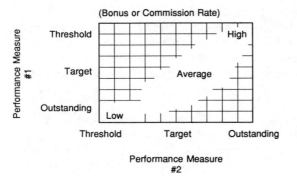

Figure 20-4. Incentive formula matrix.

Administration of Sales Compensation

The final step in the sales compensation design process is implementation of the final and approved plan design. We have found that this effort is most effective when it follows the four-step plan outlined below.

1. Field managers who administer the incentive plan must be fully knowledgeable about the plan's philosophy, design, and administration. A special training program for these individuals will contribute significantly to the plan's success. Calculation examples, announcement collateral, typical questions and answers, and documented impact on the sales personnel provide field managers with the necessary tools to implement and support the new compensation plan.

2. Once the field managers are trained, they should introduce the new program to their sales representatives. Appropriate communication material is needed, including formal plan documentation, an announcement brochure (and video, if the sales force is large), and conversion procedures comparing the old plan to the new plan. A group presentation to the sales unit should be followed up with one-on-one meetings with each sales representative. Full communication is the key to successful acceptance by the field sales organization.

3. Sales personnel need succinct reporting of how the incentive was cal-

culated. The calculation of the incentive payment relies on information from various data processing systems, such as the order processing system and the sales reporting system. The results must be timely and accurate.

4. To ensure the ongoing success of the incentive plan, a formal assessment process needs to report on the results of the incentive plan. A renewal process, involving key management personnel, should review the results of the plan and make suggestions for changes. This review process should occur on an annual basis, more frequently if necessary.

Management of Sales Compensation in the Future

For most companies, the essence of business success is the ability to attract and keep customers. Because the sales force is a vital link between a company and its customers, it holds the key to business growth and profitability. A properly directed, motivated, and rewarded sales force will make a significant contribution to the achievement of these business measures. We believe that the sales compensation plan is one of the more powerful tools available to management to achieve optimal sales-force motivation and performance.

In the future, we believe that top management will continue to ask for increased sales performance and profitability. This will require many companies to examine and rethink the assumption upon which their sales compensation plan is based. The concepts, principles, and techniques described in this chapter are intended to help the designer of a sales compensation plan address this management challenge. Our belief is that, in the future, the sales compensation plans that reflect the results of the process in which the design of it is carefully and closely linked to the business plan and related elements will be the ones that most contribute to high-achieving, excellent sales forces.

PART 4

Executive Compensation

21

Executive Compensation: A Changing Landscape

John M. Linton

Chicago Office Practice Leader
Executive Compensation
TPF&C, a Towers Perrin Company

Over the years, executive compensation programs have evolved in response to changing economic trends and government actions. Tax policy, low inflation rates, and executives' desire to accumulate capital were major drivers in the 1950s and 1960s. The 1970s saw the emergence of new vehicles, such as multiple-year performance plans, in response to a sluggish stock market. The perception existed that while company financial results were good, the stock market failed to provide executives with appropriate rewards. As a result, multiple-year performance plans, which provided rewards based on achieving corporate financial goals rather than stock market performance, became widespread.

The 1980s saw three major factors affect executive compensation planning. Deals and financial restructurings exerted a pronounced influence on the design and amount of executive pay. Tax policy featured reintroduction of preferred capital gains followed by reduced personal income tax rates. And a strong bull market for stocks restored their prominence as an executive compensation vehicle.

The 1980s has been characterized as the "deal era" and has been characterized by pressure upon executive teams to maximize returns for shareholders. This translated into executive compensation programs keyed to the achievement of immediate financial objectives and to a longer-term emphasis on the appreciation of company shares. Compensation planners responded with increased leverage in annual incentive plans, larger grants in stock-based plans, and a continuing search for the correct financial measures to forecast and create company value.

Financial restructuring also resulted in many organizations' going private with heavy debt loads. Postdeal incentive plans focused almost exclusively on cash flow as a means of retiring the debt incurred in leveraged buyouts. In the LBO environment, senior executives often hold in the range of 10 percent to 20 percent of the new organization's equity. These positions established the basis to acquire significant wealth when leverage works.

Another subtle but observable influence of the deal era was the size of fees earned by investment bankers and attorneys. Executive perceptions of appropriate compensation levels were no doubt enhanced when executives compared themselves with financiers and lawyers.

Executive protection became a pressing issue for compensation planners as the deal era intensified. Financial restructurings threatened future executive earnings and fulfillment of career goals. One result was greater use of contracts defining termination provisions. Once a comparative rarity, contracts have become commonplace throughout industry. By 1989, about half the Fortune 100 firms reported use of golden parachutes, while in 1981 only two used them.[1]

Favorable tax legislation establishing incentive stock options (ISOs) gave them a boost in the eyes of most executives. The reintroduction of preferred tax treatment for capital gains made ISOs a favored weapon in the executive compensation arsenal. Subsequent legislation diminished the tax effectiveness of ISOs and caused a shift to greater use of nonqualified options. In recent years, restricted stock, perhaps in response to the 1987 market collapse, has become a more important vehicle. Among the Fortune 100, for example, 62 companies reported restricted stock plans in 1989 versus only 8 in 1979.[2]

As the bull market persisted, many companies shifted their compensation programs toward an even greater emphasis on stock-based long-

---

[1]TPF&C, *1989 Top 100 Executive Compensation Study*, p. 3.
[2]TPF&C, *1989 Top 100 Executive Compensation Study*, p. 11.

term incentives. Jumbo or megagrants of options and restricted stock became a means of providing dramatic income opportunities and focusing executives' attention on building shareholder value. During the latter part of the 1980s, over one-quarter of the 100 largest firms made grants to senior executives that exceeded $1 million in value.[3]

For the 1990s, a central question will be how much will executives earn and for what performance achievements? The first time a Fortune 100 CEO received over $1 million in annual compensation was in 1980.[4] That year, five crossed the threshold. By 1989, 68 of the 100 were beyond that once magic seven-figure mark.[5] Public discussion of the appropriateness of executive pay levels increased as the 1980s drew to a close. Business publications and an occasional politician or social critic question the relationship of pay to performance and the efficacy of seven- or eight-figure pay levels. Likely, the 1990s will see more intense scrutiny of executive pay packages.

Other factors affecting executive compensation design will include actions by the Securities and Exchange Commission to liberalize insider trading regulations. Actions by the Financial Accounting Standards Board, as well as tax policy, will influence how compensation professionals design their programs. Continuing globalization of business and the unification of the European Community in 1992 will present new challenges to the compensation planner. The search for the ultimate performance model to use in incentive plans will continue. Perhaps incentive design will address issues related to "workouts" or the recovery of firms for which financial leverage failed. Yet, the most pervasive influences on executive compensation programs may well come from economic forces of change not yet identified.

This section on executive compensation explores both the conceptual and technical foundations required to implement a sound executive pay-for-performance program. Since the new world of executive compensation is so strongly influenced by the relationship among a firm's business strategy, external competitive environment, and interaction of stakeholder groups, no treatment of this subject would be complete without contrasting the two theoretical approaches to understanding motivation and job performance—expectancy theory, which focuses on the motivational effects of reward systems on executives, and agency theory, which stresses the contractual relationship between executives and stakeholders.

[3]Speech researched by TPF&C, Mega-Grants (Trend or Fad), John M. Linton, April 13, 1989.
[4]TPF&C, 1981 Executive Compensation Study, *500 Largest Industrials, The Top and Bottom*, p. 1.
[5]TPF&C, *1989 Top 100 Executive Compensation Study*, p. 2.

Perhaps the disproportionate amount of written information dealing with executive compensation is the result of the breadth of the group's long-range influence rather than the size of their numbers; they also heavily influence the commission of professional firms to deal with these issues.

Except for those covered under labor and professional athlete contracts, senior executives are virtually the only group with documented protection in their employment agreements. We discuss in this section the art and science of supporting the development of these contracts, an essential knowledge base for compensation professionals. In its broadest sense, we can almost view top executives as baseball players, a small group of free agents bound to their companies by a web of agreements designed both to retain talent and to encourage top performance.

Despite the global marketplace, the technical development and implementation of executive pay programs will be based on the linkage of strategy, performance, and the enhancement of shareholder values.

22
Designing Total Compensation Programs

Alan M. Johnson
Managing Director
Executive Compensation Practice
Handy Associates

In designing the total compensation program, one of the most important considerations is maintaining the proper perspective. Essentially, that means approaching the problem of design not from the direction of the individual components of pay, but rather from the perspective of the total program. This applies to issues such as how much we should pay our executives, as well as to the issues of what the compensation program is supposed to achieve and what the purpose of the program is.

One way to begin is to think in terms of a compensation philosophy, the guiding principles that underpin all the elements of the design. At the same time, it is important to understand the issues and trade-offs involved, the role of the human resources adviser, and, not unimportantly, the mistakes that others have made.

The Compensation Philosophy

There are a seemingly endless number of details that must be attended to in designing the total compensation program for the executives of any company, large or small. These range, for example, from the relatively simple questions of how much base salary to the more arcane considerations of the potential impact of a proposed change in SEC section 16(b) regulations. Although all the details are more or less important to the development of a sound, well-designed executive compensation program, probably the most important detail is to make sure that there is absolute clarity on the purpose and objectives of the total program.

One of the many steps a company can take to achieve that clarity of purpose is to articulate a compensation philosophy. The compensation philosophy is an embodiment of the beliefs and values of an organization in the area of compensation practices, but it is also a practical guide that links those values to the strategy and direction of the business, as well as a way to coherently link the various elements of compensation, such as base salary, annual and long-term incentives, perquisites, and executive benefits.

Most compensation philosophies that I have encountered in dealing with clients have been so broad and noncontroversial that they fail to identify and address the key issues that should guide the design and administration of the total compensation program. For example, a company may state that it believes in pay for performance, but what does that really mean? How much should pay vary between the top performer and the average performer? Are we willing to use forced ranking techniques to ensure that there is some dispersion in performance ratings? The following example, which focuses on only a small aspect of a compensation philosophy, may better illustrate the kind of specificity I would urge companies to strive for.

Original Version.   The mission and goals of our company will be achieved by attracting, developing, and involving the highest quality people. The objective is to provide highly competitive and excellent compensation.

Revised Version.   The purpose of our compensation programs is to help the company achieve its mission and goals (for example a 15 percent return on equity) by attracting, motivating, and retaining the highest quality people. Pay opportunities will be fully competitive (for example, targeted to the median opportunities provided by the appropriate comparator groups) for average performance, and above-average pay opportunities (for example, 75th percentile pay for 75th percentile performance) will be provided for superior performance. Variable components of pay, including both annual and long-term incentives, will be a significant element of compensation and will be truly variable on the basis of performance. They are not an entitlement.

In short, the fatal flaw that I've seen in most compensation philosophies is that they fail to be sufficiently specific. By not addressing the issues, by not fully understanding their implications, and by not taking a stand one way or the other, companies end up with compensation philosophies of little or no value and compensation programs that don't do what they're supposed to because nobody really knows what they're supposed to do.

A Link to Business Direction

By insisting on specificity, the compensation philosophy becomes the link to the direction that management intends the business to take. For example, by identifying return on equity relative to a selected group of comparator companies as the key measure for the long-term performance plan, management makes a statement about the progression of the company's culture. That is, what's important is not how the company did versus budget or whether this year is better than last year; what's important is how the company is doing versus the competition.

As another example, the compensation philosophy might address the mix between fixed and variable pay. In a fairly stable or highly regulated environment in which results are largely predictable and in which company results won't change much regardless of individual efforts, having a highly leveraged annual incentive plan tied to business results makes little sense. For a company in transition, however, trying to adapt and change from a highly regulated or protected environment to a more competitive one, such a highly leveraged plan, might make sense. In such a case, the compensation philosophy can specify the importance of having a significant variable component that can be a valuable tool in bringing about the cultural reorientation needed to survive in the new business environment. That is, it clearly identifies the link between the business direction and the program design.

The Total Program Perspective

One of the trickiest questions that needs to be dealt with in designing the total compensation program is, How much money is enough? Many of the programs I've seen are very good at getting annual pay right in terms of some target competitive position. They are less effective, however, when it comes to integrating the value of long-term incentives, benefits, and perquisites with annual pay in the context of a fully competitive total pay program.

For example, median salaries and a median annual pay opportunity (base salary plus bonus) earned for average performance is fairly straightforward. On the other hand, data on long-term incentives are much more difficult to obtain and interpret, particularly when multiple vehicles are in use among competitors. How should stock options be valued relative to restricted stock or performance units, and how does that relate to target annual pay levels? Another question is, How does the company want to position itself with respect to the competition in terms of the total pay opportunity? If the answer is that the company wants to pay its executives at the 75th percentile in terms of total compensation, does that mean paying out the 75th percentile long-term incentives on top of 75th percentile base and bonus? In reality, as Table 22-1 shows, it does not, because such an approach would probably position a company close to the 90th percentile, or better, in total compensation.

Using the survey data from Table 22-1, it would be correct to add the $50,000 median long-term pay opportunity directly to the $100,000 median annual pay to arrive at the correct $150,000 median total compensation opportunity. Adding a $70,000 long-term opportunity—representing the 75th percentile of the survey data—directly to the $130,000 75th percentile salary however, yields $200,000 in total compensation opportunity. This is a subtle and often misunderstood point. The "correct" long-term opportunity to achieve a 75th percentile total compensation target ($175,000) on top of a $130,000 salary would be $45,000. This mix of pay profile is, of course, completely different from that achieved at the median total competitive level and sends a quite different message about the relative importance of the long-term versus the short-term pay.

Benefits and perquisites are another area in which problems can arise with valuation and integration into the complete program. What alternatives are available to a company that believes in a competitive total compensation opportunity and simultaneously wants to have as few perks as possible (to promote egalitarian values, for example), yet is in an industry in which extensive perks are considered the norm? One way to deal with the situation is to simply convert a typical perk package into a fixed dollar amount that the executive can take as cash compensation or spend on cars and clubs, if that is what he or she thinks is valuable. This is an especially effective (and administratively simple) way of han-

Table 22-1. Total Pay Positioning: An Illustration

Survey Data (Assumed)

	Annual pay	Long-term pay	Total pay
Median	$100,000	$50,000	$150,000
75th Percentile	$130,000	$70,000	$200,000

dling the issue, given that there are practically no tax advantages for company-provided perks.

Benefits are more complicated, and although most companies would agree that it is important to have a competitive benefits package, whether executives should have something extra is an important issue. For example, should executives have a pension formula that is more attractive than that provided to the broad employee population? Are there trade-offs that might be attractive between additional benefits versus current compensation? Another important factor to consider is the safety and security of unfunded benefits-related liabilities. What type of protection should be provided against loss of benefits in the event of a change in control? These are all complex problems that need to be addressed with the total compensation program in mind.

Issues and Trade-Offs

One of the important things I have learned in dealing with many different companies with a wide variety of compensation-related problems is that there is not just one way to run the show. Design alternatives make profound statements about how an organization is going to be managed. One of the most important roles of the human resources professional is to make sure that management is aware of those alternatives and fully understands their implications.

The issues to be addressed and the trade-offs to be resolved extend to all elements of the compensation program. For example, the choice of job evaluation systems can send a powerful message about what the firm's priorities are. Is it primarily concerned with internal equity, that is, getting the internal hierarchy of jobs right? If so, then one of the "analytical" job evaluation systems (for example, point factor or factor comparison) would probably best fit its needs. On the other hand, if the organization is, or wants to be, more externally oriented with a greater focus on what the competition is doing than on "what so-and-so in accounting is paid," then a market pricing job evaluation system would probably be more appropriate. There are, of course, shades of gray between these two extremes, and only top management can decide which is more important.

In the area of annual incentives, examples of the issues and trade-offs abound. For example, are performance measures set primarily with respect to last year's actuals, or do they take into account what the competitors are up to? Should performance be measured primarily at the corporate level (to encourage team performance), or do we want our division managers to operate largely as independent business units or profit centers (the "entrepreneurial" approach)? Although both approaches are valid, and someone will surely have an opinion as to which appears more appropriate in the situation at hand, only the CEO and his or her advisers can decide what kind of environment they want to encourage.

Other issues that typically need to be addressed and whose implications need to be explored include the following:

- Should annual incentives be a makeup for low salaries or a reward for outstanding performance?
- Should the plan be highly leveraged or not?
- Should the plan pay out based on "first dollar" of achievement, or should there be some threshold?
- What, if any, should be the nonfinancial business objectives of the annual incentive plan?
- What is the role of individual, as opposed to business, performance?

The issue of business versus individual performance is a particularly interesting one in light of the way many companies have been handling it over the years. At the urging of many compensation consultants, companies have often decided that 20 percent, typically, of an executive's target bonus would be variable on the basis of individual performance. The balance would be derived from company or business unit results. Although the intent, in most cases, was that a $50,000 target bonus (to illustrate) could vary from at least $40,000 to $60,000 based on the individual's efforts assuming full achievement of business objectives (see Alternative A in Table 22-2), what has often happened in practice has

Table 22-2. Potential Variability of Pay Based on Individual Performance*

Compensation element	Target/est. value	Variable for individual performance	Alternative A: ± 20% of annual income		Alternative B: ± 20% of ind. perf. component	
			Minimum	Maximum	Minimum	Maximum
Benefits	$ 45,000	No	$ 45,000	$ 45,000	$ 45,000	$ 45,000
Perquisites	5,000	No	5,000	5,000	5,000	5,000
Long-term incentives	50,000	No	50,000	50,000	50,000	50,000
Annual incentives	**50,000**	**Yes**	**40,000**	**60,000**	**48,000**	**52,000**
Base salary	150,000	No	150,000	150,000	150,000	150,000
Total	$300,000		$290,000	$310,000	$298,000	$302,000

*Assumes full achievement of business objectives.

been very different. Often companies will identify 20 percent of an individual's target bonus as the "individual performance component" (in this case $10,000), and that component could vary by plus or minus 20 percent, or $2000. In the illustration given, and assuming full achievement of business objectives, the potential variability of the bonus is reduced to a range of $48,000 to $52,000 (see Alternative B in Table 22-2). In the context of a total compensation program, including base salary, long-term incentives, benefits, and perquisites (none of which are typically tied to individual performance save base salary via the annual merit increase), such a narrow band of pay variability shrinks to insignificance. This sends an important, and often unintended, message to employees about what the company does or does not value.

In the area of long-term incentives, all the preceding issues apply as well as a few others—what the balance between the long-term and short-term pay should be, for example. The central issue here is how to structure the reward system so as to encourage the executive to properly weigh the trade-offs between what may be "right" in the short term with what he or she knows to be in the long-term best interests of the organization. Many companies, intentionally or unintentionally, put an excessive amount of emphasis on achieving what are essentially short-term objectives, often to the detriment of the long-term health of the business.

One of the most important issues in designing the long-term component of the total compensation program deals with the trade-off between risk and reward. To what extent is an executive's long-term compensation truly at risk for poor performance? For example, stock options are probably the best vehicle for capturing an element of risk, because a deteriorating stock price will have an immediate impact on the value or potential value of an executive's holdings. Companies, however, often question the ability of the stock market to fully appreciate their company's true worth and have decided to grant performance units along with their options. If the market fails to reward executives, the performance units can provide a form of insurance. Although such programs can reduce an executive's exposure to market risk, a protection that shareholders do not typically enjoy, they do represent a valid way of running a business in certain circumstances.

A similar example was seen in the wake of the October 1987 stock market crash when many executives found some of their stock options under water. A few companies felt it necessary to cancel underwater options and reissue them at a lower exercise price, in effect, providing a "safety net" for executive pay.

Restricted stock provides another analogy. Like options, restricted stock responds immediately to fluctuations in the company's stock price.

It is clearly less risky than options, however, because its value will almost certainly be greater than zero, whereas options can easily be under water. At the same time, by providing the immediate tangible rewards of ownership (voting rights and dividends), restricted stock is probably a more effective retention device than options. Indeed, a recent survey of CEO views, conducted by Hardy Associates, confirms this perception. Thus, the trade-off between options and restricted stock involves more than the risk/reward issue. It also includes value judgments regarding the importance of executive stock ownership and the need for additional retention features.

Other issues and trade-offs that need to be addressed with respect to the long-term plan include:

- Real shares versus phantom shares
- Incentive stock options versus nonqualified options
- Accounting costs and tax issues vs. resources available for compensation programs
- Broader participation versus more restricted participation
- Importance of executive and employee ownership of company stock

Another area in which there are important issues and trade-offs that can have a significant morale effect—as well as an impact on hard and soft dollar costs—is in the area of executive perquisites. Although very few, if any, executive perquisites are particularly tax-efficient these days, many companies still maintain elaborate perk programs. This may or may not be intentional, but there are valid reasons for having executive perquisites. For one thing, they can be an effective symbol of power and authority, and for companies that maintain those things as important, they can be useful.

In summary, there are many important issues that must be addressed in designing the total compensation program that deal with how the business is going to be run. These issues involve trade-offs between competing and totally valid ways of running a business, and they cannot be settled by the human resources professional alone. Rather, these are issues and alternatives whose implications should be fully explored with the CEO, but whose ultimate resolution lays with senior management.

Common Mistakes

Even when companies do a good job of defining the purpose and objectives of their compensation program, there are still a number of mistakes that they make that can destroy the effectiveness of a well-designed total compensation program.

One of these mistakes is poor communication. Companies regularly fail to communicate to employees what the intent of the program is, how the program is suppose to work, and why the program is designed the way it is. An example of this can often be found with stock option plans. There are very few sound reasons to employ stock options unless one of the objectives the company wants to achieve is increased ownership of company stock by executives. If that is not desired, then there are lots of other ways to achieve some of the objectives a company may have for its long-term compensation programs. The problem is that even when companies recognize ownership as an important objective, they fail to communicate it adequately. As a result, executives simply treat stock options as another form of compensation, exercise the option when the time is right, and sell the stock. One of the important features of an articulated compensation philosophy is that it can serve as a vehicle for clearly communicating to executives that stock ownership is a desired, and expected, objective of the stock option program.

One of the real life situations that I have seen repeatedly occurs with companies that determine stock option awards as a multiple of annual pay. For example, a company may determine that a $150,000-per-year executive has a long-term opportunity equal to 33 percent of annual pay, or $50,000. At a $50-per-share stock price, the executive will receive 1000 options. If the stock price goes up to $75 per share, however, next year's grant will only be 667 shares. Unless communicated properly, executives will wonder, and with good reason, what they did wrong to merit a cut of this sort. This may seem like an easy-to-avoid problem, but I have dealt with many companies that have stumbled over what is essentially a communication problem.

Another common communication failure happens when companies have a lot of good things to say about their compensation programs, but just don't say it. For example, a company's benefits package may be just terrific by objective standards, but no one knows about it. Or a company may have a policy pay line set at the median of a competitive group and at the same time have a policy of targeting pay to a 1.05 compa-ratio. What that means is that, on average, employees are paid above the market, but if that message never gets out, the company loses a lot in terms of employee goodwill. In short, poor communication probably means you're not getting the most for your money.

The Role of the Human Resources Adviser

In many companies, compensation programs have developed piecemeal over the years. Annual incentives were added on as an afterthought on top of a salary administration program developed for a hierarchical organization that rose up in a different environment. Long-term incentives were added later because everyone seemed to be doing it. In many companies, no one has ever had the vision to provide a comprehensive view of the total compensation program. I have found that one of the important contributions the human resources adviser can make is to provide that comprehensive perspective. There are additionally three key roles the human resources adviser can play.

The first, and perhaps most important, of these is to articulate the issues and strive to keep the issues and trade-offs in focus. Many companies have problems with their compensation programs not because top executives are particularly ill-willed or shortsighted or selfish; they simply have never had anyone explain to them the real implications of their actions. This often happens because companies have a tradition of not making the best use of their human resources professionals, but even outside consultants are often guilty of not telling it like it is when confronted by a grizzled, opinionated CEO.

The second important role the human resources adviser can, and should, play is that of the advocate. Given the unique knowledge and experience base of the top human resources professional, it is inevitable that his or her opinion will be solicited in weighing and resolving the trade-offs involved.

A third role, and this probably applies more to the in-house professional than to the outside consultant, is that of "product champion," with the product being the compensation program. As an important disseminator of information on design issues and the intent and purpose of programs, the human resources professional can play a crucial role in building the kind of consensus needed to ensure the success of a new compensation program. In short, much of the burden of communication and of the success of the program falls on the shoulders of the human resources professional.

Summary

There are four keys to designing a successful total compensation program. First, articulate the compensation philosophy. By defining the purpose and objectives of the compensation programs, and by identifying specifically how those translate into the strategy and direction of the business, many of the problems companies have with their compensation programs could be avoided.

Second, it is important to have a total program perspective. This is crucial not only as it regards the question of "how much" but also as a key to helping top management understand the issues and trade-offs involved in the various design alternatives.

Third, stress the importance of good communication, not only so that the purpose and objectives of the compensation program are clear but also so that the good news will get out.

Fourth, remember that human resources professionals have a crucial role to play in developing the total program. Part of that role comes from the perspective they bring, part from their advocacy of a certain way of running the business, and part from being key disseminators of information about how the programs will be managed and in building a consensus to support those programs.

23

Annual Incentive Compensation for Executives

Peter T. Chingos

National Practice Director
Performance and Compensation Management Consulting Services
KPMG Peat Marwick

Each year, more and more companies replace their discretionary annual cash compensation plans with performance-oriented incentive pay programs. This trend results from a desire to use compensation as a management tool to motivate and reward executives for achieving desired financial results. Organizations are making an effort to determine appropriate internal performance measures, combining the direction from senior management, information from the budgeting and financial planning departments, and the performance management expertise of the human resources department. This activity is creating a new generation of annual incentive compensation programs that are more responsive to executive, company, and shareholder interests.

Annual executive incentives are widespread in U.S. industry, as shown in Figure 23-1. Although almost universal in large publicly held financial and industrial companies, annual executive incentive plans are increasingly used in private industry and not-for-profit organizations as well.

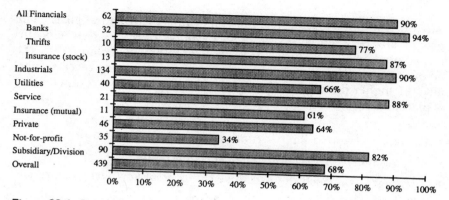

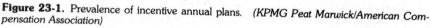

Figure 23-1. Prevalence of incentive annual plans. *(KPMG Peat Marwick/American Compensation Association)*

Compensation Strategy

To design an effective annual incentive compensation program, an organization must start with a well-defined compensation strategy. Defining a compensation strategy involves three steps. The first step is to identify the business objectives for the coming year, taking into consideration competitive pressures, economic conditions, and the current position of the company with respect to its products and services versus where it wants to be. Management must analyze what internal financial performance measures best support desired performance and how results can be measured on a timely and accurate basis. The second step is to identify the executives within the organization who can directly affect the desired performance. These individuals will vary by level in the organization and will include corporate as well as business unit executives. The third step is to design an incentive plan to reinforce desired behavior. This design could be structured in such a way as to create a strong identification with the company overall, the operating unit alone, individual executive performance, or a combination of all three. The weightings could vary depending on where management wants to place emphasis.

One additional objective of a compensation strategy is to strike a balance between salary and incentive compensation. Although salary plays an important role in attracting and retaining executives, it is less powerful as an ongoing motivating factor. Incentive compensation fills the gap by rewarding executives for achieving performance goals. The proper mix between base salary and incentive compensation opportunity should be determined for each level of management, with the amount of compensation at risk varying by responsibility level. Generally, the higher the organization level, the more incentive compensation is placed at risk. Other considerations are:

- Bottom-line responsibility or influence on operating results
- Responsibility for executing tactical action plans
- The degree to which the executive can control key performance elements
- The ability of the company to measure results
- Competitive practice

An organization should consider implementing an incentive plan when the following conditions exist:

- The organization is willing and able to identify and measure financial performance goals
- The decision/result cycle is relatively short and related to the performance period recognized by the incentive plan
- Critical factors affecting short-term results are within the control of plan participants and traceable to them
- Most important, top management must be willing to judge performance, that is, compare and rate each participant's output and make awards accordingly

Designing an Annual Incentive Plan

In designing an annual incentive plan, companies must address six basic issues: eligibility for participation, the funding mechanism and size of the incentive pool, the choice of performance measures, the allocation of funds to participants, the setting of goals, and the size of individual awards.

Eligibility

Eligibility to participate in the annual incentive compensation plan should be restricted to employees who have a measurable amount of direct influence on the company's performance. Typically, the number of employees eligible for the incentive plan may range from 10 to 15 percent of the exempt employee population. Other types of incentives are designed for those below the executive level, such as sales/commission plans, middle management plans, gain sharing, and productivity or team incentive plans.

Because smaller companies often have more employees who can affect overall business results, they often include a larger percentage of their population in the executive annual incentive plan. The opposite is true in larger companies. Also, participation in the annual incentive plan may vary depending on whether the company is labor- or capital-intensive. A service company with many levels of management employees may have a greater percentage of employees in the annual incentive plan than a manufacturer of heavy equipment with a fairly small management group.

Because no one criterion for determining eligibility is entirely satisfactory, companies usually use a combination of factors to decide who will be eligible for the annual incentive plan. A typical approach is to use salary plus some other criterion, such as management level. In a recent study conducted by KPMG Peat Marwick and the American Compensation Association, minimum eligibility levels for management incentive plans were identified (shown in Figure 23-2). In most companies, base salary eligibility for the annual incentive plan ranges from about $30,000 to $90,000, with an average of about $60,000.

Basic Funding Mechanism and Size of Incentive Pool

There are many ways in which companies go about creating an incentive pool or fund to pay incentives. Basically, they fall into four approaches: the use of a fixed formula, a measurement of prior year's performance, a peer group comparison, and attainment of specific goals.

Fixed Formula.   A fixed formula plan requires that a minimum level of financial success be achieved before an incentive pool is established

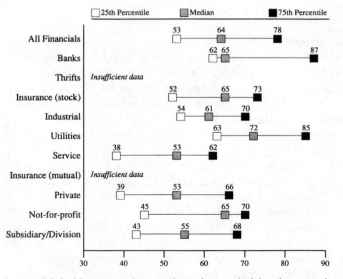

Figure 23-2. Minimum salary grade midpoint eligibility for annual incentive plan participation. *(KPMG Peat Marwick/American Compensation Association)*

for the benefit of plan participants. Figure 23-3 illustrates how a typical fixed formula ap proach would work. Here, return on investment (ROI) is specified as the single index of performance. Management has decided that the incentive pool will be equal to 3 percent of after-tax earnings in excess of the 7 percent after-tax return on investment (stockholders' equity plus long-term debt). That is, net earnings must exceed the 7 percent return on investment threshold before an incentive pool is established. If ex-

Incentive pool = 3% of net earnings in excess of a 7% return on investment.		
Net earnings		$120,000,000
Threshold	7% ROI	
Investment	$742,000,000	
Threshold percentage	7%	51,940,000
Excess of earnings above 7% threshold		68,060,000
Percentage allocated to incentive pool		3%
Incentive pool		$ 2,041,800

Figure 23-3. Fixed formula plan.

cess earnings above the 7 percent threshold equal $68,060,000, the total incentive pool would come to $2,041,800 ($68,060,000 × 0.03).

A fixed formula approach is most often found as a first-generation plan in growth companies not yet able to forecast financial results accurately. It may also be found in mature companies with a mixed portfolio of businesses in which overall, consolidated financial performance goals are desirable. Once a credible financial planning process is in place, companies often move from a fixed formula approach to one of goal attainment (to be explained later in this chapter). Nonetheless, in industries in which business cycles or financial performance are not predictable, fixed formula plans may be the most appropriate approach.

Because the terms of the plan need not be reestablished annually, a fixed formula approach is simple to administer and does not rely on the planning process to establish performance parameters. One concern, however, is that a fixed formula is implicitly a profit sharing approach with little direct correlation to the business planning process or industry results. Another is that fixed formula plans tend to stay in place for many years. A fixed formula plan designed in the early 1970s, based on a 5 percent return on equity, may have been realistic at that time but would be viewed as low today. Also, the formula typically relates to corporate performance and may not reflect differing performance opportunities and strategies of business units.

The most positive characteristic of a fixed formula approach is that it usually provides a fixed return to shareholders first before management participates in an incentive. In the example in Figure 23-3, the company must achieve a 7 percent return on investment before an incentive pool is created. The 7 percent threshold is roughly comparable to a risk-free rate of return on investment. This characteristic is well received by boards of directors and stockholders.

Prior Year's Performance. The incentive pool is determined by comparing the company's performance with either the previous year or the last few years. The performance level required to generate an incentive compensation pool is usually based on a fixed increase (which normally does not vary from year to year) in one or a combination of financial indexes, such as earnings per share, return on equity, or net income.

A typical plan might specify that an incentive pool will be established when annual revenues and net income increase by greater than 8 percent and 15 percent, respectively, over the preceding year. These two criteria serve as thresholds to ensure that a minimum acceptable level of growth and profitability will be attained before an incentive compensation pool is established. The amount of the pool increases on a sliding scale depending on the amount by which the level of performance attained exceeds the last year or the average of some defined period, for example, the last 3 years. The strengths of this approach are that it motivates management to achieve sustained, consistent profit improvement and provides a strong linkage to securities markets, which reward consistently improving results.

One problem is that a too heavy focus on growth may conflict with other strategic objectives, such as market segmentation or investable cash flow. There is also the possibility that a previous year's financial performance might not provide a meaningful basis for establishing the threshold. Outstanding performance in one year may penalize management in subsequent periods owing to higher performance thresholds. Also, it may be unrealistic to expect a company to increase profitability consistently year after year. Maintaining profitability equal to last year in some situations may be good performance. In these situations, management might wish to consider modifying the threshold by basing the threshold on an average of the past two or three years' revenue and profits.

Peer Group Comparison.   The size of the incentive pool is determined by comparing the company's performance for a given year with average industry results or with the results of a selected group of competitors. For this approach, it is assumed that outside forces have an effect on company performance that is similar to that of the comparison group. A company with results that are better than those of the comparison group is assumed to have demonstrated above-average performance.

Table 23-1 illustrates a peer group comparison plan in which the incentive pool is determined by comparing the company's return on equity with the average return on equity of a peer group of companies. If

Table 23-1. Peer Group Comparison

Company's return on equity (as a % competition's average)	Individual incentive opportunity (% base salary)
70	5
80	10
90	15
Target 100	**20**
110	25
120	30
130	35
140	40
≥ 150	50 (ceiling on incentive award)

the company's return on equity is 18.2 percent and the average for the comparison group is 14 percent, the incentive compensation pool generated would be sufficient to award all plan participants 35 percent of base salary (18.2 ÷ 14 = 130 percent, which generates a 35 percent incentive opportunity). The plan may also specify individual performance criteria to determine how much incentive will be paid to each plan participant.

Peer group comparisons are often the basis, or a significant part, of how management incentive pools are created in cyclical, interest-sensitive, or highly regulated industries (for example, utilities, thrifts). The strengths of this approach are that it provides an objective measure of performance and factors out industrywide economic events beyond the company's control. Like the fixed formula approach, however, a peer group comparison deemphasizes the importance of a well-defined planning process in determining executive awards. Also, a peer group may be difficult to define, and valid information may be difficult to obtain on a timely basis, thus delaying awards and eroding the linkage to performance. In addition, in public companies, shareholders may object if an incentive is paid to executives when industrywide results are modest, even when the company has done relatively better than its peers.

Goal Attainment.   The amount of the incentive pool depends on the attainment of specified performance targets. Before the performance period begins, the company establishes performance targets, giving consideration to various factors, such as the company's annual business plans as well as industry trends and general economic conditions. Targets may be keyed to a single index of performance, such as net income, return on sales, return on equity, or to several indexes, and may also include nonfinancial targets.

A typical goal attainment plan that uses a single index of performance, in this case return on equity, is illustrated in Figure 23-4. If the company's return on equity is 100 percent of plan, the incentive pool would generate sufficient dollars to pay plan participants 100 percent of their target incentives. That pool would then be allocated to plan participants on the basis of how they contributed to overall performance.

The matrix displayed in Figure 23-5 gives the percent of a targeted incentive award at each level of financial performance involving two indexes of performance—a targeted sales level and a projected return on sales. If, for example, the company's net return on sales is 120 percent of plan and sales growth were 120 percent of plan, the incentive pool would provide for 200 percent of the target incentives needed to fund plan.

Goal attainment is most effective when the corporate management

Incentive Pool

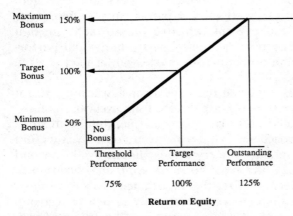

Return on Equity

Figure 23-4. Goal attainment plan with "straight line" payout.

Incentive Pool
(% of Target Award)

80%	0	0	50	75	100
90%	0	50	75	100	125
Net Return on **Sales** (% of Plan) 100%	50	75	100	125	150
110%	75	100	125	150	175
120%	100	125	150	175	200
	80%	90%	100%	110%	120%

Sales Volume
(% of Plan)

Figure 23-5. Goal attainment using two performance measures.

style is based on financial planning and forecasting performance targets has been proved to be accurate. It is less viable in emerging or early-growth-stage companies in which management style may not be planning-based or forecasting may be difficult. One of the strengths of a goal attainment funding mechanism is that it can be applied on a centralized or decentralized basis to group, divisional, or profit center operations, thus helping to reinforce the unit's planning process.

Concerns about a goal attainment approach center on the integrity and sophistication of the planning process and the ability to forecast results accurately. Obviously, goal attainment will not work if goals dictated by the planning process are too high or inconsistent with the company's long-term plans. And the opposite may occur. Companies that consistently show outstanding results may stretch goals and then pay merely an average incentive when these goals are met.

Because each of the funding approaches described has the goal of driving desired behavior and performance, they obviously share basic similarities. It is important to consider the merits of each and combine the characteristics that best meet organization objectives without, however, making the final incentive plan unduly complex. Simplicity is important, especially when the reward system applies to hundreds of executives or key employees. The final product should clearly communicate the message senior management is trying to send to the team.

Performance Measures

Determining performance measures usually encompasses a variety of organizational considerations. Performance measures must be consistent with strategic business plans and annual operating plans. In particular, a balance must be struck between short-term and long-term results so that the long-term well-being of the company is not jeopardized by short-term business decisions, and vice versa. Also, the performance measures adopted must not only be within the control of the individuals concerned but also measurable during the year through the financial reporting system. These performance measures and goals should be communicated and agreed upon before the plan year begins.

In practice, most companies use a combination of performance measures that best reflects their business and stage of development. These may be financial measures, such as return on equity, return on assets, earnings per share, operating income, and net income before or after taxes, or nonfinancial measures, such as new product development, inventory control, accounts receivable management, and development of an operating plan.

A centralized company competitive within one industry with consolidated profits may be able to adopt a single corporatewide measure of performance. A decentralized company with different marketplaces and products may need incentive plans based on divisional performance or a combination of measures.

Figure 23-6 illustrates how three different annual incentive plan designs could be used within a single corporate environment. A start-up division operates in an entrepreneurial environment in which the stra-

Business Stage:
Start-up

Key Performance Criteria:
**Product Development
Progress**

Management Style:
Entrepreneurial

Strategic Timeframe:
Short

Forecasting Abilities:
Low

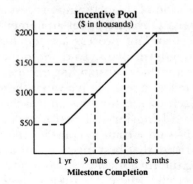

Incentive Pool
($ in thousands)

Business Stage:
Growth

Key Performance Criteria:
Market Share/Earnings

Management Style:
Informed & Controlled

Strategic Timeframe:
Medium

Forecasting Abilities:
Moderate

Incentive Pool
($ in thousands)

Market Share					
30%	100	130	150	175	200
25%	90	100	130	150	175
20%	75	90	100	130	150
15%	60	75	90	100	130
10%	50	60	75	90	100
	$3.0	$3.5	$4.0	$4.5	$5.0

Earnings
($ in millions)

Business Stage:
Mature

Key Performance Criteria:
Cash Flow/ROE

Management Style:
Strategic Management

Strategic Timeframe:
Long

Forecasting Abilities:
Advanced

Incentive Pool
($ in thousands)

Cash Flow ($ in millions)					
$1.8	100	130	150	175	200
$1.6	90	100	130	150	175
$1.4	75	90	100	130	150
$1.2	60	75	90	100	130
$1.0	50	60	75	90	100
	10%	12%	14%	16%	18%

Return on Equity

Figure 23-6. Performance measures by unit.

tegic time frame is short and the forecasting abilities are low. Key performance criteria have to do with product development and achieving increased market share. A division in the growth stage has moderate forecasting abilities and a medium strategic time frame. Here, where the environment is more informed and controlled than in a start-up company, key performance criteria are typically sales and earnings growth, return on net assets, and return on sales. In a mature division in which forecasting abilities are advanced and the management style is focused on strategic management, such performance measures as cash flow, expense control, and return on equity are typically used as performance measures in the incentive plan.

Also, some performance measures are often found in divisional rather than in corporate incentive plans. Earnings per share can only be measured at the corporate level; a division or separate business unit, however, could measure actual earnings from operation or return on controllable assets or return on investment.

Allocation of Funds

Once the amount of the incentive pool has been determined, management must decide how to allocate the pool among the participants. There are three basic methods:

- *Team performance only.* A participant's incentive is based on overall company or unit performance and is paid automatically once target levels are achieved.

- *Individual performance only.* A participant's incentive is based on his or her contribution to overall results, measured by achievement against predetermined goals and/or a more subjective performance appraisal.

- *A combination approach.* Part of the incentive is automatically paid to a participant when overall company or unit performance target levels are reached and the other part is paid after the individual's performance has been appraised.

Each of these methods has distinct advantages and disadvantages. Paying awards solely for team performance fosters a strong sense of company unity among participants, because they must work together to achieve overall results. Therefore, this method may be most appropriate when the overall objective is to encourage a strong sense of team identification. A team performance approach may also be desirable when individual goal-setting and performance appraisal systems are not well developed, or where substantial overlapping of responsibilities exists.

Allocation based only on individual performance works best in environments with firmly established pay-for-performance cultures. This approach is effective only when there are accurate objective-setting and appraisal processes. In most cases, it is based on the premise that the company will pay awards to good performers even during lean times, when overall results may be poor. Some companies may require a threshold level of performance before individual awards are paid.

When the combination approach is used, the relative weight assigned to team versus individual performance should depend on the level of responsibility and influence over results. For example, a CEO's annual incentive may be based entirely on overall corporate performance. The incentive for the head of a business unit may be split between corporate (30 percent) and business unit performance (70 percent). A divisional manager's incentive may be split equally between divisional and individual performance. Companies generally prefer combination awards because they help strike a happy medium by stressing both team identification and pay for individual performance. Obviously, this approach demands attention to performance appraisal and goal setting.

Goal Setting

Because those eligible for an incentive need to understand clearly where their efforts are to be directed to receive their targeted incentive award, goal setting is an important activity in designing and maintaining an effective incentive plan. Goals, which apply to teams as well as to individuals, should be measurable, related to specific objectives, simple to understand and communicate, and supported by a limited number of subgoals. In addition, goals should be challenging, achievable, and, most important, within the control of the individual or team being evaluated.

In most well-conceived incentive plans, goal setting is the foundation for determining the amount of an individual incentive award. The underlying assumption is that the whole is greater than the sum of the parts. The objective in setting well-thought-out goals is to get all the parts moving in the desired direction, reinforcing the appropriate financial and/or nonfinancial results. When setting goals, it is important to adhere to the following points:

- Identify approximately three, and no more than five, goals that represent the most significant performance sought from the individual. One weakness of a goal-setting plan is the creation of a laundry list with as many as 20 goals with value weightings that are insignificant.

- Select goals that make the greatest improvements on the department, operating unit, or company, and develop appropriate weightings. This can be done effectively by weighting goals according to their overall value to the company.

- Select goals that complement each other and create a balance so that the attainment of one goal does not affect other goals (for example, the goal of increasing sales should not conflict with the goal of increasing customer service).

- Consider all resources at your disposal when setting goals (for example, human resources, financial reports, information systems). Critical to the success of goal setting is the ability for the organization to track accurately the desired performance on a timely basis. It is equally important that both evaluators and employees being evaluated come to the same conclusion at the end of the performance period.

- Consider also whether or not performance from other departments or other individuals is needed to complete the goals. If this is so, management must be satisfied that the organizational structure, reporting relationships, and financial reporting are in place to allow the desired results.

- Separate goals with more than a 1-year performance period into annual milestones that can be measured as to their successful completion.

The single most important success factor in goal setting is that senior management be committed to the process. Senior management's involvement in tracking desired results and setting appropriate rewards can go a long way to changing behavior.

Size of Individual Incentive Awards

The size of an annual incentive award is usually expressed as a percent of base pay and typically increases with salary and organizational level. A CEO's annual incentive may be targeted at 50 to 60 percent of salary, with a maximum incentive opportunity from 75 to 100 percent of base pay. Other plan participants are given the opportunity to earn target awards that represent smaller percentages of their base pay, in line with the scope of their responsibilities.

The practice of using salary or salary grade midpoint is fairly mixed. Some maintain that the actual salary is the best measure of a person's level of responsibility and that the most equitable approach is to base incentives on salary. Others hold that the salary grade midpoint represents the market average and that if incentives are paid on midpoints regardless of where employees fall within the range, they will not be penalized or unduly rewarded.

Companies usually specify a target or "normal" annual incentive opportunity as well as a maximum incentive opportunity as a percent of salary. For example, if the range midpoint of a certain job is $80,000, the targeted or "normal" incentive opportunity could be $20,000, or 25 percent. The maximum award could be set at 1.5 times the target, or $30,000. Targeted total cash compensation would be $100,000 ($80,000 + $20,000) with a maximum potential of $110,000 ($80,000 + $30,000).

The term *normal* means that if the company or business unit has achieved but not exceeded its targeted financial objectives and the employee or team has similarly achieved but not exceeded targeted objectives, then the incentive will be paid. If the company and employee exceed the target, a greater amount will be paid on a sliding scale until a designated maximum has been reached. Some companies will not use a cap and provide unlimited upside opportunity. Obviously, what is normal in one industry, company, or division may not be normal in another, and the range of incentive opportunities depends on many factors that management must address.

Industry Practice.   Companies must look at competitive industry practice, which provides an external barometer as to the size of individual awards. These considerations also include the size and location of the company as well as varying practices by job level. Not to take external competitive data into account when setting incentive award levels may cause problems of retention and recruitment.

Business Strategy.   A company's business strategy can affect the size of annual incentives. In high-risk, entrepreneurial environments, management will often place a significant percent of cash compensation at risk by means of lower-than-average salaries and substantial bonus opportunities. In low-risk environments, companies will typically pay above-average salaries with more modest annual incentive opportunities.

Compensation Strategy.   The company's compensation strategy also affects the size of targeted incentive amounts, particularly the desired balance between annual and long-term incentive opportunities. Because senior executives are responsible for the long-term success and strategic direction of the company, they are often given long-term incentive and capital accumulation opportunities that, as a percent of total compensation, exceed those of the annual incentive. For the middle-management ranks, a balance of annual and long-term incentives is often desirable. A compensation plan heavily weighted on the side of annual incentives is suitable for those who principally affect short-term results.

Development Stage. Stage of development can also affect the size of annual incentive awards. In start-up companies, the focus is usually on long-term incentives in order to preserve cash for capital investment. As a company grows, it will put emphasis on increased cash compensation (including annual incentives) to attract and retain the management team and motivate shorter-term results. In mature companies, annual incentives are often stressed to reward maintaining market position and current earnings results.

Administrative Issues

Administrative issues concerning annual incentives have to do with the form and timing of payment. Payments may be made in cash, stock, or a combination of both. Cash paid at the time the award is earned is obviously the simplest way to administer an annual incentive plan and the most common. Payment in stock is useful if a company has a cash flow problem or wants to create a greater sense of stockholder identification. When payments are made in both cash and stock, the objective is to use the cash to pay taxes, allowing the executive to retain the stock.

Deferred Arrangements

Some executives prefer to defer income recognition until a future date, so many companies provide deferred payment arrangements for their annual plans. These may be short-term deferrals in which the payment is made at the employee's option over several years following the award, or deferrals until retirement.

To ensure that the deferral falls within Internal Revenue Service (IRS) provisions, the executive should elect to defer the incentive (or a portion of the incentive) prior to the period in which the service is rendered and indicate over what period the incentive is to be deferred (e.g., 1 year, 5 years, or until retirement). To ease administrative burdens, some companies limit the choices on how long the deferral period can be. The company would then pay interest on the deferred amount.

Interest may be based on a formula (for example, prime less 2 percent, or the long-term Treasury note rate), or it may be tied to the greater of the company's earnings growth, return on equity, or an interest rate. This latter approach serves to link the deferral to company performance, thus providing an additional incentive. Because funds are invested on a pretax basis, relative returns on deferred funds can be very attractive. For stock deferrals, stock units are determined at the time the bonus is earned based on the stock price at that time. Typically, dividends declared during the deferral period may be paid out as earned or reinvested into more deferred shares. If paid out when earned, they would be taxable at that time at the appropriate tax rate.

In developing deferral arrangements, it is important to understand when there is a taxable event. Employees participating in deferred compensation arrangements are generally not required to report deferred amounts for income tax purposes until "actually" or "constructively" received. Actual receipt occurs when payments are made to the employee; constructive receipt occurs when amounts are credited to the employee's account or set apart for the employee to be drawn at any time. It should be noted that to gain favorable tax treatment, deferred amounts must be unsecured, that is, unsegregated from the employer's other assets. The IRS will issue a favorable advance letter ruling concerning whether an unfunded deferred compensation arrangement results in immediate taxation if the plan meets one of two requirements: (1) If an election to defer income is involved, the election must be made before the beginning of the period of service for which compensation is payable; (2) if elections are made after the beginning of the service period, the plan must contain substantial forfeiture provisions that remain in effect throughout the entire deferral period.

Conclusion

Properly designed incentive plans can enhance an organization's performance and serve as a powerful management tool to affect behavior in a positive way. Designing, implementing, and administering an annual incentive plan for executives, however, are technical activities that can only be undertaken with the full cooperation of top management and the human resources department. Human resources professionals can provide top management with expertise on how compensation can be used as a management tool to support business objectives. To do this, human resources personnel must be knowledgeable about their company's products and services and must be familiar with the principles of financial management. In addition, they should be well informed as to the corporate legal, tax, and accounting issues that affect incentive compensation plans. In public companies, they must know SEC requirements for disclosure and any special rules in effect at the stock exchange where company stock is listed. When human resources professionals work with company management to create incentive compensation programs tied to business strategy, they contribute in a real way to the future direction and success of the organization.

24

Long-Term Incentives

Jeffrey S. Hyman
Partner, Hewitt Associates

Overview of Long-Term Incentives

Over the past decade, companies have been challenged continually by foreign competition, corporate raiders, and shareholders' demands for enhanced investment value. Organizations mindful of these threats are discovering that their traditional short-term performance orientation no longer is adequate for managing the decision-making process to support the long-range strategic planning necessary in today's operating environment. Consequently, corporate America is placing a new emphasis on the importance of maximizing performance beyond the current fiscal period. In doing so, companies increasingly have turned to compensation as one of the primary means of orienting their executives toward the long term. As a result, long-term incentives have become one of the most popular—and certainly one of the most publicized—forms of executive compensation today. No treatment of executive compensation is possible without a comprehensive review of long-term incentives.

To understand how widespread long-term incentives are, consider a recent Hewitt Associates survey that found that over 90 percent of companies offer their executives at least one long-term incentive opportunity—up from 85 percent two years ago.[1] Furthermore, organizations with more than $2.5 billion in sales generally offer three different plans, and it is not at all uncommon for executives in these firms to participate in multiple opportunities, whether in a tandem relationship or independent of one another.

Not only is the prevalence of the long-term component growing, but its relative value in the total executive compensation package has adjusted too. What was once considered a relatively incidental fringe benefit has developed into a substantial and integral part of the corporate executive's overall pay opportunity. Studies indicate that while the long-term incentive component was just 16 percent of a senior executive's total pay in 1982, it contributed 31 percent in 1989—almost double the impact in seven years.[2]

Characteristics of Long-Term Incentive Plans

Before choosing a long-term incentive program, careful thought should be given to the overall corporate strategy driving the plan implementation. Like all management systems, soundly designed compensation programs should not be structured in a vacuum, so it is essential to understand the purposes for which the long-term incentive plan is being implemented and the specific objectives the program is expected to help satisfy. Well-articulated compensation objectives are instrumental in the process of selecting the long-term incentive program design that best supports the organization's business and human resources needs.

Most often, long-term incentives are designed to:

- *Share the company's success with executives.* By allowing executives to share in the company's success, long-term plans serve to focus executive attention on certain key aspects of the company's performance.

- *Promote long-term thinking.* Long-term plans effectively balance the short-term focus of annual incentive plans.

- *Align executive interest with that of shareholders.* By making a portion of an executive's compensation contingent on company performance, long-term plans help correlate management's personal interests with those of shareholders, thereby promoting decision making that enhances the value of the firm's capital investment.

[1]Hewitt Associates private survey.
[2]Hewitt Associates private survey.

- *Attract and retain talented executives.* Long-term incentive awards often represent a sizable percentage of an executive's total compensation. When these awards are structured so that they vest over a period of years, they can act as an effective retention device. Additionally, the prevalence of long-term incentives in American industry makes it increasingly difficult for companies without such plans to attract and retain talented people.

- *Supplement broad-based, tax-qualified employee retirement income programs.* As tax laws continue to limit the benefits that can accrue on behalf of the highly paid, many companies implement long-term incentive plans to supplement the capital accumulation opportunities available to executives under broad-based, tax-qualified retirement programs.

Since the effectiveness of a long-term plan depends largely on how well the program suits the intended objectives, it is important to be familiar with the full range of program designs. Keep in mind, however, that unlike the broad-based benefit programs typically offered to all employees, executive long-term incentive plans generally are not tax-qualified (with the exception of incentive stock options) and, therefore, are not usually restricted to a format that complies with stringent legislative regulation. The range of possible program structures really is limited only by the creativity and resourcefulness of those challenged with developing the overall plan.

Notwithstanding the flexibility permissible in executive incentive plan design, the format of a long-term program typically falls into one of three categories, depending on the company's primary considerations. Plans that are *market-based* relate incentive earnings opportunities to increases in the price of a company's common stock. *Performance-based* arrangements, on the other hand, correlate payouts with more internally focused performance targets. *Hybrid* formats incorporate elements of both internal and external performance in determining the value of the earnings available to the plan participants.

Whether a market-based, performance-based, or hybrid plan is right for an organization depends entirely on the operating objectives, overall corporate strategy, and underlying management philosophy of the company itself. Remember, the long-term incentive plan is best characterized as a communication device through which the company identifies for its executives the mission it expects to fulfill, the strategy by which it will do so, and the goals that, when accomplished, will indicate the satisfaction of the corporation's purpose. Consequently, the structure of the long-term incentive is impossible to separate from the objectives it is expected to support.

Also important when choosing an appropriate long-term incentive plan are the related tax and financial accounting implications. Given the magnitude of long-term incentive awards and the breadth of participation in the plans, the impact of charges to the financial statements, the potential for earnings dilution, and the timing and characterization of income and deduction, all must be considered in the program selection process.

Still, the primary consideration when choosing a long-term incentive plan is whether the plan structure supports the organization's objectives. Understanding how these programs can work to deliver the right messages probably is accomplished best by considering the mechanics of specific program formats. The remainder of this chapter, therefore, presents characteristics (and associated tax treatment) of the most frequently used long-term incentive plans, followed by a discussion comparing the different approaches.

Market-Based Plans

Stock Options

Stock options are by far the most popular form of long-term incentives found in American industry. Roughly 80 percent of all major companies have an option program in place. Stock options provide employees with the right to purchase company stock at a stipulated price over a specific period of time. If the stock value appreciates within that time frame, the employee then has the right to acquire the stock at a price below its market value.

Nonqualified Stock Option. One type of executive stock option plan is a nonqualified stock option. While the mechanics of both types of plans are similar, they each have distinct characteristics. Nonqualified plans are the more flexible of the two kinds of stock option programs. They are unfettered by statute or regulation concerning minimum price requirements, maximum grant periods, or maximum exercise and holding periods. This absence of regulation enables companies to tailor their plans to fit their individual objectives (for example, some companies may wish to offer options at below fair market value, others may wish to extend the term of an option over an employee's career, and so forth).

On the accounting side, if the option is granted at 100 percent of the market price at date of grant, the employer incurs no compensation expense for accounting purposes. If the employer grants a nonqualified option at a discount (for example, at a price below market value at date of grant), the excess of the market value over the exercise price is deemed a compensation expense for accounting purposes and must be charged against earnings. Note, however, for several years the Financial Accounting Standards Board (FASB) has been considering a change to the accounting rules that would require an expense for all options at time of grant, but it has been unable to gain agreement on how such a charge to earnings would be calculated.

Generally, the employee who receives nonqualified stock options has no tax liability at the time of grant. However, at the date of exercise, the excess of the stock's market value over the option price is taxable as ordinary income. Any subsequent appreciation that is realized at the time of sale is taxed as a capital gain. While there is currently no difference between capital gain and ordinary income rates, it is important to note that the technical distinction between the two types of rates remains and might once again become significant if the rates are changed in the future. Figure 24-1 presents a graphic representation of the employee's tax consequences with nonqualified stock options.

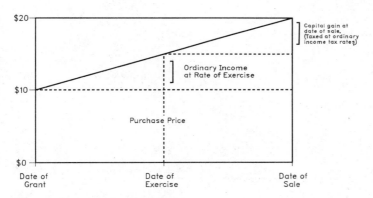

Figure 24-1. Nonqualified stock option.

With a nonqualified stock option plan, the employer receives a business expense (compensation) deduction in the amount and at the time the employee realizes ordinary income.

Incentive Stock Option. The second type of executive stock option plan is the incentive stock option. It is designed to be a tax-favored way to deliver stock to employees. The mechanics of incentive stock options work the same way as those of nonqualified stock options, except that the employee and the plan itself must comply with more restrictive tax law provisions than those pertaining to nonqualified stock options. Essentially, if the rules are adhered to, employees can avoid taxation at the time of exercise, and any gain ultimately recognizable will be capital in nature rather than ordinary income.

Specifically, an employee incurs no income tax liability upon the grant or exercise of an incentive stock option. However, the "bargain element" (the difference between the option price and the market price) at exercise is a tax preference item subject to the alternative minimum tax. If the stock is held for at least one year following the date of exercise and two years from the date of grant, then when the stock is disposed of the aggregate difference between the option price and the sale price is taxed as a long-term capital gain. But since there is currently no favorable tax treatment for long-term capital gains, the primary tax advantage employees receive from incentive stock options, as opposed to nonqualified stock options, is that tax can be deferred until the date of sale.

The tax effect of incentive stock options on the employee is shown in Figure 24-2.

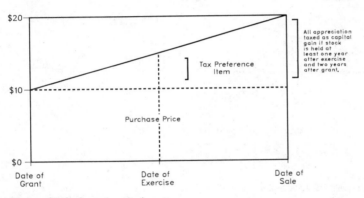

Figure 24-2. Incentive stock option.

On the other hand, since all appreciation on an incentive stock option is taxed as capital gains and not as ordinary income and the option price cannot be less than the fair market value on the date of grant, the employer generally earns no business expense (compensation) deduction unless the employee fails to meet the requisite holding-period requirements. In that case, the employee will be forced to recognize any accrued appreciation as ordinary income, and the employer then will become entitled to an offsetting tax deduction. As indicated in connection with nonqualified options, however, the FASB is exploring the idea of mandating an expense for options to be charged at the time they are initially granted.

Stock Appreciation Rights

Stock appreciation rights (SARs) allow an employee to realize the appreciation in value of a specified number of common shares without requiring the employee to make a cash investment in the stock or causing dilution of the employer's shareholder equity. SARs work like this. Suppose an employee is granted 1000 stock appreciation rights when a single share of the company's stock is selling for $20. If the price of a single share appreciates in value by $10 during the exercise period and the employee exercises all 1000 stock appreciation rights when the market value of the stock reaches $30 per share, the employee would receive an award equal to $10,000. It's at this time, when the stock appreciation right is cashed out, that tax ramifications arise.

On the exercise date, the employee must recognize ordinary income in the amount received in satisfaction of the stock appreciation right. Sometimes the stock appreciation right is satisfied in the form of shares of the company's common stock. When this happens, the recipient becomes, in effect, an investor in the company, so at the time the acquired shares are sold the amount received is subject to tax in accordance with the rules governing the sale of a capital asset. These results are displayed graphically in Figure 24-3.

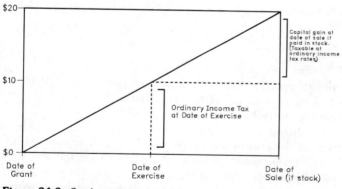

Figure 24-3. Stock appreciation rights.

Because the employee is taxed at ordinary income rates at the time the stock appreciation right is exercised, the employer may claim a business expense (compensation) deduction equal to the amount of the employee's ordinary income in the year that the employee first incurs a tax liability. The employee's subsequently earned capital gain or loss on the disposition of acquired shares has no effect on the company.

Stock appreciation rights may be granted alone or in conjunction with nonqualified stock options and/or incentive stock options. When stock appreciation rights are granted in tandem with stock options, the number of shares covered by the appreciation rights normally equals the number of shares granted to the employee under stock options. The exercise of an option typically cancels a stock appreciation right and vice versa. In this manner, the stock appreciation rights act as a tax offset or financing vehicle for the exercise of options. When stock appreciation rights are granted independently of stock options, any appreciation in company stock that occurs between the date of grant and date of exercise may be payable to the executive in cash, stock, or a combination of the two.

An accounting consequence associated with stock appreciation rights, however, greatly distinguishes them from stock options. Remember that options usually generate no earnings change. But the estimated expense of appreciation rights has to be accrued quarterly from the date of grant to the date of exercise, and the expense is generally considered to be equal to the amount of appreciation realized during each quarter. If the plan is a combination plan permitting a choice between options or rights, the compensation cost is measured according to the most likely choice. Because of the volatility of this accounting treatment, however, many companies have severely restricted the number of executives eligible for stock appreciation rights and, in some cases, have eliminated the plan altogether.

Restricted Stock

Restricted stock programs allow for the transfer of employer stock to an executive, usually free of charge to the employee. In this sense, restricted stock plans are outright equity grants. Full rights to stock acquisition are conditional, however, and are predicated on the occurrence of certain events, such as the continued employment of the individual for a specified period of time. Some plans provide for restricted stock to vest when certain corporate or individual performance goals are met. However, imposition of these types of conditions is relatively uncommon.

In most restricted stock plans, the executive enjoys full shareholder rights during the restricted period, except for the right to sell or transfer the stock. If the conditions placed upon the transfer of stock are fulfilled, at the end of the restricted period the executive owns the stock outright. However, if the conditions are not met, theoretically, the executive must forfeit the stock completely.

A variation on restricted stock is a TARSAP feature. TARSAP stands for "time-accelerated restricted stock award plan." The time-accelerated feature allows restrictions to be removed faster than originally scheduled if the executive or the company meets certain performance goals. In this sense, the TARSAP constitutes a hybrid format.

For example, if XYZ company awards restricted stock to executive A, the stock becomes A's outright if A is in the employ of the company at the end of a ten-year period. However, the company sets up certain income goals for the corporation and its business units. If executive A's business unit achieves 110 percent of its budgeted pretax income each year, the vesting period will be shortened by three years (for example, if the 110 percent goal is reached in the first year, the restricted stock will vest to executive A at the end of seven years, rather than ten years).

Another variation on restricted stock is a restricted stock performance plan which offers restricted stock in the traditional manner but also sets forth a performance schedule that can generate a cash payment related to the restricted stock award. The cash payment often is intended to pay taxes on the restricted stock when the shares vest.

As with a time-accelerated plan, a restricted stock performance plan awards restricted stock to executive A, with full rights conditioned on A's being employed with the company four years later. If executive A's business unit achieves, on average, 105 percent of its budgeted pretax income over the four-year period, the plan also will make a cash payment large enough to pay all taxes due on the restricted stock, which becomes vested in the fourth year, and on the cash itself. Performance, to a lesser or greater degree than target, likewise will provide a lesser or greater cash payment.

A third variation on traditional restricted stock is a plan that bases restrictions primarily on performance rather than continued employment with the company. For example, an executive may be granted restricted stock that becomes vested in four years only if the company achieves an average earnings per share of $2 over the four-year period and the executive is employed at the end of those four years. If the performance goal is not satisfied, a smaller number of shares may be vested, or none at all.

The compensation expense associated with restricted stock is recognized as of the date of initial grant and is not affected by any subsequent appreciation or depreciation in the stock. The amount of the expense is the difference between the fair market value on the date of the grant and the price paid for it by the employee (if any). This amount is amortized for accounting purposes over the restriction period. The accounting treatment differs if full rights to the restricted stock depend upon meeting performance goals or if a TARSAP is used. When goal achievement is a prerequisite to payment, compensation expense for the restricted stock is not based on the value at the time of the grant but instead on an estimate of its full fair market value when the restrictions are scheduled to lapse.

Contrast this treatment with that accorded TARSAPs. For these, the amount of the compensation expense is measured based on the market value of the shares on the date of the grant, but the timing of the financial statement charges depends on the timing of the accomplishment of performance goals that accelerate lifting the restrictions.

Ordinarily, an executive who gets some kind of restricted share incurs no tax liability at the date of the grant. When the restrictions lapse, however, ordinary income needs to be recognized on the current fair market value of the stock less the employee's cost to acquire the shares, if any. After restrictions lapse, the executive is viewed as an equity investor in the company, so, for tax purposes, any subsequent appreciation is treated as capital gain.

Alternatively, the employee may elect to pay tax on the initial bargain value of the restricted grant within 30 days of the grant date. When this election is made, the income recognized is taxed as ordinary income, but any subsequent appreciation is capital gain. Prior to tax reform, this election, called a Section 83(b) election, sometimes was made in order to take advantage of favorable capital gains rates when it was expected there would likely be a substantial increase forthcoming in the market price of the shares. However, as the tax law no longer offers material advantages to recognizing capital gain in lieu of ordinary income, the only real advantage to making this election would be to recognize ordinary income in a low-income year for tax planning purposes. Figure 24-4 depicts the tax consequences for an executive who receives restricted stock.

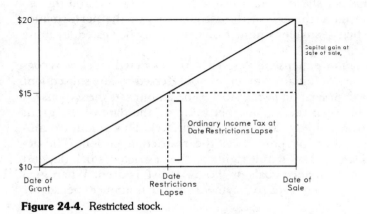

Figure 24-4. Restricted stock.

As is the case in all other instances pertaining to nonqualified compensation plan design, the employer granting restricted stock becomes entitled to a deductible compensation expense for tax purposes at the same time, and in the same amount, as the employee realizes taxable income. Typically, this means that the employer gets a deduction when the restrictions on share transferability lapse. In addition, any dividends paid on the restricted shares are also tax deductible.

Note that to obtain this deduction the company must withhold income taxes on the shares granted. However, the nature of a pure restricted stock program is such that there may be no cash payment from which to withhold. Consequently, the company must either ask the recipient to make a cash payment to the company for the withholding taxes, or the company must withhold taxes from other sources, such as salary or bonus compensation. Also consider that because the employer obtains a tax deduction equal to the value of the stock at vesting, while the accounting charge is limited to the value of the share on the grant date, companies whose stock has appreciated will accrue a tax benefit that is disproportionately high relative to the accounting expense. Any such excess benefit cannot be added to income, however, but instead must be charged to capital.

Phantom Stock

This form of long-term deferred compensation uses the employer's stock as the measuring device for calculating the value of the ultimate award payment. Designated executives are given units called "phantom stock," which incorporate a value equal to the price of shares of common equity. Unlike real shares, however, the phantom stock does not represent any true ownership interest in the company. The employer simply credits these phantom shares on its books, and as the company's stock price rises and falls, so does the value of the phantom stock. Typically, phantom shares are "put" back to the company after a stipulated time has elapsed, and the amount of any accrued appreciation during the holding period is paid out in cash. A variation on this theme pays out the full value of the stock plus any accrued appreciation, as opposed to appreciation alone, after the stipulated time frame.

As a rule, the value of one phantom share at any point in time equals the market price of one share of the company's stock. Nonetheless, when a public market for the company's shares does not exist, the employer may relate phantom-stock values to the firm's book value per share. Note also that phantom-stock accounts may be credited with any dividends declared on a number of shares of stock equivalent to the number of phantom shares in an executive's phantom-stock account.

Sometimes phantom-stock plans are used to defer compensation earned from an annual incentive plan. The employee's incentive dollars are used to purchase a number of phantom shares at the then current value of the employer's stock. At the end of the deferral period, phantom shares are revalued and final payments are made in cash, in stock, or in a combination of cash and stock. Dividend equivalents may be either credited to the executive's account or paid directly upon declaration.

The estimated expense of phantom-stock grants needs to be accrued quarterly by amortizing the appreciation in award value over the maturity period. The payment or crediting of dividend equivalents is expensed at the time of payment or credit.

The tax treatment of phantom-stock plans closely resembles that of stock appreciation rights. Participants incur no tax liability on the initial grant of phantom shares. However, final payments in satisfaction of the award accrual are deemed ordinary income in the year paid out, and it is at that time that the employer sees an offsetting deduction. Sometimes dividends are paid to holders of phantom shares. When this happens, the payments are treated as additional compensation and are subject to ordinary income tax when received by the employee. If final phantom-stock redemptions are made in stock, subsequent appreciation represents capital gain subject to ordinary income rates (see Figure 24-5).

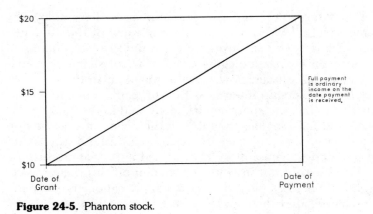

Figure 24-5. Phantom stock.

Performance-Based Plans

Performance Shares or Units

Performance shares or units plans typically provide awards to the extent that the organization meets preset, long-term performance objectives.

Generally, an employee receives a grant of units or stock at no cost. The employer then designates some objective measure of company growth or performance and relates the individual executive's reward to the level of achievement relative to the specified goal. This yardstick is typically based on the performance of the entire corporation, but it could also relate to group or division performance. Commonly, performance is measured over a multiyear time frame in terms of return on equity, return on assets (or capital employed), or compound growth in earnings. Sometimes, however, it is defined relative to a standard set by the performance of other companies.

The employee then earns the right to receive some or all of these units at the end of a specified period. The number of performance shares or units to be received depends on the employer's long-term performance. The value of the units is a fixed dollar amount determined at the time of initial grant. The value of the shares, however, is based on the market value of the employer's stock at the conclusion of the performance period. Regardless of how the value is determined, the full amount of all payments made to plan participants needs to be fully amortized and charged to earnings throughout the performance period on an as-accrued basis.

Taxation of performance shares or units is a function of cash-basis accounting. Employers get no deduction until they pay out awards, which also is when participants realize ordinary income on the full value of all amounts received. If final payments are made in stock, then the recipient is an investor with respect to those shares, and any subsequent appreciation in stock price is treated as a capital gain. Figure 24-6 presents a graphic representation of the recipient's tax consequences.

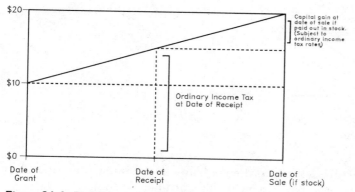

Figure 24-6. Performance share/unit.

Formula-Value Shares

The formula-value share plan is a variation on the previously discussed phantom-stock theme that has special application at private companies or at the divisional level of public organizations. Like the phantom-stock concept, the formula-value share plan awards participants with stocklike units priced to reflect a unit value of the company or division.

Generally, the unit price is defined in terms of a valuation formula relating to earnings, revenues, cash flow, or other combination of measures that the market might be expected to consider in assigning value to the company or division. Units generally are valued at the time of grant and again after a stipulated performance period at which point any accrued value is paid to the executive in cash. The variable accounting rules associated with stock-appreciation rights also apply to formula-value shares. Reserves need to be created over the performance period to reflect post-grant appreciation in award value as it accrues.

Recipients of formula-value shares incur no tax liability when they first receive their shares. When the shares are redeemed at the completion of the performance or measurement period, however, the participants realize ordinary income on the amounts received. Figure 24-7 illustrates how an employee is taxed on the receipt of formula-value shares.

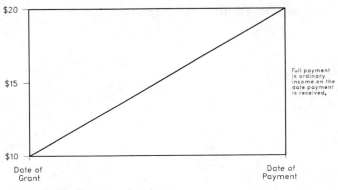

Figure 24-7. Formula-value shares.

A tax deduction accrues to the company in the same amount and in the same year as the participant realizes ordinary income.

Market-Based Versus Performance-Based Plans

After considering the mechanics associated with the variety of commonly used long-term incentive plan formats, it should start to become clear that the selection of a design format really depends on balancing the company's objectives in implementing the program with the realities of the operating environment in which the executive group serves. For example, an organization whose management philosophy exhorts executives to continuously maximize the value of its shareholders' investment might quickly conclude that any of the market-based programs are well suited for implementation since the value of the participant's earnings directly relates to increases in the price of the company's stock. This is a logical conclusion to draw, yet it ignores many compelling arguments that suggest stock prices move in response to many stimuli wholly unrelated to individual executive decision making. If we believe that factors pertaining to macroeconomic events, market psychology, industry cyclicty, and other external factors strongly impact share value, then introducing a long-term compensation system that relates individual earnings opportunities to stock-price appreciation alone may amount to an overzealous and futile attempt to encourage executive activity that enhances shareholder value.

Certainly, the effort to match executive rewards with shareholder value enhancement is an admirable goal, one from which the human-resources professional ought not to be distracted. But while market-based plans such as stock options and stock appreciation rights can be very effective systems for sharing organization success as defined by appreciation in shareholder return, they tend to reward plan participants through a retrospective, after-the-fact view of performance. In this sense, they are passive arrangements that, because of the uncertain connection between management decision making and stock-price movement, represent ineffective instruments for communicating the specific goals that are within management's grasp and that the company wants its executive team to achieve.

In many instances then, performance-based arrangements, such as performance units or formula-value shares, or even the hybrid formats (for example, performance shares or TARSAPs), might offer better approaches to plan structure when the company is clear about its performance targets and confident that goal achievement eventually will drive stock-price appreciation. Under this assumption, it is incumbent upon the organization to identify those measures of internal performance that correlate well with share-price movement.

As noted earlier, when selecting performance targets, most companies identify earnings, return on assets or investment, or some other reflection of financial performance founded on traditional accounting principles. However, at the frontier of performance-measurement thinking are the advocates of economic-based planning who argue persuasively that of all the common yardsticks of success, it is inflation-adjusted cash flow and asset growth, in tandem, that correlate most directly with stock-price appreciation. Consequently, those organizations that utilize sophisticated planning techniques and information systems are recognizing the inconsistency of promoting a management philosophy that advocates shareholder value creation while it rewards management for maximizing traditional accounting measures. Those organizations are moving away from the more common focus on book earnings and returns on equity and capital, and instead they are beginning to relate long-term incentive opportunities to value creation models whose foundations rest in discounted cash flow analysis.

Conclusion

Long-term incentive usage has grown extensively over the past decade, and expectations are that the trend will not abate any time soon. As long as management continues to emphasize long-term thinking in an effort to combat the threats of competition from overseas and unwelcome ownership transitions, then one can anticipate that the long-term incentive component of the executive compensation package will only grow in importance.

For the human-resources professional, it will become increasingly important to possess a clear understanding of how long-term incentives work to help organizations accomplish their operating objectives. Part of the challenge will be to ensure familiarity with the mechanics of plan design. But equally critical will be an ability to discern how the workings of each program will fit within the organization's culture, how effective they will be in promoting the firm's business and human-resources objectives, and how well they will support the company's overall management philosophy.

25

The New Performance Measures

Monroe J. Haegele, Ph.D.

Institutional Funds Group
Provident National Bank

Introduction

The top management of most corporations would probably agree that they follow a philosophy of paying for performance. They would also readily admit that the practical pursuit of this philosophy is difficult. It is difficult to find the appropriate linkage of reward components to performance measures, and perhaps even more difficult to identify the appropriate performance measures themselves. In fact, a casual examination of the evidence indicates that explicit pay for performance arrangements throughout most of corporate America does not exist. Obviously, a spectrum of reward systems from pure job content compensation to commission-based pay systems are present in the modern corporation. The vast majority of middle- and upper-management positions, however, are rewarded primarily on factors only vaguely related to corporate performance.

In the past decade, a number of trends and crosscurrents have begun to put tremendous pressure for change on historical reward mechanisms. Large institutional shareholders, acting more as investors than owners, are questioning management's role as it relates to the company's financial market performance, and indirectly questioning the corporation's entire reward and performance measurement system. Globalization, financial product innovation, slower economic growth in the mature industrial markets, and an aging managerial work force are causing a complete reexamination of reward and performance measurement systems.

The purpose of this chapter is twofold: to critically review existing reward-performance mechanisms and the forces not producing change in these mechanisms, and to suggest a simple framework for developing, if not creating a greater emphasis on, performance measures that align management's interests with those of the shareholders.

The Lack of a Pay-for-Performance Linkage

The reward-performance mechanism is complex in practice because people are paid for a variety of reasons. Notions of equity, legal and contractual issues, and corporate culture, in addition to labor market conditions, all come to play in compensating managers for the work they perform. As financial markets carefully scrutinize the value being created for shareholders by these managers, however, many of the components of existing reward-performance mechanisms are being questioned and will eventually change.

Performance Appraisals

In a *Journal of Finance* article dealing with compensation and incentives, three academic economists, George Baker, Michael Jensen, and Keven Murphy, questioned the prevalence of noneconomic factors in compensation systems.[1] From their perspective, the economic models of reward are incomplete and organizational inefficiencies exist. Judging from the radical restructurings taking place throughout corporate America, organizational inefficiencies, caused in part by unspecific reward-performance mechanisms, may indeed be pervasive.

Baker, Jensen, and Murphy contend that monetary rewards are not closely tied to performance. They cite two studies done within the last 10 years that show very little relationship between salary differentials and individual performance appraisals. This statistical finding should

---

[1]George P. Baker, Michael C. Jensen, and Keven J. Murphy, "Compensation and Incentives: Practice vs. Theory," *Journal of Finance*, Vol. 43, No. 3, July 1988, pp. 593–616.

be no surprise to line managers or human resources executives who have lived with a salary administration program composed of a job evaluation system layered with a performance appraisal device. The job evaluation system, based on some concept of job size and horizontal equity, determines the major reward component. Performance appraisal has only a minor influence on total monetary rewards.

Performance appraisal systems also lack clear objective measures that relate to monetary rewards; the linkage is not only small, but it is also vague. Anyone who has ever tried to install significant incentive compensation throughout an organization knows how difficult it is to develop rewardable objective performance measures. Usually, objective measures with a significant reward component are difficult for management to clearly identify, and they can also put the organization at risk. People will do precisely what they are asked to do if the reward is significant. To get the right results for the total organization, management needs to clearly specify these objective measures. This requires an understanding of the strategic direction of the company, which often times does not exist. Other management processes, such as financial information systems, may not be evolved enough to be able to control an objective performance measurement system. Paying incentives to loan officers at a commercial bank is a classic example of this problem.

Variable Pay Schemes

Profit-sharing plans are popular and have many desirable characteristics. By shifting some of the fixed-cost compensation risk to the employee and away from the shareholder, the employee can take normal economic adjustments in wages and not put his or her entire job at risk. The shareholder sees a reduction in the underlying riskiness of his or her cash flows, if the profit-sharing component is significant enough, and should reward management through a higher share piece.

At an individual level, however, profit sharing is usually not a direct reward-performance linkage. Individual participation in group or corporate profits will, in most cases, be linked to some collective measure, or even job size, as reflected in the salary administration system.

Executive compensation plans tend to reflect performance measures most akin to shareholder interest. Direct grants of stock, stock options, or phantom shares to senior management reflect a desire to bond management's and shareholder's objectives. Presumably, the key decision makers, as holders of residual claims to corporate cash flow, will act in their own best interest and, therefore, that of the shareholders as well.

The amount of the related awards, however, are rarely associated with individual performance. More likely, the amount of the stock-related award is a function of job size. People in key decision-making jobs get stock, and successful corporate performance produces gains in stock price, which is supposed to act as a reward.

Perhaps most visible in the reward-performance mechanism of executive compensation is the CEO's pay. Baker, Jensen, and Murphy cite evidence of the high correlation between corporate sales and CEO salaries. This should not surprise most compensation consultants, because this is precisely one of the key variables they use in setting salaries at the top. Again, however, sales levels may have very little relation to increases in shareholder value. The specific performance linkage is weak, and this observation is made all the more important because CEO pay level and mechanism drive the remainder of the corporate hierarchy.

Implications

The lack of a pay-for-performance linkage in a corporate structure, indeed in the entire structure of corporate America, makes it vulnerable to external shocks and resistant to change. As technological and world market developments change, the corporation's ability to adapt is limited. People do not focus on the right things. Ultimately, the financial condition of the business can be placed at risk. Large hierarchical pay systems with little reward-performance linkage are self-perpetuating, even in the face of change. There is little incentive for the manager to eliminate positions or radically change compensation when his or her own compensation is not affected by this behavior.

Forces of Change

The vulnerability of corporations to recent trends is already producing change. Leveraged buyouts totaled $1.3 billion in 1979, and rose to $62 billion by 1989. Increased debt associated with the buy-out resulted in the downsizing of the companies involved and a radical changing in the reward-performance linkage. Management-led LBOs have, of course, significantly increased the equity holdings of management and aligned their interest more closely with that of the remaining shareholders.

It is difficult to trace all the major forces at work today, but a few of the more important ones that are likely to continue through the 1990s are worth cataloging.

Slower Economic Growth

The secular decline in the growth rate of the U.S. economy and the maturation of most industrial markets has produced difficulties in reward mechanisms not based primarily on performance. Large hierarchical salary administration systems that do not discriminate closely on performance produce rewards through promotion within the system; a bigger job means bigger pay. When these types of organizations stop growing, promotion-based rewards become limited. Younger, talented managers leave, and the organization becomes populated with people who have no incentive to change.

Managerial Demographics

The baby boom population is now well into the management ranks of most corporations. This inordinately large group of people are seeking top management positions at a time when few of these positions exist. Clearly, a reward system that does not discriminate heavily on performance, and at the same time has cut-off, promotion based rewards, cannot serve organizational efficiency very well.

Financial Product Innovation

The decade of the 1980s saw an explosion of new financial instruments and market structures. The growth of the high-yield or junk-bond market allowed many projects to attract financing that would have not been formerly possible. This debt financing of takeovers, LBOs, and public-to-private-ownership transactions made it possible for managers to identify companies that seemed to be undermanaged. Michael Jensen argues that free cash flow in excess of what profitably can be reinvested by management should be disgorged to shareholders.[2] Reward mechanisms that are not performance-based provide no real incentive for management to behave this way. In fact, job-size pay systems encourage managements to make suboptimal investments and seek growth at the expense of profits. As a result, debt was created that helped finance a

[2]Michael C. Jensen, "Agency Costs of Free Cash Flow, Corporate Finance, and Takeovers," *The American Economic Review*, Vol. 76, No. 2, May 1986, pp. 323–329.

change in management, and debt covenants replaced the less formal shareholder-agent relationship.

The Reward-Performance Equation

A Need to Shift Emphasis

Reward-performance mechanisms can be generalized in the following simple form:

$$\text{Reward} = \text{function (performance, systemic factors)}$$

Reward should be identified as total reward so that all elements of bonding management to the organization are considered. Practically speaking, however, monetary rewards are what need to be emphasized in the future because they represent a command over real resources and are most closely associated with financial market structure. The systemic-factors variable should be thought of as the collection of all types of noneconomic factors that affect rewards, for example, hierarchical salary administration systems, culture, the nature of the production management process, and so on. Performance is the vector of specific outcomes that result in monetary payoffs. The functional form mapping reward to performance and systemic factors is the linkage that needs to be specified. The functional form is likely to be much more complicated for systemic factors than for performance.

Although this chapter is titled "The New Performance Measures," what is really needed is a new emphasis on performance; there is a real need to emphasize specific performance over the systemic variables in the reward equation. This shift in emphasize should improve the development of performance measurement systems and provide a better linkage of performance with reward.

The Economist's Approach

The design and administration of most large-scale reward-performance mechanisms has been, primarily, the domain of the human resources professional. Issues such as pay equity, legal compliance, corporate culture, and psychological factors dominate the theory and practice of reward systems. Because recent trends emphasize shareholders' wealth, it might be worth exploring what economists have to say about this issue. A central approach to their discipline is discovering conditions that maximize organizational efficiency.

In its simplest form, economic theory prescribes that wage rates (rewards) be equal to marginal revenue product. An additional unit of labor should be paid the value of the firm's output attributable to that unit of labor. In this purely competitive world, reward and performance are directly and inextricably linked by competition in the markets for labor and the company's product. This model has been adapted to include more realistic conditions, such as less-than-perfect competition, different labor-skill sets from investments in human capital, and labor immobility. But the central approach of the economist remains: A company seeking to maximize profits will reward its workers on their ability to produce output that can be sold. There is no doubt that the practical administration of a reward system must encompass more factors than those in the economist's predictive models, but the lack of a significant emphasis on performance in many corporate reward programs must be seriously questioned.

Shareholder value maximization has been incorporated into the economist's models. Again, in its simplest competitive form, a firm will maximize shareholder value by employing labor at a wage equal to marginal value product or the increase in shareholder wealth associated with increased output. This approach introduces conditions in financial markets (both debt and equity markets) along with the labor and product market influences. In short, workers' rewards are influenced directly by stock prices and interest rates. There is, no doubt, a chasm between these optimization models and real world practice, but the many corporate restructurings now occurring may well be narrowing this chasm.

In the past decade, economists have introduced related theories that are beginning to address the central performance issues. If shareholders are seeking to maximize wealth, they must rely on top management to achieve this result, because management is acting as an agent for the shareholder. Agency theory, although not practical enough to be immediately implementable, shows the need to bond management's interest with those of the shareholders. Agency theory provides a sound basis for demonstrating that management's decision-making outcomes will better serve the shareholder if share price is introduced into management's reward-performance equation.

Performance-Measurement Systems

Peter Drucker, along with many other popular commentators, is questioning the accountability and legitimacy of big-company management. He also has recognized the need to focus on the shareholders' interests, but he readily points out that this focus alone may be too narrow. In an article in *The Economist*, Drucker stated:

> The (corporate) raiders are surely right to assert that a company must be run for performance rather than for the benefit of its management. They are, however, surely wrong in defining "performance" as nothing but immediate, short-term gains for shareholders.[3]

Drucker underscores two important considerations in the construction of better reward-performance mechanisms: the time frame problem and multiple stakeholders.[4]

The Time Frame Problem

Every management process has a time dimension. Quarterly results make up annual operating budgets, which roll into long-term strategic plans. Performance needs to be assessed in some time dimension, and compensation needs to be delivered in some time dimension, although the time dimensions need not necessarily be the same. The convention in most top management performance measures is to use one year as short term and a multiyear time frame as long term. This is nothing more than convention. It was the accountants who decided that fiscal years were important units of observation. There are, however, some critical factors to be considered in arriving at the appropriate time frame for management's performance measurement in any one specific situation—namely, the underlying risk of the business, the experience of the management team, and the real or implied management contract.

The inherent risk of the business and how it is being financed should be expressly considered in establishing time frames. Risky business or projects have less predictable outcomes. Therefore, at least before the fact, management's ability to control outcomes is reduced when com-

---

[3]Peter Drucker, "Peter Drucker's 1990s," *The Economist*, October 21, 1989, pp. 19–24.
[4]Much of the discussion in the next two sections of this chapter were excerpted from my previous article, "A Framework for Top Management Performance Standards," *Topics in Total Compensation*, Panel Publishers, Inc., Greenvale, N.Y., Vol. 1, No. 1, 1986, pp. 23–36.

pared with the control it has over less risky, more predictable businesses or projects. This is the nature of risk. Longer time frames are needed for management not only to understand the dynamics of the business but also to learn how much impact it can have on outcomes.

Management's experience is another important factor to consider in deciding on time frames. It should seem obvious, but often is not in practice, that the more experienced the management team is, the less likely that it will need to focus only on the short term. Experience in either an industry or a specific company gives managers a better ability to know their capabilities. Experienced managers should be assessed on longer time frames. They are more aware of what impact their actions will have on the outcomes of the business. They are also in a better position to know what actions will improve short-term performance at the expense of longer-term results, and they should be measured, and given incentive to behave this way, only if that is the desired result.

The real or implied management contract also must be taken into account for performance time horizons. Obviously, a formal, negotiated contract with a given term should be consistent with the time frame of the performance measures. What is often overlooked is the importance of the contract that is implied in the corporate culture. Those corporate environments that produce stability and little turnover can often produce an environment in which management is encouraged to focus on the long term. Failures or mistakes that do not violate the cultural standards of the company are encouraged as learning devices. Setting the time frame for performance measures in this type of environment should clearly favor the longer term.

Multiple Shareholders

A corporation has many stakeholders. The shareholders are the principal stakeholders as owners and suppliers of equity capital. Suppliers of debt capital are also stakeholders, and so are employees, customers, and key suppliers of raw materials or services. At any one time, the objectives of these stakeholders could be different. They can also vary over time, and they can each have very different time horizons. Top management has to consider and balance the objectives of all these stakeholders.

The shareholder as the owner presents a complex situation. It is easy to assume that management, acting as agent for the shareholders, should maximize share price. This ignores some major problems, such as the shareholders' total portfolio objectives (that is, share price maximization at what risk and over what time period). Increased institutional holdings of equities as well as arbitrage activity raise some difficult issues as to what shareholders are really trying to achieve and how management should represent them. Arbitragers looking for overvalued or undervalued stocks, in most cases, are going to have significantly different objectives and time frames than other stakeholders such as employees or customers.

Nevertheless, the shareholders own the company and it has to be taken as given that top management's performance measures must be driven with this central fact in mind. Share price, and the components that make it up, are imperfect measures, but they represent the most direct link between the owners and their agents—top management. The competing claims of the other stakeholders must be balanced as constraints on management's achieving the satisfaction of the shareholder.

The Shareholder Value Chain

A useful way of evaluating key management performance measurements is to start with the shareholder as the prime stakeholder and consider those factors that work to build value—the shareholder value chain. Top management must ultimately build value for owners of the company through its planning and implementation of key decisions. It must make these decisions by considering the objectives of the company's other major claimants—the customers, employees, and suppliers.

The shareholder value chain, shown in Figure 25-1 attempts to relate the major performance measures to share price and in this way connects shareholder value with the objectives of the other claimants. The links in the chain, and their interrelationship, are discussed in the following sections.

Cash Flow/Dividend Stream. The limitations of using share price maximization alone as the key indicator of management's performance

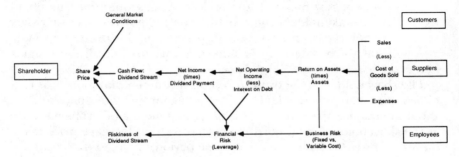

Figure 25-1. Shareholder value chain.

for shareholder value creation have already been discussed. The next link in the chain is to evaluate the immediate determinants of share price. There are numerous theories behind the specific determinants of stock price. Regardless of the specific functional form used, they are all based on a current and expected future cash flow to the investor, which has certain risk characteristics associated with it. In general, a company's stock price is based on the market's assessment of these cash flows as well as general market conditions.

The cash flow to the investor primarily takes the form of dividends. A company's dividend record is a critical measure of management's performance. Changes in dividend payments, up or down, send important messages to shareholders about the performance of their agents. The underlying riskiness of these dividend streams, however, is not often explicitly measured. Other links in the chain need to be examined, such as financial leverage or the deployment of the company's assets.

Net Income. The link to the dividend cash flow is a company's net income and its dividend payout rate. The dividend payout rate is not a useful performance measure. Management must balance the need for internally generated capital and help manage financial risk through leverage. This strategy sends a positive message to shareholders by continually increasing cash dividend payments. Net income, therefore, becomes a central link in the value chain. Net income is the most commonly used measure of top management's performance. It is not influenced by some of the extraneous factors that affect share price. It measures performance before any dividend payout decision is made. Management should decide whether dividends need to be retained in the business or paid out to shareholders. The shareholder will adjust his or her holdings of the company according to his or her need for current cash or future growth and expected price appreciation.

Net Operating Income. Net operating income, or net income before interest on debt and extraordinary items, is a good measure of a company's underlying earnings power. It measures management's performance in deploying the company's assets. Net operating income separates management's performance in deploying the company's assets from the way it finances them. When interest on debt is held aside, the financial risk of leverage can be seen in a better perspective. The company's assets can be finances from equity (externally generated by selling more shares or internally generated from retained earnings) or debt. Top management's performance for financing company assets is its cost of this financing—the paid earnings multiple for capital and interest for debt. Except under severe conditions, such as a Chapter 11 bankruptcy situation, financing costs are rarely focused on as a performance measure in themselves.

Financial Risk.   Financial risk, as measured in a company's leverage, is an important measure in assessing the quality of earnings or cash flow. Cases of excessively high leverage may require explicit measures to focus attention on correcting a problem, such as asset sales. Cases of very low leverage may result in greenmail. Investors' concerns about management's ability to deploy capital force them to borrow and increase leverage to buy back accumulated stock or lose control.

Business Risk.   Business risk is that risk associated with how a company has employed its assets. It can take the form of large fixed noncash charges to earnings, such as depreciation, if the assets are heavily employed in plant and equipment. It is also related to the underlying market conditions of each business in which the company has invested and the overall portfolio of businesses. Business risk is difficult to measure explicitly and is rarely used as a performance measure. The return on a company's assets, net operating income per dollar of assets, should, however, be related to the amount of business risk that a company is willing to assume. Securities and Exchange Commission (SEC) requirements for line-of-business reporting in financial statements attempt to keep investors informed of the underlying business risk of the company. If net operating income is to be used as a performance measure, then the nature and deployment of assets must be explicitly considered.

Deployment and Use of Assets.   The deployment and utilization of assets represents the final link in the shareholder value chain. Asset usage generates sales and commensurate costs, which result in cash flows to the other major stockholders. Costs of one type or another, usually normalized on sales, are often used as performance measures. Many types of manufacturing businesses have developed standards for cost of goods sold or other measures of investor's turnover. These performance measures have long been used by bankers in assessing management's short-term performance and its ability to pay down working capital lines of credit.

Conclusion

There is clearly a need to emphasize performance more directly in the compensation structure of most corporations. Market forces will dictate this change if managements are not proactive enough.

The focus of emphasis presented in this chapter is the creation of shareholder value—an emphasis dictated more by financial analysis than by the human resources function. The simple model of the shareholder value chain presented shows the various subcomponents that produce shareholder value. The intent is to illustrate that there are interrelationships of other variables that, if used appropriately, can serve as alternatives or compliments to stock price.

The specific application of models, such as the shareholder value chain, to reward systems will not be easy. Factors such as industry type, organizational structure, and company strategy will have to be considered when trying to apply these approaches to compensation plans. Managements that continue to try to keep a close fit between share price dynamics and reward-performance mechanisms, however, should be in better position to deal with the market trends of the 1990s.

26
Executive Compensation Systems: Pay Follows Strategy or Strategy Follows Pay?

Johannes M. Pennings

Department of Management
The Wharton School, University of Pennsylvania

There has been a great deal of controversy about the connection between executive pay and performance. Criticism in the popular business press abounds about top executives being overpaid, particularly in the face of less-than-outstanding results of their corporation. Numerous academic researchers have countered such criticism by their findings on the link between pay and performance. Yet, there remains a great deal of skepticism about the feasibility of tying compensation to performance. This skepticism becomes even more profound if the focus is on strategic performance. There are issues to address, such as what constitutes executive compensation and strategic performance and how to construe their connection. This chapter reviews these issues.

An overwhelming proportion of U.S. corporations have an executive compensation system or plan. Usually, it covers a comparatively small number of executives, although in some cases this number might exceed 50 persons. The underlying assumption is that these top managers have a disproportionate influence on corporate performance and have the leverage to direct their firm's strategic destiny. Executive compensation plans, therefore, can be labeled as "strategic reward systems." Most of these plans have been devised by compensation consulting firms. Although each firm's system might have its own unique attributes, there is also an increased convergence among corporations in the manner in which these systems are designed. The mechanical features and the formal attributes for making compensation decisions should be distinguished from the behavior and attitudes among those involved. This chapter examines both.

Conceptual Issues in Executive Compensation

Linking executive pay to performance is surprisingly difficult, because it is not easy to define the proper terms. Executive pay includes a myriad of elements, some of which defy attempts to assign them to a specific time period. For example, the pay associated with stock options can be measured at the time they are granted, at the time they get exercised, at the time the exercised options are sold by the beneficiary, the stock or cash dividends associated with those stock options during the time they were exercised but not yet sold, and so on. Similar problems exist in the interpretation of "deferred" compensation, pension contributions, and golden parachutes, where one or more executives are to receive a generous cash payment in the event of being forced to resign by a corporate raider. Even more difficult to interpret are perks, whose cash value may be small but whose symbolic meaning is highly salient. This latter aspect cannot be sufficiently emphasized. Compensation is only one of a variety of incentives. Power, status, and achievement rival compensation in their prominence for executives. In European and Pacific Basin cultures, such nonpecuniary outcomes may even exceed pay in their importance to top executives.[1] Furthermore, one should not only look at the level of compensation, but also at the profile. The profile represents the relative size of base salary, bonuses, long-term incentive compensation, stock options, and the perks' cash value. The profile is often depicted with a pie chart, showing the relative magnitude of the various compensation components.

Performance in general, and strategic performance in particular, are even more difficult to delineate. Firms resort to financial, short-term operational and accounting indicators, such as return on investment or return on equity, in choosing the criteria for decisions regarding executive compensation. When trying to endow performance with some strategic meaning, they tend to stretch such indicators over a multiyear period, the assumption being that elongating the time frame renders such performance measures strategic. It clearly substitutes accounting performance measures for (capital) market measures and draws executives' attention from short-term to long-term time horizons. Whether such pay bases deserve the label "strategic" is not quite evident. Examples of such long-term pay systems are those whereby cost of capital is related to return on equity over a 5-year period—the so-called par line—and the executives are given some long-term bonus (phantom stocks or performance shares) based on the latter's exceeding the former. Such procedures tend to blur the meaning of performance and can be challenged on their strategic relevance because the essence of "strategic" may reach farther than merely the time frame under consideration. The matter becomes far more nebulous and complicated when the issue of tying pay to performance pertains to the marginal contribution to (strategic) performance, which can be attributed to the CEO or any other executive. Economists consider the marginal productivity of labor to be equivalent to compensation: The higher an executive's marginal productivity, the greater his or her pay. It is particularly this issue that confronts the practice and research on executive compensation systems.

The link between pay and corporate strategy can be examined in two distinct ways. Compensation plans might emanate from a firm's strategy, or they may be a key antecedent through which strategic objectives get realized.

Linking pay to strategy, therefore, can be decomposed into two questions: (1) What is the meaning of executive compensation derived from or as part of the firm's strategy? and (2) What role does it play in the implementation of strategic objectives? For example, the adoption of

[1]Johannes M. Pennings, "Strategic Reward Systems: A Cross-National Comparison," working paper, The Jones Center, The Wharton School, University of Pennsylvania, 1990.

golden parachutes can be construed as part of the firm's strategy to fend off hostile takeovers and to further tie executives to their firm. Yet those golden parachutes may result in conservative choices and discourage executives from taking risks or being innovative.

In this chapter we view strategy broadly. Strategy formulation entails the long-term decisions about markets, products, customer segments, technology, and human resources. Strategy represents an effort to match corporate resources with environmental opportunities. The strategic choice to operate in a given market with a given technology and other resources is relatively enduring and long-lasting.[2] For example, committing vast resources to a new technology, establishing a solid tradition of lifetime employment and promotion from within such that the firm becomes an "internal labor market," or diversifying to overseas markets all represent significant decisions with profound strategic implications that are mirrored in decisions about executive pay. Compensation practices are part and parcel of such a long-lasting strategic posture.

Strategy implementation represents a set of decisions to preserve ongoing strategic commitments but also to succeed in turning a firm's strategic trajectory around. The reorganization of a firm's design, changes in culture and human resources, and the use of compensation as a lever of strategic change are elements of strategic turnaround. Of course, they can also function as a vehicle for preserving the strategic status quo. The point is that executive compensation systems can have profound strategic, unanticipated consequences regardless of whether or not those practices emerged from a given strategic posture. The implication is that executive pay may be the result of a given strategy, or it may be the cause of a strategy.

To better grasp this paradox, it is useful to consider the contribution of Chandler. In his classic monograph, *Strategy and Structure*, Chandler advocated the argument that strategic changes—such as the move from single-product to multiproduct offerings—necessitated changes in organizational structure, planning processes, and staffing; in short, structure follows strategy. In the absence of such restructuring, the firm's strategic turnaround would falter.[3] Others have criticized this thesis. Hall and Saias suggested that it is the change in structure, personnel, planning, and other organizational practices that enable a firm to change its strategy; strategy follows structure.[4] Both views might

---

[2]John Child, "Organizational Structure, Environment and Performance: The Role of Strategic Choice," *Sociology*, Vol. 6, 1972, pp. 1–22.

[3]Alfred Chandler, *Strategy and Structure*, MIT Press, Cambridge, Mass., 1962.

[4]D. J. Hall and M. A. Saias, "Strategy Follows Structure," *Strategic Management Journal*, Vol. 1, pp. 149–163.

Pay Follows Strategy:	Strategy Formulation:
	• Discretion
	• Proactive/Reactive Posture
	• Diversification
	• Industry Factors
	• Labor Markets
Strategy Follows Pay:	Strategy Implementation:
	• Motivation
	• Decision-making Patterns
	• Operational/Strategic Performance

Figure 26-1. Antecedents and consequences of executive compensation.

have a kernel of truth in that the firm's strategic posture sets the stage for various decisions regarding people, structure, and planning. Yet, the results of those decisions often acquire their own momentum and have their own consequences.

A similar argument can be developed on the role of executive compensation and strategy. Compensation practices might trigger certain strategic behaviors on the part of those who are governed under a certain compensation system, but those very systems may mirror strategic decisions that are an integral part of the grand strategic design. Separating cause and effect may be tenuous.

This chapter further reviews these issues. On one hand, we explore questions on the design of executive reward systems, particularly how such designs may reflect a strategic frame of mind. On the other hand, we review the strategic implications or consequences of executive compensation. In the first case, one might say that executive pay emerges as part and parcel of the intended or formulated strategy, whereas the consequences of pay can be construed as elements of the strategy as realized or implemented. Figure 26-1 lists some of the most important strategic antecedents and consequences of executive pay.

Strategic Determinants of Executive Compensation

The strategic posture of the firm and the sort of markets in which it has chosen to compete are crucial to shaping the level and profile of executive compensation. The pay profile is also a function of the degree of strategic diversification and the competitive conditions in the industry. The compensation practices vary a great deal depending on whether firms compete in a discretionary versus constrained industry, and on whether they are proactive versus reactive in the strategic orientation they assume. Firms reveal different compensation profiles. Those in discretionary industries have a proactive posture stressing variable and continent pay, such as bonuses and long-term incentive compensation. In contrast, more passive firms in constrained industries tend to stress fixed and noncontingent pay, such as base salary.[5] Ironically, even so-called variable forms of pay, such as bonuses or profit sharing, may be set in such a way that they become a fixed feature of executive pay. In 1982 *Fortune Magazine* mentioned a firm which promised bonuses if return on equity exceeded 6 percent, even though the firm was accustomed to a level exceeding 11 percent! The implication is that these bonuses were not at risk, and construing them as "variable" would be deceptive.

A discretionary industry is one in which the firm enjoys a great deal of latitude in crafting its own strategy. Whether or not firms operate in a discretionary industry hinges on their ability to measure and anticipate market developments. Thus, marketing research and geopolitical forecasts enable some firms to tune in to strategically important trends and to take anticipatory action. Furthermore, they may enjoy some leverage in shaping consumer demands or diffusing product innovations. Commodity markets or public utility firms tend to have little discretion, whereas firms in the financial services, cosmetics, and entertainment industries have selected relatively free markets. Particularly in such free markets, one would expect strategically aggressive firms to adopt compensation practices with high variations in levels of pay and to differentiate the profile of pay. For example, it has been found that pay levels or pay profiles vary considerably among firms in discretionary industries with a proactive posture.[6]

Diversified firms have the potential to tailor an executive's compensation package to the very market to which he or she has been assigned. This lies at the heart of so-called strategic reward maps, as drawn by strategic compensation consultants such as the Boston Consulting Group and Booz Allen.[7] The strategic product matrix of the firm is

[5]Johannes M. Pennings, and David T. Bussard, "Strategy, Control and Executive Compensation: Fitting the Incentive Plan to the Company," *Topics in Total Compensation*, Vol. 1, 1987, pp. 101–112.

[6]*Ibid.*

[7]Louis J. Brandisi, *Creating Shareholder Value: A New Mission for Executive Compensation*, Booz Allen, New York, N.Y., 1984.

mapped on to the compensation plan. Its fixed and variable pay components dovetail with the strategic imperatives of the various product markets. They propose to design the compensation profile in such a way as to reflect the riskiness and time horizon of the different marketplaces together with the corresponding strategic intent of the firm. For example, Booz Allen distinguishes between the risk posture (ratio of contingent pay to salary) and time focus (ratio of long-term to short-term variable compensation). As dichotomies, they furnish a two-by-two matrix that is to match the strategic mandate of various divisions. A cash cow division (large market share, low-growth) requires a package with low risk posture and short time horizon; the bulk of its executive pay could consist of a salary. The evidence to date suggests, however, that firms are reluctant to strongly differentiate compensation practices by divisions; rather, they adopt a uniform system.

Compensation Norms in Industries and Executive Labor Markets

A relevant part of a firm's strategy for compensation considerations centers around the recruitment and retention of members. Firms prefer to conform to industry norms of compensation but, as with strategy in general, human strategies can also be compared on their reactivity. It is likely that conformity to compensation norms is stronger when firms resort to a great deal of external recruitment of executive talent. A strategy of bolstering an internal labor market might render a firm somewhat immune from such norms, which are a key ingredient in strategic choices about human resources and executive labor markets. Compensation consultants such as Booz Allen, Towers, Perrin, Forster & Crosby, and the Hay Group have a great impact in promoting and institutionalizing certain compensation plans. They solidify existing practices or disseminate novel ones, thereby setting certain trends. There are both industry norms and compensation norms for various societies. Compensation innovations proliferate, but, as in the world of fashion, the compensation consultancy industry has its own designers of pay systems whose diffusion reflects the eagerness of companies and their boards to stay competitive. For example, the adoption of long-term incentive compensation plans by American corporations reveals a certain degree of faddishness.[8] Organization theorists would argue that such

---

[8]David Larcker, "The Association Between Performance Plan Adoption and Corporate Capital Investment," *Journal of Accounting and Economics*, Vol. 5, 1983, pp. 3–30.

imitations are less induced by the desire to create an optimum incentive for strategic behavior; rather, they should be attributed to pressures to conformity in order to acquire legitimacy and to convey the illusion of sound management.[9] Sophisticated compensation plans, disseminated in 10-K or proxy statements, confer public credibility and preserve the competitiveness in attracting and retaining high-level executives. An even more sharp standpoint would hold that compensation plans represent fossilized practices that have become uncoupled from the actual compensation, but serve to placate the external audience.

For high-level executives, such plans disclose how well the firm is in tune with the marketplace for executive talent. The numerous executive compensation surveys have contributed to the specification of the price of managerial labor—both the level and the proportion that is fixed versus variable. They permit a firm to set a pay range with relative, precise bounds for executives in certain industries. A great amount of research remains to be done here, however. For executives as a labor pool, there are issues such as who is in it and who is not, especially if we define the pool to coincide with a firm's industry or its strategic group. Executive search firms, together with compensation consultants, may assist firms in their human resources strategies, but they themselves may blur the boundaries between industries. Also, many firms are reluctant to go to the external labor market;[10] they prefer to bolster internal succession. In this case, the firm is more likely to resemble an *internal* labor market. At the present time we do not know to what extent internal versus external labor markets affect the level or profile of executive compensation. As suggested before, when the firm represents a well-established internal labor market (and its executives have high-quitting barriers because their human capital is vested in and idiosyncratic to their firm), compensation may be modest or below the industry norm. Yet, compensation is likely to exceed the level that would be required to retain its executives.

Strategic Consequences of Executive Pay

It seems more interesting to consider the strategic implications of the level and profile of executive compensation. After all, executive com-

[9]Paul J. Dimaggio and Walter W. Powell, "The Iron Cage Revisited: Institutional Isomorphism and Collective Rationality in Organizational Fields," *American Sociological Review*, Vol. 48, 1983, pp. 147–160.

[10]Dan R. Dalton and Idalene F. Kesner, "Organization Performance as an Antecedent of Inside/Outside Chief Executive Succession: An Empirical Assessment," *Academy of Management Journal*, Vol. 28, 1985, pp. 749–762.

pensation can be paraphrased as strategic reward system. Top executives, in general, and the CEO in particular, are governed by a reward system that is usually segregated from the general compensation systems affecting other employees. The reasons for establishing a separate compensation system are numerous. Presumably, executives have an undue impact on the strategic results of the firm. Furthermore, as we have seen, such reward systems are often linked to long-term performance criteria, such as the spread between return on equity versus the cost of capital over a 5-year period. Although such criteria are financial and reflect the vicissitudes of the market, many view them as strategic in that the choice behavior of senior executives might be conditioned by such criteria.

There has been a greater deal of research done on pay as a motivator of job performance, but virtually all this effort has been confined to lower-level employees. Thus, we do not know whether executive motivation is different from that of other occupational groups, nor do we know much about the motivational efficacy of executive compensation systems. Theoretical developments among management researchers have also failed to come up with comprehensive statements on these issues.

To fully explicate this state of affairs, it may be helpful to highlight two theoretical traditions that are deemed crucial in understanding work motivation and job performance. They are expectancy theory and agency theory.

Expectancy Theory

Expectancy theory originates in organizational psychology and holds that a person's motivation is a function of two expectancies. The first one is the expectation that a certain level of effort will lead to a given performance level (for example, "If I try, it is very likely that I will succeed in meeting my sales quota."). The higher this subjective probability, the greater the level of effort.

Performance should be viewed in very general terms. It includes both job performance, such as productivity and return on investment, as well as membership performance. *Membership* includes decisions about joining or staying, but also other commitment-revealing behaviors such as long working hours.

The second expectancy consists of the subjective belief that performance results in outcomes or rewards having an attractive value to the person. They include pay, but also the earlier-mentioned rewards of power, status, and challenge. Crucial is the assumption that individuals differ in their values such that each and every individual may not be equally motivated by the same rewards. Executives might value rewards that are different from those of other groups of employees; even among themselves, there may be differences in values. Yet, most executive compensation systems treat executives in a standardized way, thereby ignoring their differential sensitivity to levels or profiles of pay. They differ also cross-culturally. It may be such differences in values that render the executive compensation systems of Towers, Perrin, Forster & Crosby and the Hay Group less effective in societies other than the United States.[11]

Apart from the fact that U.S. compensation practices may have limited applicability elsewhere, there are two other issues to consider. First, it is essential that strategic performance criteria be unequivocally related to executive pay. If the time lag between effort and performance is long, the individual is less likely to perceive a clear relationship. Furthermore, under such conditions, factors other than those related to an executive's effort or business acumen may be perceived to affect strategic performance. They may include acts of God, government intervention, technological breakthroughs, executive labor markets, or business cycles. Furthermore, executive compensation plans, including golden parachutes, cover a group of executives in spite of performance accruing from an individual effort. It may be an opportunity for a free ride. These considerations go also at the heart of the question of "whether the CEO makes a difference"—a question that involves a great deal of contemporary research on executive succession and, by implication, executive compensation.

The second issue involves the expectancy that strategic performance is related to pay. As was already mentioned, strategic performance is a complicated phenomenon. Apart from financial performance indicators that have been stretched out over a long time period, most firms have tried little to expand the criteria by which strategic performance can be gauged. Financial performance bases of compensation are tied to either accounting measures, such as the efficient use of corporate or divisional assets, or to market measures, such as those that link shareholder wealth with equity cost of capital to the well-being of the executives. Other nonfinancial criteria could include the development of successors, the creation of embryo businesses, or a sustained level of technological innovation and the nurturing and commercial introduction of new products or services. Such performance yardsticks are not

[11]Johannes M. Pennings, "Strategic Reward Systems: A Cross-National Comparison," working paper, The Jones Center, The Wharton School, University of Pennsylvania, 1990.

necessarily embedded in short-term or long-term measures of financial performance.

"Corporations get the sort of behaviors they reward" is an often heard lament of expectancy theorists, and in principle, this should also hold for executives. If corporations like to entice executives to certain types of behavior and performance, they should make sure that such performance is feasible and convey a clear connection between certain performance criteria and pay. Also crucial is the assumption that pay itself should have a strong inducement or "valence"—whether symbolic or by virtue of its buying power. Accounting criteria-based incentive plans tend to direct managerial motivation to short-term behaviors to improve performance on the indexes chosen. Furthermore, such indexes are susceptible to accounting bias and manipulation. In contrast, market-based performance indicators, such as 5-year earnings per share, could induce executives toward high-risk decisions, particularly those involving external debt financing. A study by David Larcker is particularly intriguing. This accounting researcher found that the adoption of long-term performance plans lead to subsequent increases in capital expenditures. The effect disappeared, however, after the first year of adoption. From an expectancy theory standpoint, this suggests several concerns. First, it is important to have a sustained and unabating link between rewards and motivated behaviors and performance. Second, it is important to preserve the immediacy and saliency between rewards and performance. Long time periods or routinization of compensation decisions may dissipate the initial trigger that a new compensation plan has brought about. Third, long-term performance plans may be flawed in that the market does not always recognize the strategic strength of the firm. Ultimately, the firm (or its board of directors) seeks to reward those behaviors or performances that it considers most desirable, which may be at variance with executives' behaviors or performances, owing to the executives' motives.

Agency Theory

According to agency theorists, executives are controlled by a "contract" drawn up between them and the board of directors. The contract can pertain to behaviors (for example, implementation of strategic budgets) or to performance (for example, maintaining return on assets for certain markets or augmenting earnings per share). Such contracts are fraught with all kinds of difficulties. For example, the senior executives may have knowledge to which the board has no access. Agency problems can be alleviated by establishing more elaborate information systems. Also, and here executive pay considerations come in, the board makes the executives part of the payoff structure in the form of contingent rewards systems. Such contracts alleviate the need for highly sophisticated monitoring devices, but they also result in the sharing of risks between shareholders and executives. The interests of shareholders and executives may not always be congruent. Unlike the former, the latter do not enjoy much flexibility in diversifying their risks. Particularly when executives hold large amounts of stock or their pay profile shows them to be heavily saddled with risk, they may be tempted to shun risky alternatives, even though pursuing them may be in the best interests of the shareholders.

Jensen and Meckling have indicated that senior executives, the CEO not excluded, often avoid risk because they attempt to preserve their status and tenure in the company.[12] By modifying the pay profile, these authors believe that risk-taking behaviors can be encouraged. In contrast, the level of pay may be dysfunctional for motivating certain behaviors or results. Although the evidence to date is scant, there appears to be support for such an opinion. Rapoport showed, for example, a direct relationship between the magnitude of long-term incentive compensation and the amount of research and development expenditures.[13] The profile of executive compensation appears to foster specific strategic decisions. Such findings suggest that under certain conditions it is possible to evoke comparatively desirable types of decisions. One should be alert about dysfunctional or strategically undesirable behaviors as well.

The research by Healey is noteworthy here. He found that executives tinkered with their information and control system to inflate the size of their bonus payments.[14] By refashioning the way financial results are reported, they were focusing their attention on the management of appearance rather than the management of performance. The research also highlighted a major example of agency problems (for example, the asymmetry of information between the CEO as "agent" and the board or stockholders as his or her "principal"), which the former may be tempted to exploit for his or her own advantage.[15]

---

[12]Michael C. Jensen and William H. Meckling, "Theory of the Firm: Management Behavior, Agency Costs, and Ownership Structure," *Journal of Financial Economics*, Vol. 3, 1976, pp. 305–360.

[13]A. Rapoport, "Executive Incentives Versus Corporate Growth," *Harvard Business Review*, Vol. 56, 1978, pp. 81–88.

[14]P. M. Healey, "The Effect of Bonus Schemes on Accounting," *Journal of Accounting and Economics*, Vol. 3, 1985, pp. 85–107.

[15]Eugene Fama, "Agency Problems and Theory of the Firm," *Journal of Political Economy*, Vol. 88, 1980, pp. 288–306.

Expectancy and Agency
Theories: A Synthesis

This discussion suggests that there is some overlap and complement between expectancy theory and agency theory. Although the former has psychological origins and focuses on the motivational effects of reward systems on the incumbent, the latter has an economic/accounting origin and stresses the contractual relationship with the incentive structure designed in such a way as to align the interest of the executives and the shareholders. It would appear that these two traditions provide enough support for some propositions on the strategic consequences of executive compensation. Expectancy research assumes that individuals are different and will respond differently to a given situation; it would answer questions such as, "What behavior is motivated by a given reward system?" and, "What values and other motivational attributes (for example, tolerance for risk, need for financial success, and so on) of various executives are present such that their response to a given reward system can be anticipated?"Agency theorists tend to have an economic/rationalistic view of people and assume that each person will respond to an incentive package in a predictable way. Its major advantage is that it forces the questions: What objectives are to be attained in this time horizon? Are they short term or long term? What milestones should be furnished to direct executives toward strategic targets? In concrete terms, such questions translate into specific statements, such as the amount of risk taking desired.

Figure 26-2 provides a simplified diagram. The firm's information and control system provides data on either operational (accounting) and/or strategic (market) performance indicators. The former includes return on equity, return on sales, return on investments, and net cash flow and might pertain to overall corporate performance or group, divisional, or strategic business unit (SBU) performance. Strategic indicators include 5-year earnings per share, book-to-market value, or other measures. Such indicators tend to apply to corporate-level performance only. In other words, they cannot easily be disaggregated to organizational subunits unless one resorts to accounting measures such as research and development/assets, new product development/assets or even "softer" measures, such as the amount of new management talent nurtured.

Assuming that information and control systems embody a variety of performance evaluation criteria, their link with pay can be represented bidirectionally. The arrows from reward to performance belong to the

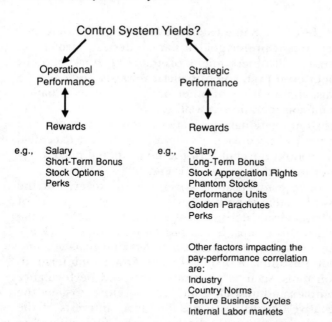

Figure 26-2. Effect of rewards on performance (expectancy theory) and specific performance requiring certain rewards (agency theory).

realm of expectancy theory, whereas the reverse arrows fit agency theory. It should be obvious that these bidirectional linkages should overlap, or should at least be consistent. Only under such conditions will the pay-strategy relationship be optimal.

Conclusion

Under the auspices of expectancy theory, a number of outcomes or rewards can be tied to these performance indicators. Conventional types include salary, short-term bonuses, long-term bonuses, stock options, stock appreciation rights, phantom stocks, and performance units. For such rewards to have a motivational impact, it is important that their connection to performance be direct, immediate, and salient. Random fluctuations of the stock price, the tightening of executive labor markets, the influence of national values in setting compensation levels, and compensation profiles tend to diminish the correlation between pay and long-term, comprehensive performance indicators, resulting in a less-than-effective motivational impact. Expectancy theories stress the importance of individual differences. Such differences suggest the necessity of pay profile differences. Some executives might prefer deferred compensation. Others might prefer golden parachutes as a protection against unemployment. Still others might prefer risky stock options. Some executives might even prefer nonfinancial rewards, such as time for family, sabbaticals, and a variety of other perks. Their tax situation might be an important consideration as well. Last, but not least, particularly when a firm is a multinational corporation, there is probably even a greater need to customize executive pay systems. Ideally, the executive compensation system should dovetail with the motivational makeup of the executive in order to render it most efficient.

Efficiency of executive compensation systems is, however, not the only issue. The reward system should also yield the type or quality of performance that is strategically desirable. Agency theory spells out the conditions under which this is most likely. Stock options and stock appreciation rights, for example, may diminish risk-taking behavior and promote a temptation to stimulate dividend yield. Other long-term incentive compensation tools, such as phantom stocks and performance units, may be too complex and unwieldy and fail, therefore, to align the direction of an executive's efforts with the long-term interests of the shareholders. Such plans require a thorough communication and coaching such that the plans become meaningful and significant. It appears that this is the major challenge of current executive compensation consulting and research.

27
Employment Agreements

Linda E. Rappaport, Esq.
Partner, Shearman & Sterling

Introduction

The employment arrangements of America's senior corporate executives have become a favorite topic for the financial press. Coverage of the details of lucrative compensation packages has become commonplace, with special emphasis being placed on the amounts earned by the executives. For example, *Business Week*'s May 1989 publication of the results of its thirty-ninth annual survey of executive compensation indicated that, for the first time ever, the average annual salary and bonus for CEOs of surveyed companies topped $1 million, and their aggregate annual compensation exceeded $2 million.[1] Also, in May 1989 *The New York Times* gave prominent coverage to the estimated $120 million compensation package given by Warner Communications Inc. to its CEO, Steven J. Ross, which, according to *The New York Times*, was set forth in his "80-odd page employment contract."[2]

[1] J. Byrne, "Is the Boss Getting Paid Too Much?" *Business Week*, May 1, 1989, p. 46.
[2] S. Bartlett, "Talking Deals: Ross's Rich Pact at Time-Warner," *The New York Times*, May 25, 1989, Section D, col. 1, p. 2.

As with the case of Mr. Ross, the terms of an executive's employment and compensation arrangements are frequently embodied in a formal, written document referred to as an "employment agreement." In its 1989 survey of trends in executive compensation, the benefits consulting firm of Mercer-Meidinger-Hansen concluded that of the U.S. companies included in its survey, 33 percent of such companies "provide a long-term employment contract to specified categories of executives."[3] According to the survey, the terms of these contracts vary depending on where the employer's business is located and whether the employer is a publicly held or private company. The terms of an employment agreement are also obviously affected by whether the employer's compensation policy emphasizes cash compensation or some form of incentive compensation, such as stock options, and by the type of position that the executive holds with the employer.

Nevertheless, the decision by the employer to offer an employment agreement to an employee, and the negotiations and contract following the decision to do so, fall into a pattern. Whether the executive involved is one of the foremost corporate leaders in the United States or a young computer whiz, certain common issues will be raised.

The purpose of this chapter is to provide a practical guide to employment agreements—both to the decision whether or not an employer should offer an employment agreement to an executive and to the principal terms commonly covered in one.

When an Employment Agreement Is Appropriate

As a general matter, employment agreements may be viewed as more beneficial to the executive than to the employer. Because they are for a specified term and generally cannot be terminated by the employer prior to the expiration of that term without the payment of monetary damages, employment agreements are an exception to the general "employment at will" doctrine. Under this doctrine, the law in most jurisdictions generally presumes that an employment relationship between employer and employee is for no set term and may be terminated at any

[3]"Trends, Issues and Predictions: Executive Compensation Planning Techniques and Strategies for 1989," William M. Mercer-Meidinger-Hansen Inc., p. 36.

time by the employer for a lawful reason or for no reason.[4] In contrast, an employment agreement obligates the employer to retain the executive for the period and under the terms set forth in the contract, unless the executive breaches the contract. If the employer terminates the executive prior to the expiration of the period of the employment specified in the agreement, the agreement typically will provide for severance benefits to the executive in the form of liquidated damages based, in part, on the compensation the executive would have earned had the executive been permitted to continue to work over the remaining term of the contract. This right to employment under specified terms, and the right to damages under contract if that contract is breached, is the hallmark of the executive's advantage under an employment agreement.

For this reason, employers generally reserve employment agreements only for their most senior or key executives. Additionally, employers generally prefer to avoid the type of arm's-length negotiation with an executive that is inherent in the preparation of an employment agreement.

That having been said, there are some benefits that an employer derives when entering into an employment agreement with an executive. Although it is true that under the U.S. legal system no one can force an individual to remain employed, the existence of an agreement to remain employed for a specified term often serves as a deterrent to the executive's walking away from his or her obligation to the employer. Properly structured terms of employment can also make it costly for an

[4]Over the last two decades, there has been a gradual erosion of the "employment at will" doctrine. In terminating an employee, an employer must carefully consider whether the facts and circumstances of the termination could give rise to a claim for unjust dismissal under any number of federal statutes, including the Age Discrimination in Employment Act of 1967, the Civil Rights Act of 1964, and the Employee Retirement Income Security Act of 1974, or under the comparable state statutes. In addition, many states have enacted laws that address certain employment practices, such as AIDS testing, the use of lie detector tests, or retaliation for so-called whistle-blowing, that may affect the termination decision. Moreover, an increasing number of state courts imply a covenant of "good faith and fair dealing" in the employment relationship between the employer and the employee, even where no written contract exists. This implied covenant has been construed by some courts as an obligation of the employer to provide employees with warning of improper behavior before any termination can take place, and, in some instances, to limit an employer's ability to terminate an employee except in situations constituting "just cause." In addition, the courts in some states interpret an employer's policy manuals and other benefits documents as a written employment contract between employer and employee. Statements in such manuals promising "lifetime" benefits or implying employment for a specified period may be construed by such courts as a written promise of employment for a set period of time. Finally, a number of jurisdictions have created "public policy" exceptions to the employment at will doctrine that prohibit an employer from terminating an employee for certain reasons, such as the employee's failure to perform an unlawful or illegal act (for example, violating a traffic safety law) or an important public duty (for example, jury duty).

executive to resign by providing for forfeitures of accrued but invested long-term compensation and benefits (a so-called golden handcuff). Last, but not least important, the negotiation of an employment agreement provides the employer with the opportunity of placing limited post-termination restrictions on the executive's right to compete with the employer following the termination of the employment relationship.

Preparation of the Agreement and Its Principal Terms

Once the decision to provide an executive with an employment agreement has been made, there are four areas that will generally be addressed in any negotiation between an executive and a prospective employer: (1) the position and duties of the executive and the term of his or her employment, (2) the salary and benefits to be received by the executive during this employment, (3) the consequences of a termination or resignation during the term of the contract, and (4) restrictive covenants, such as agreements not to compete and not to solicit the employer's customers or employees. Certain of these areas, such as position and compensation, typically will have been agreed to prior to the preparation of a written agreement, although their clarification in writing sometimes brings out certain failures in the "meeting of the minds" of the parties; others, such as rights upon termination and restrictive covenants, often result in spirited negotiations prior to the execution of the document. These negotiations can sometimes lead to uncomfortable moments, because they require the executive and the employer to focus on the end of the employment relationship at a time when both parties are justifiably focused on its beginning and its prospects. The negotiators for the principals consequently should bring a good measure of finesse to the proceedings. For this reason, it is helpful to enter the process with a feeling for the objectives of the principal terms of an employment agreement and the parameters within which the provisions of most such contracts generally fall.

Position, Duties, and Term

As an initial matter, the employment agreement typically states the executive's title and reporting obligations. In the case of the CEO, it is not uncommon to have the contract provide that the executive will report directly to the employer's chairperson or board of directors.

The degree of specificity provided in the description of an executive's duties is a function of the negotiation process. Inasmuch as a breach of a term of the employment agreement commonly provides the executive with the right to resign but recover damages under the contract, it is in the interest of the executive that the agreement define duties precisely. By the same token, the employer will be interested in obtaining some flexibility in the determination of the executive's duties to permit the employer to respond to unforeseeable situations without necessitating a renegotiation of the employment agreement.

In situations in which the employer has a number of subsidiaries and affiliates, it is advisable to state in the contract that the executive will serve for no additional compensation as an officer or director of such entities. Frequently, such titles are necessary only for corporate governance purposes, with the duties of the actual positions being within the ambit of the executive's ordinary duties. In addition, if travel will be required as part of the executive's position, it is usually advisable to refer to this fact in the section concerning the executive's duties.

The initial section of the employment agreement will also specify the term of the executive's employment under the contract. Senior executives' employment agreements typically provide for terms of 3 to 5 years, although shorter or longer periods are possible. As a general matter, however, agreements with terms in excess of 7 years are unusual, possibly because of the corporate governance and corporate waste issues that are raised in such situations. Agreements sometimes contain self-executing provisions, commonly referred to as "evergreen provisions," which automatically extend the term of the agreement by specified intervals (usually 1 year), unless advance notice is given by either the employer or the executive not to extend.

Although the term is usually not the subject of protracted discussions in the initial negotiations between the employer and the executive, it is one of the most important provisions in the contract. Employment contracts are written so that upon completion of the term the parties are free to end the employment relationship without penalty or the need to renegotiate the employment relationship for an additional period. The length of the term is also frequently used as the period during which an executive will have the opportunity to earn any applicable incentive compensation. During the term, employers are substantially restricted in their ability to terminate the executive, and, moreover, the damages for any such premature termination typically will be measured by the salary the executive would have earned over the remaining term. If the term is too short, the employment relationship may not be long enough for the parties to achieve the desired business objectives for the employer, but if the term is too long, the employer may be incurring too much risk of liability in the event it becomes necessary to terminate the executive for unanticipated reasons. Consequently, some careful thought should be given to the nature of the services of the executive and the requirements of the employer before a term of employment is set.

Salary and Benefits

The second principal section of the employment agreement establishes the compensation and benefits that the executive will receive during the term. The executive's base salary is typically expressed as a minimum annual rate, and provision is frequently made for its periodic review. Consideration is sometimes given to providing that the minimum annual rate of salary will rise automatically at stated intervals, either by a specified percentage or in relation to a specified measure, such as a particular rate of inflation or consumer price index.

The terms governing the executive's incentive compensation can be extensive and often are the subject of the most protracted discussion. Incentive payments for senior executives generally take two forms: short-term incentive compensation, or the annual bonus, and long-term incentive compensation. Although incentive compensation schemes are infinitely flexible and can be crafted to fit almost any set of circumstances, they commonly fall into a pattern in employment agreements for senior executives. Bonuses are most commonly earned on the basis of both subjective and objective criteria, although an employment agreement will sometimes provide for a guaranteed minimum bonus (however, such guarantees are more into salary than bonuses). When profits are utilized, it is important that the contract specify the precise formula for measuring the criteria and the measurement period used by the employer. It is significant to note that such measurement periods may not coincide with the 12-month periods ending on each anniversary of the executive's employment. When this is the case, the contract will need to provide for *pro rata* or delayed payment of bonuses.

Long-term incentive compensation refers to compensation intended to reward the executive for performance over a period longer than that addressed by the annual bonus, typically 3 to 5 years. An in-depth discussion of long-term incentive compensation programs is beyond the scope of the chapter, but the programs can take many forms. The standards by which the amount of compensation is determined may be pegged to the value of the employer's stock, the employer's earnings, or any other applicable measure. Awards may be objective only, or may have an aspect of subjective evaluation of an individual's performance. The manner of payment may be cash, stock, or other securities, and the time of payment may be spread over several years. Some typical long-term compensation programs include stock options, restricted stock, phantom stock, and various types of performance units. Often, an employer will have already established a long-term compensation plan, and the employment agreement will guarantee the executive's participation in such a plan, sometimes at specified levels of grants.

The benefits section of a contract typically provides that the executive is to participate in all applicable pension, medical, dental, and other insurance programs maintained by the employer for the benefit of executives of similar status. If pension of other benefits accrued with a previous employer were forfeited to join this employer, the employment agreement will sometimes reflect the employer's willingness to make the executive whole. Additionally, the executive may wish to negotiate for supplemental retirement benefits or other special insurance benefits, such as extended medical coverage or special disability or life insurance coverage.

A disproportionate amount of time is often expended on the section of the agreement devoted to perquisites, or so-called fringe benefits, such as automobile allowances and club memberships. These benefits often play a key role for the executive, but the adviser does well to remind his or her principal of the taxable nature of most of these items. The mechanism for the reimbursement of business expenses is also typically addressed, with some attention paid to the manner of business travel and the extent of business expense accounts. If the employment position requires an executive to relocate, the employment agreement often will enumerate which relocation expenses are reimbursable. Where top executives are involved, some employment agreements also provide for housing loans, guarantees, and other assistance in purchasing a new residence.

Termination

Definitions of Termination for Cause and Resignation for Good Reason.

The termination provisions of an employment agreement define the rights of the parties to the contract when the term of employment is cut short, either by action of the employer or the executive. An employment agreement will preferably deal with this subject—even though it is distasteful to most executives and employees embarking on an employment relationship—to provide clarity if the unpleasant situation arises and to attempt to avoid costly litigation over damages. That having been said, it is the unusual agreement that can foresee every set of circumstances that might trigger an early termination of an employment relationship. Therefore, sometimes the best that the termination provisions of an employment agreement can do is establish relative bargaining positions.

The termination provisions delineate in detail those situations in which an employer is permitted to terminate, without incurring an obligation to make severance payments, an executive's employment prior to the expiration of the term. In the parlance of employment agreements, such a termination is referred to as a termination for "cause." In addition, the termination provisions may also set forth those circumstances in which the executive is entitled to resign without forfeiting incentive compensation and, in certain circumstances, collect severance payments. In employment agreements, such a resignation is commonly referred to as a resignation for "good reason." Although it is true that, notwithstanding the definitions of *cause* and *good reason*, an employer can always fire an executive and the executive can always quit, the definitions of *cause* and *good reason* determine the financial consequences to the parties of such a termination or resignation. It is advisable that the employment agreement set forth the definition of both *cause* and *good reason* to clarify the legal positions of the parties.

Almost all employment agreements permit an employer to terminate an executive for cause without triggering any payments to the executives. The definition of what will constitute cause, however, is typically a subject of negotiation and is ultimately determined by what the contract defines as "cause," and not by the legal or moral connotations outside the contract that color the meaning of that word. As a result, the executive will endeavor to narrow this definition, and the employer will argue for a definition that retains maximum flexibility with respect to the termination decision.

At a minimum, cause will typically include the executive's conviction of a felony and any willful act or omission by the executive that is materially injurious to the financial condition of the employer. Occasionally, injury to the reputation of the employer is included. From the employer's point of view, a more appropriate definition of *cause* would include the commission of a felony (not requiring a conviction) and any breach by the executive of the employment agreement or any act or omission by the executive that is injurious to the financial condition or reputation of the employer, its affiliates, or subsidiaries. The definition can be narrowed further to be more protective of the executive by giving the executive the opportunity to cure the situation purportedly giving rise to cause (assuming the situation is possible to cure) and, in the case of most senior executives, requiring a resolution of a supermajority of the members of the employer's board of directors finding that cause exists after the executive has had an opportunity to be heard.

The definition of *good reason*, which sets out the cases in which an executive may terminate the employment relationship prematurely and still receive specified payments, may be seen as the functional mirror image of the definition of *cause*, although, because of unequal bargaining positions, good reason is often more narrow in its scope. It will generally include a material breach of the employment agreement, but the employer may negotiate to limit those provisions whose breach will give rise to good reason. At the very least, those provisions should include a reduction or a failure to pay the stated compensation and benefits and a change in the executive's duties or reporting responsibilities. It may also include a relocation of the executive's principal place of employment and will sometimes reach situations in which the corporate control of the employer is sold. As with the definition of *cause*, the definition of *good reason* should be carefully drafted not to be so broad as to give the executive an unfettered right to resign and collect severance benefits, while at the same time not to be too narrow so as to deprive the executive of any protection against unwarranted adverse changes in employment circumstances.

Consequences of Termination. Whether an employer fires an executive with cause or the executive resigns without good reason, the result is usually the same: The executive forfeits all future claims to salary, bonus, and benefits after the termination or resignation. In addition, the executive will also usually forfeit immediately any unvested long-term incentive compensation, and restrictions may be placed on the vested portions of such compensation.

When the executive is terminated by the employer without cause or when the executive resigns with good reason, however, the executive will generally be entitled to specified severance benefits. Severance benefits are generally based on the compensation the executive would have earned over the remaining term of the contract, including salary, bonuses, and long-term compensation. Severance benefits may also take into account the cost to the executive of loss of coverage under the employer's pension and welfare benefit plans. The severance amounts can include the full amount of such lost earnings and benefits, or even a multiple thereof in certain circumstances involving changes of corporate control (which will be discussed later), or only a portion of such earnings and benefits. If such amounts are paid in a lump sum, the payments are often discounted to their present value.

One question that must be considered is whether the severance payments received will be subject to mitigation—that is, will they be reduced in the event that the executive obtains employment with another employer before the end of the period that was originally part of the term of the employment agreement? The concept of mitigation originally stemmed from the legal principle that contract damages would only be enforceable by a court if they were reasonable as liquidated damages and did not act as a penalty. It is not uncommon today, however, for senior executives' agreements not to be subject to mitigation, relying on another legal precept that contracting parties dealing with one another at arm's length can agree on any damages for breach of a contract, as long as the amounts are supportable in light of the facts and good corporate governance, are not unconscionable, and do not act as a penalty.

Death or Disability.   The termination provisions of the employment agreement should also specify the obligations of the employer in the event that the executive dies. It should also permit the employer to terminate the employment relationship if the executive becomes disabled and should set forth the consequences of such action. In this area, the definition of *disability* can be subject to substantial negotiation, especially when the executive will forfeit long-term compensation in the event of such a termination. What should be kept in mind is that the purpose of this provision is to permit the employer to act only when the executive has experienced a long-term disability. It is important from the executive's point of view that the agreement be drafted so as to prevent the employer from claiming that a termination is for disability in order to avoid paying amounts that would otherwise be due if the termination were one without cause. For this reason, the decision whether or not a long-term disability does, in fact, exist is sometimes left to an independent physician agreed upon by the parties or some other arbiter.

It is most common for payments on death or disability to be limited to those amounts payable under the employer's insurance policies covering these eventualities, although employers will occasionally agree to some additional payments or benefits, such as limited salary continuation. It is advisable to make a special provision in the contract for the disposition of the annual bonus that the executive would have earned for the year in which the death or disability occurs. Frequently, this is accomplished by providing for a *pro rata* bonus for such year.

Restrictive Covenants

As noted earlier, one of the benefits an employer may derive from an employment contract is the agreement of the executive to remain subject to certain restrictive covenants following the end of the employment term. Common restrictive covenants prohibit an executive from disclosing confidential, nonpublic information and trade secrets. Additionally, covenants restricting executives from competing with the employer and from soliciting customers or employees of the employer are sometimes sought. What is most common is the employer's remedy for a breach of a restrictive covenant, which is to seek injunctive relief in a court, although monetary damages are sometimes provided for instead.

The enforceability of covenants not to compete and not to solicit customers or employees will depend on the facts involved and the jurisdiction in question. As a general matter, the common law has taken a dim view of covenants that purport to prohibit an individual from earning a livelihood and upholds these provisions only when some particular, special expertise or circumstance is in question or when the agreement is given by the executive in the context of selling his or her business. It is important that these covenants be narrowly written and limited to a specified period of time (seldom more than 1 or 2 years), activity, and geographic location (in both cases, those in which the executive was engaged within a recent period for the employer). They will seldom be upheld unless they can be shown to protect a legitimate interest of the employer.

In spite of the fact that the enforceability of a covenant not to compete or solicit customers or employees will be in doubt in a particular setting, these covenants continue to be included in employment agreements and to play important roles. The executive cannot be fully certain that the covenant will not be enforced, and this *in terrorem* effect will frequently prevent the activity in question or result in the executive's and the employer's "coming to the table" and negotiating. In addition, contracts that provide for payments to an executive for a period of time after the term (for example, for limited consulting services) may be written to ensure that such payments and services terminate if one of the restrictive covenants contained in the employment agreements is breached. This mechanism can also serve as a method of enforcement.

Special Consideration

Disclosure Obligation of Public Companies

Publicly traded companies that are subject to the proxy rules and the periodic reporting and disclosure requirements under the Securities Exchange Act of 1934 must, as a general rule, publicly disclose the content of their employment agreements with their senior executive officers. The proxy rules require, in connection with the election of a director or the approval of any benefit plan, that such companies disclose to shareholders the current compensation of their five most highly compensated officers and all executive officers as a group. The rules also require disclosure of the material terms of each plan pursuant to which compensation is to be paid to any such officer and, the proxy rules define *plan* broadly enough to include an individual employment contract. The proxy rules also require express disclosure of employment arrangements with directors and executive officers that provide for one or more payments upon a change in control of the employer if such payments in the aggregate exceed $60,000. A company subject to the proxy rules should carefully assess the impact that the specific disclosure of such change-in-control arrangements will have on its shareholders prior to entering into an employment agreement containing such provisions.

In addition to the disclosure required by the proxy rules, Form 10-K, which prescribes the rules for annual disclosure for reporting companies, requires that "material" contracts be attached as exhibits to Form 10-K. The rules define a material contract to include any management contract for a director or one of the five most highly compensated officers of the company and each other management contract for any other executive officer of the company unless immaterial in amount and significance.

Public companies, therefore, must consider as part of the negotiation process the impact of this required disclosure on shareholders in specific and on the public in general. Even if no official public announcement is made with respect to these contracts, it is a virtual certainty that they will be carefully scrutinized by shareholders and the financial press. As noted in a story in *The New York Times* covering employment agreements that provide change in control benefits, companies "do not announce [these agreements]; they simply file them as part of lengthy documents sent to the Securities and Exchange Commission, hoping they go unnoticed. But reporters watch for them avidly because they often disclose multimillion-dollar employment contracts."[5]

Arbitration

Employment agreements sometimes contain an arbitration clause that requires the parties to the agreement to resolve disputes before an arbitrator rather than a court. There is little consensus, however, among companies regarding the choice of forum for dispute resolution. Some companies feel that courts, and especially juries, are often inclined to be

---

[5]R. Cole, "Talking Deals: Job Contracts After Takeovers," *The New York Times*, September 7, 1989, Section D, col. 1, p. 2.

"pro-employee" and prefer, therefore, to require arbitration. Other companies feel that by retaining the right to go to court, they lessen the likelihood that an executive will pursue a claim because of the prohibitive expense of protracted litigation. Yet, because arbitration is usually an expedited and, therefore, a more cost-effective procedure, both parties may prefer to resolve their differences quickly in that forum.

Directly related to the question of arbitration is the issue of who bears the cost of dispute resolution. Some employment agreements provide that the employer must reimburse an executive for reasonable attorney's fees if a dispute arises concerning the interpretation of the contract. Often, this reimbursement is contingent on the executive's prevailing on any claim that is brought. Needless to say, the inclusion of a reimbursement provision will significantly increase the likelihood that an executive will press a claim (consequently increasing the employer's cost) which, in turn, may increase the likelihood of a settlement between the parties.

Change-in-Control Situations

An employment agreement can provide an executive with some protection if the employer is the subject of a change in control, even if the executive's employment agreement does not have specific change-in-control provisions permitting the executive to resign for good reason after a change in control. As a legal matter, the enforceability of most employment contracts against an employer does not change, even though there has been a change in ownership of the employer, when the employer undergoes a merger or its stock is purchased. Furthermore, employment agreements often include provisions that state that good reason will be deemed to exist, and the executive, consequently, will be permitted to resign and receive severance benefits under the contract, if all or substantially all the employer's assets are sold and the buyer does not expressly assume the employer's obligations under the contract. Consequently, the executive may receive the same protection regarding his or her employment relationship with the new owner as he or she had with the original employer. In addition, the presence of an employment agreement with generous severance benefits that become payable in the event of an executive's termination without cause can increase the executive's leverage in negotiations with a new owner. It should be emphasized, however, that payments made to certain executives following a change in control may be subject to the "golden parachute" provisions of sections 280G and 4999 of the Internal Revenue Code. Executives, therefore, should consult carefully with their regular tax advisers to determine the impact of these sections before triggering payments under their employment agreements.

Conclusion

An employment agreement may be viewed as offering more benefits to an executive than to an executive's employer. An employment agreement establishes minimum compensation and benefit levels for an executive but does not ensure any level of performance on the part of the executive. In addition, an employment agreement limits the employer's ability to terminate the executive without incurring an obligation to pay severance benefits but does not provide any guarantee that the executive will continue to work for the employer. For these reasons, most employers have concluded that it is advisable to offer employment agreements only to their most senior executive and key employees.

Nevertheless, having determined to provide an employment agreement to an executive, an employer can derive certain benefits from the contract. The ironing out of initial misunderstandings and the clarification of certain terms in the beginning, when the goodwill of the new relationship is still fresh, can serve for a smoother road in the future. Also, the negotiation of the scope of cause and good reason can often lead to an expansion of the employer's rights beyond what the employer might have otherwise expected. Finally, provisions including restrictive covenants, although not always enforceable, can give the employer some sense that the benefit of the bargain will be realized.

PART 5

Computers and Compensation

28

The Use of Computers in Developing Job Documentation

George G. Gordon, Ph.D.
Associate Professor of Management
Department of Business Administration
Rutgers University

Anyone who has undertaken the task of studying the jobs in an organization has probably encountered a very frustrating situation. Although managers in most organizations agree that job analysis is a useful and sometimes indispensable tool, a search for the existing job documentation usually yields either woefully outmoded documentation, owing to the inability of the documentation system to keep up with changes in jobs as they occur, or no documentation at all.

Traditional Job Description

Typically, producing a job description involves a number of time-consuming steps. First, the incumbent, a sample of incumbents, and/or immediate supervisors are interviewed by a trained job analyst. Then the analyst writes the job description, has it read by the initial interviewees, and makes changes in cases of misunderstandings, omissions, or misinterpretations. Once the description has been rewritten, it typically is reviewed and approved by higher levels of management. Depending on the backlog and current work load of the job analysts, this process may take many months to complete. Thus, it is not surprising that when a manager wants to fill a position or reorganize a unit, he or she does not hold off action until appropriate job descriptions can be produced.

An exciting development in the job evaluation area has been the application of computer technology to the production of job documentation. Through the computer processing of data obtained from questionnaires or inventories, information can be developed relatively quickly from large numbers of incumbents and supervisors at a relatively low cost. Furthermore, questionnaires can be organized specifically to provide information not only for job evaluation, but for a variety of other purposes such as training needs analysis, productivity analysis, or performance evaluation.

Questionnaires/Job Inventories

Using the computer, however, does not eliminate all problems, because the questionnaire/computer approach creates its own set of problems. Questionnaires can be expensive and time-consuming to develop. Thus, except for high-density jobs (jobs with many incumbents), companies normally will not wish to invest the time and effort required to produce questionnaires that will have limited usage. Fortunately, academics and consulting firms have recognized this state of affairs as a market opportunity and have produced questionnaires and computerized databases that are applicable to a wide variety of companies. However, such questionnaires and databases vary greatly in the nature of their content, and care must be taken that the particular instrument or system chosen will fit the purposes for which the company wishes to develop job documentation.

Questionnaires, sometimes referred to as job inventories, vary in at least three fundamental ways. First is the degree of detail with which individual items are written. Certainly the description "uses drafting instruments to produce drawings" is a more specific description than "conducts feasibility studies for new manufacturing processes," yet, both may be part of a single job. Each might be named an activity, a task, or a job element because there is little agreement among writers in this field on the terminology used in relation to job specificity. Yet, it is obvious that mixing such disparate levels of detail in the same questionnaire would either give fragmentary, uncoordinated results as the description vacillates from precise to vague, or it would result in a ponderous, redundant description if all possible items at all degrees of detail were included in the questionnaire. Thus, in developing or choosing a questionnaire, one must ensure that the coverage of activities is at a reasonably consistent level of specificity, and that the level relates to the purpose for which the information is being collected. For instance, if one were trying to develop information about specific skill training needs, one would not use a questionnaire designed for broad areas of responsibility.

A second major way in which questionnaires vary is in the scales used to measure the elements listed. In the 1950s and early 1960s the U.S. Air Force funded a good deal of research about the properties of scales used for job measurement. It generally was found that questionnaires were a reliable method for collecting job data for a variety of job families and working environments. People were most consistent in reporting whether or not they performed a task, the amount of time spent on each task, the frequency with which the task was performed, task importance, and task difficulty. It was also found that gathering more information about tasks tended to yield more reliable responses. Thus, the research demonstrates that the use of job questionnaires is a viable method for collecting job information, and that a variety of information can be obtained by this method. Table 28-1 lists some typical scales used to measure jobs and the extreme values for each.

There are some clear relationships between the applications for job analyses and the nature of the scales used. For instance, if one wanted to reorganize a work flow unit in which many people dealt with similar content, sorting out the differences with a time-spent and/or an authority-level scale would be helpful. On the other hand, in designing training programs, the use of a difficulty or learning-time scale in ad-

Table 28-1. Scales Used for the Collection of Job Information

Scale name	Typical extremes
Occurrence	Do not perform...Do perform
Importance	Unimportant...Crucial
Difficulty	Far below average...Far above average
Time spent	Much less than average...Much more than average
Amount of time spent	Extremely small...Extremely large
Frequency	Rarely...Almost continuously
Part of the job	Minor part...Most significant part
Authority level	Assists...Directs others
Learning time	One day or less...Six months or more
Current skill level	Minimal...Expert

dition to a current-skill-level scale probably would produce the most worthwhile information. The concept of learning time has often been used in job evaluation of low-level jobs, whereas importance, time-spent, or part-of-the-job scales might be most appropriate for evaluating higher-level jobs.

The third, and perhaps most important, way in which questionnaires vary is in the extent to which they deal with specific job content, defined as the expected outputs for which the job exists. Some questionnaires focus on content-oriented tasks that clearly differ from job to job. An example of this type of task might be "reviews and approves or disapproves requests for credit." This same activity might be covered in another approach in a content-free task such as "gathers and reviews readily available information and decides on the best course of action." This latter type of task description is not tied to a specific job or job family. Tasks such as "conducts performance reviews" that are more content-oriented yet applicable to many different jobs, might be found in either approach. The "worker-oriented" approach, described later in this chapter, goes furthest in divorcing itself from content by entirely dealing with what the incumbent does and not with what is accomplished.

There are clear trade-offs with different emphases on specific job content. The freer a questionnaire is from specific content, the more applicable it can be to a wide variety of jobs. Although some applications require specific content, others, including job evaluation, can be accomplished adequately without job-unique information. The following sections will illustrate how these issues have been addressed in the evolution of computer technology for job documentation.

Evaluation and Availability of Computer-Based Systems

Since the 1950s the U.S. Air Force has been conducting research about the use of questionnaires and computers to develop and analyze job information. Questionnaires have been developed for a wide variety of military occupations and analyzed with a variety of statistical routines under the heading of Comprehensive Occupational Data Analysis Programs (CODAP). Such routines are able to produce a myriad of reports, from a simple listing of tasks in order of time spent to a clustering of jobs in terms of the similarities of their task profiles. Following this line of research, a number of organizations have developed versions of both questionnaires and statistical routines for use within their own companies or to offer as a service to other companies.

Work Performance Survey System

One such system, the Work Performance Survey System (WPSS), was developed within the American Telephone & Telegraph Co. (AT&T) and the Bell Companies. The process, which is based on customized task inventories, has been described in detail by Sidney Gael in a book devoted to the system.[1] The WPSS system provides three statistics for every task, the proportion of individuals that perform the task, and the variability of individual responses around the average. It also provides the capability for producing cross-tabulations based on two or more information items, such as job level, tenure, department, and so on. Sample reports are presented for task significance, percent of time spent on tasks, job tenure by location, and company tenure by location, as well as a description of the way in which the system can be used to redesign jobs.

Gael's book covers the entire process of developing questionnaires, administering them, and analyzing the results. Thus, this approach is quite useful for firms that have jobs with hundreds or thousands of incumbents. However, because it involves complete questionnaire development, it would be of limited utility for modest-sized firms or low-density jobs. The computer programs upon which the system is based are available under a licensing agreement with AT&T.

Also pursuing a CODAP-type of approach, Control Data Corporation spent nearly a decade developing a system for measuring and evaluating managerial jobs. The system, HR Focus, is designed around a questionnaire covering core management activities to which regression analyses are applied in order to provide evaluations. Job descriptions list the relative time spent on tasks, which are organized into a series of categories developed through an extensive research program. Also available through HR Focus are the numerous types of reports typically available in CODAP-type systems.

The HR Focus, geared primarily to managerial jobs, has provided a significant start in terms of the development of a generic questionnaire of managerial activities. Such a development holds the promise of being able to considerably lower the cost of job evaluation through improved technology; however, the system has been criticized by Milkovich and

---

[1]Sidney Gael, *Job Analysis: A Guide to Assessing Work Activities,* Jossey-Bass Inc., San Francisco, Calif., 1983.

Glueck[2] for the heavy costs involved in some of its early applications. In 1987 the HR Focus system was acquired from Control Data Corporation by Personnel Decisions Inc., of Minneapolis, Minnesota, through which the system is currently available.

Position Analysis Questionnaire

Probably the most widely used computerized system is the Position Analysis Questionnarie (PAQ). Professor Ernest J. McCormick of Purdue University began a program of research in job measurement in the 1950s and, with a succession of graduate students, evolved a generalized system to measure "worker-oriented" job variables. Unlike other approaches, this system focuses on what the worker does, rather than on what is being accomplished. For instance, one such worker-oriented behavior, "using verbal sources of job information," might be involved in such diverse job content as taking an order from a customer over the phone or evaluating a presentation of a proposed advertising campaign.

A lengthy and systematic program of research has identified a relatively comprehensive list of such variables as found in the world of work. In conducting a job analysis, each variable is rated on one of a variety of scales by a trained analyst who interviews incumbents or supervisors to obtain the basic information. These variables have been subjected to factor analysis, and a number of job dimensions have been identified. The numerical basis of the job analysis lends itself to regression analysis, a technique which is commonly applied to the determination of point or dollar values of jobs.

The worker-oriented approach, in addition to its application to job evaluation, is also potentially valuable for such applications as employee selection, career planning, and training needs analysis. This approach, however, does neither provide a flavor of what the job or the unit in which the job is located is trying to accomplish or how the jobs in the unit are put together to achieve its objectives. Thus, the PAQ is limited in its applications to such areas as worker orientation, organization design, or performance evaluation. A number of companies are conducting a content-oriented task analysis prior to making the PAQ ratings, which may be a way to get around some of the shortcomings, but at the present time such an approach has not been computerized. A microcomputer program entitled Enter-Act is available for preparing and processing PAQ data and allows for the production of a wide variety of

[2]George T. Milkovich and William F. Glueck, *Personnel-Human Resource Management: A Diagnostic Approach*, Business Publications, Inc., Plano, Tex., 1985, p. 113.

summary reports. The PAQ and its related materials are distributed through Consulting Psychologists Press of Palo Alto, Calif.

Some of the major U.S. human resources consulting firms, such as Towers, Perrin, Forster and Crosby (TPF&C), the Hay Group, and Wyatt, also offer questionnaire-based computerized systems geared primarily to job evaluation. Each has developed proprietary questionnaires and computerized scoring systems that are available to clients. The offerings from two of the companies will be discussed here only as they offer separate and unique solutions to the job documentation problems.

Hay VALUE

Although most of the systems discussed in this chapter were developed primarily to produce job evaluations, the Hay Group has also produced a separate job description system that produces an output more closely parallel to those produced by conventional job analysts. This approach has been applied to job evaluation, training needs analysis, reorganization, and performance evaluation.

The system is organized around functional areas such as finance, engineering, personnel, secretarial, or crafts. Core questionnaires have been developed and are available for a wide variety of functions. By orienting each instrument to a specific functional area, it has been possible to include a great deal of specific job content. These core questionnaires are modified to fit a particular company by a process of internal review and tryout. Final questionnaires are then filled out by individual incumbents, and descriptions are produced either for each incumbent or, through a series of computerized decision rules, for each job title.

Figure 28-1 presents a portion of a description produced by the system, along with annotations on the derivations and purposes of the different elements. "General Information" includes information on the extent to which the job involves working with people, information, or machines; the nature of contacts the incumbent has; the nature of any typing/data processing requirement; and the amount of experience required for competent performance in the job. "Nature and Scope" indicates the position to which this job reports and the other jobs reporting to that same position, thereby giving some indication of the immediate organizational environment. Also, the description lists the job activities under summary headings in order of learning difficulty. There is also some indication of criticality and relative time spent on the activities. Other than the identifying information at the top of the page, the entire document is constructed from algorithms keyed into questionnaire items checkmarked by respondents.

INCUMBENT: Rita Brown
JOB TITLE: Claims Processor
DEPARTMENT: Claims Processing   ← From the cover page
POSITION CODE: C10007
SUPERVISOR'S NAME: Len Larson   Position Code: optional
SUPERVISOR'S TITLE: Supervisor, Claims
DATE: 09/04/87   Date: run date

SUPERVISOR'S APPROVAL   ─────────   Supervisor approval line: optional

GENERAL INFORMATION   **General Information**

                                                   From Job requirements and Responsibilities
                                                   Section
Approximately 20% of the job involves communica
with machines or equipment and 40% with informa   ← Question One

This job involves frequent communication with pe
customers and guests and occasional communica   ← Contacts

This job requires typing or data entry, but speed is
Approximately 90% of the work must be carried ou   ← Question Two
its confidentiality.   and Question Three

Competent performance in this job requires at lea
experience.   ←Question Four

                                                   ← If additional questions are added, they would
                                                     be placed here

NATURE AND SCOPE   **Nature & Scope**

The Claims Processor reports to the Supervisor, C   ←cover page, subordinates and peers
Claims Processor (5) and Senoir Claims Processo

Note: The activities in bold-faced type are the mo
activities marked with an asterisk (*) are those on ←This note is required
most time. Activities under each function are liste   Purpose:
learning difficulty.   -critical is bold-faced
                                                      -(*) most time activities
                                                      -explains the order of the activities

General Responsibilities

Resolve inquiries/complaints from assigned clients
Research problems relating to customer complain
Look up and code information in tables, charts co   ←Activities are listed under the functional
Trace proper route of forms to locate or determine heading
Answer questions from others which require searc
Gather information from individuals outside the off
policyholders, agents, medical personnel etc.
Collect/assemble information for use by others
Contact company employees and outside parties
information

Figure 28-1. Job description, XYZ Company.

Answer nonroutine questions for information after obtaining supervisor approval
Obtain appropriate internal approvals/signatures on documents
Complete standard forms

Claims Processing

* Collect or record documentation for claim evaluations
* Check for coverage in claim situations
   Contact claimants, witness, police, etc., to facilitate claims processing

ADDITIONAL INFORMATION

Level of Communication

> **Additional Information**
>
> The comments are printed after the activities; they are printed in the same order as they appear on the questionnaire

Occasionally a policyholder complains about a rejection and I try to explain the reason for the rejection; if they are upset the call is forwarded to the Supervisor.

Examples of Problems Faced

Gathering information from external agencies to process claim for policyholder is a difficult problem. Completing processing of claim in timely fashion if data is missing from original claim.

NE630.2
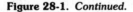
> *Version number*
> ←this is printed at the end of the job description for reference

Figure 28-1. *Continued.*

Job Description Manager

An interesting hybrid approach to producing a "conventional" job description has been created by TPF&C under the title of Job Description Manager. This approach has the user (incumbent, manager, or job analyst) write in the job summary, duties and responsibilities, and specific responsibilities after the software produces the rest of the description. The system is based on a questionnaire developed for TPF&C's computer-aided job evaluation system, WJQ. The questionnaire used is generic insofar as it covers compensable factors for a wide variety of jobs and can be applied either in generic or in customized form. The questions are not job-content specific, dealing with such factors as the level of problem solving and the nature of contact with others. The instrument used, therefore, bears similarities to the HR Focus system. In this case, however, responses are not scored for job evaluation purposes only; they are also read and converted to paragraphs to produce a job description. Figure 28-2 presents a portion of a description of a regional sales director produced by computer from questionnaire responses. Although the sample represents a relatively high-level job, the system has been developed for both exempt and nonexempt jobs.

Identifying Criteria for Success

Development Dimensions International has taken a unique approach to offering a microcomputer-based, interactive job documentation service under the title of Identifying Criteria for Success (ICS). This program is designed to produce a list of dimensions consisting of those job-related behaviors necessary for success in the position. The program is intended for use by job content experts to produce a content-valid, behavioral-oriented job description.

The system is based on a database of dimensions and behaviors that have been culled from many thousands of job analyses conducted by the company. These dimensions have been categorized into six broad job families: manager, professional, supervisor, sales representatives, clerical, and hourly. Operationally, the system makes a tentative selection of dimensions based on built-in criteria, and incumbents and managers respond to the resulting behaviors in terms of frequency and importance. Managers then rate and rank dimensions according to importance, and the computer provides the guidance to produce a final dimension list. Support materials are provided to adapt the output to a comprehensive job description, a dimension-based selection system, or a customized performance appraisal form. Although the system has not been applied to job evaluation, it would not be surprising to see such an application appear in the future. Development Dimensions International, however, has produced a microcomputer-based job documentation process built on an extensive database of job activities.

Conclusion

Job analysis, the process of obtaining and organizing information about a job, has taken enormous strides within the past two decades. Computer-based technologies are now at the point at which they are certainly appropriate for use in high-density jobs and can be cost-effective for many low-density jobs as well. Companies have begun to enter the field through the use of microcomputer software, and we can

---

JOB TITLE: Regional Sales Director	JOB CODE: 5120441
REPORTS TO: VP Sales & Mktg Div A	CODE: 5120981
PROFILED BY: Supervisor	Date: 06/07/89

Job Summary

Develop, maintain, and serve new and existing accounts in a designated territory and establish new accounts that parallel company developments to meet division sales objectives.

Duties and Responsibilities

1. Manages the development of new and existing business in an assigned territory by meeting with customer's production, purchasing, and engineering personnel to promote company image and services in relation to customer's need to increase sales and profit margins.

2. Maintains sales/technical information by preparing technical service reports, sales reports, action plans, and customer correspondence to document and retain accurate information.

3. Promotes positive company image and relationship with customer by attending business/trade functions and by entertaining customer to maintain and improve business.

4. Performs additional duties as required.

Specific Qualifications

A candidate for entry into this position is likely to possess a bachelor's degree with limited experience with specialized skills to perform complex administrative and/or technical work.

This job category is for persons with expert knowledge within the field in the company, and may function as the final authority to experienced personnel.

Specialized Study

Bachelor's degree

Figure 28-2. Job profile summary.

Scope of Responsibility

The Regional Sales Director under the executive guidance of the VP Sales & Mktg Div A and with little or no technical guidance, exercises official control responsibility for annual net sales of approximately $5.01 million and exercises official control responsibility for a net expense plan of approximately $716,000. The nature of the assigned work is such that failure to perform satisfactorily would result in failure to accomplish Company goals or objectives, resulting in losses that have a significant negative impact on the success of the total Company.

Reporting directly to the Regional Sales Director are the following positions:

    5220403—District Sales Manager
    5220404—District Sales Manager
    5220405—District Sales Manager
    5220406—District Sales Manager
    5220407—District Sales Manager
    5220408—District Sales Manager
    5220409—Sales Administrator
    5220410—Secretary

The position has direct management responsibility for 8 employee(s) and indirect management responsibility for 35 employee(s).

The work assigned to this position mostly involves solving problems by gathering and reviewing information that is generally readily available and selecting the best solution or course of action. However, solving problems by researching and reviewing information that is not readily available and selecting the best solution or course of action is an important aspect of the job. The majority of the work assigned to this position involves modifying work practices and techniques to solve problems. But a secondary aspect of the job requires the incumbent to improve upon ideas, products, or processes.

Internal Contacts. The position has contacts with:

- Senior Management that involves convincing those contacted to cooperate, grant approval, or take action of a certain kind.
- Supervisors/Managers that involves explanation and discussion of difficult information so that the other individual(s) can understand it.
- Staff that involves giving or receiving straightforward information only.

Figure 28-2. *Continued.*

External Contacts. The position has contacts with:

- Business or professional representatives of customer or competing organizations, governmental agencies, or media that involves convincing those contacted to cooperate, grant approval, or take action of a certain kind.

- Business or professional representatives of outside companies, agencies, or organizations that involves convincing those contacted to cooperate, grant approval or take action of a certain kind.

Figure 28-2. *Continued.*

anticipate much wider availability of generic questionnaires and software to service them. The amount of potential reporting and analysis of not only job evaluation data, but also job characteristics, requirements, families, and other data has multiplied enormously as different organizations have built upon the early CODAP beginnings.

With microcomputers growing rapidly in power and capacity, the capability to produce job information and link the data to sophisticated organizational analyses will be cost-effective for any size organization. The days of spending large amounts of time and money on describing jobs for the sole purpose of job evaluation are rapidly drawing to a close. Entering is the era in which large amounts of up-to-date job data will be immediately available to the organization for making informed, timely decisions on compensation, organization, performance, training, and selection.

29
Using the Computer in Job Evaluation

Trudy Downs

School of Communications, Information and Library Studies
Rutgers University

Computerized Job Evaluation

Job evaluation systems, used for rating a series of jobs within the value structure of an organization, have multiple uses in most organizations. Although the initial purpose is usually for creating salary programs with a focus on internal equity and external competitiveness, job evaluation supports organizational effectiveness in a number of other ways, including organization analysis, performance management, and staffing. Given the pervasiveness and multiple uses of job evaluation, organizations have continued their efforts to increase precision and efficiency of application. The recent focus of these efforts has been computer technology. There are several compelling reasons for this movement:

> *Natural evolution.* Job evaluation is well established, not just throughout the U.S. business and industry, but throughout the world. Automating the process is a natural next step that is available

412

now because of the acceptance of job measurement and computer technology.

Responsiveness. Organizational change can occur more rapidly today than ever before. In many situations, from inventory control to personnel practices, only the computer can help organizations keep up with the changes.

User friendly. Technology is fast losing its mystique as personal computers pop up on the desks of data processors, line managers, and CEOs. Previous resistance to a technological intervention in job measurement systems is eroding quickly as computers become day-to-day work tools.

Cost. Human resources functional costs come under closer scrutiny each year. Quickly and inexpensively describing and evaluating jobs, particularly in merger or acquisition situations, can save money, both in the evaluation process itself and in subsequent salary administration programs.

Computers have been used to support job evaluation in several different ways. Two obvious uses are to keep records and to perform calculations. For example, when multiple evaluators are used to compare jobs, the computer may be able to combine their judgments more quickly than a manual calculator.

Another use has been to let the computer substitute for people in repetitive, high-volume preliminary analysis and simple judgment tasks. This use frees people to deal with the refinements of job evaluation and with the consideration of their organization's unusual job needs.

The fourth use has been to refine the statistical foundations of job evaluation. Some efforts have used computers to investigate and change weightings for factors in job evaluation based on elaborate mathematical criteria. These criteria confirm or deny the use and weighting of factors that people who develop, use, and accept the evaluations think should be important.

The job evaluation scores derived from computerized systems can be developed from algorithms or heuristics. Algorithms produce the evaluation according to a specific set of programmed instructions, somewhat like a recipe. These are generally quite rigid, and changes may require extensive reprogramming. Heuristics are rules of thumb and are used within expert systems. Expert systems consist of two parts: the knowledge base and the inference engine. These systems are designed for ease of modification to the knowledge base and the rules used in manipulating that knowledge. Expert systems use these rules of thumb in the way a human expert might in solving a problem. Both systems can provide explanations to the user of the system so that he or she can trace the method used by the system to arrive at the job evaluation solution. No matter which type of system one chooses, it is important that the user be able to trace back and understand how the job evaluation is arrived at.

Factors in Selecting a Computerized Job Evaluation System

Computerized job evaluation systems are available using a number of different job evaluation methods. There are systems that use ranking, classification, point factor, statistical methods, or some combination of these for arriving at the job evaluation score. The primary consideration in choosing which system is right for your company should be the compatibility of the job evaluation methodology with the company's value system; these two elements must be in accord.

Just as in choosing a manual job evaluation system, a company must believe in and understand the methodology behind the derivation of the job evaluation. If the methods used to obtain the job evaluation are not easily understood and explained, it is unlikely that the employees will think the system just. Initially, some may think that a computerized system is an impartial, fair administrator of job evaluation. But upon reflection, one realizes that this depends on the methods used by the system to evaluate jobs. The computer output can be no better than the underlying philosophy and value that go into its software. The values that your company deems important should drive your system of evaluation.

Does your organization value jobs based on the external marketplace only? If so, you might derive your evaluation of the worth of jobs to your organization based strictly on the "going rate" for a series of benchmark jobs that can be matched to the external market. This approach might be suitable if these jobs are easily filled, the learning curve is quite rapid, and turnover of personnel is not problematic. It might be that you value jobs based on the internal relationship of the jobs—that is, your own organizational value structure is important to how you measure your jobs. In this case, you would take a different approach to measurement hierarchy that reflects the values your organization deems important. This would be particularly important in a company that promotes from within, has a strong sense of loyalty to its employees, and for which the external market in not a major factor in retaining or motivating employees. Of course, for most companies there is a blend of these two internal and external values. Again, this can be reflected in the method used for evaluation. The internal values can be used to develop the measurement hierarchy and the external market used to price these jobs once values are assigned. Again, the computer programs used to develop job measurement values will reflect these methods; they are not value free. It is important when using a computerized job evaluation system that one question the value system used to derive the output.

Why do companies want to use a computerized job evaluation system? Why would these systems be preferred over present manual systems? Computers have entered the human resources function in various ways that have eased the record keeping and reporting functions necessary to provide information to management, employees, government, regulatory agencies, and others that require information on the human resources of an organization. Most companies have a computerized human resources information system (HRIS) that provides various levels of information—from the very basic to the very complex and complete. Once aware of the power of these systems, the human resources manager realizes that many of the time-consuming functions in the human resources area can benefit from the use of the computer.

One of these functions is job evaluation. The task of selecting, installing, and maintaining a job evaluation system is formidable. Jobs continually change as a result of mergers, acquisitions, divestitures, downsizing, reorganizations, and so on. This puts a strain on the human resources function to keep up with the changes in jobs; thus, computer job description and job evaluation systems provide a useful tool.

A computer job evaluation system must be understood as a tool for management to use. The system itself should serve management, not direct it. It is important that those who use computerized tools recognize that when the output from a system does not seem appropriate, they have the power to override the computer tool. The tool is designed to assist the human expert manage large tasks in a timely manner. It is not designed to replace the expert. The design of that tool is an important aspect to keep in mind when selecting the right computerized job evaluation system for your company.

There are a variety of methods for achieving the job evaluation output from the job evaluation system. The human resources manager needs to evaluate how each of the systems arrives at the evaluation.

Some systems are statistically driven, using multiple regression to determine the value of the jobs within a company. This method is effective if there are no "yes, buts" in your job environment. That is, the answer to each question asked in determining job size can be answered with an absolute, unambiguous response; no qualifications are necessary, and there is no need to respond to the question and then add a "yes, but" to the response. For some types of jobs this option may be very desirable; for others it may be less so. For example, it may be desirable for jobs, which are measured strictly on output, such as sales dollars, number of units produced, carrying charges for inventory, and so on, to be measured using a purely statistical methodology. But most jobs are not measured only on quantitative, output variables. They include more qualitative measures, such as responsibility for building customer relationships, guiding junior staff, servicing customers, and other tasks that must be carried out to successfully perform the job. Once jobs become more complex with measurement, including both the quantitative and the qualitative measures, these statistical relationships do not hold up as well because the questions now have ambiguous answers that must be factored into the analysis.

Some systems derive evaluations from assigning points to various job factors, weighting these factors and then adding them up to derive the evaluation. Other systems might derive the overall job evaluation structure by using a paired comparison methodology. Whatever method is used, the human resources manager must be comfortable that the method represents the best fit between the values of the company and the values internalized by the job evaluation software.

As has been mentioned, it is possible that the job evaluation software may not be useful for all jobs. The domain covered by the system is important. Many expert systems are quite accurate for a specific domain, but when they are applied outside the defined limits of that domain, they lose their accuracy of prediction. For example, they may cover a particular family of jobs—accounting, data processing, engineering, and so on—and they may cover a particular strata of jobs—nonexempt, professional/technical individual contributors, supervisory, middle management, top management, and so on. One should be cautious and rigorously test the boundaries of job evaluation systems with particular care to see how they hold up, both within and outside the boundaries described by the system. It is difficult for a system to be all things to all people, and sometimes those with range limits are the most appropriate. One size does not always fit all.

If the computerized job evaluation system does not cover all jobs within the company, it is important that the computerized system fit well within the framework of the overall job evaluation system and that it be integrated. One does not want to have multiple job evaluation systems within an organization. Multiple methods of achieving the same overall system are useful, but multiple systems are not desirable. These require a good deal of explaining to justify to employees, to management, and, at times, to regulatory agencies.

Where the Input Originates

There are many ways of obtaining the data used for input to the computerized information system. A questionnaire can be developed in a number of ways. It may be developed by the designers of the system with little input from the client company. This assumes that the questionnaire developers are experts in job content and measurement and that the client's jobs do not differ significantly from similar jobs in the world of work. Questionnaires may also be developed with the client so that any uniqueness of the client organization is captured in the questionnaire. And, of course, a blend of the two methods may be used, allowing the tailoring or modification of a basic set of questions to capture the uniqueness and value emphasis of the client organization. Some systems recommend that data be gathered directly from the employees. Some systems suggest that it come from the supervisor. Others suggest that it come from the specialists in the human resources function. No matter where the data come from, it is important that they be accurate. How accuracy is determined can be varied also; it may be checked prior to entry into the system, or the system may check the data and flag information that is inconsistent.

In many instances, no matter who completes a job questionnaire that is used for input to the job evaluation system, there is a second level of review with discussion and resolution of any items in disagreement. This is good practice because it clarifies the job in the minds of the parties involved. This practice would also hold in a manual system. There are some systems, however, that recommend gathering data from the employee and submitting it to the system, which checks the data for reasonableness and accuracy. This is efficient but must be approached with caution because it can lead to a misunderstanding of who has control of the system. When the system rejects information because it is not reasonable relative to the job being evaluated, it is important to go back to the source of the data and clear up the ambiguity. If the data is changed in order to provide the answers the computer will accept as appropriate without going back to the source, the system is driving the evaluation. Computers should not tell management what to do; management tells computers what to do! Thus, your computerized job evaluation system must have a way to handle jobs that do not fit within the system. It may be that these are handled by manually evaluating them or slotting them into the list of evaluations developed by the computer, but there must be a way of dealing with jobs that do not fit the mold.

A computerized job evaluation system must provide sufficient benefits for the effort required in using it. This may seem obvious, but many systems fail because, although the output is accurate and acceptable, the work required to achieve that output is more than the user is willing to expend. We all know of cases of computers sitting unused in offices because the systems require so much learning or so much effort to input data.

User Interface

The system should be designed so that users can operate it with little instruction; users should not have to be computer experts to enter data into the system, to produce reports, or to produce an output file on a disk that will provide input information to other programs. All these functions should be built into the user interface.

It is also important for the system to have the ability to transport file information in and out so that data entry can be minimized. It may be that basic information can be loaded into the system from the company HRIS system or that information from the computer job evaluation system can be transported back to the HRIS system. Whatever the need, there should be a procedure for accomplishing these tasks.

Off-the-Shelf Versus Custom-Tailored Systems

For some companies and jobs, an off-the-shelf system fits just fine. But for others, the evaluation factors and weightings must be modified, or even built, to meet the needs of their particular organizational environment.

Because job evaluation is a very important aspect of any human resources function (and most certainly important to each employee of the company), the process of developing a job evaluation system that reflects the company's values cannot be underestimated. In addition, an effective way must be found to integrate these values with the market pricing of jobs so that a company maintains internal equity and external competitiveness.

Communication Is Important

Companies should be careful to avoid the "black box" effect in their computerized evaluation systems. This is the concept that something magical happens inside the computer that is known to no one, but the output is accepted because the computer produced the answer. One of the major considerations in early expert systems expressed by Buchanan and Shortliffe is that explanations were crucial if users were to accept the system.[1] They were dealing with systems that give medical advice, but their belief would apply to other systems as well. They felt that one of the main reasons for the rejection of systems was their use of statistical approaches to arrive at solutions. Explanation systems that provide the user with an understanding of the system's method used in deriving a solution are important. The system must be understood in order to engender trust in the system. In job evaluation systems, this trust is important not only to the primary user of the system, the compensation department, and managers requesting evaluations, but also to the secondary user as well—the population of employees whose jobs are being evaluated by the systems. Output with no sound foundation is suspect.

Computerized evaluation systems must provide an audit trail or explanation system to help the users of the system understand how the system arrives at the evaluation. This should enable the user of the evaluation system, through directly questioning the system or through printing out the factors used, to understand how the system arrived at the value given. One of the primary values of "human to human" interaction is trust, and this trust must also be carried over to "human to computer" interaction. The system must be able to explain how it arrives at its answer in the language of the user or this trust will be in jeopardy. It is not necessary for a system to arrive at a solution in exactly the same manner as an expert in the field, but it is necessary that the method of deriving the solution be fully explained and capable of being checked by the human using the system.

Conclusion

When a company is considering the investment in a computerized job evaluation system, it is necessary for that company to consider the sys-

---

[1]B. G. Buchanan and E. H. Shortliffe, *Rule-Based Expert Systems—The MYCIN Experiments of the Stanford Heuristic Programming Project*, Addison-Wesley Publishing Company, Reading, Mass., 1984.

tem as a tool to support human experts. Thus, consideration must be given to the methods used to derive the evaluations and whether or not these are compatible with those of the company.

Data input must be completed with relative ease. The system shouldn't require more energy to use than it saves in producing the evaluations. The system must be reliable and integrative with other methods of job evaluation unless it is designed to cover all jobs within the company.

The system must be understood by those who use it and those who are affected by it. It should provide an explanation or audit trail so that the methods used to arrive at the evaluation are apparent to all concerned. The system should serve as a tool; it should not become the driving force in evaluation. The human expert should still have the ability to question and override a system output.

Ideally, a system should provide a linkage to the external marketplace for pricing jobs. It is desirable for this to be an easy conversion so that system job evaluation output can be used directly. It may be necessary, however, for this to become a multistep process requiring conversion from the internal value system to an external value system used by the market to price jobs.

Computerized job evaluation systems are tools to serve management and as such require careful selection to ensure that they are the right tool for your company's environment.

30

Organizing and Retrieving Compensation Data for Competitive Salary Programs

Thomas W. Jacob
Vice President
Compensation Information Center
Hay Group Inc.

John Yurkutat
Senior Survey Consultant
Compensation Information Center
Hay Group Inc.

Unprecedented change in the "art" (and science) of compensation planning transpired in the 1980s. Several forces, following on the heels of one another, brought about this radical change. First, rapid inflation strained pay policies and practices designed for periods of much greater stability. Second, draconian downsizing of the white-collar work force dramatically changed the nature and security of these jobs, and essentially created a new breed of salaried worker; a worker who is more specialized, more short-term-oriented, more technically skilled, and more conversant in financial and statistical disciplines. All in all, this complex of changes adds up to a present demand for greater and more varied forms of compensation.

As for the future, the 1990s will be the age of the global economy; a time when we truly witness the beginning of the Information Age. Compressed time frames and heightened competitive pressures on all enterprises will be the norm for this decade. Undoubtedly, change will occur at an ever-increasing pace.

Few will disagree that the field of compensation is much more complex today than it has ever been. Although internal equity (as measured by systems that determine relative job contribution) remains an important pay-setting factor, it is no longer the only factor. Rapidly changing pay markets, which value new and scarce skills in a period when the pool of professional and salaried workers is expected to shrink, make it essential for companies to constantly monitor a whole host of new factors when setting competitive pay levels.

Having provided the framework necessary to begin our discussion, we will now examine the nature of these factors and suggest ways to organize them into a database that provides a usable, computer-based information system. In addition, this chapter provides examples of some of the uses of these new, sophisticated market monitoring tools.

Pay Determinants

A company reaching a decision on a compensation question usually is faced with analyzing data on some subset of a number of factors categorized as "pay determinants" or pay markets composed of comparator companies, job characteristics, and incumbent information. As a matter of fact, historical evidence suggests that differential pay practices evolve as these factors change. Although these factors are quite numerous, they are all descriptive attributes of companies, jobs, or incumbents. A more detailed look at each of these major pay determinants follows.

Companies

A very important determinant of pay is other companies' pay practices. Companies form pay "markets" when grouped according to industry, size, or financial performance. In many cases, a pay market must be defined by looking concurrently at some or all of the following criteria:

Industry. Frequently indicated by Standard Industrial Classification (SIC), the industry in which a company operates forms a natural competitive market.

Size.　The sales volume or asset size of a company usually has an important bearing on pay levels. Within the same industry, the total employee population often indicates organizational complexity, and this complexity may be linked to pay levels.

Performance.　Although the financial performance of companies is another determinant of pay levels, a consistent relationship between pay levels and financial performance does not exist. High-performing companies are not necessarily also high paying, so it is necessary to choose companies very carefully when constructing a pay market based on financial criteria.

Jobs

Job characteristics are another very important determinant of pay, and in some cases these can be more important than company determinants. Why? Because the unique nature of a job can elevate it to its own pay market independent of any industry. The best example of this was the market for electronic data processing jobs created in the 1970s and early 1980s.

Several of the most important characteristics of jobs include:

Job title.　Although less important than in the past, and not a primary determinant of pay because of the wide variability of jobs sharing the same title, job title, nevertheless, is an important information item about any job. In the absence of other pertinent information, job title can contribute to an understanding of pay levels.

Organizational unit.　There are definite and significant differences in pay patterns for jobs in different organizational units, such as corporate headquarters, divisions, or subsidiaries. Jobs in corporate headquarters tend to be staff or internal consulting positions; jobs in subordinate units often are heavily line-oriented. Many times, these differences require a company to develop different pay programs that adequately recognize job differences at the parent and subsidiary levels.

Area of activity and functional skill.　Another key characteristic of a job is the area of the company in which it operates (for example, marketing, accounting, engineering) and the function it performs in that area. For example, a lending officer in a bank (job function) can be paid quite differently depending on whether he or she works in commercial, retail, or specialty banking (area of activity).

Management level.　Pay practices vary widely based on the management requirements of a job. Paradoxically, job title is a very poor indicator of the true management responsibility of a job. Other than significant levels, such as CEO, senior executive, manager, or supervisor, a job usually is an individual contributor (even if the title is vice president of paper clips!).

Compensation plans.   The type of pay plan used by companies is another important determinant of pay levels. That is, is the job eligible for a bonus or other incentive payments? Frequently, these types of jobs receive relatively moderate base pay. They provide the incumbent, however, with an opportunity to earn up to 20 percent more through bonus payments.

Job size.   High-quality compensation databases use objective measures to define what the job does. Because these databases have a specific job content measure for each job they track, data can be retrieved on the basis of job content, thus ensuring that pay levels are reported for similar jobs. The highest quality databases put the most effort into quality control and data collection programs that group jobs of similar content.

Target salary.   Target salary represents a company's planned level of pay for a job based on the company's pay policy. Targets are usually set by salary midpoints or some other construct.

Incumbents

The actual characteristics of job holders themselves are the final determinants of pay for a job. These elements include:

Base salary.   The actual compensation of the job is, of course, the most important piece of information about the job holder. When compared to the target salary for the job, actual pay data yield important information about how much companies are actually paying for a job versus how much they are prepared to pay.

Bonus or other payments.   Information about bonuses and other payments, which includes cash bonuses, incentives, commissions, and profit-sharing awards, is a necessary element in determining competitive pay levels.

Location.   An incumbent's location, usually indicated by ZIP Code, is another big determinant of what the job is paid. Job holders in high-paying areas, such as New York and Southern California, usually are paid more than incumbents who hold the same job elsewhere.

Tenure.   Another significant influence on an individual job holder's pay is the length of time in a position. Pay for jobs in the legal, engineering, and scientific fields particularly are influenced by the individual's level of experience.

Other factors. The incumbent's breadth of experience, as measured by means other than length of service and certain demographic characteristics, also can contribute to pay differences.

Contemporary Computerized Pay Information Systems

All the data about jobs are useless to the compensation professional unless he or she possesses a system that can make the data readily available and applicable. Powerful information systems do exist and are needed to answer questions that involve some or all these pay determinants. The four most commonly asked questions are:

- How do companies in a particular industry with revenues greater than $X million pay their incumbents?

- What premium does the X job function get paid in the Y industry relative to the A, B, and C industries?

- How much should this particular job be paid in location Z?

- What is the mix of base and bonus compensation for this job function in this industry?

Answering these questions in the early 1980s was practically impossible; the data, for the most part, did not exist. More important, the computer hardware and software systems needed to develop a system capable of answering these questions would have been very expensive to develop and maintain.

As we enter the 1990s, however, the required computer systems are commonplace and relatively inexpensive. The perfection of software systems using relational database technology has made it much easier, cheaper, and faster to build databases capable of organizing, storing, and retrieving complex data. As the power of mainframe computers and microcomputers has grown, and as the costs of these invaluable tools have fallen, new pay information systems have mushroomed. Powerful relational databases now can be built on personal computers in a fraction of the time it would have taken to build less powerful mainframe systems during the early 1980s.

Aside from these significant technological advancements, another important development for compensation professionals is the addition of flexible and powerful report-writing capabilities. Although relational database technology and fast computers enable one to store and retrieve large volumes of data, these new easy-to-use report writers make it possible for individuals to analyze and display data in highly customized ways. Pay patterns of peer groups, organizational units, job functions, geographic regions, and specific types of pay plans can be studied in ways that were never before possible.

Case Studies

To get a sense of organizations' exploding data needs during the 1990s, let's follow a hypothetical organization through a series of business changes that prompt a need for changes in salary policies. From this example, we will see how the questions and issues become considerably more complex over time, and in response to this, the compensation database that provides pay market barometers must grow accordingly in both size and flexibility.

In 1984 Jay Manufacturing Co. was a small (about 75 employees and $10 million in revenues) manufacturer of electronic components used in further assembly by a number of diverse high technology companies, and headquartered in a northern New Jersey suburb of New York City. Although the organization had experienced very slow growth in 1982 and 1983, it was primed to increase rapidly. This prompted Jay's CEO to decide that more engineers would be needed if the organization was to meet its future growth requirements. Because engineers were to be the focal point, the key question from a compensation perspective was: Should engineers be paid any differently than other jobs and functions within Jay that were at the same grade and level? (See Table 30-1.)

Jay's review of the marketplace pay practices as shown in Table 30-1 revealed that engineers were indeed being paid a premium relative to other jobs. Thus, if Jay wanted to attract the best and brightest engineers to fuel its growth strategy, some type of differential, at least for individual contributors, seemed to be warranted.

By 1988 the company had grown large enough to open a second

Table 30-1. 1984 Engineering Jobs Relative to All Jobs

| | Average annual salaries | | |
Job level	National all jobs	National all engineers	Percent engineering premium
Entry-level	$24.4	$27.0	+9.7%
Intermediate	28.7	31.0	+7.4%
Senior	36.6	38.4	+4.6%
Supervisory	45.2	46.5	+2.8%
Managerial	58.3	56.9	−2.4%

SOURCE: 1984 Hay Engineering Compensation Comparison.

manufacturing facility in suburban Chicago, and this development raised two additional compensation questions:

- Was the general salary marketplace in Chicago different enough to merit a separate pay structure?
- If so, how should the engineers in Chicago be paid? According to a special "Chicago structure"? In line with the overall structure for Jay, or perhaps according to something else?

Analysis of the available market data contained in Table 30-2 showed that the overall market in Chicago was not substantially different from the national marketplace. The market data in Table 30-3, however, revealed that Chicago engineers were paid less than those in New York. Thus, if engineers in Chicago were left on the New York engineering structure, the company could attract enough well-qualified candidates to staff the new facility. One drawback, though, existed: Suppose the organization, at some time in the future, wished to back away from the New York engineering structure for Chicago engineers?

Jay Manufacturing also decided to move some of its product marketing people to Chicago to support greater product diversity. This decision, however, prompted a new question: What salary structure should be used to pay these employees competitively?

As the market information in Table 30-4 reveals, the number of marketplace choices had increased with the complexity of the business. At lower levels, marketing jobs in Chicago appear to have a lower salary marketplace than the "all jobs in Chicago" market levels. Yet, at the fully qualified and higher levels, the Chicago pay market was not adequate to attract and retain marketing professionals. Undoubtedly, Jay needed to decide whether the differences in the salary marketplace warranted separate salary structure treatment. Furthermore, Jay needed to make this decision in light of a number of factors including the business

Table 30-2. 1988 Chicago Area Salaries Relative to National Salaries

	Average annual salaries		
Job level	National all jobs	Chicago area all jobs	Percent difference
Entry-level	$29.2	$28.2	−3.4%
Intermediate	37.7	38.4	+1.9%
Senior	48.5	48.8	+0.6%
Supervisory	59.2	57.3	−3.2%
Managerial	84.8	87.3	+2.9%

SOURCE: 1988 Hay ACCESS Database.

Table 30-3. 1988 Engineering Average Annual Salary Comparison

Job level	National all engineers	Percent difference all engineers	
		New York	Chicago
Entry-level	$31.4	+4.8%	+1.6%
Intermediate	37.9	−8.2%	−1.6%
Senior	47.1	−1.1%	−4.0%
Supervisory	58.3	+5.5%	−8.6%
Managerial	80.3	−1.5%	+1.0%

SOURCE: 1988 Hay ACCESS Database.

Table 30-4. 1988 Marketing Average Annual Salary Comparison

Job level	All jobs		Marketing	
	National	Chicago	National	Chicago
Entry-level	$29.2	$28.2	$26.2	$26.8
Intermediate	37.7	38.4	35.0	33.9
Senior	48.5	48.8	47.9	49.3
Supervisory	59.2	57.3	59.9	59.0
Managerial	84.8	87.3	86.6	90.6

SOURCE: 1988 Hay ACCESS Database.

strategy of the organization, the number of employees affected, the cost of paying a premium for the high-level jobs, the administrative costs of implementing the premium, and other considerations. This dilemma greatly underscored the possibility that, in response to appropriate competitive salary conditions, different functions in the same location would be treated differently.

As of early 1989 Jay Manufacturing had grown into Jay Technologies, an organization with over $50 million in revenues and several hundred employees. The company's product line had evolved into two parallel product groups: one specializing in components for medical systems and the other continuing to serve the more generalized light manufacturing high-technology market. At this critical juncture, several organizational issues with significant compensation implications had to be addressed. The engineering function was now large enough that a separate research and development function needed to be created. This raised another key question: Should these individuals be paid differently than manufacturing or product development engineers? In addition, many of the engineers who were with the company in 1984 had stayed and continued to grow and develop, yet all of them could not be accommodated in the supervisory and managerial ranks. The body of knowledge and talent provided by these individuals was a valuable asset. Therefore, should a dual career ladder be developed? What pay levels would be appropriate? Jay Technologies, once again, examined available pay market data.

The market data presented in Tables 30-5, 30-6, and 30-7 (and summarized in Table 30-8) showed that in general industry, supervisors and managers in engineering and research and development were worth more than individual contributors, but exactly the opposite was true in the medical equipment and light manufacturing areas.

By mid-1989 Jay Technologies was evaluating compensation against roughly 15 marketplaces just for engineering and marketing jobs. And the organization was basing its evaluation on industry sector, function, location, job level, supervisory/nonsupervisory status, and subfunction within the engineering area (for example, manufacturing engineering, product development engineering, research and development engineering). In five short years, the company had come a long way from a single structure and a "one size fits all" program that worked for it when it was smaller and less diverse.

Table 30-5. 1988 R&D Engineer Salary Premium

| Job level | Average annual salaries | | R&D percent premium |
	All engineers	All R&D	
Senior	$47.1	$51.1	+8.5%
Supervisory	58.3	59.1	+1.4%
Managerial	80.3	82.9	+3.2%

SOURCE: 1988 Hay ACCESS Database.

Table 30-6. 1988 Engineering Salary Comparison: Managers to Individual Contributors

| Job level | Engineers (all industries) | | Percent difference |
	Supervisor/ manager	Individual contributors	
First-level supervisor and equivalent engineer	$53.5	$50.1	−6.4%
First-level manager and equivalent engineer	59.2	58.1	−1.9%
Second-level manager and equivalent engineer	74.3	62.9	−15.3%

SOURCE: 1988 Hay ACCESS Database.

Table 30-7. 1988 Engineering Salary Comparison: Light Manufacturing Versus Medical Equipment Industry

Job level	Engineers light manufacturing			Engineers medical equipment		
	Supervisor/ manager	Individual contributor	Percent difference	Supervisor/ manager	Individual contributor	Percent difference
First-level supervisor and equivalent engineer	$48.4	$52.2	+7.8%	$50.1	$54.1	+8.0%
First-level manager and equivalent engineer	54.5	58.9	+8.1%	56.4	60.7	+7.6%
Second-level manager and equivalent engineer	64.5	59.9	−7.1%	66.4	67.8	+2.1%

SOURCE: 1988 Hay ACCESS Database.

Table 30-8. Percent Relationship of Nonsupervisory to Supervisory Engineer Pay Levels in Various Environments

Job level	All industry*	Light manufacturing†	Medical equipment†	R&D‡
First-level supervisor/equivalent	−6.4%	+7.8%	+8.0%	−6.8%
First-level manager/equivalent	−1.9%	+8.1%	+7.6%	−16.8%
Second-level manager/equivalent	−15.3%	−7.1%	+2.1%	−6.3%

*From Table 30-6.
†From Table 30-7.
‡Not shown in other tables.

SOURCE: 1988 Hay ACCESS Database.

Conclusion

In this chapter we have reviewed some of the forces making the science of compensation more complex than ever before. This complexity causes the compensation professional to look much more closely at pay determinants when establishing pay practices. Advances in technology, particularly in computer hardware and relational database software, have made possible new, powerful databases with very detailed salary marketplace data. This chapter has demonstrated how such a database can be used by a company as its own needs change as a result of business growth.

31

The Use of Computers in Compensation

Marsha Cameron Haller

Principal, National Practice Leader
Salary Management
TPF&C, a Towers Perrin Company

No development in the 1980s has had greater impact on human resources management—particularly in the area of compensation—than computerization. By 1988, according to one survey, about three-fourths of all responding U.S. companies had automated at least a portion of their compensation function.[1] Considering that there are computer applications for virtually every component of compensation management, from costing a salary budget to evaluating a job to administering a stock option program, this finding isn't surprising. But, availability of appropriate applications is only part of the reason for reliance on the computer. The fact is, as the compensation function changes, the need for computer support expands.

Toward Greater Efficiency

Before the 1980s the compensation function was viewed as primarily administrative. Typical tasks included getting pay increases processed

[1]Morton E. Grossman and Margaret Magnus, "The Growing Dependence on HRIS," *Personnel Journal*, September 1988.

431

on time with a minimum of errors and conducting occasional special studies. Many organizations undertook some form of job evaluation and participated in annual surveys. Their most complex project, usually, was determining the size of annual merit budgets and salary structure adjustments.

In the last decade, however, a variety of factors have changed this environment. Increasing competitiveness has caused organizations to look for more effective ways to manage their greatest expense: payroll. This focus on cost control, coupled with an emphasis on productivity improvement via pay for performance, has created a partnership between line management and compensation professionals that was rare in the past. To manage a business effectively today, organizations recognize that they need more comprehensive information, faster than before, as well as innovative compensation programs to ensure a motivated, productive work force.

The drive toward productivity improvement has also affected how work is conducted within the compensation function itself. Leaner staffing requires more efficient ways of working. Manually dealing with administrative tasks such as updating salary information, recording re-evaluations, planning and implementing salary structures and merit budgets, and providing special reports is not feasible if compensation departments seek to provide strategic guidance and a high level of support to their organizations.

Yet, another factor contributing to the attractiveness of the computer is decentralization. As organizations decentralize, they often find it more difficult to maintain and analyze up-to-date compensation information. This task can be simplified greatly if all locations store information electronically, using similar computer systems that "guarantee" consistent application of pay policies and procedures.

In addition, legal and employee relations issues have set the stage for widespread use of computers in compensation. Although there have been no major legislative developments in the compensation area during the 1980s, there have been a number of judicial challenges, federal and state legislative proposals, and pressure from women's rights groups. In such a climate, it has become more and more important for employers to ensure greater objectivity and consistency in setting pay policies and programs.

At the same time, employees have come to expect more consistency and objectivity in their grade assignments and in the pay determination process. And, for the most part, the types of analyses required to ensure consistency can really be performed only with the help of a computer. This focus has, in fact, been one of the prime movers in what may be one of the more significant compensation developments of the decade: computer-aided job evaluation.

Along with these factors has come a series of dramatic technological improvements in the accessibility and "user-friendliness" of computers. When computerization of the human resources function first began, most employers had a mainframe system that typically housed payroll and, sometimes, other human resources information. Access to the system was restricted, primarily to the data processing staff, and flexibility was extremely limited. Thus, compensation professionals were not always able to answer simple questions easily (for example, How many employees in a certain location make more than $50,000?). Anything beyond standard reporting required special programming, and human resources applications usually were not top priorities in the data processing department.

The advent of the personal computer, however, gave compensation and other human resources professionals the ability to function almost independently. Personal computers quickly appeared in compensation departments across the United States and Canada. Although, initially, many simply accumulated dust, in time they became an integral part of the compensation function. Machine power increased (streamlining analysis of larger databases), hardware and software prices decreased, and menu-driven systems made use easy for nontechnical compensation staff.

The Current Scene

Today the personal computer touches most aspects of compensation management. Some systems, such as a human resources information system (HRIS), contain components for the administration and analysis of pay, but serve far broader purposes. Others are designed with more specialized objectives in mind.

Regardless of function, however, all computerized compensation systems have certain common features. These are data entry, analysis, and reporting. Data entry allows users to enter and edit information such as salaries, market pricing data, job-evaluation ratings, structured questionnaire responses, and so on. Typically, this information can be entered in a variety of ways: using optical scanning, using a data input screen within the system itself, or electronically transferring a file from another system.

A system's *analysis* capabilities let users mathematically manipulate entered data. In this way, users, for example, can calculate a compa-ratio, analyze the number of employees outside the salary range, update a salary structure, predict a job-evaluation score, and so on. As for *reporting*, most systems have both standard and ad hoc reporting features. Standard reports generally are produced in a set format, using preselected data items. Ad hoc reporting allows users to customize a report, selecting from among any number of data items.

What follows is a look at some broader salary management computer applications, with particular emphasis on the common system features of data entry, analysis, and reporting.

Salary Administration

With a computerized salary administration system, activities that used to require days or weeks (and an overwhelming supply of paper) to accomplish—such as budgeting, pay planning and tracking, and salary structure development—often can be completed in a matter of hours or even minutes. Further, as noted, many computerized systems are menu driven and extremely easy to use. This ease of use, coupled with the time savings that computerization fosters, enables compensation professionals to approach their jobs much more proactively than ever before. Not only can they play "what if" games, but they can also analyze data in greater detail and audit the use of the pay system to identify and correct deficiencies. Table 31-1 shows the components of a typical automated salary administration system.

Data

The importance of careful data selection and collection can be summarized in the statement, "You can't analyze what you don't have." In selecting a commercially available software package or installing an internally developed system, it is critical to assess what type of data can be collected as well as how easily information can be entered. In addition, consider whether the system allows for data importation from other sources—for example, PC to mainframe, mainframe to PC, or transfer of files from other PC-based systems.

Analysis

The analytical capabilities of a computerized salary administration system can greatly reduce the time needed for tasks such as forecasting

Table 31-1. Salary Administration System Components

Data	Analyses	Reports
• Employees	• Compa-ratios	• Compa-ratio report
Current base pay rates	• Salary increase guidelines	• Job evaluation summaries
Pay history	• Budgeting	Factor ratings
Annual incentive	• Cost analysis	Points by factor
Performance ratings	• Pay lines and salary struc-	Total points
Date of last increase	tures	• Employees due for salary
Job classification		action
Race		• Salary planning worksheets
Sex		• Ad hoc reporting
Employment status		
Service		
Age		
Tenure		
Education		
• Salary grades and ranges		
Current		
Planned		
• Market data		
Base salary		
Bonus		
Total cash		
• Jobs		
Job evaluation		
Ratings		
Point scores		
Grade assignments		
• Organizational data		
Organizational units		
Locations		
Reporting relationships		
• Miscellaneous data		
• Blank fields for optional		
use		

and budgeting, analyzing payroll increase costs, and developing or adjusting salary structures. The following example illustrates how computerized analyses can be used to modify a salary structure. Assuming that all the necessary data were in a computerized system, the following steps could be completed in an hour or less.

Step 1.　Request a regression of total job evaluation points against market data. Plot the resulting pay line as shown in Figure 31-1.

Step 2.　Plot the existing salary structure against the new pay line. In this example, the resulting graph (Figure 31-2) would show that the

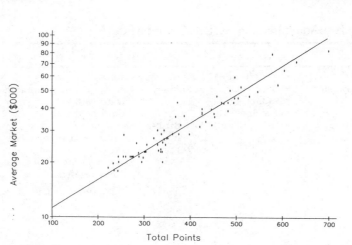

Figure 31-1. Step 1.

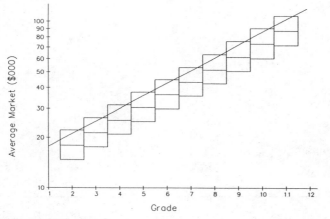

Figure 31-2. Step 2.

current pay structure is too low if the organization seeks to track the market.

Step 3.   Calculate new ranges by entering the market pay line equation and desired range widths. Plot the new ranges (Figure 31-3).

Step 4.   Plot actual employee pay rates against the new ranges and determine the cost of bringing all employees to the grade minimum (Figure 31-4).

Step 5.   Explore variations on the planned salary structure—for example, increasing midpoint differentials, changing the number of

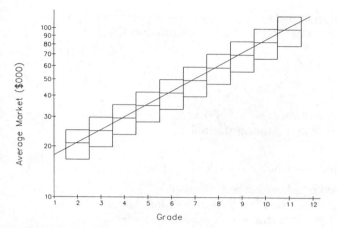

Figure 31-3. Step 3.

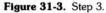

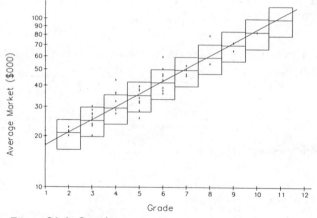

Figure 31-4. Step 4.

grades, pricing the structure differently in different locations. Conduct impact analyses to determine the change in the relationship of the grade structure to market data and the cost to the organization.

Step 6.   Assign employees to new salary grades and ranges.

Beyond tasks such as this, a well-designed system allows users to conduct analyses on subsets of stored data, such as all employees in a particular location, all jobs in a specific function or department, all employees above a particular pay rate, or some combination thereof.

Reporting

Computerized salary administration reports assist compensation professionals in a variety of ways. Among them are:

- Providing a method for tracking and controlling pay increases
- Ensuring that pay is administered consistently—for example, that particular departments don't have compa-ratios that are always high or always low, or pay rates that are consistently under the range minimum or over the maximum
- Conducting special studies at the request of management—for example, establishing the market competitiveness of current pay practices in a particular fashion.

Figures 31-5 and 31-6 provide examples of the types of reports that most computerized systems can produce.

INCUMBENT	JOB CODE	JOB TITLE	LEVEL	CURRENT SALARY	MINIMUM	CURRENT MIDPOINT	MAXIMUM	COMPA-RATIO	$ UNDER MINIMUM	$ OVER MAXIMUM
EMPLOYEE A	5606001	TECHNICAL SUPPORT SPEC.	EX 4	$ 27600	$ 23203	$ 29004	$ 34805	95.2%		
				$ 27600		$ 29004		95.2%	$ 0	$ 0
EMPLOYEE B	5101951	CUSTOMER SERVICE REP	EX 3	$ 25400	$ 20035	$ 25044	$ 30053	101.4%		
EMPLOYEE C	5626295	PROGRAMMER I	EX 3	$ 23750	$ 20035	$ 25044	$ 30053	94.8%		
EMPLOYEE D	5331574	BUDGET ANALYST	EX 3	$ 24500	$ 20035	$ 25044	$ 30053	97.8%		
				$ 73650		$ 75132		98.0%	$ 0	$ 0
EMPLOYEE E	5321674	COMPUTER OPERATOR	EX 2	$ 22500	$ 17301	$ 21627	$ 25952	104.0%		
				$ 22500		$ 21627		104.0%	$ 0	$ 0
		OVERALL ==>		$ 123750		$ 125763		98.4%	$ 0	$ 0

```
TOTAL RECORDS PROCESSED -    5
# INCLUDED IN SUMMARIES -    5
```

Figure 31-5. Compa-Ratio Report. *(Derived from Salary Manager Plus, a proprietary product of TPF&C. Reproduced with permission.)*

EMPLOYEE NAME	JOB CODE/JOB TITLE	LEVEL	LAST INCREASE	CURRENT SALARY	SALARY RANGE	COMPA-RATIO	PERF APPR	-- PLANNED INCREASE -- DATE / AMOUNT	COMPA-RATIO
EMPLOYEE A	5606001 TECHNICAL SUPPORT SPEC.	EX 4	$4199.00 17.9% 01/01/89	$ 27600	$ 23203 $ 29004 $ 34805	95.2%	2	01/01/90 $2208.00 01/01/90 $2760.00 (12-12 MOS) (8.0-10.0%)	102.8% 104.7%
						INCREASE #1: INCREASE #2:		__/__/__ $_____ TYPE:__ __/__/__ $_____ TYPE:__	
EMPLOYEE B	5101951 CUSTOMER SERVICE REP	EX 3	$ 400.00 1.6% 01/01/89	$ 25400	$ 20035 $ 25044 $ 30053	101.4%	6		
						INCREASE #1: INCREASE #2:		__/__/__ $_____ TYPE:__ __/__/__ $_____ TYPE:__	
EMPLOYEE C	5626295 PROGRAMMER I	EX 3	$2023.50 9.3% 01/01/89	$ 23750	$ 20035 $ 25044 $ 30053	94.8%	3	01/01/90 $1425.00 01/01/90 $1900.00 (12-12 MOS) (6.0- 8.0%)	100.5% 102.4%
						INCREASE #1: INCREASE #2:		__/__/__ $_____ TYPE:__ __/__/__ $_____ TYPE:__	
EMPLOYEE D	5331574 BUDGET ANALYST	EX 3	$4370.00 21.7% 01/01/89	$ 24500	$ 20035 $ 25044 $ 30053	97.8%	4	01/01/90 $ 122.50 01/01/90 $ 122.50 (12-12 MOS) (0.5- 0.5%)	98.3% 98.3%
						INCREASE #1: INCREASE #2:		__/__/__ $_____ TYPE:__ __/__/__ $_____ TYPE:__	
EMPLOYEE E	5321674 COMPUTER OPERATOR	EX 2	$1831.60 8.9% 01/01/89	$ 22500	$ 17301 $ 21627 $ 25952	104.0%	2	01/01/90 $1350.00 01/01/90 $1800.00 (12-12 MOS) (6.0- 8.0%)	110.3% 112.4%
						INCREASE #1: INCREASE #2:		__/__/__ $_____ TYPE:__ __/__/__ $_____ TYPE:__	

Figure 31-6. Salary Planning Worksheet 1. *(Derived from Salary Manager Plus, a proprietary product of TPF&C. Reproduced with permission.)*

Job Evaluation and Analysis

Computer-aided job evaluation (CAJE) came into its own early in the 1980s. The primary impetus was employers' frustration with some of the limitations of traditional job evaluation. Specifically, organizations were concerned about:

- The time and resources needed to conduct job evaluations (for example, to develop narrative job descriptions or evaluate jobs in committees) and to administer and maintain the program
- The need for ongoing support from consulting firms
- Employees' and line managers' negative views of their existing evaluation systems
- The tedious task of replicating evaluations on a large number of similar jobs

With CAJE, organizations have an opportunity not only to reduce time spent on evaluations, but also to create a defensible, objective approach to pay. Table 31-2 displays the typical features of a CAJE system.

Table 31-2. Components of a Computer-Aided Job Evaluation System

Data	Analyses	Reports
• Structured questionnaire	• Data verification	• Evaluation rationale
Compensable factor-related items	Data validity and consistency	• Evaluation documentation
Tasks	Inter-rater reliability	• Comparison of results by factor
Skills	• Job evaluation	• Total points summary
• Job information	Factor ratings	• Ad hoc reporting
Average salary	Factor points	
Market data	Total points	
Job evaluation scoring results	Predicted pay rate	
Grade assignments	Predicted grade assignment	
• Salary ranges	• Graphics and statistics	
• Organizational data	Factor weights	
Organization units	Total points against market (pay line analysis)	
Reporting relationships		

Data

Data collection is accomplished through a "structured" questionnaire that replaces traditional job analysis. The questionnaire is structured in that it provides for closed-ended responses to multiple-choice questions or numerical or quantitative items. Questionnaires typically are based on recognized compensable factors, with questions that are designed to capture traditional measures of job value, such as skill, effort, responsibility, and working conditions. The structured format also allows responses to be entered directly into a computer.

Analysis

Once the questionnaire is administered to knowledgeable job respondents—for example, incumbents, supervisors, senior functional managers, job analysts—data are entered into the computer and data verification begins. This first analytical stage involves checking the accuracy and consistency of a single questionnaire. Generally, this is done through messages built into the software that flag invalid or inconsistent data. The former include responses that are not legitimate and items left blank. The latter are identified when there are widely divergent responses on two items that are logically or statistically correlated.

After preliminary data verification, questionnaire responses are processed through job-evaluation scoring routines. Although these routines vary from system to system, they typically produce evaluation ratings by factor, points by factor, total points, a job's market rate, midpoint, or grade assignment.

The development of scoring routines is most frequently based on heuristics methods such as regression analysis, although some systems use algorithms or templates against which an employee's score is compared. Questionnaire responses for benchmark jobs are regressed against the data that ultimately will be predicted (for example, factor ratings, factor points, market data, current pay rates). The resulting equations are "hard-coded" into the system software and used to score responses for both nonbenchmark positions and new jobs. Some organizations develop the scoring routines to replicate their current job evaluation results and pay rates, thereby maintaining their existing hierarchy but automating their system to streamline the administrative process. Others are more interested in tracking the market when setting up a salary structure.

Reporting

The second stage of data verification investigates the reasonableness of the evaluation results. Figure 31-7 shows how reports can be used to assess the results for an individual compensable factor. This report lists factor ratings and displays the underlying questionnaire data for a se-

JOB CODE	JOB TITLE	FORM #	EVALUATOR	FACTOR LEVEL	FACT-FINDING AND ANALYSIS				SUB FACTOR LEVEL	ORIGINALITY AND CREATIVITY				SUB FACTOR LEVEL
					07	08	09	10		11	12	13	14	
5214412 - 0	DIR MARKET RESEARCH	101	SUPERVISOR	16.35	C	B	A	C	9.07	C	A	B	C	7.58
5204931 - 0	VP GENERAL MANAGER DIV B	91	AUDITOR	15.90	D	B	A	C	9.07	D	B	A	D	7.20
5606001 - 0	VP INFORMATION SVCS DIV	123	INCUMBENT	15.90	C	B	A	C	9.07	C	B	A	D	7.20
5120921 - 0	ASSISTANT VP SALES DIV A	34	AUDITOR	14.40	D	B	A	D	7.20	D	B	A	D	7.20
5120981 - 0	VP SALES & MKTG DIV A	33	AUDITOR	14.40	D	C	A	D	7.20	D	B	A	D	7.20
5214951 - 0	VP OPERATIONS DIVISION B	102	AUDITOR	14.40	C	B	A	D	7.20	C	B	A	D	7.20
5224941 - 0	VP SALES & MKTG DIV B	65	AUDITOR	14.40	D	C	A	D	7.20	D	B	A	D	7.20
5101921 - 0	VICE PRESIDENT GOVT RELS	35	AUDITOR	12.61	B	B	A	D	7.20	C	A	B	D	5.71
5101971 - 0	VP BUSINESS DEVELOPMENT	31	AUDITOR	12.61	D	B	A	D	7.20	D	A	B	D	5.71
5101991 - 0	VP PLANNING & DEVELOPMENT	40	AUDITOR	12.61	C	B	A	D	7.20	C	A	B	D	5.71
5112981 - 0	VP OPERATIONS DIV A	18	INCUMBENT	12.61	C	B	A	D	7.20	B	A	B	D	5.71
5122442 - 0	DIR MARKETING SERVICES	57	AUDITOR	12.61	D	B	A	D	7.20	D	A	B	D	5.71
5616012 - 0	DP CONTROLLER	120	SUPERVISOR	12.61	B	B	A	D	7.20	B	A	B	D	5.71
5626022 - 0	DIR INFO SVCS DIV A	121	SUPERVISOR	12.61	B	B	A	D	7.20	B	A	B	D	5.71
5626032 - 0	DIR INFO SVCS DIV B	122	SUPERVISOR	12.61	B	B	A	D	7.20	B	A	B	D	5.71
5224453 - 0	ACCOUNT EXECUTIVE		AUDITOR	11.42	D	A	B	D	5.71	D	A	B	D	5.71

Figure 31-7. Factor comparison problem solving. *(Derived from WJQ, a proprietary product of TPF&C. Reproduced with permission.)*

ries of jobs. It can be used to check the results by factor in much the same way as would be done under a traditional job evaluation system. Figure 31-8 shows one way to display overall results.

CAJE offers organizations a number of advantages. First, a computer-aided system definitely speeds up the evaluation process. It diminishes the time that line management must spend in evaluation committees and that employees or supervisors must give to writing job descriptions. Computerized scoring routines produce results automatically, and data verification procedures enable reviewers to focus only on potential discrepancies, rather than the whole job.

Second, a computer-aided system eases the administrative burden associated with traditional job evaluation. Computerized maintenance and administration provide the ability to document and analyze results automatically.

Third, use of a computer-aided system helps limit the potential for system manipulation and, hence, cuts down on battles between line management and compensation staff. The structured questionnaire facilitates an *objective* analysis of job content, and the variety of comparisons available also provide the job evaluator with more comprehensive information to respond to management's questions and concerns about rankings and grade assignments.

Fourth, computer-aided systems can greatly enhance the credibility of the job evaluation process. Because they tend to create the impression of objectivity, there is greater likelihood that employees will "buy into" the process and the results.

Notwithstanding the attractiveness of CAJE, there are issues compa-

JOBCODE	JOB TITLE	LEVEL	MIDPOINT	TOTAL	SKILL & KNOWLEDGE LVL PTS	PROBLEM SOLVING LVL PTS	CONTACTS LVL PTS	SCOPE LVL PTS	WORKING CONDITIONS LVL PTS
5204931	VP GENERAL MANAGER DIV B	EX	9	62370.00	630	12 177	15 188	11 70	15 190	0 5
5606001	VP INFORMATION SVCS DIV	EX	9	62370.00	626	14 193	15 188	9 61	14 179	0 5
5224941	VP SALES & MKTG DIV B	EX	8	52181.49	590	12 173	14 170	11 69	13 172	0 6
5120981	VP SALES & MKTG DIV A	EX	8	52181.49	578	11 163	14 170	11 70	13 170	0 5
5214951	VP OPERATIONS DIVISION B	EX	8	52181.49	570	11 158	14 170	15 94	11 143	0 5
5112981	VP OPERATIONS DIV A	EX	7	45059.14	529	11 163	12 147	9 61	11 153	0 5
5120921	ASSISTANT VP SALES DIV A	EX	7	45059.14	528	10 145	14 170	10 65	11 143	0 5
5214412	DIR MARKET RESEARCH	EX	7	45059.14	510	10 150	16 194	5 38	9 123	0 5
5101971	VP BUSINESS DEVELOPMENT	EX	7	45059.14	504	11 163	12 147	5 39	11 150	0 5
5101991	VP PLANNING & DEVELOPMENT	EX	7	45059.14	504	11 158	12 147	5 36	12 158	0 5
5616012	DP CONTROLLER	EX	6	38904.17	496	10 145	12 147	9 57	10 142	0 5
5626022	DIR INFO SVCS DIV A	EX	6	38904.17	488	11 158	12 147	9 57	9 121	0 5
5626032	DIR INFO SVCS DIV B	EX	6	38904.17	488	11 158	12 147	9 57	9 121	0 5
5224453	ACCOUNT EXECUTIVE	EX	6	38904.17	453	9 131	11 132	10 63	9 121	0 6
5122442	DIR MARKETING SERVICES	EX	6	38904.17	452	10 145	12 147	4 34	9 121	0 5
5101921	VICE PRESIDENT GOVT RELS	EX	5	33592.11	402	0 18	12 147	11 70	12 162	0 5

TOTAL RECORDS PROCESSED -   16

Figure 31-8. Evaluation Summary Report. *(Derived from WJQ, a proprietary product of TPF&C. Reproduced with permission.)*

nies should be aware of. For instance, the computer cannot make decisions about the reasonableness of evaluation results; human judgment is also needed to ensure a workable end product. There is also a perception that CAJE is a "black box"—complicated and mysterious—which reduces the system's credibility. Here, however, employers can demystify the process by building as many traditional job-evaluation elements as possible into a CAJE system. Indeed, the most effective computer-aided systems generally incorporate the main features of traditional factor-based job evaluation, including compensable factors, degrees, points, and so on. Using these basic elements in a CAJE system makes it easier to communicate the system to both line management and employees, thus helping to eliminate the "black box" perception. Finally, organizations need to recognize up front that they probably will not realize any time and cost savings from CAJE in the implementation phase. In most cases, the payoff comes with ongoing maintenance and administration. In this context, it is obvious that an organization must have a sufficient number of employees to make CAJE worthwhile from a productivity perspective.

Market Data Analysis

The computer has had a major impact on the way employers access and analyze market pay data. With PC-based software that facilitates both the entry and review of survey data, organizations can:

- Store job matches and pricings from different surveys and generate market rates
- Input survey data on diskettes and/or receive output diskettes for use in analysis

Generally, the first application is made possible by a module within a computerized salary administration system and includes the types of components listed in Table 31-3. Data entry allows users to match a job against one in a given survey and enter survey results. These are then "aged," weighted, and statistically analyzed. They can be displayed as part of a detailed report on each job (see Figure 31-9), included in a listing with other data, or plotted as a data point in a graph.

The second computer application typically is part of the process of participating in an externally sponsored salary survey. Diskettes are provided to expedite the data submission process and often contain software that conduct some simple accuracy checks while the data are being entered. These PC diskettes may also be used to update data submitted in prior years. In some cases, the survey sponsors also provide

Table 31-3. Survey Analysis System Components

Data	Analyses	Reports
• Survey source • Effective date • Company job code • Survey job code • Number of cases by job code • Market bonus • Market total compensation • Market salary • Degree of match	• Aging survey data • Weighting survey data • Regression of job scope, and so on, against market • Survey statistics (for example, percentiles)	• Competitive comparisons • Ad hoc reporting and graphics • Audit systems

```
Job Code 5101921    VICE PRESIDENT GOVT RELS    Source   1
                                                TPF&C CDB
Survey Code    12                               01/01/88
Survey Title   TOP EXEC REL GOVT                In Use
Use Job? (Y/N) Y In Use
Modifier       2%
Cases          15
Period         A Annual

               Raw Data     Aged to 01/01/90
MKTBONUS       83232.00     91763.28
MKTTCOMP       70000.00     77175.00
MKTSALARY      90000.00     99225.00




                        F3 Save   F4 Cancel   F10 Help
```

Figure 31-9. Survey matches. *(Derived from Salary Manager Plus, a proprietary product of TPF&C. Reproduced with permission.)*

output diskettes that display survey results and allow users to change assumptions (for example, increase the revenue value) and receive new results on-line.

Other Computer Applications

Many organizations have started to use the computer to maintain records and conduct analyses on incentive compensation, particularly stock option administration. Data typically stored in such an administration system include:

- Year of grant
- Amount of grant
- Amount vested
- Number of shares exercised
- Date of exercise
- Option price
- Market value at exercise

These systems can also be used to report option status to employees and to assist organizations in meeting statutory requirements and determining eligibility for tax benefits (benefits that have often been overlooked in the past because of the administrative burden of providing the necessary documentation).

Still another increasingly common application is storage of job documentation information used for purposes such as job descriptions, job classification, career development, training, job evaluation, performance appraisal, and broad-scale human resources planning. The development of high-density diskettes and CD-ROM has made this an easier task.

Although these systems vary in setup and use, all begin with job analysis typically based on the tasks and activities associated with a job, data related to compensable factors, or a combination of these. Here, data are usually collected through a structured (that is, closed-ended) questionnaire to facilitate electronic recording of the responses. Sometimes, open-ended information is collected as well. More recently, organizations have begun to look at ways to incorporate skill requirements into job analysis.

A major advantage of a system based on compensable factors is that it can be linked to the job-evaluation system. If job evaluation is computer-aided, this link may also be mechanized. But, this type of system can also be too generic for the needs of many organizations. This is because a compensable-factor-based-structured questionnaire ignores specific tasks that are not comparable from job family to job family. Some organizations, therefore, have sought to combine a compensable-factor approach with task information collected through open-ended questions and then entered into a computer system via a menu-driven word processing and editing facility. The resulting job documentation is then submitted to job incumbents and/or managers for review and modification.

In selecting or developing computer-based job documentation, an organization must focus on the purpose of the information. If it will be used simply for job descriptions, for example, a compensable-factor approach combined with task and responsibility statements may be sufficient. If a formal productivity analysis is planned, a task- or activity-based system is more appropriate.

Issues to Consider

Organizations need to evaluate a number of basic issues before deciding to automate their compensation function. One is whether the system should reside on a PC or a mainframe. Advantages of a PC include flexibility, ease of access, cost efficiency, and, typically, greater user-friendliness. In addition, technological changes and enhancements have made PCs increasingly powerful. Some machines can now accommodate several thousand cases (that is, employees, jobs, and so on). Overall database storage and reporting capabilities, however, are still somewhat more advanced on a mainframe. Thus, many organizations find the best approach is to use both mainframes and PCs—each for what it does best.

Organizations also need to consider the degree of automation that makes sense for them. At the most basic level, a system would cover administrative activities such as salary or incentive administration. Today there are many commercially available computerized salary administration systems that can meet an organization's administrative needs. And, by building on an ad hoc report-writing capability, an organization can greatly increase system flexibility. In addition, of course, it is less expensive to purchase a system than to develop one or pay an outside vendor to build one.

Automation of the job evaluation process creates more complexity and more risk. This is because the success of a CAJE system depends on subjective factors such as organizational culture and sophistication, as well as on the ability to provide sufficient internal staff support in the implementation phase. In the long run, however, a CAJE system requires less stable support than a traditional system. Before deciding to automate job evaluation, organizations must take into account their size, values, culture, level of technical sophistication, communication style, and the level of commitment to a rigorous process. They must also consider whether to use a customized or general system.

Generic CAJE systems are based on predetermined factors and a standard questionnaire design. Thus, organizations have the assurance of knowing they are relying on tested factors—questionnaire and software. This typically reduces cost and development "debugging" time. Furthermore, generic systems may be semicustomized through factor weighting procedures and wording changes to the questionnaire. Custom systems, by contrast, allow organizations to select their own factors and to create a fully tailored questionnaire. This can be a decided advantage if an organization has a unique value system to communicate.

Conclusion

Computerization will ultimately change the face of salary management; it is clearly not a fad. Use of computers has grown so rapidly precisely because automation meets employers' needs, enabling them to perform a range of salary management activities faster, more inexpensively, and more efficiently than before.

To realize these advantages, however, initial planning is essential. Modifications after the fact may be expensive and difficult to implement. Thus, organizations must take the time to determine their needs up front—and *then* put in the system that best supports those needs.

32

Salary Budgeting and Planning: Enhancing the Process Through the Use of the Computer

Charles H. Fay

Associate Director, Institute of Management and Labor Relations
Rutgers University

Salary budgeting and planning processes have always been constrained because end products have had short lead times and the process has been almost entirely a manual one. These constraints have made it necessary to pursue a centralized, aggregated approach. This has led to the adoption of top-down resource allocation systems, characterized by superficial consistency across organizational levels and departments.

Access to computers, and particularly to sophisticated human resource information systems, has allowed compensation managers to re-

Mr. Fay acknowledges the contributions of Jeff Knapp of InSci in preparing this chapter.

think the planning and budgeting process.[1] It is now possible to plan and budget for compensation programs differently and better[2]—to pursue a distributed nonaggregated approach based on precise human resource information and projections, tied to organizational objectives and business plans, allowing for differentiation across organizational levels and departments according to need and contribution to meeting organizational goals.[3]

Most organizations currently prepare salary increase budgets as an allocation process. Under this approach, the organization takes a fixed total salary increase budget and allocates it across members of the organization. This dominant process is characterized by (1) a blurring of the distinction between merit, market, and other adjustments; (2) a top-down control perspective; (3) general ignoring of known and projected human resources changes such as retirement, reorganization, expansion, and downsizing; (4) a static budgetary (rather than a dynamic cash flow) perspective; and (5) minimal responsibility on the part of most managers for truly planning and budgeting compensation needs in support of strategic objectives.

In addition, this approach to compensation planning is not suitable for the "new compensation" practices (for example, gain sharing, lump-sum bonuses) and allows little opportunity for meaningful audit and control. More recently, a number of leading-edge organizations (mostly business units of larger organizations), utilizing the power of computers and the human resources information system HRIS, have begun to approach compensation budgeting in a different manner.

These companies have begun to treat compensation budgeting in much the same way as most organizations treat other forms of operations budgeting: as a key managerial task to be carried out in support of organizational objectives. The American Compensation Association discusses this as a useful alternative to more traditional matrix-driven planning systems.

The alternate approach to compensation budgeting is characterized by (1) a sharpened distinction between merit, market, and other adjustments; (2) a "bottom-up" aggregational perspective; (3) careful consideration of known and projected human resources, changes such as retirement, promotion, expansion, and downsizing; (4) a dynamic cash flow perspective; and (5) routine integrated responsibility on the part of

[1]Dennis Wirtz, "Spreadsheet Software and Salary Policy Development," *HR/PC*, Vol. 2.7, August 16–September 30, 1987, pp. 4–12.
[2]William Howe, "Manage Salaries With a Goal-Seeking Spreadsheet," *HR/PC*, Vol. 3.3, February 16–March 31, 1988, pp. 4–12.
[3]Marc J. Wallace, Jr., and N. Fredric Crandall, "Data-Based Compensation Decisions," *Topics in Total Compensation: Compensation Database Management*, Vol. 3, No. 3, Spring 1989, pp. 213–221.

most managers for truly planning and budgeting compensation needs in support of strategic objectives. This approach also allows for alternate forms of compensation such as lump-sum bonuses and can be integrated with a meaningful audit and control system.

Salary Budgeting Practices Based on Allocation Approaches

Description

Under current salary budgeting practices, a finance department typically requests the compensation department to provide an estimate of the percentage increase to salary budget needed for the following year. Typically, this figure is requested in mid-summer to fall.

Compensation develops a matrix (see Table 32-1) that managers can use as a guideline in allocating the budget increase. When done by hand, the development of the appropriate matrix for an employee population may take as long as 2 weeks. Much of this time is spent in collecting data on employee populations; distributions of performance and of compa-ratios must be calculated.

These two factors determine the percentage increase given to employees. Thus, an employee judged to perform at a higher level will receive a larger percentage increase. If no constraints were placed on this process, however, an employee who consistently performed at a high level would end up above the maximum of the salary range to which he or she is assigned. To prevent this, employee position in range (as measured by compa-ratio) is also taken into account. Thus, an exceptional employee in the upper third of his or her range will receive a lower percentage increase than an employee who is also exceptional but in the

Table 32-1. The Fay/Wallace Corporation
Nonexempt Employees Performance Matrix

	Compa-ratio				
Performance rating	80–84	85–94	95–104	105–114	115–120
Outstanding	14	12	10	8	6
Exceeds standards	11	9	7	5	3
Meets standards	9	7	5	3	0
Needs improvement	4	2	0	0	0
Unsatisfactory	0	0	0	0	0

middle or lower third of the range. If matrix guidelines are followed, aggregate salary increases under this system should net out to a percentage increase to salary budget equaling the increase percentage developed in the planning period.

Based on expected market movements, the compensation department also develops adjusted salary structures for the upcoming year. These structures are typically developed in October to November. In December packets containing the revised salary structures, the merit matrix, a payroll calendar for the coming year, and a salary planning worksheet (with instructions) are sent to supervisors and managers. Because different budget increase numbers may be assigned to different groups of employees (for example, exempt and nonexempt), there may be more than one matrix.

Managers can use the worksheets to plan for salary adjustments, but these worksheets contain only current employees and limited actions. The salary planning worksheets are primarily for the use of the managers who receive them; they are not reviewed or approved by the compensation department. Their use in individual line units in the organization typically varies.

Problems With the Current Salary Budgeting Process

Because technology and time have limited organizations to this (or an equivalent) approach, it has become part of most organizations' "compensation philosophy" as an appropriate technique for planning and budgeting. There are several problems with this approach to salary budgeting. Some are conceptual and could be corrected only by a major restructuring of the process. Other problems are more a matter of implementation, and the current process might be improved in such a way as to resolve those problems.

Conceptual Problems. The most severe problems in the current approach to salary increase budgeting arise from the concept of the salary increase budget as a means of allocating a predetermined fixed resource across the employee population. Salaries are predominantly seen as an expense to be controlled rather than as an investment to be deployed. This viewpoint works against the strategic use of compensation and handicaps the organization in a variety of ways:

1. A top-down control perspective in salary budgeting processes reinforces the notion that, at least when it comes to salaries, managers are not to be trusted to make decisions that are based on business needs.

This does not suggest that managers can make salary judgment decisions without the specialized market knowledge resident in the compensation department. It does propose, however, that managers should have the same role in salary planning that they have in other expense budgeting and in capital budgeting, where proposals based on business needs are generated and aggregated upwards, subject to senior management's final decision.

2. A top-down control perspective creates a mindset that individual departments should have some predetermined distribution of performance to make the matrix come out right. This puts pressures on managers to rate the performance of their subordinates against the desired distribution rather than against appropriate performance standards. The system operates against outstanding managers who manage the performance of their direct reports to produce a high level of performance across the board, and provides no incentive for less competent managers to gain across-the-board increases of excellence among their direct reports.

It also promotes salary budgeting "gamesmanship" among managers who wish to reward direct reports according to their contribution rather than to some theoretical performance distribution. (In one Fortune 50 company, managers get together and "trade" merit ratings so that the organization as a whole will have a distribution that supports the budget.)

3. The typical salary budgeting approach does not allow for differentiation of the adjustments to salary made for a variety of reasons: merit, market, promotion, additional employees, or other human resources activities. Instead, all salary changes are lumped into a "merit" budget. This practice weakens links between pay and performance. It is little wonder that employee attitude surveys ordinarily report little perceived relationship between performance and pay.

4. This salary budgeting approach does not sufficiently take into account known or projected changes in all human resources allocations. It is possible to take into account expected changes in grade for current employees as a result of reclassification, promotion, or entry into/exit from a training program. The approach does not require managers to practice comprehensive human resources planning and translate those plans into salary costs.

5. This salary budgeting process, because it is based on a percentage increase to aggregate payroll, tends to reinforce the importance of base pay and adjustments to base pay. Organizations are beginning to move

toward a decreased dependence on base pay and toward the "new" pay, with more of the individual's total pay being "at risk." Multiple targeted earnings opportunities with lump-sum payouts are replacing base pay with annual adjustments to base. Salary budgeting processes that support this approach toward pay are necessary if the new pay is to work.

6. The greatest shortcoming of the current system is its lack of sensitivity to the strategic needs of the organization. Basically, salary adjustments are driven by a single aggregate percentage increase number rather than by the strategic goals of the company. All human resources processes ought to be designed to support managers in achieving the goals set forth in the business plan. Compensation processes, in particular ought to do this, because pay is the most powerful tool available to the manager for affecting performance of direct reports.

Implementation Problems. Most systems using this approach have additional flaws in their implementation, even if it is decided that a top-down cost control approach is appropriate for the organization:

1. A cross-sectional budget that does not take cash flow into account does not provide sufficient information for good decisions. In addition, when sufficient controls are absent, managers can utilize "surpluses" based on cash flow (for example, salary increases budgeted for the end of the year) for salary actions not in line with organizational policy.

2. The process does not allow for much audit or control of the salary adjustment process by the compensation department. A key service the compensation department can serve (in conjunction with other human resources department functions) is to audit the effectiveness of human resources programs and decisions. An ancillary function is ensuring that the equity goals of the compensation system are met, particularly with respect to practices that might form the basis of a fair employment practices charge.

Optimizing Current Practice

Making the current salary increase budget process better is possible by concentrating on the current problems of implementation. Utilizing computers and HRIS data can speed the process and allow the compensation manager to inspect alternative programs for their impact on the organization.

Data can be retrieved from the HRIS showing performance distributions and employee compa-ratios against the new structure.[4] Rather than determining distributions at the margins of the matrix and assuming even internal distributions, the compensation manager can calculate the more or less precise distribution of employees in each cell of the matrix.

Even with a simple spreadsheet program, a matrix can be set up and the total payout calculated based on percentage increases assigned to each cell. This allows the compensation manager to model a number of percentage increase patterns and see the impact on the total salary budget. Other "what if" possibilities include varying assumed performance distributions, providing a range of increases (for example, high performers in the middle of the range get between 6 and 8 percent), and varying time of increase (for example, low performers above midpoint are not eligible for another increase for 18 months, whereas high performers below midpoint may be eligible for another increase in 9 months). The software required for this last task goes beyond the "flat" spreadsheet and requires either linked spreadsheets or a three-dimensional matrix. Likewise, the feed-in from the HRIS is somewhat more complex.

A second change that can be made is to take cash flow into account. The budgeting process should specifically note when projected changes are to take place and limit increases in total budget to amounts that will cover those adjustments only for the time periods in which they are effective. The matrix used by most organizations ignores cash flow effects completely; again, with more sophisticated software, cash flow can be taken into account when calculating payout and increase percentages adjusted accordingly.

Associated with this is the need to implement a greater audit and control function in the salary budgeting process. Salary plans should be aggregated so that better projections of actual expenditures in the upcoming plan year can be made. Likewise, variances between planned and actual expenditures should be tracked. Adherence to fair employment practices can be audited and corrections can be made, if necessary. These audit and control functions require a fairly complete HRIS, because a large variety of demographic (for example, race, gender) and process (for example, turnover, start dates) variables may be critical.

These changes would enhance the effectiveness of the salary increase budget process based on a top-down allocation approach, allowing for more accurate planning in light of market movements and the organi-

[4]Joan Wilder, "Downloading from PC-Focus to Lotus 1-2-3 for Salary Planning," *HR/PC*, Vol. 1.7, August, 1986, pp. 5–8.

zation's needs, while ensuring that the implementation of the salary increase budget is more closely in line with organizational plans. In essence, these changes would make the salary budgeting and planning process faster and more accurate. They would not take advantage of the power of the computer or the software currently available to make the process substantially better; these changes would not provide the opportunity for the salary increase budget to become a fully integrated part of the human resources planning process or strengthen links between salary management and fulfillment of business goals.

Compensation Planning as a Managerial Function: Using the Power of the Computer

Purpose

Automating the current system may not be enough.[5] A different approach to salary increase budgeting, which would build on those parts of the current system that support a strategic approach to compensation, could be instituted. Some organizations are beginning to take this approach, at least in part.[6] The basic premise of this approach is that individual managers are in the best position to develop draft plans for salary expenditures for the coming year that will support those managers in achieving the goals set for them in the business plan. This approach is similar to the planning approach used by most organizations for capital budgeting and other expense budgeting. Those managers responsible for achieving specific business objectives are also responsible for estimating the resources necessary to do the job.

The role of the compensation department, under this approach, is to serve as an internal consultant to managers and as an internal auditor for senior management. The compensation department lends its expertise to managers through the provision of wage structures that are sensitive to relevant labor markets and reflective of the best estimates of the dynamics of those markets for the coming year. The compensation department also audits and controls compensation practices to ensure equitable treatment of employees and to guarantee the effectiveness of

---

[5]Jill Kanin-Lovers, "Automated Evaluations Can Help, But Can't Decide Compensation," *Computers in Personnel*, Vol. 1 No. 3, Spring 1987, pp. 18–24.

[6]Randolph W. Keuch, "Automating Flexible Compensation," *Computers in Personnel*, Vol. 3, No. 3, Spring 1989, pp. 12–17.

compensation programs in attracting, motivating, and retaining high-performing employees.

Description

The salary increase budget should be a plan aggregated from the individual salary budgets of individual managers, as approved up the line of authority. An individual manager should be responsible for human resources planning for his or her unit and base salary needs on that planning. The human resources plan should be based on the manager's unit performance plan and business goals and the current employees in the unit.

Unit Plans

Managers typically plan for unit performance. The performance management process supports the manager's translating unit goals into the performance requirements for each of the direct reports in the unit. The performance management system thus supports a more sophisticated approach toward compensation planning. Given the goals of the unit, it may be clear that current staffing levels are inappropriate, whether they are too low or too high. Plans for expansion or contraction of activities, reorganization of existing units, and other business plans may likewise make it probable that current levels of human resources available to the unit are inappropriate. Under any circumstances, a comparison of human resources needs must be compared to the projected supply within the unit.

Unit Human Resources

For both business and salary planning purposes, it is important to recognize that the unit's human resources are not a fixed supply but a group with its own dynamics. Individual employees retire, quit, and are terminated. In most cases, these transitions are fairly predictable to the unit manager. Some employees perform well above job requirements and are ready for promotions. Others are likely to remain on the job as fully satisfactory employees. Still others will require skill training or special action plans. Again, the unit manager is in the best position to make estimates about the dynamics of the human resources supply in the unit. To the extent that these human resources dynamics result in salary adjustments, it is the manager who is most capable of developing a salary budget plan.

Salary Budget Plan

The salary budget plan consists of two parts: one deals with current employees and the other deals with projected additional employees (see Figure 32-1).

Current Employees.   The basic salary budget plan should begin with current employees in the unit. A salary planning worksheet can be developed to serve as the basic salary planning document. For each current employee in the unit, the manager would receive a listing of:

Name

Social Security number

Current year's actions
  Change date
  Change type
  Weekly/hourly salary increase amount
  Compa-ratio

New salary data
  Weekly amount
  Annual amount
  Salary grade

Projected salary range data
  Minimum
  Midpoint
  Maximum

Review date

Space should be provided for any planned change in the employee's status during the coming year (see Figure 32-2):

Status change
  Retirement
  Transfer
  Promotion
  Entry into/exit from training program
  Dismissal
  Job reevaluation

Name	SS#	Current actions		Increase amount	Compa-ratio	New salary data			Projected salary		
		Change date	Change type			Weekly amount	Annual amount	Salary grade	Range data		
									Minimum	Midpoint	Maximum

Figure 32-1. Salary planning worksheet. *(Information Science Incorporated)*

Review date	Status change	Effective date	Salary change	Perform. rating	Projected increase	Effective date	Addt'l comp.	Target I.C.	Total estimated compensation		Notes

Figure 32-2. Salary projection worksheet. (*Information Science Incorporated*)

Effective data

Salary change

Additional space should be provided for actions not based on status changes:

Performance rating (with automatic calculation of recommended increase)

Projected increase

Effective date

Additional compensation (for example, performance pay not rolled into base, such as a lump-sum bonus)

Target incentive compensation

Total estimated compensation

Notes

Proposed Staffing Plans. The same form should provide space for additional employees the manager expects to add during the year. Considerably less information is required (see Figure 32-3):

Job title

Salary grade

Entry salary

Hire date

199X compensation

Comments

System Implementation

The compensation planning system should be a computerized system. If the organization has an HRIS on the mainframe and managers use work stations or PCs with electronic mail or other information systems, a special managerial salary planning module can be developed.[7] Fortu-

---

[7]Michael J. Kavanagh, Hal G. Gueutal, and Scott I. Tannenbaum, *Human Resource Information and Decision Support Systems* (in press), Chapter 9, PWS-Kent Publishing Company, Boston, Mass., 1989.

Job title	Projected information				Comments
	Salary grade	Entry salary	Hire date	199X compensation	

Figure 32-3. Proposed staffing plans. *(Information Science Incorporated)*

nately, reviews of available PC software related to compensation are available.[8]

Lacking such a system, the organization can achieve much the same end result utilizing a spreadsheet program such as Excel. The compensation department should create the basic spreadsheet design and include appropriate macros that calculate monthly salary cash flow, total compensation expenditures, beginning and year-end budget, unit compa-ratios, and so on. There should be a "what if" facility for the manager so that he or she can see the impact of different salary actions. It is important that whatever software is chosen, it should be user-friendly and menu-driven so that any manager who can turn on a PC can operate the salary planning spreadsheet successfully.

The compensation department should distribute disks (where on-line distribution is not feasible) with appropriate unit information already entered into appropriate cells on the spreadsheet. For those managers who may not have access to a spreadsheet or the computer skills to use this format, a hard copy option should be available in the early stages of implementation; with training, these managers can migrate to the automated system.

The compensation department must be available during this period as an internal consultant to managers who need advice on market levels for projected new hires or added jobs, compensation policies of the organization, and adjustment guidelines. Much of this material can be available on-line or published to accompany the planning spreadsheet.

Compensation plans should be approved by appropriate levels of management within the unit manager's department. Completed plans can be aggregated by department to the division level to develop a total compensation budget and cash flow projection. At this point, senior management can make a decision as to the feasibility of the total compensation budget. Over-commitment of salary resources can be dealt with on the basis of proposed programs by different units; compensation plans can be more closely tied to the strategic initiatives of the organization. Again, senior managers can tie salary budgets to organizational plans and do "what ifs" linking different organizational strategies with projected salary expenditures.

System Strengths

The strengths of this system closely parallel the problems inherent in the current system.

---

[8]Richard B. Frantzreb, *Microcomputers in Human Resource Management: A Directory of Software*, Advanced Personnel Systems, Roseville, Calif., pp. B-5-1 to B-5-29, 1989.

1. It is clearly every manager's responsibility to make salary decisions related to business unit needs.

2. The system bases appropriate reward recommendations on accomplishment rather than on a preconceived notion of a distribution of performance; by tying salary recommendations to accomplishment of the business plan, the performance management system is strengthened.

3. This approach to salary budgeting explicitly recognizes a variety of different adjustments that might be appropriate, and thus lends itself to total salary planning.

4. This system allows for salary planning regardless of the staffing level expected during the year, provides explicitly for changes in staffing levels and composition, and thus allows a better estimate of total salary costs.

5. This system is more flexible than a top-down allocation system and lends itself readily to the introduction of forms of pay that are not adjustments to base, such as lump-sum payments.

6. Making managers responsible for salary planning based on business need forces an awareness of compensation as a strategic tool and allows senior managers to allocate scarce resources in ways that support the strategic plans of the organization. Compensation planning is integrated into their strategic planning processes.

7. A cash flow perspective to salary planning is emphasized, giving a more realistic picture of costs incurred by salary increase decisions. The ability of managers to play games is reduced.

8. Audit and control of the compensation process is enhanced for both senior managers and the compensation department.

9. Salary planning and budgeting can be done in a much tighter time frame. At the same time, it is possible to study a number of different plan configurations for their impact and to choose one based on expected utility rather than the need to get something in place.

System Costs

The key costs inherent in the system relate to bringing managers up to speed to do this kind of planning. Because most managers do some salary adjustment planning now, and should be doing general budgeting and other planning, this cost should be minor.

The compensation department has to take on additional roles as an internal consultant to managers. Basically, most of the expertise and information needed is present in most compensation departments already, but the proposed system requires a wider dissemination of information and helps in interpretation and application.

With increased responsibility placed in the hands of managers, there is some risk of game playing. This calls for careful audit and control by senior management and by the compensation department.

If the organization does not currently have an HRIS, the full benefit of this planning and budgeting process will not be achieved. The implementation requires some start-up costs in any organization for appropriate software; this is likely to be offset by the ease of integrating salary planning with other planning processes and aggregation and transfer of approved salary actions to the HRIS. The increased control over salary budgets should also offset any costs incurred in implementation.

Conclusion

As a major expense to any organization, salaries and salary adjustments need to be carefully planned. Organizations have traditionally used a top-down resource allocation process for salary budgeting and planning because by using manual (or even semiautomated) systems they have had little alternative. The introduction of computers and HRIS software has given organizations two choices. One choice is to increase the speed of the old manual system and (possibly) increase its accuracy. The second choice is to rethink the salary budgeting and planning process and take full advantage of the potential of the computer in improving the salary planning and budgeting process. This planning should be integrated with other planning done by managers and based on the business plan of each unit. The compensation department, with its specialized knowledge and resources, can serve as an internal consultant to managers in this planning process and as internal auditors for senior management.

PART 6

Performance and Compensation

33

Performance Management Systems

Lyle M. Spencer, Jr., Ph.D.

President, McBer & Co.
Partner and Technical Director
HRPD Practice Worldwide, Hay Group Inc.

Performance management systems describe the cycle of performance planning (definition of job responsibilities, performance expectations, and goal or objective setting at the beginning of a period); performance management (feedback, "coaching" development, and positive or negative reinforcement during the period); and performance appraisal (formal performance appraisal at the end of the period) conducted between managers and employees to track and improve individual and organizational performance and provide information for one or more personnel functions:

- Compensation—for example, determining fixed or variable (performance-based) pay
- Succession planning—identifying candidates to replace incumbents in other (usually higher) jobs
- Discipline—for example, probation or dismissal actions

The author acknowledges with appreciation the contributions of his colleagues Annabelle Bennetts, Toronto; Anton Fishman, London; Miles Meyer, St. Louis; Ron Page, Minneapolis; and Signe Spencer, Boston, to the preparation of this chapter.

- Development—for example, training, job assignments, or mentoring relationships designed to increase employee competencies
- Career pathing—plans for future job assignments designed to give employees specific experiences and competencies

Background

Management theories that have influenced the development of performance management systems include management by objectives, research on achievement motivation, goal setting and self-directed behavior change, scientific behaviorism, and general systems theory.

Management by objectives, first articulated by Peter Drucker and popularized by such authors as George Odiorne, argues that management goals should be stated in terms of specific, measurable, time-phased objectives, such as "increase product *A* sales 15 percent, to $24 million, by December 31, 1991." All employees should have objectives and receive regular feedback on performance against their objectives; rewards and other management decisions should be based on "objective" performance.

Achievement motivation is a strong individual concern with *doing better* against a standard of excellence. Thoughts characteristic of achievement motivation include outperforming others (competitiveness), unique accomplishment (doing better by finding a new way to do something), and long-range plans for goal accomplishment. People high in the achievement motive set challenging but realistic goals, take personal responsibility, and seek and use feedback to improve their performance.

Self-directed change research holds that adults change their behavior when three conditions are present:

- Dissatisfaction with an existing condition ("actual")
- Clarity about a desired condition ("ideal" or goal)
- Clarity about what to do to move from the actual to the ideal ("action steps")

Actual ◄────► Ideal

"Discrepancy":
Energy and direction for change

People change only when they feel it in their own best interests to do so. Adults cannot be "changed" except through a process that leads them to feel personally dissatisfied with their current performance, personally clear about what their own goals for performance are, and personally clear (and confident) about how to accomplish these performance goals.

Research on goal setting and self-directed behavior change have tested elements of the management by objectives and achievement motivation theories empirically. Variables that increase the likelihood of goal attainment include criteria for goals (specific, measurable, challenging but moderate risk, time-phased) setting goals with employee participation and reinforcing actions toward goal attainment.

Scientific behaviorism holds that human behavior is learned. Antecedent stimuli provoke behavior responses that are followed by consequences (a stimulus → response or ["ABC"] antecedent → behavior → consequence model). Responses that are rewarded (positive reinforcement) increase in frequency. Behaviors that receive no response (extinction) or are punished (aversive consequence) decrease in frequency. Human behavior can be shaped toward desired performance by careful use of reinforcement consequences.

General systems theory holds that organizations can be described as input → process → output systems. Every individual, work unit, department, and the organization itself is a "process" system that converts inputs (supplies) to outputs (products or services) delivered to a "receiving" system (see Figure 33-1).

Employees' outputs sum to their manager's/work unit's output, work units' outputs sum to their department's output, and departments' outputs to the output(s) of the organization as a whole. Managers (theoretically) can monitor and evaluate every component system's output

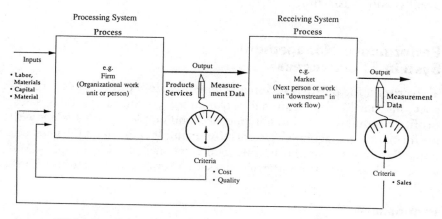

E.G. The Quality Concept: "Next Organization as Customer (NOAC)"

Figure 33-1. General systems model.

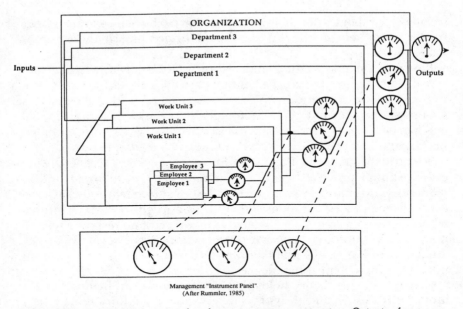

Management "Instrument Panel"
(After Rummler, 1985)

Figure 33-2. An ideal organizational performance management system: Outputs of every system component can be monitored and evaluated so that performance problems at any level can be identified and fixed. *(Management "instrument panel" after Rummler, 1985.)*

against its performance objectives to troubleshoot any performance problem (see Figure 33-2).

These theories and research findings underlay many of the process principles found to increase performance management system effectiveness and satisfaction.

Performance Management System Effectiveness

Two criteria for performance management system effectiveness are impact on "hard" organizational *performance* outcomes (such as sales, profits, productivity and quality metrics) and employee *satisfaction* with performance management systems (for example, perceived fairness and impact on motivation and morale, which in turn predict "people problems," such as turnover and grievances, that represent costs to the firm).

Performance

Performance management systems work. Many studies concur that performance management systems that include goal setting increase the likelihood of goal accomplishment between 5 and 20 percent without goal setting and 60 to 70 percent with it.[1] Goal setting results in an average increase in productivity of 19 percent.[2]

Satisfaction

The most frequently cited problem with performance appraisals is employee dissatisfaction and perceptions of unfairness (especially as performance appraisals relate to compensation) which may lead to some concerns about lowered productivity. The highest reported rating of employee satisfaction with the fairness of a performance appraisal system was only 68 percent.[3] Managers in a sample of Fortune 500 firms were even less positive, with 47.3 percent rating their firms' performance management systems as "slightly ineffective or worse," 37.1 percent as "moderately effective," and only 15.6 percent as "extremely effective."[4]

Employee satisfaction and the perception of fairness appear to be increased by:

- Separation of interviews for feedback and performance improvement ("coaching") from interviews for evaluation ("judging") for purposes of compensation and promotion. A good suggestion is to hold the compensation interview first and the improvement interview some weeks later.

- Improvements in any combination of feedback process variables: more individualized, participative goal setting; more specific, behaviorally based feedback; more frequent feedback; more attention to training needs and career development; and so on.

- Employee training, pamphlets, and explanations on the functions and purposes of performance evaluation.

- Decoupling of compensation from performance appraisals for most employees. For example, use only three ratings (performance problems; good, solid performers; exemplary performers) with the vast majority of employees receiving a rating of "good."

[1]Herbert H. Meyer, Emanuel Kay, and John R. P. French, Jr., "Split Roles in Performance Appraisal," *Harvard Business Review*, Vol. 43, 1964, pp. 124–129.
[2]G. P. Latham, and E. A. Locke, "Goal Setting: A Motivational Technique Which Works," *Organizational Dynamics*, Autumn 1979, pp. 68–80.
[3]Michael L. Smith, Edward J. O'Dowd, and George M. Christ, "Pay for Performance—One Company's Experience," *Compensation and Benefits Review* May/June 1987, Vol. 19, No. 3, pp. 19–29.
[4]J. Kane, *A Survey of Performance Appraisal Effectiveness in Fortune 500 Firms*, School of Management, University of Massachusetts, 1989.

- Training of managers to be more effective when giving feedback. For example, Gomez-Mejia & Page describe a comprehensive plan for implementing a performance management system that increased employee and management satisfaction. This plan included development of training materials for both employees and managers, individual training and group discussions with managers, and a tracking and diagnostic feedback system for managers.[5] Harry Levinson advocates training sessions to address the manager's emotional reactions to performance appraisal.[6] Mo Cayer, Dominic DiMattia, and Janis Wingrove describe in detail a type of cognitive therapy for managers (called rational effectiveness training) intended to help managers deal with the emotional difficulties of confronting employees about performance.[7]

A Generic Performance Management System: Process Variables That Increase Performance Management System Effectiveness

A generic performance management system is shown in Figure 33-3. The three "prerequisite steps" are not usually considered part of a performance management system, but probably should be. Employees' work objectives should flow from and be consistent with the organization's strategy and objectives and with their immediate supervisors' objectives for their work group.

The three steps in the performance management cycle, and "process" variables that can influence effectiveness at each step, are as follows:

[5]Luis R. Gomez-Mejia, and Ronald C. Page, "Integrating Employee Development and Performance Appraisal," *Training and Development Journal*, June 1983 pp. 138–145.

[6]Harry Levinson, "Appraisal of *What* Performance?" *Harvard Business Review* (reprint), No. 76405, 1976 pp. 30–46.

[7]Mo Cayer, Dominic DiMattia, and Janis Wingrove, "Conquering Evaluation Fear," *Applications and Research*, MacMillan Publishing, New York, N.Y., 1973.

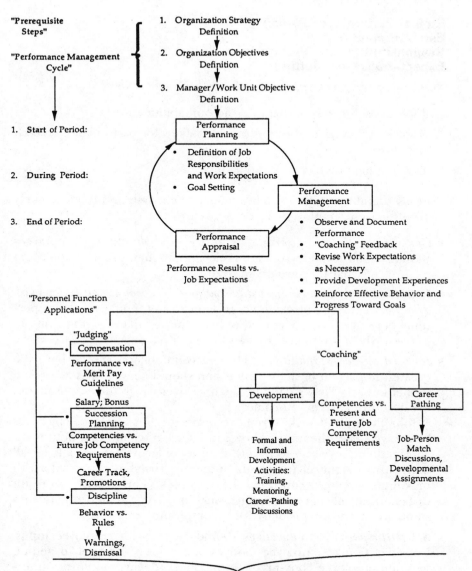

Figure 33-3. A generic performance management system.

Step 1: Performance Planning: Establishment of Job Responsibilities and Performance Expectations/Goal Setting

Managers negotiate the following issues with employees:

1. Job duties and responsibilities ("accountabilities")

2. Specific, measurable objectives or expectations for performance on each objective

3. Developmental objectives and actions

Process Variables.   Performance management systems are more likely to be effective if employee objectives are:

- *Consistent with the organization's strategy and objectives.*   Employees should be able to understand the relevance to their organization's "big picture" of what they are asked to do.

- *Related directly to their immediate managers' accountabilities or work group objectives.*   For example, in Figure 33-4, employee 1 has personal objectives directly related to his or her manager's work unit objectives, which are to cut costs and increase sales.

- *Focused on accountabilities.*   Those accountabilities should have the greatest impact on business results and should be weighted according to that impact. They should be the ones over which the employee has greatest influence on outcomes.

    John Stokes and Vicki Wright recommend that employee objectives be arrayed as in the matrix shown in Figure 33-5 and that both manager and employee try to restate as many objectives as possible to fall in the upper right cell (maximum impact on firm business results with maximum employee control of the outcome).[8] This process can result in beneficial managerial changes, such as giving a subordinate substantially more responsibility for accomplishing objectives.

- *Set participatively.*   Objectives should be set with employee input. Consideration of employee motives and values is critical to getting genuine employee "buy-in" or ownership. Ideally, employees internalize their objectives; that is, they feel them to be not only the organization's but their own. Self-directed change research has identified other variables that increase the probability of goal attainment: public

---

[8]John Stokes, and Vicki Wright, *Q4 Total Performance Pay—Reinforcing the Link Between Performance and Pay.* Hay Management Consultants U.K. Annual Client Issues Meeting, London, 1989.

Result accountability	Objective	Measure	Result	Rating	Weight	Total	Develop-ment
		Manager/Work Unit					
1. Manage budget 2. Manage sales	Cut costs 20% Increase revenues 10%	Dollars below budget Revenues					
		Employee 1					
1. Manage head count 2. Sell	Cut staff by 1 person Increase sales 10% Make 50 cold calls Open 3 new accounts	# staff cut Dollar/sales # cold calls made # new accounts opened					Take sales course

Figure 33-4. Accountability/objective measures matrix.

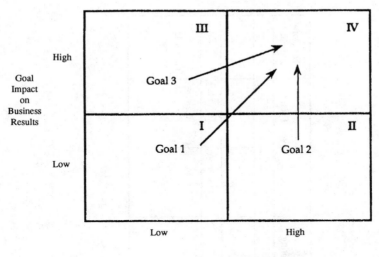

Figure 33-5. Accountability matrix: business results by employee control.

commitment to the goal; support from important others and reference groups; anticipation of obstacles; contingency planning; and frequent, specific feedback from a variety of sources.[9]

- *Challenging but attainable: moderate risk.* For example, have approximately a 50 percent probability of accomplishment similar to goals set by persons naturally high in achievement motivation.[10] Large, long-term goals should be broken down into attainable subgoals to give employees frequent opportunities for positive feedback and reinforcement.

Behaviorists, interestingly, dissent from this principle. Aubrey Daniels argues that "challenging" goals motivate only persons already high in achievement motivation.[11] For most other people, objective setting has been an antecedent for punishment; people have felt forced to set goals they could not achieve, then were criticized or denied a bonus or promotion because of their "failure."

[9]D. A. Kolb, and R. E. Boyatzis, "Goal Setting and Self-Directed Behavior Change," *Human Relations*, Vol. 23, No. 5, 1970, pp. 439–457.
[10]D. C. McClelland, *Human Motivation*, Scott Foresman, Glenview, Il., 1985.
[11]Aubrey C. Daniels, and Theodore A. Rosen, *Performance Management: Improving Quality and Productivity Through Positive Reinforcement*, Performance Management Publications, Inc., Tucker, Ga., 1982.

Behaviorists recommend a "shaping" strategy in setting objectives: Start with very easy goals that employees are almost certain to attain, praise them lavishly for their success and performance improvement (positive reinforcement), then get them to set a slightly higher but still easily attainable goal. Employee behavior is gradually shaped toward the desired level of performance, encouraged and sustained by positive reinforcement every step of the way.

- *Explicit, with agreed-upon standards and measures.* Standards are most reliable when set by the same person who will assess the performance. For performance-based pay applications, the "payoff matrix" (amount of incentive pay for specific performance levels) should be explicit and agreed upon between manager and employee. Table 33-1 shows an incentive plan payoff matrix for a professional service firm.

- *Accompanied with "how to" advice, training, or other development opportunities.* These help employees learn behaviors needed to achieve their goals. For example, in Figure 33-4, the employee's objectives of making 50 cold sales calls and opening three new accounts is supported by taking a "how to make a cold call" sales training course.

- *Made the employee's responsibility.* Employees should be given substantial responsibility and autonomy in deciding how to accomplish their objectives. Numerous studies show that letting persons take responsibility arouses achievement motivation. Conversely, authoritarian direction and bureaucratic "red tape" restrictions (for example, many approval levels) suppress it.[12]

Step 2. Manager's Ongoing Observation and Documentation of Employee Performance: Feedback to and (Positive) Reinforcement of Employees

During the performance period managers:

1. Observe and document employee performance against objectives
2. Renegotiate employee accountabilities and objectives as required by changes in organizational objectives or in the external environment
3. Give employees feedback on their performance against objectives

[12]George Litwin, and Robert Stringer, *Motivation and Organizational Climate*, Harvard University Press, Boston, Mass., 1968.

Table 33-1. Incentive Plan Payoff Matrix

Component	Percentage	Threshold	Competent	Target	Maximum	Notes
Billing/utilization	30%	80% of budget = $247,296 $5,922	90% of budget = $278,208 $7,896	100% of budget = $309,120 (Util. % = 71%) $9,870	120% of budget = $370,944 $11,844	
Sales/business development	30%	80% of budget = $600,000 $5,922	90% of budget = $675,000 $7,896	100% of budget = $750,000 $9,870	150% of budget = $1,125,000 $14,805	
Office/unit profit (gross margin)	20%	80% of budget = $1,036,000 $3,948	90% of budget = $1,165,500 $5,264	100% of budget = $1,295,000 $6,580	150% of budget = $1,942,500 $9,870	
Regional profit	20%	80% of budget = $5,137,600 $3,948	90% of budget = $5,779,800 $5,264	100% of budget = $6,422,000 $6,580	150% of budget = $9,633,000 $9,870	
Total incentive	100%	60% of bonus = $19,740 $19,740	80% of bonus = $26,320 $26,320	100% of bonus = $32,900 $32,900	120% of bonus = $39,480 150% of bonus = $49,350 $46,389	
Total opportunity		$93,340	$99,920	$106,500	$119,989	

4. Positively reinforce effective behaviors or improved performance with praise, attention, or other incentive rewards

5. Coach, counsel, and provide problem-solving assistance or training to employees on how to improve their performance

6. Provide warnings and/or state specific behavior expectations and the consequences if the expectations are not met (for example, probation or dismissal); if behavior or performance is below expectations and feedback, positive reinforcement, and development efforts have not been successful

Process Variables. Performance management system effectiveness is increased when:

- *Employee behavior and performance against objectives is systematically observed and documented.* Keep written records of critical incidents in which an employee behaved effectively, or ineffectively, and present them in a positive, helpful, goal-oriented manner.

- *Employees are given frequent, behaviorally specific feedback on their performance.* The ideal frequency of the feedback varies according to the nature of the job and the employee's experience and confidence. It is generally agreed, however, that feedback should be given far more frequently than at an annual or semiannual review, and in some situations should be as often as daily. One caution is that managers should avoid over-supervising by giving too much feedback, which may lead employees to feel mistrusted or patronized.

  Several researchers note that goal setting and feedback are inseparable—two components of the same cognitive process; goal setting without feedback on whether or not progress toward the goal is being made is meaningless.[13]

  Feedback is best if presented in a clear, simple, visual form, such as a graph related to a baseline (see Figure 33-6). Feedback data is most effective if compiled by the employee because this produces maximum feelings of employee ownership and responsibility. Less effective is feedback data compiled by a supervisor and laid on the employee. Least effective is feedback from a third source, such as a quality control or inspection group. Some writers suggest the use of feedback from several sources (including peers, subordinates, and clients) to avoid problems of bias and incomplete observation by a single evaluator.

  There is strong consensus that feedback should be individualized,

[13]H. J. Klein, "An Integrated Control Theory of Motivation," *Academy of Management Review*, Vol. 14, No. 2, 1989, pp. 150–172.

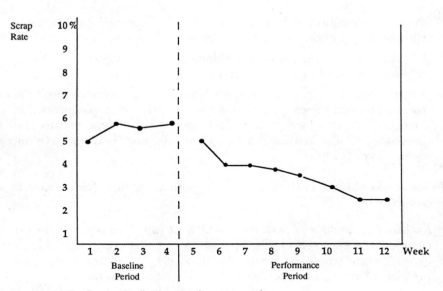

Figure 33-6. Graphic feedback on performance goals.

objective, and based on specific data or on behavior: for example, "your scrap rate increased 2 percent last week." Conversely, feedback should avoid comments on traits ("you were careless") or attitudes ("you don't seem motivated"). To help supervisors achieve specificity, Frederick Hills, et al., suggest using behaviorally anchored rating scales (BARS) especially for more subjective behaviors that may sound like traits, for example, innovation (see Figure 33-7).[14]

Behaviorist research indicates that positive feedback is most effective if given just after a successful performance; negative feedback is most effective if given just before the next opportunity to perform the behavior.

- *Employee behavior results in positive or negative consequences that are immediate and certain.* Effective behavior and outcomes and performance improvement can be positively reinforced by giving the employee something he or she wants, such as praise, merit pay, or a promotion (positive reinforcement), or removing something he or she does not like, such as filling out time cards for an employee with a perfect attendance record (negative reinforcement). Ineffective behavior can be lessened by not giving the employee something he or she wants or giving him or her something he or she doesn't want.

[14]Frederick S. Hills, Dow Scott, Steven E. Markham, and Michael J. Vest, "Merit Pay: Just or Unjust Desserts," *Personnel Administrator*, September 1987, pp. 53–59.

Critical Incident Example(s)

−1   Resists or Is Slow to Adopt Innovations

 0   Neutral: Neither Resists Nor Supports
     Innovation

 1   Supports or Is Among the First to Adopt
     Innovations

 2   Suggests Innovations

 3   Has Identified and Implemented a Significant
     Innovation (New Product or Service to Market,
     or New Policy, Process, or Procedure Within
     the Organization)

 4   Has Implemented Two or More Significant
     Innovations

Figure 33-7. A behaviorally anchored rating scale (bars) for "innovation."

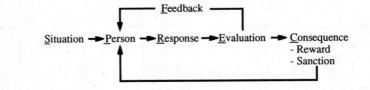

• Situation: Are performance objectives (measures) clear? the right ones? Are "how to do it" instructions clear? (training?) Does worker have resources: tools, information, etc.?

• Person: Best for the job: job-person "match" given worker's motives, values, skills?

• Response: Worker behavior and output.

• Evaluation: Are behavior and output monitored? against performance objectives (measures)?

• Feedback: Is worker told immediately after response how behavior and/or outcome deviated from performance objectives?

• Consequences: Rewards; incentives: is worker rewarded for good performance outcomes (e.g., "gain sharing"), suggestion rewards, merit pay, performance bonuses?

                  Sanctions: is poor performance punished?

Figure 33-8. Behavioral "specific" model.

A Stimulus → Person → Response → Evaluation → Feedback and Consequences (SPREC/FB) model is often used to summarize thecomponents of the performance management cycle and to analyze performance problems (see Figure 33-8). With the evaluation, feedback, and consequence parts of the model, an employee does not receive timely information or incentive to alter his or her behavior.

■ *Employees receive coaching or counseling help to learn behaviors needed to improve their performance.*   A full counseling sequence is shown in Figure 33-8.[15] Employees must be listened to before they can understand their behavior, feel a discrepancy between their actual performance and the objective, and be motivated to identify and carry out action steps to close the gap between actual and ideal behavior.

These process principles provide tools for managers to do their managerial jobs better. For example, an employee by accountability

[15]R. E. Carkhuff, *The Art of Helping*, Carkhuff Associates, Amherst, Mass., 1973.

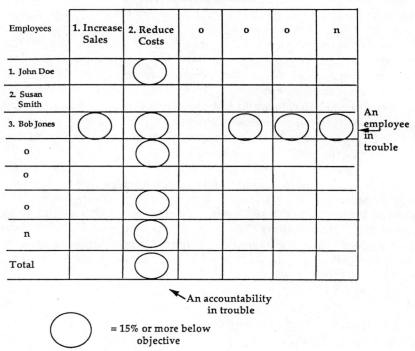

Figure 33-9. Employee by accountability matrix.

matrix (see Figure 33-9) can help managers identify the appropriate managerial actions to address performance problems with any accountability (over all individuals) or individual (for any accountability).

Step 3. Formal Performance Appraisal and Documentation

At the end of the period, employee results are measured against the accountability objective measures (including development objectives) set at the beginning of the performance management cycle. These results and behavior competencies demonstrated in work areas should be summarized, documented, and discussed with the employee.

Process Variables

- *"Hard" data (when available) and behaviorally specific observations (for example, critical incident) should be documented using forms.* See

Figure 33-7 for an example of a "competency-based" performance appraisal form that requests critical incident evidence of an employee's competence in "innovation."

Many writers on performance management observe that if the manager is doing step 2 (observing and documenting employee performance) well, most of the data needed for step 3 (appraising employee performance) will already have been collected. The formal performance appraisal should hold no surprises for either the manager or the employee, because all performance data will have been discussed many times in feedback, coaching, and reinforcement sessions during the period appraised.

Specific, detailed documentation of performance, or performance problems, should help avoid or defend against legal issues that may arise from personnel decisions, such as equal opportunity or dismissal actions. Ratings should be used sparingly. Subjective ratings and forced rating distributions cause employee resentment. Unless ratings have a specific use (for example, to allocate bonus funds or identify employee skills or job skill requirement gaps), ratings are best avoided.

Application of Performance Management System Data to Personnel Functions

Herbert Meyer, Emanuel Kay, and John French, in their classic article "Split Roles in Performance Appraisal," observed that performance management systems require managers to assume two conflicting roles: that of a "judge" and that of a "coach."[16] Judging functions are unilateral decisions made by management regarding how much employees get paid, what their career opportunities will be, and how they will be disciplined, for example, warnings, probation, or dismissal.

Coaching, or performance improvement, functions are development and career-pathing discussions designed to help the employee develop his or her skills and find the best job match for his or her unique skills and preferences.

Process Variables

Process variable prescriptions differ somewhat for the judging and coaching functions, but most researchers agree on the following principles:

---

[16]Herbert H. Meyer, Emanuel Kay, and John R. P. French, Jr., "Split Roles in Performance Appraisal," *Harvard Business Review*, Vol. 43, 1964, pp. 124–129.

- *Give managers training,* ongoing support, and diagnostic feedback on their implementation of performance management systems.

- *Give employees written materials,* that clearly explain the performance appraisal system in use.

- *Set goals* that are clearly related to organizational missions, challenging but realistic, and created with input from employees.

- *Give performance feedback* frequently with specific details relating to behavior and results rather than to character or traits.

- *Separate the announcement of management's judgments about compensation and succession planning from coaching discussions about employee development.*

Ideally, performance appraisals should be conducted for coaching and developmental purposes, and should be separated from compensation and promotion decisions by at least a month.

The proper relationship between performance management systems and compensation remains an unresolved issue. Saul Gellerman and William Hodgson describe a system successfully separating compensation from performance.[17] Dean Takahishi reports that many firms are considering performance management systems with compensation elements: gain sharing; profit sharing; lump-sum bonus; and individual, small team, and all-salaried merit pay and pay-for-performance incentives.[18] Aubrey Daniels observes that employees eventually stop paying attention to performance feedback once they realize that improved performance is not compensated.[19]

The Future of Performance Management Systems

Emergence of "Mixed Models" of Performance Management: Appraisal and Reward of Performance and Competence

The dominant trend in performance management systems has been pay for performance—an attempt to move away from pay based on job accountabilities or personal characteristics toward pay based strictly on

---

[17]Saul W. Gellerman and William G. Hodgson, "Cyanamid's New Take on Performance Appraisal," *Harvard Business Review,* May–June 1988, Vol. 66, No. 3, pp. 36–41.

[18]Takahishi, Dean, "New Ways to Pay," *Times Herald,* Dallas, Tex., June 20, 1988.

[19]Aubrey C. Daniels and Theodore A. Rosen, *Performance Management: Improving Quality and Productivity Through Positive Reinforcement,* Performance Management Publications Inc., Tucker, Ga., 1982.

numerical results, such as dollar revenues or costs cut. Recently, a backlash against pure pay-for-performance systems has begun as a result of doubts regarding their applicability to the rapidly changing, team-oriented "knowledge worker" work environment of the future. Characteristics of future work environments include:

- Rapid change in jobs, accountabilities, and objectives, which render performance objectives obsolete. It makes little sense to appraise a worker in four different "task force" jobs in a year against objectives set for the first job at the beginning of the period.

- For much of the work done in temporary ad hoc teams, links between accountabilities and results measures may not be clear under a specific individual's control. Who performed which task will not be obvious, making appraisal of individual team members difficult.

- A tight labor market that forces employers to give more consideration to individual employees' motives and work preferences, thus allowing for person-to-job matches to place workers in jobs they naturally like and do well, as opposed to jobs they don't like and aren't likely to do well.

- Longer-term development objectives are more important. That is, more jobs are "developmental assignments" or include development as an objective equal to or more important than performance.

- "Fuzzy" qualitative skills or competencies (underlying characteristics of an individual that predict effective or superior performance in a job). Employees' ability to contribute to a new multicultural team quickly, or employees' future value to the organization, based on unique competencies, may be more important than their performance in past jobs. Organizations with a future orientation are moving to balance pay-for-performance with pay-for-skills. Figure 33-10 summarizes how pay-for-performance and pay-for-competencies differ on such key variables as short-term versus long-term perspective, past versus future employee value, and performance versus development objectives.

Appraisal of Team (as Opposed to Individual) Performance

American automakers are moving to the Japanese (and Swedish) approach of appraising and rewarding team performance. Individual employees are evaluated on such process competencies as teamwork and

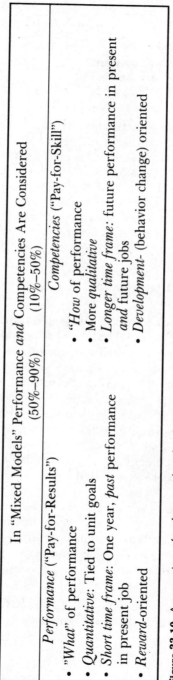

In "Mixed Models" Performance *and* Competencies Are Considered	
Performance ("Pay-for-Results") (50%–90%)	*Competencies* ("Pay-for-Skill") (10%–50%)
• "*What*" of performance • *Quantitative:* Tied to unit goals • *Short time frame:* One year, *past* performance in present job • *Reward*-oriented	• "*How*" of performance • *More qualitative* • *Longer time frame:* future performance in present and future jobs • *Development-* (behavior change) oriented

Figure 33-10. A comparison of performance-based and competence-based appraisal approaches.

the ability to work collaboratively versus adversarily with fellow workers.

Use of Performance Management Systems to Communicate and Reinforce Business Strategy and Culture

Organizations are making increasing, explicit use of performance management systems to communicate and reinforce overall strategy and culture, such as focus on quality improvement or customer service. Performance management systems accomplish these objectives by ensuring that employee accountabilities and objectives relate directly to organizational strategy and objectives—for example, by linking employees' objectives through their immediate managers' accountabilities (see Figure 33-4) to the larger organizational goals.

Computerization of Performance Management Systems

Organizations are moving toward integrated human resources management information systems (IHRMIS) in which all personnel functions use a central database that contains data about all jobs and people in the organization. Performance management system data are included in both the job and person data files. Performance management system job-related data are the accountabilities, objectives, measures and average performance results, and job competency requirements (characteristics needed by individuals to do the job well) for each job. Person data include assessment and performance appraisal data on each individual's competencies or competency gaps. Now available are sophisticated artificial intelligence expert systems that can:

- Identify all employees with accountabilities related to a specific strategic objective: where employees' accountabilities overlap or conflict, the extent to which employees sharing a strategic objective interact effectively, and the quality of each employee's performance on his or her part of the strategic objective and its impact on accomplishment of the overall objective.

- Optimally match people with jobs on the basis of individual competencies and job competency requirements.

Diagnostic or Contingent
Approaches to Employee Work
Assignment, Motivation, and Reward

Contingent approaches to performance management argue that individual workers' motives, competencies, and work preferences should be considered in making work assignments, giving feedback, and rewarding and reinforcing desirable behaviors. For example, persons high in achievement motivation should be given entrepreneurial or creative tasks with considerable challenge and responsibility, and reinforced with frequent feedback on performance. Employees high in affiliation motivation (a strong individual concern with liking and being liked, and with friendly, social relationships) should be assigned work in collaborative teams affording many opportunities for personal interaction.

Contingent performance management systems require managers to diagnose employee motives and preferences, and they involve considerable employee participation, including open discussion of alternatives, solicitation of employee input, and negotiation leading to genuine agreement between employee and manager on work tasks and performance rewards.

34
Performance Measurement

Michael E. Hora,
Vice President, A. T. Kearney, Inc.

Marvin Schiller, Ph.D.
Managing Director, North America
A. T. Kearney, Inc.

Introduction

A. T. Kearney has measured performance and productivity for almost the 65 years it has been providing management consulting services to commerce, industry, and government around the world. Over that long period of time, and among an incredibly diverse set of business environments, we have been involved with the subject of *measurement*. Many people say that if you measure performance and project expectations, you almost certainly can ensure results. If we have seen one single failure in terms of measurement over the years, it has been the mistake of measuring the *wrong thing*. This misdirection has probably been a result of emotional blindness and untimely perspectives. To illustrate the problems resulting from measuring the wrong thing, four examples may be helpful.

Direct labor costs. At one time, measuring direct labor productivity was very important to improving company profitability. But today direct labor plays a relatively small part in the total cost picture. Either because people don't realize that, or because they're emotionally attached to getting more out of the hourly work force, they haven't changed their key measurement. Today, however, measuring direct labor productivity is not very useful in most industries. As many have learned recently, understanding the impact and linking performance of direct labor to cycle time, quality, and total cost is what really counts.

Supplier relationships.   Some companies are absolutely committed to developing long-term relationships with quality vendors. This action supports just-in-time production schemes and generally results in improved cycle times and better customer service. Clearly, this kind of activity is a linchpin in a zero-defects quality program. Nonetheless, those same companies often use purchased price variance as the prime measurement for their buyers, encouraging the buyers to focus on the wrong result.

White-collar productivity.   It has also become popular to point to white-collar workers as examples of improved productivity in recent years. But frequently, white-collar productivity measurement focuses on activities rather than on the contribution to earnings. Interest tends to focus on how many purchase orders can be handled per day, how many loan applications can be processed per week, and how many customer service complaints can be dealt with per period. But those are activities. When you try to link some of them to the bottom line, the link is tenuous at best.

Maintenance management.   Similarly, maintenance management is a subject of increasing operational concern as we move to a more technological manufacturing environment. Management tends to measure maintenance performance in terms of work orders completed per person, preventive maintenance tasks completed per period, and worker performance against engineered standards. But what about uptime, throughput, quality, and total cost? These are the arenas in which maintenance can have the greatest impact and yet very few companies monitor these critical dimensions of improved performance. The paradox is that we measure the wrong things, not that there is anything innately wrong with our measurement methods. We measure what we know, we measure what we like, and we measure what people have always measured. Therefore, the question is: "How can we measure what we need to measure to guide us in changing behavior so company profitability, market penetration, and the future security of the enterprise will be enhanced?"

That's what this chapter is about: the relationship between bottom-line results and behavior and measurement. Our objective is to create a focal point around which you can consider the important issues associated with measurement and changing what counts in your business.

Measurement: Myths and Realities

Activity Versus Results

The first step in building any measurement system is to understand what behavior you want to change. To do this requires a clear understanding of the business, the role of the measurement system in the business, and the roles of the people or equipment whose behavior or function you want to change. That doesn't mean a supervisor in the metal-forming department of a major automobile company needs to understand the total business picture of the automobile industry. But that supervisor should understand that the least cost production of consistently in-specification product, delivered as promised, may not be a function of the lowest piece part cost.

Many direct labor-incentive systems are based on the concept of producing the lowest piece part cost. In many cases, we have found that these kinds of systems have driven total product cost much higher than required, rather than lower as desired. Some people suggest it is impossible to install a high-quality, just-in-time program in the midst of a system that rewards lowest piece part cost.

Still another constructive example might include measuring sales performance. Compensating salespeople for dollar volume performance is very common. And yet, when you discuss this issue with salespeople and company executives, frequently you find no awareness of which products provide the highest profit margins and the highest future market penetration potential. Salespeople sell what appears to get them the highest individual rewards. No surprise there! But good sales force effectiveness programs measure contribution, not just gross dollars.

Although most people intellectually understand the difference between activities and results, it is surprising how often measurement systems deal with activities alone. The reason given is that activities are easier to understand and measure. The unstated fundamental from such a discussion is that linking activities to results is so difficult that we often don't even try. The reality is quite different. A classic example, still found in the sales force effectiveness arena, has to do with measuring and rewarding sales performance based on the number of calls made in a period of time. Fifty calls, randomly generated, might not be anywhere near as valuable as five calls thoroughly planned for, executed, and followed up.

Reward for Performance

There is a pervasive belief throughout industry that there is a direct relationship between measurements and rewards. But nothing is further from the truth. Too many company reward systems have a compensation spread between the best performer and the worst performer of 5 to 10 percent. This is hardly adequate to ignite the winners to greater glory and to get the losers worried.

As management consultants, we encourage clients to link desired results, behavior change, measurement, and the applicable reward systems. Reward systems do not have to follow measurement programs. We suggest, however, that if you claim that performance is rewarded and then maintain a measurement system at variance with your demonstrated rewards, you've created a situation that does not work to improve your business results. It becomes counterproductive. Many businesses are managed on a relatively simple basis. On one side, there is the need to manage and minimize the cost of producing a quality product or service on time. On the other hand, there is a need to provide or increase revenue, that is, sales. The very best approaches to measuring the performance of people, departments, or units link behavior to one of these two fundamental results—cost or revenue. The measurement system is not only a vehicle to modify behavior, it is also a way to provide a clear understanding of the link between performance and results.

Over the last 10 years, the world has seen a substantial increase in "alphabet soup" solutions to manufacturing and service provision. A string of magic formulas have come along that are assumed to make the world a better place for business: CAE (computer-aided engineering), CIM (computer-integrated manufacturing), CIM (customer-intensified manufacturing) CAD/CAM (computer-aided design/computer-aided manufacturing), JIT (just in time), and SPC (statistical process control) are just a slice of the list that has affected manufacturing, for instance. From our perspective, there have been impressive gains in linking real time information to providing manufactured products and services, but only 20 percent of all the capital invested in the alphabet soup programs have paid off. In many cases, companies got so excited about investing in technology and reducing the size of their work force that they closed their eyes to the marketplace implications. A classic case is a midwestern manufacturer that spent a fortune to build the most productive high-tech manufacturing plant in the world. Soon afterward, the demand for the product dropped precipitously and never returned to the volume level required to make that plant pay off.

Where computerized information management systems have worked the best, they've been combined with intelligent and motivated people. Witness what happens when you call L. L. Bean Inc., the direct-marketing apparel company, to place an order. It is clear from the responses you get that the person you are talking to is sitting at a computer terminal with tremendous capability to respond to requests for information. At the same time, however, you are aware of being treated in a friendly way. That combination of powerful technology and friendly people makes all the difference in results.

Measuring nonproduction people is the toughest measurement task. It is a problem all management will have to deal with because approximately 80 percent of our working population is involved in nonproduction areas. Of course, measuring production activities is relatively easy and the reasons for doing so are obvious. The number of widgets produced readily converts to sales. The cost of making the widgets is easily monitored, and therefore, on a day-to-day basis we can tell roughly whether we are making money or not. It's also easy to count widgets and people. But the output per hour in nonmanufacturing has been relatively stagnant over the last 20 years, whereas manufacturing output per hour has almost doubled.[1]

Some suggest that the reason for this is the significant investments made by manufacturing companies in technology and new capital equipment. But many companies have made major investments in expensive equipment for nonproduction employees. The sophisticated computer system used at L. L. Bean doesn't come cheap. Voice mail, artificial intelligence, interconnected work stations, and a plethora of other productivity improvement devices have been placed in the nonmanufacturing workplace with relatively little result. It sounds as though some measurement might be in order.

To do that, we need to go beyond the traditional thinking that divides people into hourly and salaried, professional staff, and support staff. We need to recognize that human beings do all kinds of jobs, and those jobs ought to be organized around achieving a business goal that enhances the performance of the overall company. Whether the job is the secretary's or the president's, an equation can be written linking that individual's performance and behavior to the end results desired for the company.

---

[1]"Working Smart: With Labor Scarce, Service Firms Strive to Raise Productivity," *The Wall Street Journal*, June 1, 1989, p. 1.

A Prescription for Action

This section is something between a grand conceptual framework and a detailed work plan for putting in place an effective measurement system. We try to use this approach to bring the lessons of this chapter to a practical level for each reader's situation without creating a boilerplate approach. The factors to be considered and the steps to be taken should take the following pattern.

1. Recognize that the purpose of a measurement system is *change*. Differentiate between monitoring conditions and measuring results.

2. Focus on a *business result*. Avoid measuring activities.

3. Understand what *behavior* needs to be changed to achieve the business result, and be sure that the measurement links to that behavior.

4. Refer to the measurement specifics *often* in your communication and conversation with members of the organization.

5. Measure a *few items*, not many items. If you are inexorably driven to measuring too much, then cluster indexes by families so that people are encouraged to think in terms of the few important areas on a regular basis.

6. Make any measurement system *visual and visible*. Don't bury it at the back of a report; print it boldly in documents that people read and post it graphically where people work.

7. Be ready to *change* the measurement system if a particular index no longer is an "A" item in your business result spectrum, or if you have achieved so much fundamental change with that item that you're convinced it has very little value left in it.

8. *Challenge* traditional measures. They're probably not right any more. An example of this is the pounds per direct labor worker hour at a food plant, which is no longer relevant because of changes in technology, the diminished importance of direct labor in the cost picture, and marketplace demand for quality and consistency. Measuring pounds per direct labor worker hour frequently weakens results instead of enhancing them.

9. If you have a lot of people or a lot of activity, measure on a *sam-

pling basis or try out the system on a personal computer first, not on the mainframe. Get the measurement system working properly and get some experience with it before you ask the data processing department to create a system for capturing data and reporting results.

10. When you design a measurement system, give the job to a *cross-functional or multifunctional team,* not a "silo" team or one person who you think understands the total picture. Few people in any company really understand the total picture, not because of any intellectual failing, but because of a natural tendency of human beings to become biased with their own area of interest or point of view.

11. *Expect quantum change* and quantum improvement. If you don't expect a measured result to go through a significant change, then why is it being measured?

12. Finally, *measure the right things*—those that produce desired results.

Getting Down to Cases

Three cases illustrate the principle already discussed. Each provides an opportunity to bring a theoretical discussion down to a practical and meaningful level. All the cases discussed involve real companies.

For a $2 billion basic metals company, we show how cash flow thinking links to organizational change and provides a way to measure what counts.

In the case of a large public utility, we look at the problem of measuring what an engineer does; the reader will observe how this concept applies to many professional and technical specialist positions.

Rounding out the examples with a giant food company, we discuss how management uses a process called benchmarking to see how good they really are and to set targets for the future.

The Basic Metals Company and Cash Flow

This basic metals company has been around for more than a century. There was a time when all the company had to do was dig ore out of the ground, process it, and sell it to domestic users. Then some things started to change. Environmental health and safety laws and concerns escalated dramatically, and the cost of processing the material started to increase. Global suppliers of this commodity developed the capability to deliver the product to the United States at a very competitive cost. Because of the change from a domestic economy to a global supply-and-demand environment, the well-understood peaks and valleys of this business started to change. Low periods that used to last for a year or two now appear to last 5 years or more. Overall, the cost of processing the material could no longer be handled without regard to competition. The marketplace became much less controlled by a few U.S. companies.

But change wasn't easy for this company. A hundred years of worship at the altar of metallurgy had been inbred to the point that metallurgical engineers were everywhere. The organizational structure grew far too many layers with far too little responsibility at almost every level. There were backups for the backups, all under the illusion of needing a deep organization.

The courageous management team has made a lot of progress. This company is in the process of significant change and is a permanently better company. The fundamental change removed 40 percent of the salaried people from the organization and guided the remaining people under cash-flow measurement.

Figure 34-1 is a copy of a one-page descriptive document for every individual in the salaried organization. You will note that it is simple,

Position		
Principal Engineer – Electrical/I&C Group – Plant Engineering		
Reports To		
Manager – Plant Engineering		
Functions Managed		
Direct activities of engineering staff in providing technical consultation and engineering services to station operation personnel		
Key Objective(s)		
Improve reliability of plant equipment and components in order to prevent catastrophic failures and improve power production		
Key Levers	**Performance Measures**	**Targets**
Maintenance practices	Required time/response	80%<30 days
Vendor manuals review	Number of procedures/year	One/60 days
Review NRC and industry problem report	Number reviewed/year	Five/month
	Number reviewed/month	100%< 45 days
Total Annual $ Approximately **Responsibility** $2 to $3 million	**Annual Personal** Approximately **$ Expenditures** $600,000	

Figure 34-1. Measurement document.

clear, and relatively devoid of the standard laundry list of activities. Activities aren't important, results are. You'll also note there are several important elements of this measurement document:

- *Key levers.* The five or six items that can be measured and represent the real performance objectives of this individual job.
- *Performance measures.* How the key lever is monitored.
- *Least cost producer (LCP) targets.* The specific target for a current time period.
- *Total annual dollar responsibility.* How much money is spent under this person's direction.
- *Total annual personal expenditures.* How much money this individual spends personally.

In summary, the LCP targets are where individuals have to be in terms of performance to be assured that the key levers of their part of the business are met.

The cash-flow indicators are particularly important. In studies we have done in many companies, we have found that no more than 8 percent of managers can tell you how much cash goes through their hands. We believe that all management people have to understand that businesses operate on a cash basis and cash flow is very important. To paraphrase an old saying, the subject of cash flow is too important to be left to the chief financial officer.

Cash flow has two dimensions. The first is the amount of cash for which we personally have responsibility. We might have 10 to 15 people under our direction, all of whom spend money, and we need to manage and monitor that spending. The second dimension has to do with our control of the spending. We need to pay attention to how much of the cash we personally spend and make sure it is not too much.

One of the best observations you can make when evaluating an organization and looking at the measurement of key players is to understand the difference between how much a person is responsible for spending and how much that person spends himself or herself. For example, in a purchasing organization, if a purchasing agent has 10 buyers and personally spends 90 percent of the money, then one has to ask what the buyers do. There is no better way to understand delegation or the lack of it than by looking at cash flows and who is spending the cash. Some even go so far as to suggest that this kind of cash flow thinking ought to be the basis for organizational development. Certainly measuring the performance of individuals in an organization on an LCP target and cash flow basis is an excellent way to begin to understand how to run the business better.

What Does a Nuclear Engineer Do?

This client was a major public utility with several nuclear power plants on stream and several coming on. They had a 600-person nuclear engineering group responsible for design, installation, maintenance, and troubleshooting on this equipment. Nuclear power plants are big business. It is not uncommon for the losses to exceed $1 million per day for each day a reactor is down or delayed in start-up. The nuclear engineering people have a lot to do with how many of those days a public utility sees every year.

This client wanted to measure the performance of the engineers to accomplish two objectives. First, they were concerned about costs. Better measurement of engineering productivity might help improve their cost picture. Second, and more important, they were convinced that a dramatic improvement in professionalism among their engineering group would lead to long-term benefits, better morale, and an overall improvement in the engineering delivery system.

Initial steps focused on measuring activities. People wanted to know how long it took a draftsperson to make a "D"-sized drawing, how long engineers spent in meetings, and what percentage of engineers' time was spent with vendors.

The reader should understand that when measurement focuses around activities, a "solution" may be a foregone conclusion. For example, knowing how much time engineers spend in meetings inevitably suggests reducing the number of meetings and their length. You don't need a measurement system to do that. That kind of action can be readily taken without precise knowledge of how much time is wasted in meetings. As we struggled with this situation, we began to ask some fundamental questions that ended up being the core of the measurement system. For example, what does an engineer do? In arriving at an answer, we might be tempted to develop a laundry list of activities. After a great deal of discussion and many collaborative interviews, however, it becomes clear that engineers do one of two things: spend money or answer questions. Spending money has to do with putting hardware, equipment, and facilities in place. For example, in this case, if an engineer was responsible for installing a $5 million capital program expanding a selected process, the money spent would be $5 million. Then, one might logically ask the question: "How much does it cost to spend the $5 million?" This becomes the divisor in a calculation that proves to be very useful. If the engineer in the preceding example spent 200 worker hours at $50 an hour, the ratio of money invested divided by investment control and management dollars (CAM) would be $5 million divided by $10,000 or $500 invested per CAM dollars spent.

So, at a simple level, we can begin dealing with the engineer's end product and how much money it takes to produce that end product. We can also now rank engineers in various disciplines or among various types of projects. Moreover, we can compare this investment-to-spending ratio to the return on investment the project was supposed to generate as well as to the return actually generated. We have begun to capture some important elements of what an engineer does. But we have only skimmed the surface.

An engineer also answers questions. That's what a feasibility study is, an answer to the question "Should we do this or not?" Troubleshooting is a form of answering a question. Trying to find a better way to organize a project or department is seeking the answer to a question. Frankly, the consultants addressing this problem had difficulty coming up with a very good way of measuring the productivity and performance of engineers who were answering questions, but knowing that all the engineers do is spend money and answer questions put them on an improvement track. This only leads to more questions. How much time do engineers invest in spending money versus answering questions? Do some engineers tend to answer very few questions whereas others answer a lot? Do we have money-spending engineers and question-answering engineers? Should we break the two categories down into specialists who do one of each? Should engineers who mainly spend money be managed differently than engineers who mainly answer questions? Is the role of a question-answering engineer a promotion from that of a money-spending engineer?

Although we didn't get answers to all these questions, we determined that a second important productivity measurement for the engineering group was how much of their time they spend putting equipment and processes in place and how much of their time they spend answering questions. Those who seem to spend half their time on each were given special attention. It appeared clear that people should be at one or the other end of the spectrum in terms of their own effectiveness.

Having done that, the nuclear utility is now in the position of making these two measurement tools more sophisticated. The initial simplified measurement of dollars invested per (CAM) dollars spent seems to suggest that the more dollars we spend, the more productive we are. In simplistic terms that's true. But, what about the engineer who finds a more effective way to get the same job done and, therefore, spends fewer dollars and invests more of his or her own time to do so? Then the

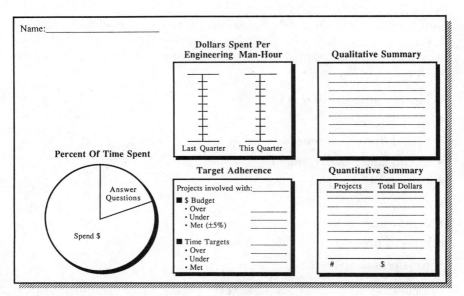

Figure 34-2. Quarterly engineer performance measurement.

ratio plummets. But, the project return on investment improves dramatically. So we have an opportunity to bring together return on investment and investment/spending ratios and separate the best engineers from those who might want to do better.

Managing the productivity of those who answer questions is perhaps a more demanding task. Our measurement system doesn't tell us how to do that yet. But it helps us identify which people are doing the more manageable thing and which people are doing the less manageable thing. The measurement has helped us pinpoint the few question-answering individuals while leaving the majority of the engineers in more measurable money-spending jobs. It has also provided an opportunity to recognize performance and promote people within the engineering group to jobs of increasing responsibility and complexity. Figure 34-2 demonstrates an overall measurement scheme in which the preceding concepts are prominent. We are convinced that the simple measurement applied here will take this company a long way to doubling the productivity of its engineering resource.

Leading the Way With Benchmarking

The concept of benchmarking as it exists today began in the mid- to late-1970s. Since that time, many companies have adopted the concept and modified it to fit their own situations. Companies such as General Electric Co., Du Pont Co., Kraft Inc., General Foods Corp., American Telephone & Telegraph Co., and others have benchmarked functions such as:

- Finance and accounting
- Data processing
- Sales force effectiveness
- Maintenance management
- Overall plant performance
- Logistics
- Senior management capital decision making
- Overall productivity establishment
- Just-in-time systems

This case study is about how very specific results-oriented benchmarking was used to bring about a 30 percent cost reduction for a major food corporation.

The people in this company thought they were pretty good. But senior management had lingering doubts. Costs were being reduced relatively slowly. Yield numbers looked so close to perfect that they were hard to believe. But there was a warning sign in the organization structure and staff size because it seemed more oriented towards bureaucracy than the actual needs of the business. Most chilling of all, when the profitability of this company was compared to similar companies, it was towards the middle of the pack.

This fine company produced a series of fine products and had an excellent reputation. Although profitability was average, everyone thought he or she was the best one could be. Something wasn't right competitively. Senior operations management knew they had to find a way to evaluate where they really stood and to get the organization to internalize the need for change and the significant potential that might be realized. The initial answer in this situation was *benchmarking*.

Benchmarking is acquiring pertinent information, setting targets and goals designed to make the company the "best of the best" in its competitive field, and acting on focused programs to change the company from its current position. Competitive intelligence and data are objectively interpreted in a way that reflects the unique differences of the company's industry, strategic emphasis, organizational philosophy, and style. In gathering competitive information, each company is ensured that the data it provides will not be released individually, but aggregated with data from the other companies in the group.

A. T. Kearney was called upon to visit one or two of the client's operating plants. The process was relatively straightforward. The steps were as follows:

1. Create a very comprehensive benchmarking guide to cover all the dimensions of the operating environments from organization, to material yields, to maintenance and energy costs.

2. Identify 10 to 20 competing companies with similar operations.

3. Send the benchmarking guide to all the client company plants to be benchmarked as well as to those competitive plants considered to be excellent (based on preestablished criteria).

4. Receive the benchmarking guides back and make telephone calls to clarify certain data.

5. Visit each plant for one day to validate data and develop subjective impressions.

6. Put the points for a wide variety of measurements on graphs. Figure 34-3 represents one of those graphs.

Percent Of Change (Annual) In Total Cost/Pound (1982-1987)

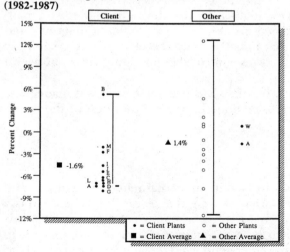

■ Client's cost per pound has dropped more than 8% during the last five years, primarily due to raw material cost.

Figure 34-3. Operations management.

7. Analyze the data points and the subjective dimensions to develop conclusions.

8. Identify the operational elements where the client company is ahead of, equal to, or behind the external sample set.

9. Set targets for the various operating parameters by using the average of the first quartile performance.

10. Convert those target gaps to benefit improvements in dollar terms.

The preceding steps got this client to the point where it had a clear understanding of what was needed in critical areas:

- Organization and people
- Operations management
- Maintenance
- Quality
- Technology
- Measurement and control

The benchmarking data helped the client immediately recognize the need to close two plants where the gap was very wide and the cost of catching up was deemed too high. They then brought all the plant managers together and explained benchmarking and what it demonstrated to them. As a result of that initial session, the plant managers led the effort to take one-third of plant controllable operating costs out over a 2-year period.

The company saw that what they had been achieving was inadequate and learned what needed to be done to become the "best of the best."

Conclusion

Measurement is not passé. In fact, in an increasingly fast-changing and technological world, it is more important than ever. But we need to pay great attention to what we measure. The important message from this chapter is that we need to break from our traditional approaches to measurement. We need to understand what our business needs to do to increase its competitive edge. That understanding of desired results must be telescoped down through the organization with the measurement system as the guide and in parallel with activities geared to improved performance.

The only good reason to measure something is to change it, to make it better. Some suggest that if you stay where you are, you're really losing ground because everyone around you is doing better. Therefore, measuring results should not be confused with monitoring conditions. Frequently, measuring the right things, all by itself, can identify 10 to 30 percent of the potential improvement available. Achieving that potential is a function of *doing it better by doing it differently*. Doing it the same way will, at best, get you the same results. A properly established measurement system can constantly keep people's attention focused on looking for opportunities to do better and do different, and focus on increasing a company's competitive edge in the marketplace.

35
Productivity in the Information Age

Richard A. Connelly, Ph.D.
Active Management, Inc.

Increasing productivity in the Information Age is a strategic management issue. Dealing with changing markets and new technologies demands that business leaders focus on changes in staffing and compensating people to perform more productively if they are going to achieve competitive growth goals. The structure of compensation programs is vital for improving productivity, because reward programs provide a critical link between people's perceptions of their self-interest and the new economics for business decisions in the Information Age. Designing compensation programs that blend rewards for individuals, organizational teams, and the business as a whole to be more productive sets the direction and the pace for making productive changes in methods and practices.

In the past, productivity and pay were based on very different issues that reflected different types of business conditions. From the earliest times of cottage industries, pay for productivity focused on setting piece-rate output incentives to raise production from individual workers. Pay and operational productivity were directly equivalent in peoples' minds. The structure of business tended to be simple. Labor was readily available. Work output was easy to count and monitor. Pay rates may not have been based on internal equity, and management goals may not always have been enlightened, but it was easy for most people to understand that their pay was based on the productivity of individual output.

As society moved into the Industrial Age, productivity management and measurement were adapted to fit the expansion of factories and assembly-line production methods. Work was scheduled centrally. Industrial engineers used work samples, stop watches, and work standards to evaluate how much work output should be expected from a job. Productivity became less personal and more dependent on the organizational structures that were set in long-term business plans and corporate reorganization decisions. Base pay with annual merit increases and multiyear labor contracts became the standard compensation practices of the Industrial Age. People expected their careers and business practices to operate similarly in long-term cycles. Most incentive pay opportunities shifted upward from production-line workers to higher management-level jobs. Management's targets and interests shifted away from dealing with markets and production cycles to an almost exclusive focus on achieving "bottom-line" financial results.

Now, in the Information Age, the deployment of computers and communication links is completely changing the importance of, and parameters for, setting productivity expectations. Productivity is becoming personal again largely because of the use of the personal computer. Because information about financial results, production flow, and people resources moves through communication networks ready to be accessed, analyzed, and acted upon, productivity decisions and results can be directly linked to individuals, teams, and organizations as a whole. People have the opportunity to have a more direct stake in their business's productivity results.

What makes modern productivity a strategic management issue is the change in the audience that evaluates and interprets productivity trends. A new generation of business analysts has emerged that understands how to look beyond financial forecasts to the operational issues that are producing results. United States accounting standards now require detailed analysis of the operational factors that underlie 10-K financial forecasts. Performance databases and research models have provided securities analysts, investment bankers, and talented professionals with the means to monitor competitive operational performance and productivity results in every industry. Productivity used to be regarded almost exclusively as a manufacturing management issue. Now there are productivity indexes produced by authoritative institutions, such as the University of Pennsylvania's The Wharton School, that comprehensively cover service industries and distribution businesses as well as manufacturers. Competitive productivity performance is ranked and reported regularly, providing analysts with an operational basis for evaluating management leadership strategies.

Businesses operate in a world in which external events such as deregulation, the introduction of new technology, and mergers and acquisitions are expected to lead to breakthrough achievements in productivity and cash flow. After such events occur, businesses that don't readjust their productive capacity and improve their resource output within a "competitive period of time" accordingly suffer a loss of reputation in the view of the marketplace.

Executive capability to manage productivity becomes a strategic issue when analyst opinions lead to stock price changes that affect company valuations and balance sheet performance. At this point, productivity is no longer regarded only as a micromanagement issue based on stop watches and work measurement standards. Productivity management requires creative leadership to adjust corporate structures, raise performance targets, and find successful ways of obtaining greater strategic value from assets, investments, and resources.

Productivity, People, and Pay

The successful transformation of business strategies and organizational structures into the Information Age depends directly on the quality of performance. The lessons learned from the past 100 years of industrial management research and analysis underscore the importance of factoring the role that people play into projections of productivity improvement success or failure. Whether the specific productivity issues involve quality improvement, customer service enhancements, or the use of new types of technology, people determine the ultimate value that will be added to work output. Much of the business success that has been achieved in the auto industry is an example of how the basic principles of productivity and quality management were put to work. Whether the application of productivity improvements occurred in Japan, Sweden, or the United States, the barriers that blocked more productive work flows were reduced by using the basic principles of accountability management, communication, and worker involvement. Improvements are more likely to be successful when people understand, endorse, and are rewarded for their participation in the change process.

The productivity lessons from the past take on even greater importance when a fundamental principle about peoples' roles in productivity is recognized in economic terms. Achieving higher productivity depends on continuously obtaining better work output from the business's "core group" of people. This core group is the base of full-time and part-time employees who are committed to working productively during economic valleys and flexibly during peak periods of business activity. As more investments are made in new technology or other productivity improvements, the quality of this core group's qualifications for changing work situations, its motivation to use new resources, and its readiness to adapt to change become the overriding factors in forecasting future productivity results.

Making productivity projections in the Information Age takes on added uncertainty because organization structures and corporate strategies continue to change so frequently. The long-term stability and structure of the Industrial Age is essentially over. Now, as competitors bring new technologies and new products or services into the marketplace, the responsibilities, performance standards, and skills mix needed by the core group to perform successfully have to be adjusted continuously. Who provides work to whom can become very different when people use new computer networks to transmit information. How much someone has to know about a particular product to answer customer questions satisfactorily can change as products or services are introduced into new markets.

Meeting the major challenge of modern productivity planning—balancing work requirements with the necessary skills and talents for performance—has caused problems for many large and medium-sized corporations. The "downsizing" experience of the 1980s provides many examples of firms that didn't understand the differences between reducing expenses and increasing productivity. When financial reductions or "freezes" are mandated equally across organizational units, short-term results at first appear to reduce expenses. But, often in the process, maintaining competitive quality and performance standards suffer when the productive alignment of resource capacity is thrown out of balance.

The use of early retirement programs to reduce staff expenses has also caused negative effects on productivity. Reductions in staff without adequate plans to maintain necessary experience and skills in the organization has caused more harm than good to performance results. There are several famous instances in the insurance industry when early retirement programs have led to larger than expected numbers of underwriters choosing retirement. Senior underwriters play a vital decision-making role in the insurance work flow. Because there were limited qualified replacements for the retired underwriters, the backlogs caused by the staff reductions cost far more than the savings initially achieved in reduced payroll expenses.

The introduction of new technology-based tools and work flow realignments are creating revolutionary changes in job requirements and staffing plans. The employment demand and pay ranges for some job groups, such as engineers, is increasing sharply, whereas the need for other jobs is being reduced or eliminated entirely. This is causing more situations in which there are vast functional salary differences between high-demand, entry-level employees and experienced, low-demand employees who must work together cooperatively in the same work flow or in the same project teams.

Designing pay plans and rewards that promote cooperation toward common goals takes on an important dimension in the Information Age because productivity depends on the quality and speed of work that flows across departments. People use compensation as a psychological litmus test of how new business strategies, organization structure changes, or new resources will affect them personally. Just as market analysts have more information about a business's results and plans for the future, people are more acutely aware in their personal planning to evaluate how changes in technology and business structure will ultimately affect their career value and personal net worth.

The use of compensation design to motivate people to increase productivity becomes an opportunity to build bridges between the needs of people and the needs of the business. Maintaining peoples' commitment to productivity improvement programs is essential for a business to remain competitive on the performance forecasts and trend curves projected by analysts for success within its industry. The design of compensation and reward programs demonstrates to people where management is placing its priorities and how people will benefit from productivity improvements that strengthen the business.

Real gains in productivity management come from plans and decisions that move beyond the use of revenue, head count, and payroll expense as the sole focuses for productivity decisions. To create greater value, Information Age goals and rewards have to be based on dynamic productivity measures that can be adjusted for changes in business conditions and linked to strategic objectives.

Strategic Productivity Analysis

The goal of strategic productivity analysis is to seek and find opportunities in which coordinating job responsibilities with work flow design will result in higher productivity and greater competitive business advantage. This analysis can use traditional work measurement techniques to examine the basis for performance standards, but the key to its success is identifying the issues that link staffing and structure to the strategic needs of the business.

The value chain framework, made popular by Dr. Michael Porter of the Harvard Business School, provides a useful method for analyzing strategic strengths, opportunities, threats, and weaknesses where productivity creates competitive business advantages. Because it closely parallels the major organizational structure and resource allocation issues used by managers in making operating decisions, the value chain makes it easier to compare strategic issues with practical decisions.

If individual departments establish budget goals, standards, and rewards that don't use value chain principles, there is a risk that overall business productivity becomes less important than satisfying local management issues. To be effective, productivity analysis needs to start at the front end and finish at the back end of a business's organizational value chain. Improving productivity involves finding the issues, whether large or small, that can cause bottlenecks in work flow or quality problems that require work efforts to be repeated.

Productivity analysis of a business's value chain is also a search for opportunities to increase organizational cooperation and performance. An organization's budgeted staffing levels and resource commitments provide the benchmarks for measuring existing productivity capacity levels. Incremental goals of individuals, teams, or groups that can contribute to increasing the total value produced by existing resources—and make the business more competitive—provide the basis for designing performance-based productivity incentives.

Productivity analysis is a search for the performance causes that lie behind business results. By establishing a strategic framework for evaluating how the functional work performed at different times by individuals, teams, and groups affects the quality and productivity of work flow, a solid foundation is established for using compensation programs and staffing plans to improve performance.

A review of the major work flow functions in a typical organizational value chain provides examples of how strategic perspectives are considered in policy decisions and productivity plans. Specific analysis of the greater value that can be achieved in overall output forms the basis for developing goals and rewards for productivity improvements.

Supplier/Distributor Productivity

A second major productivity improvement focal point in the value chain deals with the performance of suppliers and distribution agents who provide materials or customers to the business. Although manufacturers need raw material supply, and service businesses focus on customer relationships, the productivity principles involved are similar.

Before modern computerized inventory management, integrated order entry systems, and network communications were deployed, there was relatively little perceived need to coordinate supplier/distributor performance with company operating plans. Management's perspective began to change in the mid-1970s; global inflation and high interest rates led financial officers and controllers to become more actively involved in reducing inventory costs and the number of suppliers or agents who were financed in the distribution system.

The productivity debates between the operations areas and financial controllers that grew out of this period were strongly influenced by examples of Japanese success in managing inventory turnover. The development of worker involvement programs, quality assurance practices, and supplier scheduling communications demonstrated how better planning could make assembly lines more productive and suppliers more responsive. Using supplier/distributor goal-setting programs and performance incentives, the leading companies in the auto industry demonstrated how production orders could be fulfilled with more limited inventory and shorter lead times than had been accepted historically as standard performance norms.

The performance strategies and productivity measures that were developed during this period are referred to as just-in-time (JIT) performance goals. The supplier or distributor who produces services consistently and adjusts specifications and delivery levels to fit changing market conditions can contribute to predictable increases in working capital. The value that the added working capital brings to the business establishes the quantitative basis for developing incentives for timeliness, reliability, and quality of performance that has direct payback to the business.

Sales Productivity

Sales performance has traditionally been the key indicator that reflects the attractiveness of a business's products and services in the marketplace. The standard form of sales productivity and reward design has been based on individual salespeople receiving commission payments. Institutional sales provide a good example of the changes taking place in sales compensation practices. But the same productivity principles apply to all selling situations.

Incentives were usually paid in institutional selling as a percentage of revenue immediately after closing a sale or after collecting a first payment. With commissions for recent sales in hand, the sales force then moved on to future selling goals with a relatively small priority being given to customer service and business renewals.

The Information Age has begun to change the sales productivity profile in many industries. Automated customer information files, also known as CIF systems, provide marketing and sales executives with the means to design their own unique information tools for analyzing target markets and developing sales strategies. To evaluate results, accounting systems offer the means to examine operational expenses through the complete cycle of a customer's relationship with the business. Modern businesses are continuously refining comprehensive product profitability performance measures from their files and evaluating selling costs in relation to business benefits.

Having more complete marketing information doesn't necessarily make sales productivity easier to achieve. Selling products in modern markets takes more time and money because making sales requires more work now than it did in the past. The management overhead in keeping pace with changes in pricing, product design, government regulations, and potential product liability exposures reduces the time available for active selling to the customer. The time needed to train a salesperson on all the issues that are relevant to representing a company's product line has become prohibitive in many industries. The costs of training one person in all the skills needed to gain and maintain product knowledge outweighs the revenues that can realistically be expected from the available time for active selling.

New structures and tactical game plans have had to be established to keep sales results high and selling costs under control. One example that marks the productivity shift in Information Age selling is the greater use of direct-marketing techniques and team-based sales strategies. The tasks and time required to identify new sales prospects, to evaluate qualified sales leads, to close sales, and to provide service after the sale involves coordinating a broader mix of organizational resources and skills. The chief marketing officer's or sales director's greatest productivity challenge is finding the right combination of people and marketing strategies that can keep revenue flowing on a profitable basis through the sales pipeline.

Sales incentives and variable pay programs have to be designed to respect the total investment in sales and service time needed to improve product profitability. This requires defining sales priorities and job goals for an effective tactical balance between generating new customer sales and increasing sales from existing customers. There are many examples in commission-based sales plans in which the lack of a coordinated sales productivity and profitability plan leads to the selling of the products that maximize commissions, rather than sell the best products for growing effective customer relationships.

Factoring product development costs and companywide sales support expenses into sales rewards changes the weightings in establishing commissions and incentives. Although there are always strategic reasons to adjust pricing for new products and new markets, there is a dramatic difference in reward design between using first-year revenue projections and full product profitability analysis.

Introducing the perspective of competitive product positioning and the expected life cycle for product sales into reward design also gives the sales force more opportunities to be involved in planning sales productivity priorities. The development costs for new products can be so high, and the risks of introduction so uncertain, that sales force performance, which extends the expected duration of an existing product's life cycle, pays back incremental productivity to the business as a whole. This is an area where the translation of strategic marketing productivity gains into product management incentives and team sales goals gives the sales force two-way participation in strategic planning.

Operations and Customer Service Productivity

The productivity plans of the senior manufacturing or operations officer used to focus on maintaining standard costs for product orders that varied little in execution. This was during a time when either operations was considered "the back office" or manufacturing was viewed as being in a world by itself. Now, as market-driven, customized sales competition increases and more sophisticated technology-based resources are brought into manufacturing and service operations areas, business competitiveness often depends on operational capability to respond flexibly to customer needs and achieve low unit cost performance.

Manufacturing and operations are the most visible, and often the most dramatic, areas where information technology is reshaping the design of work and productivity standards. The business capabilities of the computer to automate repetitive tasks, store needed information for future retrieval, and speed communications were developed in the 1970s. Employees in the largest organizations were the first to experience the significant redesign of work and jobs around the interface with the company's central computer system.

The widespread deployment of the personal computer and distributed processing networks during the 1980s dramatically extended the use of computers as standard equipment in offices and retail stores throughout the modern world. The inexpensive personal computer gave local organizations in large and small businesses direct control over their own technology to schedule and control work according to local ideas about how to increase productivity. Output capacity exploded upwards in basic functions such as preparing correspondence, scheduling, bookkeeping, spreadsheet analysis, and standard report preparation.

Computer software began to change the shape of productivity standards and job design requirements throughout the operations and administrative areas. Career experience in using software programs became an essential qualification to gain or hold many different jobs. Secretaries needed to know word processing systems. Design engineers had to use computer-aided design/computer-aided manufacturing (CAD/CAM) programs. Technology became the productivity driver in establishing expected work rate standards. Establishing pay levels based on knowledge became easier to differentiate and justify because of technology skills.

The 1990s is the decade when the combination of new software applications, artificial intelligence, communications, and robotics will have even greater impacts on the design of job duties and overall work flow productivity. The most fundamental objective being pursued in organization planning is the examination of how the productivity rates of every job on the table of organization can be increased by designing links to supporting information systems. The potential to use the computer to have more employee questions answered, perform better diagnostic tests, make faster calculations, and analyze results more effectively changes productivity expectations and the very nature of work itself within a business.

Technology and productivity design changes in operations are reshaping strategic competitiveness in the 1990s. Examples from two industries show how new strategies and work structures are reshaping staffing strategies.

Transportation Productivity. Truck mechanics in the United States Army are using voice-activated, artificial intelligence computers as diagnostic tools in performing preventative maintenance on truck fleets. Using the technology as a job aid, the mechanic can inspect three trucks for every two that were inspected without the benefit of advanced information support. The computer diagnostics not only guides the mechanic faster to the correct area for repairs, but it also sends out electronic inventory orders for needed repair parts and fills out administrative forms that document the steps and quality checks on the work completed.

This use of Information Age technology and change in work design does even more than create faster repair time standards. It addresses a labor supply situation in which there are not enough skilled mechanics available in regional labor pools to meet industry demands for truck repair. As more sophisticated integrated truck engines are introduced, the use of job-based computer support helps to train entry-level people faster. And it plays a major role in retraining veteran mechanics to qualify them for work on new electronically based truck component designs.

Financial Services Productivity. Several major financial services institutions are moving ahead aggressively to install end-user computing. This involves creating different levels of direct information access between customers and transaction processing operations areas. When the connections are made, the standard hours required to process a transaction or respond to an inquiry shrink to a small portion of what was required when work flowed through a branch bank, a brokerage office, or an agency.

Businesses that establish these types of work flow changes gain major productivity advantages over their competitors. When these breakthroughs are implemented, competitive performance moves up a plateau where the leader's results take off and followers fall further behind. Until it can close the productivity gap, a follower organization spends more resources producing services that are less responsive and more costly than the industry's leaders. The competitive disadvantage in operations puts the future of the entire business at risk.

Research and Development/Professional Productivity

The key to the success of changes that create more productive value chains often lies in setting priorities and creating incentives for research and development projects. Productive research and development performance, when new products, technologies, or market changes are introduced quickly and effectively in low-overhead organizations, is a sign of competitive strength. The R&D-oriented projects are the means that white-collar professionals have to demonstrate the greater value that they can add to the business as a whole. Monitoring the programs and the results involved in implementing timely, cost-effective improvements to strategy, structure, or resource positioning provides an opportunity to reward people who are playing key roles in introducing change.

The need for research and development programs applies in every functional area of business that is undergoing Information Age transformation of its resources. The effective design of research and development rewards and incentives follows from an investment perspective that is set at the level of the CEO and the board of directors. The fundamental issue in setting research and development rewards deals with establishing accountability and performance criteria that follow the flow of capital invested in projects that improve productivity as a strategic issue.

Strategic productivity issues, which are monitored and rewarded at the highest level of the organization, provide a composite picture of tactical programs that increase competitiveness. Here are some examples:

- Introducing computer networks closer to the marketplace to gather faster input and develop more timely and effective pricing decisions
- Implementing improvements in sales and marketing strategies to make a more effective use of advertising expenditures and sales force size relative to sales revenue
- Improving the cost-effectiveness and timing of product development projects and new product roll-outs
- Introducing practical improvements in the quality of tools and technologies used in production
- Making effective changes in the proportion of flexible staff to per-

manent staff in business operations to match seasonal productivity cycles

- Using training resources more effectively to increase performance skills and customer service attitudes of employees
- Improving the business's track record in attracting and retaining talented staff in key operations

Using a strategic productivity investment perspective changes the traditional perceptions that professional staff and research and development units have in many organizations. In the past there were often strong cultural boundaries separating line operating areas and the staff organizations. Isolating line areas from research and development and staff was viewed as being necessary in some businesses in order to maintain independent judgment. What has become more apparent in the Information Age is that the performance value of research and development depends as much on shared accountability between line and staff for integrating the results of research and development as it does on the research and development work itself.

The Executive Role in Productivity Management

The large number of functional changes taking place across the different areas of modern business underscores the importance of the executive role in Information Age decision making. Each area involved in total business performance—marketing, distribution, operations, finance, human resources, and research and development—is going through major operational changes. But, in the final analysis, achieving a more productive structure and more competitive strategy depends on synchronizing the plans that make the whole organization greater than the sum of its parts. Success in the executive role requires vision and leadership to identify the creative solutions and common goals that help people in different areas understand how changes for the future can be more attractive than accepting current operating norms and standards.

Studies of corporate valuation and stock price conducted at Northwestern University's Kellog Business School point out that the stock market places premium value on companies that are positioned to restructure their assets and shift their markets quickly to deal with changing conditions. A business's current financial performance and cash flow fundamentals justify only a portion of a company's market price. Establishing the residual value of a business depends to a great extent on the perception of executive leadership capability to increase productivity in response to changing conditions.

The stakes in executive compensation have risen accordingly to reflect the risks and rewards for individuals who have the ability to productively restructure organizations, improve cash flow, and increase shareholder value. The mergers, acquisitions, and leveraged buyouts of the 1980s are, in effect, part of the strategic productivity challenge. Through corporate restructuring, boards of directors evaluate proposals from CEOs to reshape a firm's assets by buying or selling units that realign marketing, supply, distribution, operations, and research and development resources into more productive combinations. Although the seller's responsibility is to increase shareholder value, the acquirer has to establish a price at which debt can be retired and competitive productivity can be achieved with reasonable market risk.

The leaders who create productivity management excellence in the 1990s need operational strategies that go beyond selling assets and issuing debt to achieve their goals. The capabilities to assemble talent and implement strategies that will apply new productivity resources effectively, adjust to market changes quickly, and establish higher standards of performance are the core specifications for executive talent.

Analysts evaluate the creativity and comprehensiveness of policy decisions and management programs that address these productivity issues. This is how executive management talent will increasingly be evaluated in the Information Age. The signs of creative leadership emerge from the specific ways at both the macro and micro levels in which organizations are increasing their flexibility and balancing work requirements with the skills needed for productive performance.

Conclusion

Each organization has its own unique strategies and style for increasing productivity and strategic competitiveness. No two business strategies are implemented in the same way because of the inherent differences in people and business conditions. But finding meaningful relationships between the compensation practices that are motivating productivity performance and the challenge in the business goals being pursued is a strategic indicator of how well a business will be rising to the standards of Information Age competition.

36

Measuring and Assessing Top Executive Performance

Craig E. Schneier, Ph.D.

Managing Principal, National Director
Human Resource and Organization Effectiveness Practice
Sibson & Co. Inc.

In recent years, top executive performance has come under closer scrutiny than ever before. With the mind-boggling dollar amounts being paid to CEOs and top executives, shareholders as well as the press and executives themselves have begun to reexamine the link between executive performance and executive compensation. In fact, a number of national business publications now compare common quantitative (financial) measures—such as earnings per share, return on investment, and dividends—to CEO earnings. The result has been a rather controversial quantitative ranking of CEO "effectiveness."[1]

But running a company is more than a numbers game. Quantitative measures certainly have a role in executive performance appraisal but, in the short term, these indicators often belie corporate reality. In-

[1]Graef S. Crystal, "Seeking the Sense in CEO Pay," *Fortune*, June 5, 1989, pp. 88–104.

creased earnings in the short run do not automatically indicate that a company's strategic thinking is on target. Financial data alone says little about the company's ability to meet growing marketing challenges abroad or improve poor productivity at home. And an impressive return for shareholders will no longer stop Wall Street's grumblings or raiders' threats based on overstaffing.

To ensure that the most complete picture of corporate and CEO performance is being created, many companies are making an effort to put their quantitative data into perspective. The method of choice: supplementing quantitative data with qualitative measures that evaluate overall corporate fitness and, more specifically, the fitness of their CEOs and other top executives to lead. A Sibson & Company survey of board compensation committee members and CEOs in 345 of the largest U.S. companies found that qualitative measures were becoming increasingly popular in evaluating executives. In fact, qualitative measures were rated "critical/very important" much more often than quantitative measures by survey respondents (see Figure 36-1). Receiving the highest percent totals were "establishing strategic direction" (86 percent) and "building the management team" (84 percent). All quantitative measures received lower percent rankings. "Businesses need a new way to assess the intangible qualities of corporate performance," Sibson &

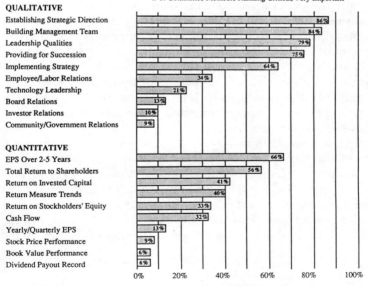

Figure 36-1. Board members ranking critical/very important.

Company concluded in its report.[2] "Committee members' emphasis on qualitative aspects of performance suggest that the pendulum is swinging...after years of quantitative decision making and dispassionate portfolio management."

In this chapter, we examine some widely used quantitative executive performance measures. We then demonstrate the increasingly important role played by qualitative measures to assess top executive performance. We also discuss the benefits of a performance appraisal system for top executives that incorporates qualitative measures and suggest how such a system should be designed.

Measuring Executive Performance in Two Companies

Acme Manufacturing was experiencing a record year in earnings and sales. Its 5-year expansion plan was beginning to produce anticipated results, with several of its recent acquisitions turning a profit for the first time. Overall, there was a winning spirit within the organization and widespread confidence that continued good times were ahead. Not so at nearby Ajax Manufacturing. Competition from abroad had obliterated the company's sales forecasts. Persistent rumors about a pending foreign acquisition were doing little to inspire key managers and other employees. So when their respective board compensation committees divvied out annual bonuses and stock options, there were few surprises. Acme's CEO and senior management team were well compensated for their efforts, with each receiving a significant incentive payout. At Ajax, the CEO and his top executives were held accountable for the company's poor performance and uncertain future. Bonuses were cut and options were not forthcoming.

Considering what has traditionally been the norm in U.S. companies, it would be difficult to argue with the actions of these two fictional compensation committees. Companies have always assessed executive performance and provided some form of reward for good results. In the past, these rewards often took the form of increased annual compensation. Today, they are typically provided as bonuses and stock options.

This appraisal method raises important questions. Consider Acme and Ajax:

---

[2]Sibson & Co., *Boards, Company Performance, and Executive Pay,* Sibson & Co., Princeton, N.J., 1988, p. 8.

- *What are the specific quantitative measures used to evaluate executive performance?* In other words, do sales, earnings, cash flow, returns, and other financial figures provide the most accurate assessment of an executive's performance? Acme's high annual earnings may indicate that its CEO and top team have managed to move the company forward. It may also mean that external forces—including government regulations, interest rates, or the mood on Wall Street—were positioned just right to produce a winning year. Therefore, a much closer evaluation is required.

- *What qualitative measures—leadership, strategy, communication skills—should be considered as part of the performance assessment process?* Because it is not uncommon for a troubled company to take several years to right itself, the performance of Ajax's top team may show little progress on the quantitative side but very positive strategic movement on the qualitative end. For example, George Foote, a former McKinsey & Company partner and member of several boards, participating in a Sibson & Company roundtable discussion on assessing CEO performance, observed that short-term profit depressants can, in fact, lead to long-term benefits. He cited a strong resistance to labor demands, a major new product development investment, and international expansion as factors that can show up negatively in the short term but then result in significant long-term gains.[3]

Quantitative Performance Measures: Necessary But Not Sufficient

Compensation committee members agree that the CEO's impact on strategy, management team building, and leadership are more critical than certain quantitative measures, particularly in the long run, but they often use measures of corporate financial performance as the criteria upon which top executive performance evaluation is based. The reasons are expediency and familiarity. Directors can easily assess executive performance based on certain "objective" (that is, quantitative) measures, but subjective (that is, qualitative) measures are another story. Quantitative measures should not be replaced completely as appraisal criteria, but they should be considered in concert with qualitative measures. For example, many people in the business community believe that the best long-term measure of top executive performance may be shareholder returns. Yet, in the short term, such quantitative measures

---

[3]As quoted in Sibson & Co., *Facts & Issues 1989: Measuring CEO Performance*, Sibson & Co., Princeton, N.J., 1989, p. 3.

as stock movement or earnings may tell very little about executive performance. More relevant is an examination of certain qualitative measures, including the "quality" of corporate strategy and success in implementing the strategy. Other useful quantitative measures could include discounted cash flow, market share, return on equity, or return on net assets. Each, as well as others, tells an important part of the story.

Qualitative Performance Measures: Telling the Complete Story

In today's company, the rapidly changing business environment makes new measures—and a new performance appraisal system—necessary for top executives. Mergers and acquisitions, leveraged buyouts, global competition and markets, deregulation, and other factors dictate a new set of performance expectations. Today's CEOs and other top executives must be able to juggle administrative, financial, strategic, and leadership responsibilities with the short- and long-term interests of their shareholders, customers, and employees in mind. In fact, instead of simply asking their top executives, "What have you done for us lately?" boards and shareholders are now trying to find out, "What do you plan to do for us tomorrow?"

The emphasis on qualitative measures doesn't represent a new way of thinking for some of the most successful companies. International Business Machines and Hewlett-Packard Company, beginning with their founders, recognize their importance, placing particular emphasis on contributions made by individual employees and initiative. More companies have followed suit. One major insurance company realized that its combined ratio and market share alone did not accurately reflect its success in implementing a new strategy and a new culture. The classic low cost and product differentiation strategies were augmented with a focus on customer service as a competitive advantage (see Figure 36-2). Other companies have been less willing to change their ways. For some, particularly those that are currently performing well, fixing a system that doesn't appear to be broken seems unnecessary. But there are a number of arguments that can be made in defense of a careful qualitative analysis.

Why Measure Qualitative Aspects of Performance?

For one thing, a company may be in trouble and not even know it. Not all problems bubble to the surface quickly. It takes a proactive company

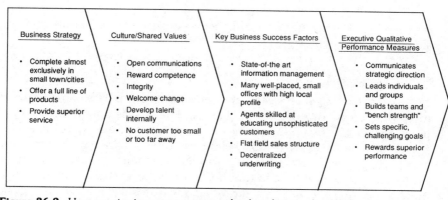

Business Strategy	Culture/Shared Values	Key Business Success Factors	Executive Qualitative Performance Measures
• Complete almost exclusively in small town/cities • Offer a full line of products • Provide superior service	• Open communications • Reward competence • Integrity • Welcome change • Develop talent internally • No customer too small or too far away	• State-of-the art information management • Many well-placed, small offices with high local profile • Agents skilled at educating unsophisticated customers • Flat field sales structure • Decentralized underwriting	• Communicates strategic direction • Leads individuals and groups • Builds teams and "bench strength" • Sets specific, challenging goals • Rewards superior performance

Figure 36-2. How a major insurance company developed a set of qualitative top executive performance measures to implement a new strategy and culture.

to look beyond the obvious—the quarterly earnings—and determine that, for example, its leadership talent is below par as it enters the 1990s, or that even though sales are coming in, the company has failed to cement supplier relationships, invest in new technology, develop the next generation of products, or anticipate customers' expectations. General Motors Corporation and Ford Motor Company provide a frequently used example. General Motors failed to see the criticality of quality in its buyers' minds nearly as early as Ford did. General Motors' top executives were no doubt not measured on their quality leadership role, but leadership in quality was a key component of Ford's executives' jobs, beginning with the chairperson. This is one reason why Ford earned 30 percent more than General Motors on sales of 30 percent less in 1988.[4]

It is safe to say that three kinds of companies exist: those that are running ahead, those that are running behind, and those that are running in place. How, then, do companies apply qualitative measures in each of these instances?

Designing a Qualitative Performance Appraisal System

Once a company accepts the fact that both quantitative and qualitative measures must be merged into an effective performance appraisal sys-

[4]*The Fortune 1988 Directory of U.S. Corporations*, published as an issue of Fortune magazine, April 24, 1989, p. 6.

tem for its top executives, it can then begin to set the parameters for such a system.

An effective top executive performance appraisal system requires six actions:

1. *Select performance measures.* Top executive performance can be measured across two broad dimensions. The first is how well the company, for which the CEO and his or her team is ultimately responsible, performs financially. Obviously, interest rates, currency fluctuations, and perhaps other factors beyond top management's control will affect performance here, at least in the short run. Nevertheless, as Figure 36-1 indicates, returns, cash flow, and other measures are obviously critical. But how well do the CEO and his or her team perform as leaders? This dimension addresses individual responsibilities for improving company performance and represents that aspect of performance largely within an individual executive's control. An example of a set of such performance areas appears in Figure 36-3. These become the basis for assessing strengths and weaknesses and provide a framework for the board to provide constructive performance feedback to the CEO and the top executives. The key is to let strategy and business goals, coupled with the requisite culture or shared values, drive these measures.

2. *Develop performance indicators.* Next, such measures as leadership must actually be assessed using some type of consistent and effective yardstick. Each performance area should contain "elements of accountability," which define the specific accountabilities within each broad area of an individual executive's responsibility. Consider succession planning, for example. The best CEOs and top executives spend a

---

- Provides leadership
- Provides strategic direction
- Proactively manages change
- Organizes, develops, and utilizes management team
- Creates an appropriate organizational environment
- Provides effective external representation
- Monitors and evaluates company performance and takes corrective action
- Maintains a positive relationship with the board of directors

---

Figure 36-3. A set of top executive qualitative performance measures for a large diversified services company.

considerable amount of time identifying and developing the "bench strength" their companies will need to succeed in the future.[5] Succession planning involvement, then, is an accountability. If viable succession is part of an executive's long-term vision, then a commitment must be made to developing those with potential in key executive positions throughout the organization. The performance areas and elements of accountability should be affirmed (or reaffirmed) by the board and CEO prior to the start of each year.

To make measurement less subjective, the board and CEO should also agree on the specific "indicators" of performance in each area, with the understanding that more than one indicator may be developed in each area of responsibility. These indicators can be either quantitative measures (for example, results of employee surveys) or observable qualitative evidence (for example, observations of the CEO's behavior in presentations to financial analysts). Indicators clearly define performance expectations up front and provide the facts needed to accurately appraise performance at year end. Of course, the board will still need to exercise considerable judgment in applying these facts. Elements of accountability and illustrative indicators for one performance measure are provided in Table 36-1.

3. *Identify resources and mechanisms.* There is a good reason why boards desire to use qualitative measures of performance but, yet, may shy away from them. They are rarely in a position to observe *how* an executive performs the job—only *what* results are obtained. Hence, in order to evaluate top executive success in each performance area, the board must determine the necessary resources and mechanisms to gather data.

The most effective systems rely on data from many relevant sources. The board should attempt to gather data in a systematic manner. After all, random comments, overheard conversations, and infrequent observations will provide a weak case if a CEO or top executive must be confronted with lackluster performance.

Suppose that the board chooses to measure a CEO's leadership style. The perception of directors, based on their direct observations, may be useful. But those perceptions should be augmented by data gathered via surveys, interviews, and focus group discussions among the CEO's direct reports, employees at lower levels, customers, suppliers, or even other directors, particularly inside directors. In addition, reviewing plans, policies, and reports can be helpful. The key is to gather enough

---

[5] A recent Sibson & Co. survey of 28 leading heavy processing companies found a strong correlation between the amount of time a CEO spends on succession planning and the effectiveness of the process.

Table 36-1. Illustration of Elements of Accountability and Performance Indicators for Performance Assessment Area: "Organizes, Develops, and Utilizes Management Team"

Element of accountability	Performance indicators
Establishes, evaluates, and as necessary, changes the management structure to improve organizational effectiveness and efficiency.	Ratio of overhead to operational costs is better than industry norms. Number of management layers is below industry norms. Management structure supports business strategy.
Attracts, selects, grows, and keeps the best available management talent.	Voluntary management turnover is below industry norms. Quality of management team, as reflected through appraisal process and financial/nonfinancial results for each business unit, consistently exceeds standards. When necessary to recruit from the outside, company is consistently able to hire leading candidates for open positions. Management development plans are in place and being executed for all management positions.
Ensures continuity in the management team through appropriate succession plans.	Management succession plans are in place for all key executive positions. Company is able to fill key positions with quality candidates from within the organization.
Successfully utilizes the management team through effective and appropriate:	Decision-making roles for key decisions have been clearly articulated in writing to executives.
1. Delegation and empowerment 2. Involvement in overall corporate decision making	Decisions are made at the lowest possible organizational level without sacrificing corporate interests (for example, as evidenced by the decision-making roles described above and a retrospective analysis of key decisions made during the prior year). Senior executives actively participate in corporate decision making (for example, as evidenced retrospectively by the degree of involvement of senior executives in key corporate decisions during the prior year).
Stimulates collaboration and cooperation among members of the management team.	Potential synergies among business units have been clearly identified and exploited (for example, joint strategies have been developed among two or more business units). Where feasible, resources are consistently shared among business units—management succession plans cut across business unit lines; where feasible, duplicative systems have been eliminated; cross-selling is the norm, rather than the exception.
Sets clear performance expectations for the management team, provides appropriate feedback and coaching, and acts decisively to terminate executives who do not meet standards.	A performance management system is in place for senior executives that establishes performance expectations in writing and formal feedback at least once per year on a timely basis (results of which are transmitted to the board). Nonperforming executives have been terminated.

data to rule out bias or overemphasis (positive or negative) on a single event.

4. *Determine the importance of measures.* Few boards weigh both financial and nonfinancial measures of performance equally; most use nonfinancial measures to "modify" the appraisal of financial measures. This is consistent with the notion that financial measures are necessary but not sufficient to describe or assess top executive performance. For example, the CEO of a large consumer goods company met financial targets but failed for a second year to develop a viable top management decision-making team, choose a successor, or deal effectively with the media. If the board chose to consider heavily the nonfinancial aspects of performance and communicated this viewpoint to the CEO, then an appraisal of that CEO's performance would result in an "adequate," or even "marginal" evaluation.

Whatever the relative emphasis of the measures, it is important that there be no mathematical system or computed weights. The reason: This would add unnecessary complexity. The critical point is setting and communicating relative priorities, not agreeing on a numerical or percentage weight.

5. *Provide for changes in priorities.* No appraisal system for top executives can work if it is too time-consuming, paper-driven, or complex. Informal discussions and candor must prevail at the top levels. In addition, no appraisal plan for top executives, no matter how detailed, will survive a year intact. Internal and external events are too numerous, complex, and unpredictable. The measures, indicators, targets, and priorities may change. To ensure that the appraisal system reflects these changing priorities, periodic informal reviews, perhaps twice a year, are advisable.

If takeover becomes a threat, if a new tax law is enacted, if an acquisition suddenly presents itself, or if financial conditions change appreciably, so must the rules of the top executive appraisal game. In a mature durable goods company, the CEO was told to look for acquisitions that would complement the company's strong national brand awareness. Halfway through the year, a proposed hostile takeover loomed. The acquisition goal was shelved in favor of a stock buy-back plan and a search for a white knight. A key nonfinancial performance measure for the CEO became his ability to negotiate effectively with other CEOs whose companies could become white knights and position the company as a solid, long-term performer in the financial community.

6. *Determine uses of results and provide feedback.* To make any attempts at top executive appraisal effective, the results of the appraisal must be linked to consequences. For the CEO, these consequences are

largely financial but, of course, could include continued employment in the most severe cases. The objectives of the appraisal process are not only to hold individuals accountable for performance, but also to foster a better working relationship between the CEO and the board, as well as the CEO and his or her direct reports. Measuring performance will focus the attention of the people at the top on those key financial and nonfinancial areas that will facilitate strategy implementation.

The assessment of nonfinancial measures should be undertaken each year by the board and/or the CEO, and feedback should be given to individuals. In those areas where improvement is needed, a goal, complete with target and indicators, can be established for the subsequent year. The attainment of this goal, along with any others, both financial and nonfinancial, should have an impact on compensation.

One CEO of a financial services company was found to have problems delegating authority, even to business unit heads. Consequently, implementation of strategy suffered. For instance, the strategy called for the positioning of its different units to provide services to specific markets. To do so, business unit heads had to understand and respond quickly to changes in those markets. By requiring all decisions to be pushed to the top, time and market share were lost in two business units. The board set a goal for the following year that required the CEO to develop and implement a plan revising the decision-making process and delegating certain marketing decisions to business unit heads. After one year, the board did not feel, based on data gathered in a systematic fashion, that the CEO had made significant progress in this area. As a result, the CEO's annual incentive was decreased, even though short-term financial targets were met. There is a moral here: If the board feels that a measure is important enough to include in a CEO's goals, it is important enough to have a bearing on compensation.

Implementing the System

Once the system has been designed, successful implementation can be carried out in four steps.

Determine timing. Boards often take the initiative to implement a top executive appraisal program as a result of a shift in strategy, a new competitive environment, growth, or some other significant event. The best case scenario would be to address performance measurement when performance is good. After all, putting off this task, especially when performance is a problem, will only worsen the situation when and if decisive action must be taken.

Determine roles/responsibilities. For CEO appraisal, those directors who will take primary responsibility for the appraisal process must be identified. Typically, this is the compensation committee. But roles for other relevant parties exist (see Figure 36-4 for general guidelines). Above all, only those with relevant data should participate in the process. The roles must be spelled out in advance of the system's implementation. For the CEO's appraisal, the normal operation of the board and its key committees will determine how much, if any, participation each director will have.

Determine relationship to other systems. As the appraisal system is implemented, its impact on compensation—and on strategic planning, succession, and other systems—must be determined. The linkage from appraisal to compensation also must be spelled out in advance. The CEO performance areas should be consistent with appraisal criteria for executives below the CEO level. Likewise, data considered by the board as it reviews succession plans and identifies "high potentials" must be consistent with CEO assessment areas. In this way, a common, well-articulated, and specific picture of success emerges for the company. What it takes to "make it" becomes less of a mystery, and the shared values that top executives must adopt to drive strategy are shaped.

Review strategy. As previously noted and shown in Figure 36-2, the appraisal system for top executives must be tied to the company's strategy. As the chief architect and implementor of corporate strategy, the CEO must have his or her goals come directly from this strategy. Each year, prior to establishing the CEO's individual perfor-

Participants*	Design System	Determine Measures, Set Targets	Gather Performance Data	Provide Performance Data	Appraise Performance	Provide Feedback	Determine Consequences
Entire Board	◐	◐	◐	◐	◐	○	◐
Board Compensation Committee	●	●	●	◐	●	●	●
Board Executive/Management Committee	◐	◐	◐	◐	◐	○	◐
CEO	●	●	●	●	●	○	◐
CEO Direct Reports	○	○	◐	○	◐	◐	○
Various Levels of Employees	○	○	○	◐	○	○	○
Outside Parties	○	○	○	◐	○	○	○

*Members of some participant categories overlap.

● Major
◐ Some
○ None

Figure 36-4. CEO appraisal: roles and responsibilities.

mance goals, a review of strategy is required. Those aspects of CEO performance that drive strategy in the nonfinancial arena (for example, how well the CEO delegates decisions, values that the CEO espouses) should be emphasized. When strategy shifts, additional goal areas surface, but each goal set for a CEO must be traced to strategy implementation.

Final Thoughts

Designing and implementing a performance appraisal system that provides an instrument to capture top executive performance, evaluate it, and feed the evaluation back to individuals is not a simple undertaking. It requires commitment on behalf of directors, the CEO, and other top executives. In the words of former F&M Schaefer Brewing Company CEO Robert Lear, "All the logic in the world says that the CEO should not be measured strictly on financial results. The trick is how to do it."[6]

Sleight of hand aside, it takes an effective performance appraisal system—one that is well designed, practical, and whose mechanisms are firmly rooted in the company's strategy and culture.

[6]Sibson & Co., *Facts & Issues 1989: Measuring CEO Performance*, Sibson & Co., Princeton, N.J., 1989, p. 3.

37

Performance Management: Chasing the Right Bottom Line

Robert H. Rock, D.B.A.
President, MLR Enterprises, Inc.

For the past two decades, calls for "pay for performance" have echoed through the halls of management. Speeches in support of pay-for-performance philosophies and practices have been delivered by board directors, top management, stockholders, special-interest groups, and management consultants. Proponents of pay-for-performance incentive plans offer a variety of rationales: attraction, motivation, and retention of people; control over variable compensation costs; recognition of contributions and achievements; and reinforcement of strategic goals and objectives.

Some managers and consultants hypothesize that incentive plans should be a process for implementing strategy, that incentive pay should be awarded for the accomplishment of preestablished standards of performance, and that the size of incentive payouts should be related to the degree of performance. In fact, there often has been only a modest correlation between pay and performance.

Most incentive plans currently focus on pay, not performance. Moreover, the plans that do focus on performance frequently do so in such an offhand fashion as to provide merely a thinly veiled justification for paying bonus awards. Cynics suggest that these so-called pay-for-performance plans devised by compensation consultants are merely elaborate schemes to sanitize the distribution of large sums of money to senior executives who hired the consultants.

Pay-for-Performance Model

Providing variable pay to managers depending on their performance is a concept that corporations have tried to implement for years. Although few corporate leaders would argue against the soundness or even the absolute necessity of a pay-for-performance system, an equally small number would attest to having been able to develop an adequate system that measures and rewards performances at multiple levels in the organization.

Basically, the 12 steps in developing a system of pay for performance are:

1. Identify corporate, unit, and individual performance measures that depend on the varying conditions and environments within the company's businesses.

2. Encourage the consideration of beyond-one-year performance standards by identifying milestones toward longer-term objectives.

3. Develop meaningful and realistic objectives and measures for individual positions.

4. Determine for individual positions the appropriate weightings among corporate, unit, and individual performance measures.

5. Provide continuity with current performance measurement systems.

6. Define eligibility criteria that specify the rationale for inclusion in the program.

7. Ensure sufficient flexibility for management discretion to accommodate changes in strategy, structure, and people.

8. Provide competitive rewards against specific pay markets on the basis of results.

9. Integrate annual incentive awards with other reward programs.

10. Recognize individual performance contributions by measuring and rewarding an individual's results.

11. Enable easy administration while allowing for flexibility to adjust the program's specifics based on changes in business objectives and external factors.

12. Ensure initial and ongoing communication of the program to the participants.

Performance Agreements

Developing pay-for-performance programs that follow the preceding 12 steps, companies are gradually moving toward more structured performance management programs that reward managers for accomplishing preestablished measures of performance. Some of these programs devise "agreements" with individual managers, specifying performance objectives, measures, and standards and relating the accomplishment of these standards to varying incentive awards.

The performance agreement for a CEO, for example, may include the information shown in Table 37-1. The CEO has the opportunity to earn an $80,000 bonus for an A + performance, which is defined as a 20 percent return on stockholders' equity (ROE) and a 60 percent market share. The CEO would earn proportionately less for achieving a lower ROE and a smaller market share.

Performance agreements can be devised for almost any position in an organization. Although these agreements define the link between pay and performance, they require substantial support systems and significant management involvement to ensure their implementation. Few companies have adopted such programs, although some are experimenting with the concept—particularly at the top-management level.

A major reason why companies fail to implement performance agreements is their inability and unwillingness to discriminate among performers. In order to relate pay to performance, it is necessary first to

Table 37-1. Performance Agreement for a Chief Executive Officer

Objective	Relative importance	Measure	Standard C +	B +	A +	Incentive awards (in thousands) C +	B +	A +
Increase earnings	75%	ROE percentage	10%	15%	20%	$0	$30	$60
Improve competitive position	25%	Market share percentage	40%	50%	60%	$0	$10	$20
	100%					$0	$40	$80

determine what constitutes performance—which, in turn, requires an understanding of the objectives, measures, and standards of the company and its underlying operating units. If realistic and meaningful objectives, measures, and standards can be determined, the resulting performance agreement could influence a manager's activities, priorities, and time frames and could be used to gauge successes and failures.

Performance Measures

Many companies have invested large sums of money and large periods of management time in developing planning processes and support systems. These processes and systems are intended to generate strategies for the overall company and for each of the underlying operating units. If an incentive compensation program is to reinforce these strategies, each strategy's goals and objectives must be translated into measures of performance that can denote good, bad, and indifferent progress toward the achievement of these goals and objectives. Moreover, this translation must be meaningful, realistic, and valid—that is, the measure or measures must chase the right bottom line.

A pay-for-performance system is only as strong as the measures it uses to gauge performance. To ensure proper focus on the right bottom line, the selection of appropriate performance measures should meet the following criteria, which are listed in order of importance.

- *Usefulness.* Can the measure appraise the most important results?
- *Sustainability.* Can the measure accurately forecast the trend of results into the future?
- *Measurability.* Can the measure be calculated from readily available data?
- *Reliability.* Would different judges make the same calculation?
- *Controllability.* Can management truly have an impact on the results gauged by the measure?
- *Communicability.* Can the measure be explained easily and clearly to internal and external audiences?
- *Universality.* Can the measure be cascaded downward from the corporate level to the operating units?
- *Timeliness.* Can the measure be applied annually even if it also can be used in the longer term?
- *Comparability.* Can the measure be related to past performances and to competitive performances?

- *Constancy.* Can the measure resist being unduly manipulated?
- *Volatility.* Can results vary widely from one measurement period to the next, so as to adequately reflect changes in performance?

Currently, many companies use only measures derived from the profit and loss (P&L) statement as standards for determining incentive awards. Thus, many incentive plans use earnings per share (EPS) or growth in earnings per share as the bonus bogey. Other companies have introduced measures derived both from the P&L statement and from the balance sheet. These companies' incentive plans use return on equity or growth in ROE as indicators of performance. Sometimes these measures are gauged according to the performance of a competitive reference group of companies.

The most direct means of linking top management's interest with those of stockholders is to relate the incentive compensation of the former to the market returns of the latter. Yet, exclusive reliance on market returns has three major limitations. First, stock price movements in any given period may be beyond management's control. Second, market return may be affected significantly by unduly optimistic or pessimistic expectations at the beginning or end of the performance measurement period. Third, performance of a particular division within a company cannot be directly tied to stock price. Despite these limitations, stock options, stock appreciation rights, and other market-based incentives can be and should be used to link management interests with those of their shareholders. Market-based incentives, however, should be and can be supplemented with more controllable, internal performance measures that are at the same time compatible with stockholders' interests.

A number of performance measurement models try to blend market-based measures with internally based ones. In general, these models use some combination of ROE or capital, cost of equity or capital, market price-to-book value relationships, and/or growth in equity or capital. The basic premise of these models is to gauge the performance of a company (or one of its divisions) in terms of its operating return versus its capital cost and/or stock market expectations. These models, however, raise numerous problems. First, ROE or capital is an accrual accounting measure, whereas the cost of equity is a capital-market phenomenon: Drawing a relationship between the two creates an "apples to oranges" comparison. Second, the models ignore the interplay of economic, industrial, and managerial factors during a specific business cycle. Third, even if the model measures performance relative to a peer group, the determination of performance standards (for example, good, bad, or indifferent performance) for a particular company in a particular time frame can be elusive.

Cash-Flow Measures

A few companies are beginning to experiment with cash-flow measures. These companies recognize the inherent shortcomings of earnings and related accrual accounting ratios, such as ROE. These shortcomings are most visibly demonstrated when comparing cumulative net income with cumulative cash flow. Companies can report substantial earnings during periods when, in essence, they are incrementally liquidating their businesses. Moreover, companies can report significant growth in earnings per share (in the order of magnitude of 10 to 15 percent per year) when, in fact, they are destroying the value being realized by their stockholders. Taking inflation into account reveals that the seemingly buoyant earnings reported by many companies over the past decade have actually diminished to the point of eroding shareholder value.

With an increasing realization that P&L statements and balance sheet figures are inadequate gauges of performance, managers are exploring the possibilities of cash-flow indicators. In times of high interest charges, high replacement costs, and high inflation, the distinction between earnings and cash flow is magnified. Earnings may show how well a company is doing at making money; cash flow can demonstrate how real that money is. Ultimately, a company's purpose is to generate cash for its investors; consequently, a measure that reflects the generation of cash flow may better reflect performance. As indicated in Table 37-2, when cash flow is tested against the aforementioned criteria, it has advantages over EPS and ROE in terms of usefulness, sustainability, and universality; its disadvantages lie in its measurability and communicabil-

Table 37-2. Responsiveness of Performance Measures

	Measure		
Criterion	EPS	ROE	Cash flow
Usefulness	−	0	+
Sustainability	−	0	+
Measurability	+	+	−
Reliability	+	+	0
Controllability	+	+	+
Communicability	+	+	−
Universality	−	−	+
Timeliness	+	+	0
Comparability	+	+	0
Constancy	−	−	0
Volatility	+	+	+

+ = "good fit"   0 = "adequate fit"   − = "poor fit."

ity. To help lessen these disadvantages, a cash-flow performance management program should plan for, measure, appraise, and reward performance at multiple levels in an organization, thereby supporting corporate, unit, and individual short- and long-term business objectives.

Cash-Flow Performance Management Model

Figure 37-1 presents a schematic of a cash-flow pay-for-performance process. The process combines a "bottom-up" determination of cash uses and sources, evidenced in a company's long-term strategic plans, with a "top-down" valuation of cash generation required by the capital markets. The bottom-up determination starts with an evaluation of each strategic business unit's planned competitive positioning and the capital requirements needed to support these plans. These requirements, in turn, reflect the potential cash uses and sources of each strategic business unit (SBU), and the aggregate of all the company's SBUs reflects the cash-flow projection for the company over its planning horizon.

The top-down approach starts with the company's stock market val-

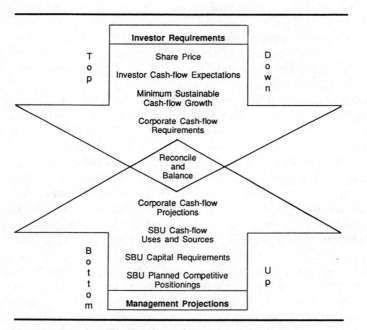

Figure 37-1. Cash flow pay-for-performance process.

uation and derives an expected growth in cash flow needed to support the stock market's expectations, as reflected in the company's share price. This growth in cash flow can be translated into a net cash-flow requirement for the overall company.

If the aggregate of the SBU's cash-flow projections derived from the bottom-up approach equals the expectation for cash flow evidenced in the top-down one, then cash-flow targets can be set for the overall company and its individual SBUs. If the bottom-up target differs from the top-down one, then the overall corporate strategy must be redefined to meet market expectations; otherwise, the company must communicate to the stock market its inability to meet these expectations (or, conversely, its ability to exceed them).

Achieving a Balance

The bottom-up approach, developed by Professors Alfred Rappaport and Carle Noble of Northwestern University, maintains that the present value of an SBU's strategy equals (1) the discounted value of all future cash flows attributable to the strategy during the plan period, plus (2) the discounted, strategy-positioned terminal value. By adjusting for the present value of the SBU's debt and equity, we obtain the so-called shareholder value contribution of the SBU's strategy. The aggregate of individual SBUs' contributions to shareholder value equals the expected contribution to shareholder value of the overall company. Some investors, particularly brokerage firms, try to estimate corporate cash flows as a basis for buying and selling corporate securities.

The top-down approach, developed by Marakon Associates and Strategic Planning Associates, maintains that a company's share price reflects investors' expectations for growth in "free cash flows" and uses the "constant dividend growth discount model" to derive the minimum sustainable growth required to support the share price. Free cash flow is defined as cash from operating (after reinvestment necessary to maintain the company's existing productive base) that is available either for investment in growth opportunities or for distribution to investors. Therefore, a company's share price can be translated into a minimum-required growth rate which, in turn, can be translated into a corporate cash-flow target.

The cash-flow pay-for-performance process combines the top-down and bottom-up approaches. The cash flows expected by investors must be reconciled and balanced with the cash flows projected by management. The process for reconciling the two approaches involves adjustments to the company's financial policies (for example, dividend policy), its profitability demands (for example, required return on net assets), and/or its investment community communications (for example, announcements regarding future performance). Once a balance between market expectations and management plans has been determined, the growth rate or the absolute cash flows can be used to establish a meaningful, realistic, and valid corporate performance target. Moreover, because cash flow is applicable throughout all levels of a company, the corporate cash-flow target can be developed into divisional and unit cash-flow targets. These targets can be used in performance agreements to reinforce management's drive to achieve the right bottom line.

38
Merit Pay and Performance Appraisal

Frederic W. Cook
Frederic W. Cook & Co., Inc.

What Merit Pay Is

Merit pay is the permanent increase in a person's salary rate based on his or her evaluated performance. By being individually driven and permanent, merit pay is easily distinguished from profit sharing and gain sharing, which are group-driven and based on company or business unit performance. General increases (which are also group-driven but based on competitive conditions or inflation), promotional increases (which are individually driven but based on moving to a new, higher-level job category), incentive or spot bonuses (which are based on individual contributions but paid in a single lump sum), and piecework

NOTE: The scope of this chapter is the administration of salaries based on individual performance. The perspective is that of a company that employs large numbers of salaried employees (exempt and nonexempt) and desires to pay them based on individual performance. The administration of salaries for executives is within the scope of this chapter, but pay for hourly employees represented by collective bargaining units is not.

(which is individually driven but based on actual output of the employee) are not merit increases for purposes of this chapter.

Because it is a permanent increase in pay, merit pay represents the best way to reflect a permanent increase in a person's value to the company. A person's singular contribution, no matter how valuable, is more suitably recognized by a reward that is also singular in nature, such as a spot cash bonus. It is very important in compensation to match the pay device correctly to the nature of the services performed so that the value of the employee's contribution is matched to the company's costs, both in amount and duration.

What Is the Purpose of Merit Pay?

Before addressing that question, three questions must first be asked:

- What is the purpose of base salaries? Answer: To attract and retain the number and caliber of employees necessary to accomplish the organization's mission.
- What is the purpose of job evaluation and job grading? Answer: To recognize and reflect the hierarchy of jobs in the company in terms of responsibilities, skills required, impact, and reporting relationship. Also, to motivate employees and reward promotions.
- What is the purpose of a salary structure (grades, ranges, and midpoints)? Answer: To align internal salaries to the competitive marketplace.

Now, what is the purpose of merit pay? This is important. Answer: To motivate and reward performance on the job *and* to result in salary levels that are significantly differentiated within the same job grade based on relative performance and contribution.

There is occasionally confusion about merit pay, so let us restate the objectives so we can proceed from a common ground: The objective of merit pay is to differentiate base salaries for employees within the same grade based on relative individual performance. The purpose of merit pay is *not* to result in pay *increases*, which are differentiated by performance. Merit increases are a tool to align base salaries for performance differences; they are not an end in themselves. The purpose of merit increases is *not* to recognize differences in performance, but to result in *salaries* that recognize differences in performance. The distinction is subtle but important. The difference is that, if merit increases are to recognize differences in performance, then existing salaries presumably are not a factor that needs to be taken into account. Excellent performance might deserve, for example, a 10 percent increase regardless of the person's current base salary. Many people believe this is how it should be. But proper salary administration requires the existing salary rate to be taken into account, as well as the individual's performance, when setting the new salary rate. For example, excellent performance may warrant a 20 percent increase if the person is paid low in the pay range, 10 percent if paid in the middle, and 0 percent if paid high in the range. This is not universally understood or accepted.

A merit increase is an adjustment between the current base salary and the new salary rate. The new salary rate should reflect the person's relative individual performance and value on the job. The size of the adjustment necessary to do this is the amount of the merit increase. The size of the increase, measured as a percentage of the old base salary, is derived from the relationship of the new rate to the old rate.

If the purpose of merit pay is to result in salaries that are differentiated by individual performance, how much of a difference do we want? There is no agreement on this within the compensation community, but if a company employed a 5-point performance rating scale (with 5 being the highest), it might find the following target salary relationships appropriate:

Performance Rating	Target Salary as a Percentage of Avg. Salary for "2" rating
5	150%
4	130%
3	115%
2	100%
1	—

Stated another way, the typical salary range is ±20 percent around the midpoint for a total 50 percent spread. This range can be broken into performance bands (or ranges within a range) to obtain the desired differentiation. If so, then the bands would be as shown in Figure 38-1. The differential chosen is less important than the fact that a company decides that it wants its salaries to be differentiated by performance and sets forth policies and procedures for getting there.

So far, nothing has been said about length of service in merit pay. Should longevity on the job affect one's level of pay? Certainly, if longevity adds value and aids performance. If it does, it should be reflected in the performance rating and in the resulting pay. If not, then there is no place for rewarding longevity, per se, in a modern salary administration program. Most would readily acknowledge that a relatively

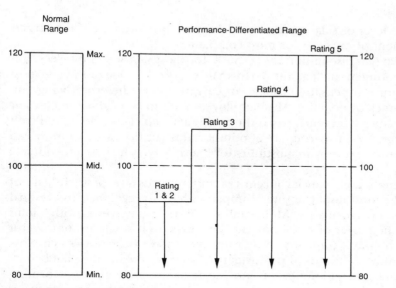

Figure 38-1. Typical salary range.

short-service employee need not, and should not, be paid at the same or higher rate as more experienced people. But after a period of time in most salaried jobs, 3 to 5 years for example, relative service should make no real difference, and performance alone should drive pay.

Is that how it is now? Unfortunately, no. Several companies have attempted to correlate the differences in salary levels within the same job grade with factors such as age, company service, sustained performance rating, or time in grade. They found no significant correlations with any factor, except a slight correlation with time in grade, meaning that the pay level was more strongly influenced by service than by performance. That is an indictment of current practices, and incompatible with pay-for-performance philosophies.

Why Is Merit Pay Important?

Base salaries are the foundation of the total compensation program, and for most employees, represent the largest component of total compensation. Many benefits, such as death and disability benefits, pension plans, and savings and profit sharing tie directly to salary level. For management, annual incentive compensation and stock options often relate directly to one's salary. So it is important that salaries are established correctly. Therefore, merit pay is important because it affects the absolute level of salary and related benefit costs, which are the largest component of expense for most companies.

Merit pay is also important because, for most salaried employees, it is the embodiment of "pay for performance," which is one of the two most significant compensation themes of current times (the other being employee stock ownership). Most employees want to be paid based on their performance, and merit pay is the traditional vehicle for doing it. Profit sharing and gain sharing are also important, but they are group-driven and, hence, are not a substitute for merit pay, which is individually driven.

Although nonfinancial incentives and rewards are powerful, merit pay is the most important way companies have to recognize and reward individual performance. Money talks, and merit pay speaks with a loud voice. The power of merit pay cuts two ways, so it is important to get it right. The way a company administers merit pay says a lot to its employees about its standards of performance, what is valued, and what behavior is rewarded and not rewarded. Turnover among higher-performing employees, the ones companies want to lose least, can be strongly influenced by a company's merit-pay policies. The same is not true of less-valued employees.

Finally, merit pay is important because in a time of slower growth, downsizings, and pressures on productivity and staffing, there are fewer promotional opportunities in large companies. This means that even high-performing people will stay in grade longer; thus, merit rather than promotional increases are the way they will be recognized and rewarded.

Requirements for Success

Despite the fact that virtually everyone is in favor of merit pay and most companies are trying very hard to make it work, it is not very successful in many companies. The problem from the company's point of view is that there is often too little spread in the size of merit increases and the resulting salary levels based on performance. From the employees' perspective, there is widespread cynicism and lack of trust, as revealed by attitude surveys, that good performance will, in fact, be recognized and rewarded.

There are two simple requirements that must be met if a merit-salary plan is to be successful in motivating and rewarding differences in performance. First, there must be a credible system of measuring and evaluating performance. Second, employees must perceive that differences in performance will be recognized and rewarded.

Performance Appraisal

Performance appraisal is the process by which a supervisor evaluates or appraises the performance of a subordinate in meeting the requirements of the job and contributing to the organization's success. The appraisal process is usually done annually and involves a discussion with the employee and written documentation that is made part of the employee's personnel file. Beyond that, there is very little commonality in approaches among companies. Each company evolves its own system to meet its own needs and philosophy. The human resources department is usually charged with developing and maintaining the performance appraisal program. In decentralized companies, different divisions may be charged with developing their own programs, or the program might remain centralized. Often, the programs adopted are different for exempt and nonexempt jobs, with the appraisal of exempt positions being more complex. Within the exempt ranks, the program for evaluating management positions may be different from that for evaluating technical/scientific positions, given the differing nature of the jobs. In many companies, formal, documented systems at lower levels give way to informal evaluations at the executive level or no evaluations at all.

Performance appraisals serve many important purposes, which include letting employees know what is expected of them; setting and communicating job standards or objectives, relating individual objectives into overall organizational needs and objectives, evaluating employees' performance of job requirements and objectives, and telling employees how they are doing, including when things are going well and when performance needs improvement.

The results of the appraisal process are used primarily as a basis for merit-pay actions, but they also are used as input to training needs, transfers, promotions, and termination decisions. Performance appraisal programs, however, do not exist just to support merit-pay or other decisions. They exist because it makes sense for managers to let employees know what is expected of them and how well they are performing against those expectations. Managers likewise benefit by getting feedback from their employees.

Types of Performance Appraisal Programs

The best performance appraisal system would be one in which an individual's performance and contribution are measured quantitatively and in an objective fashion. Unfortunately, this is not possible for most salaried positions. Qualitative assessments are required because of the nature of "white-collar" work. But if the program is to be perceived as effective, these judgments must be seen by employees to be valid, germane to the job, and free from bias, discrimination, or favoritism.

There are three basic types of performance appraisal programs for salaried employees:

- Job requirements
- Management by objectives (MBO)
- Trait

A performance appraisal program that focuses on job requirements relates directly to the employee's job description and evaluates the employee on how well each of the assigned responsibilities has been performed. Under an MBO system, finite (often quantitative) objectives are set for the employee each year. These objectives often relate to, but are more specific than, the job requirements set forth in the job description. Often the employee will be involved in setting the objectives, but ultimately the manager must ensure that the objectives tie into the overall objectives of the business unit or company. In some quantitatively oriented companies, the individual's objectives are weighted in terms of importance, with performance scales built around the objective so that overachievement or underachievement can also be assessed. At year end, a precise numerical evaluation of total performance can be enumerated. Whatever the degree of precision, an MBO appraisal process requires the annual resetting of objectives.

Trait appraisal systems are not currently popular, although they may be making a comeback as part of a more comprehensive appraisal program. Traits include judgmental and difficult-to-measure concepts such as leadership, communication skills, quality of work, adaptability, diligence, interpersonal skills, and dependability. Trait appraisals fell into disuse by professional managers because they were highly subjective, did not directly relate to job performance, were not under the control or ability of the employee to affect, and were used to justify actions that could be perceived as discriminatory or biased. On the other hand, personality traits are important characteristics that often lead to success or failure on the job and define promotability. So, can they be totally disregarded? There is a place for trait appraisal in a modern performance appraisal system, but in a supportive rather than a dominant role.

Frequency of Appraisal

An individual's performance should be formally appraised at least once a year by his or her supervisor, typically at year end. More frequent appraisals should be given to newly hired employees, typically at the end of a 3- or 6-month probationary period. At time of transfer, promotion, and change of supervisor are also times for performance appraisal. This is a matter of good housekeeping and planning, so that the new requirements and objectives are set for the rest of the performance period under a new supervisor. Finally, off-cycle appraisals are appropriate in cases of performance deterioration; they can identify areas in which the employee needs to improve and lay the groundwork for dismissal if the employee does not do so.

A formal, yearly performance appraisal does not replace the need for periodic "coaching" or interim reviews as needed. Instances of good or poor performance should not go unnoticed or unmentioned until the year-end appraisal. On the other hand, frequent coaching does not replace the need for an annual comprehensive evaluation that considers performance during the past year and planning for performance for the next. Both are necessary characteristics of a good appraisal program, which helps the employee improve performance, avoids surprises, is seen as fair by the employee, and provides valid input for personnel decisions.

Many managers dislike giving performance appraisals. They regard them as time-consuming and awkward, and they dislike being placed in a judgmental role that has such an important effect on a person's career. It is likely that, unless required to do so, many managers would not give annual appraisals at all. That is unfortunate because employees want feedback on how they are doing. Indeed, employees have a right to know how their supervisor views them. To relieve the time burden on managers, some suggest that evaluations be spread throughout the year. But there is overriding merit in doing them all at once at year end, when performance can be evaluated relative to others similarly situated and with respect to business achievements for the year.

An important development that would improve performance appraisals is management training in their use. Of particular benefit to managers would be training for evaluating employees who are acceptable but who have the potential to do better. The problem is not evaluating top performers; that's easy and even fun. The issue is also not evaluating the failing employee who is on the way out; that is neither easy nor fun, but most managers know how to do it when necessary. The issue is with employees who are good, solid contributors, but who have the potential to improve; the difficulty is in delivering criticism in a way that motivates rather than demotivates the employee. Most of us do not like to be criticized and do not respond well to criticism. Delivering criticism in a way that evokes a positive response is not a skill most of us have. If managers could get help in this critical aspect of their job, the leverage for improving organizational performance would be immense.

The Performance Appraisal Process

The process of doing a performance appraisal can be as simple as filling out a form once a year about an employee's performance and sending it to whomever it is supposed to go. Or it can be as complex as the following multistep approach:

Start of year.
1. Review with the employee the requirements of the position for the forthcoming year, reach an agreement on qualitative and quantitative objectives for the year, and identify areas of weakness that the employee should work on.
2. Ask the employee to summarize the discussion in writing on an appropriate form.
3. Review the completed form, sign it, return a copy to the employee, retain a copy, and send a copy to the next higher level of management.

During the year.
4. Conduct periodic review sessions with the employee to track progress, offer assistance, and make changes in objectives as appropriate.

End of year.
5. Arrange a meeting with the employee at which he or she will be asked to do a self-appraisal of the year's performance.
6. At the meeting, listen carefully to the employee's review and offer comments and your own perspective on the employee's performance (this is also a good time to ask the employee to evaluate your own performance as a manager and to identify your strengths and areas in which you could do a better job).

7. After the meeting, commit to writing your evaluation of the employee's performance and contribution, taking into account the employee's self-appraisal but giving more weight to your judgment of the real accomplishments.

8. Give a copy of the completed appraisal to the employee before you sign it so that the employee has another chance to give you his or her perspective in an area in which you might disagree.

9. Ask the employee to add any amplifying comments he or she wishes and to sign the completed form.

10. Sign the form yourself, give the employee a copy, keep a copy for yourself, and send a copy to the next level of management for review and approval.

There are many variations between the extremes of the one-step and the 10-step processes. But there are good reasons to recommend the multistep approach in our complex industrial society, when jobs, pay, and performance are of critical importance to a person's self-esteem and the company's performance.

Overall Performance Rating

Most, but not all, companies with formal performance appraisal programs require that the supervisor provide an overall performance rating for the employee at the end of the process. Overall ratings exist despite the fact that it is somewhat simplistic to sum up a whole year's performance in one word or number. Furthermore, single ratings are not a necessary ingredient in appraising someone's performance and deciding how much his or her pay should be. The reasons for ratings seem somewhat bureaucratic and include simplifying record keeping, aiding in analyses of performance distributions, providing comparison and trends, forcing managers to be specific in evaluating and categorizing performance, simplifying the sorting process when selecting people for transfer or promotion, and facilitating the application of merit matrices in merit-salary systems.

Ratings take many forms and carry many definitions in different companies. The simplest is a five-rating scale of outstanding, excellent, satisfactory, below average, and poor. Because few employees want to be "satisfactory" or "average," companies go to great lengths to define the middle rating in positive ways, such as "meets high standards." Employees catch on quickly, however; the more astute employees want to be rated no lower than the second category from the top no matter how it is labeled or defined.

Some companies use four-rating scales (instead of five) to force managers to categorize employees on one side or the other of average. Five choices, however, seems the most common. Some companies create subcategories within the overall five, such as a "high 3" or a "low 4," or permit rating along a continuum, such as 3.2.

If a company feels the need to have an overall rating, then it should define the middle categories broadly and positively. Otherwise, the rating distribution will become excessively skewed to the high side. (Some skewing is to be expected; the best that can be hoped for is to keep it within reasonable bounds.) Here is a five-part rating scale that meets the preceding definition:

Rating	Definition
5	Exceeds all requirements
4	Exceeds most requirements
3	Meets all and exceeds some requirements
2	Meets most requirements
1	Does not meet requirements

These definitions evaluate performance in terms of job requirements or standards that are established for a particular job but which are common for all people holding that job. In other words, the requirements are not tailored to the particular individual's abilities. Under the definitions listed, job requirements are established with the expectation that they will be met by most people. They are minimum but nonetheless solid standards of job performance; they are not "stretch" objectives.

Forced Distributions

Most companies find that managers skew the ratings to the high side, particularly in small groups and at upper levels. There is a natural tendency by managers to rate most people positively as long as things are going well. This need not be a source of concern unless it becomes excessive, such that the rating definitions lose their meaning.

Companies have two choices in controlling skewed ratings: require forced distributions or communicate encouraged distributions but do not require rigid adherence. The distribution chosen as appropriate might vary from one company to another, depending on the number and definition of rating categories and employee dynamics. Without trying to promulgate a single standard for all, the following might be an expected distribution for a large population:

Definition	Rating	Percentage in Category
Exceeds all requirements	5	10%
Exceeds most requirements	4	25%
Meets all and exceeds some requirements	3	50%
Meets most requirements	2	15%
Does not meet requirements	1	—

Forced or encouraged distributions are artificial and potentially harmful to teamwork because they mean that, for one to get ahead, someone else must fall behind. This is inconsistent with what most people understand the term *performance* to mean. Specifically, performance is not a zero-sum game. If someone performs well, someone else does not have to fail; both could perform well, in which case total performance expands. Employees know this and, hence, tend to resent forced or encouraged distributions. Forced or encouraged distributions have nothing to do with absolute performance; rather, they are measures of comparative performance among employees.

The ultimate in forced distributions is ranking, a process whereby employees in the same job level or category are ranked from high to low in terms of performance, value, and contribution. In ranking, there are no performance categories or ratings; rather, each individual's rating is his or her place in the rank order. In large units, managers must get together to discuss and merge the relative rankings of their employees. This leads to concerns about favoritism, politics, and the relative strength or weakness of a manager's ability to argue for and against the rank ordering of his or her subordinates.

Communicating Performance

It is unarguable that an employee should know how his or her performance is viewed by the company. But does it necessarily follow that an employee has a right to be told his or her performance rating, to see the appraisal form completed by one's managers, to sign it, to add comments, or to appeal it to a higher authority? The answer is apparently "yes," because the trend in large companies is clearly in that direction.

The reasons for openness are logical and compelling. Performance evaluations and ratings have an important influence on the employee's career, which includes pay and promotion opportunities. Employees who are performing poorly have a right to know it so that they can either work hard to improve or leave for better opportunities. Employees who are strong performers also should know that their work is valued so that they will be motivated to stay and do even better. And good performers who can improve should know the areas in which they are weak so that they can decide whether these are areas they want to work on.

Another reason is that, if merit pay is to be based on performance ratings, it makes sense for employees to know their ratings so that they can see the connection between their pay and performance.

A final reason for open communication is often not stated. Requiring supervisors to tell employees their ratings and to let them see their completed appraisals prevents supervisors from deceiving employees about their performance. The specific problem is a supervisor who submits a negative evaluation of an employee but who is not willing to discuss it with the employee. Not only is this fundamentally wrong, but it can cause legal problems if the employee is terminated for poor performance and subsequently sues for wrongful dismissal.

So, the best solution is to encourage accurate evaluations of performance and open discussion of results with employees. Having performance ratings and requiring that employees be told their ratings and sign the completed evaluations is a check on the supervisor that the appraisals are being accurately communicated. And encouraging a relatively normal distribution of ratings (if a company has ratings) forces the supervisor to be discriminating in the evaluations, so as not to mislead the employee.

Merit Pay: How Much?

Earlier in this chapter, I defined merit pay, discussed its purpose, and described a target spread in salaries for employees at different performance levels. Having now discussed performance appraisal, let us look at the details of actually administering merit pay.

Conventional wisdom says that a merit increase should be no less than 4 percent, if it is to be meaningful to the recipient, and that an increase of 10 to 12 percent would be outstanding. Of course, this range is subject to a number of variables. For example, in times of high inflation and competitive movement, the range might shift to from 6 to 15 percent. At the other extreme, in times of severe economic hardship when there is very little money available for merit increases, a 2 percent increase may be regarded as outstanding, perhaps if only for its symbolic, recognition value. Other variables include the time interval between increases and the actual pay level of the person receiving an increase.

How Often?

Most companies award merit increases on an annual basis (12-month intervals). This does not mean they grant increases all at the same time. Many do, but perhaps an equal number spread the increases throughout the year, using the anniversary date of the person's employment or promotion as the time to grant salary increases. Although there are great advantages to evaluating employees' performance once a year at year end (for purposes of making comparisons; also many objectives are defined in fiscal-year terms), it does not necessarily follow that salary increases have to be made at the same time.

Annual salary reviews may be the norm for a company, but more frequent reviews and salary increases (if warranted) should be given to newly hired or promoted employees, for example, 3 or 6 months after hiring or promotion. The reasons are to give rapid feedback on the performance of a new person's duties and to recognize the person's progress through the learning curve.

Conversely, it is also common practice for the interval between salary increases to be stretched out to 18 or 24 months once the person becomes mature in the job and is paid well into the range. This is quite logical and easily explained because, after a person has become experienced and proficient in performing the responsibility of the job, incremental changes in job value become smaller. Some companies keep everyone on an annual-increase cycle, but grant smaller increases (as a percent of salary) to those who are experienced on the job and well paid. This accomplishes the same objective of slowing down the rate of growth in salary once growth in performance slows down. On balance, however, the stretched-out interval has advantages because it permits the increases, when granted, to be healthier and more motivational in amount; it dampens the sense of entitlement and peer competition that builds if companies grant increases at regular 12-month intervals.

Salary Increases and Inflation

The rate of inflation and competitive movement obviously have a lot to do with the frequency and size of merit increases. In times of high inflation, such as were experienced in the late 1970s and early 1980s, merit budgets of 8 to 10 percent were the norm, and the 12-month merit interval became common (some companies granted increases even more frequently). In times of lower inflation and smaller competitive movement, merit budgets of 4 to 5 percent are more common, and it makes a lot of sense to lengthen the merit interval.

Despite this general connection, companies should avoid linking salary movement to changes in the cost of living, because this creates entitlement and reduces the amount of money available to differentiate for performance. Specifically, cost-of-living allowances (COLAs), once common in union contracts, are not appropriate for salaried employees. They are nothing more than general increases that are outside the company's control; they are not based on performance. A company has no obligation to increase its employees' salaries as inflation rises. Its obligation is to pay them competitively and in line with their performance and the company's ability to pay.

Merit Pay Versus Promotional Increases

A promotion moves an employee to a new salary grade with higher responsibilities. A promotion calls for a special salary increase, which is different from normal merit treatment. It is larger, often at least to the minimum of the new grade range, and occurs at the time of promotion rather than at the normal merit interval. It is only appropriate to combine a merit and promotional increase if the promotion occurs at about the same time as normal merit treatment; otherwise, it is best to keep them separate.

Some companies do not give promotional increases. They pay the employee at the level appropriate for the old job until the employee has proven himself or herself in the new job. But this is a minority practice and should be discouraged unless the promotion is, in fact, a trial appointment.

An interesting issue is title promotions in which job responsibilities do not change but the employee, for example, is elected or appointed a vice president. On the surface, a title promotion would not seem to justify an increase as would a job promotion. However, it may be even more important because title promotions reflect individual performance on the job and should only go to the best contributors in that grade.

Linking Merit Pay to Performance

Merit pay is for improved performance on the job, not for taking on new job responsibilities. The size of merit increases, and the resulting salary levels should relate to performance as defined and evaluated by the performance evaluation system discussed previously.

If all employees in the same job grade started out at the same salary rate, then the size of each employee's merit increase could be a direct function of his or her evaluated job performance, with higher-rated people getting the higher increases. However, the starting point is rarely equal, and, therefore, the size of the merit increase must take into account the employee's relative salary rate as well as his or her evaluated job performance. The reason for this subtle, but important, complexity is that the purpose of merit salary administration is to result in salary levels that are differentiated by performance. Merit salary increases are the means by which salaries are differentiated, not the end in themselves.

The common tool for taking into account both the employee's performance and his or her current salary rate is the merit matrix. The example shown in Figure 38-2 is fairly typical. It is designed to move the employee who performs well up to the midpoint of the range, which should be the competitive going rate. Better-performing employees can move past the midpoint up to the maximum of the range under this matrix.

A problem with the merit matrix shown is that the ranges (and mid-

Sustained Performance Rating

Position in Range	1 + 2	3	4	5
4th Qtl. (110–120)				4 - 6%
3rd Qtl. (100–110)			4 - 6%	5 - 8%
2nd Qtl. (90–100)		4 - 6%	5 - 8%	7 - 10%
1st Qtl. (80–90)	0 - 4%	5 - 8%	7 - 10%	8 - 12%

Figure 38-2. Sample merit matrix (built around assumed 5 percent merit budget and performance ratings).

points) in a typical company increase every year in response to inflation and competitive pay movement. Thus, the employee needs an increase every year that is at least equal to the range change as his or her compa-ratio deteriorates. An annual range change of 4 percent and a merit budget of 5 percent would be common in the early 1990s. If everyone gets an increase each year equal to the range change, how much can be left for true merit, which many would define as moving up in the range? Answer: Not much! One of the problems with salary systems, which try to target employees' salaries to various positions in a range and which also increase the ranges every year, is that most of the merit money is spent keeping up, and little is left over to differentiate for per-formance. Thus, salaries become differentiated more by time in grade than relative performance.

A different type of merit increase matrix is shown in Table 38-1. Here, the size of one's increase is a function of performance and one's salary versus others in the same grade. It is designed to achieve within 5 years the following percentage relationship between salaries:

Sustained performance rating	Target salary as a percentage avg. salary for "2" rating
5	150%
4	130%
3	115%
2	100%
1	—

Position in a range is not a factor in the preceding target pay-differentiation system. But naturally, the compensation administrator would want to audit the average salary by grade, in relation to compet-itive pay levels, so that the company's pay program remains competitive.

The Merit Budget

Merit matrixes take many different forms, but all are built around the concept of spending a certain amount of money called the merit bud-get. This is the amount the company has decided it can spend for merit increases that year. The purpose of the merit matrix is to help manag-ers allocate the available merit funds in a pay-for-performance fashion.

Where does the merit budget come from? It is a combination of three factors: (1) the company's current salary position versus the market

Table 38-1. Sample Performance-Salary Merit Increase Matrix*
5-Year Matrix

Percent of current salary to level 2 avg.	Sustained performance level (in percents)			
	2	3	4	5
150				2.5
145				3.0
140				4.0
135				4.5
130			2.5	5.5
125			3.5	6.5
120			4.0	7.0
115		2.5	5.0	8.0
110		3.5	6.0	9.0
105		4.5	7.0	10.0
100	2.5	5.5	8.0	11.0
95	3.5	6.5	9.0	12.5
90	5.0	7.5	10.5	13.5
85	6.0	9.0	11.5	15.0
80	8.0	10.0	13.0	16.0

*Calculated to achieve desired performance-salary level in 5 years, assuming a 2.5 percent annual movement in a level 2 average salary.

(that is, average company salary divided by going market rate), (2) anticipated competitive movement for the forthcoming year, and (3) the point at which the company wants (and can afford) its average salary position to be at year end versus the market. For example, if a company's current salaries were 100 percent of market averages, it anticipates a 5 percent movement in competitive averages, and it wants to still be at 100 percent of the market by year end, then it would authorize a 5 percent merit budget for the year.

How does one go about projecting competitive salaries ahead to some point in the future? First, you have to know where you are now. This involves taking the latest and best competitive survey data you have and bringing it forward to the present time using anticipated competitive pay movements (for example, 0.5 percent a month). Then you project ahead to a future point using survey estimates of what other peer companies are planning to do in the same time period. The sources of survey data on projected pay movements include industry associations, various consulting firms that survey their clients, and an annual survey conducted by the American Compensation Association (ACA) for its numerous members. The ACA survey shows projected merit budgets for various classifications of employees. It also shows how much was spent in the previous period versus what was projected.

Care must be taken in using these survey projections to derive your own merit budget because they are often biased upward. They are estimates of what compensation professionals in various companies are planning to *recommend* as merit budgets; they are not approved merit budgets. Top management may knock down the compensation manager's recommendations once business realities are taken into consideration. Even if accurate, they are projected *merit* budgets, not projections of competitive pay *levels* to some future point. The difference is changes in population, which typically means lower-paid individuals entering the grade (through promotion and new hires) and higher-paid people leaving the grade (through retirements and promotions). Hence, merit increases for those staying in grade may be offset by a decrease in average salaries through population changes. A 5 percent merit budget may result in a 3 to 4 percent increase in average competitive rate. Of course, if you anticipate the same population changes as others, this factor may be disregarded.

Two final notes of caution. First, adopting the same merit budget as the survey average assumes that everyone is starting at the same point. However, your company's average paid rate may be lagging or ahead of the market. Varying the size of your merit budget versus the merit budget of others is a way to make fine-tuning corrections in market rates. Second, in a large, complex organization, it is overly simplistic to adopt a single merit budget. Employees in different job classifications, functions, or levels in the company may be at widely varying positions versus their own relevant markets and the company average. Hence, different merit budgets and different merit matrixes may well be appropriate within the same company to achieve a competitive result. Avoiding a focus on a single number also prevents a situation in which large numbers of employees feel unappreciated and demotivated if they do not get an increase at least equal to the company average, even if they are well paid to begin with.

Communicating the Merit Program

There are two schools of thought on communicating a merit-pay program. The first, called the open-salary system, believes that employees have a right to know and should be told their salary grade, their salary midpoint and range, when the salary range is changed and by how much, the merit budget, the merit matrix or increase guidelines, and the average merit increases. Proponents say open-salary systems build trust and motivate employees to improve their performance because they will see clearly that above-average performance leads to above-average pay increases.

The second, called the confidential-salary system, believes that employees should be told the company's pay-for-performance philosophy and how it works, the performance factors that are important in determining raises, and the employee's performance rating. But the employee should not be told his or her range, the amount of range movement, the merit budget, the merit matrix, or the average increase. Proponents of confidential-salary systems say it reduces the focus on and sense of entitlement to the average increase, maintains the average employee's self-esteem, reduces conflict and disgruntlement, and results in a wider dispersion of merit increases and resulting salary levels by performance.

Some companies that have confidential-salary systems will let an employee know his or her grade and range if asked. Most large companies employ open-salary systems, whereas smaller organizations tend to employ confidential-salary systems.

Some Perennial Issues

Range Minimums and Maximums

Should range minimums and maximums be treated as absolute limits, below and above which salaries are not permitted to go? Or should they be treated as guides that can be violated for good reason? I strongly prefer the latter because it is consistent with the merit concept. To illustrate: Should someone who is a poor performer paid at the minimum receive an increase just because the minimum is increased? Obviously not. Any salary increase that is not earned by performance undermines the merit principle. And should an outstanding performer be denied an increase just because he or she happens to be paid above the maximum? Again, obviously not. Arbitrary rules should not supersede common sense.

Performance Deterioration

Assume that a properly paid employee's performance deteriorates. Should that person's pay be cut? Most would say no. A clear warning combined with no increase is sufficient punishment. But this devalues the current salary and creates the sense of entitlement to an increase so long as performance does not drop. And it provides no means to reward the employee if he or she reverses the performance deterioration. What's wrong with a pay decrease if it is justified by a performance deterioration? Does an employee own his or her salary? If pay was decreased to match a decrease in performance, the employee's attention would be clearly riveted on performance, and the employer then would have a way of rewarding improved performance. Also, decreased salary would be clear evidence of prior notice if performance does not improve and the employee is subsequently terminated.

Demotions are the reverse of promotions. They are the downgrading of a job or a person's responsibilities such that a lower salary grade applies. Demotions, while rare, do occur. They may result from the individual's just not being able to handle the new responsibilities of a previously granted promotion, or they may result from the elimination or downsizing of a job in a reorganization or consolidation. What should happen to a person's salary? Should it go down as well?

Here we are not talking about a performance deterioration, but either a lack of performance coming up to a new standard or a job elimination or downgrading. In either case, the individual is less at fault, and companies do not commonly reduce salaries in cases of demotions. Instead, they "red circle" the current salary if it is outside the new-range maximum. This means the individual will not be eligible for an increase until the new-range maximum moves above the current salary through range movements. Most would think this is fair. But is it motivational?

For the same reasons discussed for deteriorating performance, the absence of a decrease removes the company's ability to reward good performance. If a promotional increase had been given in the expectation that the individual would perform well in the new job assignment, is it wrong to take it away when it proves not to have been justified? Is it not better and more honest to reduce salary to the new expected performance level, thereby giving the employee an incentive for performance improvement, than to freeze the salary for multiple years until performance and value comes back into line with paid salary?

Upward Migration

Should unused merit money be allowed to migrate from one level to another? Specifically, if a company has a 5 percent merit fund, should each grade (or grouping of grades) be limited to 5 percent or is it enough that the total company be limited to 5 percent, with some grades receiving more and some less? A reasonable answer would seem to be that if monies are not needed or deserved at a particular level, they could be used at another level where larger increases are more justified. But it would not seem to be reasonable if the migration is always upward to the higher grades, which is what happens in many companies.

Do higher-level people perform better than lower-level people? Are they deserving of larger increases as a percentage of their salary? Certainly it is to be hoped that higher-level people perform better than lower-level people. Otherwise, how did they get to be higher-level people? The real issue is, do they perform better *in their jobs* than lower-level people do in their jobs? Some would argue that this is a statistical impossibility, so the answer is no. But if the natural skewing in performance ratings gets worse at the upper levels, the answer would seem to be yes. If merit increases are tied to performance ratings, an organization with a 5 percent merit budget may find its executives getting 8 percent with very little left for anyone else. If forced or encouraged ratings by level are not used, then some delineation of merit pools by level may be needed to prevent upward migration.

Merit Increases and Company Performance

Should the size of merit increases relate to how well the company is performing? If the company has just concluded a poor (or great) year, should this affect the size of the merit budget going forward? Generally, no. Merit increases affect future salary levels and are not an appropriate vehicle for recognizing a prior year's performance. Bonuses, profit sharing, or other forms of variable pay are a better vehicle for rewarding for past performance.

But should a company's future outlook affect the size of its salary increases? A reasonable answer is yes, because these salary increases would be paid for by future performance. Whether the outlook is poor or great, however, the effect on salary increases should not be great. The reason is that base salaries should be kept reasonably competitive over time if they are to be effective in attracting and keeping good people. Some lagging and leading is acceptable, but wide swings are not appropriate. Even in a disaster scenario of layoffs and shutdowns, when a company has to tighten its belt, a company should retain the ability to recognize and reward those who are significantly underpaid in relation to their contributions.

Achieving Job Objectives

Should merit increases be granted for achieving job objectives? On the one hand, this seems quite reasonable, and many companies do it. But on the other hand, it is not logical to do so because the costs of the reward are not aligned with the economic values created. A salary increase is a permanent increase in costs. Considering benefits roll-up, the present value cost of a $1 increase in salary is probably $10 to $12.

Achieving a job objective is a finite event that may have no residual value to the company. It is better recognized and rewarded by a bonus. Salary increases should be for permanent increases in job value, based on how well the individual performs the ongoing responsibilities of the job, not special events.

Entitlement

Everyone in the compensation community is against the concept of "entitlement" when it comes to salary increases, bonuses, and other variable rewards such as stock options.[1] Entitlement is bad when it comes to variable rewards because the absence of a reward when one is expected is a disincentive and demotivator. If the reward is only what one expected, then it is taken for granted and devalued. When entitlement exists, positive motivation is only created when one receives more than one expected (or was entitled to).

Why does entitlement exist and what can be done about it? Entitlement is caused by two factors at work in an organization's environment. The first is administrative systems that we in the compensation community create and which result in regular delivery of rewards at periodic intervals, with minor variations. Once the pattern is established, the employee logically expects it to continue, and entitlement has been created. The answer is to break the pattern of expectancy and use much more variability in the amount and timing of rewards, but always based on performance.

The second factor is the language of entitlement—the words that have evolved for expressing the delivery and receipt of rewards. Words such as *you have been "granted," "awarded,"* or *"given"* an increase or a bonus imply power in the hands of the giver and subservience in the receiver, which leads to entitlement. The phrase *you have "earned" a salary increase or bonus* would be far better because it transfers a sense of control over the reward to the employee, where it belongs, based on the employee's performance.

Merit Versus Promotion

Most companies that have pay-for-performance philosophies have only two types of salary increases: merit or promotion. A minor exception is a salary increase to induce a relocation to a higher-cost area. Everything

---

[1]No one is against entitlement when it comes to employee benefits because these are something that the employee is *entitled* to as a condition of employment.

that is not a promotional increase is presumably based on merit and justified by improved performance. But there are many types of increases, masquerading as merit, that are not really merit increases at all, such as general or cost-of-living increases, equity adjustments such as when two organizations or units are merged and the pay levels of one are brought up to the higher level of the other, competitive adjustments to reflect a pay survey that shows the company has fallen behind, seniority adjustments such as when recently hired college graduates receive increases to keep them ahead of escalating rates for new graduates, retention adjustments to keep someone who has received a competing offer, and "nonperformance" adjustments for when the employee's performance does not really warrant an increase but the supervisor grants one anyway to avoid a confrontation, to protect the employee's self-esteem, or because he or she thinks no increase will demotivate rather than motivate the employee to do better. These types of increases may or may not be justified; that's not for us to discuss here. The point is they are not based on merit and should not be labeled as merit increases, because to do so demeans the term and devalues the achievements of those who receive real merit increases.

If these other types of increases are justifiable, they should be labeled for what they are and dealt with outside the regular merit cycle and budget.

Dollars Versus Percentage

Should merit increases be communicated in dollars or as a percentage of the old salary? Most communicate the increase as a percentage, and employees seem to like it this way because it makes it easier to make comparisons with others and judge whether one is keeping ahead of or falling behind the range changes or inflation. But communicating increases as a percentage encourages employees to take their existing pay level for granted and to think of themselves as working for their increase, to think of merit increases as a zero-sum game in which, for one to get more, someone else must get less. It also encourages one to make comparisons to the average, which means the average employee is likely to be disappointed and not believe his or her pay is based on performance.

It would be far better to calculate and communicate the increase in dollar terms, particularly in times of low merit budgets. This is not an attempt to deceive the employee—it reflects the reality of how an increase should be determined. Specifically, an employee's salary should be evaluated in terms of his or her performance and pay relative to others in the same job grade or level. An improvement in performance and value to the company warrants a new salary level. The merit increase is the dollar amount representing the difference between the new and old salary rate. The *percentage* change is derived by dividing the dollar increase by the old rate. If the increase stated as a percentage is important to employees, they will calculate it for themselves.

Confidentiality

Finally, a word on salary confidentiality. Most compensation professionals believe employees talk about their salaries, and they accept this as a fact of corporate life. I doubt this is true, but whether it is or not, open communication of salaries should be discouraged by strong statements of corporate policy. An individual's salary, just like his or her performance appraisal, should be a strict matter of confidence among the employee, the supervisor, and others with a valid need to know. Companies that condone open communication of salaries and merit increases are condoning practices that will lead to employee unhappiness and undermine merit-pay practices to differentiate salary levels by performance.

PART 7

Corporate Culture and Compensation

39

Culture and Compensation

Michael R. Cooper, Ph.D.
President and Chief Executive Officer
Opinion Research Corporation

As more national companies globalize and international work forces continue their trend toward demographic differentiation, successful implementation of compensation programs will become even more difficult and demanding for practitioners. Managing this complex set of problems can begin with the recognition that a compensation system is really a communication vehicle for reinforcing management's expectations for employee business behavior.

In Part 7, we seek to stimulate a behavioral and organizational orientation to compensation, highlight an approach to diagnostically link compensation and culture, and emphasize the need for employee involvement in developing a communication channel and gaining support for compensation programs.

Very specifically, the chapters in Part 7 go beyond the design characteristics of compensation and move into what is required to make compensation programs effective. Implementation of these programs is too often focused on technical issues. Yet true effectiveness is dependent on issues that deal with integrating the program and organizational, cultural, and human characteristics into the firm's strategy.

The keys to the effectiveness puzzle include whether the program has clear objectives, whether the reward system is tailored to these objectives, whether the organization and culture are compatible with the reward system, and whether there is clear communication of the program. Each of the chapters in Part 7 deals with a different piece of the puzzle.

Ira Kay's chapter (Chapter 40) presents compensation readiness, which focuses on various aspects of culture needed to support contingent compensation. Although culture influences compensation effectiveness, the reward system itself also influences culture. He concludes that there is a need for strong cultural attributes to support specific compensation programs.

George Gordon, in Chapter 41, presents cultural factors that affect the success of compensation programs. These are the same dimensions that serve as the basis for the compensation readiness chapter by Ira Kay. Gordon presents the conceptual overview that contains the links between various aspects of culture and various contingent compensation programs.

Placing this chapter in perspective, it clearly presents a case for a conceptual, organizational, cultural, and human resource set of attributes as needed to be able to manage and maximize the effectiveness of specific incentive compensation plans. Certainly one way to identify these attributes is through the readiness audit. Once information from an audit like this is secured, analyzed, and understood relative to the strategy of the firm, movement into implementation can begin. A communications thrust is a necessary first implementation step, and if the correct attributes are managed and the communication plan is clear, this can lead to greater employee motivation and organizational effectiveness. How all these cultural, communications, and motivation aspects can be tied together is best depicted in Gordon's chapter, which represents both the beginning and ending phases for consideration or implementation of sustainable compensation plans in support of a firm's strategy.

Edward Lawler's chapter (Chapter 42) explains how compensation can be used as a tool for motivation by securing employee involvement. Lawler further discusses the influence of compensation on retention, development, culture, structure, and cost. The critical point is made that reward systems, such as long-term incentives, can be extremely powerful in securing employee involvement. As such, compensation is a powerful but undermanaged tool for shaping organizations.

Finally, Claudio Belli, in his primer on compensation communication (Chapter 43), focuses on the process of communication, stressing the criticality of pay and benefits communications as part of a systematic plan. He stresses the importance of obtaining information directly from the work force in preparing for the communication process. Most important, he discusses the critical role of informal leadership and line management as the primary conveyors of the firm's compensation philosophy.

40

Ensuring the Success of a New Compensation Program

Ira T. Kay

Director, U.S. Compensation Practice, and
Worldwide Director, Compensation Design
Hay Group Inc.

Peter Gelfond

Director, U.S. Operations
Research for Management
Hay Group Inc.

Jesse Sherman

Vice President, Research for Management
Hay Group Inc.

When compensation professionals introduce a new program—especially in the contingent or variable compensation arena—they worry about how it will be received. This is because many of the new compensation programs that companies are installing to boost productivity or control costs fail to live up to their potential. Why? Often, the problem is not that a particular program is flawed, but rather that an organization's internal environment is not "ready" to accept the principles and procedures that make the plan work. The result: wasted time and money and lost competitive ground. Although your competitors use innovative pay techniques to help them become more productive, you may be saddled with a program that fails to influence the performance of your work force.

Before implementing a new program, there are three basic questions that must be answered:

1. Will the program reflect and reinforce the appropriate business and organizational direction?
2. Does the work force have the skills to respond to the requirements of the reorganization?
3. Do we have the correct culture to allow the program to be as successful as possible?

These are all difficult and highly important questions, but we believe that the third has been the least explored and leaves companies highly vulnerable to failed compensation programs. Intuition suggests a number of specific ways that employee culture of an organization could be critical to the success or failure of a *contingent* compensation program. For example:

- Incentives could be totally ineffective in improving performance in an organization that cannot set goals.
- A profit-sharing program might be less effective in an environment that discourages risk taking or makes it unsafe for employees to show initiative.
- Incentive pay based on team performance may not work in an organization that is highly focused on the individual contribution of employees.
- A culture that discourages active employee participation could dramatically reduce the effectiveness—especially given the large cost of an employee stock ownership plan (ESOP). Recent research has shown, for example, that the most successful ESOPs have occurred when employees have been given a major role in management and day-to-day operations in addition to stock ownership.

An understanding of the internal environment could be critical to the overall success of the program for the following types of plans:

- *Gain sharing.* Gain-sharing plans are unitwide bonus systems designed to reward all eligible employees for improvements in unit productivity.

- *Profit sharing.* Profit-sharing plans provide all eligible employees with bonuses or shares based on unit or corporate profit performance.

- *Group incentives.* Group incentive plans encourage performance by basing rewards on various measures of group accomplishment.

- *Individual incentives.* Individual incentive plans tie all or part of an employee's pay to specific elements of his or her own performance.

- *Subjective performance bonuses.* Subjective performance bonuses are bonus plans linked to management's evaluation of performance but not to specifically prevalued individual or group performance targets.

- *Pay for knowledge/skill.* Pay for knowledge and/or skill programs increase the base rate as an employee masters additional skills.

- *Key contributor programs.* Key contributor programs provide special cash awards to ensure retention of individuals who make unique contributions to the organization.

Our research has shown that organizations continue to look for new and creative ways to reward their employees. The extent and success of the preceding plans vary widely by industry. All the organizations, however, have the same goal: to create competitive advantage. We believe that measuring the internal culture and modifying that culture or the compensation program can improve the probabilities of a successful program.

Measurement Methodology

To measure those factors that might influence the success of a contingent compensation plan, we developed a new diagnostic questionnaire, the "Compensation Readiness Audit," which assesses sensitive key elements of organizational culture. The Compensation Readiness Audit compares your company's internal environment with those that successfully implement contingent compensation programs. The result is a guide to:

- Which programs will work for you now
- Which programs can work in the future
- How your culture must be changed to increase the effectiveness of specific contingent compensation plans.

The readiness profile audits your organization's culture to determine its compatibility with each pay system. The audit relies on results of a culture questionnaire administered to management and employees.

The questionnaire provides information on four general topics covering a total of eight specific factors. These are:

1. How focused is the organization?
   - *Individual versus group orientation.*

     Individual orientation.   The degree to which accomplishment of objectives depends largely on individual effort and expertise, and teamwork is not emphasized.

     Group orientation.   The degree to which accomplishment of objectives depends largely on integration of effort among employees and work units.
   - *Clarity of direction.*   The extent to which the organization has a clear business focus along with consistent goals and direction.

2. How demanding is the organization?
   - *Pressure for performance.*   Whether the organization holds people personally accountable for meeting high standards of performance.
   - *Encouragement of initiative.*   The extent to which people are encouraged to use their initiative to take actions, to take risks, and to suggest better ways of doing things.

3. Are people willing and able to change how they do things?
   - *Trust.*   The extent to which employees trust the organization and various levels of management and supervision.
   - *Achievement motivation.*   Whether most employees are motivated more by the desire to get the job done or by the fear of making mistakes.

4. Do systems exist to support performance planning/measurement?
   - *Individual performance measurement.*   How effectively the organization measures performance on most jobs.
   - *Current compensation.*   Whether most employees view the current compensation system as equitable and as rewarding good performance.

A pilot survey of 138 diversified companies was conducted to evaluate their culture and their experience with contingent compensation plans. Extensive analysis of the results showed statistically significant differences between the culture scores of "successful" and "troubled" plans.

Table 40-1. Percentage of Favorable Responses

Item	Successful plans	Troubled plans	Interpretation
1. Group orientation	43%	30%	The result for group orientation, described in the text, is an interesting one. It basically shows that even individual incentive plans are aided significantly by the need for an integrated effort.
2. Clarity of direction	45%	39%	The better employees understand where the organization is going, the more successful its incentive plans will be.
3. Pressure for performance	67%	50%	As hoped, plans work better when people are held personally accountable for outcomes.
4. Encouragement of initiative	48%	22%	Incentives work best in an environment that encourages risk taking.
5. Trust and commitment	52%	22%	A culture in which employees trust management is very helpful.
6. Achievement motivation	28%	55%	This is a paradoxical finding. One possible explanation is that some negative motivation (fear) is helpful in an otherwise supportive environment.
7. Performance management	72%	39%	This largest differential shows the absolute criticality of being able to measure performance.
8. Current compensation	31%	20%	Incentive plans work in an environment in which employees already feel fairly compensated. Contingent compensation is not best used to make up for past shortfalls.

Table 40-1 shows the percentage of employees responding favorably to questions measuring different aspects of organizational culture, as seen in Figure 40-1. The results show, for example, that employees working for companies with successful incentive plans have a greater "group organization" (43 percent favorable) than employees in companies with troubled plans (30 percent favorable).

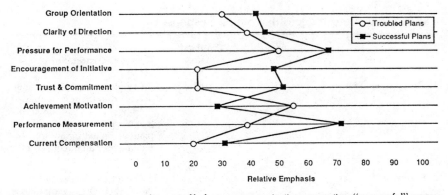

Figure 40-1. Difference in culture profile between organizations reporting "successful" versus "troubled" contingent compensation plans.

Causality

The way we have reported the data shows our interpretation of the causality. That is, we are assuming that organizations with these specific types of environments make the best "homes" for successful contingent compensation plans. The alternative explanation is that these plans have helped to create those types of environments in their organizations. Both types of causality are possible and useful. The newness of many contingent compensation programs makes it harder to conclude that the programs have improved the culture. Therefore, we interpret the data as previously outlined. As these plans become more established within companies and industries, we will be able to explore their impact not only on culture but also on the more important outcome: financial results.

Potential Responses by Individual Companies

The impact of this audit on a specific company can be dramatic. Cultures and pay systems can be tested for compatibility throughout these three phases of the diagnostic process:

Information collection. The Compensation Readiness Audit is administered to employees and used to generate a profile of a company's culture. A second questionnaire, relating to the types, longevity, rationale, and effectiveness of existing compensation plans, is completed by a senior human resources executive.

Analysis and feedback. A comparison is made between your company's profile and benchmark profiles of companies that have successfully implemented programs.

Recommendations. Reports provide recommendations on the types of plans that will work now and/or later, and prescribe specific actions to help prepare for future plans. There are four basic strategies for proceeding:

1. Choose the programs that will work best for you now.
2. Plan for the programs that may work in the future.
3. Change your organization to set the stage for desired programs.
4. Fine-tune existing plans to get better results.

Case Studies

Case I

Company A, caught in a 3-year productivity slump, has already frozen hiring and kept merit increases to a bare 3 to 4 percent. It is now considering a gain-sharing program to improve performance, in large part because a similar program seems to have worked for its biggest regional competitor. A Compensation Readiness Audit analysis, however, shows that such a program might not work immediately in company A's current culture. (See Figure 40-2.) Trust and commitment within the organization are low, suggesting that many employees would not readily accept the concept of gain sharing. And because this reward mechanism requires initiative and clear direction, management must improve these areas before launching a full gain-sharing program.

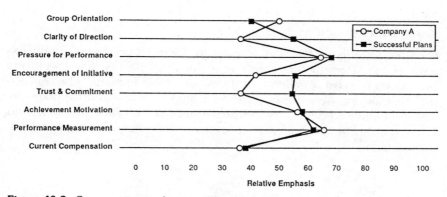

Figure 40-2. Compensation readiness profile: gain sharing.

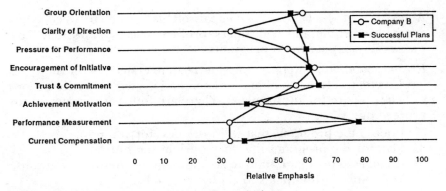

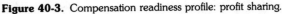

Figure 40-3. Compensation readiness profile: profit sharing.

Case II

Company B felt that its ESOP plan, which was implemented 2 years ago, was not achieving desired results. A Compensation Readiness Audit was conducted, and it identified two problems: (1) poorly understood goals and objectives of the company, among other things, as reflected in its profit sharing plan, which was essentially subjective rather than tied to substantive measures of company performance; and (2) an employee performance evaluation system which was also overly subjective and weakly related to actual on-the-job performance. (See Figure 40-3.) In response to these findings, the company identified measures of performance at the company, business unit, and individual levels; revised its performance appraisal system; and tied its profit-sharing plan to understandable aspects of company performance, over which employees had greater control.

Conclusion

Compensation payrolls today account for 25 to 50 percent of total company costs. As companies continue to focus on profits, few employers can afford the cost of failed incentive compensation plans. The compelling relationship between internal environment and incentive plan success or failure underscores the importance of advance planning and focused cultural assessment in incentive compensation design and implementation.

41

Cultural and Psychological Implications for Compensation

George G. Gordon, Ph.D.

Associate Professor of Management
Department of Business Administration
Rutgers University

Although compensation, or reimbursement to an employee for services rendered to the organization, is often thought of in financial terms, there is a powerful psychological component to it as well. What appears to one person to be a very generous bonus, to another may seem like less than a fair share. Thus, it is important in designing compensation plans to take into account the way in which different psychological environments interact with compensation. By different psychological environments, I mean the ways in which employee perceptions of compensation issues vary systematically from situation to situation.

As the following data demonstrate, such systematic variations do exist. The reasons for these variations depend on the particular subject under discussion, but some of the roots are very understandable. They include:

Job level.   The higher one moves in the organization, the higher the overall pay becomes. People at the lowest pay level may have trouble meeting basic food, clothing, and shelter requirements. At higher levels, the income has strong implications for luxury and prestige rather than basic living requirements. It, therefore, would not be surprising to find different perceptions of compensation at the different salary levels.

Industry sector.   It has been shown that industry sectors differ in their internal corporate cultures, including the role that monetary rewards play.[1] This may not merely be a function of how the companies are managed, but also may be a function of the people themselves. That is, because industries have very different competitive characteristics, they may attract people with different motivations and, in turn, different compensation desires.

The remainder of this chapter pursues these and related ideas and their implications for compensation planning.

Aspects of Compensation

For some time, both researchers and practitioners have been concerned with at least three aspects of compensation—internal equity, external competitiveness, and relationship to performance. It is abundantly clear that the perceptions of these factors are far more complex than the direct relationship to gross dollars. For instance, Edward E. Lawler found that although managers agree that merit should be an important determinant of pay, they also think that factors on which they themselves are strong should be the most important ones on which pay is determined.[2] This would be fine if their strengths were in the areas most critical to the performance needs of the company. If not, one could expect to hear a good deal of complaint.

In a related vein, Basil Georgopolous, Gerald Mahoney, and Nyle Jones found that better performers perceived stronger relationships be-

---

[1]George G. Gordon, *The Relationship of Corporate Culture to Industry Sectors and Corporate Performance.* In Ralph H. Kilmann, Mary J. Saxton, Roy Serpa, and Associates (eds.), *Gaining Control of the Corporate Culture,* Jossey-Bass, San Francisco, Calif., pp. 103–125.

[2]Edward E. Lawler, "Managers' Attitudes Toward How Their Pay Is and Should Be Determined," *Journal of Applied Psychology,* Vol. 50, 1966, pp. 273–279.

tween pay and performance than did poorer performers.[3] Thus, if we were to hear complaints about the company not paying for performance, it would be important to ascertain whether the complaints were coming from the better or poorer performers.

Perceptions of fairness are at least as complex. J. Stacey Adams and William Rosenbaum found that on a piecework basis, those who were overrewarded, for instance, actually slowed down so that they received what they believed to be the "fair" pay for the job.[4] In a follow-up study conducted by Lawler and Paul O'Gara, those who were underrewarded on a piecework basis sped up their production to achieve the same "fair" pay but in the process reduced the quality of what they produced.[5] Robert Pritchard, Marvin Dunnette, and Dale Jorgenson determined that not only was underpayment related to general dissatisfaction with the job, but that overpayment had more negative effects on satisfaction than equitable payment.[6] With such an array of potential negative effects, it is important that people be paid in ways that they perceive to be fair.

Survey Data Results

A variety of data collected by Hay Management Consultants through its culture surveys shed light on some of the factors that seem to condition compensation perceptions. The data were collected from over 17,000 people in professional and managerial jobs between 1981 and 1985.

Compensation Characteristics

Table 41-1 presents responses concerning various ways to look at a person's compensation. Scores are averages on a seven-point scale ranging from very negative (1) to very positive (7).

Obviously, all questions are not answered equally favorably. The question that asks how competitive compensation is with outside com-

[3]Basil S. Georgopolous, Gerard Mahoney, and Nyle W. Jones, "A Path-Goal Approach to Productivity," *Journal of Applied Psychology*, Vol. 41, 1957, pp. 345–353.

[4]J. Stacey Adams and William E. Rosenbaum, "The Relationship of Worker Productivity to Cognitive Dissonance About Wage Inequities," *Journal of Applied Psychology*, Vol. 46, 1962, pp. 161–164.

[5]Edward E. Lawler and Paul W. O'Gara, "Effects of Inequity Produced by Underpayment on Work Output, Work Quality and Attitudes Toward Work," *Journal of Applied Psychology*, Vol. 51, 1967, pp. 403–410.

[6]Robert D. Pritchard, Marvin D. Dunnette, and Dale O. Jorgenson, "Effects of Perceptions of Equity and Inequity on Worker Performance and Satisfaction," *Journal of Psychology*, Vol. 56, 1972, pp. 75–94.

Table 41-1. Mean Scores on Compensation
Issues

	Mean score*
Internal equity	3.63
External competitiveness	3.47
Compensation related to performance	3.73
Satisfaction with compensation	4.31

*On a scale of 1 (very unfavorable) to 7 (very favorable).

panies gets the lowest response (3.47), about half a scale point below the middle of the scale (4.00). The highest average response (4.31), about one-third of a scale point above the midpoint, has to do with the satisfaction with compensation. Interestingly, all three aspects of compensation—equity, competitiveness, and relation to performance—are below the midpoint of the scale, but satisfaction is higher. Clearly, factors other than comparisons with each other or relationship to performance condition peoples' "bottom-line" feelings toward their pay.

If a company obtains the preceding results on the first three variables but has no norms through which to interpret the data, the survey may well conclude that the compensation system has serious flaws, when in fact the company is "average." What actually appears to be happening is that when people think of compensation, they tend to think they are worth a little more than they get, both in comparison to others and in relation to their performance. What is most surprising and puzzling is that despite these feelings, professionals and managers are relatively satisfied with their compensation. The data seem to indicate that we may think we're worth more, but are reasonably happy with what we get.

Management Level

For much of the data, information was available to code responses into three management levels—senior, middle, and lower. Decisions about coding titles and levels were made in relation to the industry involved and the size of the company. For instance, a divisional vice president in a large insurance company was classified as middle management whereas a vice president of marketing in a $100 million manufacturer was classified as senior management. Lower management almost always consisted of the first two levels of supervision/management.

In Figure 41-1 (and Figure 41-2), the data are reported in percentiles rather than averages. In light of the differential response tendencies toward specific items (Table 41-1), percentiles were used to adjust all the

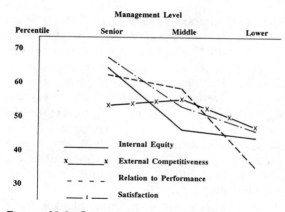

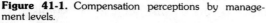

Figure 41-1. Compensation perceptions by management levels.

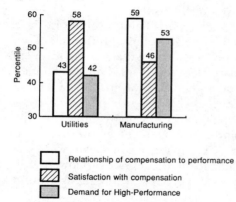

Figure 41-2. Comparison of utilities and manufacturing concerns.

items to the same basis. A percentile measures where a group or individual stands in relation to the population. A percentile of 50 is at the middle of the population. The higher the percentile, the higher the standing of the group in the population and the more positive or favorable it is on the item in question. Clearly, from Figure 41-1, senior managers are more positive in their perceptions of compensation characteristics than are lower managers. Middle management, depending on the particular issue, sometimes respond more like the senior group and other times more like the lower group.

The greatest overall spread is in the perception of how closely compensation is related to performance. Both senior and middle managers are very favorable in their responses (around the 60th percentile), whereas lower-level managers drop all the way to the 35th percentile—a very low response. This may reflect the existence of more incentive plans at higher levels or perhaps other factors that we have not yet uncovered. The result, however, is striking. Unlike the relationship of compensation to performance in which senior and middle management are similar, internal equity is perceived very favorably (64th percentile) by senior management and very close to average (45th percentile) by both middle and lower management.

External competitiveness shows the least differentiation, and even a reversal, at the middle management level. Senior management at the 53rd percentile is quite close to the all-industry median or average, while middle management is not significantly above that level (55th percentile). Because lower management is at the 47th percentile, there is a total spread of only 6 percentile points on this item. In effect, all three groups see external competitiveness as about average, with no one group having an unusual perspective on this issue.

Interestingly, this phenomenon of all groups being average in their perceptions of competitiveness may well be an accurate reflection of reality. In another study currently in progress, the actual competitiveness of compensation for different management levels was being examined company by company. In these data, a good deal of difference among levels within a company was not unusual. That is, in a particular company, senior management might be paid at the 70th percentile of equivalent jobs in other companies, middle management at the 50th and lower management at the 30th. The opposite results, however, were just as likely to have been observed. Thus, if the perceptions followed reality, one would expect to find each of the groups averaging at around the 50th percentile.

Finally, satisfaction with compensation is sharply different from group to group, ranging from the 67th percentile at senior management to the 50th at lower management. It almost appears that satisfaction is more a function of gross earnings than a function of how those earnings compare with others at the same level, whether inside or outside the firm.

Industry Sectors

As indicated in Figure 41-2, different industry sectors seem to have unique characteristics concerning how people perceive and feel about compensation issues. In utilities, satisfaction is much greater than the relationship to performance, whereas in manufacturing, just the opposite is true. Speculating on the reasons for this reversal across the industries leads to some intriguing possibilities.

Previous work indicated that there is greater focus on the management of performance in manufacturing environments than there is in utilities.[7] Indeed, perceptions of demand for performance, also plotted in Figure 41-2, are significantly higher in manufacturing.

The opposite of the performance demand concept, job security, also differs between the two industries. Managers in utilities perceive a much greater degree of job security than their counterparts in manufacturing.[8] There is also a very significant difference in compensation satisfaction between the two industries that does not stem from parallel differences in actual compensation. Indeed, at all but the lowest management levels, the utilities sector pays significantly below the manufacturing sector.[9] It is possible that the greater pressure for performance found in manufacturing companies may lead people to expect more on the reward side, whereas the opposite may be true for utilities. Regrettably, the present data do not allow for further probing of this possibility.

What is clear is that industry sectors differ in the extent to which they are able to relate pay to performance—at least through the eyes of their management. If a manufacturing firm were to attain a percentile score of 50 on the extent to which managers perceived that compensation was related to performance, it would be inaccurate to draw the conclusion that the company was doing as well as its competitors in that area. If such a conclusion led to a lack of attention toward spurring performance through compensation reinforcement, the result could have negative implications for the competitiveness of the business.

Implications for Contingent Compensation Plans

In developing compensation plans in which pay is contingent upon some type of performance, an understanding of the cultural and psychological environment is critical to their success. There are at least four cultural areas to consider. These are:

- Focus
- Performance
- People
- Systems

[7]"How's the Weather Inside?" *Electrical World*, Vol. 186, 1976, pp. 107–110.
[8]George G. Gordon and Walter M. Cummins, *Managing Management Climate*, Lexington Books, Lexington, Mass., 1979.
[9]*Hay Compensation Comparison*, The Hay Group, Philadelphia, Penn., 1985.

The remainder of this chapter discusses these areas and their implications for compensation planning.

Focus

The extent to which people actually understand where the company is headed and what it is trying to accomplish is a limiting condition of how well their energies can be harnessed. A company that frequently changes its emphases, begins projects and abandons them, and has units attempting to achieve competing objectives, is hardly one in which a payout based on corporate performance would maximize individual contributions. On the contrary, as people perceive the changes and conflicts hindering the accomplishment of corporate objectives, the fact that it may cost them money can only serve to create frustration, resentment, and possibly a "what's the use" attitude. For a program to effectively harness peoples' energies, it must be tied to an organizational level, whether corporate, division, or department, where the business focus is clear and in which they can relate their own activities to that unit's success.

A second and related concept of focus is whether performance is individually or group-based. A classic example of an individual focus is found in many sales jobs. In such cases, the individual brings product know-how, market knowledge, personality, and a great deal of effort to bear on accomplishing the objective—the sale. The general manager is also in a position in which all the means of success are focused in an individual job.

On the other hand, most accomplishments in industry depend on the successful integration of efforts among peers or peer units. Even in many complex sales situations, a team consisting of an account manager and technical and administrative support people shares responsibility for achieving the sale. Yet, in spite of this more widespread requirement for teamwork, many companies create a culture that emphasizes individual accomplishment. Pepsico Inc., for instance, has been known for its individualistic, internally competitive spirit that top management is loathe to undermine.

Many companies that espouse internal cooperation actually create structures and systems that strongly reinforce internal competition. When managers and professionals are asked to what extent the company's success depends upon individual or group performance, responses consistently shade toward the group side. Yet when these same people are asked what the reward systems encourage, the results consistently shade toward the individual side. These results are in agreement with the findings of a review of studies that concluded that "despite our cherished belief in the virtues of competition, study after study shows that nothing succeeds like cooperation."[10]

The implications for compensation are clear. If the desired results depend on cooperation, the compensation system should be designed to foster that cooperation. Executive pronouncements about "one big family" are not enough. The objectives, measurement systems, structures, and compensation must follow, to actually reach the minds and hearts of employees.

Performance

Just as people are not able to maximize their contributions if the organization is not able to provide the appropriate focus, they are unlikely to perform at maximum levels if they do not perceive the organization as demanding such performance. Although this may seem to be a very simplistic concept, it is one that is frequently not implemented in an organization. In particular, companies vary considerably in the extent to which they hold their people accountable for results. Without such accountability, it is difficult to ensure that extra efforts are being put forth to meet the organization's objectives.

In the same studies described earlier in this chapter, managers responded to the question, "To what extent are managers held personally accountable for the end results they produce or fail to produce?" Most managers responded in a positive fashion, but more than one-third gave responses in the low to neutral range, which might be considered "poor" to "fair" performance in this area. In utilities and insurance companies, this proportion approached half the respondents (44 percent). Thus, accountability, whether individual or group, is far from a universally implemented concept in industry.

Closely related to the concept of accountability is the extent to which people are encouraged to use their initiative or to adhere to established policies and practices. Holding people accountable for results when they are expected to adhere to very well-defined policies or procedures is a very different phenomenon from that in which they have a very wide latitude in which to operate. In the first instance, the accountability for choosing the appropriate strategic or tactical directions rests at a higher level in the organization. In this case, individuals are really only affecting day-to-day operating characteristics, such as manpower utilization, variable cost control, and so on. Concepts such as market penetration, profitability, and so on require much greater latitude in choos-

---

[10]Alfie Kohn, "How to Succeed Without Even Vying," *Psychology Today*, September 1986, pp. 22–28.

ing appropriate strategies or tactics and also require one's initiative to react to developments both within and outside the organization.

In designing and implementing compensation, these concepts of accountability and initiative are extremely important. They are strong and pervasive attributes of the culture—too pervasive to rest on compensation alone. A compensation plan can only reinforce, not create, the broader aspects of the culture. The company's history, external environment, and senior management styles of operation are much more powerful in creating the images of the type of behavior required to succeed. Compensation should be designed to fit and push to the limits of these forces. But, to create plans that are in conflict with the culture will, at best, have little influence on behavior, and, at worst, will create confusion and decrements in performance.

People

One of the key issues concerning contingent compensation is the motives of the person in the program. Victor Vroom postulates that motivation is a function of:

E = The *expectancy* that one's effort will result in performance

I = That performance will be *instrumental* in achieving rewards

V = The *valence* or value a person places on a reward

Mathematically, these variables are related by the formula $M = E \times I \times V$. Therefore, according to Vroom, each of the elements must have some positive value if the program is going to tap the positive motivational resources of its participants.[11] A zero for any one variable would render the program useless. The first two elements have already been touched upon under "Focus" and "Performance," but it is the third factor that is often overlooked.

Is the reward equally attractive to all employees? As seemingly universal as promotion might be as a reward, the desire to be promoted is far from universal among people we have surveyed. Incentive plans in which the individual payouts can vary considerably from period to period can well be demotivating for people with high needs for security. In these cases the valence of the rewards (promotion, incentive payout) may be close to zero for some people, and even if the focus and performance factors are high, the program may not work.

Yet another "people" variable that can have a very significant impact

---

[11]Victor H. Vroom, *Work and Motivation*, John Wiley and Sons, New York, N.Y., 1964.

on the success of a particular program is the trust that people have in the company and its management. In an ideal world, compensation level, raises, incentives, and bonuses could be based on objectively measured, indisputable criteria that are accepted by all involved. In reality, however, there are decisions and judgments involved in almost every aspect of compensation. Even something as seemingly objective as corporate profitability depends on many accounting decisions relating to depreciation, capitalization, write-offs, and so on. Thus, in almost all instances, the credibility of compensation depends on the trust people have that their superiors will apply appropriate judgments and measurements to the issues that affect their compensation.

The issues of trust play very heavily in gain-sharing programs, for example, in which:

- A high level of participation by employees is necessary for effective gains
- Gains depend upon cooperation and concerted effort of a large part of the organization
- Measures are on an organizationwide (usually plant) basis, as opposed to a piecework system, and are, therefore, impossible for individuals to track personally.

(A Scanlon plan is probably the most typical example of such a plan, although many management incentive plans also share these same characteristics.)

In such plans, trust must extend both laterally and vertically. Laterally, people must feel comfortable in relying on their peers to "hold up their end of the bargain." This is certainly true at the production-line level where it has been evident that peer pressure has a very powerful effect on performance. In such cases, it is important for management to create an environment in which cooperation can be directed toward organizationally desired outcomes. This is best accomplished by giving the work group considerable authority in developing the work processes and setting objectives. To do so also requires managers or supervisors to place a great deal of trust in their employees. Such environments are probably less typical than more traditional hierarchical environments in which the boss retains the lion's share of the authority.

In many management incentive programs, the trust element is also extended vertically and horizontally. Marketing must depend on manufacturing to produce the correct mix, quality, and cost of products to meet its sales goals. The management information systems (MIS) department is dependent upon timely and accurate inputs from throughout the organization in order to produce the sensitive and timely information that will allow the line units to make appropriate adjustments to their operations. Yet, data from the Hay culture surveys discussed earlier indicate that only 40 percent of the managers surveyed report that there is a good deal of cooperation among units. Thus, an incentive that relies on such cooperation might not, in many instances, offer the prospect of immediate effectiveness. This is one area, however, in which compensation could play a very significant role in moving companies toward such an environment. Of course, this would require the desire and commitment of senior management to see such an environment established. In other words, compensation cannot break down "fiefdoms," but can help a determined top management to do so.

Systems

In this final area, there are two key issues to consider: the way in which compensation is currently administered (before new programs are introduced) and the extent to which the company creates and disseminates performance information.

Any alteration to or replacement of an existing compensation program does not stand on its own, but rather is perceived in relation to what currently exists. Change itself is a negative to many people, especially those who place a high value on security. Some companies have had the experience of improving their programs—that is, implementing programs that resulted in higher total compensation costs—only to experience negative reactions from employees. This has been particularly true in benefit programs, such as denial coverage, because many employees focus on the deductibles, exclusions, and co-payments rather than the fact that certain expenses are covered that were not covered previously. If such a program is instituted in conjunction with other changes, there is a tendency to believe that the company has somehow gotten "the better of the deal." This, of course, would be heightened in companies in which the general level of trust in management is low.

A second consideration in instituting change is the adequacy of the current compensation plan. For instance, if managers perceive that the current salary plan produces gross inequities among jobs, introducing an incentive plan that works off a percentage of base pay will only serve to heighten the feelings of unfairness. Yet, many companies do just that, in many cases to overcome an uncompetitive base salary without adding fixed costs.

In both types of situations cited, the company must back off and consider its objectives. Is it attempting to enhance commitment to the company, keep valued employees, spur greater performance, or attain any of a number of other objectives? Keeping in mind the reactions of employees to current aspects of compensation, the level of trust, the motivations of employees, the performance expectations of the company, and so on, it is critical to design and communicate changes that will build upon, rather than decrease, the current levels of acceptance. For instance, when a company wishes to improve performance through introducing incentives but finds strong feelings of current inequity, a restudy of the basic salary program and a program of phasing in adjustments where needed would give the incentive plan a greater chance of accomplishing its objectives. Such a blending of business purposes and employee psychology can maximize the impact of compensation.

Last is the issue of the systems that the company currently has in place to define and measure performance at all levels. A wealth of research has demonstrated that performance is enhanced when results are measured and fed back to the individual or groups involved.

Companies normally produce an abundance of data at the operating level; this is true whether considering manufacturing (pieces produced, scrap), finance (transactions processed, errors), mining (tons loaded), or any other industry. At a corporate level there is also a wealth of data, such as revenues, return on investment, and so on. In the myriad of support functions, such as law, market research, or personnel, the situation is often quite different, with few objective performance or productivity measures customarily employed. Even in some of the major operating areas, certain key information, such as product profitability in a life insurance company, is often not isolated, measured, and communicated.

As in the case of corporate objectives it is critical to create clear understandings about performance. It is equally necessary to create measures in some of the "softer" areas if these are critical to successfully implementing corporate objectives. For instance, many companies are now stressing the need to become "customer-driven" but have not created the backup measures to give people specific targets to aim for. Yet, this is entirely possible as some companies have demonstrated by elevating measures, such as "time needed to settle claims" or "average response time to inquiries," to a position of prominence. The basic message in this area is that a powerful spur to performance can be obtained through a focus on appropriate measures, and that this focus can provide a ready level on which to apply compensation reinforcement.

42
Employee Involvement and Pay System Design

Edward E. Lawler III, Ph.D.
Director, Center for Effective Organizations
University of Southern California

The most prevalent approach to designing work organizations calls for features such as hierarchical decision making, simple repetitive jobs at the lowest level, and rewards based on carefully measured individual jobs and job performance. This "control approach" appears to be losing favor.[1] Numerous articles and books have recently argued that organizations need to move toward a more involvement- or commitment-oriented approach to management. In the involvement approach, information, knowledge, rewards and decision-making power are moved to lower levels in the organization.[2] The advantages of the involvement approach include higher quality products and services, less absenteeism, less turnover, better decision making, better problem solving, and lower overhead costs—in short, greater organizational effectiveness.[3]

[1] Edward E. Lawler, Gerald E. Ledford, and Susan A. Mohrman, *Employee Involvement in America*, American Productivity and Quality Center, Houston, Tex., 1989.
[2] Edward E. Lawler, *High-Involvement Management*, Jossey-Bass, San Francisco, Calif., 1986.
[3] Edward E. Lawler, Gerald E. Ledford, and Susan A. Mohrman, *Employee Involvement in America*, American Productivity and Quality Center, Houston, Tex., 1989.

Employee involvement approaches to organization design generally argue that three features of an organization should be moved to lower organization levels. Briefly the features are:

1. *Information* about the performance of the organization and the ability to bring information about needed organizational changes to the attention of key decision makers
2. *Knowledge* that enables employees to understand and contribute to organizational performance
3. *Power* to make decisions that influence organizational direction and performance

Information, knowledge, and power are the central issues in all organizations.[4] How they are positioned in an organization determines the core management style of the organization. When they are concentrated at the top, traditional control-oriented management exists; when they are moved downward, some form of participative management is being practiced.

Pay in Organizations

Reward systems are an important part of the very fabric of organizations. As such, they must fit with the overall management style of the organization and must reinforce and support the kind of behavior and culture that is desired. How organizations handle rewards is as important as how they handle information, knowledge, and power. Indeed, the literature in organizational behavior is replete with examples of their functional role as well as their dysfunctional role in organizations. The underlying assumption in this chapter is that, when properly designed, the reward system of an organization can be a key contributor to its effectiveness.

The first step in discussing the strategic role of reward systems is to consider what behavioral impact they can have. That is, we need to first address the outcomes that one can reasonably expect an effective reward system to produce. The research, so far, on reward systems sug-

[4]Jay Galbraith, *Designing Complex Organizations*, Addison-Wesley, Reading, Mass., 1973.

gests that potentially they can influence six factors, which in turn influence organizational effectiveness.

Attraction and Retention

Research on job choice, career choice, and turnover clearly shows that
the kind and level of rewards an organization offers influences who is
attracted to work for an organization and who will continue to work for
it.[5] Overall, those organizations that give the most rewards tend to attract and retain the most people. Research also shows that better performers need to be rewarded more highly than poorer performers in
order to be attracted and retained. Finally, the way rewards are administered and distributed influences who is attracted and retained. For example, better performing individuals are often attracted by merit-based
reward systems.

Motivation

Those rewards that are important to individuals can affect their motivation to perform in particular ways. People in work organizations tend
to behave in whatever way they perceive leads to rewards they value.[6]
Thus, an organization that is able to tie valued rewards to the behaviors
it needs to succeed is likely to find that the reward system is a positive
contributor to its effectiveness.

Skill Development

Reward systems help determine the type of skills that individuals develop because of their influence on the motivation to learn and the legitimacy of learning. Just as is the case with performance motivation,
individuals are motivated to learn the skills that lead to important rewards.

Culture

Reward systems are one feature of organizations that contribute to their
overall culture or climate. Depending on how reward systems are devel-

---

[5]Edward E. Lawler, *Motivation in Work Organizations*, Brooks/Cole, Monterey, Calif.,
1973.
[6]*Ibid.*

oped, administered, and managed, they can cause the culture of an organization to vary quite widely. For example, they can influence the degree to which it is seen as a human resources-oriented culture, an entrepreneurial culture, an innovative culture, a competence-based culture, and a participative culture.

Reinforcing and Defining Structure

The reward system of an organization can reinforce and define the organization's structure.[7] Often this feature is not fully considered in the design of reward systems. As a result, their impact on the structure of an organization is unintentional. This does not mean, however, that the impact of the reward system on structure is usually minimal. Indeed, it can help define the status hierarchy, the degree to which people in technical positions can influence people in line management positions, and it can strongly influence the kind of decision structure that exists. The key features are the degree to which the reward system is strongly hierarchical and the degree to which it allocates rewards on the basis of movements up the hierarchy.

Costs

Reward systems are often a significant cost factor. Indeed, the pay system alone may represent over 50 percent of the organization's operating cost. Thus, it is important in strategically designing the reward system to focus on how high these costs should be and how they should vary as a function of the organization's ability to pay. For example, a reasonable outcome of a well-designed pay system might be an increased cost when the organization has the money to spend and a decreased cost when the organization does not have the money. An additional objective might be to have lower overall reward system costs than business competitors.

Overall, reward systems in organizations should be looked at from a cost/benefit perspective. The cost can be managed and controlled and the benefits planned. The key is to identify the outcomes needed in order for the organization to be successful, and then to design the reward system in a way that these outcomes will be realized. Because it represents a different management style, employee involvement requires a different approach to rewards, one that produces an identifiable set of

[7]Edward E. Lawler, *Pay and Organization Development*, Addison-Wesley, Reading, Mass., 1981.

benefits.[8] It requires an approach that supports a low level of turnover; motivates team and group performance; motivates individuals at all levels to develop a broad range of skills; creates a culture of open communication, power sharing, and a focus on human resources; reinforces a structure that is flat and developed around lines of business; and relates the costs of a business to its ability to pay.

Features of Pay Systems

Reward systems in organizations are made up of core values, structures, and processes. Often in organizations the emphasis is on the structures. The structures are tangible and often easy to manipulate. They include things such as the merit pay delivery system, the job evaluation system, the pay ranges, and so forth. Associated with the various forms and procedures are a number of process issues that concern communication and decision making. In the area of communication, organizations vary from being highly secretive to quite open. As far as decision making is concerned, companies can use a participative strategy that allows a number of people to be involved in decision making or they can use a top-down strategy. Finally, organizations have core values with respect to their pay systems. These may be explicitly stated, as they are in some corporations, or they may simply develop over time and be generally shared as part of the culture. Core values usually concern key process issues (for example, communication) and key structural issues (for example, pay for performance). They guide what is done in these areas.

In reviewing how a pay system can be aligned with an employee involvement approach to management, consideration will be given to how it should affect core values, processes, and structures. As will be seen, employee involvement calls for specific approaches in all three areas.

Core Values

To support employee involvement, pay needs to be driven by a clearly articulated, well-accepted set of core values. These core values should not be a temporary commitment of the organization but, rather, fundamental beliefs that will be unchanged for decades.

There is a set of important core issues that the values ought to address. These include:

---

[8]Edward E. Lawler, *High Involvement Management*, Jossey-Bass, San Francisco, Calif., 1986.

1. Job security
2. How pay levels will compare to those of other organizations
3. The major determinants of an individual's pay, that is, whether it is performance pay, seniority-based, and so on
4. Individuals' rights concerning access to information and involvement
5. The relationship of pay levels to business success
6. The degree to which the system will be egalitarian
7. The degree of support for learning, personal growth, and involvement

There are no "right" core values; a part of the employee involvement process might, in fact, be developing them. It is possible, however, to make some statements about the general orientation that is congruent with the major principles of the employee involvement approach to management. In particular, the core values need to emphasize the relationship of pay to the success of the business, individual rights, due process, open communication, egalitarian approaches, pay rates that are competitive with similar businesses, and an emphasis on rewarding individual growth and skill development. An organization's core values should be supportive of a management style for which the organization depends upon people to both think and do and that stresses broad scale business involvement on the part of all employees.

Process Issues

Employee involvement suggests some specific process approaches to pay administration. In particular, it suggests greater openness of communication about pay practices and broader involvement on the part of all organizational members in the development and administration of pay and reward system practices. Greater openness is a prerequisite for understanding the business as well as for broader involvement and participation in the development and administration of pay practices. Openness and participation are congruent with the emphasis on moving power downward and having individuals involved in both the thinking and doing sides of the business. For a reward system to be effective it has to be both understood and designed in ways that lead to individuals accepting it. Participation in the design and administration process helps ensure this. It also ensures that the system will fit the situation, because it allows the people who will be affected by the system to influence its design.

With openness and participation, widespread ownership of the reward system should develop so that it is not simply the responsibility of the compensation or human resources department. Instead, it becomes the responsibility of everyone in the organization to see that it operates effectively and fairly.[9] This is a particularly important point, because in traditional management structures all too often the reward system becomes the property of the human resources department, and as a result, it ends up being ineffectively and poorly supported by line management. It almost goes without saying that in the absence of broad support in the organization, the reward system cannot support particular business objectives and strategies.

Pay System Structure

Here are some structural mechanisms that fit particularly well with employee involvement. Many of them represent important changes in the way pay is currently administered in most organizations.[10] In particular, the following structural approaches to rewards are appropriate for organizations practicing employee involvement.

Decentralized. In a large corporation, a centralized compensation approach is incongruent with the idea of business involvement and with targeting structure and reward system practices to the business strategy. By their very nature, most large corporations are engaged in multiple businesses that have quite different needs and that compete with organizations that pay differently. Having a single approach to pay that emphasizes a corporatewide approach to market position, to merit pay performance measurement, and so forth, makes it impossible for particular business units to structure their reward system effectively. Business units end up being forced to adopt a corporate structure that often is not congruent with what is needed to compete in their particular environment. Smaller organizations tend not to have this problem because they often face a single external environment. Some large organizations that are in a single business may not need to decentralize because they also face a single external market. In most cases, however, organizations that have multiple businesses need to decentralize compensation practice.

Decentralized pay argues for a dramatically different role for the corporate compensation staff. In a centralized system, they are the design-

[9]Allan M. Mohrman, Susan M. Resnick-West, and Edward E. Lawler, *Designing Performance Appraisal Systems*, Jossey-Bass, San Francisco, Calif., 1989.
[10]Carla O'Dell, *People, Performance, and Pay*, American Productivity and Quality Center, Houston, Tex., 1987.

ers and controllers of the corporate-driven system. In effect, they administer, in a centralized manner, a single compensation system that is monolithic within the corporation. Decentralized pay requires locally driven and designed plans, and needs a central compensation function that is capable of taking on a support and consulting role to the different business units. Carrying this out effectively requires a knowledge of the business's strategy, the determinants of a business effectiveness, and alternative pay system approaches. It also requires consulting skills.

Business-Based Rewards for Performance. If people are to be concerned about the success of a business, then their rewards must be driven by the success of the business.[11] This is not to say that individual pay-for-performance systems should be eliminated because they may still be appropriate if performance can be measured at the individual level.[12] Organizations need many systems that reward organization and business unit performance. Indeed, organizations need to be riddled with performance-based reward systems so that individuals' pay is driven by such things as their own performance, the performance of their business, and total corporate performance. For example, at the plant level, gain sharing plans as well as corporatewide stock ownership and profit-sharing plans could cover every employee. This combination can help push both power and information downward because it gives rewards for business performance to lower-level employees and legitimizes their getting information and power.[13] It also, of course, can influence motivation and create a team culture.

At the management level, emphasis needs to be placed on long-term performance. Particularly in the case of executive compensation, this suggests the importance of replacing or supplementing many of the current short-term profit-driven incentive plans with 5- to 10-year incentive plans. It also argues for paying managers based on the organizational units they managed in the past as well as on the performance of their current units. This can help to ensure that when managers leave a position, they cannot simple walk away from their past decisions.

Choice-Oriented. Traditional approaches to compensation provide the individual with a fixed package of benefits, cash, and perquisites.

---

[11]Edward E. Lawler, *Pay and Organization Development*, Addison-Wesley, Reading, Mass., 1981.

[12]Allan M. Mohrman, Susan M. Resnick-West, and Edward E. Lawler, *Designing Performance Appraisal Systems*, Jossey-Bass, San Francisco, Calif., 1989.

[13]Carl F. Frost, John H. Wakeley, and Robert A. Ruh, *The Scanlon Plan for Organization Development: Identity, Participation, and Equity*, Michigan State University Press, East Lansing, Mich., 1974.

This approach is inconsistent with the substantial individual differences that exist in the work force and with the idea that individuals can, and should, be able to make decisions concerning their own lives. Some organizations are already giving individuals greater choice. Initially, this was evident in the popularity of flexible working hours, and, more recently, it is evident in the growing popularity of flexible benefit systems. In flexible benefit systems, individuals are given the opportunity to choose the mixture of benefits they feel best fits their needs.

Individual choice does not need to be limited to fringe benefits and hours of work. Ultimately, organizations taking the employee involvement approach could allow individuals to have tremendous flexibility in determining their own total reward package. Flexibility could extend, for example, to the kind of perquisites and benefits offered and to the mixture of cash, stock, and bonuses. This has the potential of benefiting both the individual and the organization, because it will help individuals to get the rewards they value and assure the organization that the money it is spending is being spent in ways that produce the maximum impact on individuals.

Skill-Based.   Traditional pay approaches emphasize paying people for the jobs they do rather than the skills they have.[14] Employee involvement suggests paying individuals for the skills they have. This has already been done in a number of high-involvement manufacturing settings.[15] In these settings, individuals are put into self-managing work teams and are cross-trained so that they can perform all the functions within the team's area of responsibility. In this situation, it is particularly useful to have individuals who understand the whole manufacturing operation. Thus, paying individuals more to learn additional job skills fits with the general management style and business strategy. Paying for skills in manufacturing situations also reinforces psychological participation and ownership of the business results. It creates an environment in which individuals are able to understand the total operating situation and feel responsible for the overall performance of the organization.

Skill-based pay represents a truly revolutionary change in the nature of compensation practice. To mention just a few of the potential changes, it might mean that an individual who is promoted would not

[14]Milton L. Rock, *Handbook of Wage and Salary Administration* (2nd ed.), McGraw-Hill, New York, N.Y., 1984.
[15]Edward E. Lawler, Gerald E. Ledford, and Susan A. Mohrman, *Employee Involvement in America*, American Productivity and Quality Center, Houston, Tex., 1989.

receive a pay raise for being promoted. First, he or she would have to demonstrate the skills associated with a new job. Once demonstrated, however, a pay increase would be awarded. It also means that individuals at lower levels of the organizational hierarchy could be paid more than people at higher levels. With an emphasis on skills, it is quite possible that a highly skilled production worker or a highly skilled specialist might make considerably more than a middle-level manager, particularly if the specialist and production worker are encouraged to learn managerial skills in order to become more self-managing. In this sense, pay would become unhinged from the hierarchical nature of the organization and be used to reinforce skills rather than hierarchy.

Relatively little use has been made of skill-based pay in nonmanufacturing situations, and even in manufacturing situations it has been limited to the lower-level employees. There is reason to believe, however, that the use of skill-based pay should be expanded. Skills are the key to effectiveness in the growing number of organizations that are emphasizing employee involvement. In addition, knowledge-based work organizations require that skills be spread throughout the organization. Skill-based pay can motivate skill acquisition and reinforce it so that knowledge-based work and high-involvement organizations can build the kind of skill base they need to be effective.

The changing demographics of the society also suggest that skill-based pay should be increasingly popular. The "baby boom" group of individuals is rapidly approaching the age when they can be expected to end up in middle management. At the same time, employee involvement calls for flatter organizational structures and leaner staff groups. This means that the number of positions in middle management will be limited, and there will be less upward mobility opportunities for the large group of individuals in the age group that typically staffs middle management. In traditional management, this would simply mean individuals would stay on a plateau or in a dead-end position for a long period of time. If skill-based pay were put into place, they could be rewarded for making lateral moves, and as a result, continue to learn.

Egalitarian. There are several ways in which the pay system can be made more egalitarian in order to match the emphasis in employee involvement on moving information, knowledge, and power downward. A number of organizations already call all their employees salaried employees and treat them the same. Treating employees the same primarily means eliminating time clocks and putting all individuals on the same benefits package. An egalitarian approach can be combined with flexible benefits such that, although individuals have differing total compensation levels, they have access to all benefits in the organization.

In those corporations that adopt a strict egalitarian approach to rewards, such things as private parking spaces are eliminated. Further, individuals can be relatively highly paid by working their way up a technical ladder and do not have to go onto a management ladder in order to gain high levels of pay. This less hierarchial approach to pay and other rewards produces a culture that encourages decision making by expertise rather than by hierarchical position, and it creates fewer status differences in the organization.

Also consistent with the idea of a more egalitarian pay treatment is lowering the level at which such things as stock option plans and profit sharing plans operate in organizations. Traditionally, incentive pay plans have been concentrated only at the top level of management. This is inconsistent with employee involvement, which suggests that pay-for-organizational performance plans be pushed much further down in the organization. The one thing that probably should vary as these plans move further down the organization is the amount of an individual's compensation that is dependent upon them. At the lower levels, individuals should participate only to a small degree in profit-sharing and stock options plans, which are based on corporate performance. At the top level, compensation should be heavily dependent upon these plans. As was mentioned earlier, long-term incentive plans may be the one type of plan that should be targeted at top management.

The employee involvement approach also brings into question the wisdom of pay plans that pay senior executives much more than lower-level employees. Large differences can be justified under a traditional management system because executives are expected to exercise considerable power and to control information. Under the employee involvement approach, however, power, information, and knowledge are pushed downward so it follows that rewards such as pay should be pushed downward as well.

The management practices and strategies that are consistent with employee involvement requires new pay practices. Because compensation is the fabric of any organization, it must be congruent with the overall management style and strategy of the business. It suggests new core values, new administrative processes, and some new pay structures. As

Table 42-1. Pay and Management Style

	Traditional management	Employee involvement
Communication	Secret	Open
Decision making	Top-down	Wide involvement
Structure	Centralized	Decentralized
Pay for performance	Merit pay	Business success-based
Reward mix	Standardized	Individual choice
Base pay	Job-based	Skill-based
Degree of hierarchy	Steep-level effect	Egalitarian

shown in Table 42-1, pay needs to be characterized by egalitarianism, local control of decision making, individual choice, and, most important, a strong performance-based system that ties to the business itself. Taken as a package, these new pay practices are congruent with employee involvement and promise to change the way work is done.

43

Strategic Compensation Communication

Claudio Belli

President and Chief Executive Officer
Europe, Middle East, and Eastern Countries
Hill and Knowlton

Introduction

For many reasons today, the relationship between an organization and its employees is more vulnerable than in recent history. Downsizing, restructuring, and automation have eliminated a vast number of jobs. As Peter Drucker has pointed out, the shift toward knowledge work has enhanced the mobility for those employees with information-based skills. Both the organizational cutbacks and increased mobility have eroded the loyalty most employees feel toward organizations. All this comes at a time when population trends have created a dramatic shortage of skilled workers in most developed economies.

Communication of compensation information has always been important. The job package of wages and benefits is the central aspect of the employee's relationship with the firm—certainly as seen from the employee's viewpoint. But, organizations today are less willing to let compensation be a static trade of dollars for work. Instead, management is demanding that compensation be linked to effectiveness, productivity, and the achievement of overall strategic direction in an unprecedented way. Employees, on the other hand, know their motivation and results are impacted by the compensation program under which they work. They also have a much more sophisticated understanding of the economics of their job packages and are searching for a richer and more subtle array of rewards—from educational programs to parenting leaves. So, a successful compensation program today hinges very much on the quality of communication that supports it. How well are all the elements explained? How effectively is compensation linked to company goals? Does the communication have strong enough emotional appeals to spur peak performance in sustained ways?

The Basic Communications Process

The classical model for communications depicts a message being sent from a communicator to a receiver. Perhaps it's a speech, a brochure, a videotape, or a phone call. Although we think of communications as a formal process using devices like these, frequently casual remarks and spontaneous comments are the most influential communication. An off-hand remark by a single high-ranking manager debunking a compensation program can have more effect—in its damage—than the hundreds of thousands of dollars spent to unveil and promote the program itself. Words themselves are not even necessary. Oftentimes, communications can be nonverbal. In organizations, managerial behavior can send strong messages. For example, when CEO Lee Iacocca of Chrysler Corporation chose to work for $1 a year in the early years of the Chrysler turnaround, that sent a powerful message about "equality of sacrifice" to that company's work force.

Communication is, by definition, a two-directional process. The flip side of communication is feedback. How was the message perceived? As with the initial communication, feedback can take many forms. A speaker whose talk is greeted by cheers and applause knows that he or she has hit the mark. When a firm conducts an attitude survey after introducing a compensation plan and finds widespread confusion about the implemented changes, it has also gotten feedback. The feedback says the plan was communicated poorly. If an organization's skilled workers don't complain about compensation but simply leave for more competitive pay elsewhere, that too is feedback—the feedback of employees voting with their feet.

The Information Age we live in today makes most workers more skilled in processing information and more demanding as well. Two decades ago, a well-designed brochure on a company's benefits or a professionally made video on compensation policy would have been an exception. Compensation communication was a routine and not very sophisticated aspect of company life. Today, in a company of reasonable size, these kinds of communication are well developed. Our video culture has also put a premium on speed. Tom Peters reports that in some manufacturing plants, "electronic scoreboards" track "quality progress by the hour." Ford Motor Company has created an internal television network that links together more than 280 facilities in North America. Ford's annual profit-sharing announcement is telecast to its employees. Employees—with their information habits shaped by television news—expect to learn important new data as soon as possible.

Conventional communications thinking pictures management as communicating downward through endless layers in an organization built on the military model. Responses then flow back upward through the chain of command. In fact, communication in even the very largest organizations works less and less that way. Managerial spans of control have become far larger. Electronic mail has shrunk the time needed to deliberate on and implement decisions. The distance between top and bottom ranks in the company has been collapsed to a large extent. The operating style of most organizations has become much less rigid and more collaborative. If compensation communication is to be successful, it will share in that style. That is, it will be more direct and more personal.

The shift toward speed and informality could lead one to conclude that communicating in large organizations has become totally informal, even chaotic. Although the style is more fluid, the principles and practices, ironically, have become more sharply defined. Legal and regulatory trends have mandated increased care and exactness in communicating to employees about sensitive personnel issues. There is also a demand that complicated benefits information be addressed in straightforward language.

Today, the compensation communicator has two chief duties in dealing with all the complexities of his or her job. First, he or she must ensure that the routine structure for communicating with employees as a group is in place and that this system is at least as good as the communications programs of those organizations with which the firm must compete for human resources. Second, and equally important, he or she must give managers throughout the organization the training and the staff support to implement the system in an ongoing way. In the end, it is how line managers interpret and utilize the program that will determine its success in any organization.

Preparing to Communicate

Most organizations spend insufficient time preparing to communicate their compensation and benefits programs and messages. No effective communication is possible without a thoughtful understanding of the audience and their concerns and attitudes.

There are many ways to communicate features of compensation and benefits programs. I have found the following checklist helpful in preparing what to communicate:

- When was the last change to this program made? How was it received? Is this a controversial issue for employees? Does the change endanger a long-standing practice that employees have taken for granted?

- Do employees believe that the present program is fair? Do they understand it? Do they understand the economic impact of the program for the organization? How will they view changes given their understanding and evaluation of the present program?

- In what way does the proposed change interrelate to the overall personnel policies of the organization? Does it have a probable impact on such issues as career planning, advancement, recruitment, organizational design?

- How does this change relate to the organization's mission and strategy? (For example, organizations that want strong entrepreneurial behavior will often install strong incentive pay programs to spur performance. Organizations needing the long-term commitment of research people may strengthen and publicize their retirement program.)

- How much total change are employees being asked to accept at this time? Does the new program come on the heels of major restructuring or reorganization? Has the timing been carefully analyzed?

- How strong or weak has the organization's recent financial performance been? How does performance compare with that of similar or competitive organizations? How will employees view the new program in the context of that performance?

- Is the economy weak or strong? Will concerns about the economy make the new program look particularly positive or negative?

- Does the change represent an innovation, given the organization's history? Given the practices of competitive or comparable organizations? If it's a breakthrough, how can the organization capitalize on that innovation and earn credit for it?

There are many channels to gather data such as this. Larger firms will systematically canvas employee opinion through the use of attitude surveys. The surveys can be used to shed important light on many of the preceding questions. In any surveying, organizations must use their best judgment so that the very raising of certain questions does not create inappropriate anxiety in advance of possible change.

An understanding of employee attitudes and expectations is indispensable. Management and human resources staff should continually be collecting and discussing input on how employees view the organization and its compensation and benefits practices. Frequently, messages will surface through the grapevine far more quickly and clearly than through formal surveys. A management that seeks input on compensation and benefits recognizes the importance of these topics and displays its willingness to listen. Employees respect both traits in their management.

It's especially important that the voices of what Hill and Knowlton CEO Bob Dilenschneider calls the "informal leadership" of the organization be listened to carefully. At every level and in every department, you will find people whose opinion counts for a good deal more than their official rank in the hierarchy. They are respected for their informal leadership and solid, practical judgment. Frequently, they are long-tenured employees with strong loyalty. Oftentimes, the views of a senior secretary, a maintenance supervisor, or a particular production engineer may have more influence on how a certain program change is accepted than all the words of management or union leadership.

Today's compensation communicator must be a student of organizational and company culture. Companies often have personalities as distinct as those of people, and these traits will determine how successful communication takes place. Do employees want simple summaries, or is thorough documentation a must? Is top management expected to announce or endorse even relatively minor changes in personnel policy? Are appeals to logic or emotion more likely to sell something new? Is a major personnel policy alteration destined for rough sailing if some sort of task force has not "blessed" the change in advance? There are fewer certain rules that can be applied to all organizations today. Rather, the emphasis must be on finding the style, the channels, and the approaches that work in each individual culture.

It is also important for a compensation communicator to monitor public policy and current events diligently. Is a major shift in the national health-care policy on the horizon? Is a change in the structure of work in your industry going to affect wage ranges for entry-level positions? Is the trend toward day-care centers so well established among other firms located in your headquarters city that it's now essential that you create a facility to remain competitive?

Every aspect of organizational behavior has become more competitive today. That includes communications staff work itself. Even a decade ago, firms fundamentally competed through their marketing departments. Today, competition takes place on every front, including computer power, distribution facilities, and, certainly, human resources administration. In an ongoing way, the compensation professional will conduct a self-audit of compensation practices compared to competitors:

- If I am in a unit of a larger organization and my compensation and benefits programs are certainly determined, are they administered in my unit as well as in other units? If each unit is administered separately, what can I learn from the other programs in my company or organization?

- Who are the standard setters for compensation communication in my industry? In my community? Do I regularly try to study samples of their communication and learn from them? In what specific ways do they use communication about compensation and benefits to enhance their performance or their competitive behavior?

- When new employees for the main organizations become my colleagues, do I talk with them to learn about compensation and benefits communication practices of their former employer? What did they like? What did they dislike? Do they spot any immediate opportunities to improve the program in our organization?

- Do I have a sound idea of comparative costs? Are the compensation and benefits communications costs of competitive or rival organizations more or less? Why? Are their organization structures similar? Do they utilize more or fewer outside service providers?

A new dimension of compensation communication is the opportunistic communication of information supporting the company's policies. Compensation communication cannot be a once-a-year exercise, nor can it be left to the traditional compensation reports and statements. Is it possible to showcase a new incentive/productivity program in the company magazine? If work forces in other countries have much higher rates of productivity than the organization's, should an article describe the situation and point out the threat? If a firm has a management newsletter to keep decision makers updated on major trends, are the breakthroughs and leading innovations in compensation regular topics? If the compensation communicator wants his or her responsibility area to receive the proper emphasis, he or she must be assertive as an active voice and "market" the importance of this aspect of management.

The Standard Delivery and Feedback Systems

No effective compensation and benefits program can exist without certain essential components and vehicles for communication. The first step is to create clear policy and procedures. Supporting the policy should be an organizational philosophy toward compensation. This should be a simple statement, probably no longer than 100 or 200 words, that embraces the company's stance toward compensation and benefits and the role they play in achieving the organization's goals and objectives. Such a philosophy statement is a worthwhile part of any organization's statement of strategy or mission.

As much as possible, the company should strive for open communication of its policy and procedures in compensation. There are obviously good reasons for not disclosing the individual details of each person's compensation package, but the proxy statements and Form 10-K filings of public companies reveal considerable data about the compensation packages of top managers, and the trend has been toward increased disclosure. Those organizations most likely to run into the greatest problems in compensation communication are ones in which employees think that there are many hidden deals and arrangements that undercut or circumvent the "official rulebook."

Most companies translate their policies and procedures on each key compensation and benefits area into a brochure or leaflet. Thus, companies will usually have separate publications on their medical plan, their retirement program, life and disability insurances, career advancement and compensation, time off, and the other highest profile human resources concerns. As part of a new employee's orientation or when a major program overhaul takes place, each of these topics is also usually the subject of a video or slide presentation.

It's important for employees to see the scope of their total compensation and benefits program, as well as to understand each element separately. For this reason, most firms publish individual compensation and benefit statements for all employees each year. These statements can be as educational as they are purely informational. For example, they can point out how much the organization contributes toward medical and life insurance benefits and state the company contributions to social security and unemployment insurance. Many firms time their annual review of potential changes in the compensation and benefits programs to coincide with the publication of their annual statements.

Company newsletters, newspapers, bulletin boards, or magazines can be used to announce changes in policy or practice. They are also good vehicles for discussing recurrent questions or problems in the administration of policy. Payroll stuffers remain an effective channel, even as many employers now offer direct deposit of paychecks. Many firms have suggestion systems that encourage employees to contribute their comments. Often, these comments will be about compensation and benefits, and many companies will answer anonymously posed, representative questions in their employee newsletter or magazine. Monitoring the suggestion system is one of the best ways to get in touch with the employees' priority concerns and potential opportunity areas.

There has been a strong general communications trend toward CEOs and other top managers holding open-ended meetings with employees at all levels. Compensation and benefits questions are among the most popular topics at such give-and-take sessions. It's very important that the compensation communicator help top managers anticipate the questions. That includes briefing them on all the aspects of the organization's compensation and benefits program. Top managements' understanding of these issues is essential to the organization's health. Employees will earnestly measure top managements' understanding of the business through its answers to the questions and will expect candor, clarity, and knowledgeability on the issues.

Almost all major compensation and benefit communications require the review by legal counsel. So many aspects of these topics are addressed in laws and regulations. Other legal concerns stem from the implied contract relationships that can exist between organization and employee and the increasingly litigious nature of our society. That means the language must often be painstakingly clear. Accepting that legal input is essential. I would also argue for the strong use of judgment in how any communication is worded. The first goal of communication is to get the message across. Language, which is continually qualified and unnaturally guarded, can easily subvert the whole goal of communication. As part of the management team, the communicator must argue for and help to attain the proper balance of clarity, accuracy, and understandability.

The announcement of new programs or a major change will most likely to take place through an audio-visual presentation. The preparation of such programs is frequently a major duty falling on the compensation communicator. To plan and execute such presentations, a methodical review of all the factors is essential:

- What was the last major presentation of this sort? The last major presentation on this topic?

- As with any communication, the style of the presentation will often be linked to the message itself. Was the style smooth and professional or choppy and amateurish? (Note that there is a big difference between "slick" and professional. An organization that makes its messages too polished or sells too hard can be distrusted as manipulative.)

- What kind of visual format will best support the nature of the presentation? If the program includes many charts or numerical examples, perhaps a sound-and-slide presentation will be sufficient. If more budget dollars are available and a strong message is needed from a top manager to endorse the programs, then videotape may be the answer.

- Can the program be produced in-house or should a media production specialist be used? I have seen even large companies invest millions in overhauling a major compensation program and then skimp on its communication. A failure to sell the program effectively can cripple even the best-designed plans.

- What related print communications material will be required? Frequently, a new booklet describing the revised program is distributed at the time of the presentation. Often, the key changes are described in a single-page highlights sheet.

- A detailed timing-and-action calendar is a must when planning any major program announcement. In large companies, that may mean that the general program is announced on paper to all employees and then is quickly followed by a series of explanatory meetings. It is important to monitor the tone of the first meetings in such a "rollout" very carefully. Audience behavior and questions may signal serious flaws or opportunities in the presentation that can be corrected in subsequent presentations. If the change is truly major, it is often desirable to have a member of top management at each of these meetings. This top officer's presence can help signal management's endorsement of the change. It's usually best if the managers are *not* solely from the human resources pyramid. It is too easy to dismiss complex compensation or benefit changes as the work of human resources "technocrats." The smartest compensation communicators find ways to sell their programs as "company programs" rather than just pieces of human resources administration. Another critical factor in a communications "rollout" is time. Communication on issues as important as these must move swiftly throughout the organization. Either the official communication will move quickly or the grapevine is bound to overtake it.

- When major program changes are announced or a new employee is being oriented, it is wisest to supplement the media presentation with a question-and-answer session. If the group is very large and many questions are anticipated, it frequently helps to break the group into smaller units. In that setting, the employee can resolve personal concerns with the help of either a personnel specialist or a general manager.

Statistical monitoring can have significant value in detecting compensation and benefits troublespots. Is a particular work unit the source of a greater-than-average-number of complaints in the employee suggestion system? Compensation is a very personal issue, and unhappiness is often expressed through personal behavior. Unusually heavy employee turnover, absenteeism, lateness, workers' compensation claims, or productivity decreases can all signal serious problems with the compensation program or its communication. Some companies also monitor issues that arise in the regular performance review meetings with employees as well as exit interviews of individuals leaving the organization.

Training Line Managers to Communicate

There has been a strong trend toward linking each employee's personal performance to the performance of the total organization. In many respects, compensation is an investment, and employers expect a competitive return on that investment. The return can be measured in many ways, such as sales per payroll dollar, units of output for each dollar of compensation, and operating profit for wages invested. Most companies don't attempt to measure the individual worker's personal performance in this way, but more and more do measure the performance of a department or work unit. The unit's performance may then be compared with that of other units in the organization and with that of competing or rival organizations.

At one time, only management saw this type of data. Increasingly, however, management has recognized that employees need to know and understand productivity data if they are to help the organization become truly competitive. It is said that everyone today manages something. That something may be one's own performance. Supervisors must be able to explain the relationship between the individual's performance and the effectiveness of the work unit and the success of the company. These explanations are important to the ongoing management of any work unit and at the time of periodic individual performance reviews.

One of the most important of a line manager's duties is to communicate compensation actions for individuals, usually in conjunction with personal performance reviews. Over the years I have observed three recurrent pitfalls that mangers must guard against and that compensation communicators must help managers avoid.

1. *The compensation message doesn't mesh with the performance message.* In order to make the employee "feel better" about a relatively small increase, the manager will inflate the performance review with superlatives about the individual's performance. These mixed messages can be dangerously misleading and are certainly unfair to the employees, who don't learn in a clear way what they must do to improve performance.

2. *The compensation discussion contains avoidable surprises.* In well-managed companies, there is solid awareness at every level of the structure of the pay ranges or whatever other discipline is used to organize compensation decisions. There is also general awareness of how well the organization and the particular work unit are meeting their respective goals. If belt-tightening, poor unit performance, an anticipated economic downturn, or other factors will reduce the amounts available for bonuses or raises, it's usually best for management to signal direction early. But, it's also critical that this communication be closely coordinated with the organization's communication to other audiences. It is, for instance, very easy for a firm to communicate a performance signal to its employees that ends up being reported and acted on in the financial marketplace. At the speed with which information moves today and the careful monitoring that takes place, one can assume that communication to any one particular audience will end up in the hands of another. Unions, as one example, are using the bullish projections some firms may make in the financial markets as evidence in wage negotiations that companies are better off than management contends.

3. *The line manager avoids endorsing the compensation.* "I would have given you a bigger increase, but the human resources department said I couldn't." That may be the most often used hedge working against modern human resources administration. If the manager doesn't demonstrate his or her belief in the fairness and integrity of the system, it is hard to expect the employee to do so. Supporting the system may mean that the manager has to deliver "bad news." Perhaps the

employee isn't measuring up against other individuals or units with which his or her performance is being compared. Maybe the employee has been shielded from the views of others in the organization who view his or her performance less positively. The line manager has an accountability to support the compensation system just as he or she must support company strategy.

A successful compensation and benefits program requires knowledgeable line managers who can communicate effectively. These mangers must be able to link individual rewards to individual performance. They must also know how to use company programs to motivate individual performance. They should be able to identify compensation problems in their work unit and know when to call in specialized help. They should have a basic understanding of compensation as a motivational aid. And they must treat compensation communication candidly and thoughtfully, for their sake as well as for the sake of the employees.

Index